Life time design
of building in urban areas

Methods, instruments and process of sustainable building design in architecture

Imprint

Publisher

Hochschule Wismar
University of Applied Sciences:
Technology, Business and Design
Faculty of Architecture and Design/
WINGS - Wismar International
Graduation Services GmbH

Editing

Prof. Dipl.-Ing. Martin Wollensak
Ing. arch. Lucia Oberfrancová

English translation

M.A. Nina-May Gill
M.A. Scott Bailey
B.Tech Arch Sci Brenton Wiebe

Layout/Revision of Pictures

Ing. arch. Lucia Oberfrancová
M.A. Adriana Ďurišová
B.A. Dominik Siebold

Final revision

Ing. arch. Lucia Oberfrancová
Ing. arch. Alžbeta Križánková

Print

Callidus Verlag, Wismar

Address

Hochschule Wismar
University of Applied Sciences:
Technology, Business and Design
Philipp-Müller-Straße 14
23966 Wismar
Germany

Phone: +49 (0) 3841 753 - 7138
Internet: www.hs-wismar.de
www.wings.hs-wismar.de

ISBN 978-3-942100-06-9
1st. Edition

The contents of the book were carefully collected together. However, they are based partially on student works, projects and are not proven in every case. For the correctness of the book's content, the authors do not assume responsibility or liability.

Life time design
of building in urban areas

Preface

Sustainable holistic planning and design, integrated design and life cycle analysis are terms which today determine the architecture and the planning process and have led to a special profile in the education of architects in Germany.

Starting with the point of view that the building design is an architectural work and so much more than a service in the construction process is a perspective that has developed in Germany since the "Bauhaus" architectural period and the creation of the "Werkbund", as it determines what an architect must do (term Building culture).

The architect is the specialist responsible for the assembly of the layers of individual building components, as well as the coordinator of construction experts. The architect holds knowledge of all the details, without being a specialist in detail. He must know something about everything but does not have to know everything about anything.

In the face of the increasing specialisation of construction, better and faster communication and social coercion to regulate and test everything is becoming increasingly significant. The people who can keep an overview, give recommendations on the classification and evaluation of complex relationships in construction, are growing in importance.

Simultaneously, against the progressive specialization and the many legal pitfalls in partial aspects of construction, it is always more difficult to have comprehensive knowledge about all special and partial fields of a building's construction. Many architects feel overwhelmed and voluntarily limit themselves to a part of the building construction industry where they can prove that they have the required knowledge.

As a result, more and more architects are withdrawing from the overall responsibility of building and leave that field of action to lawyers and engineers; people even less trained and incapable to taking full responsibility.

In Germany, the architect has been demoted from a construction manager to a construction controller. In the general jurisprudence he still has far-reaching responsibility for the implementation of the technical, economic and design aspects of a building. His scope of action is becoming increasingly limited and replaced by additional experts, calculations and standards.

It would be interesting to study whether this far-reaching change of responsibility is connected with the rising costs of the construction industry.

Why does this loss of ability to act exist?

The architect has made a large contribution to this development because he /she feels overwhelmed by the multitude of new requirements and no longer attempts to possess comprehensive knowledge because of the increasing complexity and thus fails to consolidate his / her proper position. Instead, the architect devotes more and more time to the design task, which continues to lose its meaning, given the increasing importance of technical and economic aspects.

In this book, we have documented our experiences in order to give the opportunity to those who want to confront the future tasks, being able to acquire the knowledge that is necessary in our view to assume overall responsibility in building as an architect, as it was before.

In our view, the knowledge and skills described have been shown to be necessary in continuing to have a say. It should not be expected that they are complete, as they are constantly influenced by change and must be continually updated.

Sustainable action requires a holistic approach to allow an overview of integrated planning.

Sustainable buildings should, if possible, be durably designed and built for a specific situation; it is rarely a series product. The importance of the environment and the uniqueness of the situation leads to new concepts that usually allow no series of buildings. A building is therefore rarely a product but rather an individually customized event or object.

Therefore, it is not possible to create general rules for everything. (European Construction Products Regulation)

We therefore attach great importance to ensuring that the examples and aspects mentioned in the book cannot be understood as a recipe but rather solely intended to provide the future architect assistance in improving his knowledge about the future in terms of a sustainable and holistic approach, so that the architect can in the future remain responsible and be able to act and keep an overview.

Prof. Dipl-Ing. Martin Wollensak

Content

Content

Key words, energy standards and norms

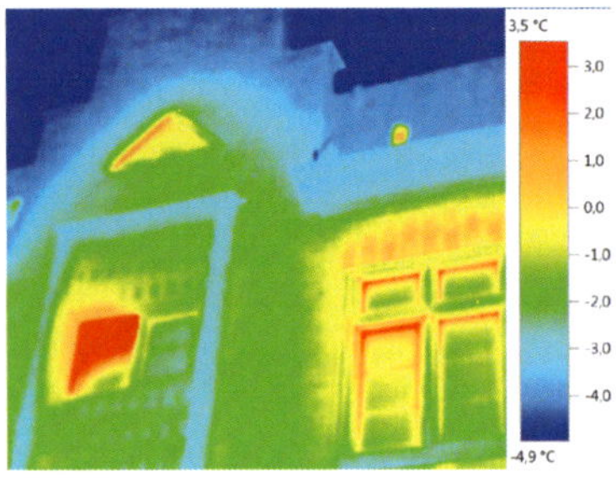

1

1 *A thermal camera recording of an old uninsulated house before renovation*
2 *The different standards and the requirements for the heating demand and primary energy demand*

Energy standard

The energy standard of a building determines how high the energy consumption may be per square meter of heated area throughout the year. In the construction industry, there are many energy standards and labels that are partly determined by regulations. Many standards have now been documented by means of certification and quality assurance services.

WSVO – "Wärmeschutzverordnung" (Thermal insulation ordinance)

The regulation for the energy-saving thermal insulation of buildings first appeared on the 1st November 1977. Its purpose was to reduce the energy consumption through structural measures due to rising energy prices.

The Thermal Insulation law was amended twice. Once on the 1st January 1984 and the second thermal regulation on the 1st January 1995. On February 1st 2002, it was replaced by the Energy Saving Law (EnEV), which for the first time combines the insulation regulations and the heating system regulation.

Low energy standard (EnEV 2002)

Low energy houses have a very low heating and hot water energy demand. The heating requirements of low energy buildings shall not exceed 70 kWh/m²a, or consume the equivalent of 7 litres of heating oil or 7 cubic meters of natural gas per square meter per year. Decisive attributes for the evaluation of a house include very good thermal insulation, prevention of thermal bridges on the basis of precise technical characteristics, a standard compliant air tightness which is also judged on the heat-resistant glazing, controlled ventilation and efficient building services. In addition, by having a compact building form and a very good building envelope will help to achieve these low consumption figures.

KfW – "Kreditanstalt für Wiederaufbau" (Credit for building reconstruction)

KfW is a public law institution and promotional bank of whom offers help with construction, housing, energy saving and a wide range of programs that are used to finance investment for residential property.

Standard	Heating demand Q_h	Primary energy demand Q_P	Heat transmission losses H_T
Un-renewed house, built in 1960-1980	300 kWh/m²a		
Average house in Germany 2002	160 kWh/m²a		
"Wärmeschutzverordnung" Thermal insulation ordinance (WSVO 77)	≤ 250 kWh/m²a		
"Wärmeschutzverordnung" Thermal insulation ordinance (WSVO 82)	≤ 150 kWh/m²a		
"Wärmeschutzverordnung" Thermal insulation ordinance (WSVO 95)	≤ 100 kWh/m²a		
Low energy house (EnEV 2002)	≤ 70 kWh/m²a		
KfW-60-House (EnEV 2004)		≤ 60 kWh/m²a	
KfW-40-House (EnEV 2004)		≤ 40 kWh/m²a	
KfW-Efficient house 70 (EnEV 2007)		≤ 60 kWh/m²a	≤ 70% highest value EnEV 2007
KfW-Efficient house 55 (EnEV 2007)		≤ 40 kWh/m²a	≤ 55% highest value EnEV 2007
KfW-Efficient house 85 (EnEV 2009)		≤ 85% highest value EnEV 2009 (approx. 50 kWh/m²a)	≤ 100% highest value EnEV 2009
KfW-Efficient house 70 (EnEV 2009)		≤ 70% highest value EnEV 2009	≤ 85% H_T, Ref EnEV 2009
KfW-Efficient house 55 (EnEV 2009)		≤ 55% highest value EnEV 2009	≤ 70% H_T, Ref EnEV 2009
KfW-Efficient house 40 (EnEV 2009)		≤ 40% highest value EnEV 2009	≤ 55% H_T, Ref EnEV 2009
Passive house (PHPP)	≤ 15 kWh/m²a	≤ 120 kWh/m²a	

2

Funding objectives are the creation of home ownership, the energy efficiency of buildings, housing modernization, the construction of fuel-efficient new buildings and PV systems. Since 2006, the federal government has provided the framework for the initiative "Housing, Environment, Growth" with an annual 1 billion € budget that is available to the program to reduce CO_2 emissions, to be attractive, and to meet the national climate change commitments under the Kyoto Protocol. Defined by KfW, lending criteria KfW-40 and KfW-60 are recognized energy standards for buildings.

3 litre house standard

3 litre houses are ultra-low energy buildings that consume only the amount of primary energy per square meter per year which includes 3 litres of fuel oil that covers about 30 kWh of energy per square meter per year. The electricity for pumps, control and burner is already included. In the late 90s, Fraunhofer IBP created this standard and protected the name under the trademark "3 litre house".

Passive house standard

Passive house standard was developed by Dr. Wolfgang Feist, who founded the passive house institute in Darmstadt. The heating demand for a passive house is less than 15 kWh/m^2a (referring to the living space). The main concept of passive house includes a high level of thermal insulation, triple-glazed windows, an air-tight building (< 0.6 h^{-1}) and a heat/ventilation recovery system (with an efficiency of at least 75 %) so the heat transmission loss is as small as possible. To plan a passive house, the software PHPP - Passive House Planning Package can be used.

Nearly zero energy standard

"A nearly zero energy building is a building that has a very high energy performance. The nearly zero, or very low amount of energy required should be achieved by using energy from renewable sources, including energy from renewable sources produced on-site or nearby." [1]

To achieve the EU target, new buildings should be built as nearly zero energy buildings by 2020, with public buildings by the end of 2018.

Zero energy standard

Zero energy house, which is also known as a zero net energy building is a building with a zero net energy consumption and zero annual carbon emissions. The zero energy house is an standard for buildings that require no external energy such as electricity, gas or oil. The energy required for heating and hot water is generated in the house itself, usually by heat pump and solar panels.

Element	U-value
Outside wall	≤ 0.15 W/m^2K
Roof	≤ 0.10 W/m^2K
Bottom slab	≤ 0.12 W/m^2K
Window	≤ 0.80 W/m^2K

3

[1] *ECEEE – European Council for an Energy Efficient Economy;* Steering through the maze #2. Nearly zero energy buildings: achieving the EU 2020 target. Stockholm/Schweden: ECEEE Secretariat 08.02.2011, page 1

3 Maximum U-values of the building components for a passive house
4 The main concept of a passive house
5 The main concept of a zero energy house

cold air
warm air

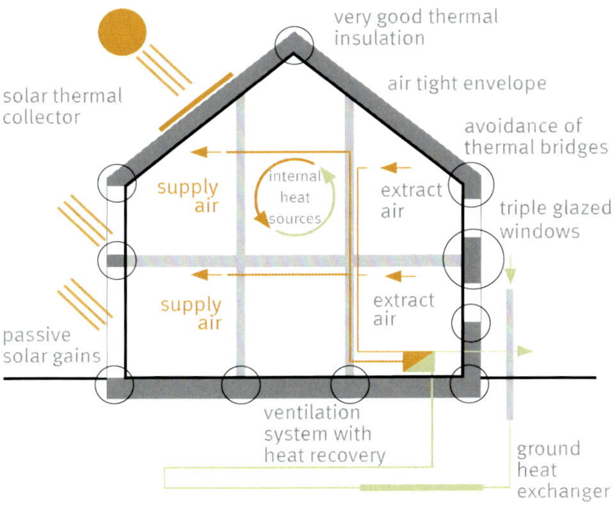

4

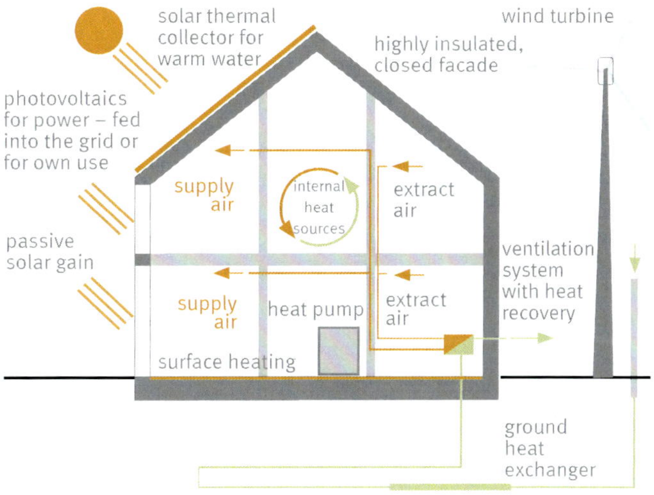

5

Key words, energy standards and norms

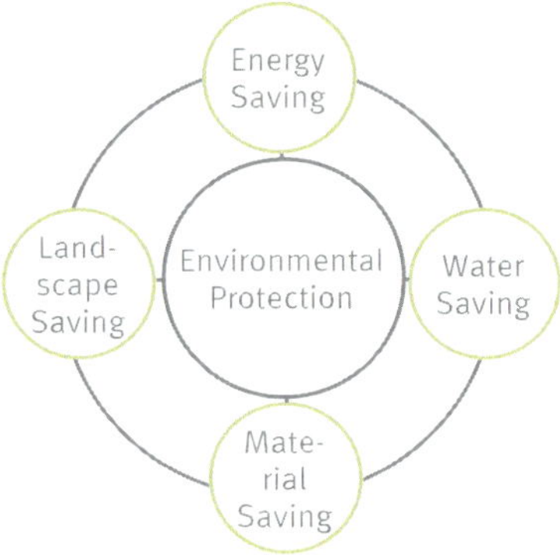

6

[2] *Werner Sobek;* Triple Zero® [http://www.wernersobek.de/index.php?page=392] (20.09.2012)

6 Four save standard principle
7 Efficiency House Plus with electromobility, outside view, Germany, architect Werner Sobek
8 Detail of floor heating in wood fibre insolation instead of EPS, Efficiency House Plus with electromobility, Germany, architect Werner Sobek

Plus energy standard

The plus energy house produces more energy than its inhabitants consume. Energy Plus uses a 100 % renewable energy supply and has an emission-free operation. In addition, an increase of clean solar electricity is produced and fed into the grid. Passive use is combined with active systems i.e. the house itself generates electricity and heat which is stored within the building and strategically used when required.

Triple zero® standard

"Triple zero® is a standard developed by Werner Sobek to define the demands a building must fulfil to satisfy aspirations regarding environmental sustainability. The name Triple zero® is protected by trademark law. R128 is a good example of a building fulfilling Triple zero® standards.

- Zero energy building

The building requires no (zero) energy. The energy generated from regenerative sources on and in the building or the immediate property upon which the building stands on is at least equal to the entire primary energy requirements of the building for heating, cooling, hot water, auxiliary power and power for all typical domestic applications.

- Zero emission building

The building produces no (zero) CO_2 emissions. The reference value is the total primary energy demand, which is then converted to CO_2 emissions. No burning processes are permitted in the building or on the property.

- Zero waste building

No waste (zero) is produced when the building is being converted or deconstructed. At the end of its life cycle all building elements can be fully recycled without any components requiring to be burnt or sent to a disposal site. The plot of land can be returned to nature without any fear of contamination or residual waste." [2]

Four save standard

Also known as the "Green Four Sections" is a standard developed in China and refers to: save landscape, save material, save water and save energy including environmental protection. It is the highest level of environmental protection standards for residential buildings in China.

Primary energy PE [MJ or kWh]

Primary energy is from the earth's naturally occurring sources. These energy sources are fossil fuels such as coal, petroleum, natural gas or minerals (Primary energy nonrenewable), and renewable energy sources such as the sun, wind, water, biomass and geothermic (Primary energy renewable).

7

8

Primary energy nonrenewable PE_{nre} [MJ or kWh]

Nonrenewable energy is energy taken from limited resources that will eventually disappear. They are becoming too expensive and too environmentally damaging as opposed to renewable energy sources which are naturally replenished in a relatively short period of time.

Nonrenewable sources of energy can be divided into fossil fuels (coal, fuel oil, natural gas) and nuclear fuels (plutonium, uranium). Nonrenewable energy sources are highly available and the technologies used to harness these energy sources are well developed. The problem is that they are limited and will be exhausted in approximately 70 years. Burning them contributes to air pollution and further health problems. Most CO_2 emissions come from industrial energy production, causing the greenhouse effect.

Primary energy renewable PE_{re} [MJ or kWh]

Renewable energy is energy that comes from naturally replenishing resources such as sunlight, wind, rain, tides, waves and geothermal heat. The term renewable energy generally refers to the energy supplied from renewable sources, such as wind and solar power, geothermal, hydropower, and various forms of biomass. These energy sources are considered renewable sources because they are continually replenished on the earth. The initial costs of these energy systems are expensive (e.g. solar panels,...) however, renewable energy technologies are clean sources of energy that have a much lower environmental impact than conventional energy technologies. Most renewable energy investments are spent on materials and the workforce to build and maintain facilities, thus bringing working opportunities. Furthermore, renewable energy is unlimited and will not run out.

Primary energy factor f_p [-]

The primary energy factor shows the relationship of used nonrenewable, primary energy (included is the energy loss through generation, transportation and storage) to the submitted end energy. The lower the primary energy factor, the more efficient the generation of energy based on the primary energy sources.

Primary energy demand Q_p [kWh/a]

To calculate the primary energy demand of a building according to EnEV (EnEV page 76), at first, the final energy demand must be determined.

There is energy loss during the transformation of primary energy into usable energy caused by the conversion and transportation processes (figure 9).

Grey energy

Grey energy is energy required for production, transportation, storage, sale and disposal of a product in consideration to the raw material extraction and energy input of all implemented production processes. This does not include the final usable energy.

Secondary energy

Secondary energy is the energy generated by the conversion of primary energy. From primary energy such as coal, natural gas, petroleum, or renewable energy such as solar power or wind energy, secondary energy is produced by the process of transformation.

The most common type of secondary energy is electricity, but also fuel oil and communal heating (thermal energy) are secondary energy sources. Only the secondary energy is available as the final energy for the consumer. Examples include coke, briquettes and petroleum products such as gasoline.

9 Different energies – primary energy, end energy, usable energy

10 Primary energy factors used for different energy sources in Germany

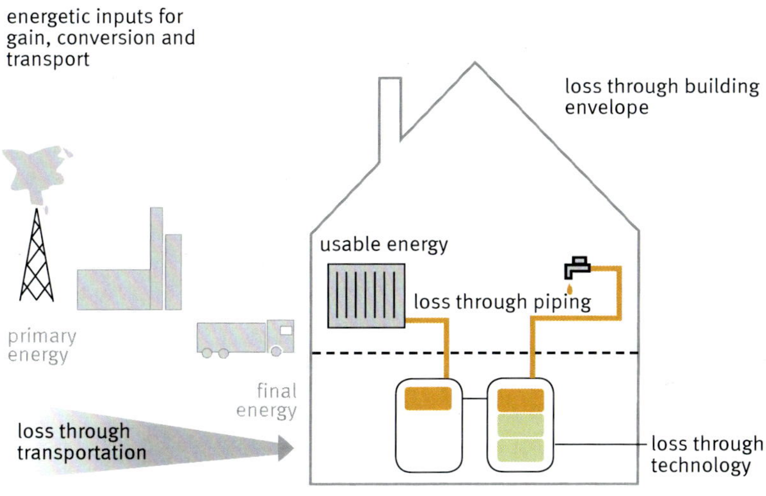

9

Energy sources		Factor f_p
Fuels	Petroleum	1.1
	Natural gas	1.1
	Hard coal	1.2
	Lignite	1.2
	Wood	0.2
	Renewable	0.0
Local or communal heating from combined heat and power	Fossil fuel	0.7
	Renewable energy	0.0
Local or communal heating from heating plants	Fossil fuel	1.3
	Renewable energy	0.1
Power	Power mix	2.4

10

Key words, energy standards and norms

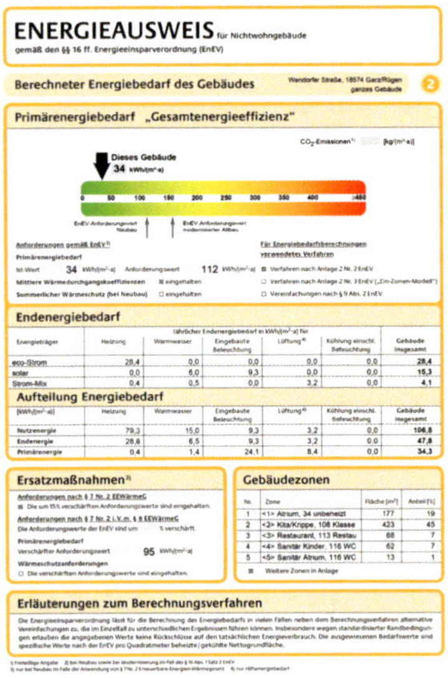

ENERGIEAUSWEIS für Nichtwohngebäude
gemäß den §§ 16 ff. Energieeinsparverordnung (EnEV)

Berechneter Energiebedarf des Gebäudes — Wendorfer Straße, 18574 Garz/Rügen, ganzes Gebäude — 2

Primärenergiebedarf „Gesamtenergieeffizienz"

CO_2-Emissionen[1] [kg/(m²·a)]

Dieses Gebäude 34 kWh/(m²·a)

0 50 100 150 200 250 300 350 400 ≥400

EnEV Anforderungswert Neubau — EnEV Anforderungswert modernisierter Altbau

Anforderungen gemäß EnEV[2]
Primärenergiebedarf
Ist-Wert 34 kWh/(m²·a) Anforderungswert 112 kWh/(m²·a)
Mittlere Wärmedurchgangskoeffizienten ☒ eingehalten
Sommerlicher Wärmeschutz (bei Neubau) ☐ eingehalten

Für Energiebedarfsberechnungen verwendetes Verfahren
☒ Verfahren nach Anlage 2 Nr. 2 EnEV
☐ Verfahren nach Anlage 2 Nr. 3 EnEV („Ein-Zonen-Modell")
☐ Vereinfachungen nach § 9 Abs. 2 EnEV

Endenergiebedarf

Energieträger	Jährlicher Endenergiebedarf in kWh/(m²·a) für: Heizung	Warmwasser	Eingebaute Beleuchtung	Lüftung[4]	Kühlung einschl. Befeuchtung	Gebäude insgesamt
eco-Strom	28,4	0,0	0,0	0,0	0,0	28,4
solar	0,0	6,0	9,3	0,0	0,0	15,3
Strom-Mix	0,4	0,5	0,0	3,2	0,0	4,1

Aufteilung Energiebedarf

[kWh/(m²·a)]	Heizung	Warmwasser	Eingebaute Beleuchtung	Lüftung[4]	Kühlung einschl. Befeuchtung	Gebäude insgesamt
Nutzenergie	79,3	15,0	9,3	3,2	0,0	106,8
Endenergie	28,8	6,5	9,3	3,2	0,0	47,8
Primärenergie	0,4	1,4	24,1	8,4	0,0	34,3

Ersatzmaßnahmen[3]
Anforderungen nach § 7 Nr. 2 EEWärmeG
☒ Die um 15% verschärften Anforderungswerte sind eingehalten.
Anforderungen nach § 7 Nr. 2 i.V.m. § 8 EEWärmeG
Die Anforderungswerte der EnEV sind um % verschärft.
Primärenergiebedarf
Verschärfter Anforderungswert 95 kWh/(m²·a)
Wärmeschutzanforderungen
☐ Die verschärften Anforderungswerte sind eingehalten.

Gebäudezonen

Nr.	Zone	Fläche [m²]	Anteil [%]
1	<1> Atrium, 34 unbeheizt	177	19
2	<2> Kita/Krippe, 108 Klasse	423	45
3	<3> Restaurant, 113 Restau	68	7
4	<4> Sanitär Kinder, 116 WC	62	7
5	<5> Sanitär Atrium, 116 WC	13	1

☒ Weitere Zonen in Anlage

Erläuterungen zum Berechnungsverfahren
Die Energieeinsparverordnung lässt für die Berechnung des Energiebedarfs in vielen Fällen neben dem Berechnungsverfahren alternative Vereinfachungen zu, die im Einzelfall zu unterschiedlichen Ergebnissen führen können. Insbesondere wegen standardisierter Randbedingungen erlauben die angegebenen Werte keine Rückschlüsse auf den tatsächlichen Energieverbrauch. Die ausgewiesenen Bedarfswerte sind spezifische Werte nach der EnEV pro Quadratmeter beheizte / gekühlte Nettogrundfläche.

1) Freiwillige Angabe 2) bei Neubau sowie bei Modernisierung im Fall des § 16 Abs. 1 Satz 2 EnEV
3) nur bei Neubau im Falle der Anwendung von § 7 Nr. 2 Erneuerbare-Energien-Wärmegesetz 4) nur Hilfsenergiebedarf

11

11 Energy performance certificate for kindergarten "Wildblume" in Garz/Rügen, Germany

12 The embodied and operational energies, emissions or costs of conventional building and green building alternative – the higher embodied energy (emissions, costs) of green building are compensated back after a few years of building operation

13 The general life cycle of a product

The conversion losses are considered to be the primary energy factor f_P. The relationship between the final energy demand Q_e , primary energy demand Q_P and the primary energy factor f_P is

$$Q_e \cdot f_P = Q_P$$

Final energy [MJ or kWh]

The final energy describes the amount of energy consumed after the deduction of conversion and distribution losses. For example, this can be in the form of power, wood pellets, heating oil or district heating. End energy is generally a base for the calculation of energy costs.

Final energy demand Q_e [kWh/a]

The final energy demand is the amount of energy required for the generation of useful energy (for example heating, generation of warm water, lighting,...) for a building. Energy losses by distribution, storing and conversion in a building are considered. It is determined for standardized conditions (for example, defined user behaviour, interior temperature,...) and separated into its required energy sources.

Final energy use [kWh/a]

Final energy use describes the amount of actual in-building energy required. It also considers for example, the users behaviour and climatic fluctuations.

Usable energy [kWh/a]

Usable energy is the energy consumed by the consumer. It is calculated from the end energy after the deduction of conversion losses.

Usable energies are in forms of heat, light, movement or sound waves. The useful energy determines the basis for the calculation of primary energy demand according to EnEV (page 76).

Heating demand Q_h [kWh/a]

The heating demand is the calculation for the amount of energy, which has to be delivered to the building during the heating period to cover heat losses. It is a result of transmission H_T and ventilation loss H_V with consideration for solar and internal gains.

Energy performance certificate

Post EnEV 2007, an obligation was introduced for homeowners and new tenants to present the energy performance certificate for their buildings. The certificate is based on the energy consumption of a building describing the measured energy use which depends on the user behaviour and climatic fluctuations.

The certificate is based on the energy demand of a building and is either calculated or theoretically determined. The energy performance certificate is valid for 10 years.

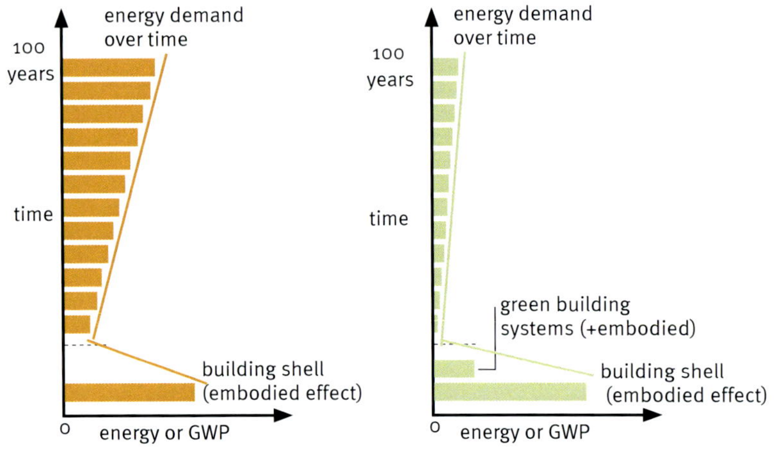

Conventional building

Green building alternative

12

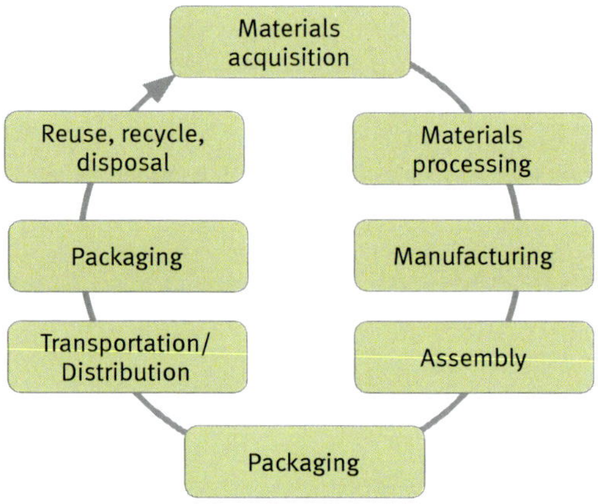

13

Life Cycle Assessment (LCA)

Life cycle assessment analysis also known as ecobalance (LCA page 72) is a technique to assess environmental aspects and potential impacts associated with all the stages of a product's (building's) process's, or service life (from raw material extraction, the processing of the materials, the manufacture, distribution, use, repair and maintenance, and disposal or recycling).

LCA results help answer numerous questions that arise during the design and construction of a green building. It allows architects and other building professionals to understand the energy use and other environmental impacts associated with all life cycle phases of a building. It also allows the architect to show to the client that the use of LCA will improve and demonstrate the "green-ness" of the project and significantly help to increase the long-term paybacks by better decision-making.

The LCA does not determine which product or process is the most cost effective or the best solution. The LCA study should be just a part of group of different analysis, which is generally known as Life Cycle Management.

Life Cycle Costs

Life cycle costs is the total costs of building over the whole building life. Typical areas of expenditure include planning, design, construction and acquisition, operations, maintenance, renewal and rehabilitation, depreciation and the cost of finance and replacement or disposal. The costs considered include the financial costs (relatively simple to calculate) and also the environmental and social costs (external costs) which are more difficult to quantify.

Life cycle costing (LCC)

Life cycle costing is a method which calculates the costs of a product, from the product idea to the demolition of a product. The main idea is to see if the saving of money in the life time operation is comparable to the higher investment costs. Using whole life costs calculation avoids the issues with decisions being made based on the short term costs of design and construction. Often the longer-term maintenance and operation costs can be a significant proportion of the whole life cost.

External environmental costs

External costs are based on the results of the LCA analysis on environmental impacts, where the amount of different emissions (e.g. greenhouse gases) are quantified and monetised so they can be considered as an additional cost input in a LCC analysis. External costs are effected by the behaviour of one or more individuals.

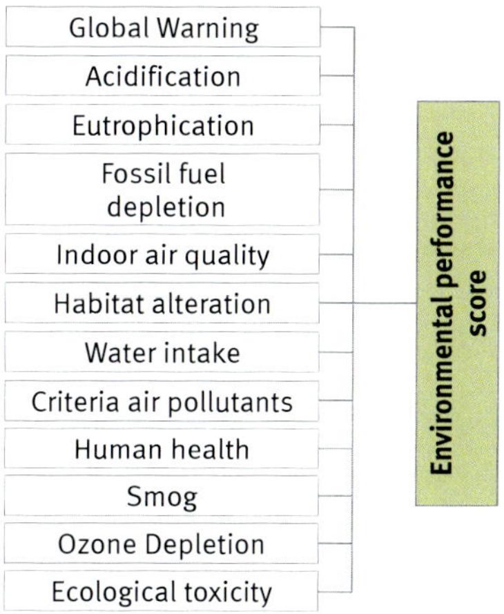

14

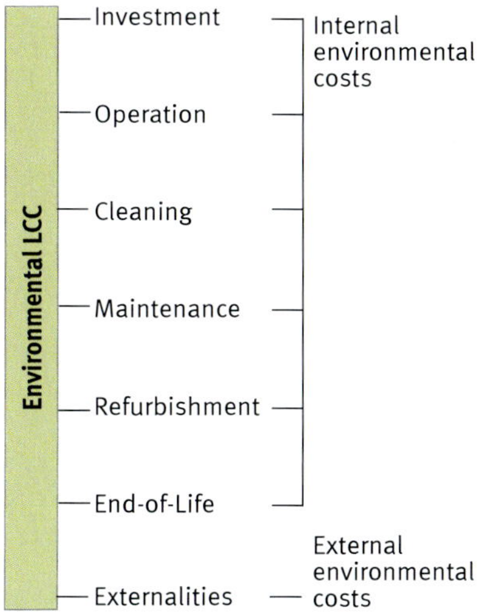

15

Emission category	External cost	Unit	Source
Greenhouse gas CO_2	70 (280 max.)	€/CO_2 equiv.	Maibach et al. 2007
Acidification potential SO_2	5,200	€/SO_2 equiv.	Maibach et al. 2007
Photosmog C_2H_4	265	€/C_2H_4 equiv.	Adesam et al. 2002
Ozone-reduction potential R11	11,850	€/R11 equiv.	Adesam et al. 2002
Eutrophication potential PO_4^{3-}	1,700	€/PO_4^{3-} equiv.	Adesam et al. 2002

16

14 Different groups of impact emission categories as a result of LCA
15 Main internal LCC categories plus external environmental costs
16 Example of external cost rates

Key words, energy standards and norms

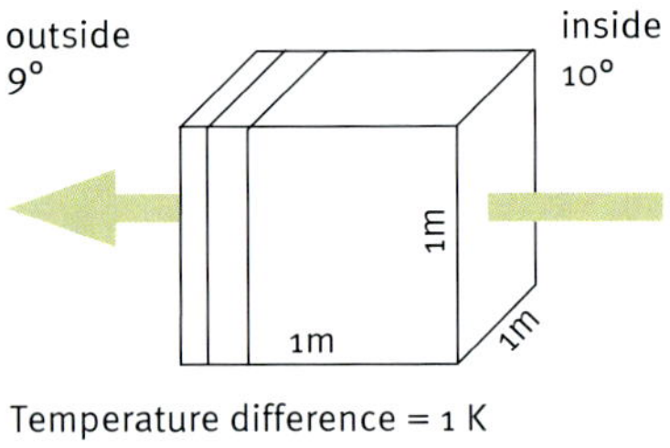

17

Building physics

Building physics is considered as scientific discipline which is the theoretical basis for the design and assessment of civil engineering structures. Requirements for building physics properties are standardized by a large set of criterion.

U-value [W/m²K]

or heat transmission coefficient is the measure for heat flow under static conditions and is determined by the heat output in Watt per m^2 of a surface and by the difference of one Kelvin between each surface of the building element. It describes the thermal transmittance across the structure. The lower the value, the better the structure's insulation properties, as less thermal energy is lost through the structure.

λ-value (lambda) [W/mK]

or thermal conductivity describes the characteristics of a material and how well it conducts heat. The higher the value, the higher the heat transfer across the material. For thermal insulation materials, the lowest λ-value is desired.

H_T-value [W/m²K]

is the parameter for specific transmission heat loss. It describes the thermal loss through a buildings envelope to the environment. The lower the factor, the lower the thermal energy loss through the building envelope.

H_V-value [W]

describes the specific ventilation thermal loss, or the thermal energy that flows out through ventilation. Ventilation heat demand is the amount of heat that is required to heat up the fresh air within the considered time period. The lower the H_V-value, the lower the thermal loss through ventilation and ventilation heat demand.

A/V – ratio

or surface area to volume ratio is the rate of the heat transferring surface of an object (A) and the heated volume of the object (V). It is used as a value to evaluate the compactness of a building. It is important to consider in connection to the thermal losses from a buildings surface – the bigger the surface area, the greater the thermal loss.

DIN V 18599

is a group of norms, which considers calculations of usable, final and primary energy demands for heating, cooling, ventilation, warm water and lighting (energy balance) of buildings (11 parts). The most current version is from December 2011.

17 U-value determines the capacity which flows through the surface of 1 m², when the difference of temperature on both sides is 1 K
18 Issues of building physics

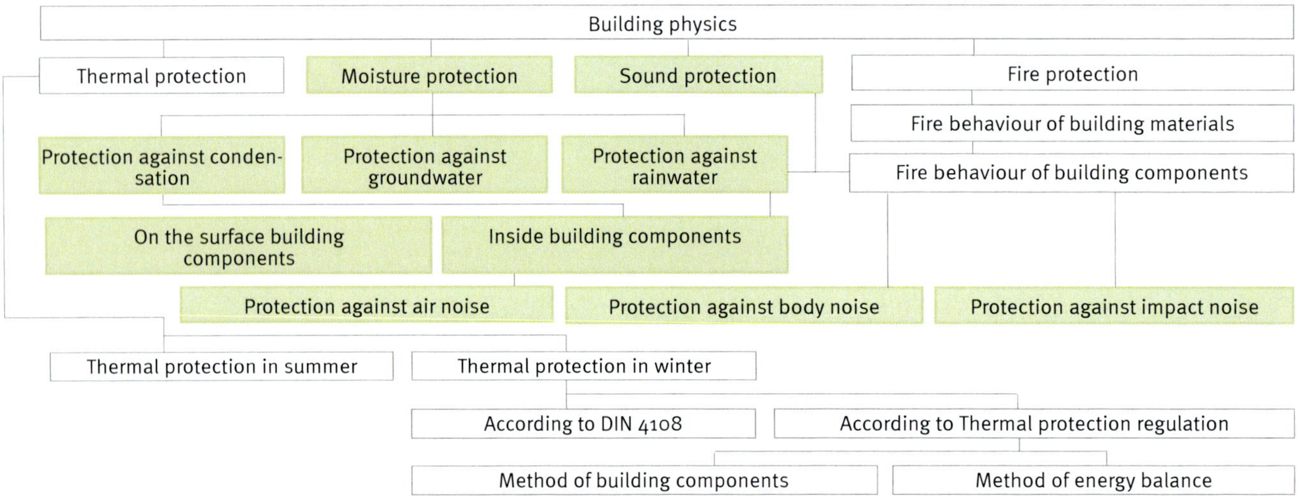

18

DIN 4108

is a norm that considers the thermal protection (winter, summer) of buildings. It is also the foundation for the German energy EnEV, however it is of less importance because updates of EnEV are based on DIN V 18599. Important still is DIN 4108 supplement 2, which considers the building's thermal bridges and regulates the design details.

DIN 276 Building costs

The DIN standard DIN 276 regulates the determination of costs in construction. Currently, only Part 1 of Construction (last updated 2008-12) and Part 4 of the civil engineering building (last updated 2009-08) are valid.

Related costs are divided into cost categories. In the first level of cost structure, the total cost will be divided into the following seven cost categories:

- 100 Building site
- 200 Infrastructure works
- 300 Building – construction
- 400 Building – tech. equipment
- 500 Exterior equipment
- 600 Equipment and artwork
- 700 Extra building costs

For a more accurate cost estimation of a building, the cost groups 200 and 300 are used. Below are the subgroups for the category 300:

- 310 Pit
- 320 Foundation
- 330 Exterior walls

(331 Load bearing exterior walls, 332 Non-load bearing exterior walls, 333 Outer columns, 334 External doors and windows, 335 Exterior wall cladding, exterior, 336 Exterior wall cladding, interior, 337 Unitised exterior walls, 338 Sun protection, 339 Exterior walls, other)

- 340 Inner walls
- 350 Blankets
- 370 Constructional installations
- 390 Other measures

DIN 277 Base areas and volumes of structures in building construction

The norm DIN 277 (last updated 2005-02/04) is used in Germany to determine surface areas and volumes of buildings or parts of buildings in building construction.

The standard is particularly applicable to the determination of surface in buildings with multiple uses. It is divided into three parts.

Surface areas and volumes are used among other things for the determination of costs in building construction and the comparison of structures.

Term	German	English	Explanation
Gross floor area	BGF	GFA	NGF+KGF
Net floor area	NGF	NFA	NF+TF+VF
Construction floor area	KGF	CFA	Sum of all structural components in floor plans of a building (walls, columns, piers, bases of chimneys, inaccessible bays, doorways, niches, slots,...)
Usable area	NF	UFA	Part of the NGF which is used for its intended purpose
Technical function area	TF	TFA	Part of the NGF, which serves the central housing of technical plants. If the purpose of placement of technical plants is to supply other buildings (e.g. boiler house),the area of technical plants is usable area.
Circulation area	VF	CFA	Part of the NGF serves the access to the rooms, the circulation within the building and also exiting in an emergency
Gross volume	BRI	GRV	Volume of the building without a foundation which is enclosed by the external boundary surfaces of structure.
Net volume	NRI	NRV	Total area of all content areas, the bases of which are NGF

20

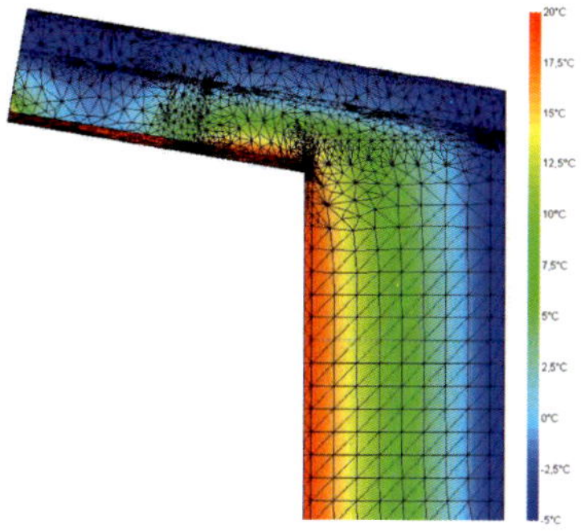

19

Ψ-value (psi) [W/mK]

The heat transfer coefficient describes the transmission heat losses through thermal bridges.
It is divided into lineal (e.g. balcony connection) or point thermal bridges (e.g. corner).
It depends on the quality of construction, dimensions and U-values of the surrounding building components.

19 Typical building construction detail with the temperature flow
20 Abbreviations for building measurements based on DIN 277
21 Minimum H_T-value

According to EnEV, Appendix 1 Chart 1:

a) nonresidential buildings with f ≤ 30 % and residential buildings with

A/V_e m^{-1}	H_T W/m^2K
≤ 0.2	1.5
0.2 < A/V < 1.05	$0.3 + 0.15/(A/V_e)$
≥ 1.05	0.44

b) nonresidential buildings with window-surface f > 30 %

A/V_e m^{-1}	H_T W/m^2K
≤ 0.2	1.5
0.2 < A/V < 1.05	$0.3 + 0.15/(A/V_e)$
≥ 1.05	0.44

21

22

22 The interlocking of architectural and functional design within the boundaries of regulations – user-friendly emergency exit for children in case of fire in the form of slides at the kindergarten "Wellen-reiter" in Wismar, Wollensak architects

Life time design

1.0 Strategies and regulations

1.0 Strategies and regulations

1.1 Introduction

Gray energy [(kWh)]	Wood building	Brick building
Basement*	308,300	317,200
Upper building**	177,400	231,700
Whole object	485,700	548,900

*110 m² cellar effective area (wood) and/or wood/brick building method 115 m² (bricks) by different wall construction
** 207 m² living effective area, energy-saving building method
23

Today, problems with energy savings and natural resources worldwide are a big question for future development. There is a need to consider these problems and search for solutions.

Highly developed countries have in total the highest energy consumption and therefore, the greatest need to save energy. Without any strategies and regulations there would be no control in future development.

The building sector is a high consumer of energy and therefore requires a great need of measures and regulations. Sustainable development leads to social change and creates new ideas and consumption habits, including a new ecological, social and economical use of materials.

Ecological aims

- reduce the primary raw material consumption
- use of renewable resources
- reduction of emission
- protection of natural spaces
- reduction of area occupation

Social aims

- social compatibility
- reduction of contaminant emission, pollution, noise
- heat, moisture, noise insulation and fire protection
- comfort, living space climate

Economical aims

- long-term sustainable, economical development
- reduction in manufacturing-, operating- and maintenance costs
- consideration of the lifetime of materials, products, buildings, etc.
- reduction of demolishing costs

Prior aims of sustainability are

- decrease of global greenhouse gas emissions
- the proportion of contaminant release does not exceed the acceptance capacity, a change is necessary
- conservation of resources
- the degradation rate of renewable energies does not exceed the regeneration rate, a change is necessary
- employment creation and retaining of existing jobs
- protection of social systems

23 Comparison of the grey energy of buildings built from different materials
24 Transformation of the environment on the earth from a wilderness to the built up planet during different periods shows the necessity of sustainable re-thinking

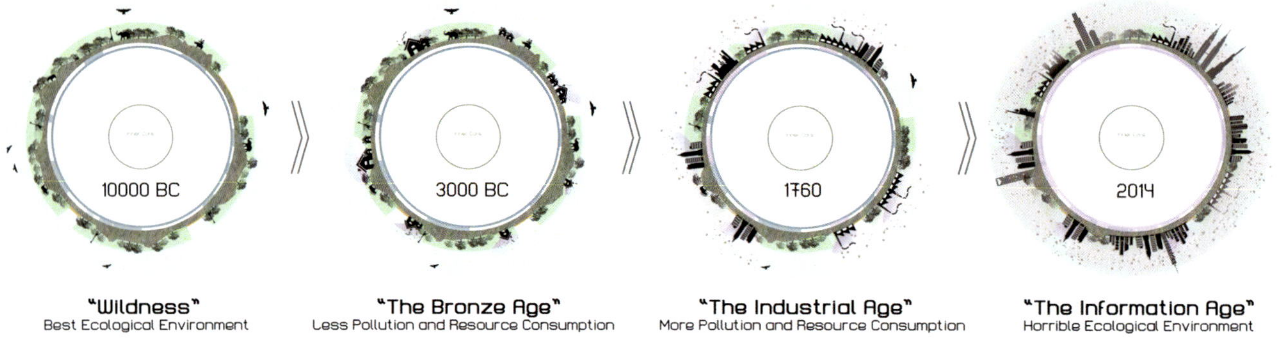

24

Grey Energy

Examples of a household with grey energy loads:

- everything that lands in the garbage pail, in particular packing material, wastes grey energy

- prior to purchasing products and devices, consider the quality, longevity and capability to repair articles, and refill or recycle products

- grey energy is considered with old, functioning equipment is replaced with new, energy-saving equipment. Energy is saved only if the new equipment uses less energy in its life span than was necessary for its production.

- each water drop from the tap is also grey energy

- the origin and season of food is crucial: exotic fruits and vegetables contain much more (grey) energy of transport or greenhouse energy than native, in-season products

- Over a ten-year span, an average vehicle also corresponds to the current consumption of a typical household

Also plants, which produce energy, need energy for production. The harvesting factor indicates how much energy is gained when compared to the life span of the plant and when the energy of production is applied.

The three fundamental phases to be considered at the beginning of an ecological design are the manufacturing phase, the utilisation phase and the disposal phase. From this the disposal expenditure can be calculated.

Building materials also contain large differences in grey energy. For example, brick production is less energy-intensive than reinforced concrete. Aluminium sheet production is twice as energy-intensive than copper. Likewise, the production of insulating materials is energy-intensive.

Hydroelectric power station	100
Wind power station	20
Heat pump	12
Solar collector for warm water generation	48
Biogas system	4
Photovoltaic system	4-21

25

25 Harvest factors of some energy systems with renewable energy, it means how much more energy the systems produce in comparison to the energy they require for their production
26 Elements of sustainable development
27 Sustainable development model

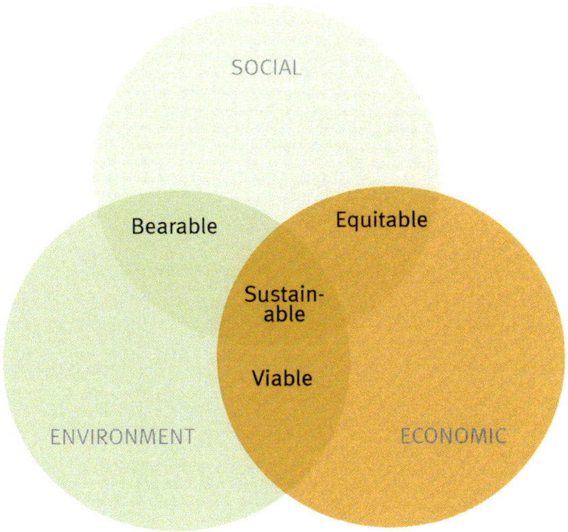

26

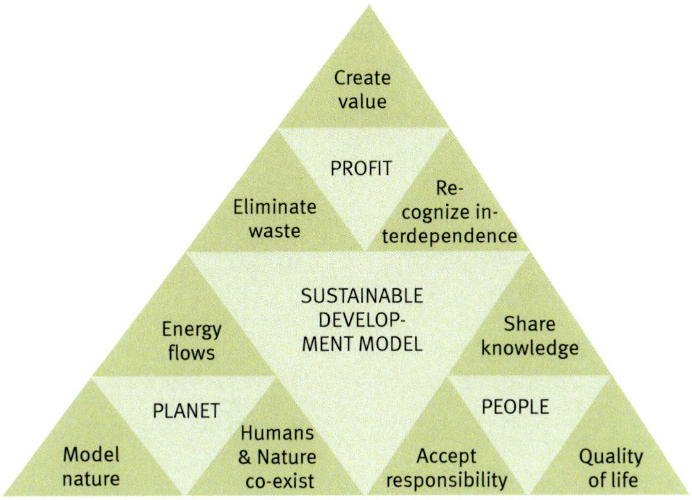

27

1.2 World Green Building Council

28

1.2.1 Introduction

"The World Green Building Council (WorldGBC) is a global member network of Green Building Councils enabling green building and sustainable communities through leadership and market transformation.

WorldGBC aims to make all building and communities sustainable, enabling us to live within the limits the planet can support. Its goal is to strengthen green building councils in member countries by championing their leadership and connecting them to a network of knowledge, inspiration and practical support.

Green building councils are member-based organisations that empower industry leaders to effect the transformation of the local building industry toward sustainability. With one hundred thousand buildings and almost one billion square metres of green building space registered, the influence and impact of this global network is a significant force for social and environmental change.

WorldGBC fosters and supports new and emerging Green Building Councils by providing them with the tools and strategies to establish strong organisations and leadership positions in their countries. Since its establishment in 2002, it has been working closely with councils to promote local green building actions and address global issues such as climate change.

By driving collaboration and increasing the profile of the green building market, WorldGBC works with its member councils to ensure that green buildings are a part of any comprehensive strategy to deliver carbon emission reductions. (...)

History

Since 1998, national Council representatives have met to review global activities and offer support for each other's efforts. This led to the founding meeting of the WorldGBC in November of 1999 in California, USA with 8 countries in attendance:

- U.S. GBC
- GBC of Australia
- Spain GBC
- United Kingdom GBC
- Japan GBC
- United Arab Emirates
- Russia
- Canada

Formal incorporation of the World Green Building Council (WorldGBC) followed in 2002 – its primary role being to formalise international communications, help industry leaders access emerging markets, and provide an international voice for green building initiatives.

In early 2007, national Council leaders identified the urgent need to establish a Secretariat for the WorldGBC that could directly respond to the growing industry interest in green buildings and communities from an international perspective." [3]

[3] *World Green Building Council;* The introduction of GBC

28 Logo of WorldGBC

Five Regional Networks of WorldGBC

Nowadays, there are five regional networks of WorldGBC:

- Africa
- Americas
- Asia Pacific
- Europe, Middle
- Middle East, North Africa (MENA)

The Africa Regional Network

Established: South Africa
Prospective: Ghana, Kenya, Mauritius, Namibia, Nigeria, Tanzania, Zambia

The Americas Regional Network

Established: Argentina, Brazil, Canada, Colombia, Peru, USA
Emerging: Costa Rica, Guatemala, Mexico, Panama
Prospective: Bolivia, Dominican Republic, Ecuador, El Salvador, Nicaragua, Paraguay, Trinidad and Tobago, Uruguay

The Asia Pacific Regional Network

Established: Australia, Hong Kong, India, Japan, Malaysia, New Zealand, Singapore, Taiwan
Emerging: Indonesia, Kazakhstan, Korea, Philippines
Prospective: Pakistan, Sri Lanka, Vietnam

The Europe Regional Network

Established: Austria, Croatia, Dutch, France, Germany, Poland, Spain, Sweden, Turkey, United Kingdom
Emerging: Bulgaria, Finland, Hungary, Ireland, Italy, Switzerland
Prospective: Czech Republic, Georgia, Greece, Latvia, Macedonia, Montenegro, Slovakia, Slovenia

MENA Regional Network

Established: United Arab Emirates, Jordan
Emerging: Lebanon, Qatar
Prospective: Bahrain, Egypt, Kuwait, Oman, Palestine

29 The map of WorldGBC

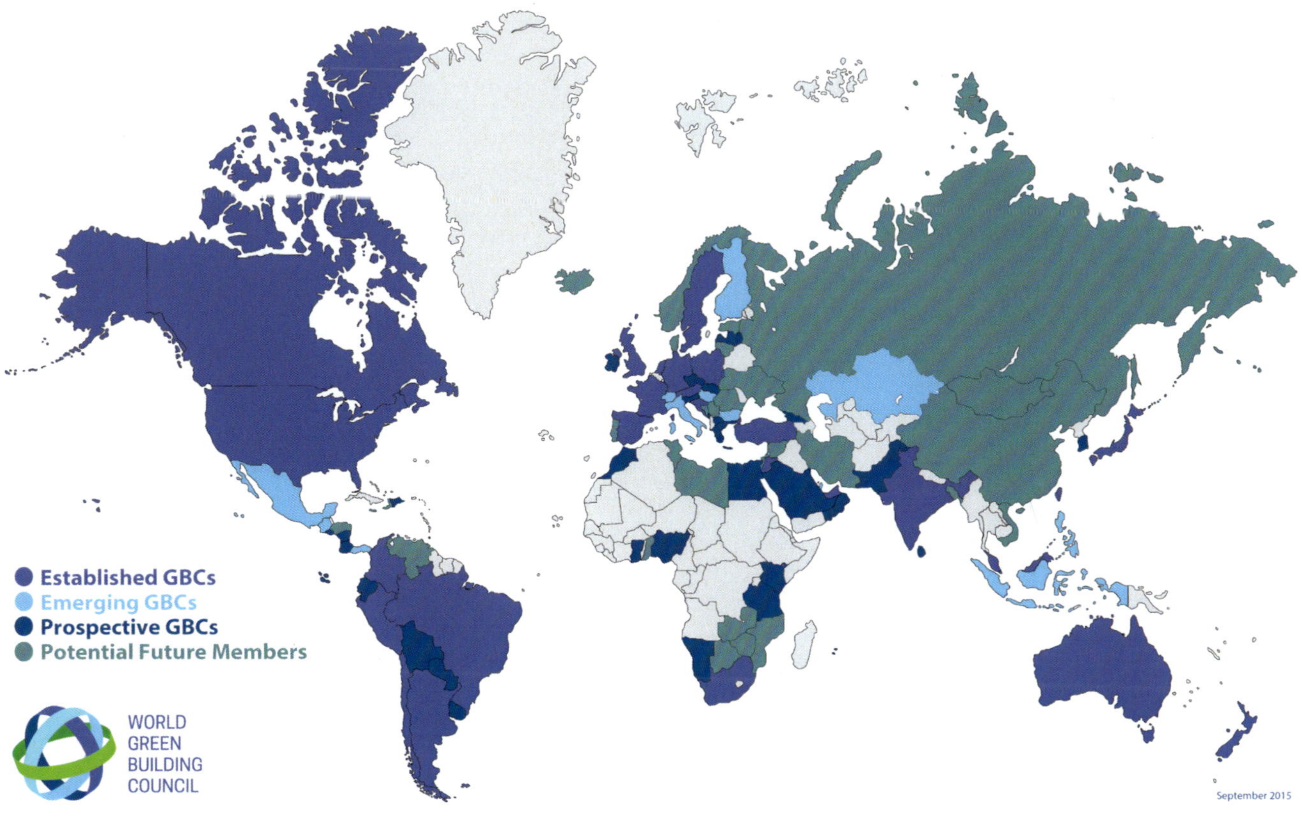

29

1.2 World Green Building Council

1.2.2 BREEAM®

Building Research Establishment Environmental Assessment Method United Kingdom, Netherlands

"BREEAM® is the world's foremost environmental assessment method and rating system for buildings, with 200,000 buildings with certified BREEAM® assessment ratings and over a million registered for assessment since it was first launched in 1990.

BREEAM® sets the standard for best practice in sustainable building design, construction and operation and has become one of the most comprehensive and widely recognised measures of a building's environmental performance.

A BREEAM® assessment uses recognised measures of performance, which are set against established benchmarks, to evaluate a building's specification, design, construction and use. The measures used represent a broad range of categories and criteria from energy to ecology." [4]

There are 8 environmental categories that are to be considered:

- Management
- Health and Well-being
- Energy
- Transport
- Water
- Land Use and Site Ecology
- Materials
- Waste and Pollution

"BREEAM® evaluates buildings according to set criteria and then concludes by providing an overall assessment score.

Anything that could have an impact on the environment at all levels of its construction and life cycle is featured in the criteria, from the building's carbon emissions and energy efficiency to its recycling facilities and location – for example a Brownfield site construction will be awarded more points than a Greenfield one.

The final BREEAM® assessment will rate a building as falling within one of the four rating bands:

- Pass
- Good
- Very good
- Excellent " [5]

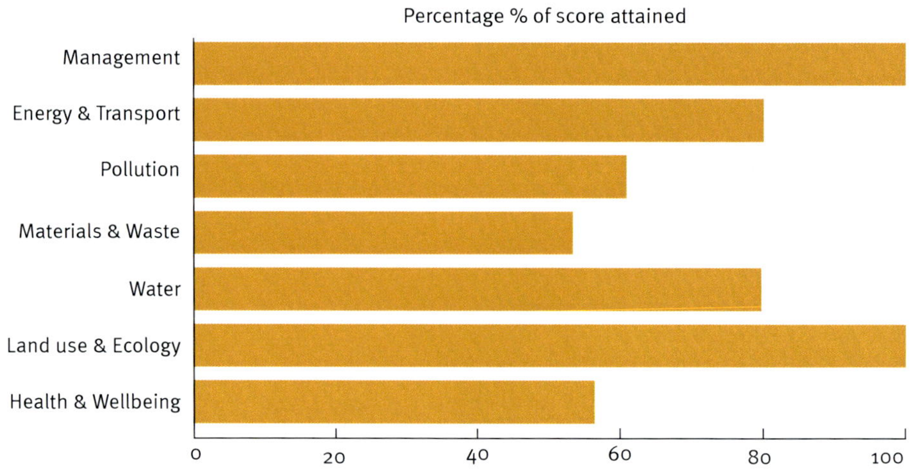

30

30 Evaluation of MH Building, University of Aberdeen, Bennetts architects

Example: BREEAM® Bespoke Award Winner: Matthew Hay Building, University of Aberdeen, Aberdeen

"Overview of environmental features:

- A highly efficient facade system
- U-values and air permeability beyond the minimum requirements of building regulations
- Exposed, reinforced concrete frame
- Natural daylighting
- Local controls for heating and lighting
- Building Management System (BMS)
- Day and night lighting modes
- Monitoring of all plant items and energy consumption
- Mixed mode ventilation strategy
- Majority of spaces being naturally ventilated
- Low carbon technologies and passive renewables
- Heating source with low NOx emissions
- Green Guide-rated materials
- All insulants to be specified with low Ozone Depleting Potential (ODP) and Global Warming Potential (GWP)
- Encourage use of public transport
- All BREEAM® construction site impacts considered and achieved
- Low water consumption fittings
- Rainwater harvesting system" [6]

[4] *BREEAM®*; What is BREEAM®? [http://www.breeam.org/about.jsp?id=66] (30.07.2012)

[5] *BREEAM®*; Evaluation with BREEAM® [http://www.qed-energy.com/breeam.html] (30.07.2012)

[6] *BREEAM®*; BREEAM® 2008 Award Winners [http://www.breeam.org/filelibrary/BREEAM%20Awards/BREEAM_Awards_2008_PRESS.pdf] (30.07.2012)

The current occupancy profiles are:

- “New office and administrative buildings
- Modernisation of office and administrative buildings
- Existing office and administration buildings
- Complete renovation of office and administration buildings
- New retail buildings
- New industrial buildings
- New educational facilities
- New residential buildings
- New hotels
- New urban district
- New business districts
- New industrial locations
- Certification of master plans for new retail buildings, new industrial buildings, new educational buildings, new residential buildings and new hotels
- Mixed occupancy: Due to the strong interest in the certification of mixed-occupancy buildings, DGNB has expanded its portfolio. Effective immediately, structures used for two or more purposes can receive a certificate. At present occupancy profiles are available for the following:
- Office and administration buildings (new)
- Retail buildings (new)
- Residential buildings (new)
- Hotels (new)” [11]

“Auditors

Auditors accompany the owners during the certification process. To be officially recognised as DGNB auditors, they must participate in a multi-day training course by the DGNB or, by educational institutions that have been accredited by the DGNB such as Universities or Chambers. The modularly structured curriculum consists of an introduction to sustainable construction; it also conveys the relevant contents for the implementation of the certification system.” [12]

Goals of the DGNB Partner Network

The primary focus is the international comparability of projects and application of the DGNB system in various countries. Also, the further development towards a European and global certification system.

The DGNB system has already been adapted for a number of different markets. Quality assurance during the adaptation and certification process is guaranteed by the DGNB with the participation of an internationally assembled committee, the DGNB International Board.

There are two existing certification systems in Germany:

BNB – Bewertungssystem Nachhaltiges Bauen (Rating System for Sustainable Building)

Promoted through BMVBS – Bundesministerium für Verkehr, Bau und Stadtentwicklung (Federal Ministry of Transport, Building and Urban Affair)

More information as well as checklists can be found under: **https://www.bnb-nachhaltigesbauen.de/**

DGNB – Deutsches Gütesiegel Nachhaltiges Bauen (The DGNB German Sustainable Building Certificate)

Promoted through DGNB – Deutsche Gesellschaft für Nachhaltiges Bauen (GeSBC – German Sustainable Building council)

41 The path to certification
42 Development of the DGNB (BNB) certification system

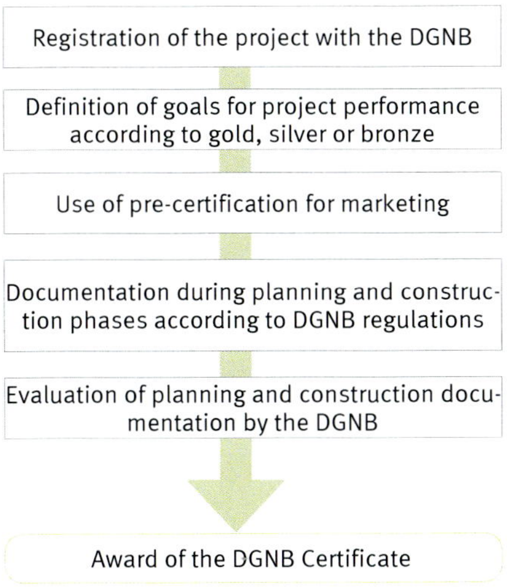

41

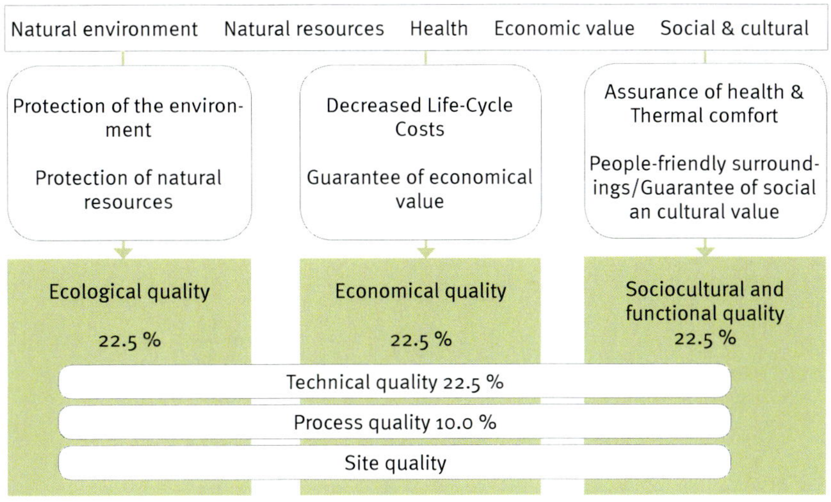

42

1.0 Strategies and regulations

1.3 DGNB

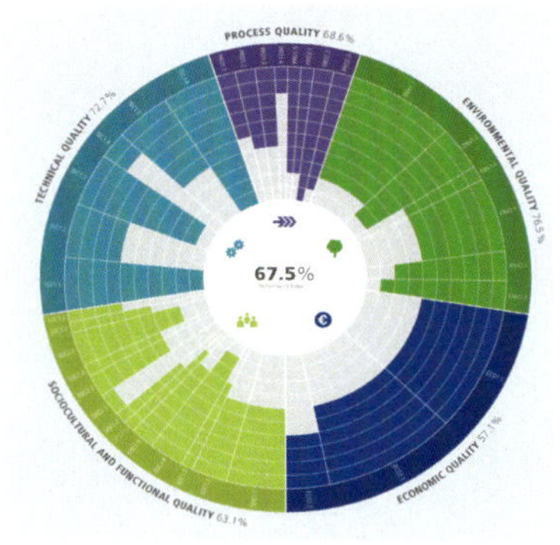

43

[13] *DGNB;* German sustainable building certificate. Structure – Application – Criteria. Stuttgart: DGNB 03/2009, page 9

[14] *DGNB;* German sustainable building certificate. Structure – Application – Criteria. Stuttgart: DGNB 03/2009, page 10

43 A Software-generated evaluation diagram – evaluation in gold
44 Stages of certification – gold, silver and bronze (DGNB and BNB)
45 AIDA company headquarters in Rostock, Germany, awarded with DGNB Gold Certificate
46 Criteria of sustainability for office building (DGNB, BNB), Version 2011

Assessment and classification

Six main topics are considered:

- Ecological quality (22.5 %)
- Economical quality (22.5 %)
- Socio-cultural and functional quality (22.5 %)
- Technical quality (22.5 %)
- Process quality (10.0 %)
- Quality of the location (0.0 %)

"The topics are weighted differently in the overall assessment of the project, depending on their relevance.

E.g., for the certificate "New Construction Office and Administration, Version 2008", both the economical and the ecological quality have the same weighting (22.5 % each). The quality of the location is not included in the final grade but is presented separately.

Conclusive individual criteria

Each topic is divided into several criterion. For instance, the energy consumption, acoustical quality, or land consumption are considered for building evaluation.

For each criterion, measurable target values are defined, and a maximum of 10 points can be assigned. The measuring methods for each criterion are clearly defined.

Detailed weighting

In addition, each criterion has a weighting factor: it can flow threefold into the evaluation of its respective topic. This way, for instance, the energy consumption of an office building is of more importance than the acoustical comfort. The weighting factor can also be zero, depending on the project, such as a motorway bridge that does not require the criteria for indoor air quality.

Clear presentation of results

Each criteria flows into the overall result in a clearly differentiated way. A software-supported computation displays the building's performance: by reaching a defined degree of performance, it is assigned the bronze, silver, or gold award. Grades are given for the total performance." [13]

"Evaluation

From a total degree of compliance of

- 50 %, the silver certificate is awarded
- 65 % for gold
- 80 % for platinum

Alternatively, the total degree of compliance is indicated by a grade:

- 95 % corresponds to grade 1.0
- 80 % corresponds to 1.5
- 65 % corresponds to 2.0" [14]

Total-Performance Index	Minimum Performance Index	Awards	
from 35 %	— %	Bronze*	DGNB
from 50 %	35 %	Silver	DGNB
from 65 %	50 %	Gold	DGNB
from 80 %	65 %	Platinum	DGNB

*This award is valid only for existing buildings

44

45

Ecological quality		22.50 %
Impaction on the global environment		
01	Global Warming Potential (GWP)	3.375 %
02	Ozone Depletion Potential (ODP)	1.125 %
03	Photochemical Oxon Creation Potential (POCP)	1.125 %
04	Acidification Potential (AP)	1.125 %
05	Eutrophication Potential (EP)	1.125 %
06	Risks to the local environment	3.375 %
08	Sustainable use of resources	
	Other impacts on the local environment	1.125 %
09	Microclimate	
Use of resource		
10	Primary Energy need not-renewable (PEnre)	3.375 %
11	Total Primary Energy need and proportion of Primary Energy renewable (PEre)	2.250 %
12	Other uses of nonrenewable resources	
13	Waste by category	
14	Potable water consumption and sewage generation	2.250 %
15	Surface area usage	2.250 %

Economical quality		22.50 %
Life cycle costs		
16	Building-related life cycle cost	13.500 %
Development of recycling		
17	Value stability	9.000 %

Socio-cultural and functional quality		22.50 %
Socio-cultural and functional quality Health, comfort and user satisfaction		
18	Thermal comfort in the winter	1.607 %
19	Thermal comfort in the summer	2.411 %
20	Indoor air hygiene	2.411 %
21	Acoustical comfort	0.804 %
22	Visual comfort	2.411 %
23	Influences by users	1.607 %
24	Quality of outdoor space	0.804 %
25	Safety and risks of failure	0.804 %
Functionality		
26	Barrier free accessibility	1.607 %
27	Area efficiency	0.804 %
28	Feasibility of conversion	1.607 %
29	Accessibility	1.607 %
30	Bicycle comfort	0.804 %
Security of design quality		
31	Planning competition	2.411 %
32	Art within architecture	0.804 %
	Quality features of use profile	
	Social integration	

Technical quality		22.50 %
Quality of technical design		
33	Fire protection	
34	Noise protection	5.625 %
35	Energetic and moisture proofing quality of the building's shell	5.625 %
36	Building services' backup ability	
37	Building services' ease of use	
38	Building services' equipment quality	
39	Durability	
40	Ease of cleaning and maintenance	5.625 %
41	Resistance to hail, storms, and flooding	
42	Ease of dismantling and recycling	5.625 %

Process quality		10.00 %
Planning quality		
43	Quality of the project's preparation	1.429 %
44	Integral planning	1.429 %
45	Optimization and complexity of planning	1.429 %
46	Announcement and awarding	0.952 %
47	Creation of conditions for optimal use and management	0.952 %
Quality of building design		
48	Construction site, construction phase	0.952 %
49	Quality of companies involved /prequalification	
50	Quality assurance of the construction activities	1.429 %
51	Systematic commissioning	1.429 %
52	Controlling	
53	Management	
54	Systematic inspection, maintenance, and servicing	
55	Qualification of operating personnel	

Site features		0.00 %
Site features		
56	Risks at the micro location	
57	Circumstances at the micro location	
58	Image and state of site and neighbourhood	
59	Connection to transportation	
60	Vicinity to usage-specific facilities	
61	Adjoining media, infrastructure development	
	Legal situation for planning	
	Extension options / reserves	

1.3 DGNB

1.3.2 Example: Student´s DGNB case study of a new office construction in Wismar, Germany

Students studying the subject "Green building" at Hochschule Wismar worked together to find the DGNB evaluation for this case study building.
It is an office building built in 2007. The entire construction is of concrete and a portion with an external wood cladding. Heat insulation is gained from the use of polystyrene and fibre insulation.
Heating and warm water are supplied by earth gas boilers. The heating is distributed via floor heating and has no controlled ventilation system. The building uses no renewable energies for operation.

Evaluation

1.3.2.1 Ecological quality

Impact on the global environment

01 Global warming potential (GWP)

Definition GWP: Shortwave UV radiation enters the atmosphere and is transformed into a shortwave infrared radiation. This is absorbed by greenhouse gases in the atmosphere and reflected which causes higher heat.
The goal is to reduce the global warming potential by evaluating the greenhouse potential of the construction, operation and structure disposal over a period of 50 years. The measurement for GWP (carbon footprint) is presented with kg CO_2-Equiv./m^2_{NFA}a.

GWP is one of the LCA results (page 15, 72) which the students calculated for all life cycles of building with Legep software (page 278). The same calculation was used for criteria 01-05, however they can also be calculated with the help of Ökobau.dat (page 243, 261). The EnEV calculation (page 274-275) is required to evaluate the energy in use.

02 Ozone Depletion Potential (ODP)

Definition ODP: The Ozone layer is produced at high altitudes where short-wave ultraviolet sun rays hit oxygen molecules. The Ozone absorbs the short-wave UV radiation and then disperses in all directions as long-wave lengths. Emissions made by man are depleting the ozone layer which is one of the elements causing the warming of the earth .
The goal is to reduce pollutant emissions that contribute to the destruction of the ozone layer. The measurement for ODP is presented with kg R_{11}-Equiv./m^2_{NFA}a.

03 Photochemical Ozone Creation Potential (POCP)

Definition POCP: Although the ozone that is within the stratosphere has a protective function, the ground-level ozone contains a highly reactive and harmful gas. The photochemical ozone near the Earth (troposphere) is also known as summer smog which damages vegetation and materials.

The higher concentrations of gas within the ozone layer are toxic for humans. Together, solar radiation, nitrogen oxides and hydrocarbons can form complex and aggressive chemical reactions. However, nitrogen oxides alone cause no increase to the concentration of the ozone because the main reaction product is the ozone itself.

The goal is to reduce the photochemical ozone creation potential i.e the mass based equivalent of destructive trace gases incl. nitric oxide and hydrocarbons. The measurement for POCP is kg C_2H_4-Equiv./m^2_{NFA}a.

47 criteria of the ecological balance in the life cycle and their evaluation, calculated with Legep software
48 Evaluation of GWP and its development in 50 years for different life cycles

construction
corrective maintenance
heating system
lighting
cooling
maintenance

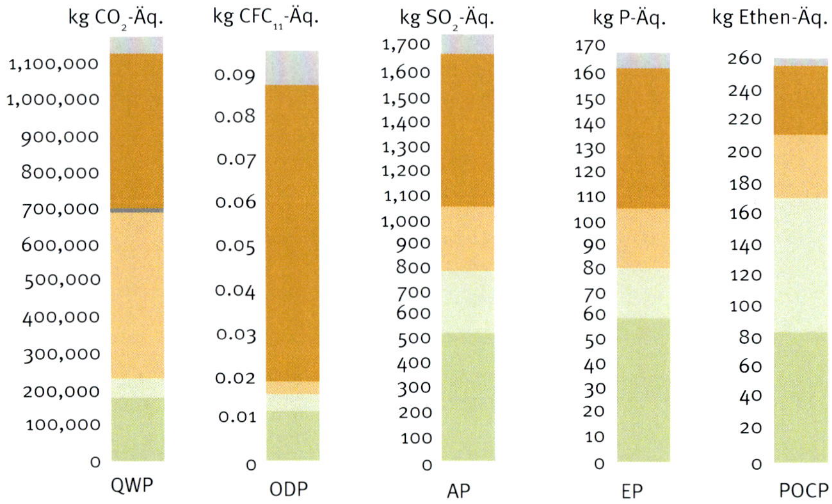

47

04 Acidification Potential (AP)

Definition AP: The transformation of air pollutants such as sulphur dioxide and nitrogen oxides in acids (H_2SO_4 and HNO_3 here) cause the acidification of soil and water. Ecosystems, and in particular our forests are therefore damaged. The damage is done, directly or indirectly by absorbing nutrients or by increased solubility of metals within the soil.
Buildings and building materials are also subject to damage. This is through the corrosion of metals and natural stones. Acidification means the rising in concentration of H-ions in the air, water and soil.

The goal is to reduce the Acidification Potential. The measurement for AP is kg SO_2-Equiv./m^2_{NFA}a.

05 Eutrophication Potential (EP)

Definition EP: EP is the 'over' enrichment of nutrients in a particular location. Nutrients found within water and the ground are distinguished differently. This over-enrichment contributes to air pollutants, sewage and fertilizer in agriculture.
Eutrophication describes the transition of water bodies and soil from a nutrient-poor to a nutrient-rich (eutrophic) state.

The goal is to reduce Eutrophication. The measurement for EP is presented with kg PO_4-Equiv./m^2_{NFA}a.

06 Risks to the local environment

The goal is to reduce or avoid the use of materials, mixtures or articles (products), which have properties and concentration that can cause harm during the construction process or by weather. Treats include potential risk to the surrounding air, soil and groundwater.

Material and substance groups with associated potential risks are to be checked individually and product-related.

The determination of the product-related information can be made with help of the GISCODE (page 286), verified declarations such as EPD (page 286), and the material database GESTIS (BGIA), as well as industry-specific regulations (i.e. RAL, VdL-Richtline) or industry-owned certification (i.e. EmiCoce).

The following material groups are to be considered:

- halogenated and partially halogenated refrigerants and propellants
- heavy metals
- materials and products, which belong to Biocide directive
- materials and mixtures which can have sensitizing, human toxic or environmentally hazardous properties
- organic solvents
- release of hazardous materials

49 Schematic of GWP
50 Schematic of ODP
51 Schematic of POCP
52 Schematic of AP
53 Schematic of EP

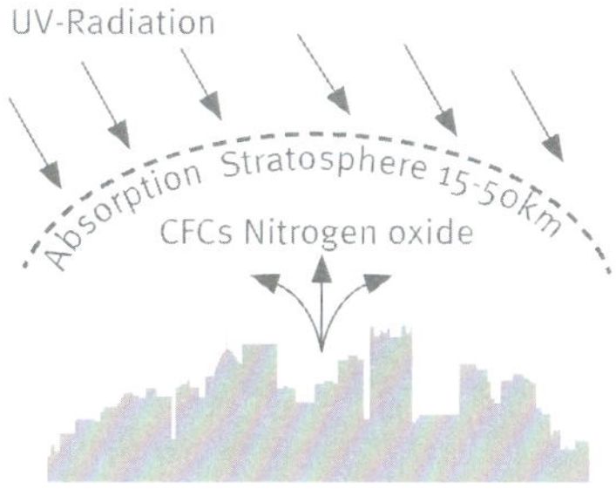

49

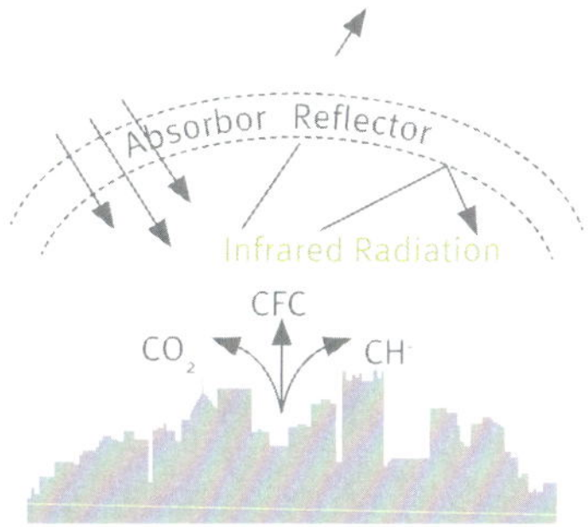

50

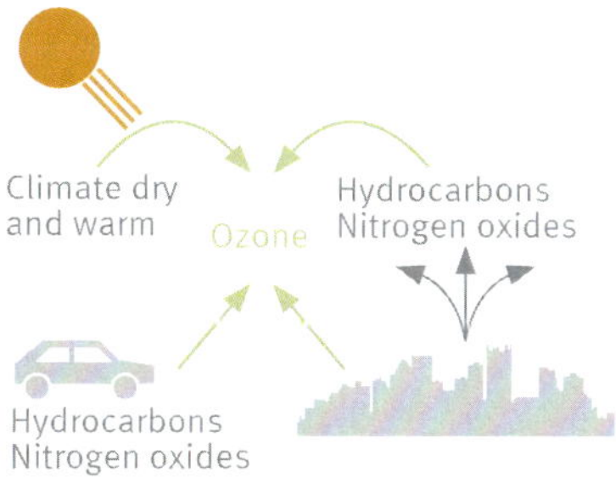

51

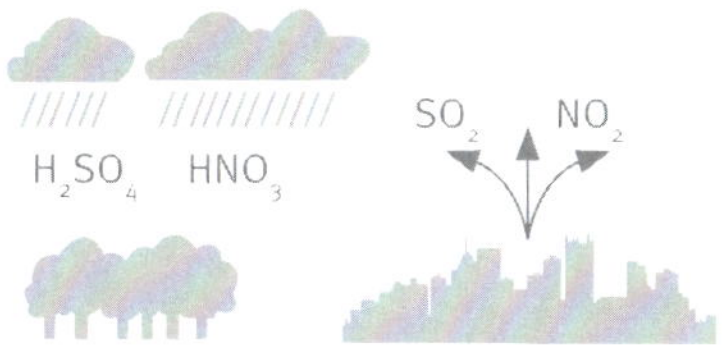

52

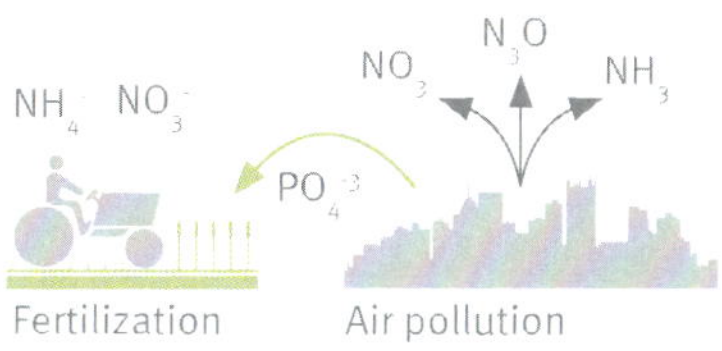

53

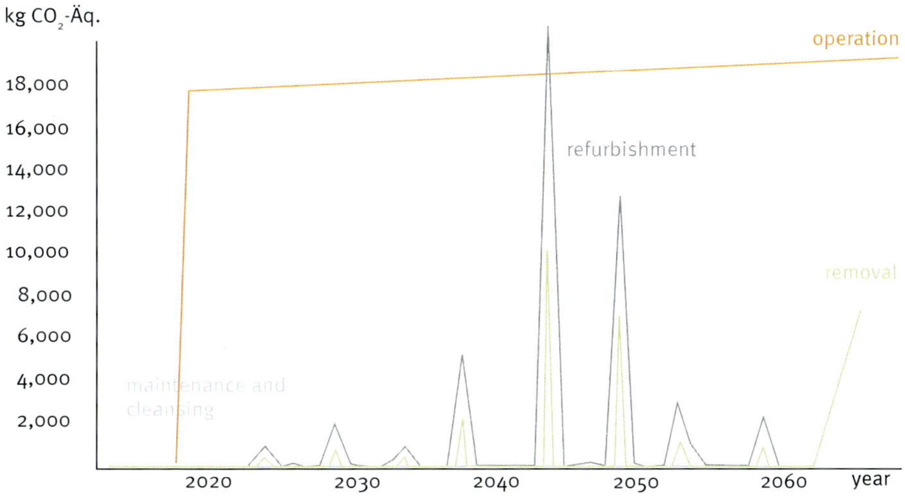

48

1.3 DGNB

In the evaluation, there are 4 defined action levels that support each other. To acquire a higher action level, the successful implementation of all prior level requirements must be obtained.

Each action-level contains a list of materials and products that should be avoided, and the more that these can be achieved, the lower the risks are for the local environment.

Due to lack of information regarding material processing in the case study building, action level 1 was chosen for evaluation.

- Quality Level 1 (limit point 1)

Documentation of the following materials and products:

- thermal insulation and the main insulating materials for building equipment
- products for surface coating of walls, floors, ceilings or roofs which contain polyurethane, epoxy resin or bitumen
- coatings, waterproofing, glue or preservatives for assignment to surfaces including walls, floors, ceilings or roofs which contain polyurethane, epoxy resin, bitumen

08 Other impacts on the local environment

The proof and use of certified woods, particularly the subtropical and boreal woods, are only allowed to be used if the supplier can certify the controlled and sustainable cultivation of the forest origin.
In the evaluation, there are 3 defined action levels that support each other. Due to limited information regarding the wood used in the case study building, the evaluation was unable to achieve higher than quality level 1.

- Quality level 1 (limit point 1)

consists of following conditions:

- The design and tender documents contain a reference in order to prevent the use of non certified tropical, subtropical and boreal woods.
- The proof of the certificates for FSC (Forest Stewardship council)/ PEFC (Programme for the Endorsement of Forest Certification Schematics) are not required at this stage.
- For all tropical wood products and/or wood-based materials of Boreal or from a subtropical origin, the FSC certification and an associated CoC certificate is required.

54 Evaluation of the first part – ecological quality
55 Percentage flow of energy and material mass during the life cycle

Ecological quality					**22.500 %**
Criteria	**Building evaluation**	**Energy supply evaluation**	**Evaluation total**	**Score**	**Importance**
Impact on the global environment					
01 GWP [kg CO_2-Equiv./m²NGF.a]	9.41	39.67	49.08	10 %	3.375 %
02 ODP [kg R_{11}-Equiv./m²NGF.a]	0.00000062	0.00000329	0.00000391	20 %	1.125 %
03 POCP [kg C_2H_4-Equiv./m²NGF.a]	0.00711	0.00380	0.01091	10 %	1.125 %
04 AP [kg SO_2-Equiv./m²NGFa]	0.033	0.041	0.074	40 %	1.125 %
05 EP [kg PO_4-Equiv./m²NGFa]	0.00337	0.00371	0.00708	40 %	1.125 %
06 Risks to the local environment	-	-	Quality level 1	10 %	3.375 %
08 Other impacts on the local environment	-	-	Quality level 1	10 %	1.125 %
Use of resource					
10 PEnre [kWh /m²NGF.a]	162.19	668.06	830.25	0 %	3.375 %
11 PEtotal [kWh /m²NGF.a] PEre [%]	193.06	712.5	905.56 8.30%	0 % 20 %	2.250 %
14 Potable water consumption and sewage generation [m³]	-	-	204 m³	10 %	2.250 %
15 Surface area usage	-	-	10 checklistpoints	10 %	2.250 %
Final score - building can not be evaluated, because it did not reach minimum for bronze rate – 50 %				**15 %**	**3.375 %**

Use of resource

[10] Primary energy need nonrenewable (PE_{nre})

The primary energy need (page 13) considers the non renewable primary energy used over the whole building life cycle from construction and building use until the end of life. The aim is to reduce the total of all non renewable primary energy claims.

The results of criteria 10 and 11 are required for LCA calculations. Students used the Legep software to calculate for a 50 year period. The measurement is in $kWh/m^2_{NFA}a$. The programme Ökobau.dat can also be used as an alternative.

[11] Total primary energy need and proportion of primary energy renewable

The goal is to minimize the total primary energy need and to raise the level of renewable energies (page 13). The measurement is in $kWh/m^2_{NFA}a$ and level of PE_{re} is in %. The goal is to reach a level of where the PE_{re} is at least 20 % of the total PE.

[14] Potable water consumption and sewage generation

Potable water (page 128) is extremely valuable. The goal is to reduce potable water consumption and sewage generation. There are different passive (page 128) or active (page 202) ways to achieve this. For example, the influence of user behaviour and the use of grey-water and rainwater should be integrated into the building during the planning process. The calculation of potable water consumption and sewage generation must be done (page 262).
The measurement of potable water usage is in m^3/a. The lower the consumption, the better the evaluation results.

There are 3 components to consider:

- potable water consumption and sewage generation created by the use of toilets, sinks, showers and kitchens
- potable water consumption and sewage generation created by cleaning (floors, glass surfaces, sanitary)
- rain water that does not percolate but flows into the sewage is considered as sewage generation

[15] Surface area usage

The goal is to reduce land use and to stop building on unbuilt landscapes. A good evaluation is obtained when land recycling (brownfields redevelopment) and the reuse of destroyed industry or army lands are used.

To compensate for developed land use, the use of green roofs should be considered. The free forest, meadow or agricultural areas should not be used at all.

Conclusions

The case study building is ecologically inefficient and could not be evaluated by the DGNB certification, receiving very few points in total.

The production of the building materials used generated high levels of emissions and used large amounts of nonrenewable energy.

The operational energy uses no renewable energy resources, only limited fuels such as earth gas which produce a high level of emissions.

The best solution would be to ecologically improve the building, to reduce emissions and nonrenewable energy, and to use other natural construction materials. Also, the use of renewable energy for operational energy use , e.g. energy from the sun and earth, would improve the LCA results.

In addition, there are no water recycling measures in the building. An improvement could include the use of rainwater for toilet splashing, so that it would not flow to the drainage but instead, would be used in the building.

Lastly, the building was built on a site which had not yet been built on before. In terms of surface area, this means that it is also very inefficient. It may have been better to build on a site that had already been built on before.

construction
operation of building
maintenance and renewal

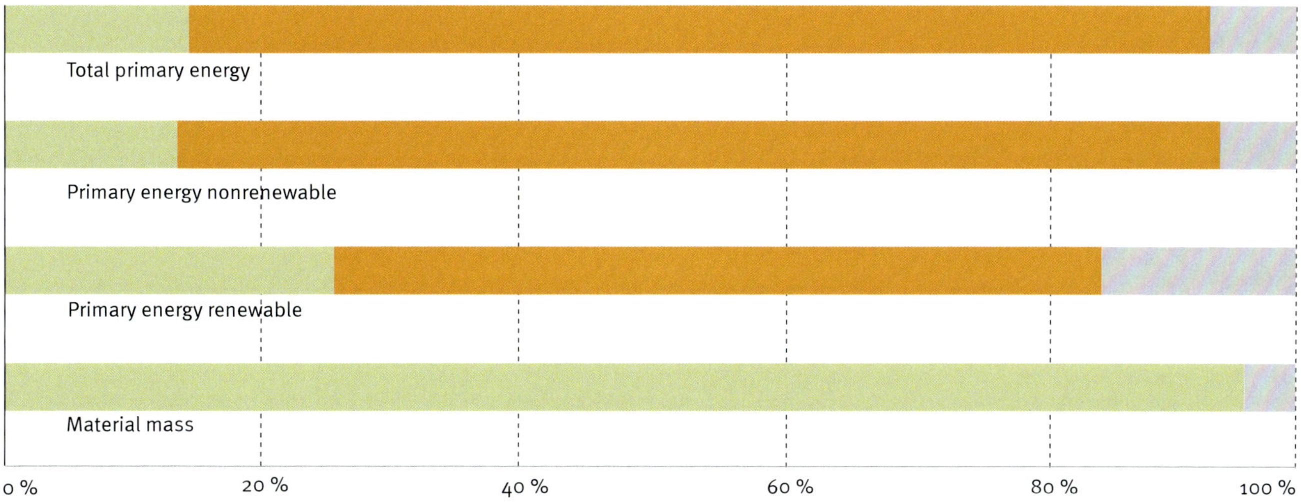

55

1.3 DGNB

Conclusion

The building achieved full point from life cycle costs, so from this point of view is building economical and well designed.

The comparison of expenses of the building process and the maintenance of the building show that the price of the initial ante is almost the same like the price for the usage. If there is more invested into a solar system or better materials for the building´s isolation, the initial price would be higher but chosen operational costs and chosen reconstruction costs would decrease. The initial investment can be higher if the money is used for technology that saves operational and maintenance expenses by the usage of the building.

The building is also not very difficult to accommodate on substantial change of purpose. It got 6 points what is over reference asset requirement. The better evaluation could be reached by reduction of poor usable areas (less space for circulation), by use of non-structural cellular elements that effectively share space and by use a BUS system – all building is controlled from one place/computer.

The building would get gold evaluation in the economical quality of DGNB certification.

1.3.2.2 Economical quality

Life cycle costs

16 Building-related life cycle costs

For the calculation of the life cycle costs, the LCC analysis should be used (page 15, 264). The analysis helps to design buildings economically because it considers the entire building life cycle and not only initial investment. It shows on going costs for the different solutions designed and chosen at the beginning of a buildings life.

Building-related life-cycle costs are determined at net present value over a period of 50 years and measured in €/$m^2{}_{GFA}$a.

Development of recycling

17 Value stability

This criterion considers the high efficiency, flexibility and changeability of a building (page 110). The building should be able to react to changing conditions, which not only change the comfort standard, but also the owner, function or internal arrangement.

The evaluation is made via check-lists divided into 3 groups:

- area efficiency (see criterion 27) – max.30 % of the evaluation
- conversion feasibility (see criterion 28) – 50 % of the result from criterion 28
- possibility to be reconfigured for other types of use – e.g., if the water supply is arranged as such that the possibility to retrofit for other types of use gains max. 20 % of the evaluation

56

Economical quality					22.500%
Criteria	**Building evaluation**	**Energy supply evaluation**	**Evaluation total**	**Score**	**Importance**
Life cycle costs					
16 LCC [€/m²BGF.a]	1,436.67	334.69	1,771.36	100 %	13.500 %
Development of recycling					
17 Value stability	-	-	60 checklistpoints	60 %	9.000 %
Final score - evaluation in gold, because of overreaching the minimum requirements for gold rate of 80%				**84 %**	**18.900 %**

57

Category according to DIN EN 15251	Heated building (offices and similar used rooms)
I	21-23 °C
II	20-24 °C
III	19-25 °C

58

Category according to DIN EN 15251	Heated and cooled building (offices and similar used rooms)	Building without heating and cooling
I	23.5-25.5 °C	$Ø_i = 0.33\ Ø_{RM} + 18.8 \pm 2$
II	23-26 °C	$Ø_i = 0.33\ Ø_{RM} + 18.8 \pm 3$
III	22-27 °C	$Ø_i = 0.33\ Ø_{RM} + 18.8 \pm 4$

59

1.3.2.3 Socio-cultural and functional quality

Health, comfort and user satisfaction

18 Thermal comfort in the winter

Building thermal comfort is important for the satisfactory of the user, and in-particular how the energy demand is generated.

A thermal simulation is important to make during the planning process in order to avoid an uncomfortable building interior.

The criterion is divided into sub-criterions which are evaluated by the following checklists:

- operating temperature
- draught – should be avoided – it depends on the air speed and ventilation system within the building
- radiant temperature asymmetry and floor temperature – describes the temperature of the surfaces including the ceiling that should not be higher than 35 °C, the floor not higher than 29 °C, glass surfaces and walls should not be less than 18 °C and not higher than 35 °C
- relative air humidity – describes the comfort through pleasant humidity in the rooms
- vertical temperature gradient – describes the temperature difference in the vertical (e.g. between the feet and head)

19 Thermal comfort in the summer

The evaluation is similar to criterion 18 and also divided into:

- operating temperature
- draught
- radiant temperature asymmetry and floor temperature – where the temperature of the ceiling should not be less than 16 °C, the floor should not be less than 19 °C, glass surfaces and walls should not be less than 18 °C, but not higher than 35 °C
- relative air humidity
- vertical temperature gradient

20 Indoor air hygiene

The goal is to improve the quality of the indoor air hygiene within and around the building and its structures, especially as this will affect the health and comfort of the building occupants. This is found within particulates, microbial contaminants or other substances that can induce adverse health conditions. Source control can be found via filtration, the use of ventilation to dilute contaminants, air samples, monitoring human exposure to pollutants, collection of samples on building surfaces and computer modelling of the internal airflow.

The evaluation is divided into:

- volatile organic compounds (VOC)

The evaluation of VOC and formaldehyde concentration can be found within the building can be found up until 4 weeks after construction. They are emitted as gases from certain solids or liquids and their concentration depends on the emissions within the building materials used. VOCs include a variety of chemicals, some of which may have short- and long-term health effects.

- perceived air quality
- microbiological situation
- personal-related ventilation rate

With the appropriate design of operable windows and/or mechanical ventilation systems, the required ventilation rate can be achieved.

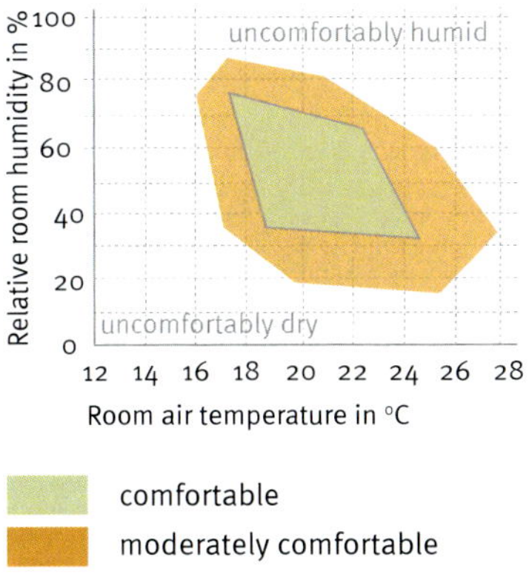

60

56 Life cycle costs for 50 years of the building's life
57 Evaluation of the second part – economical quality
58 Categories of operating temperature in winter in office buildings
59 Categories of operating temperature in summer in office buildings
60 Comfort zone in building depending on humidity and temperature
61 Quality of the indoor air in dependance on CO2 concentration
62 Evaluation table of VOC and formaldehyde concentration in the air of rooms

Indoor air category	Description	Absolute CO_2 concentration in the indoor air [ppm]
IDA 1	High room quality	< 800
IDA 2	Middle room quality	800 - 1,000
IDA 3	Moderate room quality	1.000 - 1,400
IDA 4	Low room quality	> 1,400

61

	Air concentration in the rooms		Checklistpoints
	VOC [µg/m³]	Formaldehyde [µg/m³]	
1	< 500	< 60	50
2	< 1000	< 60	25
3	< 3000	< 120	10
4	> 3000	> 120	0

62

1.3 DGNB

[21] Acoustical comfort

The goal is to have a suitable indoor acoustical quality which depends on the room function. For example, in an office building, a high level of clear conversation and a low level of noise is important. In large open offices it is important to minimize sound travel between working areas.
The evaluation is based on the reverberation time T [s] in the empty rooms and it is divided into room types:

- individual offices
- shared offices
- meeting rooms
- canteens

[22] Visual comfort

The visual comfort in a job forms the basis for efficient and performance enhancing work. In addition, creating good natural daylighting can save the energy need for artificial lighting and cooling. Lighting that is constantly required in all interiors must be sufficient and uninterrupted.
Visual comfort is achieved by balancing the lighting with minimal disruption from direct or reflected glare, a sufficient level of illumination, and individual adjustment to ones respective needs.
The requirements generally apply to daylight and artificial lighting, where the assessment of the dynamics of daylight illumination and change in the light conditions play a major role.

For the evaluation, daylight simulations must be done. The evaluation of visual comfort is made via checklists divided into:

- daylight availability for the total building

The evaluation is based on the daylight factor DF, which is defined as the ratio of illumination at one point on a given interior plane to the outdoor illumination level, excluding direct sunlight. The goal is to achieve daylighting for the entire net surface area.

- daylight availability for permanent working place

The annual relative daylight supply factor for standard office use times is determined according to DIN V 18599 Part 4.

The daylight supply factor represents the daylight provision on the use of time and gives a good indication about the daylighting indoors depending on the building design, the location, the facade and the solution sunscreen or anti-glare systems.

- view to the outside

The clear view to the outside is important and should not be limited by the activation of anti-glare or the sun protection.

- glare-free daylight

63 Evaluation table of daylight factor DF – partial criterion of visual comfort
64 Evaluation table of annual relative daylight supply factor – partial criterion of visual comfort
65 Daylight examination of the case study building

	50 % of the UFA has a DF	Evaluation	Checklist-points
1	> 2 %	very well	16
2	> 1.5 %	medium	12
3	> 1 %	low	8
4	< 1 %	no	0

63

	Annual relative daylight supply factor	Evaluation	Checklist-points
1	> 80 %	very well	14
2	60 - 80 %	medium	10
3	45 - 60 %	low	7
4	< 45 %	no	0

64

65

In order to avoid glare within the working place, an anti-glare device should be considered.

- glare-free artificial light
- light distribution of artificial light

A combined direct-indirect lighting is preferable to pure direct lighting. A higher acceptance rate is also achieved with an additional lamp on a single working space. A combination of lighting and individual lighting also has the advantage of flexibility in switching work.

- colour rendering

The colour reproduction in daylight and artificial light conditions have an impact on the perception and acceptance of users.
Both artificial light sources as well as sun protection, anti-glare and daylighting systems can vary greatly in colour reproduction and the resulting colour spectrum of daylight.
By applicable rules and regulations for colour reproduction in artificial light, constantly used rooms should have a colour rendering index of at least R_a 80. An improvement is accordingly positively evaluated.

The final evaluation is a sum of the points gained from all checklists.

23 Influence by users

The aim is to maximize the influence of the user on areas including ventilation, solar shading, glare, and outside temperatures during the heating season, and the management of natural and artificial light at work.
For assessing the influence of users, a checklist was developed that maps different criteria and end results in a final grade.

As part of the checklist, the following criteria are evaluated:

- ventilation
- sunscreen
- antiglare
- temperatures during the winter
- temperatures during the summer
- daylight and artificial light
- user control friendliness

24 Quality of outdoor space

Lounges serve the common good and encourage user uptake. The integration of the building-related external surfaces in the overall design of the building and its environment promotes the development of a three-dimensional urban environment. By harnessing this area may contribute to the reduction of CO_2 emissions and improve the microclimate.
In addition to planning the creative integration of useful areas in patios, courtyards and open spaces, roofs and facades (i. e. balconies) can also be used by design for the public good. The possibilities in outdoor areas for people and the public to be seated is desired. The sustainable use of land resources considers the high quality development of open space in the foreground to enhance the amenity value to the users.

The evaluation is based on the checklist.

66 Evaluation of the third part – socio-cultural and functional quality

Socio-cultural and functional quality			**22.500 %**
Criteria	**Evaluation total**	**Score**	**Importance**
Health, comfort and user satisfaction			
18 Thermal comfort in the winter	65 checklistpoints	65 %	1.607 %
19 Thermal comfort in the summer	35 checklistpoints	35 %	2.411 %
20 Indoor air hygiene	50 checklistpoints	50 %	2.411 %
21 Acoustical comfort	10 checklistpoints	10 %	0.804 %
22 Visual comfort	36 checklistpointS	36 %	2.411 %
23 Influences by users	50 checklistpoints	50%	1.607 %
24 Quality of outdoor space	50 checklistpoints	50 %	0.804 %
25 Safety and risks of failure	14.5 checklistpoints	14.5 %	0.804 %
Functionality			
26 Barrier free accessibility	0 checklistpoints	0 %	1.607 %
27 Area efficiency F_{eff}	F_{eff} = 0.73	90 %	0.804 %
28 Feasibility of conversion	68 checklistpoints	68 %	1.607 %
29 Accessibility	0 checklistpoints	0 %	1.607 %
30 Bicycle comfort	100 checklistpoints	100 %	0.804 %
Security of design quality			
31 Planning competition	10 checklistpoints	10 %	2.411 %
32 Art within architecture	0 checklistpoints	0 %	0.804 %
Final score - the building can not be evaluated, it did not reach the minimum points to receive a bronze rating of 50 %		**36.55 %**	**8.220 %**

66

1.3 DGNB

25 Safety and risk of failure

Aims are to ensure that the users feel safe, and that the environment is safe and easy to direct in the case of an emergency. The evaluation is based on checklists divided into:

- a subjective feeling of safety and protection from abuse

including a clear layout, visibility and direction, illumination, accessible parking spaces with short routes for women, technical safety devices, ...

- damage extent reduction in the case of an emergency situation

including evacuation plans, materials containing substances (such as halogens) that lead to fire and caustic or corrosive fumes should be avoided, a rapid discharge of combustion gases must be ensured, escape routes, ...

Functionality

26 Barrier free accessibility

Provides all persons (children, disabled, blind and deaf) with the opportunity to use equally, all parts of the built environment.
The evaluation is based on the checklist, where the highest value of 10 points can be gained. Ten points can only be achieved when the whole building (higher than 95 %) and the exterior spaces are barrier free.

The main entrance must be barrier free including several other special requirements such as an audio guiding system for the blind, or tactile devices.

27 Area efficiency

Area efficiency is the measure to calculate and utilize the buildings interior spaces, to optimise space usage, operating and running costs.
The higher the amount of usable area in the gross floor area, the more points the building will receive. To calculate the quotient one must divide the usable floor area by the gross floor area (page 17).

28 Feasibility of conversion

Describes how flexible and adaptable a building structure can be, and if it is possible to change the building function. A conversion should be made only when the additional resource consumption and effort is low.

The evaluation checklist:

- building modularity

The height of each room should be no less than 2.75 m.

- spatial structure

The flexibility of rooms elements and technology.

- provision of electricity and media
- provision and disposal of heating and water

67 Visual comfort provided by passive lighting systems in Science and graduate school of health building designed by Durbach Block Jaggers in Sidney, 6 stars in Green Star
68 Influence by users – relationship with the street art
69 Bicycle comfort depends on the building function, e.g. for school building, large area is required
70 Checklistpoints for the partial criteria of bicycle comfort – number of bicycle parking spaces

67

68

29 Accessibility

The aim is that a building should be open to the environment and the society containing various spaces for public use. Public accessibility improves the acceptance and integration of a building. The more that the buildings parts and exterior spaces are accessible to the public, the better the evaluation result.

The evaluation checklist:

- public accessibility of a building
- open outside public spaces
- internal facilities open to the public, e.g. coffee shops, library, ...
- rental opportunities for building spaces
- internal spaces providing variety of use

30 Bicycle comfort

Bicycle comfort contributes to an environmentally and energy-efficient mobility.

The evaluation checklist:

- number of bicycle parking spaces(based on usable floor area)
- realization of the qualitative aspects, e.g. distance of bike spaces to the entry, weather protection, conformity of service offer to the function of building, changing rooms for users, ...

Security of design quality

31 Planning competition

Aim is to ensure high quality of design and urban planning through competition. An organised and judged competition as a planning tool is used to find the best solution for the architectural and structural design tasks.

Evaluation method is to identify whether a planning competition was carried out, and if so, to what extent and quality. If not, than alternatively, buildings can be recognized for their high artistic quality. It is evaluated with the help of a checklist.

32 Art within architecture

Buildings are constantly in the publics eye, therefore art plays an important role to enhance the peoples experiences. The federal benefits are awarded to visual artists to place their art within buildings provided the purpose and significance of the structure warrant it. For office and administrative buildings, this is usually the case. Private developers should evaluate the opportunity for art within their buildings in the same way.
The evaluation confirms the art within the architecture, if there was a competition, if the artists were promoted, and what percentage of building costs were spent on the art. The "Guidance of art within architecture" from BMVBS must be considered.

Conclusion

The case study building was unable to be certified because it does not receive enough points in the socio-cultural and functional qualities. A low acoustical quality had resulted due to high sound reflection of the concrete walls and ceilings – this could be improved by placing acoustical panels as wall and ceiling linings.
The visual comfort was insufficient due to large openings situated in the spaces where daylighting was not needed. These should have been located near the office areas, where natural daylighting was required. In addition, the building has no shading for sun and glare.

There are no measurements for safety and risks of failure, and the building is not barrier free. The building is not accessible for the public and has no art within the architecture. It wasn't designed as part of a competition.

The criterion stated above require improvements to gain higher points in order to make the building more sustainable from a socio-cultural and functional point of view.

Two criterion that were acceptable included the area efficiency and bicycle comfort.

69

Description	Checklist-points
Less than 1 space per 200 m^2	10
1 space per 200 m^2	30
1 space per 140 m^2	40
1 space per 80 m^2	50

70

1.3 DGNB

1.3.2.4 Technical quality

Quality of technical design

33 Fire protection

The occurrence of fire should be expected at virtually any time. Prevention is to prevent the occurrence, spread and smoke of fire. Furthermore, to ensure that fire-fighting operations can be performed to rescue endangered persons and animals. Office buildings require a special fire protection system.

For the assessment of fire protection, a checklist has been developed. Minimum requirements follow the standard fire safety requirements however additional fire protection measures will increase the criterion rating.

The following facts are validated, if they go beyond the national technical capacity required:

- avoidance of the incorporation of materials/products that when exposed to fire develop toxic fumes, or a faster spread of fire
- implementation of an increased fire resistance rating
- realization of enlarged cross sections for smoke extraction
- achievement of smaller fire/ smoke sections
- installation of automatic fire/ smoke detectors or others
- installation of an automatic fire extinguishing system (e.g. sprinkler system), automatic fire/smoke doors and other alarm systems

34 Noise protection

Noise protection in the working spaces is important to serve the pleasant working atmosphere. Minimum acoustical requirements for components to foreign workspaces are defined in DIN 4109.

Recommendations for higher noise protection to foreign workspaces and recommendations for normal and higher noise protection for sound transmission from work areas in office buildings are found in supplement 2 DIN 4109.

Evaluation checklist:

- airborne sound insulation against external noise
- airborne sound insulation against foreign work spaces and private work areas (partitions, partition ceilings, staircase walls)
- step sound insulation against foreign premises and own workspaces (partition ceilings, stairs,...)
- soundproofing against building services (plumbing system, other building services)

35 Energetic and moisture proofing quality of the buildings shell

The goal is to minimize the heat demand for space conditioning, while ensuring a high thermal comfort and avoidance of structural damage. To evaluate the criterion, different input variables are required. Basic requirements are in accordance with the Energy Conservation Ordinance, the DIN 4108 and DIN EN 12207.

For certification, the following values are evaluated within the checklists:

- component related average heat transfer coefficient U [W/m²K]

71 Evaluation table of average heat transfer coefficient as partial criteria from technical quality
72 Evaluation table of thermal bridge surcharge as partial criteria from technical quality

	Component	Maximum values of the heat transfer coefficient U based on the average value (by considering of all components)		
		Limit	Partial target	Target
1	Opaque exterior components, not included in the components of the lines 3 and 4	U=0.35 W/m²K	0.28	0.20
2	Transparent outer parts, not included in parts of lines 3 and 4	U=1.90 W/m²K	1.50	1.30
3	Curtain wall	U=1.90 W/m²K	1.50	1.40
4	Glass roofs, skylights, domes	U=3.10 W/m²K	2.60	2.20
Checklist items		**15**	**20**	**30**

71

	Limit / Reference value	Partial target	Target
Thermal bridge surcharge ΔU_{wb} in W/m²K	0.10	≤ 0.05	≤ 0.01
Checklist items	**2**	**8**	**15**

72

- thermal bridge surcharge ΔU_{WB} [W/m²K]
- class of air permeability
- constr. condensation m [kg/m²]
- air exchange n_{50} [h^{-1}] and possibly q_{50} [m/h]
- sun entry parameter S [-]

40 Cleaning and maintenance ease

Cleaning and maintenance friendliness has a high impact on the environmental and cost components of a building during the use phase. Structures exposed to optimal maintenance receive the maximum possible life span. Surfaces that can be cleaned easily require low cost cleaning agents and overall low cost cleaning. The expenses for cleaning and maintenance should be minimal during operation.

Maintenance comprises of inspection and repair. Inspection is a measure designed to identify and assess the actual state of the technical means of a system. Maintenance is a measure for the preservation of the target state of a system. Repairs are measures to restore the desired state.

Cleaning: removing impurities using auxiliary media, e.g. water purification with additional air additives. In the "Sustainable Building Guide", clamping ranges for the applicable stage of life at LCC and LCA analyses of components and component layers are added. Cleaning and maintenance are parameters that significantly affect the service life of components and component layers.For the evaluation checklists, the building is divided into the following three types of components:

- supporting structure
- non-load-bearing exterior structure including windows/exterior doors
- non-load-bearing interior construction

42 Ease of dismantling and recycling

The target aim of dismantling and recycling is the prevention of waste, in particular by reducing their amount and harmful properties. The easier the building can be broken down into components, the higher the evaluation for "deconstruction". The higher the quality of the individual building elements and their recyclable properties, the higher the evaluation points. The higher the result of both properties, the better the performance of the criterion in terms of sustainable construction.

The checklist divides the building into four sections to assess the properties of:

- technology
- nonconstructive components
- non-structural building structure
- supporting building structure

For each area, the following issues are examined and assessed:

- effort required to dismantle and disassemble into 5 steps
- effort required to separate the disassembled parts into 5 steps
- is there an adoptable recycling/disposal concept that addresses the future life of the components of the design?

73 Evaluation of air exchange rate as partial criteria from technical quality
74 Evaluation of the forth part – technical quality

	Limit	Reference value / Partial target	Target
Buildings with an internal volumes ≤ 1500 m³			
Air change rate n_{50} in h^{-1}, without controlled ventilation	3.0	1.5	1.0
Air change rate n_{50} in h^{-1}, with controlled ventilation	1.5	1.0	0.8
Additionally for buildings with an internal volume > 1500m³			
Air permeability q_{50}	3.0	2.5	2.0
Checklist items	**2**	**8**	**15**

73

Technical quality			**22.500 %**
Criteria	**Evaluation total**	**Score**	**Importance**
Quality of technical design			
33 Fire protection	-	-	-
34 Noise protection	100 checklistpoints	100 %	7.500 %
35 Energetic and moisture proofing quality of the building's shell	40 checklistpoints	40 %	7.500 %
40 Ease of cleaning and maintenance	50 checklistpoints	50 %	7.500 %
42 Ease of dismantling and recycling	-	-	-
Final evaluation - evaluation in bronze		**63.00 %**	**14.250 %**

74

1.3 DGNB

1.3.2.5 Process quality

Planning quality

43 Quality of the project's preparation

The tasks for optimal project preparation which should be made prior to project planning are described here. Evaluation is made via checklists divided into 4 main parts:

- requirement planning

Describes the needs from building owner and building users.

- goal agreement

Fixes concrete planning goals.

- architectural competition

Ensures project quality.

- influence on the user-related energy requirements

Considers the users behaviour and related equipment use because it is an important part of the power demand of a building.

44 Integral planning

The integral planning team, together with the building owner, develop a complex and sustainable strategy in order to minimize the energy demand and loads on the environment and to maximize the comfort and economy through high-quality planning.
The evaluation is based on checklists divided into:

- integral planning team

Consists of at least three professionals of different disciplines and one coordinator.

- qualification of planning team

All planners in the team should be members of an architecture or engineering chamber whom continue to encourage further educations in sustainability.

- integral planning process

The certification criterion should be integrated in all planning and construction processes.

- user participation
- public participation

45 Optimization and complexity of planning

Evaluation is through checklists divided into:

- SiGe (safety and health) plan

Considers the safety and health protection plan which must be prepared and followed on the building site.

- energy concept

Focuses on the use of alternative energy generation systems and renewable resources.

- water concept

The goal is to minimize potable water use and to support the use of grey water, rainwater and rainwater infiltration.

- optimization of day and artificial light

The goal is to optimise the daylight use based on daylight simulation.

- waste concept

The goal is to avoid, minimize or re-use waste and to save resources.

- monitoring concept

Is the monitoring process of technical equipment for 2 years after construction in order to optimise further building operation.

- concept for reconstruction, deconstruction and recycling
- concept for cleaning and maintenance ease

To support the reduction of life cycle costs during the buildings operation.

75 Integral planning and participation in practise – designing and building of a lecture class "clima design" during summer school in park Lingezegen, Holland

75

- planning documentation proving via an independent third party

To ensure the planning quality.

- implementation of alternatives

The best planning can be made only by proofing different alternatives.

46 Announcement and awarding

The evaluation is based on checklists divided into:

- integration of sustainable aspects in the announcement

The goal is to ensure that chosen materials and products fulfil sustainable criteria.

- integration of sustainable aspects found within the chosen companies

47 Creation of conditions for optimal use and management

The evaluation is based on checklists divided into:

- creation of object documentation/building passport
- creation of maintenance, refurbishment and the operation manual

The documentation should ensure efficient building operation and the reduction of life cycle costs.

- adaptation of building planning documentation and finished building calculations
- creation of user handbook

The users find here important information to building use.

Quality of building design

48 Construction site, construction phase

Sustainable building endeavours, in all phases of the life cycle of buildings, to minimize the consumption of energy and resources. The building site and building processes are particularly important as it is during these phases that the main effects impact the environment.
The goal is to minimize the impacts on the environment while protecting the health of all concerned.
The assessment of the site and building processes occur via checklists including the following criteria:

- low waste construction site

The planning and execution shall comply with the requirements of the Recycling and Waste Management Act. The aim is to conserve natural resources and to prevent waste including waste material which is to be separated.

- low noise construction

Any construction site should be planned, set up and operated so that noise may be prevented. The noise is to be measured throughout the building phase.

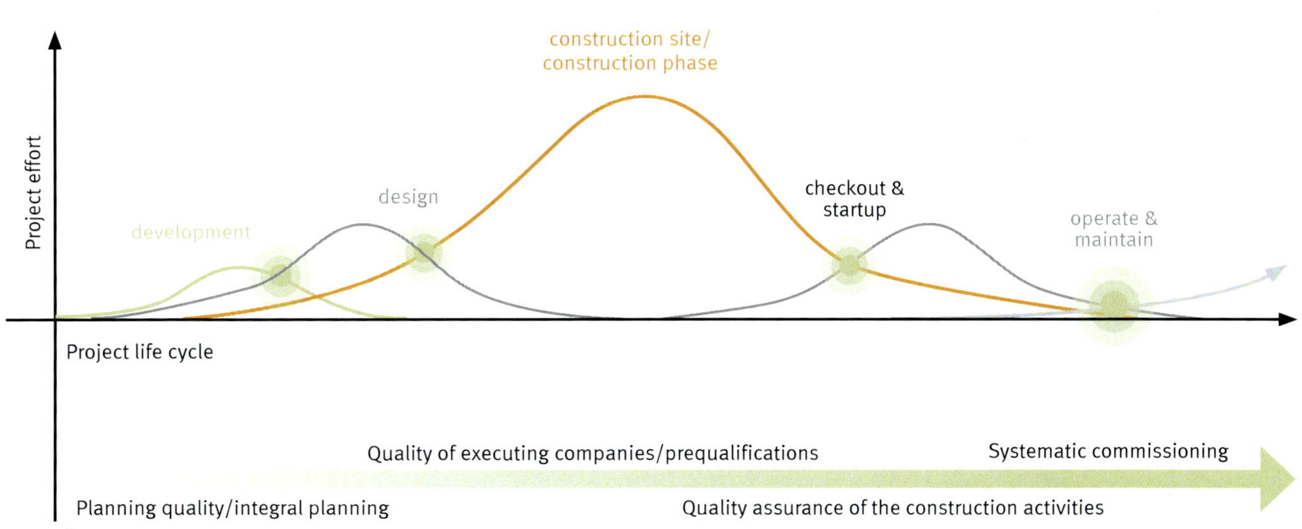

76 Importance of the process quality (planning and construction process) in the building life time, because during this stage the future of the building is determined

1.3 DGNB

- low dust construction site

The prevention of dust on site contributes to the protection of workers, and to other persons involved. Machines and instruments should have effective dust-proof equipment with wet or sucking processes to eliminate dust.

- environmental protection on the construction site (soil protection)

The soil and groundwater must be protected from harmful material inputs, chemical uncleanliness and mechanical damage.

49 Quality of companies involved/prequalification

Construction companies should be pre-qualified in writing for public, private, and other contracts to verify their credibility, professionalism as well as the actual production capacity.

By awarding the contract to one with a PQ procedure "certified" construction company, this prevents the client from potential risks, such as insolvency of a participating company.

The evaluation is based on the checklist which describes the qualification of the companies involved.

50 Quality assurance of construction activities

The aim of building a detailed documentation is to restore market transparency, to deliver a unified information base and to improve the quality of presentation.

The evaluation of the documentation is based on checklists including the following criteria:

- documentation of materials, auxiliary materials and the material safety data sheets

A documentation of the used/built-in materials during construction is important to the following life-cycle phases.
The safety data documents contain the nature of the product, possible hazards, safe operation and preventative measures as well as measures to respond to hazardous situations.

- quality control measurements

The quality of construction can be documented and evaluated through various measurement techniques. Examples of required measurements: Proof of the building tightness (Blower door measurements), Thermographic method (thermal imagery), sound protection measurement, ...

51 Systematic commissioning

The systematic commissioning make an important contribution to the optimization of the technical equipment functions.
The evaluation is based on checklists which evaluate the systematic commissioning with the optimization of operation and its documentation.

1.3.2.6 Site features

Site features

56 Risks at the micro-location
57 Circumstances at the micro-location
58 Image and state of site and neighbourhood
59 Connection to transportation
60 Vicinity to usage-specific facilities
61 Adjoining media, infrastructure development

Final evaluation

The overall evaluation shows, that the building could not be certified with DGNB systems because it does not fulfil sustainable requirements in ecological quality, sociocultural, functional and process quality.

Possible ways to improve the ecological quality would be to chose more sustainable materials for the building construction, and to consider renewable resources for the buildings operation.

Greywater or rainwater reuse could also be considered.
To improve the sociocultural and functional quality, different measurements to improve the acoustical qual-

77 Public participation on the planing and construction process is important for good process quality
78 Evaluation of the fifth part – process quality
79 Final DGNB building evaluation

77

ity, visual comfort, safety and failure of risks, art within architecture, barrier-free design and public accessibility should be considered.

To achieve certification in process quality, the evaluation and certification processing should have begun during the planning phase. There are different sustainable criterion to be fulfilled in the planning and construction phase.

On the other hand, the building received good ratings in the economical quality. The building is of a high quality in the view of the life cycle costs and the long term value stability.

The evaluation of technical quality received bronze, however these could be better optimised within building operation (as cleaning, maintenance) and the physics quality which would help to improve ratings.

Site features were not evaluated because they have no value in the overall evaluation. Nevertheless, a buildings location should be considered as it is very important in the view of sustainable planning.

Criteria Process quality	Evaluation total	Score	Importance
Planning quality			
43 Quality of the project's preparation			1.304 %
44 Integral planning			1.304 %
45 Optimization and complexity of planning			1.304 %
46 Announcement and awarding			0.870 %
47 Creation of conditions for optimal use and management			0.870 %
Quality of building design			
48 Construction site, construction phase			0.870 %
49 Quality of companies involved /prequalification			0.870 %
50 Quality assurance of the construction activities			1.304 %
51 Systematic commissioning			1.304 %

78

	Score	Maximum	Partial score	Certificate
Ecological quality	3.375 %	22.50 %	15.00 %	-
Economical quality	18.900 %	22.50 %	84.00 %	Gold
Sociocultural and functional quality	8.220 %	22.50 %	36.55 %	-
Technical quality	14.250 %	22.50 %	63.00 %	Bronze
Process quality	-	10.00 %	-	-
Site features		0.00 %		
Total	**44.745 %**	**100 %**	**-**	**-**

79

Conclusion

The certification process begins at the first stage of the building planning. It is during the planning process where there is the highest opportunity to design and improve the sustainability of a building in all life cycles, and thus it is important that the certification process accompanies the building from its earlier planning stages.

All planning and construction processes should be checked continually according to criterion in order to improve all parts of sustainability. This suggests that when a building is already finished, it is therefore impossible to evaluate, especially in regards to the "Process quality" section of the DGNB criterion.

It is not possible to evaluate process quality checklists due to a lack of information regarding the planning and construction processing when the building is already finished. It is not possible to influence the planning and construction phase and improve the processing.

It is only possible to assume that the building would not reach the DGNB certification in process quality because it was not following the sustainable advice provided in the criterion and thus presumably not built with respect to sustainability.

1.3 DGNB

80

1.3.3 DGNB – Sustainable urban districts certification (DGNB Zertifizierung nachhaltige Stadtquartiere)

The DGNB certification system was originally used only for single buildings however, recent changes now provide analysis methods to be used for urban districts. The urban districts play a central role in the sustainable development of our society.

The DGNB certification for sustainable city districts is divided into:

- Environmental quality (22.5 %)
- Economical quality (22.5 %)
- Sociocultural and functional quality (22.5 %)
- Technical quality (22.5 %)
- Process quality (10.0 %)

For the certification of urban districts, the public space and the environment must be considered. The buildings are included, however, only of basic value.

There are three certification phases:

- Planning (Pre-certification)
- Development (Certification)
- District (Certification)

Similar to the assessments for a single building, the LCA is required to certify a sustainable urban district. Included are criterion for soil and water conservation, resource-saving and efficient waste management, as well as the life quality in public spaces, the range of uses and the noise protection. There are also studies on economic characteristics such as the LCC, space efficiency and value stability.

80 Potsdamer Platz, Berlin
81 Potsdamer Platz, Berlin
82 The criterion to be considered within the DGBN Certification for sustainable new urban districts, version 2012

81

Certification requirements for sustainable urban districts:

- the minimum size of a city quarter is 2 ha of built land in total
- the urban district must be made up of several buildings and at least two building plots together including public or publicly accessible spaces and related infrastructure
- the residential area is at least 10-20 % – no more
- In all phases of the certification, the authority is responsible for ensuring that there is no contradiction against the certification, between the owners (private property) of the area.

During the pilot phase of the DGNB certification for sustainable urban districts, twelve projects participated. Two projects, the Dom Aquarée and the Potsdamer Platz in Berlin, were certified a “Silver Quarter”, and the Le Quartier Central in Dusseldorf was certified with the award of “Silver Development”.

Example: Potsdamer Platz, Berlin

Certification in silver

Owner: SEB Asset Management AG

The Potsdamer Platz district includes 17 buildings, 10 streets and two squares. The total of 550,000 square meters of gross floor area is divided by different types of use including office, administrative, retail, residential, hotel, entertainment and gastronomy. The neighbourhood receives up to 100,000 daily visitors.

As early as the first planning considerations for the Potsdamer Platz in 1991, the issue of sustainability played a major role.
Drees & Sommer were the general managers controlling the project that year with an ecological budget of approximately 3 % of the total budget. At only 3 %, specific measures were already included to implement systems such as green roofs and rainwater recovery.

Although the neighbourhood opened in 1998, to communicate the economic and environmental benefits effectively in the market, Drees & Sommer supported the client, SEB Asset Management, to complete the certification of the DGNB sustainable urban district. In 2011 Potsdamer Platz received the Silver Certificate.

The certification makes the economic, environmental and sociocultural strengths of Potsdamer Platz transparent. It shows that a well-developed district may also provide good quality for a longer period.

Overall, the planning focused on health, providing environmentally friendly building materials, minimizing energy consumption and emissions.

There was a number of measures to ensure the environmentally friendly supply and careful use of water and soil. This included rainwater optimization, e.g., to water the plants and for flushing toilets within the individual buildings.

For energy consumption, air conditioning was omitted, and replaced by the use of windows and a sophisticated ventilation and wall system creating a natural climate. The supply and waste transport is completely underground and the dehydration plant for wet waste significantly reduces waste shipments.

Environmental quality		22.50 %
Global and local environmental impact		
ENV1.1	Life cycle assessment	2.700 %
ENV1.2	Water and soil protection	1.800 %
ENV1.3	Changing urban microclimate	2.700 %
ENV1.4	Biodiversity and interlinking habitats	1.800 %
ENV1.5	Considering possible impacts on the environment	1.800 %
Resource consumption and waste generation		
ENV2.1	Land use	2.700 %
ENV2.2	Total primary energy demand and renewable primary energy share (PE_{re})	2.700 %
ENV2.3	Energy-efficient development layout	1.800 %
ENV2.4	Resource-efficient infrastructure, earthworks management	1.800 %
ENV2.5	Local food production	0.900 %
ENV2.6	Water circulation systems	1.800 %

Economical quality		22.50 %
Life cycle costs		
ECO1.1	Life cycle cost	6.800 %
ECO1.2	Fiscal effects on the municipality	4.500 %
Value development		
ECO2.1	Value stability	4.500 %
ECO2.2	Efficient land use	6.800 %

Sociocultural and functional quality		22.50 %
Social qualities		
SOC1.1	Sociocultural and functional diversity	1.800 %
SOC1.2	Social and commercial infrastructure	1.800 %
Health, comfort and user satisfaction		
SOC2.1	Objective and subjective safety	1.800 %
SOC2.2	Public space amenity value	1.800 %
SOC2.3	Noise protection and sound isolation	1.800 %
Functionality		
SOC3.1	Open spaces offer	2.700 %
SOC3.2	Inclusive accessibility	1.800 %
SOC3.3	Flexibility of use and development structure	1.800 %
Security of design quality		
SOC4.1	Urban integration	2.700 %
SOC4.2	Urban design	1.800 %
SOC4.3	Use of existing structures	1.800 %
SOC4.4	Art in public space	0.900 %

Technical quality		22.50 %
Technical infrastructure		
TEC1.1	Energy technology	2.600 %
TEC1.2	Waste management efficiency	2.600 %
TEC1.3	Rainwater management	4.000 %
TEC1.4	Information and telecomunication management	1.300 %
Technical quality		
TEC2.1	Maintenance, upkeep and cleaning	2.600 %
Transport, mobility		
TEC3.1	Quality of transport systems	4.000 %
TEC3.2	Quality of motor transport infrastructure	1.300 %
TEC3.3	Quality of public transportation	1.300 %
TEC3.4	Quality of bicycle infrastructure	1.300 %
TEC3.5	Quality of pedestrian infrastructure	1.300 %

Process quality		10.00 %
Participation		
PRO1.1	Participation	1.700 %
Planning quality		
PRO2.1	Concept development process	1.100 %
PRO2.2	Integral planning	1.700 %
PRO2.3	Municipal participation	1.100 %
Quality of the management and construction		
PRO3.1	Management	1.200 %
PRO3.2	Construction site and construction process	1.200 %
PRO3.3	Marketing	1.200 %
PRO3.4	Quality assurance and monitoring	1.200 %

1.4 Eco-city

83

Cities represent an important relationship between humans and nature. Its dependence on one another can determine whether or not the society is sustainable or unsustainable.
An unsustainable relationship cannot sustain over a long period, otherwise the society will have no future. Examples are industrial cities and urban lifestyles. They consume large quantities of fossil resources, produce high rates of waste and emissions.
The task is to create/change such cities for a sustainable future – what will they look like? Ecological urban development is an important field of study for the future.

An eco-city can be defined as an ecologically healthy city. Here are some main principals regarding an eco-city:

“An eco-city is...

- An ecologically healthy human settlement modeled on the self-sustaining resilient structure and function of natural ecosystems and living organisms.
- An entity that includes its inhabitants and their ecological impacts.
- A subsystem of the ecosystems of which it is part — of its watershed, bio-region, and ultimately, of the planet.
- A subsystem of the regional, national and world economic system.” [15]

Each city is different, so there are also different ways how to reach this goal.

However, eco-cities share some basic characteristics, as consideration of environmental impacts and minimization of required inputs of energy, water, food and waste output of heat, air or water pollution. It uses renewable local resources, creating the circular material and energy flow in itself. The renewable energy sources are e.g. wind, sun, bio-gas from sewage.

The different methods to reduce air conditioning demand, e.g. planting trees, natural ventilation systems, water features, green roofs, green spaces at least 20 % of the city´s surface. It is called climate architecture and help to avoid the “heat island effect” in cities, which is cased by building or city operation resulting in higher temperature in urban area as in surrounding rural areas.

The important topic of eco-city is transportation. The goal is to reduce the car emissions (zero-emission transport), providing good possibilities for pedestrian, bicycle or public transportation. Roads may be designed to make driving difficult. Also optimal building density can support the efficient public transportation.

The concentrated mixed-function building system should be prioritised, by allowing people to live closer to the workspace, avoiding to create suburban centres with long way to the work in the city centre.

[15] *Eco-city Builders;* Why Eco-cities? [http://www.ecocitybuilders.org/why-ecocities/] (10.10.2012)

best
very good
good
medium
bad

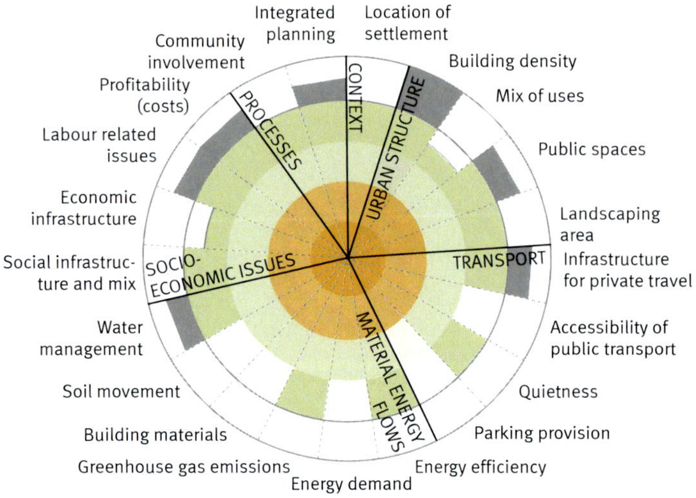

84

85

Other features are sustainable urban drainage systems, energy conservation systems, zero energy buildings, xeriscaping - garden and landscape design for water conservation, ...

Urban gardening

Urban gardening, also known as Guerilla gardening is a modern trend trying to bring different agricultural systems into cities. People can plant flowers, vegetables or fruit within public spaces in the city and within the centre or suburban areas.

The goal is to not only improve a cities microclimate but the relationship between the cities people and their food production. This reduces the distance of travel for food from the farm fields to people and improves social relationships and communities. The growing may be done within either small scale/private farming plots or through larger scale agriculture (e.g. farmers).

Urban gardening and urban agriculture are ideas that are becoming increasingly important as our world becomes more urbanized and developers transform agriculturally fertile lands and open spaces into sprawling suburbs.

Many examples of urban gardening have been developed in Germany over the past few years, in particular in Berlin.

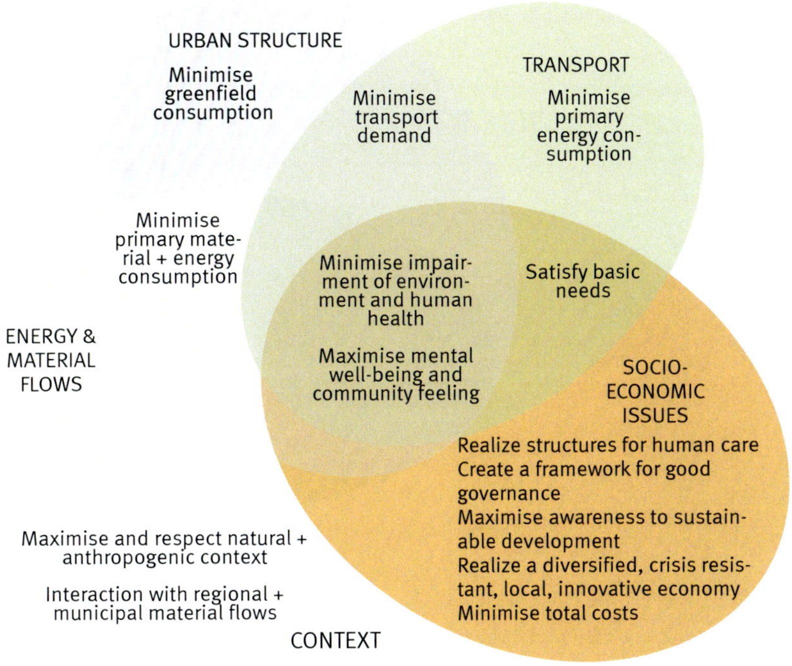

86

83 Prinzessinnengärten – urban gardening in Berlin, Germany
84 Example of energy evaluation and certification pass for an Eco-city in Thüringen
85 Example of an Ecocity project – Solar plus neighbourhood, Vauban in Freiburg, Germany (2000-2006)
86 Overall Eco-city goals according to five elements of Eco-city planning (2002-2005)
87 Principles of Eco-city – EU research and development (2002-2005)

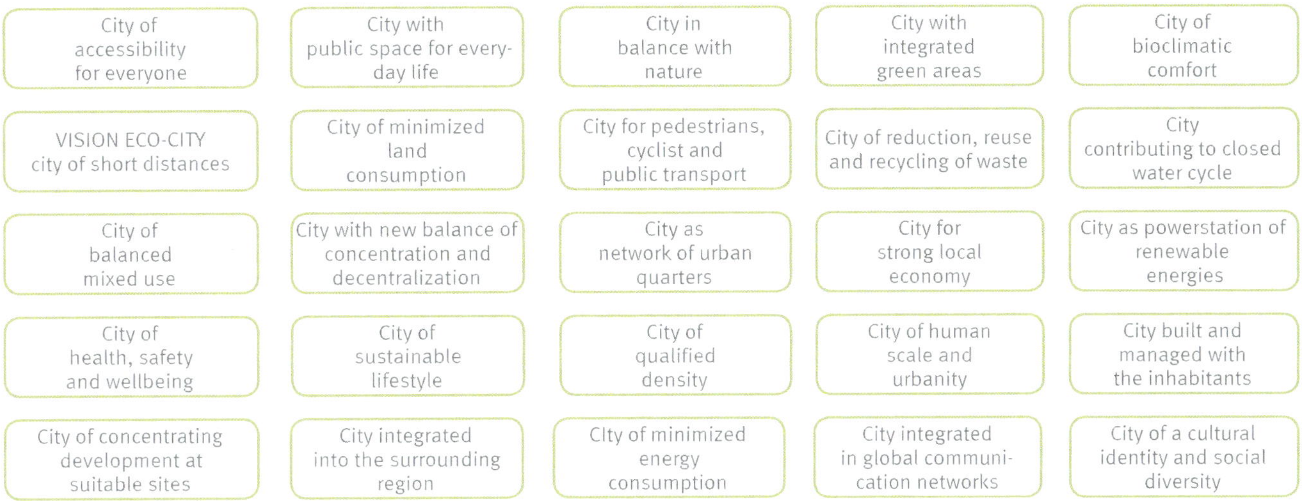

87

1.5 EnEff:Stadt

"Energy Efficiency in Communities

45 % of the global population lives in cities. In 2020, this figure will be 62 %. National and global climate protection, indisputably necessary, is therefore based on energy consumption and the resulting emissions of pollutants in our cities and conurbations. For centuries, cities have been both social and cultural centres. The development in cities has a global effect and set trends for entire generations. This also holds true for technological innovations, which are often initiated in cities. The energy savings and pollution reduction requires a significant increase in energy efficiency.

The EnEff:Stadt Research Initiative

Increasing efficiency is the focus of the "EnEff:Stadt" research initiative of the German Federal Ministry of Economics and Technology. This initiative is intended to reveal ways of increasing the energy efficiency via optimised efficient energy supply and use concepts. In doing so, it considers typical city districts and focuses on the key urban development tasks of our future – from refurbishment of historic areas via conversion of former industrial and commercial spaces to innovative supply solutions including modern storage technologies.
Pilot projects in different communities and typical city districts will provide examples and indicative findings for widespread application. The projects include innovative planning concepts, implementation of the concepts in buildings and evaluation via scientific measurements." [16]

Example: Climate-neutral campus at Leuphana University Lüneburg

"The plan is to further develop Lüneburg's university campus in the Scharnhorststrasse and Bockelsberg area in terms of both the urban development and energy use. Measures to the existing buildings, the integration of a new building as a central facility for the university and the conversion of the energy supply are being jointly examined. It is planned to convert the energy supply to renewable energy sources and, in so doing, incorporate the low-energy heating system in the new building as well as seasonal heat storage. Since the 1990s, the site has been supplied with a local heating system comprising CHP waste heat. This solution was chosen during the redevelopment of the site, which was previously used as army barracks. As part of the refurbishment of the barrack buildings, which date back to the 1930s and are used by the university, the heating system will be converted to renewable energy sources and optimised in energetic terms, whereby the planned energy-efficient new building for the university central building will be incorporated in the energy system. The corresponding concept plans to use cascaded heat and a seasonal heat storage tank." [17]

88 Project EnEff:Stadt Luckenwalde – urban redevelopment areas
89 Project EnEff:Stadt Luckenwalde – renovation plan of city centre

88

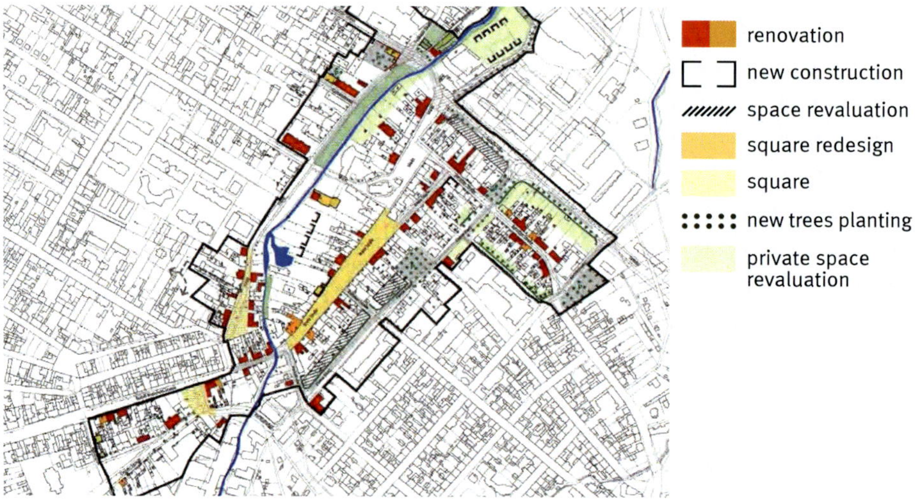

89

1.6 EnEff:Wärme

"The EnEff: Wärme Research Initiative

Local and district heating networks open up multiple energy saving opportunities. On the other hand, they are associated with complicated technology and are complex to operate. Their energy efficiency cannot be increased unless options such as industrial waste heat utilisation, cogeneration and renewable energy sources are taken into account system-wide.
Heat distribution costs can also be substantially reduced through new concepts, networks and technologies. Given this background, the BMWi's EnEff:Wärme research initiative focuses on new network concepts and the development of innovative technologies. The aim is a substantial energetic, economic and ecological improvement of heat supply.
EnEff:Wärme promotes specific network optimisation with the aim of further increasing the share of local and district heating and integrating less densely populated areas into the supply network.
This could be the future of central heat supply systems. District heating networks, so-called smart grids, are to become central building blocks in local energy management. Low-exergy technologies (LowEx) help reduce transmission losses.
Furthermore, new adaptive cooling and heating networks offer starting points for the integration of renewable energy. Thermally-driven micro cooling systems, latent heat and cold storage facilities, ORC technologies or thermally-driven heat pumps: The use of modern building technology and the development of distribution technology and system components represent important aspects of the EnEff:Wärme initiative - just like intelligent control and measuring technologies. Together, they form a fundamentally new heat supply concept." [18]

Example: Intelligent network of urban infrastructures – Smart Power Hamburg

"SMART POWER HAMBURG wants to take a new approach to energy efficiency: How can a network of real estate properties become more efficient via a combined heat and electricity generation system while also offering additional energy services to others?

This requires that the urban infrastructures in the form of energy generators, loads and storage systems are intelligently combined. In this regard, the energy forms electricity, heating, cooling and gas are being examined with the aim of integrating renewable energy sources.

The urban infrastructures and regulatory provisions provide the underlying framework. This is intended to provide a stimulus for planning cities and urban districts." [19]

[16] *EnEff:Stadt;* EnEff:Stadt. Forschung für die energieeffiziente Stadt [http://www.eneff-stadt.info/en/research-initiatives/] (10.10.2012)
[17] *EnEff:Stadt;* Pilot projects: Climate-neutral campus at Leuphana University Lüneburg [http://www.eneff-stadt.info/en/pilot-projects/project/details/climate-neutral-campus-at-leuphana-university-lueneburg/] (10.10.2012)
[18] *EnEff:Stadt;* EnEff:Stadt. Forschung für die energieeffiziente Stadt [http://www.eneff-stadt.info/en/research-initiatives/] (10.10.2012)
[19] *EnEff:Stadt;* Heating and cooling networks: Projects: Intelligent network of urban infrastructures – Smart Power Hamburg [http://www.eneff-stadt.info/en/heatingcooling-networks/project/details/intelligent-network-of-urban-infrastructures-smart-power-hamburg/] (10.10.2012)

90 Energy bunker – energy generation and storage in the quartier
91 Wind power plants situated nearby the highways, California, USA

90

91

1.7 Strategies in Europe and Germany

92

1.7.1 EU SDS - EU Strategy for Sustainable Development

"The goal of the EU strategy for sustainable development, adopted in the summer of 2001, is to improve the quality of life on earth of both present and future generations. In particular, it is intended to ensure that economic growth, environmental protection and social integration go hand in hand.
The strategy adds the environmental dimension to the Lisbon Strategy and is conceived as a supplement to the European Union's commitment to economic and social renewal. In its first step, the sustainable development strategy addressed four topics of central importance for sustainable development: climate change, transport, health and natural resources. Moreover, it contains statements on issues of global environmental protection. For the review of the strategy, the European Commission carried out a broad public consultation between August and October 2004. The new, more complete and more ambitious EU sustainable development strategy with objectives, indicators and an effective monitoring procedure should be based on a long-term positive vision and fully include the external dimension.

On 13th December 2005 the commission presented its review of the sustainable development strategy. On the basis of this, the ECl adopted the renewed EU sustainable development strategy on the 15th/16th June 2006.
The renewed EU sustainable development strategy names clear goals and priority measures for the seven key challenges in the field of sustainable development:

It confirms key goals and planned measures in the field of **climate change and clean energy**. These include the 2 °C target, the 2010 targets for renewable energies, the 9 % reduction in energy consumption by 2017, EU support for climate targets for 2020 and (indirectly) for 2050, and the strategy for biomass. The EU sustainable development strategy makes it clear that energy policy must be consistent with the goals of competitiveness, security of supply and ecological sustainability, and that energy policy is of key importance in mitigating climate change.

The strategy confirms the building blocks of a **sustainable development of the transport sector**, including decoupling economic growth and the demand for transport, the goal of shifting from road transport to environmentally friendly transport modes, controlling demand for transport through costs including the internalization of external costs, reduction of noise and pollutant emissions from traffic and measures for reducing the environmental impacts of mounting air and maritime traffic.
In the field of **sustainable consumption and production**, by 2010 the

[20] *BMU;* EU Strategy for Sustainable Development [http://www.bmu.de/english/sustainability_globalisation/current/doc/35355.php] (10.10.2012)

92 A European Union Strategy for Sustainable Development – cover
93 Gender inequality index value

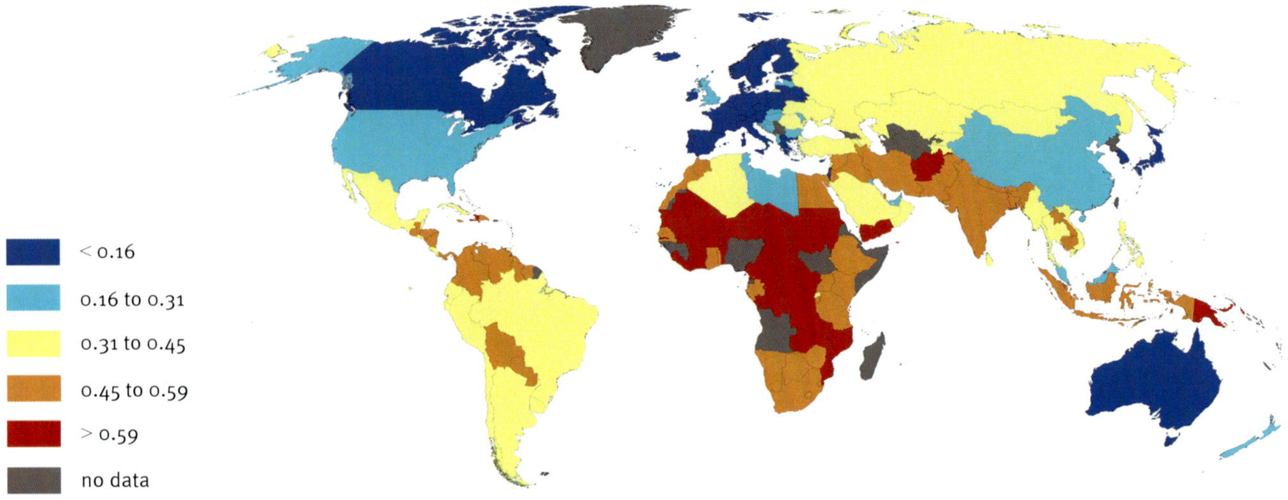

93

strategy aims to reach an EU average level of green public procurement equal to that currently achieved by the best performing Member States. A benchmarking has been introduced for this. For setting environmental and social performance targets, a dialogue process will be initiated between the European Commission, Member States and trade and industry. The labelling of products with high environmental impacts will be extended. The strategy contains a mandate for the Commissions to propose an Action Plan for sustainable consumption and production, which was carried out in July 2008.

For the **conservation and management of natural resources** the renewed strategy calls for targets and measures in the framework of the thematic strategy on the sustainable use of natural resources.
In the field of **public health**, the European Union is required, inter alia, to propose a strategy for improving indoor air quality.
With regard to the **global challenges relating to poverty and sustainable development**, strengthening multilateral environmental agreements should contribute to improving international environmental governance. The EU should use trade agreements to improve environmental and social standards.
In the field of **social inclusion, demography and migration**, improving the quality of life is a priority goal. Specific environmental topics are not addressed in the context of these challenges.
Furthermore, the renewed strategy calls on the Member States to take further steps to shift taxation from labour to resource and energy consumption and to pollution. It is confirmed that relative to the Lisbon Strategy, the two strategies complement each other. However, the EU sustainable development strategy represents the overall framework, within which the Lisbon Strategy will serve as a driving force of a more dynamic economy.
The revised EU strategy for sustainable development also strengthens the relationship with the national sustainability strategies, for example through voluntary peer reviews and streamlined progress reports based on existing reports.

The strategy also lays down a new monitoring process for reviewing implementation: the European Commission will submit a progress report every 2 years, on the basis of which the European Council will review the implementation of the strategy, also at 2 year intervals." [20]
The last review of the EU SDS was in July 2009. It underlines that in recent years the EU has mainstreamed sustainable development into a broad range of its policies. The review overseas the EU policy measures in the areas covered by the EU SDS and has launched a study into the future and its relation to the Lisbon strategy.

Lisbon strategy

The Lisbon Strategy was introduced in 2000 and was set as a target for 2010 by the European Union – the most competitive and dynamic knowledge-based economy in the world – a global economy capable of sustainable economic growth with more and better jobs and to achieve greater social cohesion.

The mid-term review of the Lisbon strategy found at best, a mixed result. It realised that the gap between Europe and its commercial partners in productivity and growth has deepened, and additionally the challenge of an aging population has increased.

Therefore, the European Council has decided to relaunch the Lisbon Strategy through a partnership for growth and jobs. The main objective of this partnership is still for sustainable development.

However, Europe has to achieve this goal while focusing on fewer priorities. Its stronger and more sustainable growth will achieve more and better jobs, to free the necessary resources so that wider ambitions in economic, social and environmental terms can be cemented.

94 Income share held by the wealthiest 10 % of the population
95 Income share held by the poorest 10 % of the population

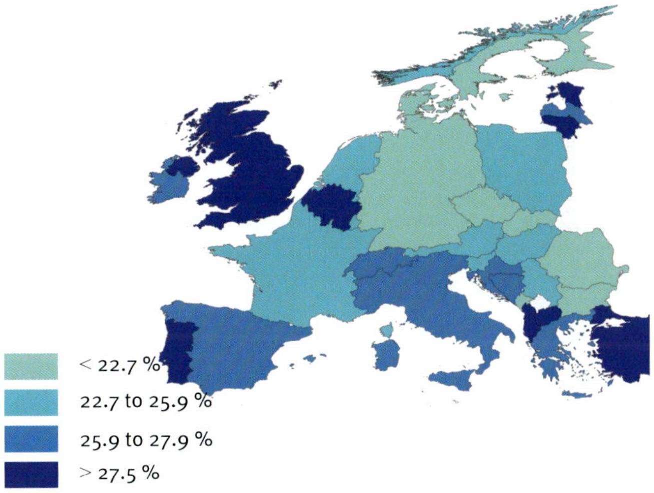

94

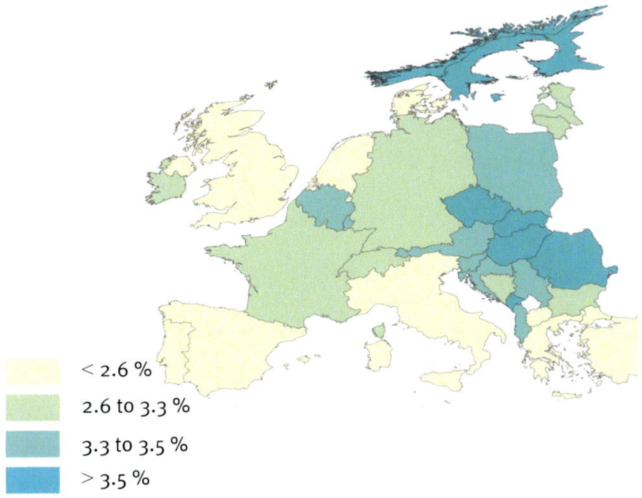

95

1.7 Strategies in Europe and Germany

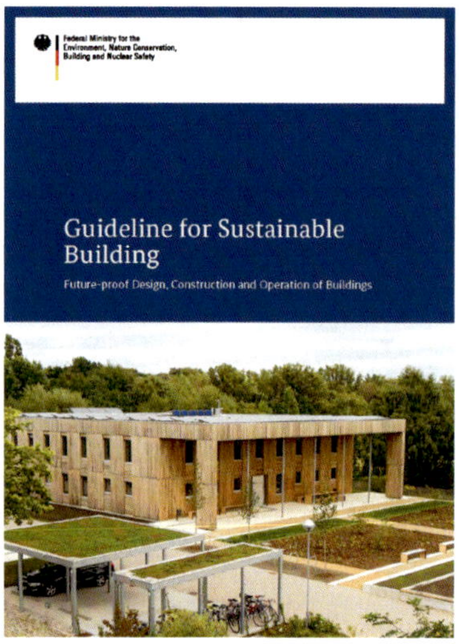

96

1.7.2 Leitfaden Nachhaltiges Bauen (Guidelines for Sustainable Building)

It was developed and published by the Federal Ministry of Transport, Building and Urban Development (BMVBS), Federal Institute for Building, Urban Affairs and Spatial Research (BBSR) and the Federal Office for Building and Regional Regulation (BBR) in February 2011 in Germany.

The guidelines represent the general principles, targets, recommendations and methods for sustainable building in accordance with the methods to be implemented for federal construction projects (RBBau).

It also offers working aid for the design, planning, construction, maintenance, operation and use of federal landholdings and buildings in accordance with RBBau.

The revision and introduction of Guidelines for Sustainable Building (2011) occurred parallel to the enforcement of the rules for the application of Rating Systems for Sustainable Building (BNB).

The guidelines consist of the following four main parts:

- Part A - general principles and methods of sustainable building

The three main dimensions of sustainability - ecology, economy and socio-culture are described. Additionally for sustainable building, technical quality, planning and construction and location features are to be considered. The goal is to optimise the building within its entire life cycle in order to minimize energy and resource consumption, environmental loads and its improvement of the economy.
Also the socio-cultural aspects for improvement of the quality of life and efficiency of users, e.g. healthiness and comfort is to be considered.

The rating system for sustainable building BNB is the German green building certificate, that is based on the principles described in this guideline. The evaluation and certification of the building with the help of BNB is also described here.

- Part B "New construction" - task-related principles, sceneries, basic planning and implementation of new projects and extensions, including the design of outdoor facilities

The focus is on the integration of sustainable principals already in the building design and planning. The structure is oriented on the planning schedule due to the RBBau (figure 99) and the working phases of the HOAI (page 89).
Here it is also described, that everything has to be considered in every planning phase in order to design a sustainable building.

96 Guidelines for Sustainable Building in Germany – cover
97 German federal environment office in Dessau, Sauerbruch Hutton architecture agency

97

- Part C "Building use and management" - the use and operation as well as the maintenance of buildings and properties

By having regular efficiency and consumption controlling, education for the operators and users in relation to how the implementing of sustainable principals and operation methods can reduce the overall operational costs.

- Part D "Existing building" the planning and implementation of modernization, reconstruction and redevelopment projects for existing buildings

Appendixes to Guideline:

- General and services due HOAI
- Minimum performance levels of federal buildings
- Pre-check BNB version 2011_1
- Specifications for energy requirements (sample)
- Health
- Indoor air quality
- Documentation required BNB
- Goal setting table
- Evaluation report on the sustainability (sample)

The guidelines for sustainable building as well as the appendixes can be found in the information portal www.nachhaltigesbauen.de under the heading "Guidance and working aids".

ES-Bau (Entscheidungsunterlage Bau) ES-building (Decision support construction)	
E.g. requirements description, explanation of the construction project, planning concept, cost estimation, cost ceiling	HOAI: LP1 partially LP2

↓

EW-Bau (Entwurfsunterlage Bau) EW-construction (Design pad construction)	
Development of the design, or approval planning, e.g. design plans, explanatory reports, evidences, cost calculation	HOAI: LP 2, 3 and 4 partially LP5

↓

Ausführungsplanung Implementation planning	
E.g. implementation drawings, performance directories with quantity calculations, tested security proofs, evidences: EnEV, sound, fire	HOAI: LP 5 and 6

↓

Bauausführung Construction process	
E.g. inviting offers, procurement of construction output, monitoring and coordinating the execution, cost determination / control	HOAI: LP 7 and 8

↓

Bauübergabe und Baubestandsdokumentation Building handing and documentation	
E.g. object supervision and documentation	HOAI: LP 9

↓

Betriebsoptimierung (zusätzlich zur RBBau und HOAI) Optimization of operation (in addition to RBBau and HOAI)
E.g. function optimization of house technical equipment, commissioning management, Commissioning

98

98 The planning process by RBBau and the corresponding working phases of the HOAI in reference to building planning and establishments, in accordance to the Guidelines for Sustainable Building 2011

99 Operational costs per m3 UFA and year (example)

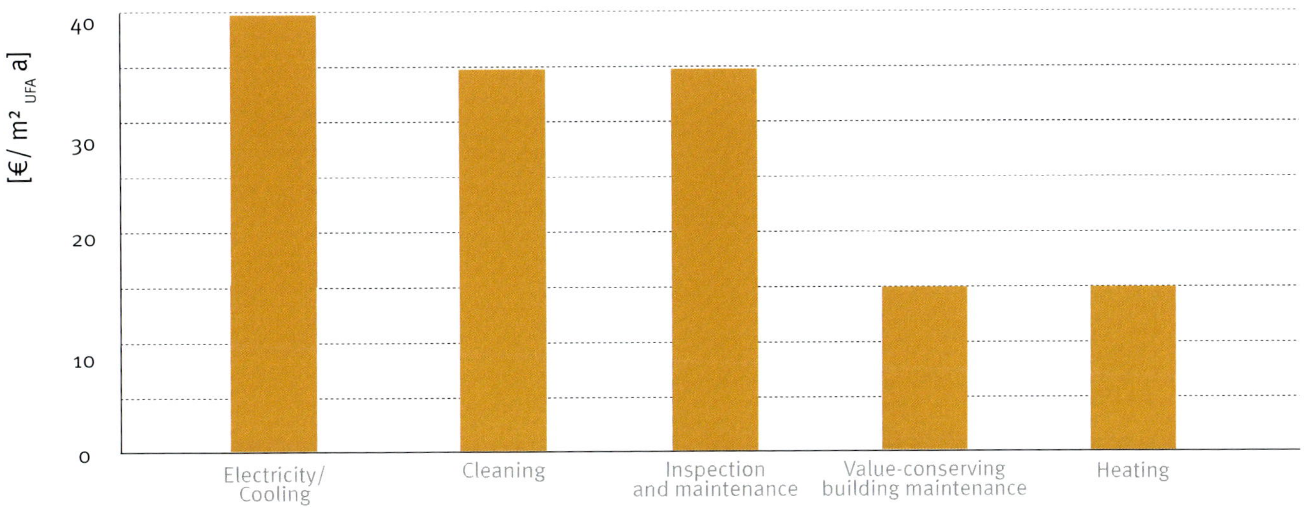

99

1.7 Strategies in Europe and Germany

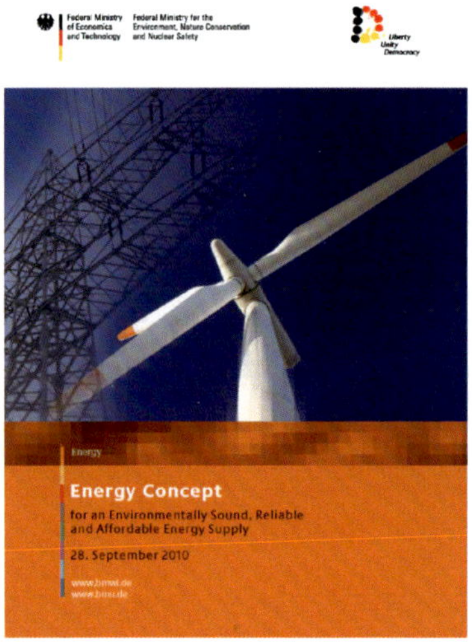

100

[21] Post Carbon Pathways; German Government: Energy Concept [http://www.postcarbonpathways.net.au/transition-strategies/german-government/] (11.10.2012), selections

100 German National Energy Concept 2010 – cover
101 CO_2 Emissions 1990-2050 based on Energy scenarios of German government

energy industry
trade and services
industry
private households
traffic
diffuse emissions

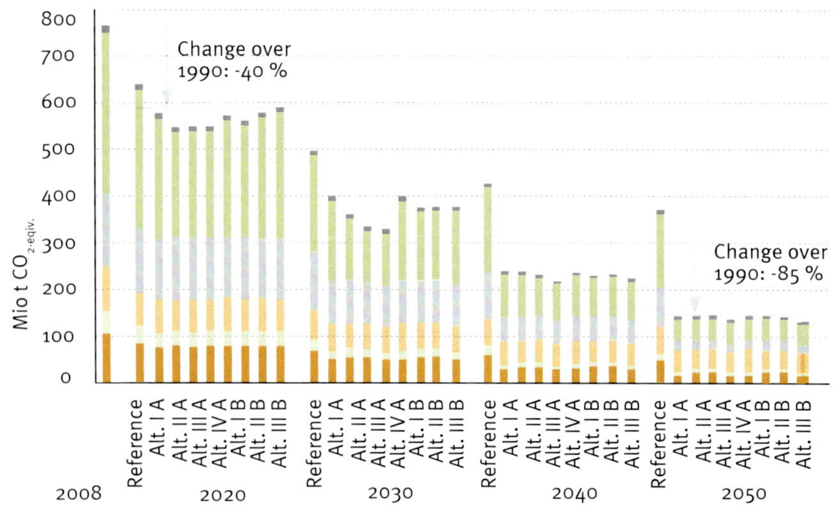

101

1.7.3 Energiekonzept der Bundesregierung Deutschland 2010 (German National Energy Concept 2010)

"Source, aims and scope

The Energy Concept was developed by Germany's Federal Ministry of Economics and Technology and Federal Ministry for the Environment, Nature Conservation and Nuclear Safety, and adopted by the German Government in September 2010. It constitutes the German Government's long-term strategy to 2050 for designing and implementing a national energy supply system that is considered environmentally sound, reliable and affordable. (...) The strategy draws on a set of scenarios that reveal different pathways and conditions under which the targets can be achieved. It describes measures, many of which are already being implemented, in a range of key components or fields of action. These include: renewable energy, energy efficiency, nuclear and fossil-fuel power plants, an efficient grid infrastructure for electricity and integration of renewables, buildings, mobility, research into innovation and new technologies, energy supply in the European and international context, and issues of transparency and public acceptance.

Emissions reduction and energy targets

Germany has a target for cutting CO_2 emissions by 40 % by 2020 and at least 80 % by 2050 (on 1990 levels). It is acknowledged that the objectives of national energy, climate and budget policies need to be harmonised, but the Energy Concept deals only with energy supply and use. It specifies targets for the amount of renewable energy as a proportion of gross final energy consumption of 18 % by 2020, 30 % by 2030, 45 % by 2040, and 60 % by 2050. Targets are also specified for gains in energy productivity so that primary energy consumption is to be reduced from 2008 levels by 20 % in 2020, and 50 % by 2050.

Assumptions and priorities
Technology and innovation (...)

Although the focus of the strategy is on the cost-efficient expansion of renewable energy sources and energy efficiency measures, it also considers the role of existing fossil fuel and nuclear power. Within the Energy Concept document, nuclear power is considered a bridging technology and provision is made for the extension of the operating lives of Germany's seventeen existing nuclear power plants by an average of twelve years. Importantly, this aspect of the Energy Concept has since been overturned by the German Government, marking a dramatic shift in their position on nuclear power as a cornerstone to Germany's transition to renewable energy. The new approach is to phase out nuclear power as fast as possible.

The Energy Concept's main policy priorities, either planned or being implemented, include:

- continued amendments to existing policies to support solar power
- improving grid integration of renewable energy sources and acceleration of the German energy grid expansion, including planning for a national target grid for 2050, integration with the European network, increasing storage capacity
- faster expansion of offshore wind farming, including investment of 75 billion € to boost capacity to 25 GW by 2030

- expansion of onshore wind farming, including improving the legal and planning frameworks
- promotion of the sustainable use of bio-energy for heating, electricity and fuel, with measures to avoid conflict with land use or issues with efficiency
- targeted energy efficiency measures for households, industry and the public sector
- termination of subsidies for domestic hard coal
- upgrading the energy performance of building stock, in particular reducing demand from heating
- promotion of electric vehicles, in order to meet the goals of one million electric vehicles on German roads by 2020 and six million by 2030, and bio-fuels
- continued development of the National Hydrogen and Fuel Cell Technology Innovation Programme." [21]

As a response to the nuclear disaster in Fukushima, the need to switch from nuclear energy to renewable energies within the German Energy Concept has been re-evaluated in the summer of 2011. Germany wants to phase out the use of nuclear energy by 2022, improve energy efficiency and accelerate the transition to renewable energies. The Federal Government has set up a concrete action program with a solid financial plan based on measures of the energy concept in September 2010. Together, the decisions of the Energy Concept of 2010 and the Energy Transition 2011, form the government's current energy policy.

In March 2012, the Federal Government released further plans to help phase out nuclear energy. In spring 2014, the German government made additional decisions in relation to the final stages to switch energies. Security of supply is an important criteria in order to switch energy supplies. The amount of electricity generated in Germany must be equal to demand from consumers.

Electrical generation from wind and solar power alone can not contribute to the security of energy supply. Therefore, for the foreseeable future the conventional power plants (brown coal, hard coal, gas) are required.

In the age of renewable energy the country requires a highly efficient and above all flexible, conventional power plants. The federal government will make the legal and financial conditions for the environmentally friendly combined heat and power (CHP) so that their share rises to 25 % by 2020. Yet in 2014, the framework conditions for cogeneration, in particular the Combined Heat and Power Act will be reviewed and adjusted.

At the latest in 2022, the last nuclear power plant in Germany will be switched off.

102 Assumed power mix in 2050 based on Energy concept of German government

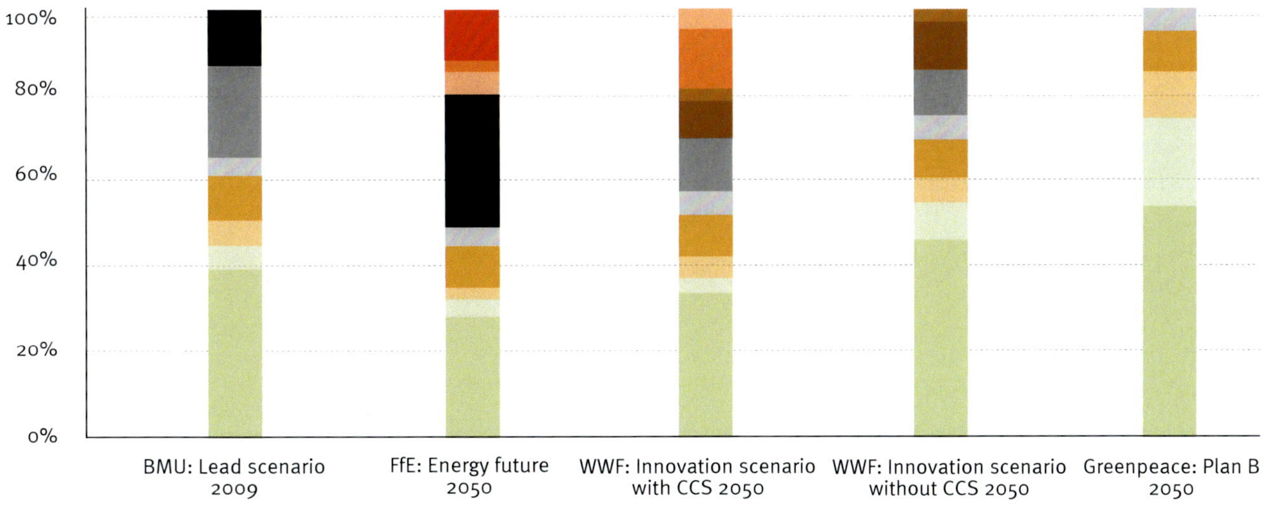

102

1.7 Strategies in Europe and Germany

IDEAS
INNOVATION
PROSPERITY
The High-Tech Strategy for Germany

103

[22] *BMBF;* High-Tech-Strategy [http://www.bmbf.de/en/6618.php] (11.10.2012)

1.7.4 HTS – Hightech-Strategie für Deutschland (The High-Tech Strategy for Germany)

"The High-Tech Strategy, which was launched in August 2006, was the first national concept to rally the key stakeholders involved in innovation around a common idea. On 14th July 2010, the Federal Cabinet decided to continue along this successful path.

The new High-Tech Strategy 2020 will ensure the continuity of the overall approach and, at the same time, set new priorities.

The aim of the High-Tech Strategy (HTS) is to create lead markets, intensify cooperation between science and industry, and continue to improve the general conditions for innovation.

We want to make Germany the leading provider of science and technology-based solutions in the areas of climate/energy, health/nutrition, mobility, security, and communication. The HTS focuses on these areas, and this is also creating growth and employment in Germany.

Forward-looking projects in selected areas will be the focus of future research and innovation policy. These projects pursue specific objectives related to scientific and technological development over a period of ten to fifteen years.

Strategies for innovation are being developed and steps towards their realization planned in concrete cases.

The High-Tech Strategy has formulated the following central examples of forward-looking projects:

- CO_2-neutral, energy-efficient and climate-adapted cities
- The intelligent restructuring of the energy supply system
- Renewable resources as an alternative to oil
- Treating illnesses more effectively with the help of individualized medicine
- Better health through an optimised diet
- Living an independent life well into old age
- A million electric vehicles in Germany by 2020
- More effective protection of communication networks
- Increasing Internet use whilst making it less energy consuming
- Making global knowledge digitally available and accessible
- Tomorrow's working world and its structure

National and European research and innovation policies are being closely linked. Europe 2020 is an ambitious process started by the European Commission and the European Council with the aim of putting education, research and innovation at the centre of European growth policy.

103 Logo of the High-Tech Strategy for Germany
104 The German Government's Cluster Strategy Structure of the German government's innovation funding for SME´s
105 Forward projects and fields of demand

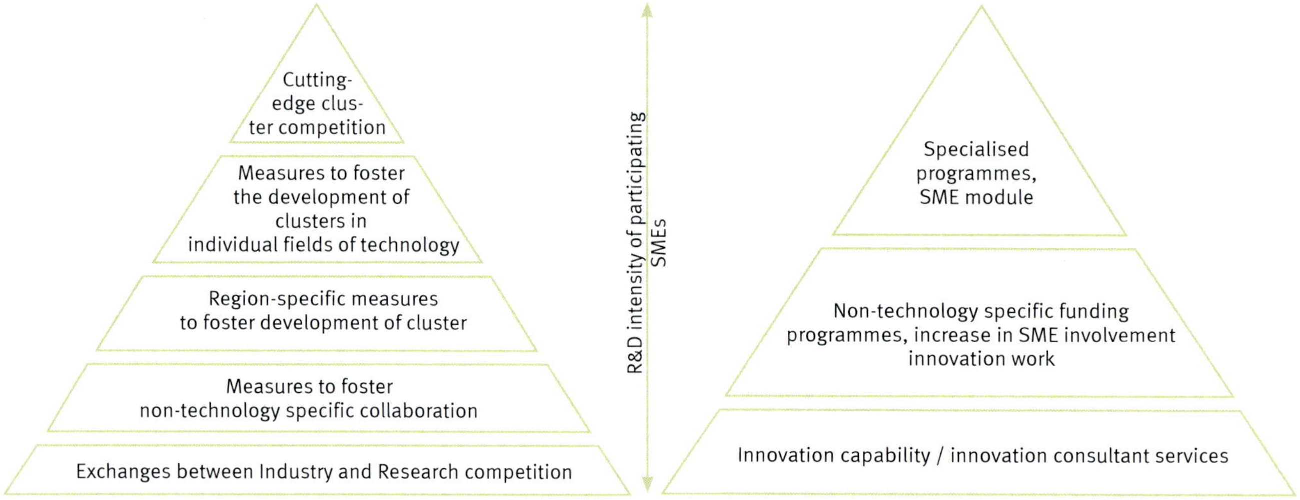

104

On this basis, Germany will contribute to a coherent research and innovation policy in Europe.

The general conditions for innovation in Germany are being improved even further. In particular, this refers to the conditions for setting up businesses, the special circumstances of SMEs, sufficient funding for innovations, and the provision of venture capital.

Not least, research and innovation depend on an intensive dialogue with society.

To this end, new dialogue platforms are being created so that the general population can become more involved and bring its own ideas into the debate about emerging technologies and research results that can contribute to meeting the great global and societal challenges of our time." [22]

Seventeen High-tech sectors of the High-Tech Strategy:

- Nanotechnology
- Biotechnology
- Micro-system technology
- Optical technology
- Materials technology
- Space technology
- Information and communication technology
- Production technology
- Energy technology
- Environmental technology
- Automotive and traffic technology
- Aviation and aeronautical technology
- Maritime technology
- Health research and medical technology
- Plants
- Security research
- Services

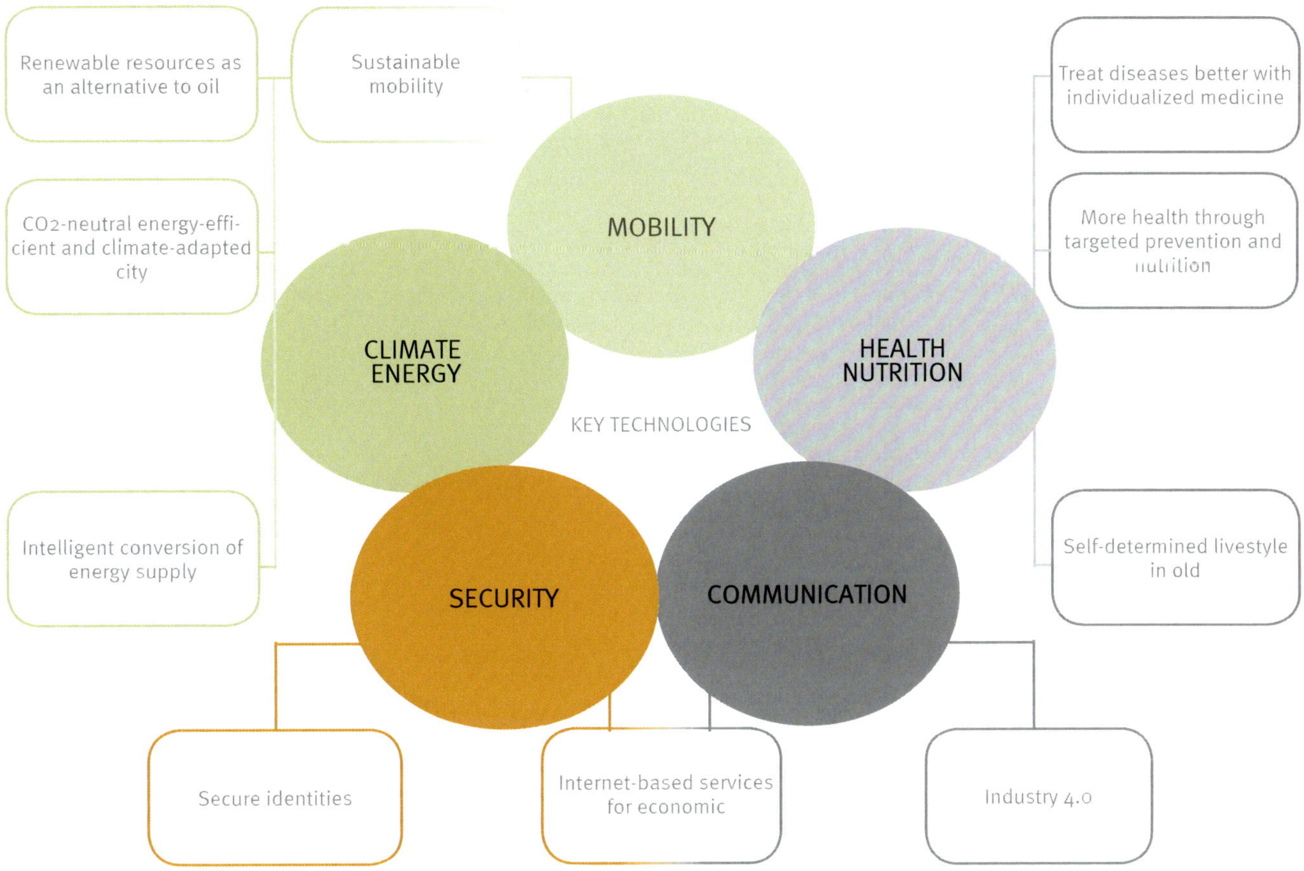

1.7 Strategies in Europe and Germany

[23] *Common Sense for the World;* Manifesto for sustainable architecture and civil engineering issued by architects, engineers and town planners in Germany. [http://www.klima-manifest.de/fileadmin/templates/klima-manifest/images/BDAKlimaManifestENGLISCH.pdf] (30.07.2012)

1.7.5 Manifest "Vernunft für die Welt" (Manifesto "Common Sense for the World")

"Manifesto for sustainable architecture and civil engineering issued by architects, engineers and town planners in Germany.

Preamble

The scientific evidence that mankind is responsible for climate change is irrefutable. The temperature of the earth's biosphere has risen perceptibly over the past one hundred years. Extreme weather conditions are an ever more frequent phenomenon. If we fail to change our attitudes and lifestyles, global warming will have a devastating effect on our lives and those of future generations.

Countermeasures can still be taken. If we combine and coordinate our efforts, climate change can be kept at bay. So far, however, attempts to achieve the far-reaching goals of sustainable development have been far too hesitant. That applies equally to societies, governments, trade and industries, and the scientific community all of which have shown a lack of interest, resolution, decisiveness and boldness. All segments of society are now called upon to act. In this manifesto we document the specific responsibility we bear as architects, engineers and town planners. The contribution we can make in the form of sustainable architecture and civil engineering is essential to bring about the changes needed in the use of our natural resources.

We must ...

place the planning and layout of our cities and buildings on a new ecological footing,

- by substantially reducing the amount of energy, material and land use,
- by avoiding emissions that are harmful to the environment,
- by planning the use of materials so that they can be recycled to form the basis for new products.

We want...

sustainable cities,

- which are structured so that people can run their lives along ecological lines,
- which are systematically reorganised to make them producers rather than consumers of energy,
- which make wise use of density to save land and take due account of demographic changes,
- in which local public transport enjoys priority over private motor traffic,
- in which intelligent systems are employed to reduce water consumption,
- in which materials usage forms part of a recycling economy that makes sensible re - use of used materials.

We want...

resource-saving architecture and civil engineering,

- in which sustainability is the dominant element in planning and execution,
- in which the physical, biological and technical properties of all systems involved
- interact to mutual benefit,
- which give priority to the use of regional materials, thereby avoiding the unnecessary transport of often superfluous imported materials,
- which rely on natural cycles rather than energy - intensive technology,
- in which regional building traditions are linked with pioneering ideas in the development of new forms of architecture and civil engineering,
- which find expression in new architectural forms and designs, yet fit in with the infrastructure and appearance of our cities, thereby providing clearly recognizable indications of the change in our attitude.

We want...

a heightened awareness of sustainable development,

- so that we no longer approach complex ecological problems with the narrow outlook of the present but with a holistic understanding,
- so that money in government research budgets is invested in the development of ideas and concepts that treat ecological building as an integrated whole comprising building construction, materials, usage and design,
- so that an all - embracing appreciation of the ecological interaction between the planning and design of cities and architecture becomes the foundation for teaching and research at all colleges and universities,
- so that Germany, as a key player with global responsibilities, acts as a pioneer of climate - friendly architecture and civil engineering.

We will...

lend credibility to our commitment through personal involvement,

- by advocating sustainable urban development with sustainable architecture and civil engineering, the special quality of which will be determined in equal degree by functional, aesthetic and ecological aspects,
- by working for global awareness to counteract climate change and, out of respect for other cultures, by devising specific solutions which will help to alleviate the effects of climate change and resolve ecological problems worldwide,
- by actively encouraging further training for architects, town planners and engineers that will enhance their awareness and improve their ability to plan and build sustainable architecture and use civil engineering accordingly,
- by co-operating with the relevant players in the public and private sectors to draw up and agree on incentives for sustainable construction and climate - friendly urban development,
- by employing evaluation techniques we ourselves have helped to develop to ensure that the sustainability of the buildings and urban neighbourhoods we have planned is made transparent,
- by intensifying research and development for specific tasks in resource - saving construction and by working together with the building materials industry to implement series solutions,
- by joining the construction industry and tradesmen in devising forms of ecological architecture and civil engineering that constitute an investment in the future.

This manifesto issued by architects, engineers and town planners is a touchstone for the fundamental ethical attitude of our professions. To document our position publicly, we will report regularly on the extent to which we have lived up to our voluntary commitment.

Architects, Engineers, Town Planners, Landscape Architects and Interior Architects are called upon to sign the 'Common Sense for the World Manifesto' and publicly to make known their aspirations.

Please sign the manifest under www.klima-manifest.de" [23]

106

106 Manifest Common Sense for the World – cover

1.7 Strategies in Europe and Germany

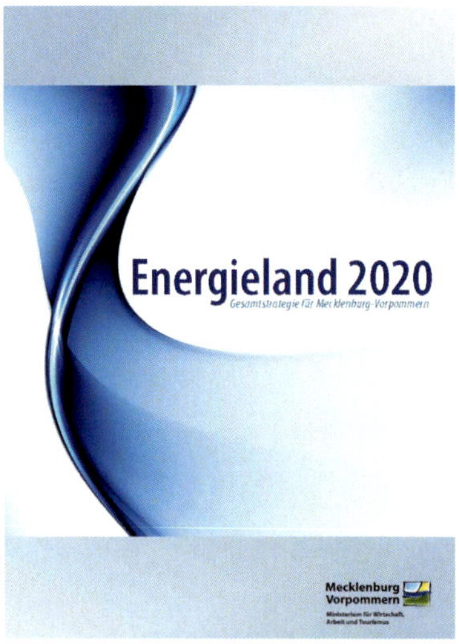

107

1.7.6 Energieland 2020 Mecklenburg-Vorpommern (Energy State 2020 M-V)

The ministry of economy, labour and tourism, the leading ministry in Mecklenburg-Vorpommern for energy and climate protection, created guidelines under the "Energy State 2020".

The energy policy goals of the state of Mecklenburg-Vorpommern are aimed towards providing the residents and businesses with the most secure, affordable, consumer-friendly, efficient and environmentally responsible energy supplies.

There are 8 main guidelines stated by the 'Energy State 2020':

- Long-term stability and low energy prices
- Expansion of the electricity and gas networks
- Energy location - Lubmin, Germany
- Renewable energy/Renewable resources
- Climate protection, energy efficiency
- Waste and energy industry
- Technology development/Innovation
- Create and secure jobs

Guideline 1: Long-term stability and low energy prices

The state of Mecklenburg-Vorpommern supports the efforts of the federal government in support of the gas and electricity markets stepping up and obtaining stable and affordable energy prices. These include measures such as the tightening of the antitrust law, improving the network connection of new power plants or the replacement of the power rate approvals by incentive, but also to participate in the discussion of further unbundling measures.

Guideline 2: Expansion of the electricity and gas networks

For the transmission of the future, especially for the off-shore wind turbines producing electricity, but also for closing choke points in the network or to covering an expanding company, extensions of the power grids are required. A comprehensive and secure supply is to be ensured for the future. By creating, in Lubmin a gas pipeline from Russia to the west and south areas of Mecklenburg-Vorpommern this will form a direct source of energy from Russia. This project is of high importance for the country and the state government of Mecklenburg-Vorpommern who are strong supporters. To allow a future supply of bio-gas into the gas distribution network, even remotely located producers are to be connected to the network.

Guideline 3: Energy location Lubmin

The key areas for energy generation are developed into central industrial sites, including a number of producers of renewable and fossil energy as well as other companies already located on site. Due to the landing position of the Baltic Sea pipeline at Lubmin, the site will be further upgraded. A concept for the creation of electricity, gas and heating networks in Lubmin is required, as well as the establishment of further heat users at the site.

Guideline 4: Renewable energy/Renewable resources

The development of renewable energies is a main focus on the political 'Energy State 2020'. The construction of a rural, decentralized energy supply structured with predominantly self-sufficiency can be used for economic stabilization, to boost employment and for security of supply. By re-powering onshore areas and with the expansion of offshore installations, Mecklenburg-Vorpommern will expand its wind power potential considerably. The materials and energy from biomass reflect both environmental protection and future security, employment and value added within rural areas. Therefore, renewable resources and the use of bioenergy for Mecklenburg-Vorpommern

107 Energy state 2020 M-V – cover
108 Power generation 2020 – scenario renewable energies, variant 1
109 Technology funding in energy sector 2000 - 2007

is of particular importance. Support should be awarded for projects that provide the most efficient and full use of bio-energy. The application of solar thermal energy for heating and for generating process heat in the commercial sector offers a significant savings potential which should be enhanced. For the increased use of geothermal energy, it is necessary for the federal government and the European Union to raise additional funds.

Guideline 5: Climate protection, energy efficiency

Improving energy efficiency and energy savings in all areas of life are particularly important parts of the climate protection measures. The state policy will continue to remedy these issues through the continuation of support measures in urban development, housing and transportation bills. Within the country there is a high level of untapped potential for efficient waste heat recovery opportunities to be found. Energy supply programs involving appropriate potential and the possibilities of creating the necessary infrastructure is therefore of particular importance. The management of the country's property is subject to the principles of efficiency and environmental compatibility and it is desired to minimize the consumption of energy and resources.

Guideline 6: Waste and energy industry

Waste management in the country will eventually become the energy industry and the economic potential is used more intensively. In addition to the traditional renewable energy sources, it may be offered together with waste industry also as an energy potential, which has not yet been exhausted.

Guideline 7: Technology development/Innovation

M-V is seen as the development of new technologies and their implementation in practice. These networks and competence centres such as the hydrogen technology initiative, the solar centre and the offshore energy expertise network will be supported. Storage technologies will be also created. Research areas include the investigation of new methods for the production of second generation biofuels and energy storage technology.

Guideline 8: Create and secure jobs

The energy industry in M-V should be able to create and secure jobs with appropriate boundary conditions such as stable and affordable energy prices, a high degree of self-sufficiency based on renewable energy sources, by applying new technologies (e.g. 2nd generation bio fuels, storage technologies), or changed location of industry.

RIS (Regionale Innovationsstrategie) Regional Innovation Strategy

The first three strategies for Energyland M-V 2020 – engineering, health, information and communication technologies – were introduced in April 2013 at a conference in Greifswald. At the following conference in October 2013 in Rostock, an additional three fields were discussed – energy, nutrition and mobility.

The future funding in the new EU program period from 2014-2020 was also the focus of discussion at the conference. The Minister spoke about the initial EU funding program from the period 2007-2013 and made clear that future collaborative research in cooperation between companies and universities will be a major focus of the new EU funding.

The future concepts developed during the conferences in Mecklenburg-Vorpommern formed the Regional Innovation Strategy (RIS) of Mecklenburg-Vorpommern. The RIS is itself necessary for the Operational Programme EFRE "European Regional Development Fund". This provides the framework for the promotion of EU funds.

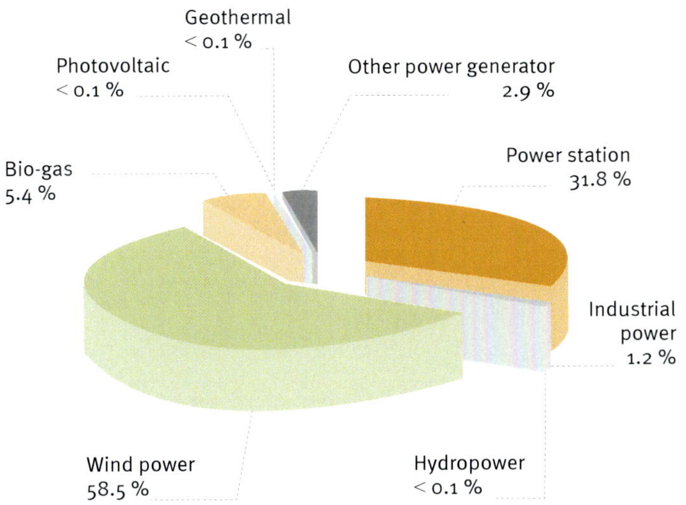

108

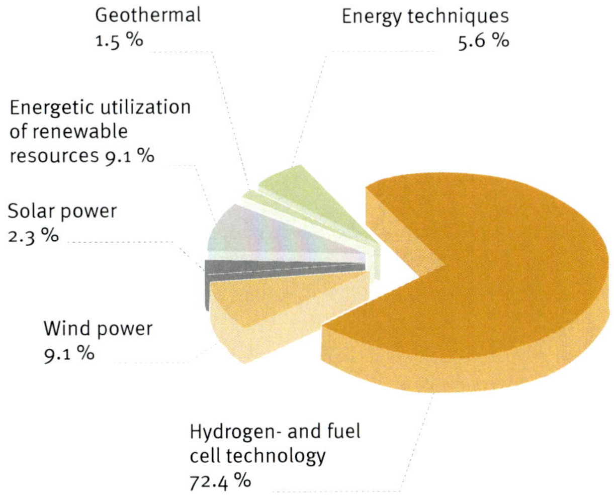

109

1.8 Regulations in Europe and Germany

1.8.1 Directive 2010/31/EU of the European Parliament and of the Council of 19 May 2010 on the energy performance of buildings

"This Directive aims to promote the energy performance of buildings and building units.

Methodology for calculating the energy performance of buildings

Member states shall adopt, either at national or regional level, a methodology for calculating the energy performance of buildings which takes into account certain elements, specifically:

- the thermal characteristics of a building (thermal capacity, insulation, etc.);
- heating insulation and hot water supply;
- the air-conditioning installation;
- the built-in lighting installation;
- indoor climatic conditions.

The positive influence of other aspects such as local solar exposure, natural lighting, electricity produced by cogeneration and district or block heating or cooling systems are also taken into account.

Setting minimum requirements

Member States shall put in place, in compliance with the aforementioned calculation methodology, minimum requirements for energy performance in order to achieve cost-optimal levels. The level of these requirements is reviewed every 5 years.

When setting requirements, member states may differentiate between new and existing buildings and between different categories of buildings.

New buildings shall comply with these requirements and undergo a feasibility study before construction starts, looking at the installation of renewable energy supply systems, heat pumps, district or block heating or cooling systems and cogeneration systems.

When undergoing major renovation, existing buildings shall have their energy performance upgraded so that they also satisfy the minimum requirements.

The following may be exempt from the application of the minimum requirements:

- officially protected buildings (for example, historic buildings);
- buildings used as places of worship;
- temporary buildings;
- residential buildings intended for a limited annual time of use;
- stand-alone buildings with a total useful floor area of less than 50 m²

When new, replaced or upgraded technical building systems such as heating systems, hot water systems, air-conditioning systems and large ventilation systems are installed, they shall also comply with the energy performance requirements.

Building elements that form part of the building envelope and have a significant impact on the energy performance of that envelope (e.g., window frames) shall also meet the minimum

[24] European Union; Europa. Summaries of EU legislation: Energy performance of buildings [http://europa.eu/legislation_summaries/internal_market/single_market_for_goods/construction/en0021_en.htm] (11.10.2012), selections

110 Member states of European Union

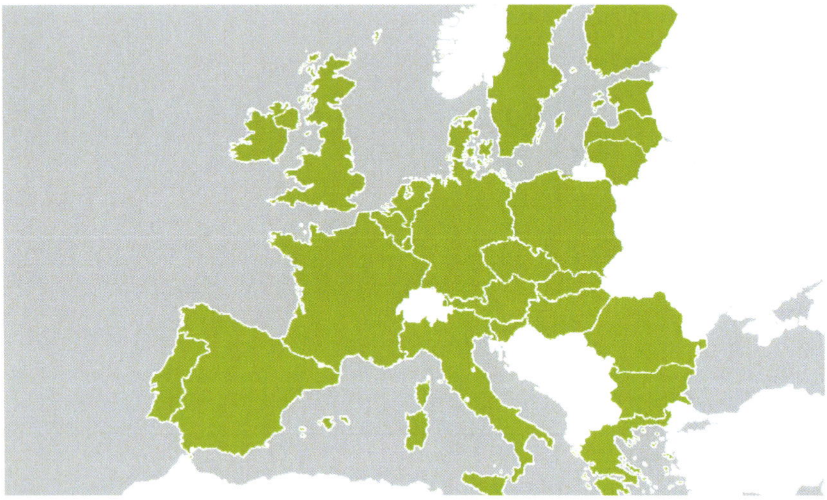

110

energy performance requirements when they are replaced or retrofitted, with a view to achieving cost-optimal levels.

This Directive strongly encourages the introduction of intelligent energy consumption metering systems whenever a building is constructed or undergoes renovation, pursuant to the Directive concerning common rules for the internal market in electricity.

Objective: Nearly zero-energy buildings

By 31st December 2020, all new buildings shall be nearly zero-energy consumption buildings. New buildings occupied and owned by public authorities shall comply with the same criteria by 31st December 2018.

The Commission encourages increasing the numbers of this type of buildings by putting in place national plans, which include:

- the member state's application in practice of the definition of nearly zero-energy buildings;
- the intermediate targets for improving the energy performance of new buildings by 2015;
- information on the policies and financial measures adopted to encourage improving the energy performance of buildings. (...)

Energy performance certificates

Member states shall implement a system for the energy performance certification of buildings. It shall include information on the energy performance of a building and recommendations for cost improvements.

When a building or building unit is offered for sale or for rent, the energy performance indicator of the energy performance certificate shall be included in advertisements in commercial media.

When buildings or building units are constructed, sold or rented out, the certificate is to be shown to the new tenant or prospective buyer and handed over to the buyer or new tenant.

With regard to buildings where a total floor area of over 500 m² is occupied by a public authority and buildings with a total floor area of over 500 m² which are frequently visited by the public, the energy performance certificate shall be displayed in a prominent place and be clearly visible (this threshold shall be lowered to 250 m² on 9th July 2015).

Member states are responsible for putting in place a system of regular inspections of heating and air-conditioning systems in buildings." [14]

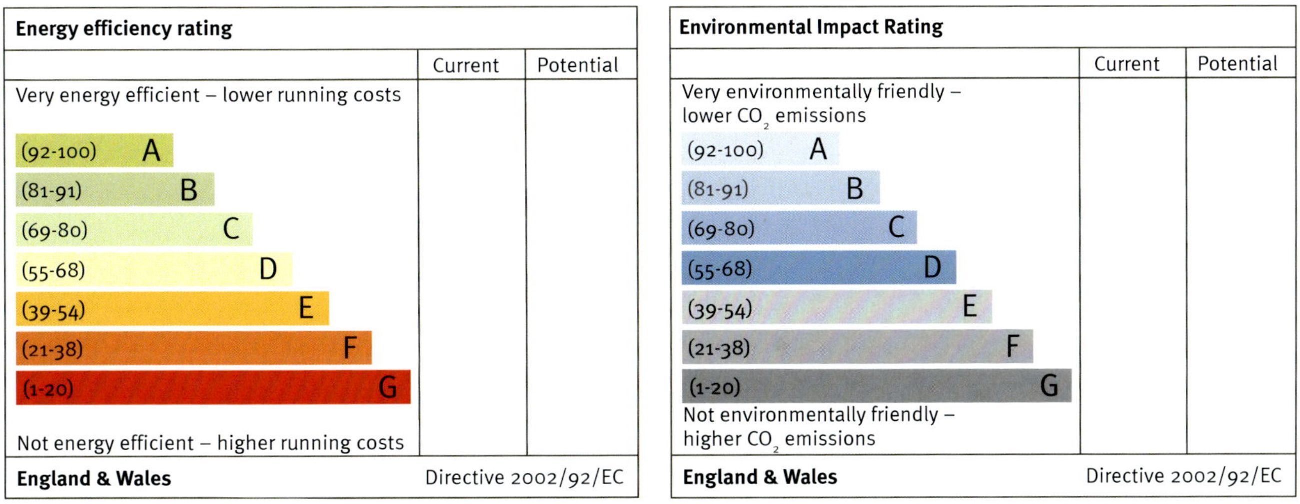

111

111 Example of Energy Performance Certificate in England & Wales

1.8 Regulations in Europe and Germany

1.8.2 CPR – The EU Construction Products Regulation

"Key concepts of the CPR

The CPR builds upon the Construction Products Directive (CPD) and aims to break down technical barriers to trade in construction products within the European Economic Area (EEA). To achieve this, the CPR provides for four main elements:

- a system of harmonised technical specifications
- an agreed system of conformity assessment for each product family
- a framework of notified bodies
- CE marking of products

The CPR harmonises the methods of assessment and test, the means of declaration of product performance and the system of conformity assessment of construction products, but not national building regulations. The choice of required values for the particular intended use is left to the regulators and public / private sector procurers at the national level. However, such required values must be expressed in a consistent manner (technical language) as used in the harmonised technical specifications.

Some elements of the CPR came into force on 24th April 2011. The first changes apply to notified bodies and technical approval bodies and the way in which they operate. The full legislation relating to manufacturers, importers and distributors comes into force on 1st July 2013, when the CPD will be replaced." [25]

"Harmonised technical specifications

Under the CPR, harmonised technical specifications are harmonised European product standards (hENs) established by Comité Européen de Normalisation (CEN)/Comité Européen de Normalisation Èlectrotechnique (CENELEC) or European Assessment Documents (EADs) produced by the European Organisation for Technical Approvals (EOTA) as the basis for issuing ETAs for products not covered by hENs. The harmonised technical specification for a product defines EEA-wide methods of assessing and declaring all the performance characteristics required by regulations in any member state which affect the ability of construction products to meet seven basic requirements for construction works. These cover:

- mechanical resistance and stability
- safety in case of fire
- hygiene, health and environment
- safety and accessibility in use
- protection against noise
- energy economy and heat retention
- sustainable use of natural resources" [26]

"Harmonised european standards (hENs)

Currently, there are over 420 hENs covering a broad range of construction products. hENs are progressively becoming the norm as conflicting national standards (e.g. Irish and British Standards commonly used here) are being withdrawn.

All hENs under the CPD have an informative annex Za. In general, this annex contains 3 parts:

- ZA.1 A list of product characteristics as well as the clauses in the standard in which the assessment or test method is set out or referred to. The list represents a compilation of all regulated requirements for the product in question across the EU,
- ZA.2 The procedures for conformity assessment, namely the tasks to be carried out by the manufacturer and the notified body. This is currently referred to as the agreed system of attestation of conformity, but will be known as the system of assessment and Verification of Constancy of Performance under the CPR, and
- ZA.3 The process for CE Marking and labelling.

[25,26,28] *Construction products association;* Guidance Note on the Construction Products Regulation [http://www.constructionproducts.org.uk/publications/industry-affairs/display/view/construction-products-regulation/] (11.04.2014, page 2-4)

[27] *Building Regulations Advisory Body;* Information Note on the Construction Products Regulation [http://www.environ.ie/en/Publications/DevelopmentandHousing/BuildingStandards/FileDownLoad,30649,en.pdf] (11.04.2014)

112 Guidance Note on the Construction Products Regulation – cover
113 The Certificate of Compliance CE (CE Certificate of Conformity)

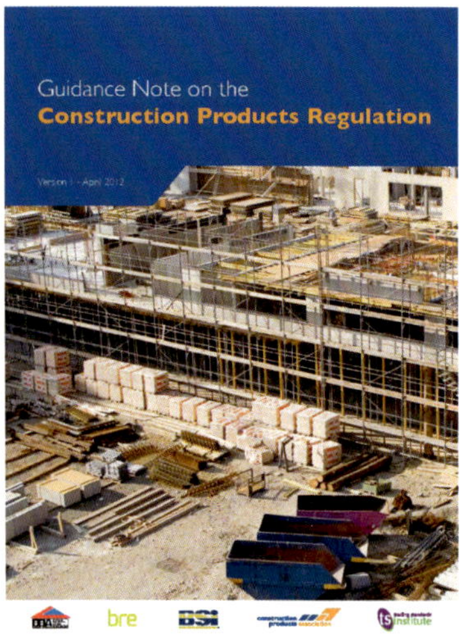

112

A list of hENs is available at the following link:

http://ec.europa.eu/enterprise/newapproach/nando/index.cfm?fuseaction=cpd.hs&cpr=YT" [27]

"CE marking under the CPR

CE marking enables a product to be placed legally on the market in any member state. However, as explained below, this does not necessarily mean that the product will be suitable for all end uses in all member states.

CE marking indicates that a product is consistent with its Declaration of Performance (DoP) as made by the manufacturer. The declaration varies according to the particular harmonised technical specification covering the product. In general there are three ways in which information can be presented for each relevant characteristic:

- confirmation of achievement of a minimum performance or threshold. This could be by satisfying a Pass/Fail criterion or simply by being eligible to be in the standard
- the actual performance (a declared value)
- a particular class of performance reached.

As such, decision makers (e.g. designers and specifiers) should understand the relevant performance requirements for the product.

How CE marking is approached for a specific product is set out in the harmonised technical specifications. For hENs this is set out in Annex ZA.3 and for ETAs in a section in the EAD." [28]

The hENs are important for manufacturers when declaring the performance of their construction product. It also helps authorities when specifying requirements for construction products but also for architects and designers when choosing the construction products.

Building product

A building product is a product or a building set, which is manufactured and placed on the market to be permanently incorporated for construction works or as parts.

Its performance has an impact on the performance of the construction works but still has to follow the basic requirements for construction works. (Regulation (EU) No 305/2011 Article 2)

CE	CE symbol with proportions of a minimum height of 5 mm, confirmed by regulation (EC) No 765/2008 of the European Parliament and by the Council setting out the requirements for accreditation and market surveillance relating to the marketing of products and the repealing Regulation (EEC) No 339/93
0123	Identification number of the notified agency
Company	Name and registered address or mark of the producer
Year	The last two numbers of the year, in which the CE symbol was first used
0123-xxxx-xxxx	Reference number of the declaration of performance
e.g. EN 12620	Number of harmonised European norms or the European technical specification
Gravel 04/16 gravel for concrete	The uniquely identifying code of the product
Product-specified characteristic (according to respective hEN)	Additional information according to appendix ZA of the harmonised European norms or the European technical specification

113

The Certificate of Compliance CE

CE Certificate of Conformity - requirements that must be complied with for CE marking according to Article 9 the EU Construction Products Regulation following, is mandatory after 1.7.2013 for all construction products placed on the market for which harmonised standards are in place – prerequisite of the CE marking is a successful run of conformity assessment procedures.

The CE marking must affix itself visibly, legibly and indelibly to the product.

The CE marking shall be applied to a construction product only by the manufacturer or his authorized representative. Marking CE means that the product complies with the European Union's Directives in the field of consumption security.

1.8 Regulations in Europe and Germany

"The results of a Life Cycle Assessment of a product can be outlined in an Environmental Product Declaration (EPD). The main purpose of an environmental declaration is to provide easily accessible quality assured data on the environmental impact of a product or process. This public document is an environmental declaration (type III) according to ISO 14025."[29]

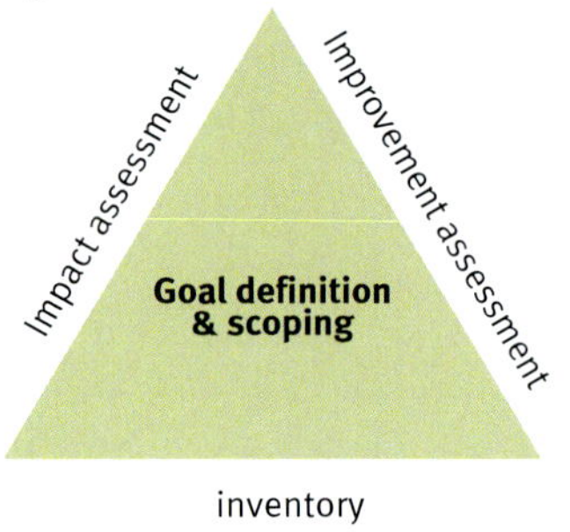

114

[29] *The Chemical Company;* Eco-Efficiency Analysis and SEEBALANCE. Quantifying Sustainability. Ludwigshafen

114 Life Cycle Assessment methodology
115 Phases of LCA
116 Inputs and outputs during the product life time
117 Different levels of building products

1.8.3 DIN EN ISO 14040:2009-11 – "Environmental management – Life cycle assessment – Principles and framework"

DIN EN ISO 14044:2006-10 – "Environmental management – Life cycle assessment – Requirements and guidelines "

The LCA according to ISO 14040 and 14044 is a method for detecting and assessing the environmental impacts of products, processes, services, etc. over the entire life cycle, e.g. from raw material extraction, to production and use, through to disposal.

The life cycle assessment according to DIN EN ISO 14040 and 14044 should be the principal form of product-related accounting today. The last version of DIN EN ISO 14040 was updated in November 2009 and DIN EN ISO 14044 in October 2006.

It turns in particular to five central parameters:

- consumption of material resources
- consumption of energy sources
- load of air by atmospheric emissions
- material load of the water
- load of the soil by wastes and direct emissions

The economics and society ranges, i.e. the economic and social effects are, however, not regarded in the life cycle analysis. Such is specified in the line analysis.

Products and services become considered with parameters over the entire product life cycle. Thus all are analysed; the dismantling of the raw materials, the supply, the production and processing of semi-finished materials and products, the use of the products, re-utilization (recycling), or disposal. Also considered, depending upon definition of the balance framework, are the supply ranges of energy, supply by auxiliary and additives, transportation and maintenance in the respective phases.

Goals of the ecological balance are to minimize the withdrawal of resources, the delivery emissions, and to maximize the direct feedback from flows of material and energy i.e. the material cycle in the building industry. In order to ensure Standardisation and concomitantly, comparability of ecological balance studies with the individual components of the ecological balance is regulated by DIN EN ISO 14040.

The four main steps of LCA:

- Goal and scope definition
- Life cycle inventory analysis
- Life cycle impact assessment
- Evaluation

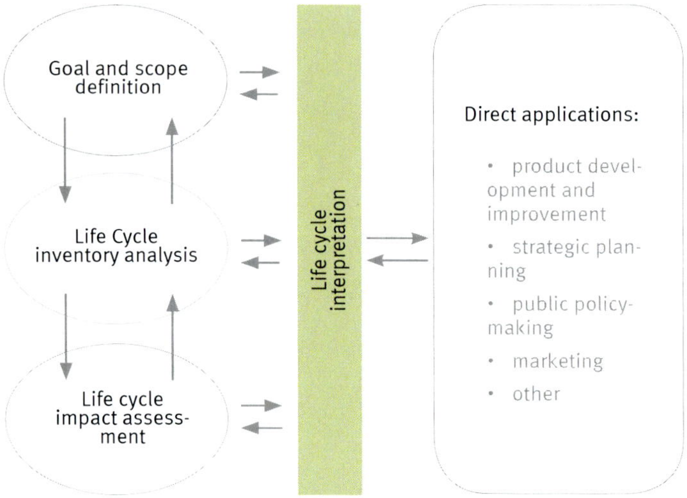

115

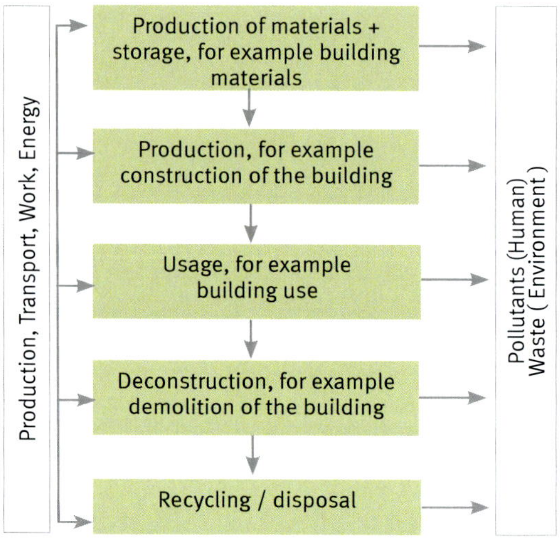

116

In order to provide a standard ecological balance, the steps specified above are necessary. As it concerns the building industry and its large material and energy flows and thus large information capacities, ecological balance can be accomplished on different levels of investigational goals:

- single substances
- building materials
- building parts (functional units)
- building and structural facilities

Single substances

Single substances such as propellants and solvents can be understood as additive. Commonly, they are a component of a constructional material solution and often noticed by planners as complex. Aside from the material characteristics, the environmental and health risks are represented with processing, transport, storage and disposal.

Building materials

Building materials and building products are used during the establishment and repair/modernization by buildings. The manufacturers' products technical and ecological characteristics are effective in the phase of processing as well as the phases of use, maintenance and disposal.

The most frequently considered life phases on this balance level are the raw material extraction and the production, as well as the recycling and/ or disposal of the product.

Building parts (functional units)

By functional units, one can understand a construction material solution in built condition, such as a brick wall or a window unit. The units concern the building parts as the combination of material (building materials, building products) and Realization (building process).

For functional units, information can be made available of technical characteristics; the building design aspect, expenditures, environmental impacts, production and usage risks, aging, maintenance, as well as disposal.

Building and structural facilities

Building and structural facilities represent the subjects of planning considerations. Particularly, the expenditures, environmental impacts, usage risks, maintenance and operation of buildings should only be measured and evaluated as a whole building. The only possible reciprocal effect between the individual functional units is shown simultaneously on this level.

Goal and scope definition

- definition and description of the target group of analysis (product, process or activity)
- clear reason for execution study, identification of boundaries and preparation of environmental impact categories (energy source, surface coverage, waste heat, etc.)
- description of life-cycle criteria (time of use, recycling, etc.)
- the goal definition gives the basic conditions for the balance process

Life Cycle Inventory analysis

- is an inventory of all relevant air and water emissions, material and energy flows (inputs and outputs), wastes and environmental releases along the life cycle of a product

Life Cycle Impact assessment

- describes the impact from the life cycle inventory on the environment
- assessment of environmental effects (resources consumption and emissions) along the complete life cycle (production, use and disposal)
- analysis and results evaluation of the life and impact balance

Evaluation

- summary of results, identification of development opportunities, weaknesses, priorities, the advantages and disadvantages of several alternatives, etc.
- conclusions and recommendations to select the preferred product, process or service

1. Level: Building material	2. Level: Building components	3. Level: Building
Functional unit		
E.g. 1 kg of building material	E.g. 1 m² of building component	E.g. 1 m² of living space
Life stages		
• extraction of raw materials and production of building materials • recycling of materials and disposal	• extraction of raw materials and production of building materials • instant bearing of considered building components • use of building components • recycling of materials and disposal	• new building • renovation • use • disposal
Targets		
• process optimising for producers • comparison of the products for customers • date bases for levels 2 and 3	• selection of aid for decisions in process of building projection e.g. in the form of catalogues of building components • date bases for next level	• selection of aid for planning • stage with the goal to optimise the building

117

1.8 Regulations in Europe and Germany

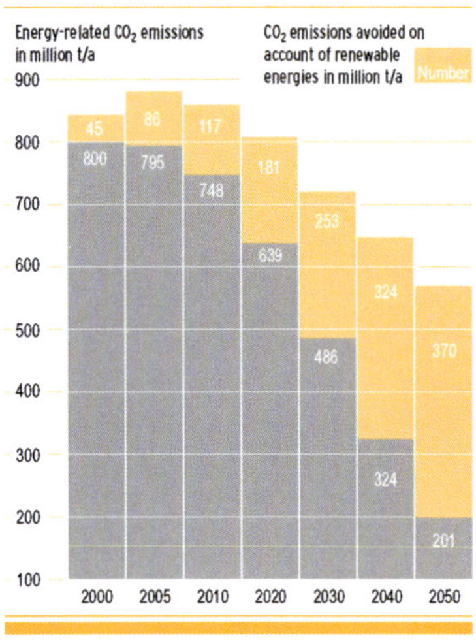

118

[30] *BMU;* EEG – The Renewable Energy Sources Act. Berlin: BMU 07/2007, page 4

[31] *BMU;* EEG – The Renewable Energy Sources Act. Berlin: BMU 07/2007, page 6

118 Energy related CO_2

119 Electricity generated from renewable energies

1.8.4 EEG – Erneuerbare Energien Gesetz (Renewable Energy Sources Act)

The EEG was formed on 29th March 2000, revised in 2009, and finally came into force on 28th December 2012. In the summer of 2014, there was an additional amendment to the Act.

The concept is to create a coalition to maintain the feed-in system and to allow the continuation of older plants. The further expansion of renewable energies will be coordinated in a statutory framework: 40 to 45 % by 2025, 55 to 60 % before 2035. It will be checked annually as to whether the objectives are being achieved (monitoring). It is also important to involve the European electricity market.

"The goal of the EEG is to speed up the market launch of technologies for electricity production from wind power, solar radiation, biomass, geothermal power and hydropower, as well as mine gas. The core element of the legislation is the duty of grid operators to give priority to electricity from renewable energy sources, and to pay for it according to fixed tariffs." [30]

"The EEG guarantees each plant operator a fixed tariff for electricity generated from renewable sources which is fed into the public electricity grid. The tariff paid is basically dependent on the technology used, the year the installation was put into operation and the size of the plant." [31]

The federal government wants to reduce the rise in costs by offering compensation Schematics and stable costs.

After many years of funding by the EEG, renewable energies cannot exist without subsidies in the market. Therefore, the coalition will continue to integrate renewable energy into the electricity market.
In the future, new installations from 5 MW should directly market their electricity. From 2017, this will apply to all new installations.

In the promotion of photovoltaic systems, the reforms over recent years have shown it as possible. For biomass systems there must be a limitation primarily on waste and residual substances. This is to protect nature and avoid the overuse of landscape for corn production.

For the future of wind turbines on land, good sites are to be used in relation to appropriate economic models. For wind generation at sea, it is realistic to expand: The 2020 expansion path is set to 6.5 GW.

In order to achieve the expansion of 15 GW by 2030, each year an average of two wind farms with a capacity of approximately 400 MW are to join the network.

photovoltaics
bioenergy
wind energy
hydropower

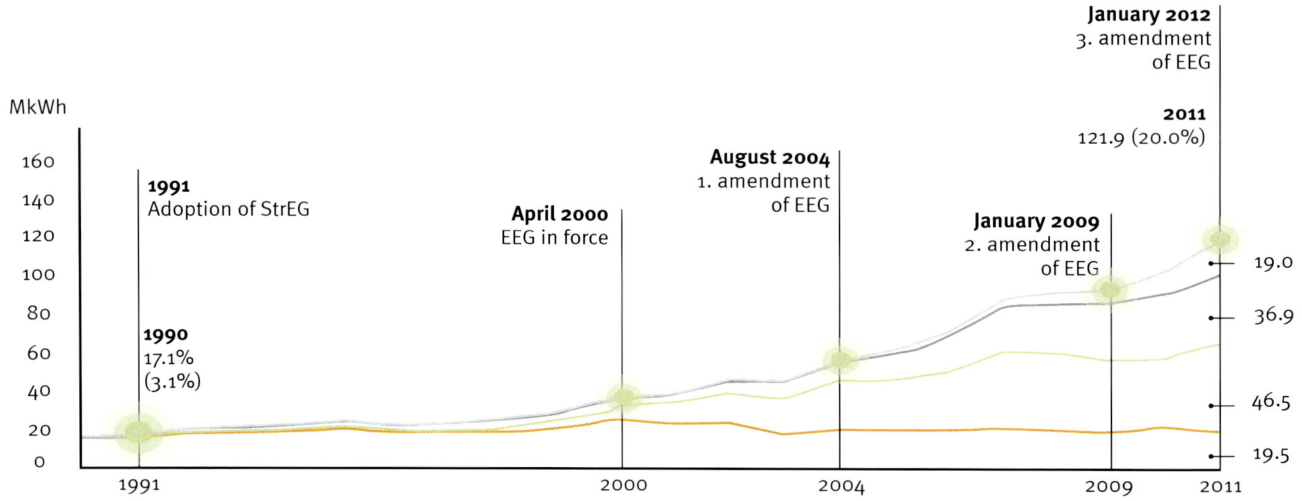

119

1.8.5 EEWärmeG – Erneuerbare Energien Wärme Gesetz (Act on the Promotion of Renewable Energies in the Heat Sector, Heat Act)

"The new Renewable Energies Heat Act entered into force on 1st January 2009. It stipulates that owners of new buildings must cover part of their heat supply with renewable energies. This applies to residential and nonresidential buildings for which a building application or construction notification was submitted after 1st January 2009.

The owner is free to choose which source of renewable energies is used. A certain technology-specific percentage of heat, dependent on the type of energy employed, must be used.

The Heat Act has been amended. The amendments arose from the "Act Implementing European Renewable Energies Legislation" (implementing Directive 2009/28/EC of the European Parliament and of the Council of 23rd April 2009 on the promotion of the use of energy from renewable sources) and came into force on May 1st 2011.

The obligation to use a share of renewable heating or cooling, previously only applied to new buildings, is now extended to existing public buildings undergoing major renovations.

The public sector must fulfil an exemplary role in using renewable energy sources for heating and cooling. This applies to public buildings being the property of, or in the possession of the public sector, and being used for legislative or executive functions, for the purpose of the administration of justice or as a public facility.

An exemplary role must also be ensured where buildings are rented or leased.

The law was created with the objective that every owner of a building should be able to find an individually tailored, cost-effective solution.

Accompanying the legal obligation for new buildings, the German government continues its comprehensive support programme, the market incentive programme for renewable energies in the heat market (solar, biomass, geothermal installations), to supplement the Act.

It assists owners of existing buildings in getting a start on heating or cooling from renewable energies, providing either capital grants for smaller installations or low-interest loans and redemption grants for larger installations or infrastructures like heat networks or large heat storages."[32]

The last amendment of the Heat Act was in December 2011 and came into force on 1st April 2012.

[32] *BMU;* The Renewable Energies Heat Act [http://www.bmu.de/english/renewable_energy/downloads/doc/42351.php] (12.10.2012)

120 Duty for all new construction since 2009 – heat from renewable energies, three examples for the heat generation in a singe family house (150 m²)

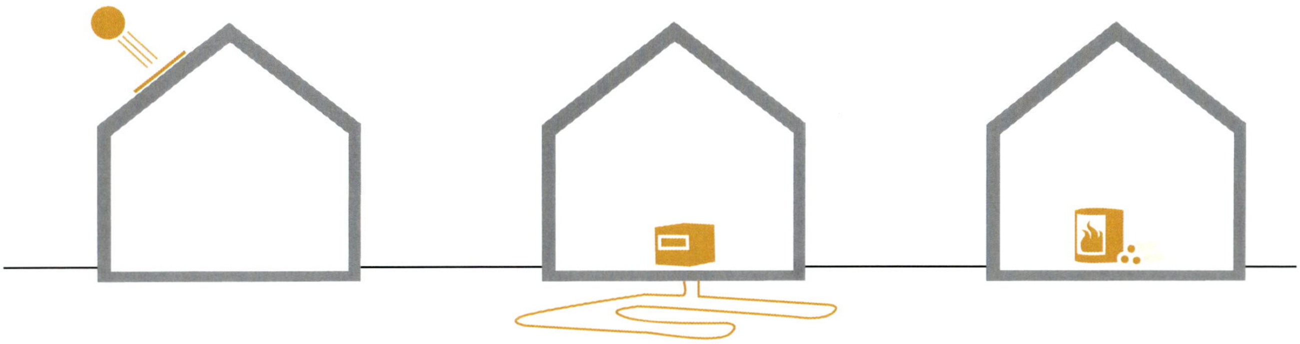

Energy from the sun
solar collector
costs: approx. 4,000 €

Energy from the earth
heat pump
costs: approx. 16,000 €

Energy from biomass
wood pellet plant
costs: approx. 12,000 €

120

1.8 Regulations in Europe and Germany

In principle, the provisions of the Energy Saving Ordinance (EnEV) are for any building, regardless of the facade design. However, there are exceptions such as heritage buildings.

Heritage protection has more importance than EnEV. In case the heritage building substance appearance would be changed or impaired through energy saving measurements, it can be deviated from the requirements of EnEV.

Since the energy saving regulation is designed to look at the house as a whole, the increased heat loss in the facade can be compensated with insulation of other components such as the roof or by using modern heating, hot water and renewable energy sources.

1.8.6 EnEV – Energie Einspar Verordnung (Germany Energy Conservation Regulations for Buildings)

EnEV is the German Energy Conservation Regulation which defines standards for insulation, fenestration, envelope, heating, ventilation and air-conditioning.

It also discusses the limitation of primary energy use, that may not be exceeded. It shows the potential of using the calculation procedures as a planning tool which offers new energy saving approaches and CO_2 reduction in buildings.

Germany's energy efficiency building code was first passed on 1st February, 2002. Since 1st October 2009, there is a new EnEV 2009 with the main goal to reduce energy use by 30 %. The new EnEV 2014 came into force on 1st May 2014 and should further reduce this by another 30 %.

It is based on the new DIN V 18599:2011-12 and describes how the new building energy passes are to be created.

After 1.1.2016, the primary energy border value from a reference building should be under 25 % for all new construction. Also included are tighter building requirements.

DIN V 18599:2011-12

The EnEV is based on existing EN / DIN standards. This means that the norms of their issue date are here cited, becoming apart of the EnEV.
DIN V 18599 Energy Efficiency of Buildings is a calculation tool for the net, final and primary energy demand of heating, cooling, ventilation, domestic hot water and lighting. The latest version is from 2011.

Content of EnEV 2014:

- General

§1 Purpose and area of application
§2 Definitions

- New building

§3 Residential building
§4 Nonresidential building
§5 Alternative power sources
§6 Airtightness of building envelope
§7 Heat protection
§8 Small buildings

- Existing building

§9 Change, extension
§10 Upgrade of existing building
§11 Quality of energy
§12 Inspection of air-conditioning

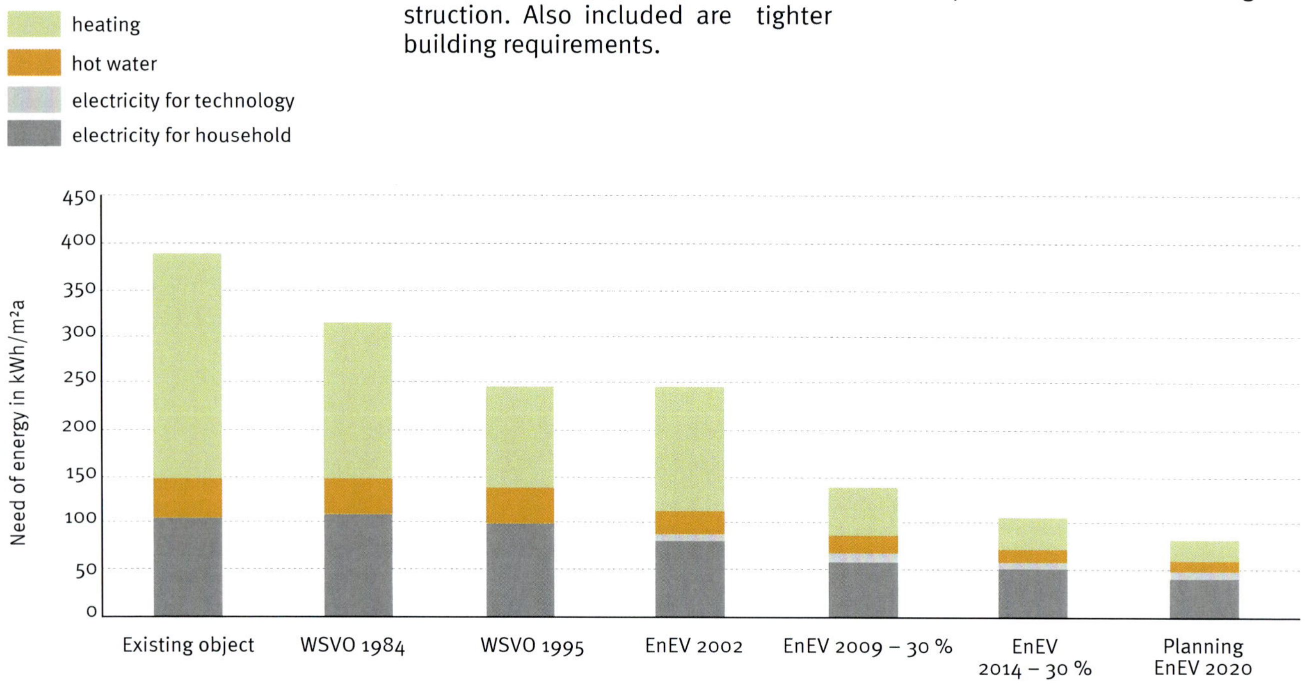

121

- Technology

§13 Installation of boiler
§14 Pipes, hot water
§15 Cooling and ventilation

- Energy Performance Certificate

§16 Aim of Energy Performance Certificate
§16a Required fields in reports
§17 Principles of Energy Performance Certificate
§18 Requirements of Energy Performance Certificate
§19 Use of Energy Performance Certificate
§20 Recommendation for modernisation
§21 Exhibitors of Energy Performance Certificate

- Common

§22 Mixed-use building
§23 Regulate of technology
§24 Exceptions
§25 Exemption from EnEV
§26 Responsible
§26a Private evidence
§26b Authorise chimney sweep
§26c Registration numbers
§26d Sample checks
§26e Data evaluation
§26f Experience reports countries
§27 Regulation offence

- Transitions, to come in force

§28 Transitional regulations
§29 Energy Performance Certificates
§30 Transitional regulation on provisional perception of implementation tasks of the countries by the German Institute for Building Technology

- Article 2: Announcement
- Article 3: Entry into force

Appendix to EnEV 2014

- Requirements for residential building
- Requirements for nonresidential building
- Requirements existing building
- Tightness, minimum of air change
- Start of heating
- Insulation of pipes, valves
- Energy Performance Certificate for residential building
- Energy Performance Certificate for nonresidential building
- Announcement for certificate of energy need
- Announcement for certificate of energy use
- Energy efficiency classes
- Content of training

Purpose of EnEV

The purpose of this regulation is to save energy in buildings, in accordance with the legal principle of economic viability. Regulations should contribute to the energy policies of the federal government, especially to reach nearly carbon-neutral building stock by the year 2050.

In addition to the definitions in the Regulations the objective may be achieved also with other instruments, especially with a modernization program for building, incentives by the funding policy and a remediation road map.

In the context of this yet to be determined requirements for the energy performance of zero-energy buildings, the federal government is also in this context, a fundamental simplification and consolidation of the instruments governing the energy saving and the use of renewable energy in buildings aspire to make the energetic and economic optimization of buildings easier.

121 Comparison of different German standards requirements for the building energy demand in accordance to EnEV
122 Comparison of different German standards requirements for the specific heat transmission losses in accordance to EnEV
123 Parts of the DIN V 18599

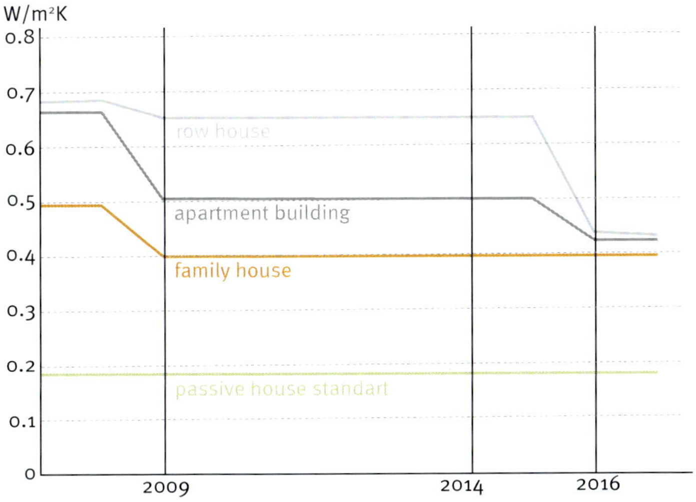

122

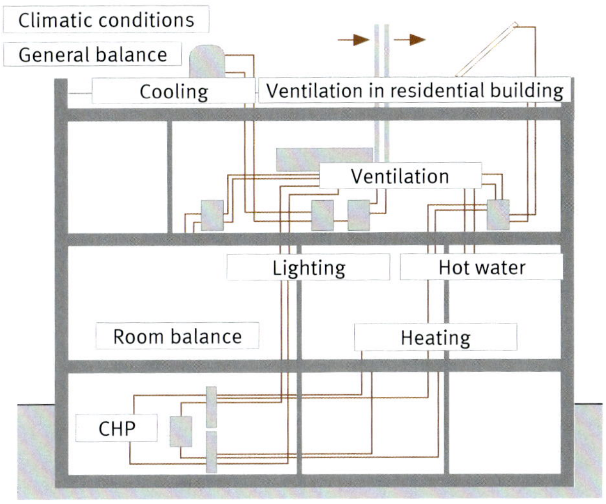

123

1.8 Regulations in Europe and Germany

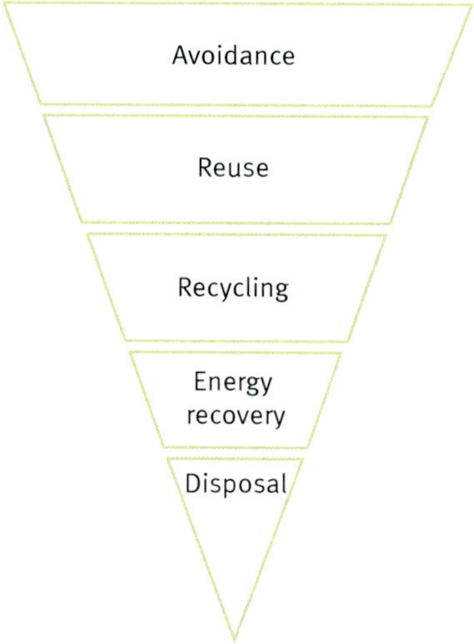

124

1.8.7 Waste directive of EU 2008/98/EG

This directive establishes a legal framework for the handling of waste in the community.

Its goal is to protect the environment and human health by avoiding the adverse impacts of the generation and management of waste.

It came into force on 12th December 2008. Until 12th December 2010, the EU member states had to consider it in their national laws.

The following items are in descending hierarchy outlining objectives for dealing with waste:

- waste avoidance, reducing its quantity and harmfulness
- preparing for recycling
- waste recycling
- other recovery, especially energy recovery and backfilling
- waste disposal

To promote this hierarchy of waste treatment, member states may adopt measures with legislative acts.
However, they must ensure that waste management is carried without endangering human health or harming the environment.
Each waste producer or other holder of waste must carry out waste treatment themselves, or it can be performed by a dealer, facility or company.
Member states may cooperate, if necessary, to build a network of waste disposal installations. This network will enable the independence of the European Union in the field of waste treatment.

The storage and treatment of hazardous waste must be carried out under conditions that ensure the protection of the environment and human health. They must not be mixed with other hazardous waste and must be packaged in accordance with applicable international or community standards and be labelled.

Establishments and undertakings intending to carry out waste treatment must obtain a permit from the competent authority. This permit is for the type and quantity of waste to specify the method used as well as the monitoring and control procedures.

Incineration or co-incineration with energy recovery is approved only with the recovery of energy with a high level of energy efficiency.

124 The waste management priority pyramid – waste prevention should always be considered first
125 Waste seperation in Plus Energy School Rostock, Germany
126 Waste management is a daily problem in a lot of countries
127 The different colours of the waste separation baskets in Germany – the orange basket is new, since 2013

125

1.8.8 Kreislaufwirtschaftsgesetz – Gesetz zur Förderung der Kreislaufwirtschaft und Sicherung der umweltverträglichen Bewirtschaftung von Abfällen (Act for promoting closed substance cycle waste management)

The Recycling and Waste Management Act is the main federal law within the German waste law. The law has been in force since 1996 and regulates the handling, securing and the sustainable management of waste.

The last amendment to the Act was made in May 2013 and came into force on 1st May 2014.

According to §1 of the recycling and waste management act, it is the purpose of the law to promote recycling to conserve natural resources and to ensure the environmentally sound management of waste.

The aim of the recycling law is to reduce considerably the accumulation of waste and to protect the natural resources by promoting low residue recycling.

Furthermore, the aim is to make consistent measures for the prevention and recovery of waste prior to the material generation and disposal of nonrecoverable waste in land fills.

Outline of the Law

The recycling and waste management act is divided into nine parts and four appendices:

- General regulations
- Principles and obligations of the producer, waste owner, and public waste management authorities
- Product responsibility
- Planning responsibility
- Promotion and waste consultancy
- Monitoring
- Waste management companies
- Business organisation, business representative of waste and unburdening for audited company sites
- Final definitions

Appendix 1: Disposal methods
Appendix 2: Utilisation methods
Appendix 3: Criteria determining the state of the technology
Appendix 4: Examples of waste prevention measures according to §33

126

Waste separation

Waste separation is the collection divided into different types of waste. It is also to be considered the waste separation of households or from industry and commercial facilities.

In Germany, the waste is separated already by the user. After the recycling law it is the user's duty to presort the trash in industry and commerce in order to make easier the separation expenditure. It will be duty for each person after 2015. There are different types of waste to be separated, e.g. paper, glass, plastics, organic waste, metals, electrical equipment and bulky waste.

The waste is to be separated into collection containers and must be disposed of in accordance to the type of waste. A Schematic was introduced by the recycling code, that can be found primarily on products made of plastic, but also on other objects.

Of the 455 kg of waste per capita in German households in 2009, 199 kg was household and bulky waste, 143 kg was recyclables and about 111 kg was organic waste.

Reusable materials

Packaging and other objects from:
Plastic
Metal
Composite material

Please no electrical appliances, energy saving lamps, batteries, textiles, and wood volume

Glass

For example:
Beverage bottles
Oil and vinegar bottles
Jars (jam, baby food, ect.)

Please no electrical appliances, energy saving lamps, batteries, textiles, and wood volume

Paper / Cardboard

For example:
Newspaper
Magazines
Brochures
Boxes
Books

Please fold or tear cartons flat

BIO materials

For example:
Fruits and vegetable left overs
Food leftovers (also cooked)
Tea- coffee filter
Flowers
Garden rubbish

Well wrap it in newspaper, or kitchen paper, do not use plastic bags

Household rubbish

For example:
Sanitary articles
Dust bags
Diapers
Wallpaper

Construction waste or pollutants not in or adjacent to the ton

127

1.9 Summary

128

Today, there are many strategies, norms and regulations. These restrictions are extremely important. Without these laws, everyone would do as he or she pleases without considering the effects on others or our environment.

However, the building requirements and various laws and regulations restrict planning and building processes and it is uncommon for them to contradict themselves.

In order to fulfil certain requirements of one law, the terms of other laws may be broken. This is due to the diversity of buildings and the particularity of its situations and conditions, which are often impossible to be considered by general norms and regulations.

Other consequences include the limiting of the design process during the building concept development as costs increase and the planning process takes even longer.

An example is the difference between architectural competitions and the implementation of the plan.

The implementation of an architectural competition in order to secure the building design quality as described in the Guidelines for sustainable planning, prevents the earlier creation of an integrative planning team during in the initial design phase, which is very unsustainable.

What are the borders of planning conditions, limitations and regulations? Which planning instruments are important in ecological planning and designing? Which limitations have to be considered in order to plan sustainably? A lot of questions in relation to sustainable and ecological planning are still open, which need to be openly discussed and answered.
All of the laws and regulations also restrict the consumer. What was once self-understanding for consumers has now been removed and therefore the responsibilities have disappeared. Therefore it is of high importance, that the consumers are made aware of this once again. The responsibility of each user is the foundation of sustainability.

It was observed, that the introduction of regulations do not lead to sustainability, but rather to the waste of energies and resources. A greater participation has to be introduced with the support of informal instruments in order to redevelop peoples own thinking in order to build sustainably.
In some communities, the modern re-thinking of self-responsibility has already been introduced, e.g. in Amsterdam, where the "play regulation plans" replace the laws.

In Germany, these are known as "master plans". The plans are important instruments for communal planning, which provides guidelines for future developments.

128 Workshop "Green Univer-City Wismar" – students' notes – analysing problems and searching for solutions
129 Workshop "Green Univer-City Wismar" – working atmosphere

129

Workshop

"Green Univer-City Wismar"

In March 2014, the workshop "Urban Ecology" together with different experts and students took place at the University of Wismar.

"Green Univer-City" was an international workshop that focused on developing concepts to benefit the city. 31 students from 10 different countries worked with 11 experts to develop ideas that could change the perception of Wismar, to make it a greener place and to provide access to areas of the town that have previously been unused.

There is a lot of potential for the city of Wismar and for the University to teach internationally and establish a pilot project for sustainable urban planning. Wismar could take the first step into the future and become a global player.

The conclusion of the workshop noted that the overall concept may be divided into the topics of connectivity, transportation and energy management. This was based on our experience and observations.
The campus will be fitted with equipment to produce sustainable energy. Solar panels that could produce at least half the current usage as well as wind-power and biogas facilities could also be added.
100 % renewable energy at the Wismar University is an exciting and ambitious plan that will cut the carbon footprint of the university while also promoting and educating the public about the importance of such Schematics. By changing the way the campus operates and utilizes new energy sources, we can all look forward to an exciting and more sustainable future.
Students also proposed new concepts to connect the city and the campus in a more efficient and attractive way. By bridging the wetland between the old city and university, there would be a much faster route and better accessibility to the wetland and its stunning landscape.
In addition, the waterways will be encouraged to flow more naturally and could provide a water-concept to link the entire campus.
Long distances in Wismar generally don't exist. It is possible to make your way around, by walking to your destination. This opens up the opportunity to propose a concept of sustainable transportation.
The main aim was to develop a comfortable and easily understandable system of mobility in Wismar. Students also developed a system of spaces, where people can enjoy beautiful vistas, different activities or pick up bikes for free.
These places will have a specific design and signage. Students also proposed a free wifi connection in the city and developed new apps for Wismar.

130

130 Workshop "Green Univer-City Wismar" – student sketches
131 Workshop "Green Univer-City Wismar" – vision masterplan

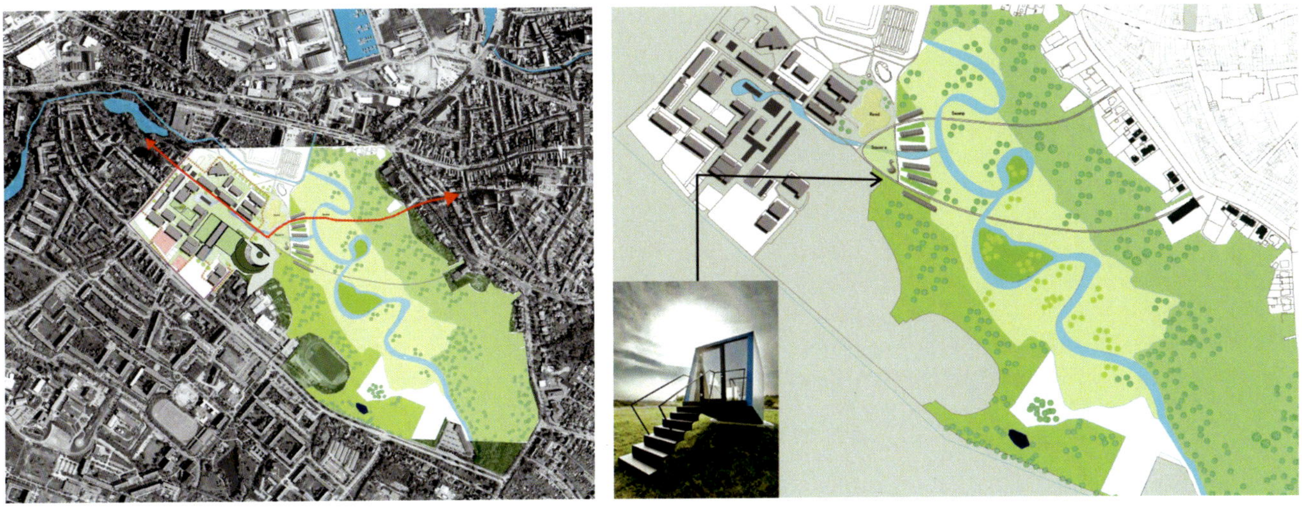

131

132 Building renovation and conversion is a large part of a building's life time design – conversion of a heritage residential house into an office building, Bützow, IGEL-Institut

2.0 Building life time

2.0 Building life time

2.1 Introduction

The life of a building consists of more steps than what are normally considered.
The life cycle design is the cornerstone of sustainable building design. The different life cycles of a building should be considered and integrated already within the designing phase in order to ensure the building is sustainable.

The planning process is very important in order to build a sustainable building. A well planned project can save a lot of energy, resources, costs and waste.

From this point of view, integral planning is the best way of planning. Integral planning considers the whole life cycle of a building, starting with the projects design to the demolition of the building. Architecture, structure and technology are connected together and can be optimised during the planning process.

The integral planning team develops together with other members of the project (owner, user, administration, etc.) a concept that focuses on resource saving and minimizing the environmental loads and improvement of comfort and economy.

The planning is a very important part because it has a major influence on the future life cycle of a building. The energy concept, water concept, waste concept, lighting concept, cleaning and maintenance concept and also the flexibility and recycling concept should all be part of it.

It is important to examine, how large the flexibility of the building is to change its use and which operating costs are to be expected due to the thermal quality of the building cover. Good planning can save additional costs in construction and other life cycles can be avoided.

Building cycles and processes

There are five fundamental life cycles to be considered at the beginning of each ecological planning:

- Building material production phase

It is important to consider how the individual building materials used in the construction contribute to the ecological expenditure of the production of the building.

Also to consider is how the resources for the building material are extracted and how much primary energy is required for the processing and manufacturing. The transportation to the building site is also important to consider. Local, natural materials are the best choice.

- Construction process phase

This phase considers the construction of the building itself. It relates to the construction processes on site (con-

133 A building life cycle consisting of the five main stages

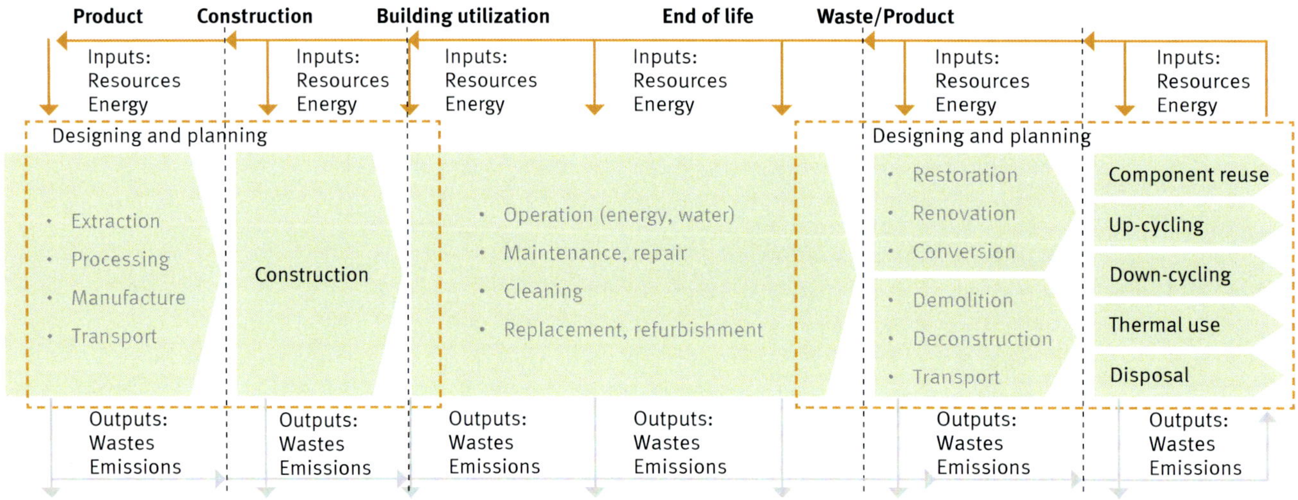

133

struction waste, noise, dust, loads on soil and environment). The goal is to minimize the loads and create a healthy environment for all participants.

- Building utilization phase

This phase generally has the longest life cycle – around 20-100 years and requires a lot of energy and resources. Here, the operation energy and water use is important. Examine the ecological expenditure of individual building materials and building materials for maintenance (repair of the building). The energy and resources for cleaning and refurbishment are also to be considered.

- End of life phase

Building end of life consists of two main possibilities: keeping the existing building or building demolition.

Keeping the existing building – restoration, renovation or conversion should always be considered as the first possibility. By renewing and reusing an existing building, waste, resources and the energy demands for a new construction can be avoided.
This also means the building life cycle can be closed, going from the end of the building's life to the beginning. Few additional resources are required to renovate a building compared to the demolition of a building and new building construction.

The case of **demolishing a building** should only be considered if the existing building is in very bad condition or if it is not possible to be reused. The demolishing of a building results in a large amount of building waste and emissions.
Examine the effects of the building materials on the environment as well as their connections:

- separable or inseparable
- re-usable (product recycling)
- material usability (down-cycling)
- composting/burn/decomposing

From this an estimate of the disposal expenditure of a construction can be derived. It is important to leave the land untouched after the end of a builds life.

- disposal/recycling phase

It is important that the buildings elements are disposed after the building is deconstructed or that they can be recycled and used again for product processing. In this way, the cycle can be closed without generating any waste.
In every cycle there are resource and energy inputs and waste and emission outputs. The goal is to reduce these as much as possible and to create a closed independent cycle.
As a tool to optimise the inputs and outputs during the entire life cycle of the building, the LCA (page 15, 72), LCC (page 15, 264) and the consideration of external costs (page 15) are to be used.

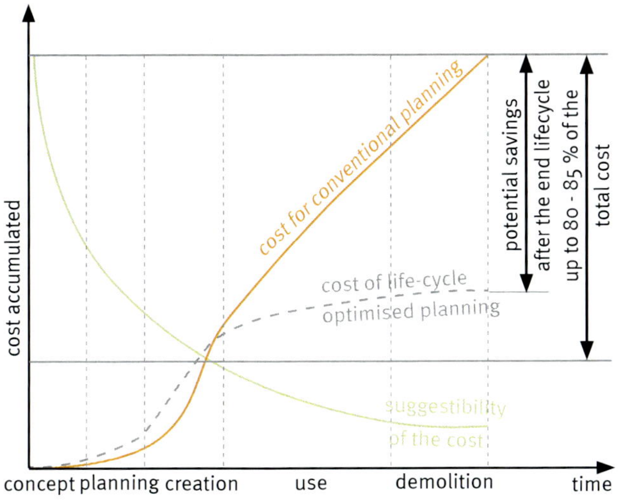

134

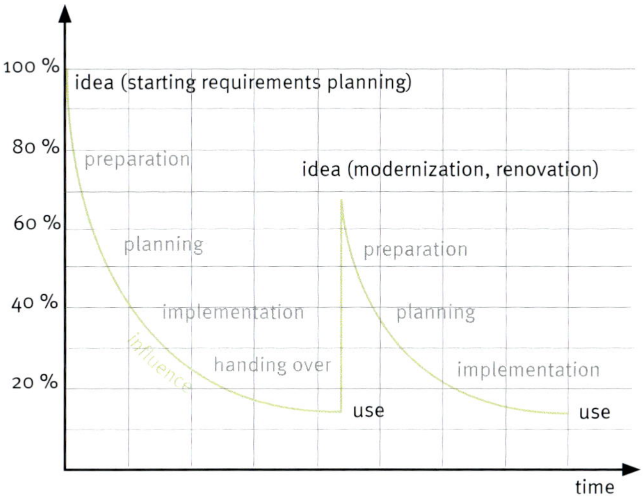

135

134 Life cycle costs relationships between building alternatives
135 The total costs during the life time of the building, costs rise over time because older buildings become increasingly expensive to operate and maintain

2.2 First building life time

Glass

A material which is particularly important for solar building construction is the glass, which is commonly used in the form of insulating glass (as double or triple glazing).

There is a number of commodities used for the manufacture of glass, for example silica sand and limestone, used in appropriate mixtures. The appropriate "mixture" is made in a mixing machine and moved by a transport device (for example conveyor belts) in the oven.

First, the rough melt is conducted in the oven heated with gas or with oil at a temperature of 1,400 °C. After, a "purification means" is completed allowing steam and gas bubbles to escape from the streaks of the products of rough melt. The own glass aggregate is achieved by cooling down to 1,200 °C.

Glass ovens typically work with heat recovery. The fibreglass used as insulation material is made from alkaline raw glass and molten shards by centrifuging. Glass can also be recycled to a certain extent.

136 CO_2 balance by manufacturing varies in dependance on the produced building material
137 Basic values of building materials

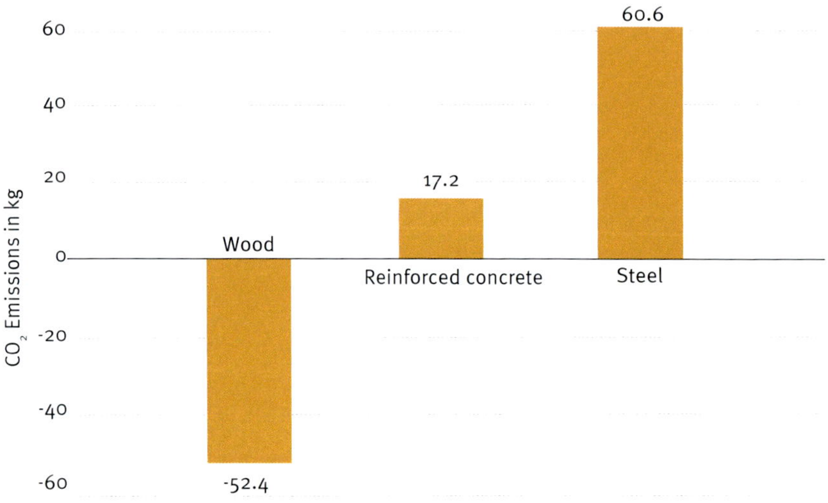

136

The first life time of the building considers the extraction, processing and manufacturing of building materials, their storage, and transportation to the building site. This life step is closely connected to material and resource consumption.

From this point of view, the considering of the primary energy content of materials is important. Also, with building materials there are large differences in the contained primary energy. Bricks, for example are less energy-intensive in production than reinforced concrete.

Various thermal insulation materials also have large differences – expanded polystyrene EPS or extruded polystyrene XPS require much more primary energy for their production than wood fibre insulation or rock-wool or cellulose. (figure 137)

Metal sheets of aluminium are twice as energy-intensive as copper. Also, waterproofing foils have high differences in primary energy required for production.

The following are examples of conventional building materials and their manufacturing:

Cement

The production of cement requires large industrial plants in which limestone is crushed and mixed with other materials (clay, bauxite, iron oxides or blast furnace slag) in a tube rotary oven at temperatures that range from 1,250 °C to 1,500 °C. The final product is again crushed into the finest material. A characteristic for the surrounding area of a cement plant is a white-gray veil that coats the vegetation.

Concrete

From the cement plant, the cement is packed in paper or plastic bags, or it is transported directly into a building materials warehouse or factory for the manufacturing of semi-finished products or building components. Both semi-finished products (such as concrete blocks and plates) and finished components (such as concrete beams and base) are manufactured in factories where first the concrete is created by mixing binders (for example cement) and aggregates (sand, gravel) with water in large concrete mixers. The concrete is poured into forms for either semi-finished products or with inlaid steel skeletons in forms for building components. Building components are then transported in truck containers when ready for distribution.

Brick

Also, the production of bricks and other ceramics require machines and energy. The raw clay or loam must be processed through coarse and fine crushing and kneading. The wet mass is then mechanically pressed into a strand and cut to a brick length. Bricks are fired at a temperature of around 1,100 °C in ovens. In order to make the bricks more dense and hard, the firing temperature must be increased. The bricks can then be coloured and glazed by adding of mineral resources. Porous bricks are produced by the mixing of sawdust or other combustible materials with clay and are therefore lighter in weight and very good at insulating heat. The same is true for a hollow brick. Pallets are used for storing the stacked bricks. Often they are wrapped in plastic foil and transported by trucks.

Material	Density [kg/m³]	Thermal conductivity λ [W/mK]	Diffusion resistance factor μ [-]	Primary energy non renewable PE_{nre} [MJ/kg]
Brick wall				
Full brick wall	1,600	0.70	10	2.7
Pored brick, width 38 cm	920	0.15	8	2.6
Concrete				
Light concrete	600	0.22	10	4.7
Aerated concrete block	420	0.13	5	4.2
Reinforced concrete	2,400	2.33	90	-
Cement screed	2,000	1.40	30	0.8
Sand, gravel				
Wet gravel	1,900	1.40	2	0.1
Natural wet sand	1,800	1.40	2	0.1
Dry sand	1,300	0.70	2	0.1
Thermal insulation				
Expanded polystyrene EPS	11 - 30	0.044 - 0.035	20 - 50	95
Extruded polystyrene XPS	25 - 45	0.034 - 0.032	80 - 200	101
Wood fibre heat insulation plate	155	0.045	5	14
Coconut	50	0.05	1 - 2	35
Cork	120	0.041	18	7
Sheep wool	20	0.04	1 - 2	16
Foamglas	105 - 120	0.04 - 0.05	dense	67
Straw	80 - 200	0.046 - 0.075	1 - 2	4
Rockwool	25 - 200	0.041 - 0.035	1.1	17
Cellulose	30 - 50	0.041	1 - 2	22
Panel cladding				
Softwood plates	600	0.15	50	3.6
Fibre cement plates	2,000	0.58	50	14
Plasterboard	900	0.21	8	5.1
Flooring				
Floorboards	500	0.14	70	4.7
Tiles	2,000	1.00	200	7
Linoleum	1,000	0.18	500	17
PVC-cladding	1,400	0.21	12,000	63
Glas, metal				
Glass	2,500	0.81	100,000	15
Aluminium	2,800	200	dense	230
Aluminium recycled	2,800	200	dense	23
Steel	7,800	60	dense	36 - 100
Vapour barrier, waterproofing sheets				
ALU-foil 125 g/m²	-	-	dense	714
Bitumen	1,200	0.17	1,200	53
Asphalt, asphalt streed	2,000	0.70	2,000	5
Plastic roofing	-	-	90,000	-

137

2.3 Second building life time

57-storey skyscraper in 19 days
30-storey skyscraper in 15 days

Construction building phase depends on several factors. The priorities are normally time, money, quality and sustainability, which can not work all together. When time is the main importance, also amazing is possible. In 2012, China´s Broad Group construction company managed to build a 30-storey, 183,000 square foot hotel near the Dongting lake, in the Hunan Province, China in just 360 hours (15 days). 3 years later, they moved further on and built 57-storey skyscraper with 800 apartments and enough office space for 4,000 people.
But is this possible also by considering the building quality and sustainability of building site?

The second life time of building relates to the construction process, which has a high load on the environment. The goal is to minimize the loads and keep the construction site healthy for all participants.

Building construction is the process of preparing and forming the building until the structure is ready for occupancy.

After the building is occupied, with the help of monitoring and by taking various measurements over a period of one to two years, the building operation efficiency and user behaviour can be calculated and optimised.

The construction is the implementation of a design envisioned by architects and engineers. Because of technological complexities and market demands, changes of design plans during construction are not uncommon.

During the construction phase, the main focus should be on reducing or recycling the building waste, reducing the noise to build, dust, and the loads on soil and environment.

Building excavation must also be considered as well as chemical processes on the building site (e.g. gluing of the foils, lacks, etc).

During the second life time, the main focus is on the use of the land. Buildings take away parts of the landscape and generally cover it up.

The built area within the world has increased rapidly with dense settlements and large cities as well as the traffic systems covering up free land, reducing the natural earth surface.

On a daily basis, expanses of vacant land are built upon all over the world, e.g. 113 hectares of free land in Germany. This means that 113 hectares of land, which was previously agricultural or forests, is covered up with new streets, parking spaces, buildings, industrial areas, etc.

It is of high importance that the built area around the world is reduced and the reuse of existing sealed surfaces used instead. The greatest solution is land reuse.

Various concepts and strategies have already been developed to save untouched land. For example, a letter from the national sustainable strategy in Germany in November 2008 focused on this issue. The goal was set to reduce the amount of land covered by buildings and infrastructure to "30 hectares" by 2020.

Until 2050, the balanced land use is to be practiced.

138 The change of the land use in the world – the wild and natural area is lowered because of expanding used area

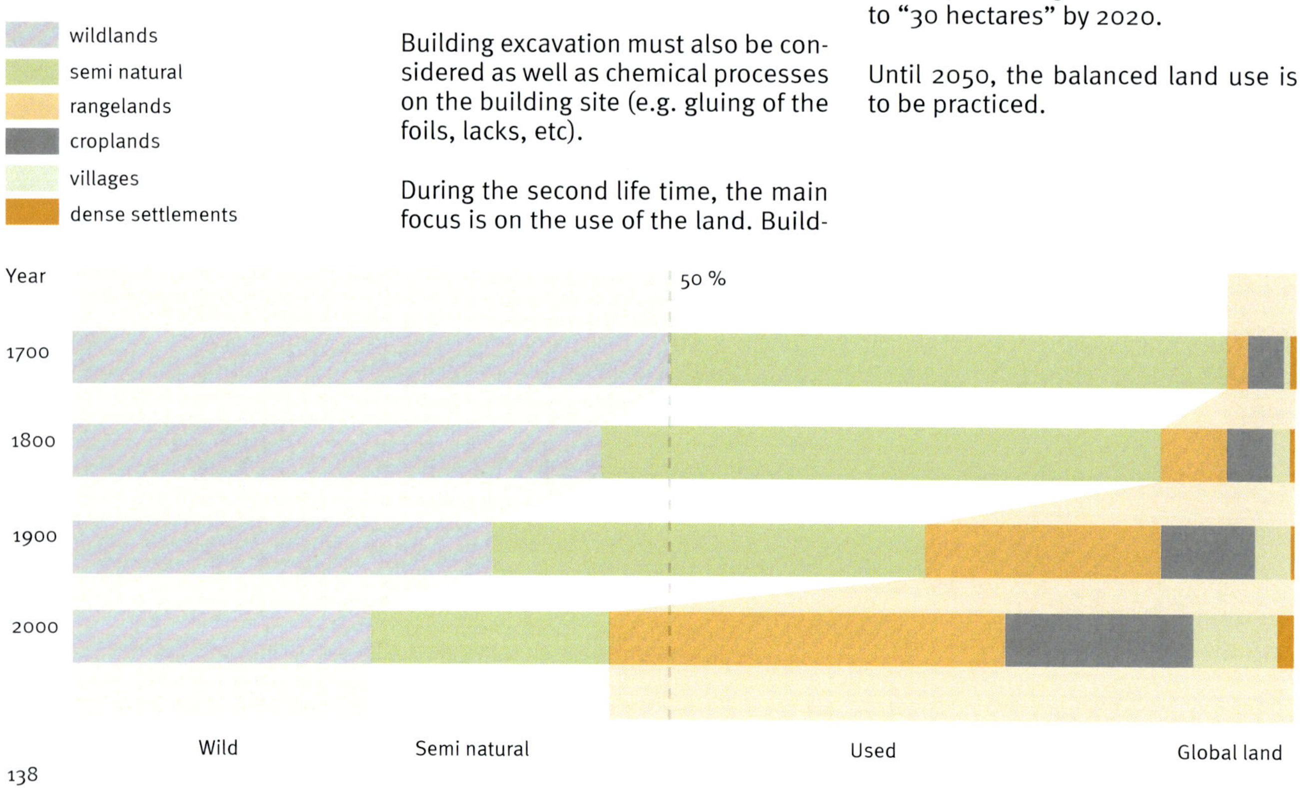

HOAI – Honorarordnung für Architekten und Ingenieure (Honorarium rules for architects and engineers)

HOAI is ordinance to regulate the honorarium for architects and engineers in Germany. The new version from 2013 regulates the planning services of architects and engineers. The main tasks for architects and engineers are divided in HOAI into 9 planning services:

- 1. Basic determination

The determination of the task based on the communication with the client, also containing building site analysis, existing building condition analysis, and planning of space and functional program.
It is preparation for the planning process by choosing all architects and engineers that should take part in the planning.

- 2. Preparation of project and planning

The fundamental analyse and preparation of the planning concept with sketches and proofing of different alternatives.

Clarification of environmental loads from urban, design, functional, technical, physical, economical, energy and landscape conditions.

Proofing of environmental structures as soil, water, climate, air, plants and animals. Costs estimation due DIN 276 (page 17).

- 3. Preliminary design

Preparing of main design by architects with cooperation with engineers and other participants, which respects all aspects and conditions and its graphical documentation. Cost calculation.

- 4. Permit application planning

Preparing planning as documents for permit application and completing the applications.

- 5. Implementation planning

Based on planning services 3 and 4 graphical documentation of objects with all needed plans and details for realization.

- 6. Preparation of tender

Documentation of measurements as a basis for preparing the services with coordination of all participants.

- 7. Involvement by allocation

Documentation and examination of offers with price comparison and involvement in the ordering.

- 8. Object (construction) supervision

Supervision of the construction of objects based on the implementation planning and coordination on the building site with a time plan. Handover of the object and documentations. Costs controlling.

- 9. Object care and documentation

In case of defects, visitation of the object and removal of defects.

139

139 Honorarium rules for architects and engineers – cover

140 Daily grow on the built and traffic area in hectare in Germany and the "30 hectare" goal for 2020

buildings and open space, plant area (excluding mining land)
recreation area, cemetery
traffic area
milestones of the UBA for 2010 and 2015
trend (moving four-year average)
goal of sustainability strategy space, plant area (excluding mining land)

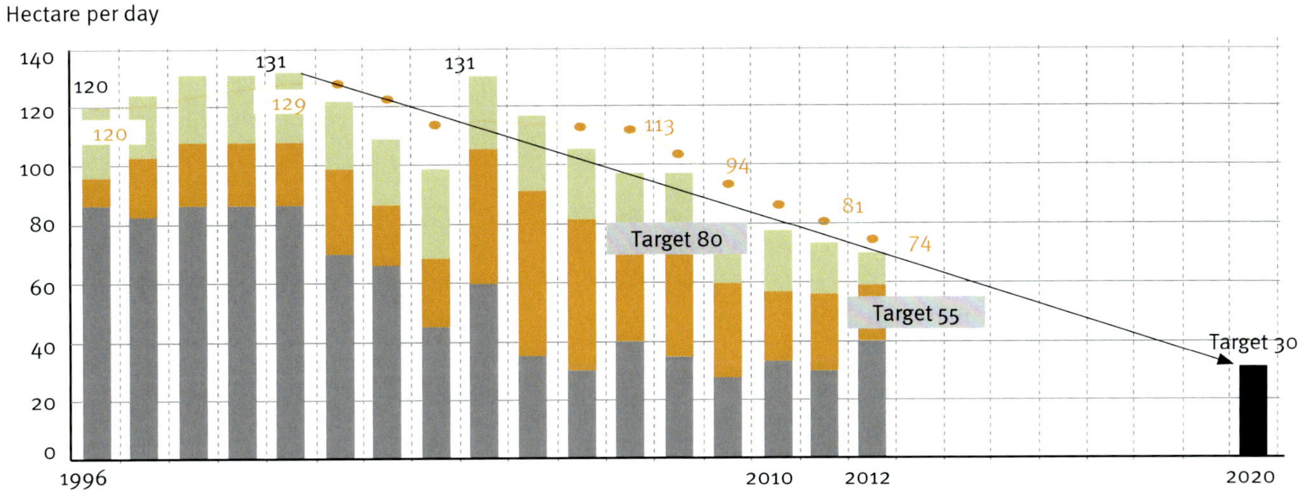

140

2.4 Third building life time

The third life time is the longest phase (approx. 20-100 years) and considers the utilization phase of the building. It considers the resources, water, energy and costs needed for operation (ventilation, heating, cooling, lighting, etc.), for cleaning, maintenance and refurbishment.

Operation

The operational energy is needed for achieving the thermal, air and visual comfort and appropriate conditions in the building. The energy needed for building operation can be reduced by both passive and active energy-saving systems.

Passive techniques are based mostly on the lowering of energy needs by reducing transmission and ventilation losses, avoidance of overheating and maximized use of daylighting, and an active search for solutions on how to generate the energy required.

When considering a building's operation, the choice of energy-supply systems makes a difference. This viewpoint underlines the importance of the primary energy factor of the energy supply system.

Uses of renewable materials, with a zero primary energy factor are better than fossil energy, with a high primary energy factor.
Primary energy factor, as defined on page 13, shows the relationship of used primary and final energy.

The goal is to use resources with the lowest primary energy factor (natural materials) and to develop new and sustainable uses, which reduces the required material for construction. In energy conversion, the more environmentally friendly the energies and resources are used, the lower the primary energy.

Plants that produce energy also require energy for production. The harvesting factor indicates how much more energy is gained during the whole life span of the plant, when compared to the input energy of energy production the entire enterprise.

EnEV (page 76) is a regulation in Germany that regulates the characteristics of building components and technology in order to save operational energy.

Monitoring and building automation also helps to optimise the building technology and confirm the energy concepts. One year after the building is finished, monitoring begins and the building operation is documented and analysed in order to correct the mistakes and improve the system. Intelligent buildings use automation systems to optimise the efficiency of building use (page 273).

Minimizing fresh water consumption

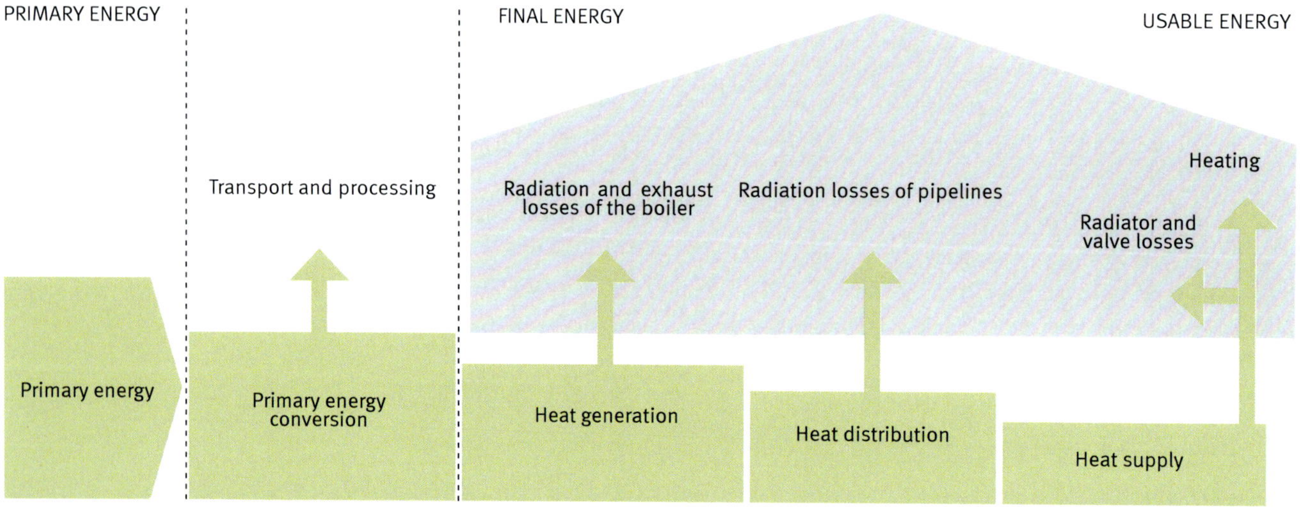

141

141 Conversion chain of conventional heating systems in residential buildings – from primary through final to usable energy – high primary energy need due to high energy losses also plays an important role during a building's operation time (sustainable water association page 128, 202).

Waste handling is also an important responsibility of building utilization. Waste prevention, separation, recycling or thermal reuse plays a significant role.

Cleaning

Cleaning depends on the building function and is commonly based on the cleaning of floors, sanitary rooms and glass surfaces.

Generally, glass surfaces are to be cleaned twice a year, outside wall coverings and sun shades once every four years, interior doors and windows four times a year, and floors depending on the function, i.e. for offices 100 days a year, floors in sanitary and entrance rooms as well as the sanitary equipment every day during usage (chapter 'building concepts').

The costs, resources and energy required for building cleaning during the whole life time is an important part in the LCC and LCA.

Therefore, it is important to design cleaning-friendly buildings with easily accessible and cleanable surfaces. The water consumption of cleaning is also very important

Maintenance

Maintenance considers the common repair and exchange of building equipment, for example the renewing of protection layers (corrosion protection, humidity protection, fire protection) and repair of building construction and technical equipment. Building elements that require minimal maintenance often have greater life duration.

The equipment should be easily maintained with basic instruments. Generally, building maintenance is approximately 0.1 % of the construction costs, every year. The growing yearly costs must be considered.

Refurbishment

Refurbishment is the replacement of the elements with a finished life time (the life time of building elements figure 145). The reparation of the old elements and what happens with them after their life time must be considered.

The goal is to reduce the material flows and waste generation by keeping them in a closed cycle. The products and materials that come to the end of their life duration should not be classified as waste, but treated as valuable resources for producing new products.

The goal of increasing the recyclability avoids waste by minimizing its quantity and harmfulness.

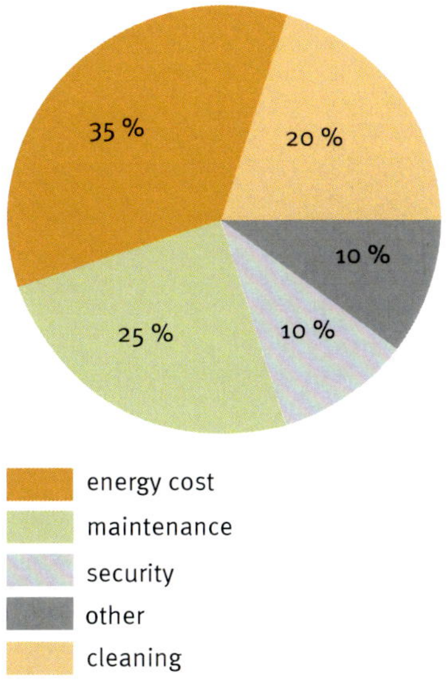

142

142 The average percentage of different costs during the building utilization
143 Energy balance between gains and losses for heating and electricity

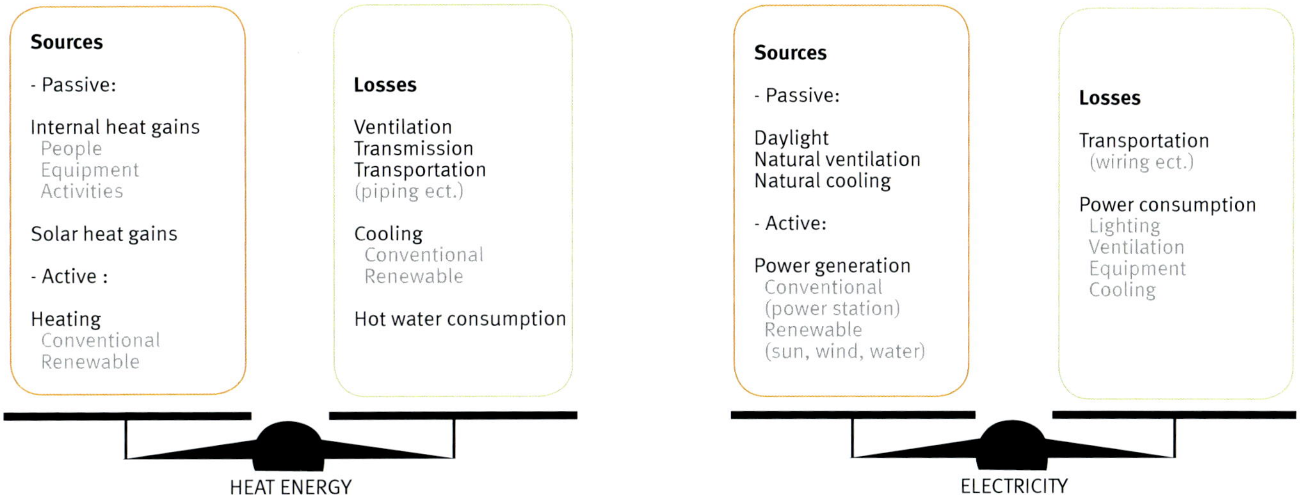

143

2.5 Forth building life time

The forth life time of a building is its end of life. It is closely related to the life span of the materials and life of the building. Different building parts have different life spans as they depend on the material and technology used. For example, a building's structure designed for a long life span, around 50-100 years, while the technology has a middle life span and the furniture must be changed every 5-10 years.

There are two possibilities at the end of a building's life time - keep the existing building or demolish it. The best solution is to keep the building and renew it, where possible. There are three main possibilities for renewing - building restoration, renovation or conversion.

Building restoration is a process where the existing building is conserved, leaving as much material untouched as possible, while restoring the building to a historically accurate condition and replacing missing elements.

Building renovation retains its original function and makes the building ready for further use through revitalization of the existing building.

Building conversion, or adaptive reuse, occurs when the original function is changed. The building is renewed in order to fulfil the new functional requirements.

When demolition or deconstruction is required, the building should be easily demountable. Next, the old building parts are transported from the building site and processed. The material after demolition must be considered to avoid any creation of waste.

Useful lives of construction parts

"For the evaluation of sustainability in buildings during the life cycle, the Useful Lives of Construction Parts to be used are very decisive, since they shed light on the frequency a construction part has been exchanged within a specified observation period. They can be used as an orientation aid or recommendations, should no exact details be available from the planners or the product manufacturers. The guidelines are based, currently, on textbook calculations, expert interviews and statements from building product manufacturers and their societies." [33]

Different building types have varied life span durations. E.g., the life span of residential and administrative buildings with a heavy construction is approximately 100 years. Industrial buildings with heavy construction have life spans of 80 years while the same buildings with wood or steel construction are 20 - 30 years. Details on life spans can influence the planning phase, which enables the appraisal of LCC and LCA.

[33] *BMU;* Assessment System for Sustainable Building: Practical Aids and Tools [http://www.nachhaltigesbauen.de/sustainable-building-english-speaking-information/assessment-system-for-sustainable-building.html] (04.05.2014)

144 Various life spans of different building components
145 The middle useful lives of construction parts as input values for life cycle calculations, the useful life details describe the time span, after which the build building element has to be changed

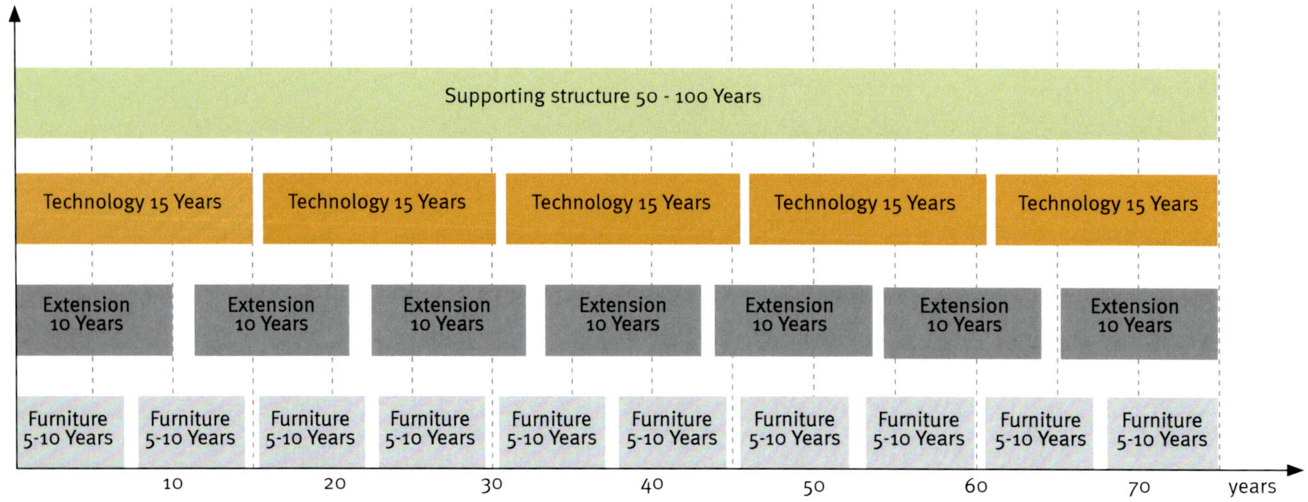

144

Cost group		Building element/material	Life time [a]	Exchange in 50 years
320 Foundation	322, 323, 324	Foundation slabs, single and strip foundations, pilotis, floor slab	> 50	0
320 Foundation	326 Waterproofing	Waterproofing against non-pressing water	35	1
330 Outside walls 340 Inside walls	331, 332, 333 341, 342, 343	Brick, concrete, wood, steel, clay, stone	> 50	0
330 Outside walls 340 Inside walls	334 Outside doors and windows 344 Inside doors and windows	Standard doors: doors from leaf three wood, metal Spetial doors: fire protection doors, noise protection doors, glass doors Window frames from aluminium, aluminium-wood-composit, aluminium-plastic-composit, treated leaf three wood and steel	> 50	0
330 Outside walls 340 Inside walls	334 Outside doors and windows 344 Inside doors and windows	Standard doors: doors from wood materials, plastic Windows from plastic and coniferous three wood	40	1
330 Outside walls 340 Inside walls	334 Outside doors and windows 344 Inside doors and windows	Standard doors: doors from treated coniferous three wood	35	1
330 Outside walls 340 Inside walls	334 Outside doors and windows 344 Inside doors and windows	Sliding doors, rotation doors, simple doors and windows	30	1
330 Outside walls	334 Outside doors and windows	Automatic doors	20	2
330 Outside walls	334 Outside doors and windows	Glass filling	20	2
330 Outside walls	335 Outside wall covering, outside	Metal covering - zinc, cooper, aluminium, stainless steel	> 50	1
330 Outside walls	335 Outside wall covering, outside	Thermal isolation from glass wool, rockwool, polystyrol, mineral wool, wood fibre, cork, cellulose, hemp Wood and galvanized steel clothing	40	1
330 Outside walls	335 Outside wall covering, outside	Plaster	30 - 45	1
340 Inside walls	345 Inside wall covering	Plaster Clothing from wood, aluminium, steel, cooper, zinc, plasterboards	> 50	0
340 Inside walls	346 Elemented interior walls	Sanitary partitions, locker room	30	1
350 Ceilings 360 Roofs	351 Ceiling construction 361 Roof construction	Concrete, metal, wood, stairs	> 50	0
350 Ceilings	352 Flooring	Cement screed, gypsum fibre plates, wood material plates, step insulation, natural and artificial stone, wood parket, wood Plasterboards, metal covering from aluminium, steel, cooper, zinc	> 50	0
350 Ceilings	352 Flooring	Ceramic tiles	20 - 50	0 - 2
350 Ceilings	352 Flooring	Linoleum, laminat, PVC, cork, natural rubber, sporting hall flooring	20	2
350 Ceilings	352 Flooring	Textiles	10	4
360 Roofs	362 Roof windows	Flat window frames from aluminium, plastic, aluminium-wood-composit	> 50	0
360 Roofs	362 Roof windows	Flat window frames from leaf three wood, treated	40	1
360 Roofs	362 Roof windows	Flat window frames from aluminium-plastic-composite	35	1
360 Roofs	362 Roof windows	Flat window frames from coniferous three wood, treated light domes	25	1
360 Roofs	363 Roof covering	Waterproofing: bitumen, plastic sheet, asphalt protection: gravel, grass, plates	20 - 40	1 - 2
360 Roofs	363 Roof covering	Brick, concrete, zinc, cooper, stainless steel, wood tiles	> 50	0

145

2.6 Fifth building life time

The fifth life time considers what happens with the waste material after the end of the building's life. There are a few possibilities – **component reuse, up-cycling, down-cycling, thermal use or disposal.**

Building demolition creates a large amount of waste, far greater than all other phases. Land filling is the most common waste treatment in Europe and is clearly the worst from an environmental perspective. Therefore, disposal must always be the last possible option.

Material recycling, waste incineration with energy recovery and biological treatment are options that all need to be considered in order to replace landfilling.

"In 2005, 331.9 million tonnes of waste were generated. The quantity of construction wastes (56 %) accounts for more than half of the amount of waste generated in Germany. The other sub-quantities of waste are mining slag (16 %), wastes from production and businesses (14 %) and municipal wastes (14 %). All types of waste contain in part hazardous wastes, amounting to a total of 18.5 million tonnes in 2005." [34]

"**Construction waste recycling** is the separation and recycling of recoverable waste materials generated during construction and remodelling. Packaging, new material scraps and old materials and debris all constitute potentially recoverable materials. In renovation, appliances, masonry materials, doors and windows are recyclable.

Most construction waste goes into landfills, increasing the burden on landfill loading and operation. Waste from sources such as solvents or chemically treated wood can result in soil and water pollution.

Some materials can be recycled directly into the same product for re-use. Others can be reconstituted into other usable products. Unfortunately, recycling that requires reprocessing is not usually economically feasible unless a facility using recycled resources is located near the material source. Many construction waste materials that are still usable can be donated to non-profit organisations. This keeps the material out of the landfill and supports a good cause.

The most important step for recycling of construction waste is on-site separation. Initially, this will take some extra effort and training of construction personnel. Once separation habits are established, on-site separation can be done at little or no additional cost.

The initial step in a construction waste reduction strategy is good planning. Design should be based on

[34] *DESTATIS;* Waste management: Much reutilisation, hardly any landfilling of waste. Wiesbaden: DESTATIS, 28.11.2007

[35] *Sustainable Sources;* Construction Waste Recycling [http://constructionwaste.sustainablesources.com/] (04.05.2014)

[36] *Energy Recovery Council;* Waste-to-Energy and Recycling Are Compatible [http://www.energyrecoverycouncil.org/waste-energy-recycling-compatible-a2975] (04.05.2014)

146 Typical construction waste composition

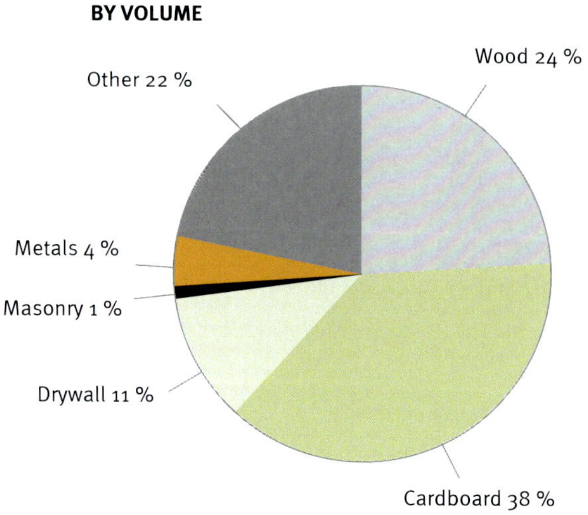

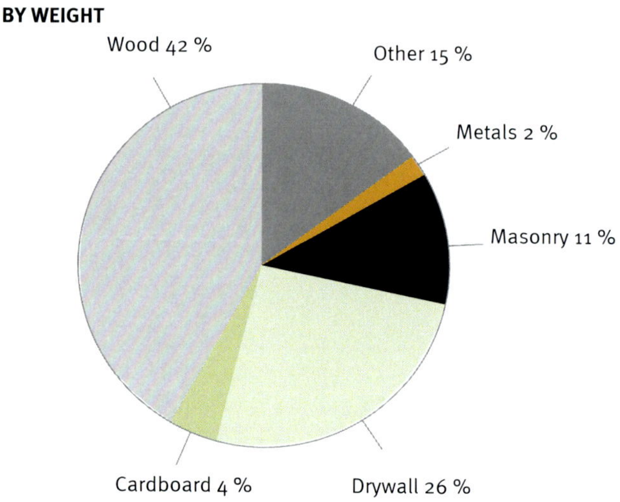

146

standard sizes and materials should be ordered accurately. Additionally, using high quality materials such as engineered products reduces rejects. This approach can reduce the amount of material needing to be recycled and bolster profitability and economy for the builder and customer."[35]

The separation of a buildings material plays an important role. In relation to the separation of building material, components are reused and recycled (up-cycling, down-cycling) as described in chapter '6.0 Active resource-saving concepts'.

The recovery of energy from waste is another way of waste utilization. Energy recovery from waste, also often called waste-to-energy, is the conversion of non-recyclable waste materials into usable heat, electricity, or fuel through a variety of processes, including combustion, gasification, anaerobic digestion, and landfill gas recovery.

By using this method, waste can be treated as a new renewable energy source and reduces carbon emissions by offsetting the need for energy from fossil sources and reduces methane generation from landfills. There are already some waste-to-energy plants all over the world, e.g. approximately 85 in the USA.

"Waste-to-energy plants facilitate the recycling of a number of materials. Many facilities provide drop-off locations for recyclable materials, including computers, white goods, and other unwanted products. In addition, many waste-to-energy plants employ metal recovery programs onsite to remove ferrous from the ash. More and more waste-to-energy facilities are also beginning to implement non-ferrous metal recovery systems for recycling." [36]

Source-separation and material recycling generally lead to lower environmental impacts than incineration. For organic waste, the options to incinerate, compost or to use anaerobic digestion are available.

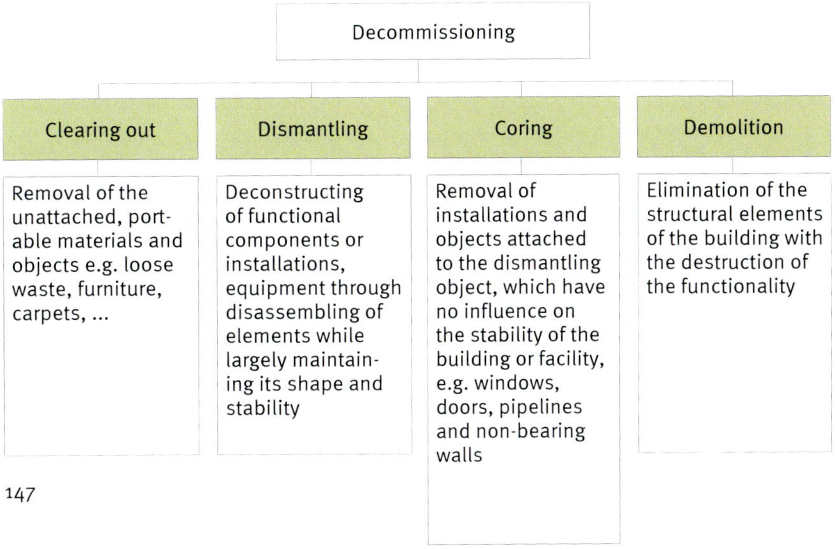

147

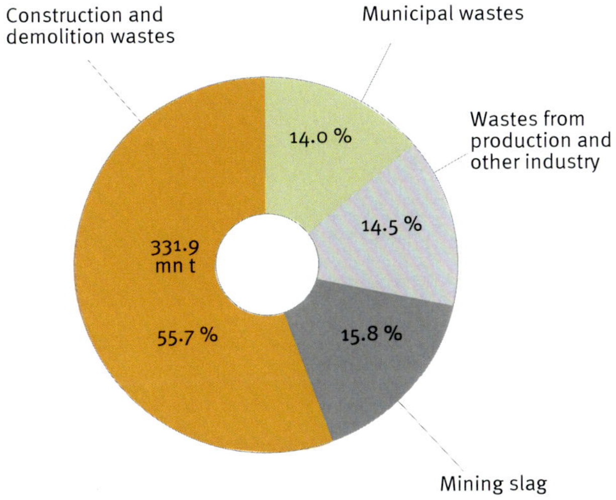

148

149

147 Process of building decommissioning – the decommissioning concept is a part of planning
148 Composition of waste generated in Germany in 2005
149 The waste separation at a demolishing site enables the recycling of materials

2.7 Summary

Five basic rules for protection of people and the environment

The five basic rules for ecological stability were introduced in 1994 as a result of the Enquete commission at the 13th German parliament (Bundestag):

1. The rate of degradation of renewable resources should not exceed their regeneration rate. This corresponds to the requirement of maintaining the environmental performance, at least to maintain the ecological functions defined by the real capital.
2. Nonrenewable resources should be used only to the extent in which a physically and functionally equivalent substitute in the form of renewable resources or increased productivity of renewable and nonrenewable resources is created.
3. Substances into the environment should be based on the carrying capacity of environmental media, and all functions are to be considered, not least the "silent" and more sensitive control function.
4. The time scale of anthropogenic inputs or interventions in the environment must be in proportion to the time scale relevant to the responsiveness of the environment natural processes.
5. Dangers and unacceptable risks to human health due to anthropogenic impacts are to be avoided (e.g. nuclear energy).

150 The material and energy flows on earth determined by people's activities

Understanding a building's lifetime is very important for sustainable building designing and planning. In every phase of construction, resource and energy inputs are required. Resources and energy are needed to acquire and process materials into building components, to build and operate the building and also to renovate or demolish it.

Each phase of the building's life produces waste and outputs in the form of emissions, which have negative effects on the natural environment.

The goal is therefore to minimize the inputs (resources and energy) and outputs (emissions and waste) as much as possible. The process, known as regional value creation, is very simple to implement.

Traditionally, **preindustrial cities** were constructed using local or regional sources because of limited import facilities. The people were dependant on local, natural materials and recycling. They had close relationships to their environment and their lifestyle and behaviour norms sustained the ecological conditions. Renewable energy was harnessed from the sun and there were short material cycles and system couplings. Highly developed cultural and spiritual embodiment of the "Five basic rules" was characterised in habits and lifestyles, in religions and the consciousness of the people.

Modern industrial cities have lost these connections to nature and regional resources due to the industrial building and transportation revolution. Here, the constant increase of open systems based on external supplies has created irreversible losses in the urban ecosystem (energy, water, material) and ignorance for the destruction of nature.

The closed-cycle of an urban eco-life has changed to a linear consumer system resulting in a high level of resource consumption and a huge amount of emissions and waste. Cities are highly dependent on fossil resources and global imports of limited nonrenewable resources based on global exchange economy replacing household economy, ignoring ecological costs. The cultural and spiritual change is characterised by believing in technical solutions and in the liberation of the restrictions of the "Five rules of ecological stability", reducing nature to just a resource base for human needs and exploitation.

Therefore it is of significant importance that the regional value and closed-cycle treatment of resources and energies are redeveloped. The main characteristics are the minimization of material loses and irreversible processes, raising system efficiency, system couplings, reducing of energy imports and compensatory climatic functions.

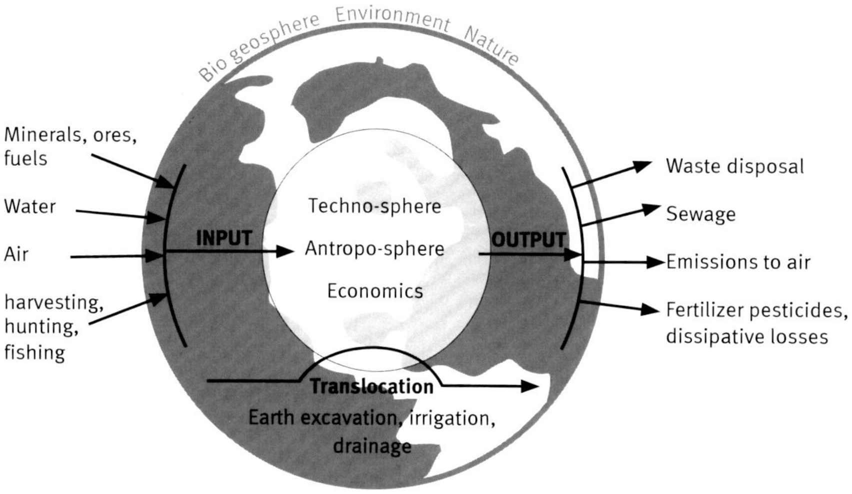

150

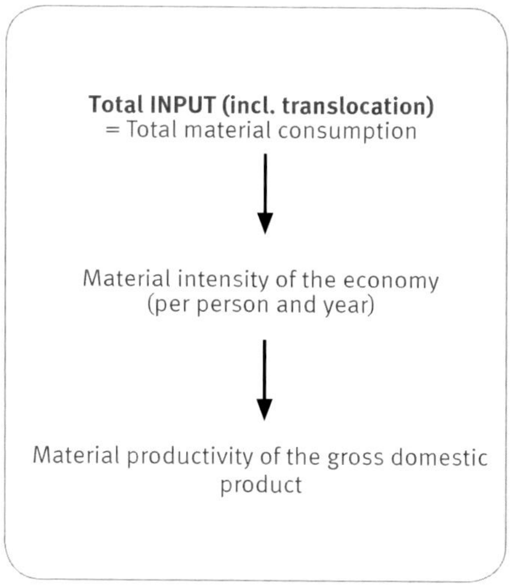

The new post-industrial city should support the reconciliation of the people with nature based on new scientific-technical concepts where the integration of urban planning and natural experience is of high importance. The new post-industrial city must begin the reduction of material losses by closing local and regional circuits, the reduction of our dependence on energy and resource imports and the redevelopment of market economies into an ecological and social household. The basic idea is to use locally available resources, techniques appropriate for small scale, cycles and networks, integrated systems of water, energy and material flows at a localized level. Local people must play a key role. Buildings should be designed following principles according to intelligent and flexible interaction between humans, technology, and nature.

Reuse or recycling is not always the most suitable solution. Every situation is different and offers various solutions and treatments. Therefore a case study analyses e.g. LCA or LCC is an important supporting tool for sustainable designing. The consideration of the entire life time of a building with each life cycle phase should be apart of every building planning.

The interest of architects and engineers to undertake the task of life cycle building design and management should increasingly grow.

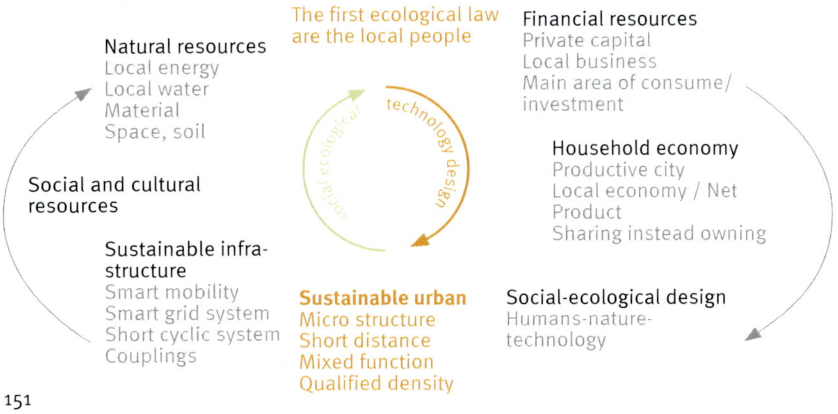

151

The building life cycle analysis that assists the decision-making process during the building design must be a part of architectural education. Therefore the architect should be responsible for the building culture of our society.

Having access to life cycle analyses (environmental or costs aspects and potential impacts) achieves the best decisions for building. Not only is the building location and function important, but also the duration of the building over its lifetime.

A building, which should stand for only ten to twenty years, has very different life time principals and priorities compared to a building designed to stand for a much longer time. The topics and methods on how to treat different buildings over various lifetimes will be discussed in the next chapters.

151 Key position of neighbourhoods and urban quarters – green urbanism is decentralised, cellular and integrated
152 The cycled material and energy flow of a preindustrial city with small inputs and outputs
153 The high demand on inputs and outputs for a modern city with little cycled flow
154 The cycled material and energy flow with small inputs and outputs as required for the future post-industrial city

input
output
recycling

152

153

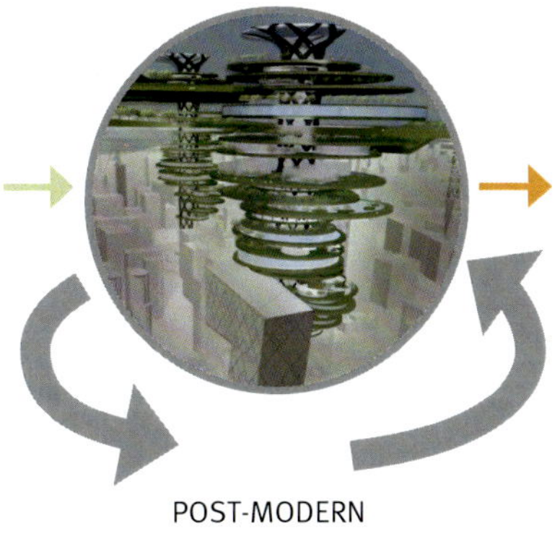

154

155

155 Entire building built up from renewable building materials - wood structure and massive clay walls for energy storing - kindergarten "Wildblume", Garz/Rügen, IGEL-Institut

Life time design

3.0 Passive resource-saving concepts (light-tech)

3.0 Passive resource-saving concepts

3.1 Introduction

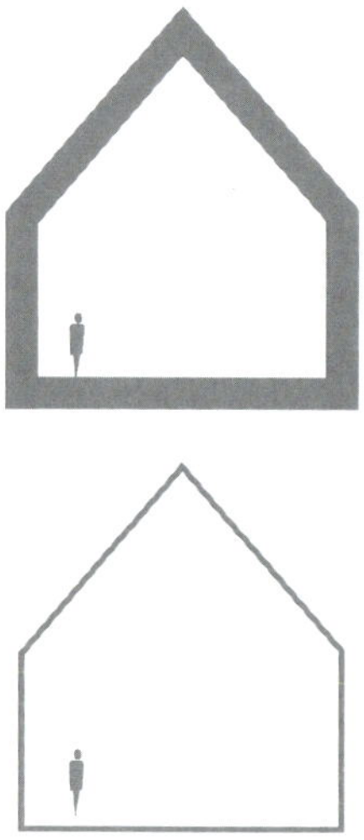

156

Passive resource-saving concepts, also known as light tech concepts, help to save energy generally in the first life time of a building. The first life time of a building considers the building materials used in the construction – how they are gained, the energy and emissions needed for their production, storage and transport to the building site.

Passive resource-saving concepts are based on the light-tech idea, which is to use as least material as possible. Fewer materials mean fewer resources and energy consumption, less maintenance and also less costs and less waste at the end of the process.

The first principal to help reduce material use is by **re-using an existing building** - by reusing parts of an existing building, which are in good condition and suitable for use or by adding new sections where necessary, a considerable amount of new material can be saved.

The basic handling of existing buildings is building restoration, renovation or conversion.

Re-use of elements or whole construction units salvaged from old buildings is also a part of the passive resource-saving concept. It is a very effective way to save resources and to protect from landfill problems.

Space management is another important principal for resource saving design. The less space we need, the less materials are required to build it. Buildings should be designed to minimize the overall space and surfaces. As an example, the reorganisation of spacial usage or incorporating double height rooms can be considered.

Also the **intelligent design of construction** brings more advantages as the mass heavy construction. Houses should be "breathable" and the structural design of the building components should follow the statical loads. By reducing the weight of a component it can be produced on the building site faster and more accurate.

Under the demand to deal with a new architectural language that deals with materials more economically, already in the fifties some architects turned again to light construction – "the world becomes easier".

The **flexibility of a building** is also very important – the tendency towards material-saving tends to lead to a design where the function is less important. However the structure should be durable and easy to adapt to any change in the future – if functional or in comfort.

Also the material choices are important in order to save resources and energy. Passive resource-saving con-

156 Bad insulated house of 100 m² built for 2 years saves more resources as the same good insulated house
157 The intelligent material-saving roofing construction of Olympic stadium in Munich, architects Otto, F. and Behnisch, G.
158 Olympic stadium in Munich, architects Otto, F. and Behnisch, G.

157

158

cepts therefore prioritise the natural materials which are renewable resources, easy to gain and do not need high energy for transformation into the building materials. Different regions have different natural material sources. By using the local materials, the energy and emissions required for long-distance transportation are avoided.

Use of renewable materials, which have a zero primary energy factor are better used than fossil energy, which have a high primary energy factor. The more environmentally friendly the energy and resources and energy conversion are used, the lower the primary energy.

Earthsheltered architecture is also an example for resource saving buildings – by using the stable temperature of the earth, many resources and energies for thermal insulating or for future heating/cooling of a building can be saved.

Land, earth and water are other important natural resources. Without these, human existence would not be possible.

Land saving in the form of avoiding sealing new land and the preferring of brownfield recycling is a very good way for land treatment. The contaminated grounds are to be recycled in order to reuse them or bring them back to the natural ecosystem.

Water is another material that is a valuable resource, which should be handled with the greatest respect. A sustainable association with water is therefore also an important part of passive resource-saving building concepts.

Water is a vital resource required for all living organisms. About 70 % of the worlds surface is covered by water but only 3 % of the earths water is fresh water, however most is frozen in glaciers and polar ice caps. In reality, only 0.3 % of all fresh water is available for use.

In many countries freshwater is highly scarce and yet developed countries with general high standard of living continue to consume high levels of fresh water while polluting water resources.

The actual handling of fresh water and wastewater results in the overuse of natural water resources. It is thus important to develop new sustainable concepts for handling water that are incorporated into the urban and architectural planning.

159

159 Headquarters of the Northern German pension insurance, example of a passive water concept – rainwater retention, Behnisch architects
160 Headquarters of the Northern German pension insurance, the "unfinished" facade design saves maintenance and refurbishment resources and costs, Behnisch architects

160

3.2 Land saving

161

Land is the most important resource. It is the essence of our daily life and makes up our surroundings.

The current growth of the building sector is unsustainably taking over free landscape. Today there are new movements and concepts to help keep the landscape free of building.
In 1998 Germany created a concept for sustainable development with the goal of reducing land use, preventing the sealing of landscape and uncovering the potential of unsealing.
The German National Sustainable Strategy from 2002 formulates the goal of **"30 hectares"** – the reduction of the daily growth of sealed surfaces to a maximum of 30 hectares until 2020, as already mentioned in the chapter above.

Other German laws and regulations for land saving are the Federal Land Protection Law adopted in 1998 and BBodSchG – Gesetz zum Schutz vor schädlichen Bodenveränderungen und zur Sanierung von Altlasten (The Federal Land Protection and Residual Contamination Ordinance) from 1999, the final edition that came into force on the 1st of June 2012 and ROG – Raumordnungsgesetz (Spatial Planning Act), the latest edition from 30th June 2009.

The goal is to reduce the amount of new landscape surfaces required for building, settlements or traffic areas. Surface recycling is one method to reach this goal – the technique reuses abandoned surfaces, e.g. surfaces that already have buildings, industry or traffic footprint, vacant lots (building gaps), brownfields. The conversions of old areas with strong or weak loaded industry or military areas are of high importance.

Other concepts support high-density areas within city centres instead of suburban extensions. Appropriate surface management within a city is fundamental for sustainable handling in relation to land management.
This is also known as **brownfields redevelopment**. Brownfield sites are generally abandoned land that was originally used for industry, commerce or other polluting operations, e.g. gas stations, oil refineries, dry cleaners, railroads. It is commonly contaminated by hazardous wastes or pollution.

The use of brownfields requires appropriate policies. The main strategies for revitalizing Brownfields are activation, reorienting, preserving and restoring nature and are linked with additional strategies of extending, disenabling, engaging and experimenting.

Generally, there are 3 principles on how to treat brownfield areas:

- to remove and deposit it
- to seal it
- to filter (remediate) it

161 Space saving equipment for parking of bicycles
162 Building foundation designed to be easily removed after building´s end of life, leaving the ground untouched
163 The reuse of abandoned industrial area to the cultural and exhibition centre in the city core of Athens, Greece

162

163

3.3 Space management

Space management is strongly connected to resource saving, but also energy saving and building economics.

In many existing buildings and building complexes there is a large amount of floor area that is unused or used very little, e.g. the university campus (concept Campus 2020 page 320) or student residential houses. The space economy can have a great influence on the resource-saving concept.

The main goal of sustainable space management is to **optimise the use of the entire floor area**. The better the space organisation and functional structure, the greater the savings. To satisfy the growing demands in an area, first all unused or misused spaces should be considered and restructured. A detailed understanding of current occupancy and the ability to forecast future space requirements is a good way to save resources.

Also important is the time in which different rooms are occupied. The **multifunctional use** of one space for the day or night time can avoid the need of new additional structures. For example, the rooms, which are used only in the morning or during the day for teaching and learning, can be used in the evening for other functions.
Space classification is also an important part of space management. Space is classified in relation to how it is used – working space, meeting areas, or secondary rooms. Consider the ratio of support space to spaces required for people to live in order to optimise space organisation.
The reduction of areas for supporting functions brings more space for the buildings main functional areas – e.g. reduction of storage space by using modern space-saving storing equipment, reducing corridors by connecting them with useful spaces, for example meeting areas.
The **density of the spaces** is also to be considered. For example, contract workers in offices only require a small space to sit with their laptops and coffee. These higher density areas help to save on resources, energy and costs.

The floor area has the greatest influence not only on the amount of resources required to be constructed, but also on the high operational costs due to the heating and cleaning, which make up more than 50 % of the building life time costs. The reduction of the building floor area to reduce the overall LCC is very important for passive energy-saving concept.
There are various software programs, where it is possible to model the functional and spatial use of a building to help reduce and optimise the floor area.

Page 240 gives instructions on how to perform space management.

164

164 Tiny Flatiron Building in New York, USA, that use with its form maximal potential of the building site
165 Concept 2020 Hochschule Wismar – using existing space efficiently greatly reduces the campus' material and energy consumption

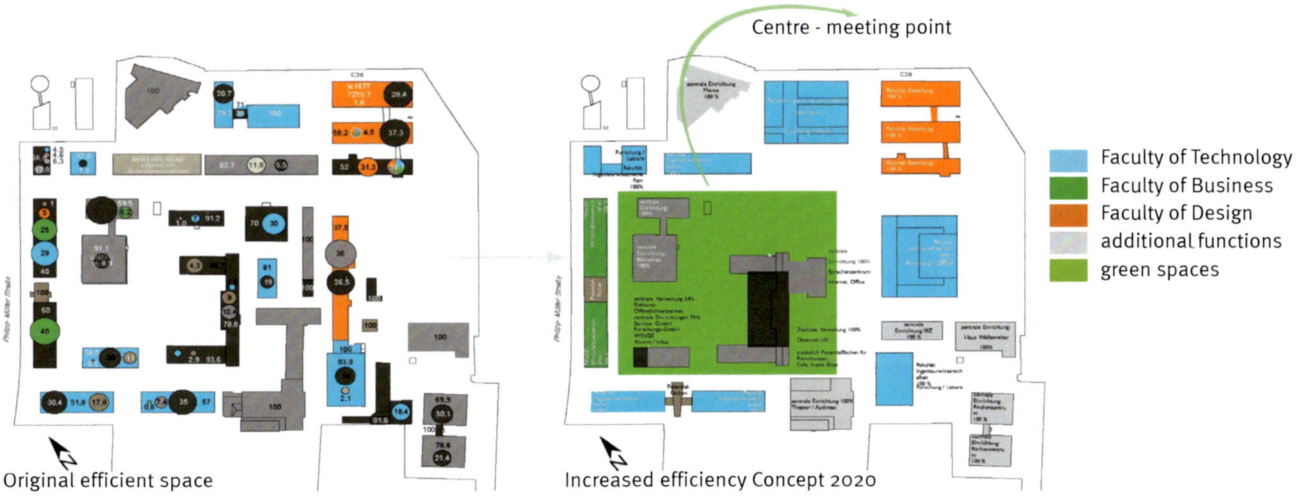

165

3.4 Building with an existing building

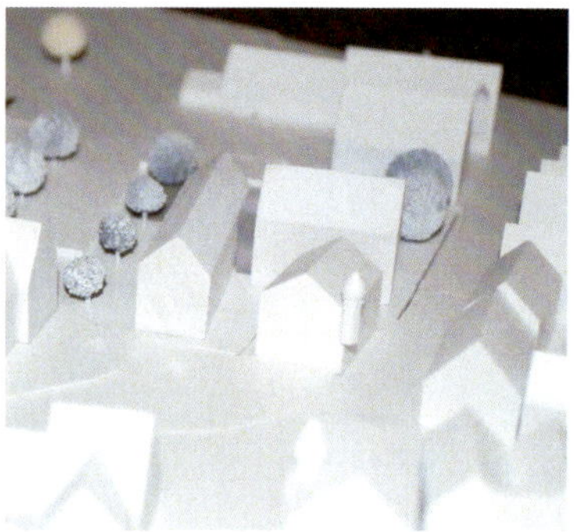

166

166 Model of the 1st price awarded design in competition city hall in Thannhausen, 2009, Schoblocher architects
167 Version renovation and enlarging of the city hall in Thannhausen – life cycle costs over 80 years
168 Version demolition and new construction of the city hall in Thannhausen – life cycle costs over 80 years
169 Version renovation and enlarging of the city hall in Thannhausen – ground floor plan
170 Version demolition and new construction of the city hall in Thannhausen – ground floor plan
171 Version renovation and enlarging of the city hall in Thannhausen – external costs
172 Version demolition and new construction of the city hall in Thannhausen – external costs
173 Version renovation and enlarging of the city hall in Thannhausen – greenhouse and acidification potential
174 Version demolition and new construction of the city hall in Thannhausen – ecological balance

Building with an existing building is another important method of resource saving. This considers building restoration, renovation or conversion, which are described also in the chapter '2.0 Building life time'.

The difference is in building restoration; the goal is to conserve the original building without trying to change it to modern standards so it remains closely connected to heritage protection.

On another hand the building renovation keeps only the original function of the building but adopts it to new modern standards. Building conversion adopts the old building and converts it to a new functional use.
The following example shows the calculation of external costs in comparison to building renovation with demolishing and building a new construction.

Example: External costs trough demolition – city hall in Thannhausen, Germany

The master thesis project shows the design of office building of city hall for Thannhausen on the location of the existing hotel Engel in two variations:

- reuse of the existing structure and enlarging new construction
- demolition of the existing structure and the whole building as a new construction

The project compares these two variants and their external costs. The comparison of the space program with both variants shows that the preservation of the existing building is of the same quality. It evaluates both building versions with the Life Cycle Cost calculation (LCC) and Life Cycle Assessment (LCA). On the basis of life cycle assessment he calculated the external costs for both building variants.

External costs calculation results:

- renovation and enlarging construction external costs 949,658.39 €
- demolition and new construction external costs 1,150,272.02 €

The renovation and enlarging construction version saves 200,613.63 € external costs. The construction costs are also 467,930.91 € lower with this version. The results show that the renovation of the existing structure is cheaper and better in an ecological point of view. The renovation is not only better from the resource saving point of view but it also causes less external costs than the new construction.
The aim is that environmental damage in all activities during construction must be reduced to a minimum. This may include the identification and consideration of the "external costs" of the planned expansion to contribute a great deal.

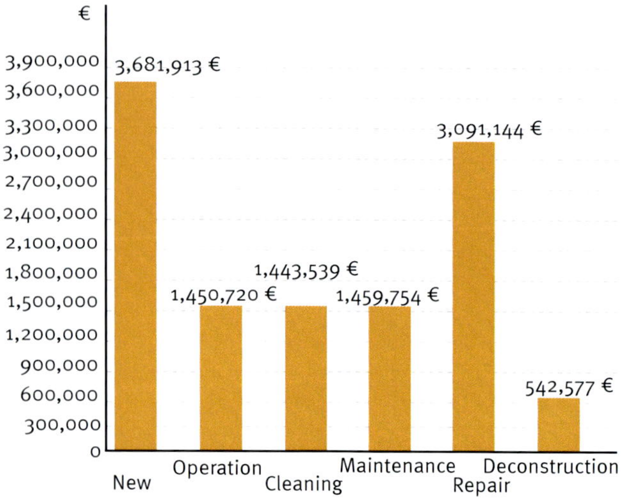

167

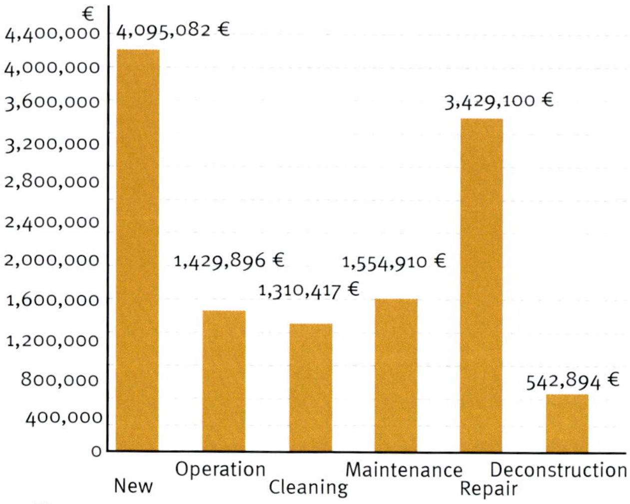

168

Ground floor

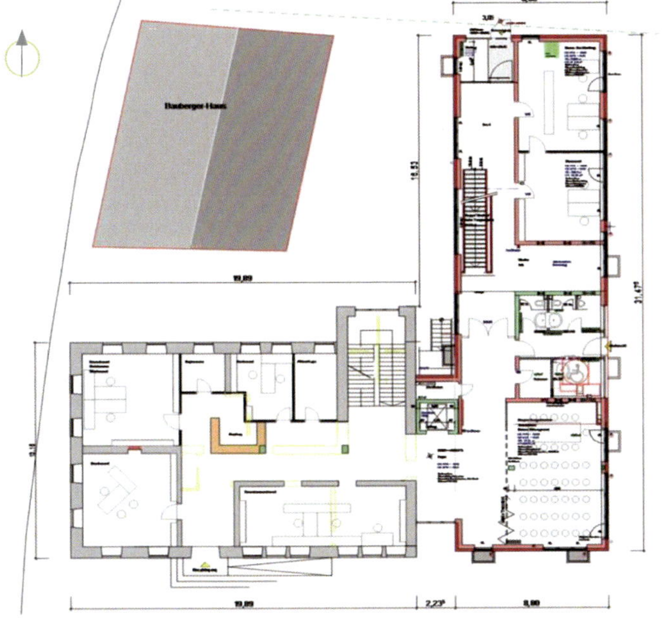

169

Ground floor

170

Version renovation	External costs
Global Warming Potential	139,069.17 €
Acidification Potential	24,607.49 €
Primary Energy	778,230.12 €
Eutrophication Potential	6,50.19 €
Ozone Depletion Potential	542.23 €
Photochemical Ozone Creation Potential	759.18 €
Total	**949,658.39 €**

171

Version new construction	External costs
Global Warming Potential	203,680.12 €
Acidification Potential	27,453.16 €
Primary Energy	910,352.80 €
Eutrophication Potential	7,187.72 €
Ozone Depletion Potential	668.83 €
Photochemical Ozone Creation Potential	928.93 €
Total	**1,150,272.02 €**

172

new construction
repair
heating
equipment
power supply
lighting

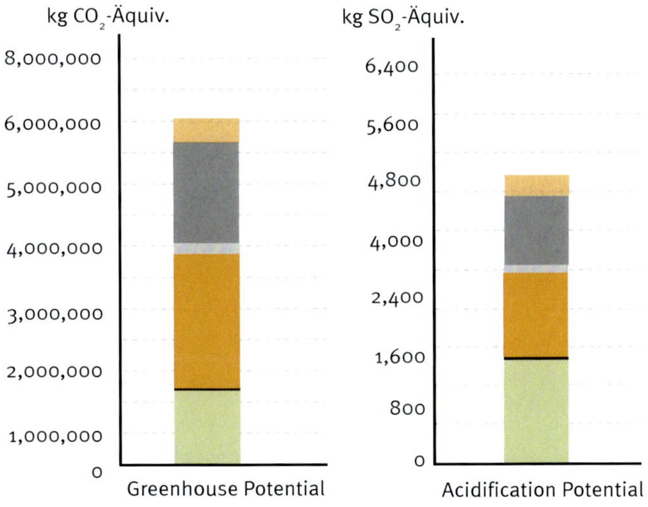

173

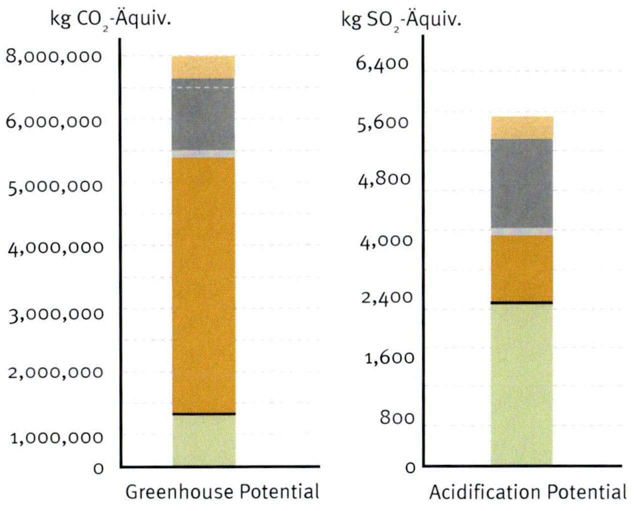

174

3.5 Component reuse

“Reuse of individual components extracted from the demolition of one project in a new building is commonly known as “component reuse.” Structural components, such as beams, columns or non-structural components, such as cladding panels, bricks or staircases, are taken from one project and used in another.” [37]

Existing buildings and infrastructure are a huge storage of potential resources and should not be simply thrown away. The demolition of a building should always be the last possible choice. If demolition is the only possibility, the next strategy should be - which parts of the building can be reused and which materials and building components from the old building can be integrated into a new structure to avoid the use of new materials.

Component reuse should always be the alternative strategy in cases where reuse of an original building is not possible.

Component reuse is always better than recycling because it brings value to the component and avoids the energy and resources required to reprocess and recycle the material. By recycling, the material is brought back to the manufacturing process.

The re-use of materials can be seen throughout history. In early times, when horses limited transportation, travel times were much higher and raw materials were less available and more valuable. Materials were commonly re-used two or three times.
After the Romans departed from the northern Alps, bricks and roofing materials were often re-used in farmhouses. After the introduction of industrial mass production and ease of transportation, building materials became more affordable. However, as a result buildings became homogeneous and lost their regional value.
Nevertheless, re-use of materials remained the first priority before something new was built. After World War II, the re-use of rubble created from damaged buildings became a critical material to regain livable conditions.

During the economical boom, re-use was disregarded as new buildings arose. This was due to the cry for modernity and the loss of value in depreciating old buildings and building materials.

Today, the majority continues to disregard old materials and chooses to build new buildings or building components. This is due to high availability, high quantity and reasonable pricing.

However, after the realization of limited fossil resources and dying forests, it is becoming increasingly important to raise the awareness of material re-use.

175

“Trümmerfrau” when translated means “rubble woman” and is the name for a women, who after World War II helped to clean and reconstruct the bombed cities in Germany by collecting and cleaning the building rubble for reuse for new constructions

[37] *Ontario Association of Architects: Gorgolewski, M.;* Reusing Buildings and Components [http://www.oaa.on.ca/professional%20resources/sustainable%20design/reusing%20buildings%20and%20component] (05.03.2014)

175 Detail of building exterior wall built from reused old bricks
176 Re:Start project in Christchurch, New Zealand, where brightly coloured shipping containers were converted into shops and cafes to bring life back into the earthquake destroyed area

176

Example Student Master Thesis

Reuse of wind rotor blades

The life span of a wind turbine is on average 20 years. Because of the fast development of technologies and lack of space, such turbines are normally changed earlier, for a new model with higher efficiency.

The wind turbine column consists of steel or concrete. Other parts include the rotor, the drive mechanism and the power generator. The drive mechanism can be dispensed by the use of Neodym. The rotor blades consist mainly of fibreglass reinforced plastic. Other materials include polyurethane foam, balsawood or carbon fibre reinforced plastic.

The deposit of rotor blades has been forbidden since 2005 because of the amount of organic material (carbon 30 %). Down cycling is also not a solution because of an oversupply of recycled plastics, so the abandoned rotor blades are stored on private sites, deposited illegally or burnt. The latter causes air pollution. There are also other concepts, e.g. energy reuse by burning the rotor blades for energy production and the remaining materials are then mixed into concrete.

Because of the problems and the scarcity of concepts about how to recycle the abandoned rotor blades, the student searched for possibilities to reuse them in architecture, and proposed different solutions.

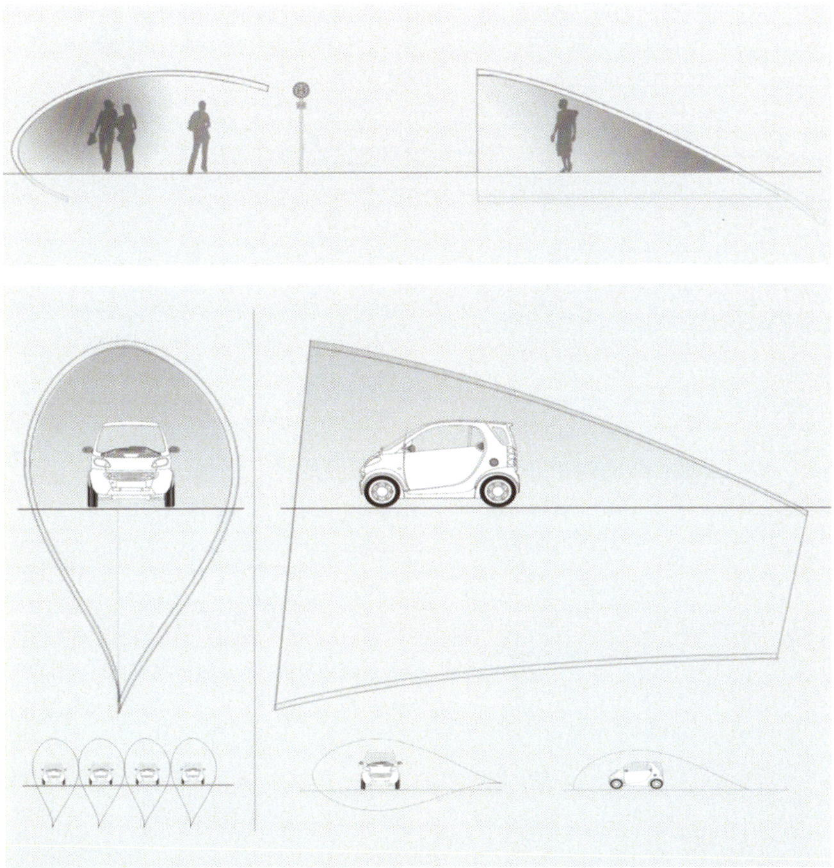

177

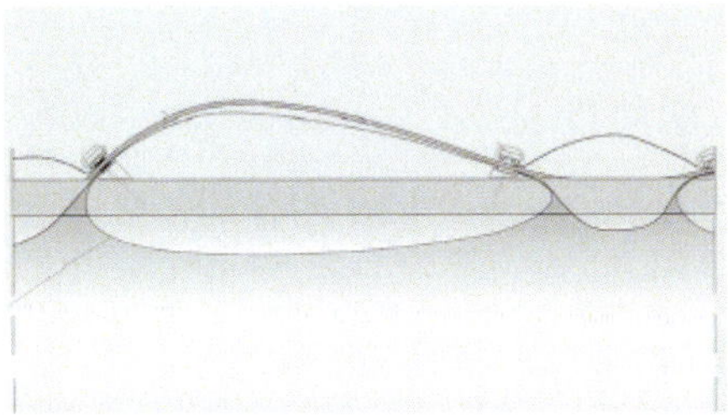

178

177 Student example – reuse designs of wind rotor blades – bus stops – carports
178 Facade and roof construction of production hall made out of reused wind rotor blades – detail
179 Facade and roof construction of production hall made out of reused wind rotor blades

179

3.6 Light building construction

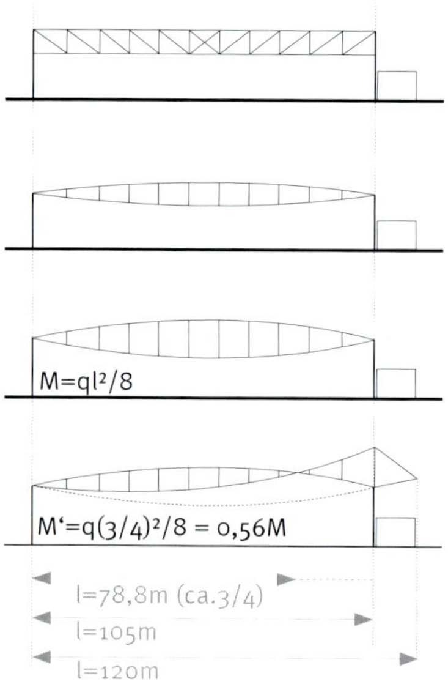

180

Light building construction with intelligent material saving design has a high potential to save resources. Construction design that follows static loads, using light building techniques and material saving methods are only a few examples.

Examples of products:

Concrete saving profiles - Cobiax® "Principles of the Cobiax flat slab

- Reduce concrete volumes as much as possible while maintaining the full strength of a slab, allowing a bi-axial load transfer.
- Maintain concrete in the structurally relevant external zones of the cross-section and create as many internal voided volumes as possible.

Materialization of the Cobiax flat slab

- Void formers positioned between the bottom and top reinforcement layers displacing concrete.
- The resulting dead-load reduction of up to 35 % has a positive impact on the whole structure and allows building material savings." [38]

"The numerous advantages of the Cobiax® technology lead to an increased value for all stakeholders involved in the design and execution process of concrete structures for buildings.

Resource efficiency leads to increased static performance, economic costing and sustainable climate friendly building structures.

Weight reduction

- Up to 35 % lighter than solid slab
- Up to 15 % less load acting on foundations
- Increased freedom for structural concepts

Large spans

- Up to 20m spans
- Flat soffits, no obstructing beam
- Up to 40 % less columns

Earthquake safety

- Reduction of mass
- Earthquake design verification
- Reduced damage risks

Cost effectiveness

- Concrete and steel savings
- Increased floor-to-floor height
- Simple retrofitting of building

Sustainability

- Resource efficiency via savings through building
- CO_2 emission reductions due to volume optimization
- Use of recycled material for Cobiax products" [39]

[38] *Cobiax®;* Concept [http://www.cobiax.ch/en/concept.html] (8.11.2012)

[39] *Cobiax®;* Benefits [http://www.cobiax.ch/en/benefits.html] (8.11.2012)

180 From the heavy to the light construction – material saving by intelligent construction design, Prof. Schulitz
181 Muster of the spherical Cobiax cage modules
182 Slim-line Cobiax cage module in ceilings before covering with concrete

181

182

Timber-saving profiles

To ensure a high level of sustainability, when using a natural material, it is desirable to reduce the material proportions.

There are many modern techniques developed to save material volumes, depending on the characteristics of the used material.

E.g., there are some interesting and sustainable material examples of wood.

I-beam (TJI-Träger) is the wood beam formed in the I shape as a steel beam. It has great static strength and uses less material than standard full-wood beams. It consists of two wooden belts jointed together with OSB plates.

It has good thermal insulation due to the reduction of the thermal bridge dimension (in this case the wood beam); also the thermal conductivity characteristic (l-value) is better.

Curved I-beam (Wellsteg) – similar system as I-beam however the connection between the wooden belts is waving wood or a metal plate.

The team at **TU Dresden** under the leadership of **Prof. Peer Haller** developed special technology which enables the bending of wood without breaking under high pressures.

The technology presses the wood pieces under a high pressure and approx. 140 °C until the tiny fibres are compressed.

The elements are half as large, stronger, denser and stiffer than the origin. The pressed wood elements are then cut into slides and glued together. The different dimensions of wood plates and boards are formed and can be bent, curved or shaped in different ways.

The wood pipe column can also be produced which saves around 70-80 % of the material in comparison to standard wood columns.

XXX-beam (XXX-Träger) is also developed by the team of Prof. Heller. It is a special mixed beam with wood belts connected together with steel screws at 45°. This method helps save resources and is a special feature of the XXX-beam.

183

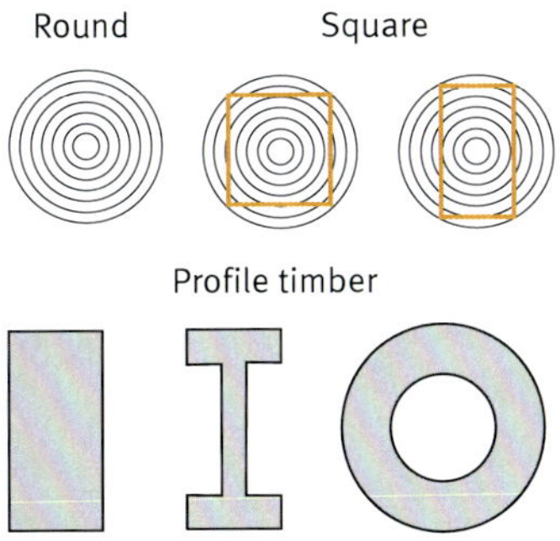

184

183 Light large span wooden construction in exhibition and congress hall in Friedrichshafen, Germany
184 Examples of different beam sections developed to save wood, Haller, P. with his team, TU Dresden, Germany
185 Examples of I-beams

185

3.7 Variability/Flexibility

186

186 Building component separation – technical elements are separated from building structure and easy to maintain
187 Six kinds of flexibility by flexible house approach
188 Three systems of building component separations: primary, secondary and tertiary system

Variability and flexibility has become a basic demand in modern architecture, and even more fundamental today. Modular lightweight construction methods permit flexibility within the spatial arrangement that can easily alter the relationship of the interior and exterior spaces at any time.

Elements can be exchanged relatively easily, particularly because they are supported by the smaller weights of new building materials.

While buildings are often designed for a sole function, there is a risk of high costs if major redevelopment is to take place. The building structures are too strongly aligned with the first function. This problem should be considered for new buildings and renovations.

The possibility of changes in the use of a building, including expanding or shrinking the required quantity of space should be part of the planning process. Here, the choices of material and technology systems play important roles. Durable materials of good quality, which require less maintenance, can be a good choice. Designing separate systems can be very helpful.

Designing an attractive building that people will love and want to keep around also promotes saving resources and is an important aspect of variability/flexibility.

Variability

Variability or changeability refers to the ability to change an object or situation. In building construction, it means the possibility of different uses. In contrast to flexibility, it is the possibility that an object can be adapted to any use or changes that occur, and also by changing the material or technology systems and parts at the required moment. The building can change designs without any additional material or financial efforts in advance. These additional resources are spent at the moment the building change is required. The variability of an object gives greater possibilities for future building changes, not only through spatial adaptations, but also through material and technology building system adaptations.

Flexibility

The term, flexibility, defines the possibility to adapt a building's components for future alterations or a change in the function. The different future uses are already planned and implemented during the construction process, therefore additional resources and investments are required. This occurs even when these changes are unlikely in future and therefore can be also understood as a waste of resources and money. Flexible planning is therefore less sustainable than variable planning. Also there is no recipe and a solution

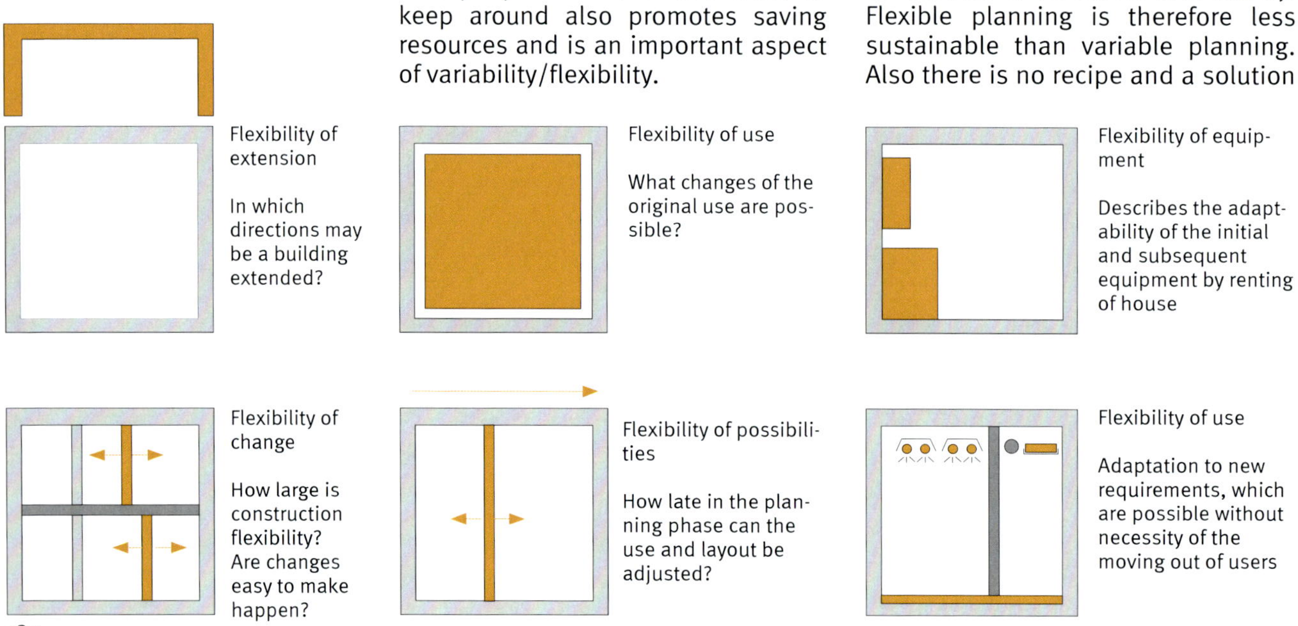

187

depends on situations, e.g. a flexible wall used to divide the conference room into two smaller rooms, which is often used is a good investment and saves resources.

Building component separation

A variable/flexible concept is based on the separation of different system stages. Building component separation is defined by the separation of building elements with different life times and use times.
Building structure and building technology have different life times. The renewal of technology installations should be possible without the interfering of the buildings structure.
The building parts and components should be separated into primary, secondary and tertiary systems and arranged in such a way that they are not fixed together. This will allow ease of interchangeability, customisation and extensibility.

- primary system

is the long term investment of 50-100 years including the structure, facade, roof, interior and exterior circulation systems, the entrances and the main structure of the building technology

- secondary system

is the investment of 15-50 years including interior elements such as walls, floors, ceilings, lighting technology, circulation arrangement and security

- tertiary system

is the short investment and should be easily changeable without any construction alterations required, e.g. furniture

Building elements with a short life time are often connected with elements of a longer life time – without any possibility to separate them. Pipelines in concrete can be renewed only with much work and high costs. The change of functions is also extremely difficult because the building structure is strongly aligned with the first function.
With system separation, building elements with different life times are separated; elements that have a shorter life time or a change in function can be easily renewed.

Variability/flexibility major parts

- Structure

The primary structure should be planned to enable different planning situations throughout its life cycle and provide space connections within the secondary system. The height of the room should be suitable for a range of different uses but should not cause high costs. The depth of the building should enable different types of plans but should not raise technology requirements (lighting, ventilation). The static loads should enable different uses and the foundations should be designed to adapt to different building functions.

Questions regarding building extensions:

Can new stories be added to the building?
How many m² can we gain through vertical extension?
Would new building stories be easily integrated within the surrounding?
Can the site carry higher loads or will additional foundations be required when additional stories are added?
Do the new stories shadow other neighbouring buildings?
Do the additional stories cause a higher cost requirement due to fire protection?
Can the current services fulfil the requirements in the case of additional stories?
Is there any possibility on the building site to extend the building horizontally?
How many m² can we gain through horizontal extension?
Would a horizontal extension be a better solution than a vertical extension of the existing building from an urban planning point of view?
Are there lower requirements for the foundation by the horizontal extension as by the vertical extension?
Do the services and circulation areas benefit with a horizontal extension?
Is the traffic area easy to organise with a horizontal extension?

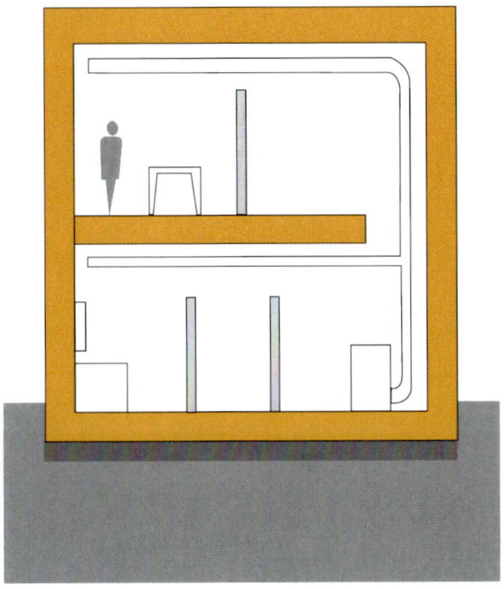

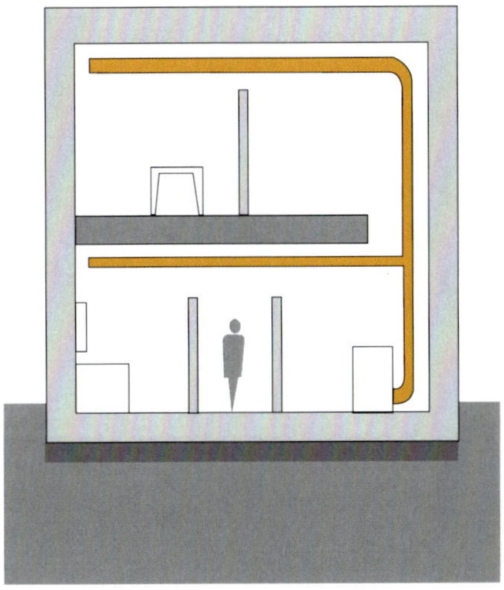

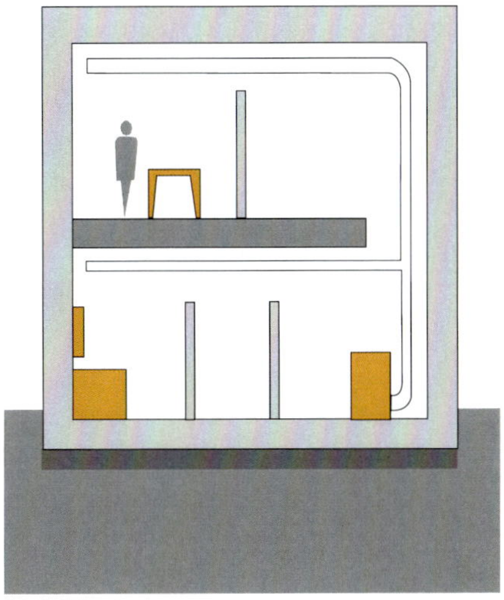

3.7 Variability/Flexibility

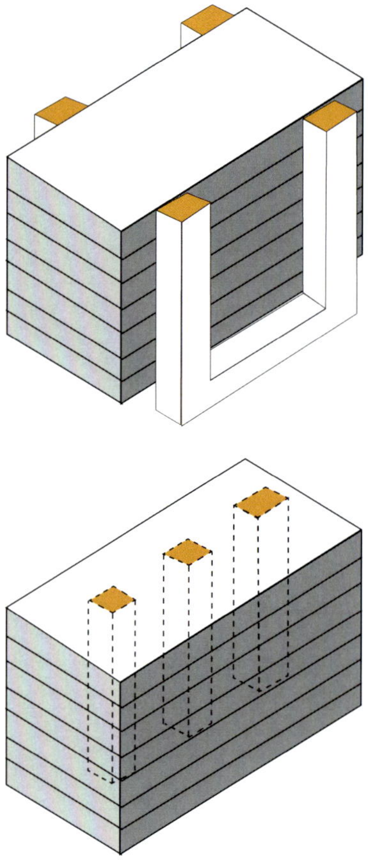

189

- Building envelope

The interior walls should allow the height extension of up to at least 2.5 m. The choice of facade should consider natural lighting, ventilation, summer and winter heat protection. The roof should be constructed to enable extensions.

- Development

The vertical and horizontal circulation inside and outside the building should be precisely dimensioned and offer a simple orientation.

- Installation concept

Considers all main vertical and horizontal fixed points and lines which must be accessible for maintenance and extension.

- Use of a neutral floor plan

A neutral floor plan is flexible, multifunctional, and appropriate for all users. It avoids large spaces which cannot be separated, and allows combinations of spaces. It offers fast and reliable orientation.

- Use of a convertible floor plan

A convertible floor plan is based on a modular system and construction. The basic module consists of building blocks, which are added and stacked, allowing variations of the geometrical arrangement, and tailored to requirements. The possibility of prefabrication results in speed of construction and favourable costs, long life and quality of architecture, changeability, sophisticated interior and exterior spaces.

The building consists of convertible parts with fixed main points. The fixed points are not so easy to change and are the core of the flexible building parts. Their placement and number should be considered very thoroughly. The goal is to have as few fixed points and as many flexible parts as possible.

From the viewpoints of flexibility and increasing the life span of the building, it is important to determine the main fixed points.

The fixed points are:

- construction
- circulation
- technical installations

These building components are very difficult, resource demanding and expensive to change and are designed from the beginning as unchangeable. Their combination allows larger, flexible spaces e.g. in the placement of vertical circulation systems (stairs, elevators) in connection to the vertical technical installations (installation shafts, toilets, kitchens etc.).

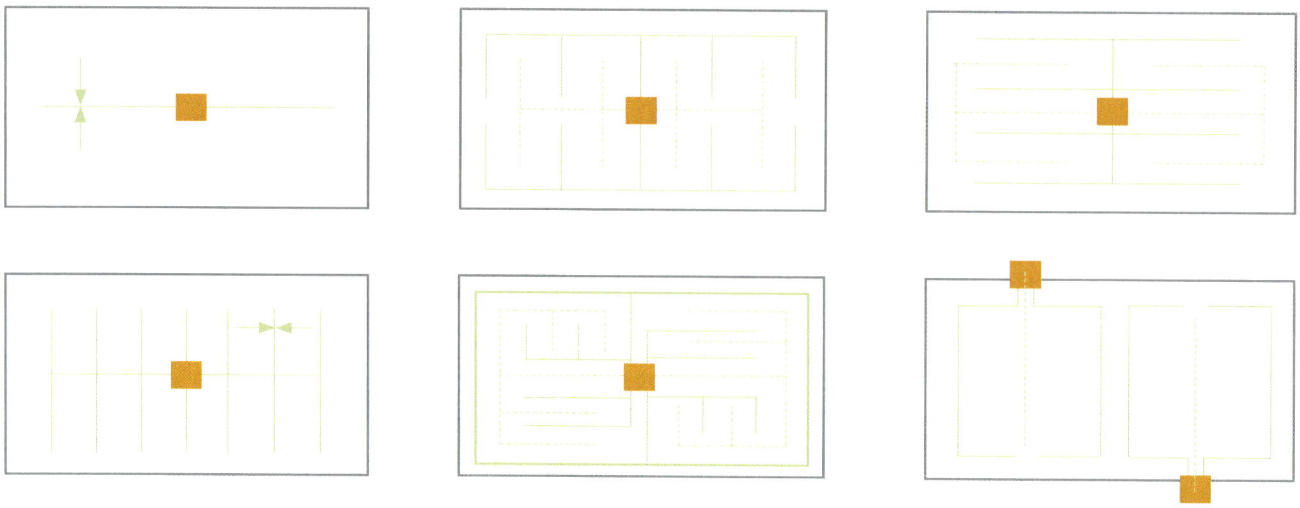

190

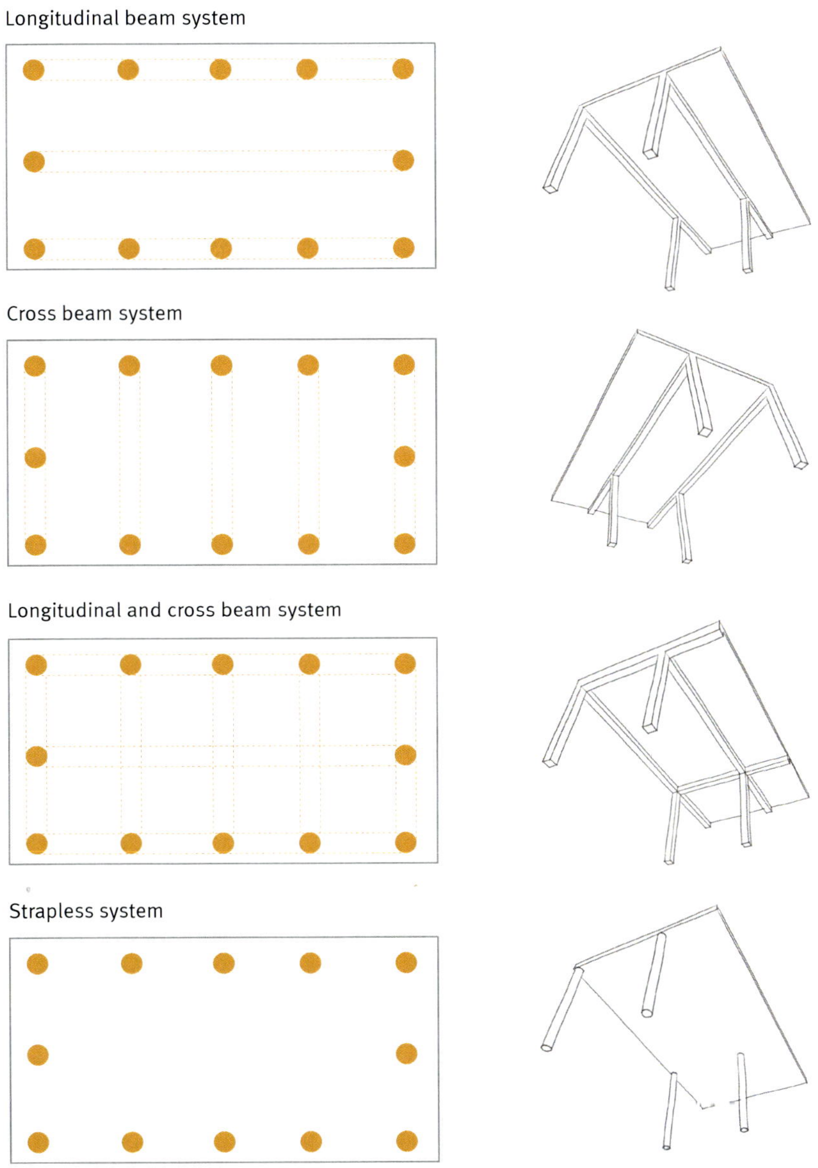

191

192

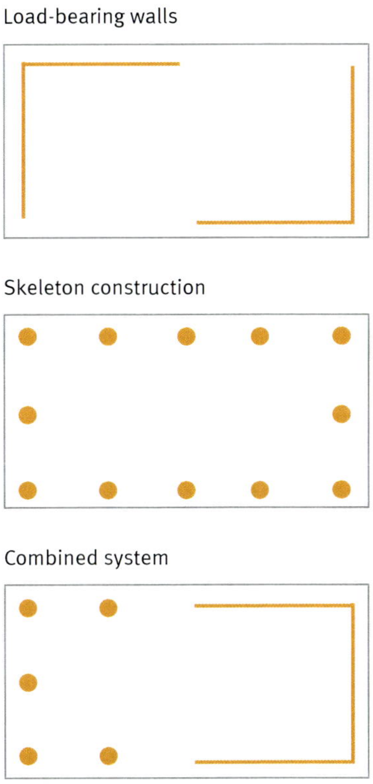

193

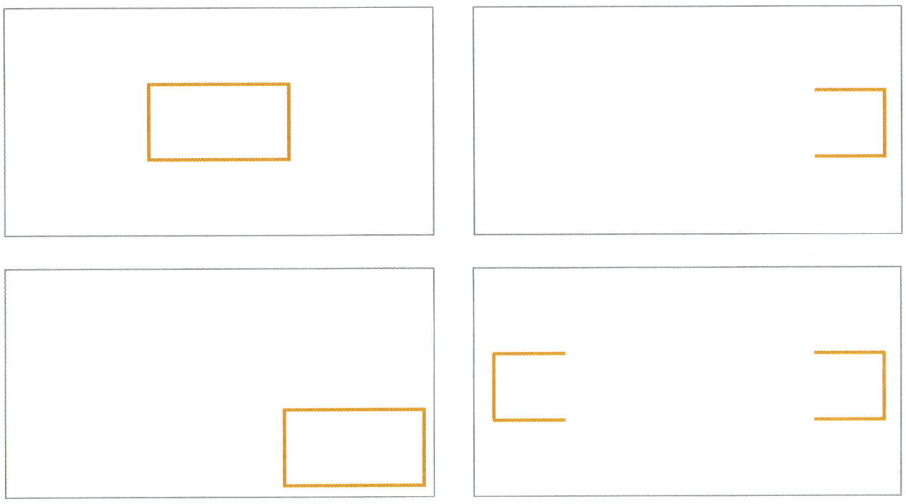

194

189 Examples of various technical fixed points (water+wiring) positions
190 Examples of various technical fixed points (ventilation – fresh air supply and exhaust air) positions
191 Construction fix points – beams
192 Example of "Smart Price House", IBA Hamburg, which consists only from the main construction – columns and ceilings, the walls are built by owners to suit their requirements and can be any time took away or changed
193 Types of construction fix points – walls and columns
194 Examples of circulation fix points – stairs, elevator and corridors

3.8 Renewable building materials

Formation of fossil resources took hundreds of millions of years.
The lignite comes from dead plant that rests that sank into the marshy ground, and was converted into peat, sand and clay covered the peat layer which was changed to lignite under elevated pressure and high temperature, this process took around 300 millions years.
The hard coal was created even after another million years, from the lignite under the sustained high pressure and elevated temperatures.
The petroleum and natural gas comes from plankton living in tropical seas about 250 million years ago, which were converted into sludge on the seabed, the sludge was covered airtight by sand and clay, by increased pressure and temperatures, the digested sludge was transformed into oil and natural gas; which, thanks to their lightweight, rose later on to higher strata.

Different evolutionary phases according to Prof. em. Dr.-Ing. Dirk Althaus based on the theories of Johann Heinrich von Thünen and Adam Smith – pre-fossil phase, where the energy was gained above earth surface, mostly from photosynthesis stored in biomass – fossil phase, where the energy is gained from under the earth surface – post-fossil phase, where the energy is gained from above the earth surface, much more efficient at high period of technical development

Renewable resources are an unlimited source of raw material and energy. Renewable materials ensure security as they can re-grow and can be found in almost all countries. Renewable materials can be produced within the local agricultural and forest industries and used as a building material. Renewable energies are solar radiation, wood, tidal, wind, geothermal, biomass and other natural elements.

The production of renewable resources along with food production has been one of the main tasks of agriculture for a long very time. Before oil, coal, natural gas and uranium were discovered, there were no other choices than to use plants in addition to mineral resources to cover needs.

Firewood, timber, wool, fibre and dye plants for textiles, food for animals (the bio fuels of yesterday) and medicinal plants were all everyday products that came from fields and forests. However, when fossil fuels begin to run out, we must enable modern methods to produce and convert more efficiently the many new products and applications.

Renewable resources contribute in many ways to the supply of sustainable energy and raw material. They help to slow down climate change, as they produce less greenhouse gas than fossil fuels in regards to energy use and conservation of carbon dioxide produced by the material.

The use of renewable resources is often associated with environmental advantages in environmentally sensitive areas. The products are often less (eco) toxic and their production is often less energy-consuming. In addition, the cultivation of renewable raw materials, on the contrary to public perception, not only risks species but also raises opportunities to develop a wider range of species through agriculture.

After all, the range of energy and raw materials is much larger than the spectrum of the now mainly cultivated food crops.

Renewable resources are found within local agriculture and forestry industries that are generated in Germany. The continuation of processing and consuming of these is of high value, as it sustains and generates new jobs.

This is particularly important for the rural people who depend on such industries, which can offer great opportunities and new perspectives. Renewable resources score high on all environmental, economic and social levels therefore can be suitable for varied sustainability concepts.

However, these should be treated as valuable materials and used efficiently. Some examples of natural renewable materials include wood, bamboo, cork, straw, stone, clay and soil.

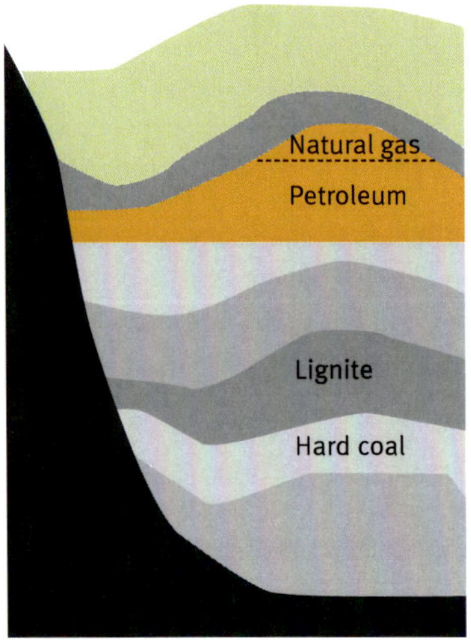

195

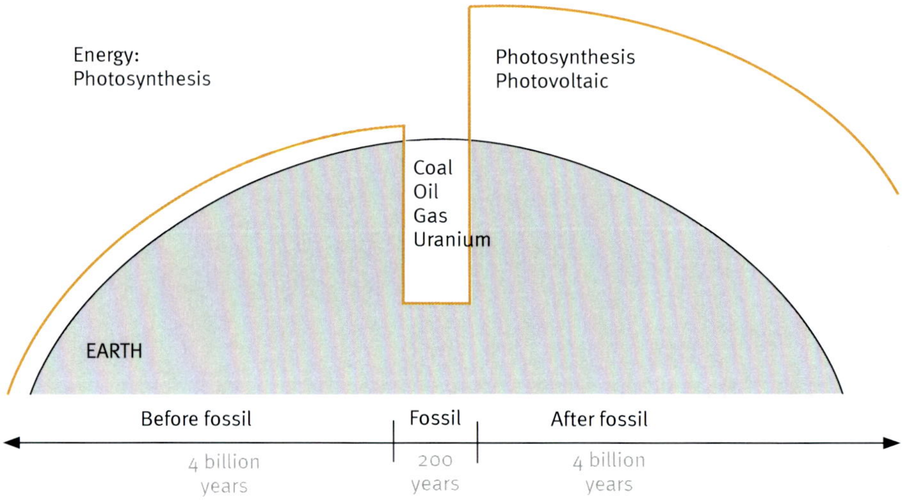

196

3.8.1 Wood

Less problematic in terms of energy than nonrenewable building materials is the domestic building material – wood, however it grows slowly.

In recent years, the interior has shifted to tropical woods (Koto, Mahogany, etc.) that are cheaper to import. This produces the absurd situation where products made from the wood of the (threatened with extinction) tropical rainforest are considerably cheaper than local spruce.
Therefore, an important aspect is sustainable forestry and the use of wood from responsible sources that ensure sustainable processing of the wood.

"Forest certification verifies the sustainability of forest management and assures customers of wood sourced from sustainably managed forests. Optional third-party chain-of-custody certification traces the steps that wood follows from its point of harvest to its end use, including all stages of processing, manufacturing, and distribution." [40]

Wood has always been an essential building product because of its strength, versatility and beauty. Wood is a 100 % renewable material and can be used for many purposes.

Trees grow naturally using energy from the sun, absorbing and storing the carbon dioxide. When wood is used as a building material, the carbon dioxide is then stored for the lifetime of the product. In this way, using wood is carbon neutral and will help to maintain carbon balance. Using wood instead of steel or concrete will also save a lot of greenhouse emissions.

Besides wood and its important role of balancing carbon, it is also a good material for cost saving, achieving energy efficiency, and a healthy, comfortable environment.

Wood helps to reduce waste because wood can be recycled or reused. In addition, for creative interior design, wood offers many advantages and possibilities. Wood has a high aesthetical value and creates pleasant indoor air quality.

Wood reflects and absorbs sound waves and is therefore a great material for acoustics. Finally, it is durable and receives high life cycle assessment results.

Understandably, wood cannot be used without power saws, transportation, sawmills and veneer plants (with hot, hydraulic presses)

197

[40] *Naturally:wood®;* Key Features of Wood [http://www.naturallywood.com/design-environment] (08.11.2012)

195 Formation of fossil resources
196 Energy and resource use in different evolutionary phases
197 Wood construction as a structural and architectural element of sporting hall
198 Development of typology of wood construction methods and systems

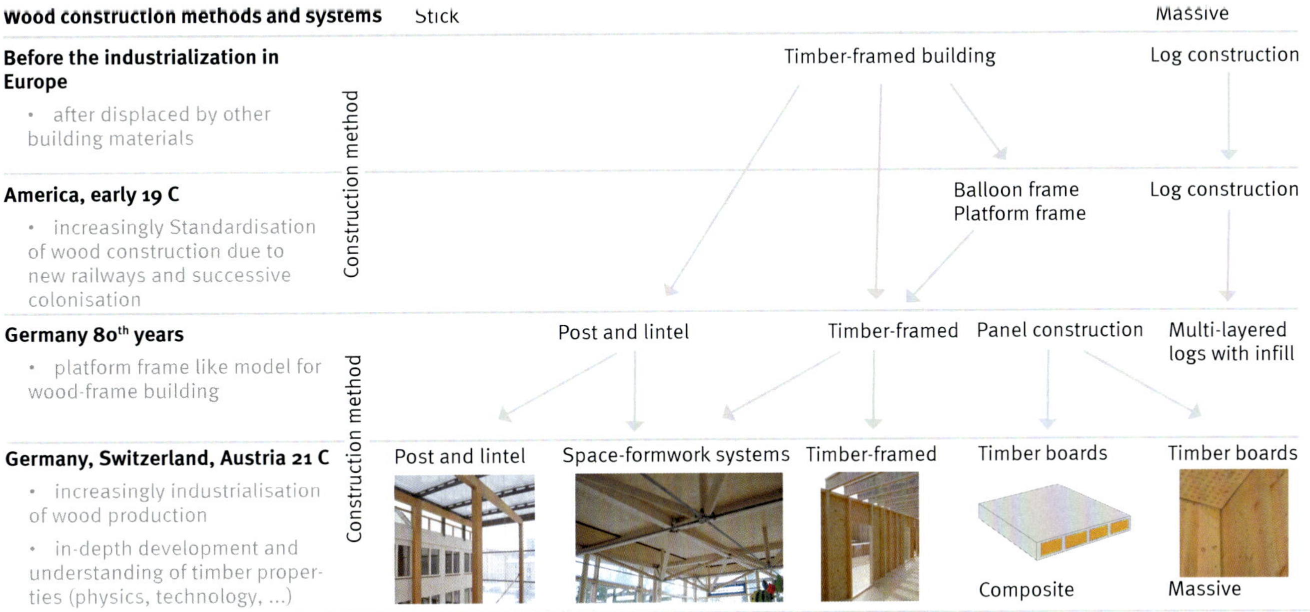

198

3.8 Renewable building materials

199

3.8.2 Bamboo

Bamboo is one of the oldest construction materials with many sustainable features. It grows fast, is extremely useful, pertains high strength, is practical and can be used in a variety of ways. It can be used to create structural panels, flooring, dimensional lumber, composite roofing, and much more.

Bamboo is highly resistant to earthquake shocks due to flexibility and strong longitudinal fibres. Boards made from bamboo resist moisture, pressure, and scratches. They are flexible and insulate against noise and heat while resisting both insects and rot. In addition to these many advantages, bamboo is also one of the least expensive building materials available.

Bamboo is a fast growing plant, as it grows one third faster than the fastest growing tree. Some species grow up to one meter per day. Its anti-erosion properties create effective watershed, they stitch soil together along fragile riverbanks, deforested areas, and in areas prone to earthquakes and mud slides.

With the shock-absorbing characteristics of natural bamboo, a bike ride over a bamboo frame would appear to be very smooth. Furthermore, some designers use environmentally friendly products such as bamboo to design cars.

Bamboo is also very good for purifying the air. With bamboo photosynthesis, carbon dioxide is drawn in, releasing oxygen up to 35 % more than trees. Therefore, bamboo can absorb much higher levels of carbon dioxide. If we were able to plant bamboo world wide, this may help to reduce carbon emissions.

Bamboo is also very beneficial for soil. Dense and fibrous bamboo roots that can firmly grasp the foot of the land and can effectively purify the soil and prevent erosion.

Traditionally, bamboo was used as a structural material in South Asia, East Asia, South Pacific and in Central and South America. In China and India, bamboo was used to hold up simple suspension bridges.

Bamboo has also long been used as scaffolding, for example in China for buildings over six storeys, and in Hong Kong for skyscrapers.

"Bamboo is useful for different things at different ages:

- < 30 days it is good for eating
- 6-9 months for baskets
- 2-3 years for bamboo boards or laminations
- 3-6 years for construction
- > 6 years bamboo gradually loses strength up to 12 years old" [41]

[41] Networkearth; Bamboo Architecture and Construction with Oscar Hidalgo [http://www.networkearth.org/naturalbuilding/bamboo.html] (13.04.2016)

199 Bamboo plants in China
200 Partial wall made from Bamboo in Kindergarten "Wellenreiter", IGEL-Institut Wismar, Germany

200

3.8.3 Cork

Cork is harvested from the cork oak tree, which can reach an average height of 12-18 m, and with a trunk circumference of 2-3 m. Most cork oak trees grow in the southwest Europe region and in northwest Africa. The most productive areas are located in Portugal's cork forests, producing half of the world's harvested cork.
When a new tree is grown, the first harvesting takes place when the tree is around 20 years old. However, if the first harvesting was of poor quality, the cork can only be used to make agglomerated cork products. The harvesting cycle typically occurs every 9-12 years over the life of a tree that spans over 150-200 years.
Cork is a light, elastic material that is impermeable to liquids and gases. It has good thermal and electrical insulating characteristics while absorbing acoustics and vibration. The products can be made form agglomerated cork or granulated cork.

"In buildings, cork has a range of uses from the foundations up. It can be used for its anti-vibrational, thermal, and acoustic absorbing properties in specific locations such as around plant rooms, sound studios, or with all these properties for more general applications such as floor, wall, ceiling tiles or underlay. It can also be used for seals, gaskets, in expansion joints and for intumescent strips. (...) When using cork tiles they are often sealed with a water based acrylic but a wax coating is also available." [42]
Cork can also be used as a thermal insulation material or for the external cladding. Granulated cork can be mixed into concrete and used as insulation for concrete slabs. Such composites have lower thermal conductivity, lower density and good energy absorption as a simple concrete.

There are also many other cork uses including musical instruments, soals of shoes, stamps, as the core of a baseball or cricket balls, as bricks for the outer walls of a house (Portugal's pavilion at EXPO 2000), in sandwich composite construction,...

Cork products, and the waste products from the manufacturing process can be reused or recycled. These by-products can be further used for example, by burning to produce energy, giving this material a high energy content.
"There is no cork byproduct that is not re-used or otherwise valued/employed.

The use of cork products is very important from an ecological point of view because it is a renewable product of long duration, promoting CO_2 fixation. Furthermore, a cork oak tree that is harvested periodically, will produce between 250-400 % more cork than what it would produce had it not been harvested, developing a higher CO_2 fixation." [43]

[42] *Green Building magazine;* Cork for building [http://www.buildingforafuture.co.uk/autumn02/focus_on_cork.php] (08.11.2012)

[43] *Gil,L.;* Cork as a Building Material: Technical Manual [http://apcor.pt/userfiles/File/Caderno%20Tecnico%20F%20EN.pdf] (08.11.2012)

201

201 Bamboo used for scaffolding in China

3.8 Renewable building materials

3.8.4 Straw

"Straw is what's left over when grains, such as wheat, rice, barley, oats, and rye, are harvested." [44]

The history of straw building runs back to the late 19th century. One of the first known straw houses is House Burke, built in Nebraska 1903. Later, straw buildings were replaced with industrial building materials. The rediscovery of straw buildings came at the end of the 1970's in the USA, and internationally this continued until the middle of the 1990's.

Straw as a building material has many advantages – it is inexpensive and is ecological because it is already a recycled local material, which saves energy. It has very good thermal insulation characteristics and, once packed densely into bales, is remarkably fire resistant.

Straw bale construction

"The most direct way to use straw in building is through straw-bale construction. During grain harvest, a baler compresses straw into rectangular bales tied with either two or three wires or polypropylene strings.

There are two primary ways to build with straw bales. In load-bearing straw-bale construction, bales are stacked and reinforced to provide structural walls that carry the roof load. With in-fill straw-bale construction, a wood, metal, or masonry structural frame supports the roof, and bales stacked to provide non-structural insulating walls. With either alternative, the bale walls are plastered or stuccoed on both the interior and exterior. (...)

There are a number of variations to standard load-bearing and in-fill straw-bale construction systems. A hybrid approach uses elements of both, such as building three load-bearing walls and a fourth (on the south) that is framed to permit more glass. (...)

A very different approach is to mortar straw bales in place as is done with concrete blocks. (...) While it produces a quite rigid wall system, it uses a lot of high-embodied-energy Portland cement, and the thermal performance is not as good because of conductivity through the mortar joints." [45]

Another way of using straw is in manufactured compressed-straw panels. When the straw is compressed under high temperature, the straw fibres connect together without any adhesives. When the material is cooled, the fibres stay in place.

These panels are mostly used for interior applications, however, several panels added together can be used as structurally insulated panels for the buildings exterior envelope.

[44-45] *BuildingGreen, Inc.;* The Next Great Building Material? [http://www.buildinggreen.com/auth/article.cfm/1995/5/1/Straw-The-Next-Great-Building-Material/] (08.11.2012)

202 Observing the straw wall construction with the architecture students at HS Wismar
203 Reed roof of traditional house in North Germany

202

203

3.8.5 Stone

"Stone has been used as a building material for thousands of years. It has long been recognised as a material of great durability and superior artistic quality, the foremost choice for buildings associated with status, power and religion.

The pyramids in Giza, burial chambers in the UK and temples in Malta were all built from stone over 4000 years ago and are still standing. The use of stone in construction has declined over the last hundred years, but it remains an aristocrat of building materials." [46]

Stone is a highly durable, low maintenance building material, which has a high thermal mass. It is available in many shapes, sizes, colours and textures. It can be easily recycled and it fits well with natural landscapes. Stone can be used as a local material gained from the immediate site.

There is a huge variety of stone types with different fields of use, including granite, sandstone, limestone, marble, slate, etc. For example, granite, sandstone and limestone can be used for building walls. But slate can only be used for roofs and floors.

Most natural stones are used to produce mineral binders or additions to the concrete and mortar production. Generally, stone can be used in buildings for: masonry, gabions, facade cladding, flooring, inside wall cladding, roof cladding.

The earliest stone style construction was dry stone or dry stacking. These are irregular shaped stones placed accordingly so that they can fit together without slipping. This type of construction has wide bases and gets thinner as height increases. There are many retaining walls, bridges and buildings known from history built with this method. These structures are durable and easily repaired.
Later, stone became more common to use for masonry walls. "Stone blocks are laid in rows of even (courses) or uneven (uncoursed) height, and fixed in place with mortar, a cement or lime mixture pasted between the stones. Building stones are normally extracted by surface quarrying then drilled and split using diamond saws or iron wedges. They are then shaped and polished according to their requirements. (...) Stones are either shaped (dressed) into a block, known as ashlar masonry, or left rough and cut irregularly, known as rubble masonry. Mortared stone structures are less durable than dry stone, because water can get trapped between the stones and push them apart. (...)" [47]

Gabions are another way of using stones or construction rubble.
Gabions are walls or structures where the stones are held together in metal cages.

204

[46-47] *Sustainable Build;* Stone Construction [http://www.sustainablebuild.co.uk/constructionstone.html] (08.11.2012)

204 Detail of the wall made out of gabions, kindergarten "Wildblume"
205 Traditional stone houses of the village Atsicholos on the Peloponnese island, Greece

205

3.8 Renewable building materials

206

3.8.6 Clay

Clay is produced into a different form when used as a building material. The clay used for building is mixed with silt and sand, formed while wet and then dried. In many regions, straw is added to the clay, which is not necessarily required, but results in a reduced density material. The added straw also means that the resulting material has better thermal insulation properties while adding reinforcing against cracking.

Within the skeleton structure, bearing capacity is taken over by timber components. Here, clay is used instead as infilling and as non-bearing walls. Clay is non-flammable and protects other flammable materials, commonly wood.

Clay surfaces are absorptive to water and exterior surfaces must be protected from weathering in order to avoid cracking. Wet clay walls are susceptible to frost. Dry clay walls, due to their low inherent moisture and high absorptiveness, extract moisture from wood and therefore act as protection. Climate in a clay building is pleasant because of the material's high heat storage capacity and temperature balancing. The humidity is stabilized as the clay retains moisture and slowly absorbs or releases. In a hot summer, the rooms of a clay house are nice and cool. In winter, the clay regulates humidity and protects against dry air.

Clay has some very positive features which makes it interesting for ecological construction:

- free of pollutants
- requires very little primary energy
- regulates humidity and is diffusible
- dry clay is antibacterial and resistant to pests
- preserves wood
- 100 % recyclable
- stores heat
- binds pollutants

The production of clay is also very easy and can often be found directly on the building site from within the ground. Clay is a cheap material but is labour intensive. Specialists in clay buildings are needed to obtain good results. Easily applied interior plasters are beneficial for creating a positive interior climate.

Clay buildings are dry, warm and regulate the internal humidity. Clay is extremely water sensitive. A clay building should begin with the roof construction. The building must be complete at the end of summer to have sufficient drying time.

Typical clay buildings technologies:

- clay brick
- stamping
- wood-light clay
- spray

206 A typical detail of the "Fachwerk" house made from a combination of wood and clay in Germany
207 Light clay brick constructions with the implementation of the clay plaster in Yazd, Iran

207

3.8.7 Rammed earth

"Rammed earth construction has its roots in Neolithic China, with evidence of rammed earth walls found in archaeological sites dating back to 5,000 BC in Yangshao and Longshan cultures of the Yellow River Valley. By 2,000 BC rammed earth architectural techniques were commonly used for walls and foundations across China.
It also became popular in other parts of the world such as Africa, The Americas and Europe. The Romans built many rammed earth structures throughout Europe. According to historians, along France's Rhone River there were thousands of rammed earth buildings." [48]

"Rammed earth is a method of building walls whereby a mixture of earth is compacted in layers between forms. Each layer of earth is approximately 15 cm (6 in) deep. As each form is filled, another form is placed above it, and the process begins again. This is continued until the desired wall height is achieved. Forms can be stripped off as soon as the form above is begun, as the compressed earth wall is self-supporting immediately. (...)
The soil mix needs to be carefully balanced between clay, sand and aggregate. The clay and moisture content of rammed earth is relatively low compared to that used for mud brick or other earth building methods." [49]
"Made from locally quarried aggregate, rammed earth buildings usually have low embodied energy and there is very little waste during the construction phase, including low use of timber as the formwork can be removed and reused.

For the life of the building, rammed earth buildings remain energy efficient. Using stabilised earth as a building material, Earth Structures houses offer outstanding thermal performance, particularly in climates with variable day-night temperatures.
The buildings have superior strength and durability, with no need for paint or other toxic finishes so that minimal maintenance is required. With no wall cavities, they are also pest proof and fire proof." [50]

Rammed earth construction offers a comfortable interior climate and regulates the interior humidity between 40 and 60 %. It is fireproof, termite-resistant, non-toxic and a good thermal mass storage.
Rammed earth construction does not have good thermal insulation characteristics, however this can be achieved with some insolating additives in the earth mixture.
The process to build the walls is time consuming and repetitious. However, nowadays more than forty percent of the population live in earth built structures. Many buildings in history used this affordable and simple method. Today, building regulations are required to enable the use of this constructions method.

208

[48] *Earth Structures;* Rammed Earth: History [http://earthstructures.com.au/rammed-earth-construction/] (11.11.2013)

[49] *Rammed Earth Constructions;* What is Rammed Earth? [http://www.rammedearthconstructions.com.au/] (11.11.2013)

[50] *Earth Structures;* Rammed Earth: Environmental benefits [http://earthstructures.com.au/rammed-earth-construction/] (11.11.2013)

208 Detail of a wall built by rammed earth construction method
209 The method of constructing a rammed earth wall

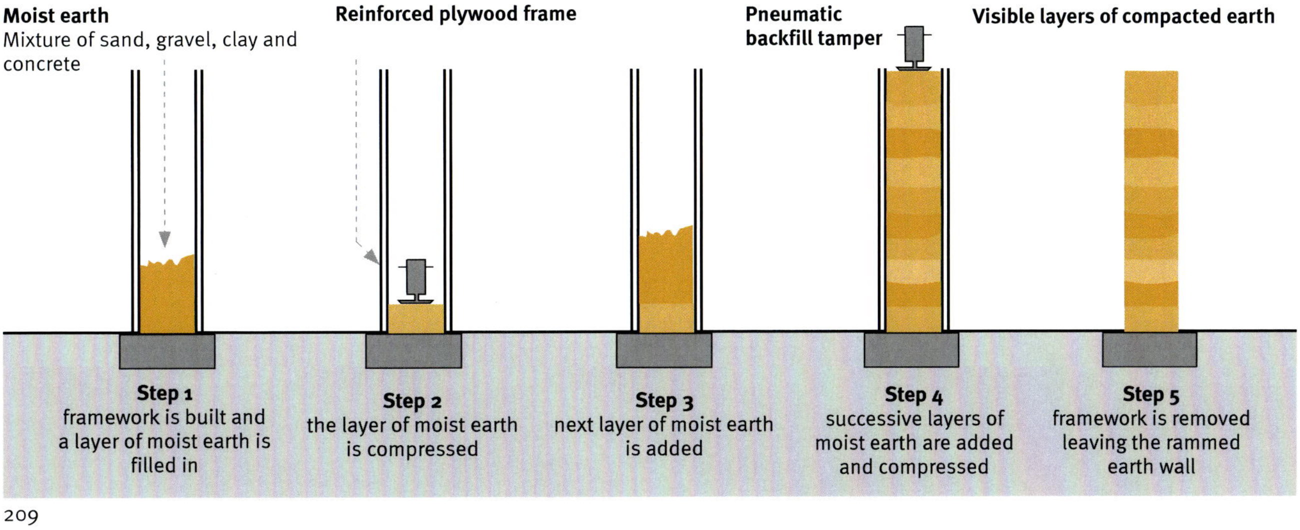

209

3.8 Renewable building materials

3.8.8 Earthbag

"Building with earthbags (sometimes called sandbags) is both old and new. Sandbags have long been used, particularly by the military, for creating strong, protective barriers, or for flood control. The same reasons that make them useful for these applications carry over to creating housing. Since the walls are so substantial, they resist all kinds of severe weather (or even bullets) and also stand up to natural calamities such as earthquakes and floods. They can be erected simply and quickly with readily available components, for very little money.

Earthbag building fills a unique niche in the quest for sustainable architecture. The bags can be filled with local, natural materials, which lowers the embodied energy commonly associated with the manufacturing and transportation of building materials. The fill material is generally of mineral composition and is not subject to decomposition (even when damp), attractive to vermin, or burnable – in other words it is extremely durable. The fill material is generally completely non-toxic and will not give off gas noxious fumes into the building.

Earthbags have the tremendous advantage of providing either thermal mass or insulation, depending on what the bags are filled with. When filled with soil they provide thermal mass, but when filled with lighter weight materials, such as crushed volcanic stone, perlite, vermiculite, or rice hulls, they provide insulation. The bags can even act as natural non-wicking, somewhat insulated foundations when they are filled with gravel.

Because the earthbags can be stacked in a wide variety of shapes, including domes, they have the potential to virtually eliminate the need for common tensile materials in the structure, especially the wood and steel often used for roofs. This not only saves more energy (and pollution), but also helps save our forests, which are increasingly necessary for sequestering carbon.

Another aspect of sustainability is found in the economy of this method. The fill material can be literally 'dirt cheap', especially if on-site soil is used. The earthbags themselves can often be purchased as misprints or recycled grain sacks, but even when new are not particularly expensive. Burlap bags were traditionally used for this purpose, and they work fine but are subject to rot. Polypropylene bags have superior strength and durability, as long as they are kept away from too much sunlight. For permanent housing the bags should be covered with some kind of plaster for protection, but this plaster can also be earthen and not particularly costly.

The ease and simplicity of building with earthbags should also be mentioned, since there is much unskilled labour available around the world that can be tapped for using this technology." [51]

[51] *EarthbagBuilding.com;* Earthbag Building [http://www.earthbagbuilding.com/index.htm] (08.11.2012)

210 Earthbag barrier for flood control

210

3.8.9 Air/vacuum

Air is also a sustainable, renewable resource that can be used in different forms within building construction. Pneumatic membranes are a good example.

Pneumatic membranes are stabilized by one another or under pressure from another medium, generally by air. The pressure-generating medium is a self-supporting construction element.

The most common form of pneumatic membranes in buildings is the air dome. Current volumes stretch to approximately 300 meters. If the membrane is reinforced with a wide-meshed network cable, self- spans of several kilometres are technically feasible.

Other forms of pneumatic membranes are pillows and hoses. The cushion consists of two membranes clamped pneumatically. Hoses use positive air pressure and behave statically as a rigid carrier.

They are used individually or in combination as a carrier, wall or ceiling. Because of the high pressure and the small volume of air they react even with the smallest leak in the diaphragm. They are therefore very sensitive and almost exclusively used for temporary constructions.
The material for membrane construction can be diverse, e.g. the ETFE foil technology (Ethylene-tetrafluoroethylene), which has many advantages – minimal weight, durability, high transparency and light transmittance, UVtransparency (greenhouse) and VU-resistant, very good tensile, tear and puncture resistance, elastic, weatherproof, hail resistant, self-cleaning, optimal chemical resistance, used in a wide temperature range, noncombustible (cost reduction by significantly lowered maintenance costs, easy to repair, etc).

Vacuum is also a resource for sustainable buildings. The idea of vacuum can be understood as an empty space without any material. On the ground, a vacuum can be produced within a closed cavity. The recipient is free of the gas contained therein, by means of suitable vacuum pumps.

Vacuums have a very good thermal conduction and a very low convection. It is therefore used as a thermal insulate, e.g. in vacuum bottles, double insulated glass windows, vacuum pipe collectors or in vacuum thermal insulation (example vacuum bottle house page 324).

Another example is Aerogel that is composed of up to 99.98 % air by volume. The gel is ultra light, low density with low thermal conductivity and is therefore a very good thermal and conductive insulator.

211

211 ETFE-foil used for the outside skin of the Alianz Arena in Munich, Herzog&de Meuron architects
212 The air domes – a typical pneumatic construction, where the membrane is fulled with air – the air cushions, where the usable space remains free from pressure differences, however requires supporting construction

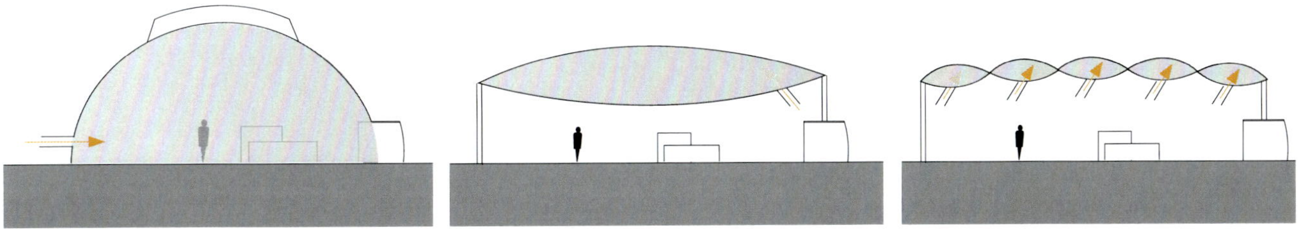

212

3.8 Renewable building materials

213

3.8.10 Water/ice

Water is a chemical combustion of Oxygen (O) and hydrogen (H). It can come in three different forms – as liquid (water), solid material (ice) and a gas (water vapour).

The application of water has many possibilities due to its diversity and properties. Water is an excellent solvent for a wide variety of materials, has a relatively high boiling point (100 °C) and melting, or freezing point (0 °C). When water freezes, it expands.

In addition, water has a high heat capacity, which absorbs heat, making it an important factor in nature and industries. Heat is absorbed when water evaporates from lakes, rivers and seas, and is released when it condenses as rain or snow.

Liquid water absorbs more energy than the ground because of its higher capacity to maintain warmth. In turn, water's high thermal mass retains a greater amount of heat and is able to provide this heat over a longer period of time.

Water is used in architecture not only because of its high aesthetical appeal, but also to create a pleasant climate and environment. Lakes or basins are formed to help cool the climate during the hot summer period, or to help clean the air of polluted cities.

An example is the research project from the Chinese capital Peking, where measurements of the city's air quality revealed much more pollution than what is allowed for human health. Experimenting with artificial rain in Peking showed that it can clean the air and help maintain the quality of air. Therefore a proposal was made to use a sprinkler system on tall buildings to water the city.

Water walls or roof ponds have a high thermal storage capacity and can be used to store heating and cooling energy for a building's interior.

Ice and snow are also basic building elements, already seen in history. Igloos are typical houses made from snow originally built by Inuits and were predominantly constructed by people of Canada's Central Arctic and Greenland's Thule area.

Snow is also used as a thermal insulation material in cold regions where houses use low pitched roofs to keep snow on it as thermal insulator.

Hotels, bars, temples, churches, even entire cities have been formed by ice as a touristic attraction in cooler regions.

213 The lite silhouette of ice buildings during the Harbin International Ice and Snow Festival, China
214 Water walls in the city of New York, used also to cool the environment

214

3.8.11 Plants

Similar to water, plants and trees help to control the climate and clean the air, as they absorb the CO_2 in the process of photosynthesis. A plant is normally composed of 72-98 % water and dry matter (mainly starch, fats, sugars, proteins, cellulose). It is important for plants to have sufficient sunshine and water in order to survive.
There are many possibilities of how to use plants within architecture – well know examples are green roofs which improve a roof's thermal insulation characteristics, help to avoid the overheating in summer, regulate the humidity, are aesthetically pleasing and act as walking terraces while also improving the city's environment.

215

Green facades work similar to green roofs. They improve a city's climate by absorbing the heat energy from the summer and preventing the heat island effect of buildings in urban areas.

Plants on a facade are also very effective as a shading system – green in summer; they shade the interior of buildings and cool the climate. During the winter the leaves fall to allow sunshine into the building to provide solar gains.

Trees around buildings also act as very good shading elements. In addition, they help to maintain the groundwater level, where building foundations and basements in built up areas destroy its original level.
However, not only freshly grown plants are used within buildings. **Dried plants** can be also be used **as a good thermal insulation materia,** for example flax, hemp or sea grass.
Another example are thatched roofs, where dry vegetation such as straw, water reed, sedge, rushes or heather are used for the roof cladding.
The plants can also have a **structural function** and carry different building loads, for example tree houses. In many native areas, the aboriginals build their houses from branches, straw or palm leaves.
Plants can be added to other materials to improve thermal characteristics.

215 Traditional turf houses, Glaumbær, Iceland
216 Examples of green facades – Copenhagen Denmark and Springe by Hannover, Germany

216

3.9 Earthsheltered architecture

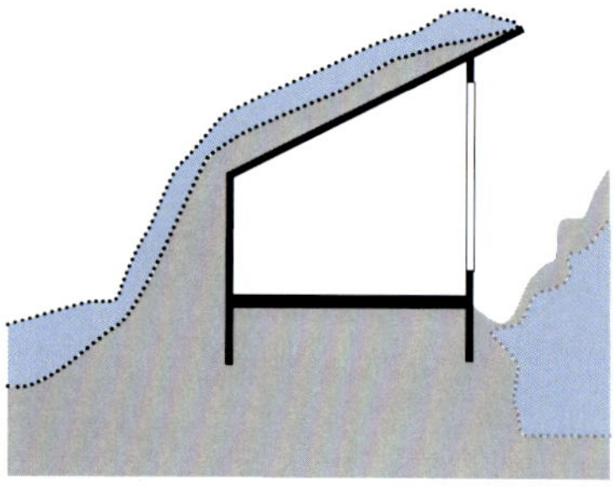

217

The earth has a stable temperature during the entire year. The deeper below the ground, the more stable the temperature. At a depth of 3-4 meters under the earth, the soil has a temperature of 5-10 °C all year.

However, soil temperature increases by 1 °C every 33 meters of depth due to the earth's excessive body heat. Soil temperature is not only influenced by geological and hydrological conditions but as well as climatic conditions.

This characteristic can be used for a fresh air supply via earth heat exchangers (fresh air supply in the building is warmed up in the earth during winter and cooled down during summer). This can also be used to stabilise the surrounding temperatures (counteracting the outside air, which changes temperature with the seasons) for the earth sheltered architecture.

Main reasons for building under the earth

- to achieve a pleasant inside environment in extreme climate
- to show the relationship between the nature and the built environment
- to save space above ground for other functions where space is lacking
- to respect the historical aspects of the site and surroundings
- to use the stable temperature of the earth to reduce heating and cooling needs
- to protect the building or the surrounding from noise and pollution
- to leave nature untouched
- to re-use old industrial underground areas such as old mines
- to reuse the earth which has been removed for foundations
- because of higher significance (for example churches, cemeteries)
- because of the building function (for example a vineyard or theatre)
- as historical city bunkers, e.g. the underground cities remaining in Turkey which were used as hiding before enemy attacks

Issues that must be considered in underground architecture

- construction and materials – the construction must be very strong because the earth bears a large weight on the structure
- lighting – it is naturally more difficult to bring light inside earth-sheltered architecture as it is for above-ground architecture
- ventilation – the ventilation systems are more complicated to solve because there is a need to bring fresh air into the underground spaces
- groundwater – underground building must have an adequate and secure waterproofing and drainage system

217 Wofati eco building – the soil around the house is waterproofed to use the thermal insulation characteristic of the dry soil
218 Umbrella house using the storage capacity of dry soil – the soil around the building is waterproofed, in summer, air enters the house through earth tube and is warmed by the sun, moving through the second tube it warms the cooler soil, in winter, cool air enters, is heated by the warm earth and passes into the house
219 Influence of solar radiation and air temperature on the seasonal course of the soil temperature

cold air
warm air

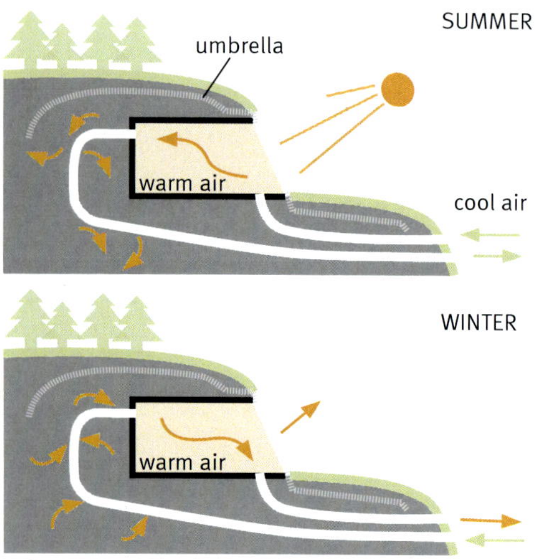

218

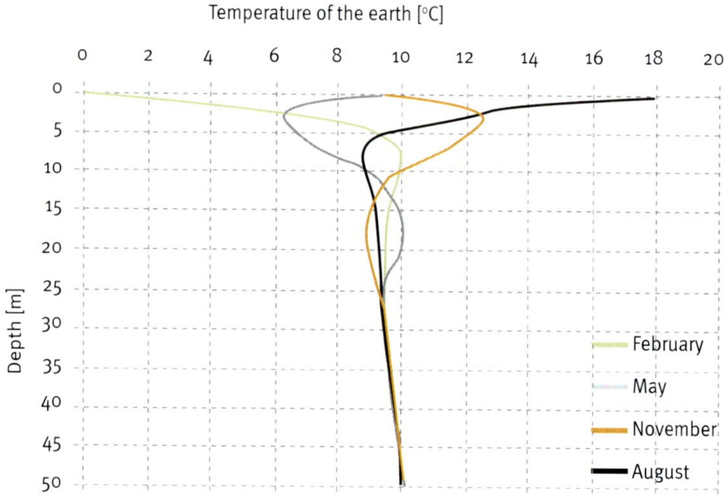

219

· flexibility – interior or exterior changes are difficult to be made, and once constructed, are hard to alter
· projection and building costs – for an earth-sheltered building costs can be unpredictable and unsteady
· negative psychological reactions – there can be negative reactions for people living or working in underground conditions because of limited visibility and lack of contact with the outside world
· radon – gas found in some areas
· sewer pipe construction and materials

Materials used in earth-sheltered architecture

The most common choice is concrete because of its strength, durability and resistance to fire. However steel, brick, stone, wood or earthbag construction can also be used.
Wood must be able to withstand the pressure exerted by a depth of only one storey. Construction made deeper with the use of wood could cause structural problems.

Important to note is the thermal insulating properties of dry soil. It has six times the insulating properties of wet soil. This particular characteristic has been used in projects where the soil surrounding the underground building was waterproofed in order to stay dry.

In this way, soil acts as a very good thermal insulator without any additional thermal support.

Dry soil can also be used for its high thermal storage capacity where warmth from the summer sun can be stored in the earth and used for heating in the winter.

Lighting in earth-sheltered architecture

There are different solutions to bring light into an earth-sheltered building:

· via windows, skylights, light pipes, light channels, atriums, ...
· with the help of a heliostat mirror

Ventilation and power in earth-sheltered architecture

There are different solutions to ventilate an underground building. One of the natural ways is by using a solar chimney, which can also be used to produce electricity with the addition of small turbines.

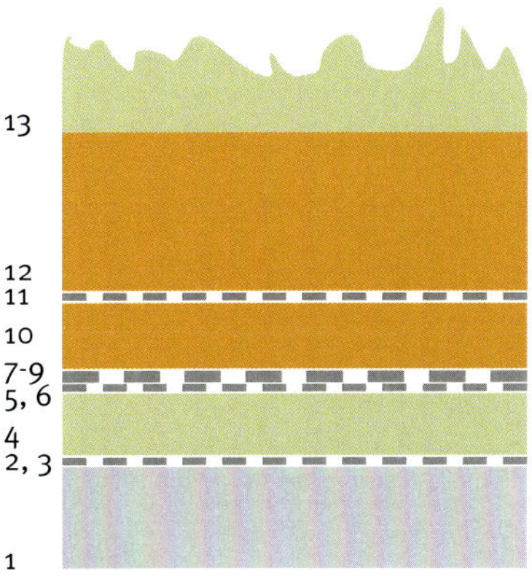

1 construction
2, 3 waterproofing layer
4 thermal insulation
5, 6 waterproofing layer and ensuring against slipping in case of a slope roof
7, 8, 9 protecting layer – mechanical, against roots
10 drainage layer (shaped foil, gravel)
11 filter layer (geotextile, sand, ...)
12 substrate (soil min. 7 cm)
13 vegetation

220

220 Composition of the green roof
221 Student project Back to Nature, Climb the tree, Burrow into the ground

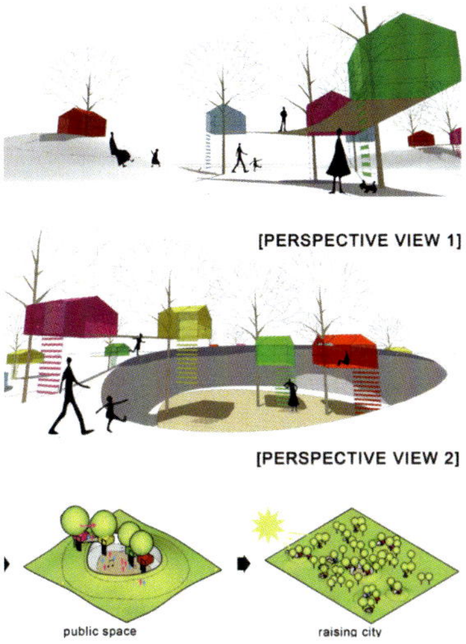

221

3.0 Passive resource-saving concepts

3.10 Passive water-saving concepts

Potable water (also known as drinking water) is water used for continuous consumption, to prepare, clean food and for personal hygiene. It is safe water, which does not contain any microorganisms or substances that could cause disease or health disorders. Drinking water is the most important and irreplaceable substance.

Rainwater (also known as storm water) is water from precipitation.

The runoff water is rainwater classified as wastewater collected by canalisation.

There are three main sustainable associations with water:

- potable water savings
- natural sewage water recycling management
- natural rainwater management

Potable water saving and natural rainwater management can be defined as a passive water saving concept.

Passive potable water savings

Passive potable water saving uses water-efficient technologies and also depends on the user's behaviour.
The most important means of reducing potable water consumption without any special active technology are:

- using water-efficient appliance technology:

(water saving fittings, water saving washing machines and dishwashers, flushing control devices and water saving WCs, water saving or even waterless urinals and separation toilettes, urine separation toilettes, vacuum toilets, compost toilettes, dry toilettes)

- responsible water saving behaviour by the consumer
- use of rainwater

Rainwater management

Rainwater in built-up areas is classified as wastewater, and must therefore be drained and treated in municipal wastewater treatment plants. Rainwater drainage has a significantly negative impact on water balance, micro-climate and the flora and fauna of cities.
Natural rainwater management methods positively influence the local water cycle and are based upon the fact that rainwater normally drains into the ground and replenishes the groundwater directly as well as flowing by means of normal channels into surface water rivers and lakes.
Under high rainfall conditions, rainwater infiltration is insufficient to deal with large amounts of water. Further rainwater management strategies are required, such as harvesting and retention.

Possible rain water management systems are:

- the use of rainwater (recycling is a part of active concepts)
- rainwater retention (green roof, collection roof, filter trench, retention pond, ditch or hollow, retention filter basin, retention basin)
- rainwater percolation (permeable surface percolation, trough percolation, basin percolation, soak-away pits, pipe percolation, infiltration ditch percolation (blind or french drain), including a combination of these different types)

222 Methods and ways for a sustainable association with water, the green colored diagrams show passive water-saving concepts

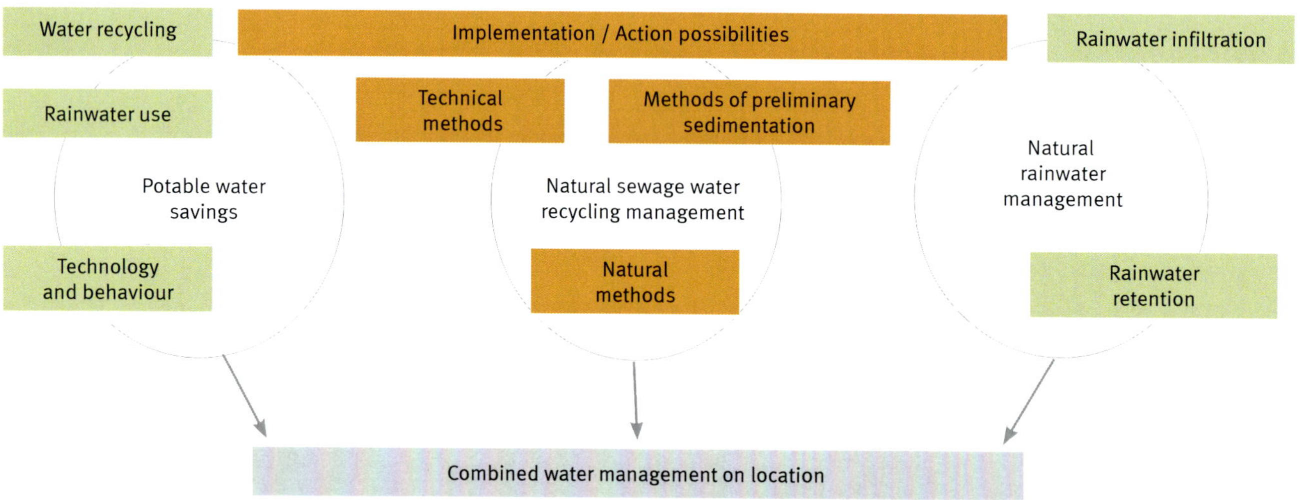

222

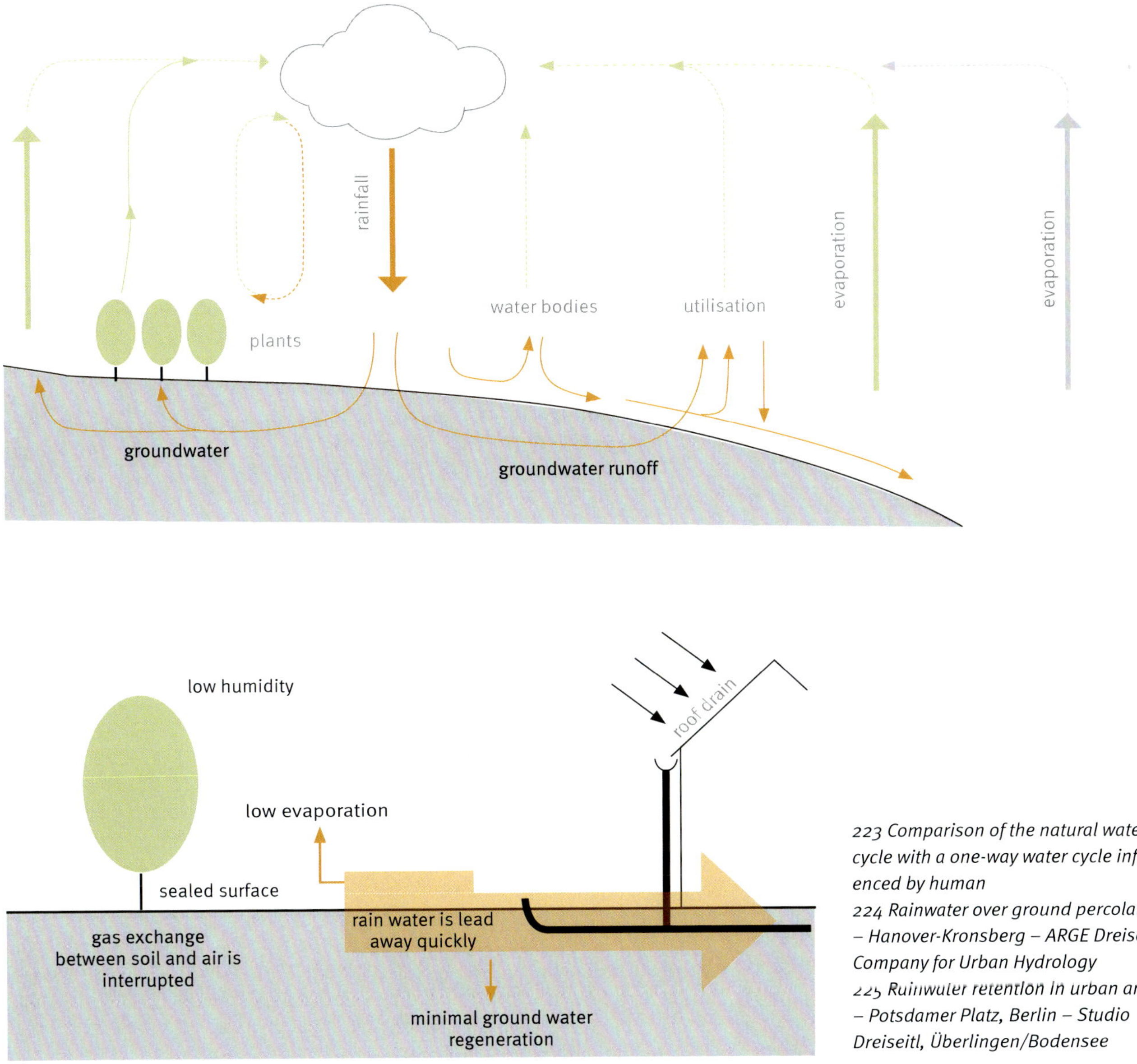

223

224

225

223 Comparison of the natural water cycle with a one-way water cycle influenced by human
224 Rainwater over ground percolation – Hanover-Kronsberg – ARGE Dreiseitl/ Company for Urban Hydrology
225 Rainwater retention in urban areas – Potsdamer Platz, Berlin – Studio Dreiseitl, Überlingen/Bodensee

3.11 Summary

"Es kann nicht sein, dass wir ein Gebäude abbrechen und den gleichen Quatsch an gleicher Stelle wieder hin bauen!

It can not be that we demolish a building and build the same crap in the same place again!"

Prof. Stefan Behnisch on 30.11.2011 at Hochschule Augsburg

Extract from the heritage Protection Act

"Heritage monuments are things or parts made by humans from history. Their conservation is in the public interest because of their historical, artistic, urban development, scientific or ethnographic significance. The owners and otherwise legal beneficial owners of heritage buildings have to keep their monuments in standing condition, repair them, treat them properly and protect them from hazards, in a way that is expected of."

The aim of heritage preservation is permanent preservation of buildings under heritage, not to destroy, damage or influence them.

The increasing demands of building planning, energy efficiency and sustainability makes the treatment of existing buildings more difficult. Special training is required, following new static requirements, use changes, treating of pollutants, warranty liability and high technical standards.

Existing buildings are increasingly being abandoned for economic reasons and replaced by new buildings.

As an example is the STARK III program from the Saxony-Anhalt model project, only two out of ten existing buildings were considered for renewing projects while the remainder became building replacement projects.

The renewing of an existing building can bring more advantages from use or an environmental point of view. Here, the consideration of a building's "external costs" for replacement in comparison to the demolition and following new construction highlights such environmental impacts.

There are also many opportunities related to an existing building that cannot be repeated with new construction. Through the reuse of an existing building, added value can be achieved, which is only possible when a considerable effort is made in the new building.

The building as a resource offers a large, hidden potential for new interpretations of the building use, e.g. loft apartments would never exist without the reuse of storage and industry buildings.

Today, the hidden potential of railway stations, storage houses, industry buildings, gas stations, mines, windmills, schools, etc. has been overlooked with the potential of discovery.

Unfortunately this task is not typical for architects. The spatial uses and possibilities to be discovered with existing structures are not connected "to build in the existing building", but "to build within the existing building".

In this way, additional qualities can be gained and resources can be saved. Sometimes the willingness to change is important. In heritage protection (restoration) the building will only be considered to be protected and restored and the exploring of opportunities for new interpretations will be lost.

Demolishing an existing building eliminates any opportunity for new interpretations and the possibility to create additional qualities. The demolition also demands additional resources and energy.

226 Building before renovation, Kindergarten "Plappersnut", Wismar, Germany

226

For the reuse and rehabilitation of existing buildings, the legal and economic constraints and barriers required must be reduced. Architects and investors must identify future opportunities and the unique values added when renewing an existing building.

Therefore it is of high importance that more architects reuse abandoned buildings and learn from existing structures the possibilities to achieve new spaces for the user with less additional resources.

It is important to keep and protect heritage buildings and the history of our building culture while also considering climate protection, resource and energy saving.

An appropriate solution should be found to harmonise both strategies. For example, that the heritage value of buildings are not destroyed by high energy standards, but a compromise that allows for heritage preservation without causing high resource demands.

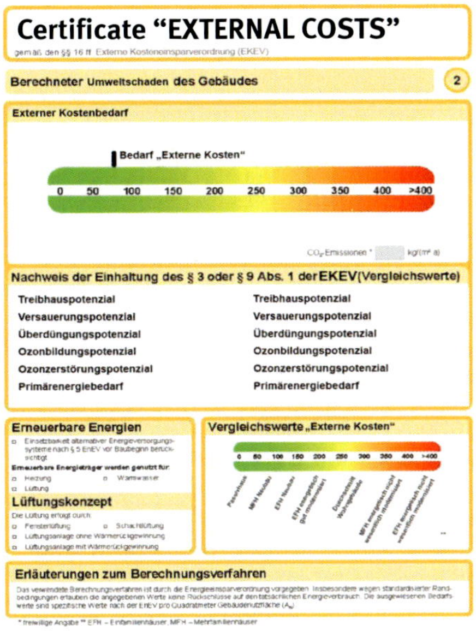
Certificate "EXTERNAL COSTS"
gemäß den §§ 16 ff. Externe Kosteneinsparverordnung (EKEV)

Berechneter Umweltschaden des Gebäudes (2)

Externer Kostenbedarf

Bedarf „Externe Kosten"

0 50 100 150 200 250 300 350 400 >400

CO_2-Emissionen * kg/(m² a)

Nachweis der Einhaltung des § 3 oder § 9 Abs. 1 der EKEV (Vergleichswerte)

Treibhauspotenzial	Treibhauspotenzial
Versauerungspotenzial	Versauerungspotenzial
Überdüngungspotenzial	Überdüngungspotenzial
Ozonbildungspotenzial	Ozonbildungspotenzial
Ozonzerstörungspotenzial	Ozonzerstörungspotenzial
Primärenergiebedarf	Primärenergiebedarf

Erneuerbare Energien

- Einsetzbarkeit alternativer Energieversorgungssysteme nach § 5 EnEV vor Baubeginn berücksichtigt

Erneuerbare Energieträger werden genutzt für:

- Heizung
- Warmwasser
- Lüftung

Lüftungskonzept

Die Lüftung erfolgt durch:

- Fensterlüftung
- Schachtlüftung
- Lüftungsanlage ohne Wärmerückgewinnung
- Lüftungsanlage mit Wärmerückgewinnung

Vergleichswerte „Externe Kosten"

0 50 100 150 200 250 300 350 400 >400

Passivhaus, MFH Neubau, EFH Neubau, EFH energetisch gut modernisiert, Durchschnitt Wohngebäude, MFH energetisch nicht wesentlich modernisiert, EFH energetisch nicht wesentlich modernisiert

Erläuterungen zum Berechnungsverfahren

Das verwendete Berechnungsverfahren ist durch die Energieeinsparverordnung vorgegeben. Insbesondere wegen standardisierter Randbedingungen erlauben die angegebenen Werte keine Rückschlüsse auf den tatsächlichen Energieverbrauch. Die ausgewiesenen Bedarfswerte sind spezifische Werte nach der EnEV pro Quadratmeter Gebäudenutzfläche (A_N)

* freiwillige Angabe ** EFH – Einfamilienhäuser, MFH – Mehrfamilienhäuser

227

228

227 *The building pass "External costs" in addition to the building energy pass*
228 *Resources protection sign in addition to the heritage protection*
229 *Double windows acting as trombe walls and integrated Photovoltaic solar shading on the south facade, Kindergarten "Plappersnut", Wismar, Germany*
230 *View inside the garden, the atrium is fitted for the special windy and rainy climate in northern Germany, Kindergarten "Plappersnut", Wismar, Germany*

229

230

231

231 Some of the passive energy-saving techniques designed in the kindergarten "Sonnenschein", Wismar; specially designed southern facade that collects heat energy from the sun and uses it to preheat the incoming fresh air in the winter, as well as usage of an in-ground heat exchanger to help preheat/precool the fresh air, IGEL-Institut Wismar

Life time design

4.0 Passive energy-saving concepts (low-tech)

4.0 Passive energy-saving concepts

4.1 Introduction

232

The saving of operation energy needed to provide required comfort in the building (ventilation, cooling, heating, lighting) is considered within the third building life cycle. There are two main concepts that deal with this topic – passive and active energy-saving concepts. In this chapter, the passive concepts are described.

Passive concepts (also known as low-tech concepts) are the simplest, cheapest and most sustainable concepts for energy saving, as they respect and use the natural conditions of the site to provide building comfort. They are designed for the users and based on the building's function.

Passive low-tech concepts reduce the energy required for ventilation, heating, cooling and lighting of the building. Using natural ventilation concepts saves the energy otherwise required for mechanical ventilation. Passive concepts help to preheat or precool a building, so that the energy required for heating and cooling is lower. In addition, passive concepts aim to receive as much daylight as possible into the interior, so that the demand of artificial light remains low.

The passive application of environmental conditions are closely linked with local meteorological conditions. Therefore, it is important to consider the local temperatures (summer/winter), the average annual radiation, the rain frequency, the average annual amount of precipitation and the wind direction and strength.

Respecting conditions in different climate zones by traditional building

Passive concepts are well known in history, when modern day technology was not yet developed and people had no choice but to use passive concepts. The history of building in different climate zones exhibits a great connection to local climate conditions.

The five main climate zones distribute themselves over the earth and are the basis of different traditional building types. – humid tropical, dry subtropical, humid temperate, humid cold and cold polar – the sixth additional group, the highland climate zone is unclassified and cannot be used as a building environment.

Humid tropical (equatorial) climate

Humid tropical is characterized by high annual temperatures and large amounts of precipitation, typical with rain forests, monsoons and the Savanna ranges. Tropical rain forest regions include countries around the equator without any dry season. Building structures are designed with good aeration possibilities and protection from sun and rain. Materials of the building structures must be able to drain and dry fast.

232 Typical narrow street in the mediterranean city in order to provide sufficient shading
233 Different climate zones of the world in respect of the Köppen climate classification system

- humid tropical
- dry subtropical
- humid temperate
- humid cold
- cold polar

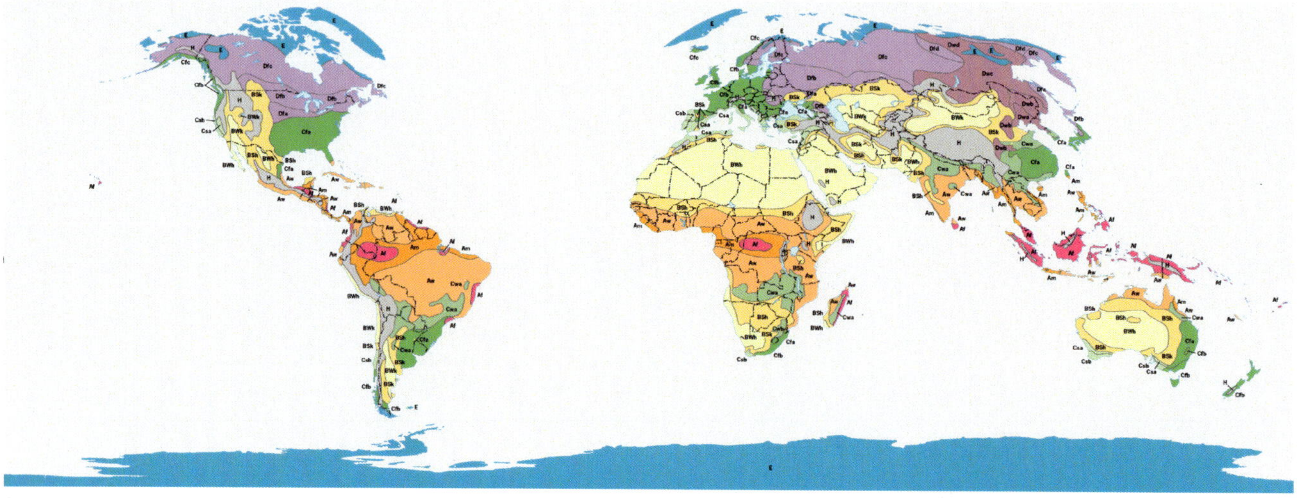

233

Tropical monsoon regions have short dry seasons and are mostly common in Southern and Central America. Typical are light dwellings for protection against warmth and rain, with good aeration.
The tropical savanna regions have a dry winter period. It has ideal climate conditions with favourable outside temperatures during the year.

These regions are typical for South America, Central Africa and India. Simple building structures are used for the protection against sun exposure and strong rainfalls without an isolating effect.

Dry subtropical climate

Dry climate zones have very little rain with a highly variant daily temperature range. Included are steppe (semiarid) and desert ranges (arid).
Most commonly found in North Africa, Central Asia, and Australia.
In the steppe ranges, the summers are damp, sultriness with mild winters. Common are simple building structures with good aeration possibilities and easy isolation for winter.

Desert ranges experience extreme heat and a large lack of water.
Mobile, light dwellings or mass buildings with few windows are used for protection against heat and sand and for the use of evaporative cooling, earth cooling, air movements and thermionics.

Humid temperate climate

Found here are warm dry summers and cool wet winters. Due to the large land/water differentiation, this zone is divided into the mediterranean (maritime) ranges and the continental ranges.

This is typical for Europe, South-East USA, and South-West Asia.

Mediterranean ranges have an ideal climate with damp and not so hot summers as well as mild winters. Building structures give sufficient shade with favourable aeration possibilities. Simple heating methods are necessary in the winter.

The continental ranges have warm summers and cold winters with a small moistening effect. Isolated building structures contest both extreme hot and cold outside temperatures, i.e. the wall structures should partially absorb heat.

Humid cold climate

The cold climate zone season has a high variation of temperatures with little rainfall. Located in the middle regions of large landmasses, for example in Canada and Russia, good insulation is required as well as high-pitched roofs, used to shed snow.

Cold polar climate

The North and South pole has less solar radiation, resulting in extremely cold temperatures with permanent ice areas, typically dominated by polar ice caps. There are two zone ranges – tundra and arctic ranges.

The Tundra ranges have moderate summers and very cold winters. Suitable housing structures are mobile and easily isolated to protect against wind.

The Arctic ranges have very cold outside temperatures with high wind velocities. Building structures should be well isolating and wind-protected. Wearing warm and well-fitted clothing is also extremely important.

Highland climate

High mountain ranges have moderate summers, very cold winters and high wind velocities. Building structures are more substantial with a well isolating form.

234 Traditional desert architecture in Yazd, Iran – thick clay walls of houses with few small windows and wind catchers provides natural cooling

234

4.2 Respecting the climate

Climate

Climate can be understood as a long-term weather mode with many peculiarities, variety and variability, which manifests itself in a particular place. The main climate-creating factors are the balance of energy, atmospheric circulation, geographical factors and human intervention.

The energy balance is mainly determined by the sum of all short and long wave radiations, which are absorbed, reflected and radiated by the atmosphere and surfaces.

Atmospheric circulation is the means of creating a climate from the predominant air flow and movement of air masses.
Geographic conditions are climate created from specific, relatively stable geographic conditions. The biggest influences on creating a climate are:

- latitude
- altitude
- distribution of continents and oceans (the locations distance from the coast)
- topography (relief of the earth's surface)
- ocean currents

Anthropogenic influences are created by man who have the greatest influence on the growth of CO_2 and other gases in the atmosphere.

Climate analysis

Respecting climate conditions is the main attitude when designing a passive energy concept. The factors that need to be considered when designing:

- climate region
- altitude
- air temperature incl. daily and annual fluctuation
- air pressure
- air humidity
- solar radiation (direct/diffuse)
- wind (strength and direction)
- precipitation (amount and temporal occurrence)
- evaporation
- fog frequency

Air temperature

The outside temperature depends on solar radiation and the height above sea level. Temperature decreases at around 1 °C for every rise of 200 meters in height.

The air temperature influences the transmission and ventilation losses in winter and possible overheating in summer. The extreme temperature frequencies should be considered in context to the efficiency of passive measures and dimensioning of the building technology.

Solar radiation

Solar energy in buildings, for passive and active use, is gained significantly from the values of solar radiation. Global solar radiation consists of:

- direct radiation

penetrating direct and unhindered on the earths surface

- diffuse radiation

penetrating after spreading through the atmosphere (i.e through clouds, water and dust particles) and then on the earth's surface

Due to different radiation angles, and varying distances to the equator, the intensity and seasonal fluctuation of available solar energy differs.

The duration of a bright day and its sun hours has a direct influence on the level of solar gain. To ensure high performance of solar energy for passive and active use it is important to know the data regarding intensity and sunshine duration, also the radiation angle and course of the sun.

Wind

Directional air movements in the atmosphere result from various air pressures of air masses. The air within the high air pressure zones flows to the zones with low air pressure until a balanced pressure is reached.
For the development of natural ventilation systems, it is important to know the static relevant wind loads, predominant wind direction, and the pressure and suction conditions.
A good natural ventilation concept can be developed through the clever arrangement of supply and waste air openings which are dependant on the building depth and height.

Buildings exposed to wind have high energy losses through the building envelope. In order to decrease the wind velocity on the building, landscaping including trees, hedges or walls can be strategically located as a barrier along the winds direction.
With an appropriate building form, comfortable outdoor spaces can be created, even in windy areas.

Air pressure

is the basic meteorological element. It is the force exerted by the weight of air that extends from the measuring point to the top of the atmosphere. Air pressure decreases with height, for every 5.5 kilometres it is halved. The cooler (heavier) the air is, the faster the pressure decreases upward. Air pressure is variable and depends on the temperature and humidity, latitude and altitude.

Precipitation

Along with the air temperature, atmospheric precipitation is considered the most important meteorological element. It is also considered to be the most changeable meteorological elements from a spatial and time perspective. Atmospheric precipitation is mostly influenced by the geographical position of the area, altitude, windward/leeward area to prevailing wind, bringing moist air masses and frontal systems. Precipitation can be in the form of rain or snow.
Water is a valuable resource that has no equivalent. Creating quality drinking water requires considerable effort and energy to bring the water to a hygienic state.
Rainwater should be considered for different functions. Not only to use for flushing toilets or watering, but also for its cooling effect.

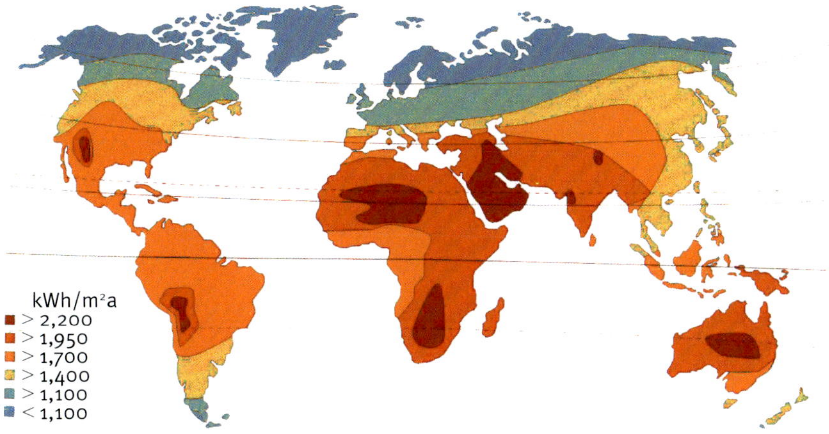

235

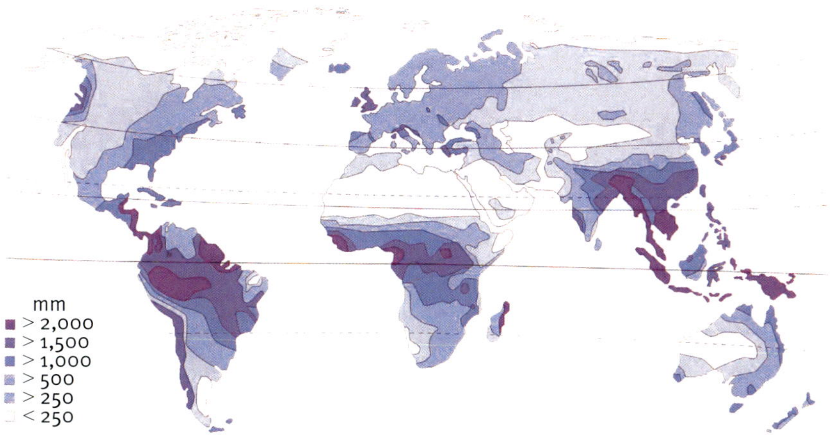

236

235 Distribution of annual global solar radiation
236 Distribution of annual precipitation
237 Influence of increasing altitude to the climate and temperature conditions

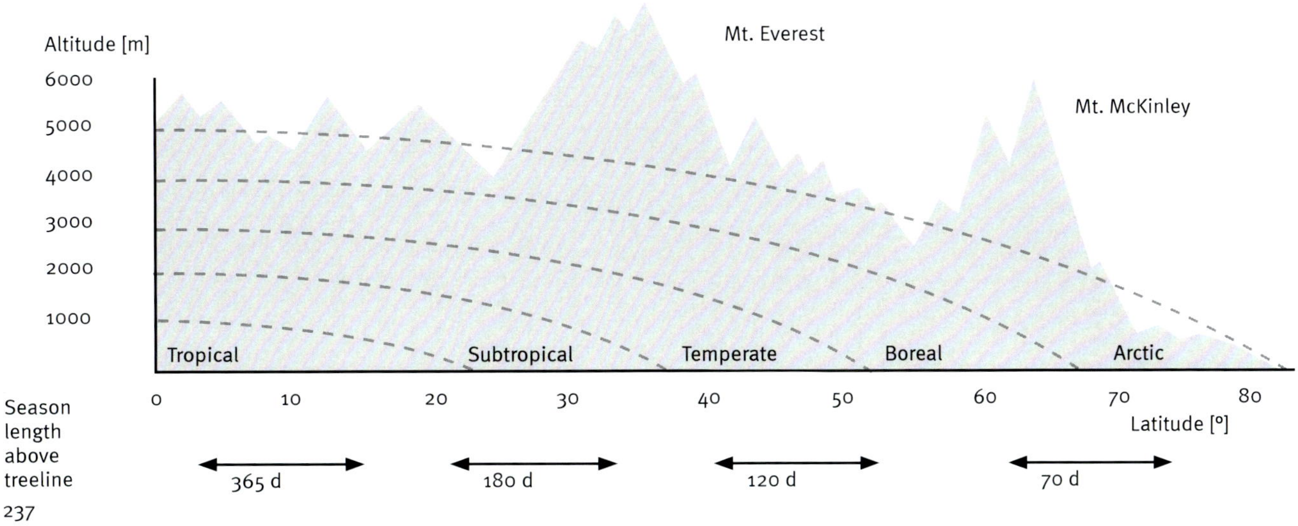

237

4.3 Respecting the terrain topography

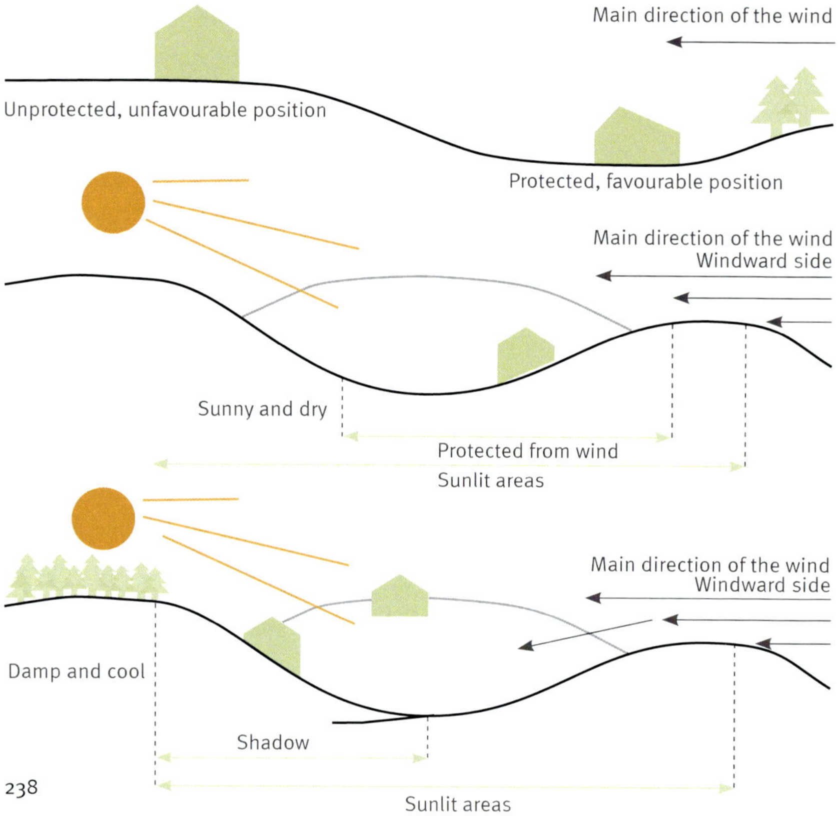

238

238 Location of a building in terrain – a building's most favourable position is on the South facing hill side, in a sunny and dry area protected from wind, a building's least favourable position is in shadow and not wind protected, however this is ideal for hot areas where cooling is needed
239 Influences on building, which depend on different topographic locations including possible solar energy gains and losses as a result of wind

Terrain topography identifies land shapes and height features as a three-dimensional surface. It is typically presented in a topographic map with the use of contour lines.

It is desirable to design a building in accordance to the environment – to locate the building with respect to the local climate, terrain configuration, vegetation, orientation to the sun and the method of surrounding the building structure.

Air temperatures in valleys and on the top of the hills are lower compared to protected areas and on southern slopes. Valleys can create cold air lakes due to the descent of cold air, especially at night. Valleys also hold pollutants and polluted air due to the lack of airflow.

Determining where to locate the building within the terrain is important. To avoid high energy losses, a wind protected location is ideal. To use solar gains, the sunny side of a slope is desirable.

Located against a hill with the south side wind protected makes an ideal building position for a tempered climate zone. This also protects the building from high energy losses in the winter.

The climate zone is essential to consider. In hot areas, where building cooling is needed, a location in the shadows and on the windy side can be ideal.

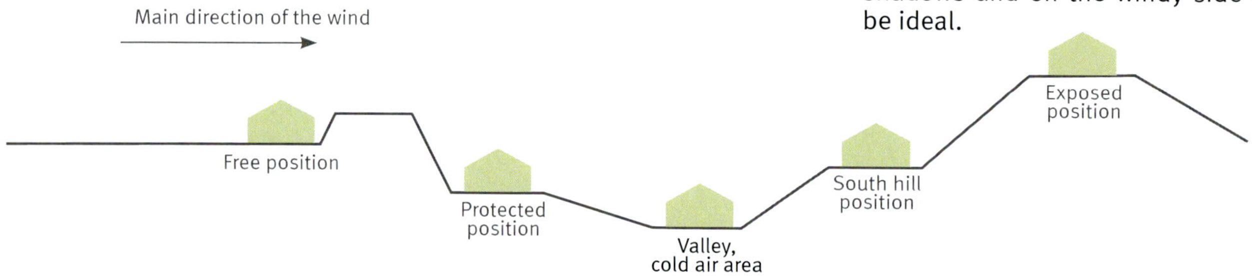

	Free position	Protected position	Valley, cold air area	South hill position	Exposed position
Difference in the ambient temperature	± 0 °C		- 3 °C	- 2 °C	- 1 °C
Temperature heat losses	± 0 %		+25 %	- 17 %	+ 10 %
Heat losses from wind	± 0 %	- 50 %		+ 100 %	+ 100 %

239

4.4 Respecting the sun

The way in which the sun is handled is an important aspect of the energy concept. Important data includes the building orientation, percentage of window area, passive sun energy use and shading systems as protection from overheating and natural daylighting.

The height of the buildings will also influence natural daylighting within the building.

Building height and distances

If the sun is to be considered as a significant source of energy, the sun must reach the building.

In general, a line showing the angle of the sun at various times of the year can be drawn to help determine distances between buildings, elements and heights in order to show that the sun can reach each building.

There are also regulations for building heights and distances between buildings. When the sun energy is required year-round, a distance between a South neighbouring building of at least twice the height is required.

As the height of the building increases, the space between buildings must also increase to provide natural sunlight to lower levels.

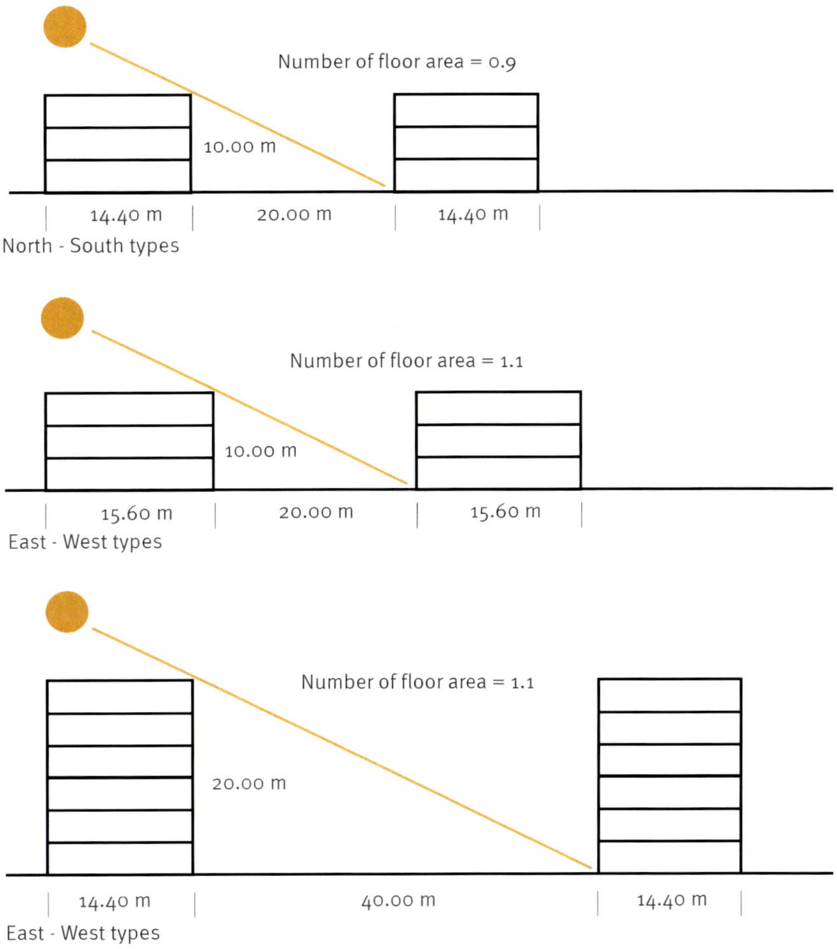

240

240 Various building depths and distances between structures depending on their orientations and heights
241 Micro climatic effective elements and their influence on the building

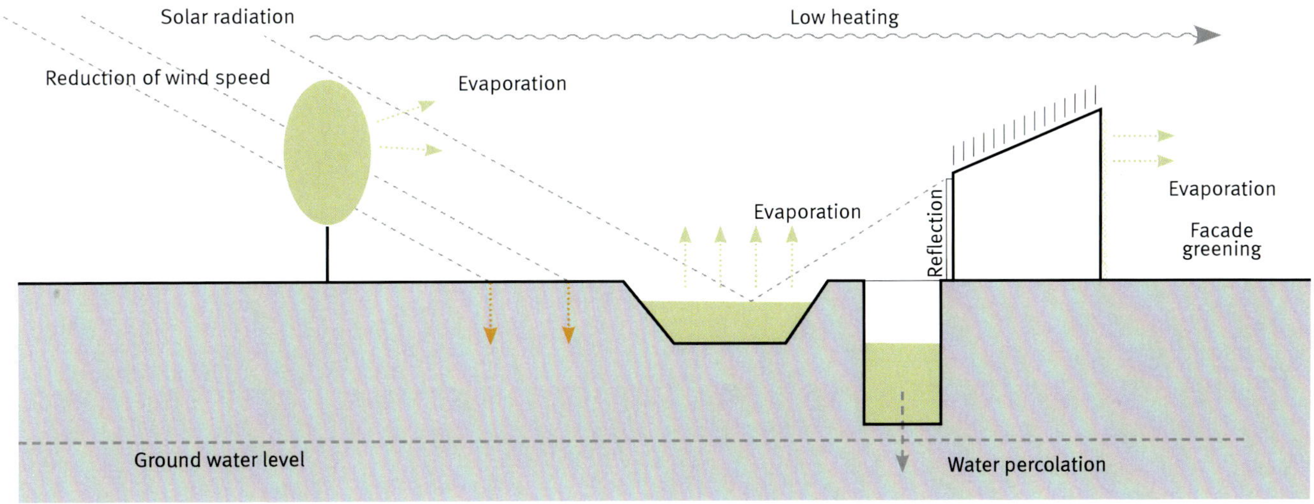

241

4.4 Respecting the sun

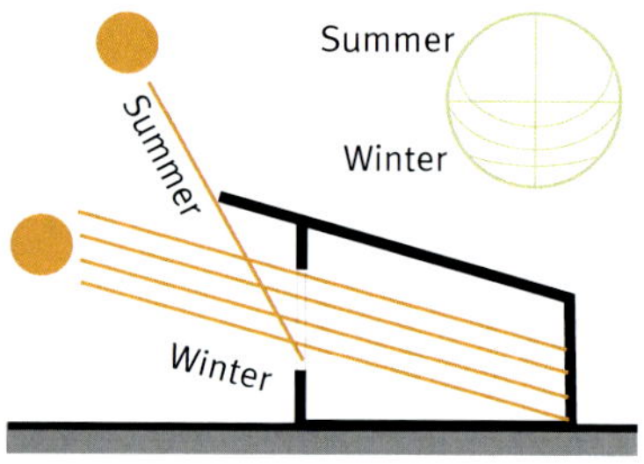

242

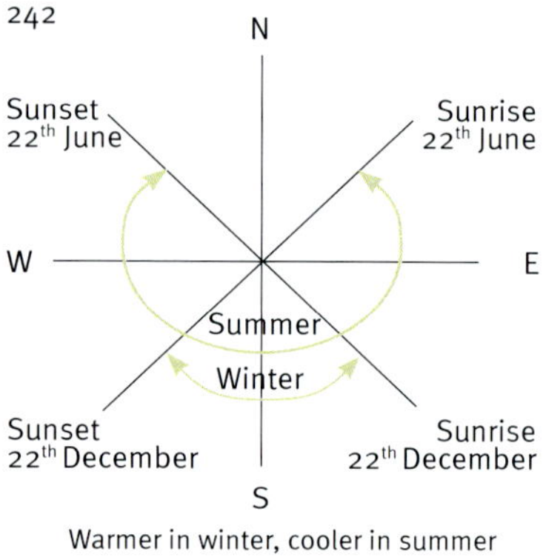

243

242 Section of the house in accordance to the orientation, location Germany
243 Movement of the sun in winter/summer, location Germany
244 Course of the sun on 21st December, location Germany
245 Course of the sun on 21st June, location Germany
246 Examples of different possibilities for sun protection of a window
247 Optimal window area in accordance to building orientation
248 Appropriate implementation of sun protection systems for different orientations – the south and north facades require horizontal shading while the east and west facades require vertical shading due to the different sun angle

Building orientation

The performance of the building in summer and winter is dependant on:

- solar azimuth angle and the facades elevation angle
- intensity of the solar radiation

There is also a correlation between the use of the rooms (i.e services placed on the darker north side), the tanning of the facade (light or dark), and the annual variations of the outside air temperature.

North orientation

- gains direct sun radiation only during the summer solstice
- it is possible to use large surface glazing however, risk of heat loss in the winter
- often no sun protection, therefore must ensure room-temperature is controlled by sun protection glazing or other sun protection means ie. timber slats

East orientation

- in the summer, high radiation penetrates at a small angle so shading must be designed to reduce solar penetration while maintaining an outlook
- 50 % of the exposure time coincides with the usage time

South orientation

- steep angle sunlight penetration
- facade receives lower radiation intensity
- efficient shading that diminishes daylight entry, often with an additional skin (e.g. fixed projections or horizontal slats)
- 100 % of the exposure time coincides with the usage time

West orientation

- sunlight penetrates at a shallow angle with high radiation and therefore makes it difficult to achieve a concept that provides sufficient natural daylighting and shading
- approx. 75 % of the suns exposure coincides with the usage time
- energy radiated in the afternoon must be dissipated during the night
- the west side is the hardest to deal with

Main facades along the N-S Axis

- arranged along the N-S axis is more efficient in the summer, because the south facade is exposed to the sun
- it is important to avoid solar radiation on the north facade
- disadvantages include different room qualities i.e. south facing spaces will gain higher qualities than north facing spaces

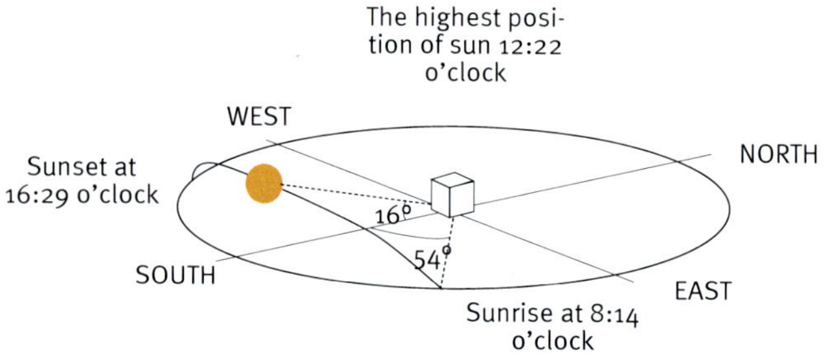

244

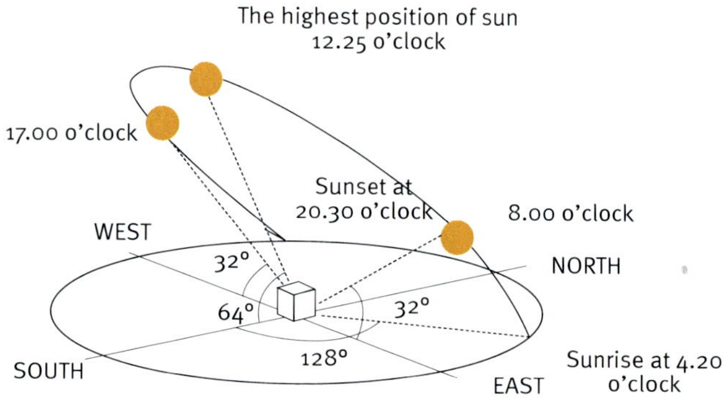

245

Main facades along the E-W Axis

- the E-W axis is more efficient, all of the rooms receive sun
- the window to surface ratio must be limited
- greater potential to use ventilation/sun protection strategies
- due to the shallow sunlight penetration angle, special attention must be aimed at sun protection

Effects of window-area ratio

- the window area ratio influences the climate in summer
- large windows on exposed facades should be reconsidered
- a large sunny space only with external sun protection
- on the N side, generous glazing is possible in the case that sun radiation transmission is limited
- the S facade allows for greater transparency than E or W facade
- the thermal dynamics increase when the window to area ratio increases, raising requirements for active cooling
- the cooling energy demand increases almost proportionally to the window to area ratio
- respect to daylighting – arrangement of the transparent areas are more important than their size, when the windows surface amount is of 50 %
- the amount of glazing on a facade for a residential building should be › 30 % and for buildings with other functions › 50 %

Preventing overheating by using sun protection systems

- energy input by a facade is determined by the total energy transmittance of the glazing and the reduction factor of sun protection
- total energy transmission can be affected in the cavity by coating the glass or sun protection measures
- reduction factor depends on whether the sun protection is on the outside or inside – outside depends on weather, inside – cost efficient, easy to maintain, depends not on weather, but less efficient
- outdoor installation reduces radiation by 75 %, inside one only by 25 %
- orientation of the sun protection is correlated with the orientation of the building
- control strategy has a significant influence on the indoor climate
- to avoid diffuse radiation, louvres are often useful to include sun protection, even if no radiation strikes facade
- trees, green facades or other planting are very effective, passive and sustainable methods for sun protection

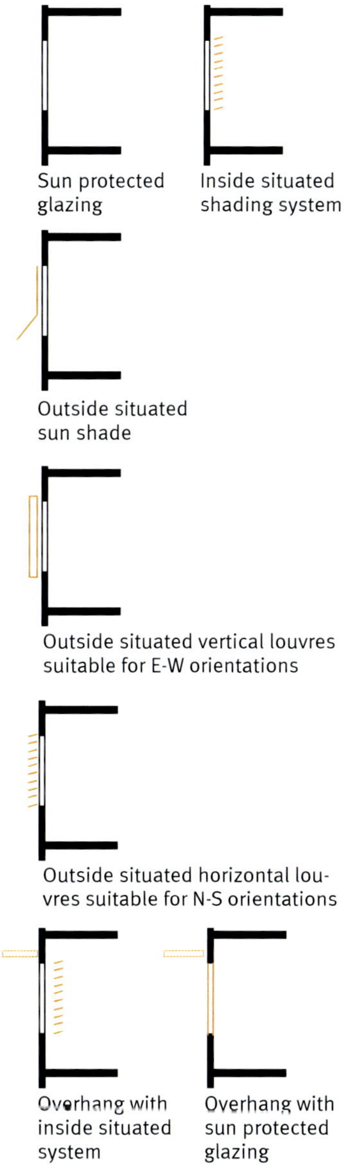

246

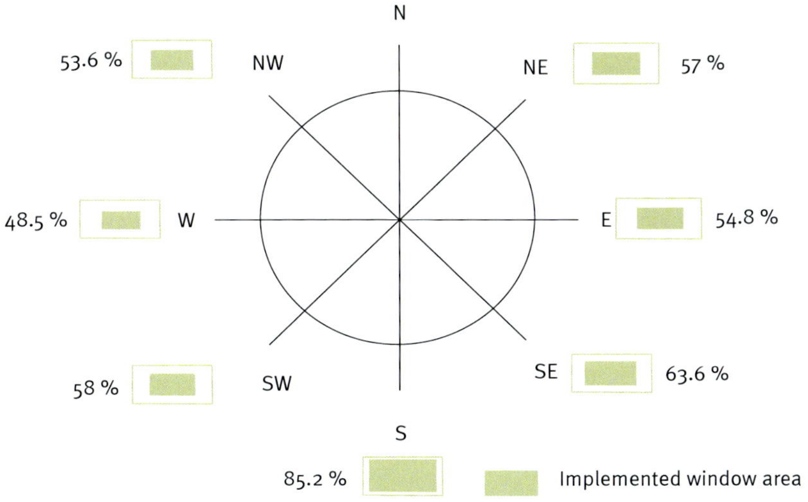

247

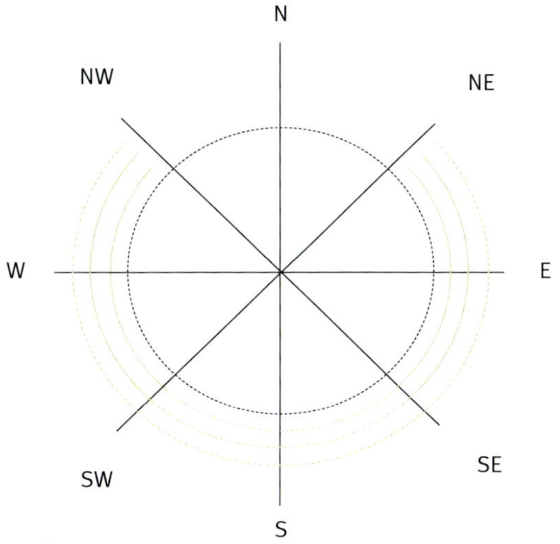

248

4.5 Respecting the function, user behavior

249

To develop an appropriate concept for the building, consideration of the building typology is important. Each building type has different optimization potentials.

The different building types should consider such factors:

- use
- operation time
- day/night operation times
- occupation density
- comfort requirements (air, light, temperature)
- building form
- design of facades
- internal organisation

An appropriate use and function for every building type can result in higher energy-savings. In regards to use and operation time, combining different functions in the same building can bring many advantages in terms of sustainability.

E.g., schools or universities which are used during the day can be combined with theatres or cinemas which are used in the night. In this way, only one building is appropriate for a range of functions and therefore resources and energy can be saved. More information in relation to this can be found in the space management section.

Lighting can become a big issue. Some functions such as schools or offices that function mainly during the day often require only natural daylighting.
If the building is designing well enough to receive daylight without overheating, it is capable of saving high levels of energy that would be otherwise required for artificial lighting.

The saving of artificial lighting energy should be used wherever possible for buildings that function at night, such as foyers, receptions, theatres and cinemas.

Different building types have varying comfort requirements, such as the comparison between office and residential buildings. Therefore, different concepts of optimization potentials must be found.

A big issue with office buildings is the summer cooling loads due to large glass facades that gain necessary natural sunlight. On the other hand, residential houses focus instead on heating energy and warm water generation.

User behaviour in different functions

While developing a concept, the user behaviour must be considered. In an ideal situation, the users should behave according to the building concept with appropriate conduct. The designer must be aware that the user is different according to the building type.

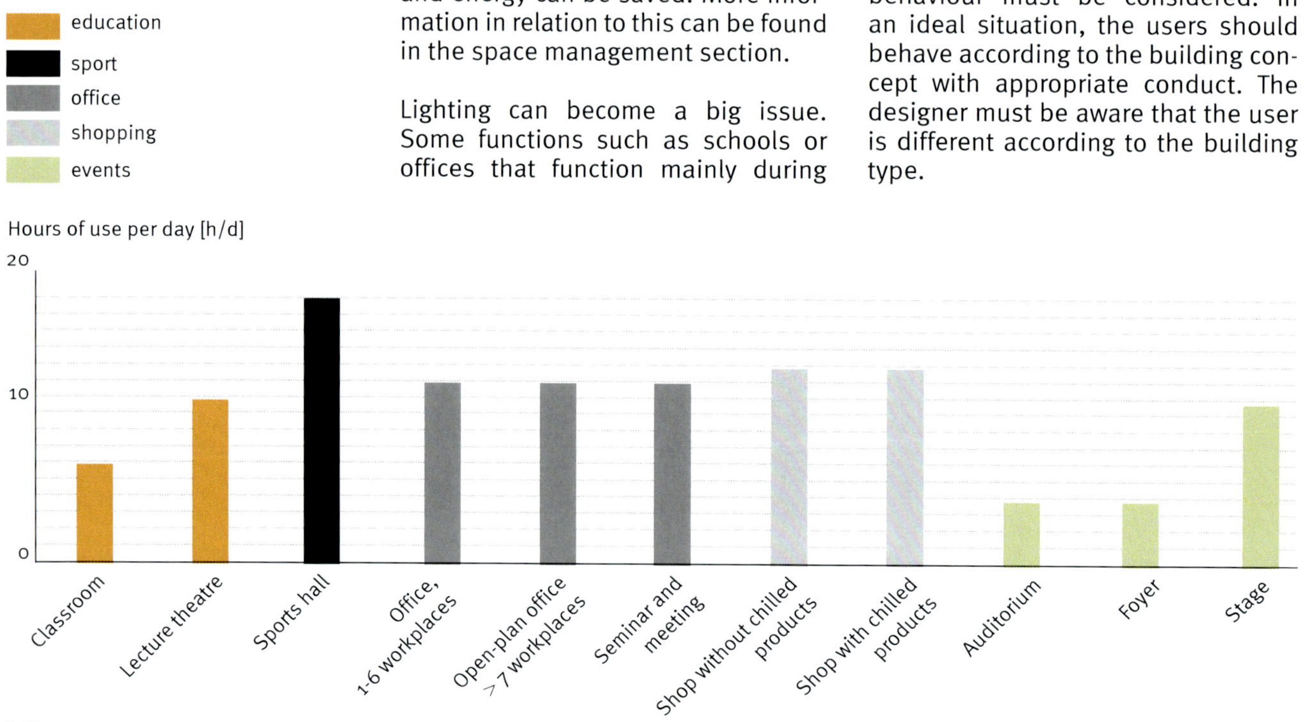

250

E.g., in a family house, the users care about costs and they will try to save energy.

However, in a hotel where people pay per night without being aware of their energy usage, users are more common to leave windows open when the heating is on. In this case, controlled ventilation would be a more effective concept.

While designing a concept, the education of the future users is very important. For this purpose, handbooks with the main energy and functional concept should be made as a manual for the users. This way the users can be informed on how to behave in the building in order to save operation energy.

249 A well thermally insulated hotel without controlled ventilation has higher energy losses than a bad insulated hotel with controlled ventilation, because of the users behaviour
250 Daily use hours for various building types
251 Internal heat loads from persons and equipment for various building types
252 Daily hours of use for various building types divided according to day and night

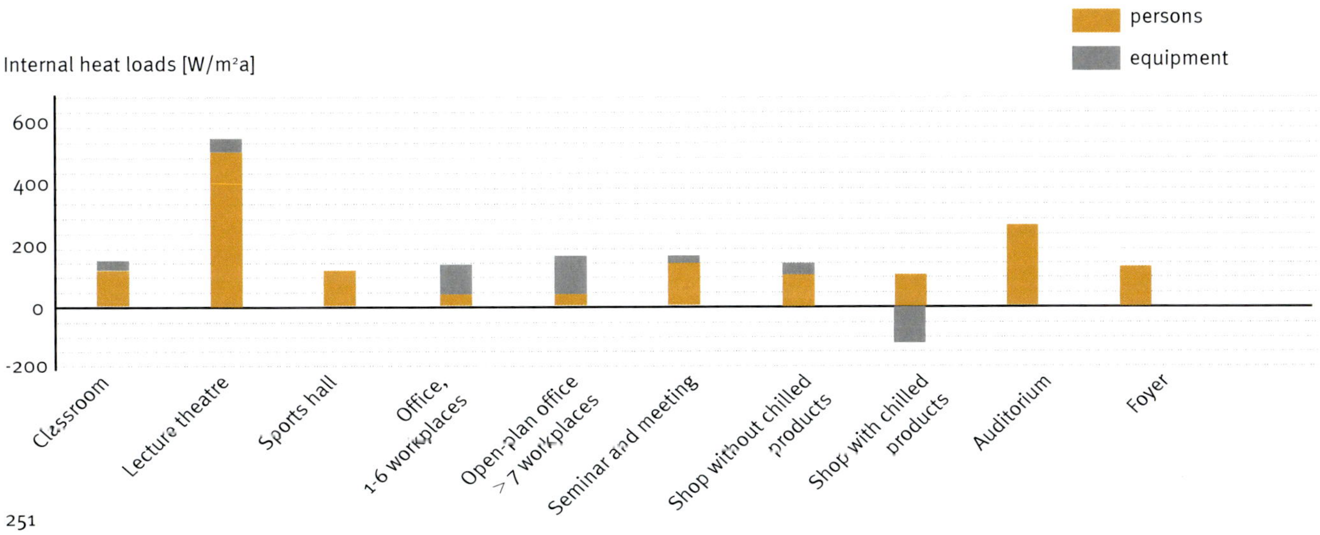

251

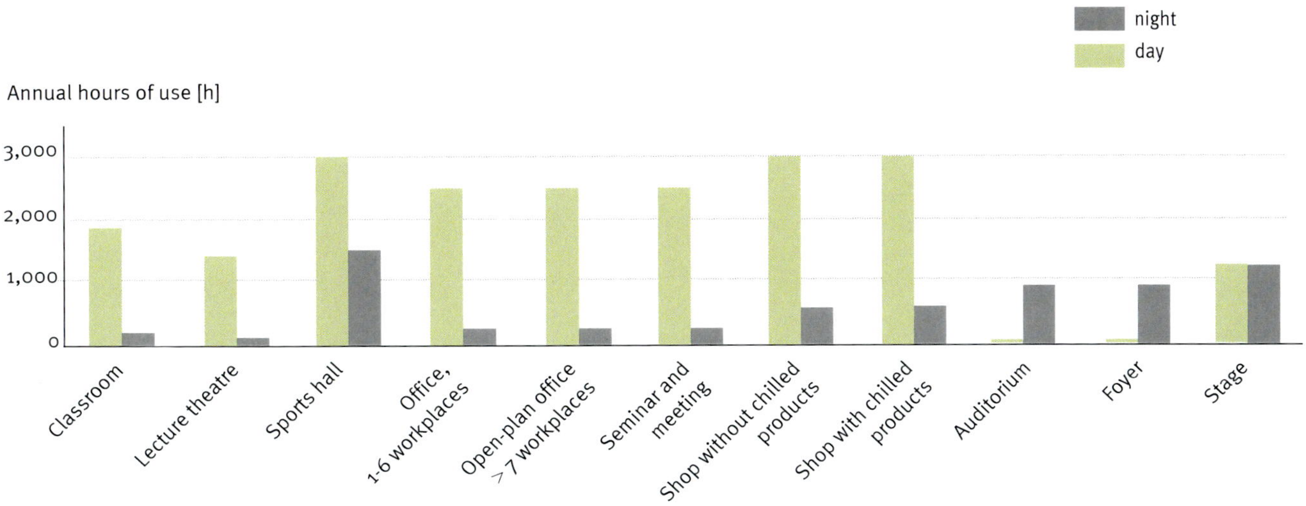

252

4.6 Heat transmission loss/gain prevention

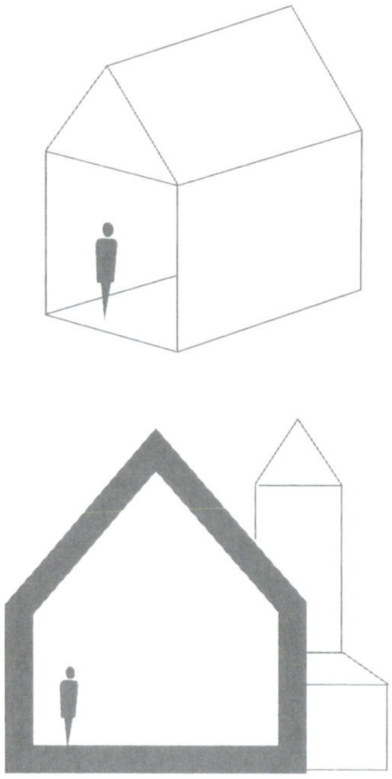

253

253 *The small glasshouse that has bad thermal insulation saves more energy and resources than the large palace that is highly insulated*

254 *Principles of thermal building zoning - concentric zoning - linear zoning - floor by floor zoning*

4.6.1 Surface optimization and geometry

By optimising the building envelope, heat loss/gains can be reduced. This concept not only considers the use of thermal insulation and the avoidance of thermal bridges, but also the compactness of the building through optimization of spatial programmes and zoning. The building dimensions are also important as smaller houses often save more energy than the bigger houses.

Compactness

A building form has a high effect on the energy requirements. The smaller the external surface area of the building, the lower the heat exchange between the interior and exterior spaces, resulting in lower heating and cooling energy requirements. Here, the A/V ratio is important to consider, as described on page 16.
Considering all geometry, the sphere is most ideal form. It has the smallest surface area in comparison to geometrical objects with the same volume.
For orthogonal forms, the cube has the best A/V ratio. Deviations of the optimal form create differences in building heat energy requirements.

In principle, compactness improves with an increasing building volume. For example, the larger volume of a multi-storey residential building has a lower heat loss transmission than a single family house with the same living area.

Plan zoning

During the planning stages of a building, functional zones can be created due to varying temperature requirements, daylight demand or the actual use time. From an energy point of view, thermal zoning is most effective where main functions are thermally protected via buffer zones or secondary usable rooms, which do not require high heat levels.
There are three principle zoning possibilities:

- concentric zoning

Enabling greater building depths and the integration of thermally stable functions which should be protected from the climate within the building core.

- linear zoning

Based on the orientation to the sun, the rooms with the highest light and heat demands are oriented to the south, east or west. The rooms which are not permanently heated or heated with a lower temperature are oriented towards the north. The South facade can be designed for example with a winter garden to receive solar gains.

- floor by floor zoning

The rooms with high temperature requirements are situated in the core of the storey stack.

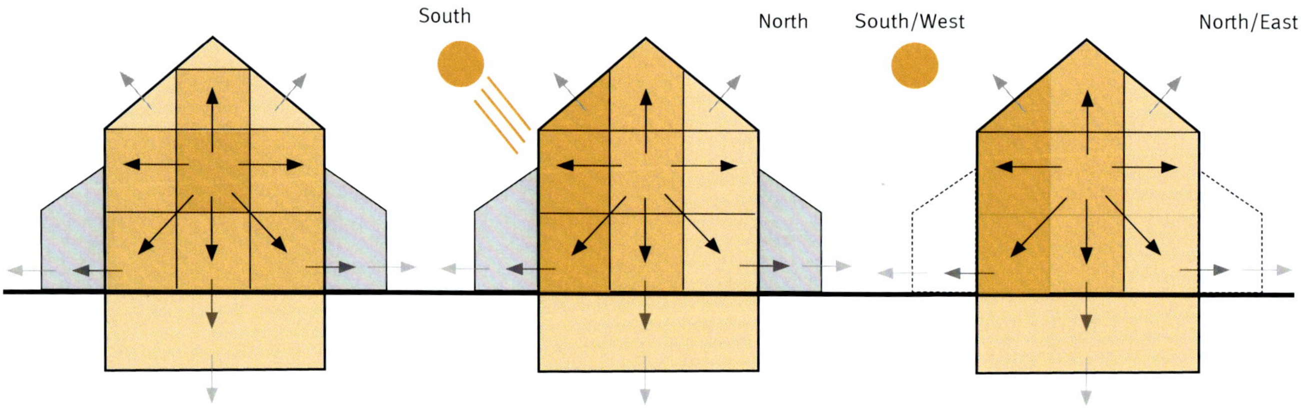

254

Buffer storage zones

Buffer storage zones are one of the most proven passive energy-saving concepts. It can have various forms depending on the building situation. E.g. a house concept within an extremely cold location is internally protected from the extreme weather conditions by the external shell creating an unheated buffer zone.

Similar effects are created like a winter garden or an unheated courtyard space, where the large air volume works as a buffer storage keeping the warm energy in winter and cool energy in summer.

Larger volumes generally need a greater time to change their climatic conditions due to their inertia and lower air change rate. The bigger the zone volume, the lower the thermal energy losses via thermal exchange to outside.

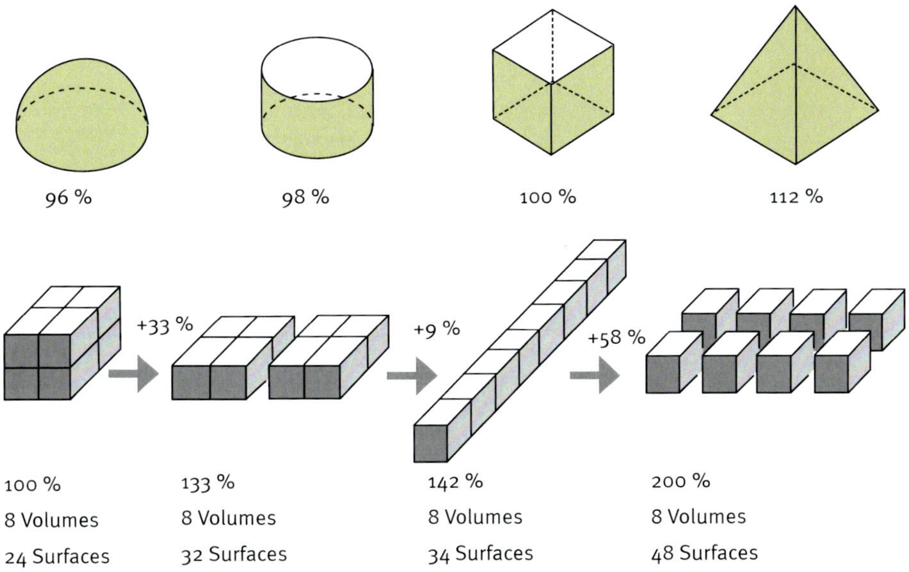

255

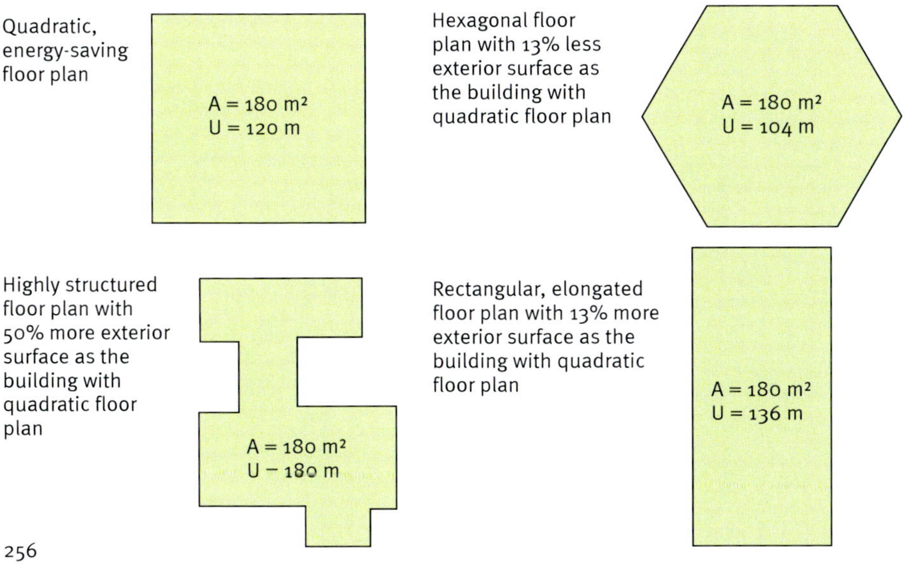

256

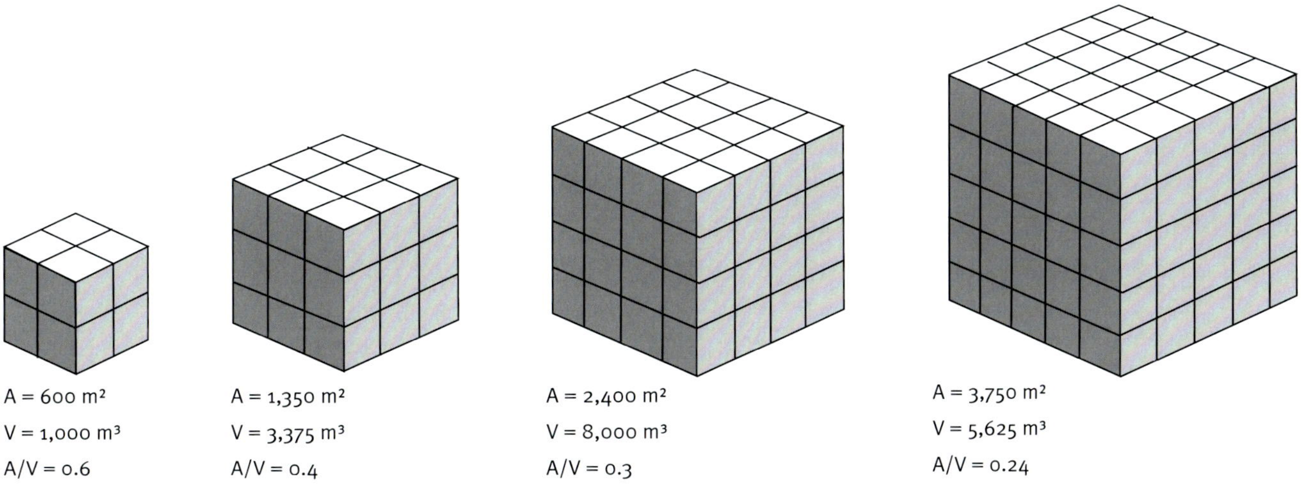

257

255 Transmission heat losses through different building forms with the same volume
256 The same floor area by different shapes – the more complicated the floorplan is, the more outside surfaces the building will have
257 Relationship between the surface and volume of the building – the bigger the building is, the better the A/V ratio will be

4.6 Heat transmission loss/gain prevention

258

4.6.2 Building envelope

The building envelope forms the separation between interior and exterior space. It functions as a form of protection, connection and communication. Its main function is to protect the building from wind, rainfall and solar radiation, however it also regulates the interior climate.
The building envelope should consist of different layers:

- base
- heat-insulation
- air and vapour barrier
- humidity buffer
- protective layer

The material choices should consider the energy inputs regarding the production of building elements as well as the expenses and operational energy used for cleaning or maintenance. Other aspects of sustainability should include noise and visual protection, material durability and the dismantling process.

A well-planned energy efficient building envelope will enable low energy inputs for the comfort of the interior climate during the whole year. An energy-optimised building envelope that reaches maximal passive efficiency creates a base for future energy concepts.

To improve the building envelope heat behaviour in the winter, the following elements are essential:

- surface optimization and geometry
- heat insulate opaque building elements
- heat insulate transparent building elements
- passive use of solar radiation
- minimize ventilation heat loss
- active solar thermal energy gain

Earth-sheltered architecture

Earth-sheltered architecture, mentioned in the previous chapter, uses the earth as a buffer zone protecting the building from external conditions.

The positioning of a building within the ground (or at least its north facade) will protect the building from high heat losses from the structure and will provide a stable and tempered environment. Therefore the building envelope is not exposed to the extreme temperature changes preventing high heat transmission losses in winter and overheating in summer.

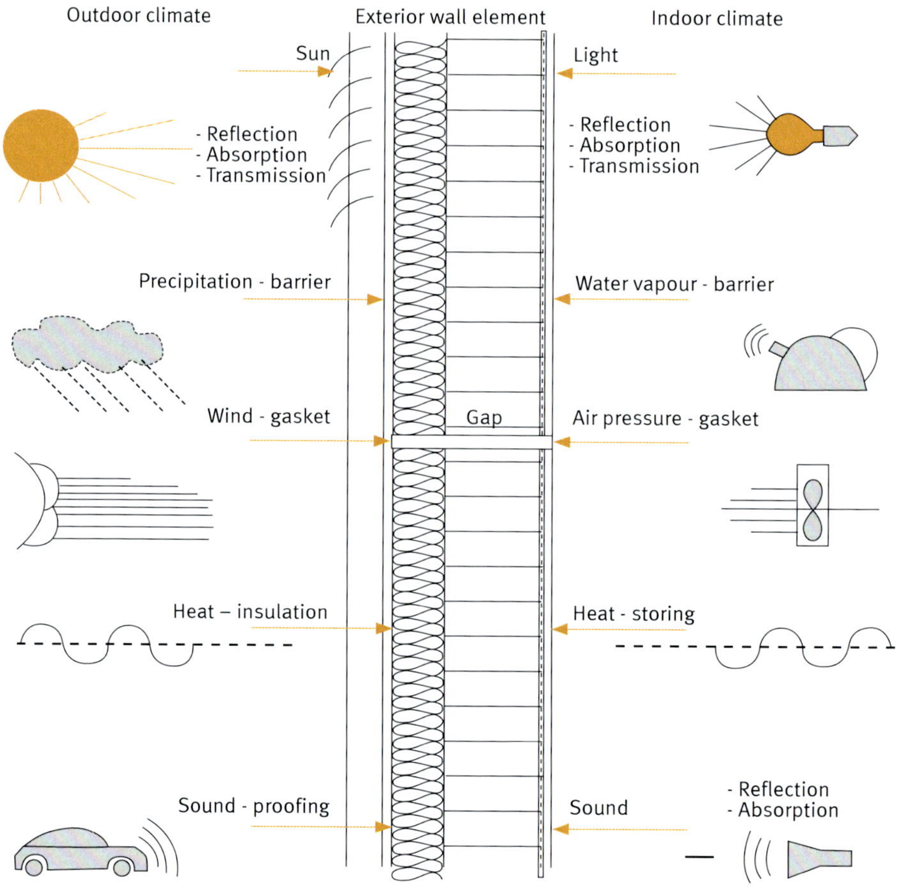

259

258 Placing of unheated zone out of the building envelope is also an effective heat transmission loss prevention
259 Influences on an external wall from the building design aspect
260 Goals, concepts and measures to energy optimization of the building envelope

Goal	Partial goal	Concept	Measures
Optimising the building envelope	Conservation and generation of warm energy	Surface optimization and geometry	Compactness, zoning, thermal envelope
		Heat insulate opaque elements	Material choice, heat insulation, thermal bridges
		Heat insulate transparent elements	Glazing percentage, glass quality
		Passive use of solar radiation	Buffer zone, transparent heat insulation, storage mass
		Minimize ventilation heat loss	Air exchange rate, heat recovery, air preheated, air tightness
		Active solar thermal energy generation	Roof collector, facade collector
	Overheating avoidance	Reduce heat transmission	Heat insulation, surface temperature, phase shifting
		Reduce solar radiation	Construction measures, special glazing, sun protection systems
		Storage mass and ventilation	Thermal storage, air preheating and precooling
	Decentral ventilation	Free ventilation	Window ventilation, wind usage, thermal rising
		Mechanical facade ventilation	Parapet elements, convectors, frame ventilation
	Use of daylighting	Geometry optimization	Building and space geometry, glazing share, glazing organisation
		Daylighting system	Transparency, translucency, reflection, deflection, light spreading, light transportation
	Power generation	Building envelope with photovoltaics	Photovoltaic facade, photovoltaic roof, solar sun protection
		Solar technology and building envelope	Integration, interconnection
		Solar technology and design concept	Addition, integration, adaptation

4.6 Heat transmission loss/gain prevention

Transparent building elements

While planning transparent building elements, different requirements regarding daylight use, clarity and anti-glare must be considered. The size and arrangement of glazing has a direct influence on the heat transmission losses/gains.

Thermal quality can vary, depending on the type of glazing, the climate zone, and the use. Systems available range from single glazing to high developed insulating glazing elements with different coatings and gasses.

Insulating windows, such as double or triple glazed windows and windows with movable insulation, protect the building from high heat losses/gains. Lighting should also be considered. The electrical energy required for lighting compared to using triple-glass windows could be more than the energy saved for heating. On the south side, when other shading is not possible, triple glazed windows can reduce the overheating while having enough daylighting.

In temperate climate zones, it is standard to use double heat protection glazing.

261 Typical thermal bridges and their factors used for EnEV calculation following the norm DIN 4150-6
262 Reference U-values for new residential construction due to the EnEV 2014, Appendix 1, Table 1

Thermal insulation

Thermal insulation reduces unwanted heat losses/gains. When the building is well insulated with reduced thermal bridges, heat losses/gains are reduced. High heat loss is also found through fireplaces chimneys therefore such constructions should be avoided.

Plants can also act as good additional thermal insulation. E.g. in cold areas, we can grow green plants in the north to prevent penetration of the winter wind.

Opaque building elements

The level of heat transmission loss for opaque building elements depends on the thermal conductivity (λ-value) (page 16) of the building element. This depends on the specific characteristics of the materials and on the construction of the building elements. The lower the thermal conductivity, the better the material insulates.

The heat transmission coefficient (U-value) (page 16) is the factor used to find the thermal quality of a building component.

Regarding heat insulation, the lower the U-value, the better the building element. High insulated buildings, for example the passive house, has opaque building elements with a U-value lower than 0.10-0.15 W/m²K.

Thermal bridges

Avoidance of thermal bridges is of extremely high importance. A thermal bridge is an interruption within the thermal envelope with a higher heat transfer into the environment, in comparison to other surfaces.
There are two main types of thermal bridges – **geometrical and structural**. Geometrical occur in places where the surface area ratio for the inner and outer surface of the structure is modified. A typical example is the corner of the building.

Structural thermal bridges occur primarily at the intersection of several materials with different coefficients of thermal conductivity to the external wall. A typical example is the combination of a skeletal system and reinforced concrete masonry infill.

In contrast to existing buildings, the planning of a new construction gives the opportunity to avoid thermal bridges. With existing buildings, thermal bridges must be evaluated and regarded as a heat loss source when calculating heat energy needs. A thermal weak point may be identified with thermographic recordings, which provide images that show information about surface temperatures. The data enables conclusions regarding heat conductivity within that zone.
The consideration of thermal bridges can be done through multiplying factors or through detailed calculation.

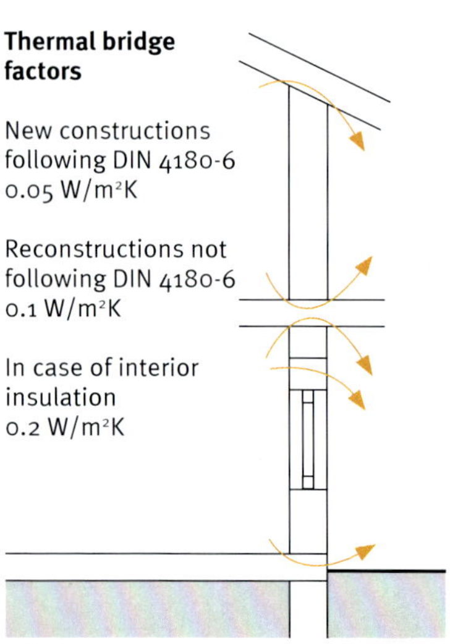

261

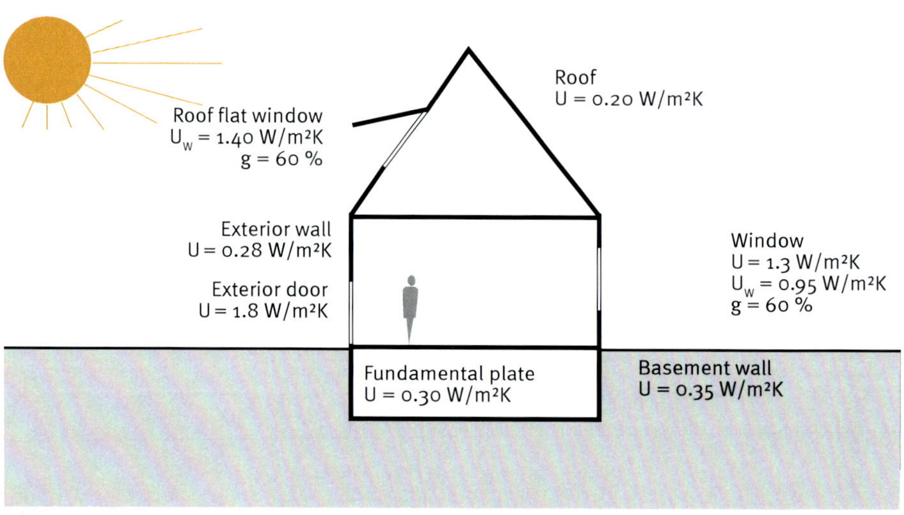

262

4.7 Heat ventilation loss/gain prevention

A simple method to prevent the building from undesirable ventilation losses/gains is to control the airtightness of the building, to avoid the airflow through the envelope.

The decisive factor for ventilation is the air exchange rate (h^{-1}). It shows how much time per hour the air within a room must be changed. There are regulated values of air change rates in order to provide a healthier internal environment.

When trying to reduce heat ventilation losses/gains, a low air exchange rate is most effective. There are possibilities to reduce the air changing for a room while maintaining a healthy environment.

One option is to have rooms with larger volumes. A room with larger air volume takes longer to pollute and therefore requires a lower air exchange rate. It also uses the buffer zone effect – storing the energy that takes longer to be changed.
Another solution is ventilation through other means such as buffer zones with more stable air conditions compared to external air. The zone can be e.g. a double facade, winter garden, ground air exchanger, etc. In this case, the incoming air is passively preheated/precooled by the buffer zone.

Another solution is to ventilate the room according to the CO_2-value. The amount of CO_2 indicates the quality of the interior air environment. It can be measured, for example by a CO_2 hanging lamp, which shows if the air is still healthy. If the CO_2 level is high, the room must be ventilated. Shock ventilation is also good method to reduce the ventilation losses for the winter. When the air within the room should be changed, the heating is quickly turned off and all openings are opened to exchange the air.

In summer, ventilation at night is beneficial. Windows opened during the night help to change and cool the air within the building.

Well positioned openings can support air change and shorten the time to ventilate by creating air flow, e.g. cross ventilation.

There are many other types of ventilation systems, which can be designed for individual situations. One example is hybrid ventilation, a combination of natural and mechanical ventilation. It takes advantage of both natural and mechanical ventilation to reduce the overall energy consumption.

A few ventilation systems mentioned in '4.8.1 Passive ventilation' can also be used to reduce heat energy needs. E.g., supply air can be preheated via air-ground heat exchangers. Ventilation via the trombe wall of a double-skin facade can also reduce heat losses.

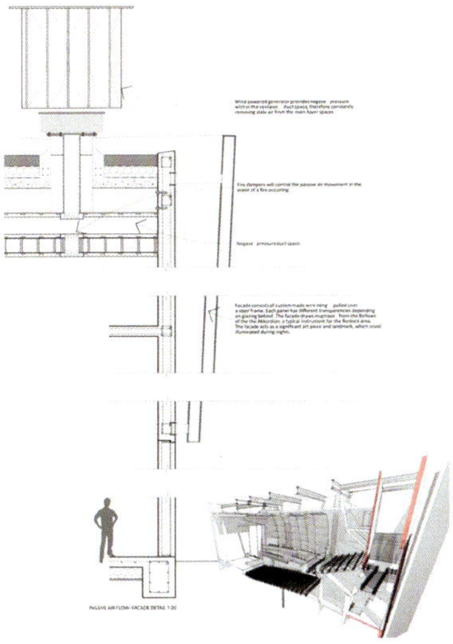

263

263 An example of a combination of different ventilation systems in the student project inspired by Council House 2 (CH2), Melbourne
264 Headquarters of the Northern German pension insurance – the cooling in summer is provided through buffer zone of an entrance atrium and solar chimney, architect Behnisch & Partner
265 The summer cooling by the help of ventilators in city Yazd, Iran

264

265

4.8 Passive building concepts

4.8.1 Passive ventilation

The interior concentration of the three most common air pollutants (i.e particle allergens, chemical pollutions and humidity) is much higher than the outdoors. Therefore, a building must have a ventilation system that takes away the internal air pollution and introduces fresh air to improve the air quality. The best and simplest way to passively ventilate a building is simply by natural ventilation. Many systems that are used for passive ventilation can also be used for passive cooling.

Advantages of passive ventilation systems:

- energy-saving

The clearest advantage is the reduction of energy consumption. With passive systems, the initial investment and operating costs are much lower than mechanical ventilation.
With a high quality passive ventilation system, the fresh air entering the rooms can be preheated in winter or precooled in summer to achieve lower needs for active heating and cooling of the building.

- improved space utilisation

As passive systems do not require large equipment or pipes, wall space is saved and internal spaces can be larger.

- comfort

With natural air circulation the internal conditions are more comfortable.

Disadvantages of passive ventilation systems

- they depend on nature
- they are independent from human control
- they are constrained by outdoor air quality

The seven types of passive ventilation concepts:

- wind driven ventilation
- stack effect ventilation
- evaporative cooling tower
- solar chimney
- trombe wall
- double-skin facade
- air-ground heat exchanger

Wind driven ventilation

This is the most simple ventilation type with high efficiency, based on the Bernoulli principle, which uses wind speed differences to move air.
"Wind causes a positive pressure on the windward side and a negative pressure on the leeward side of buildings. To equalise this pressure, outside air will enter any windward openings and be drawn out of leeward openings." [52] This ventilation depends on wind behaviour, the building envelope interaction and openings.

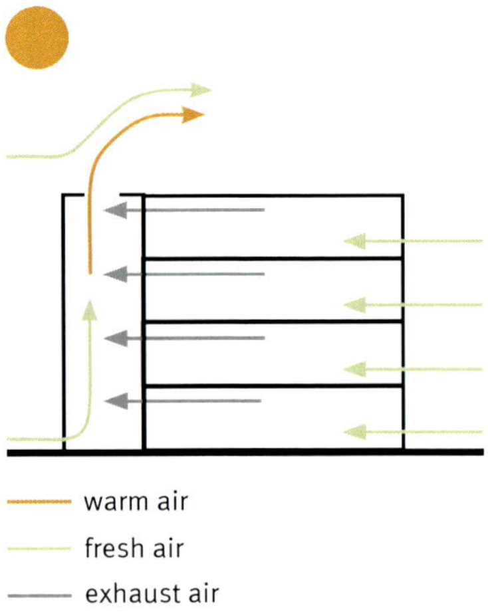

266

[52] *Autodesk®, Inc.;* Autodesk Sustainability Workshop: Concepts and tools for sustainable design [http://sustainabilityworkshop.autodesk.com/resource/passive-ventilation-strategies] (08.11.2012)

[53] *Autodesk®, Inc.;* Autodesk Sustainability Workshop: Concepts and tools for sustainable design [http://sustainabilityworkshop.autodesk.com/] (08.11.2012)

[54] *Greenplanet–solarenergy;* Solartower [http://www.green-planet-solar-energy.com/solar-tower.html] (08.11.2012)

266 Schematic section of a stack effect ventilation
267 Cross wind driven ventilation depending on the surrounded trees and placement and size of the openings

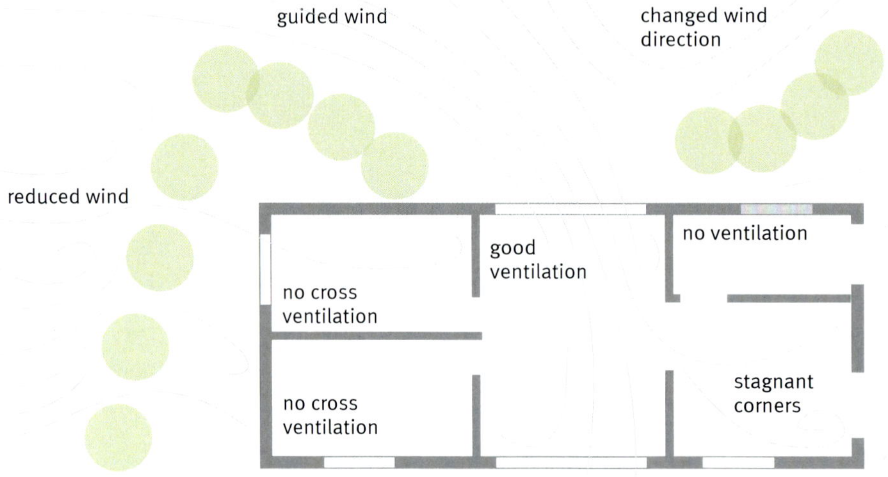

267

However, this type has some disadvantages including uncertainty of wind direction and strength. Zero wind and extreme winds can cause problems and limit ventilation.
It is possible to design an increase of wind speed throughout the building to form a negative pressure zone. The negative pressure sucks air into the internal spaces bringing fresh air through the openings. This system can also be used for passive cooling.

Stack effect ventilation

Due to air density differences, hot air rises because of its lower pressure, and cold is pushed down to the floor. Hot air gathers in the ceiling spaces before pushing out into the atmosphere. This is also called buoyancy ventilation.
Stack effect depends on the temperature difference and not on natural wind pressures. This ventilation method is therefore more suitable for hot climates where there is little wind. This system can also be used for passive cooling.

Evaporative cooling tower

In hot and dry areas an evaporative tower can be used. The tower has a water tank inside the top of the tower which in reaction with the hot outside air, water starts to evaporate. After the water evaporates, the heat of the air is absorbed creating cool air which sinks down into the building achieving the effect of both cooling and ventilation.

Solar chimneys

"A solar chimney uses the sun's heat to provide cooling, using the stack effect. Solar heat gain warms a column of air, which then rises, pulling new outside air through the building. They are also called thermal chimneys, thermosiphons, or thermosyphons. (...) Solar chimneys need their exhaust higher than roof level, and need generous sun exposure. They are generally most effective for climates with a lot of sun and little wind; climates with more wind on hot days can usually get more ventilation using the wind itself." [53]

The solar tower is a type of solar chimney to produce power which combines the passive and active energy system. "Sunlight falls on the glass cover surrounding the solar tower itself. The sunlight becomes heat and the air gets hotter. As we know, hot air rises and so the air is forced towards the centre of the structure. By the time the heated air gets to the turbines, its temperature has increased by 50 °C and the estimated speed at the turbine is 15 metres per second. The spinning of the turbines generates electricity." [54]

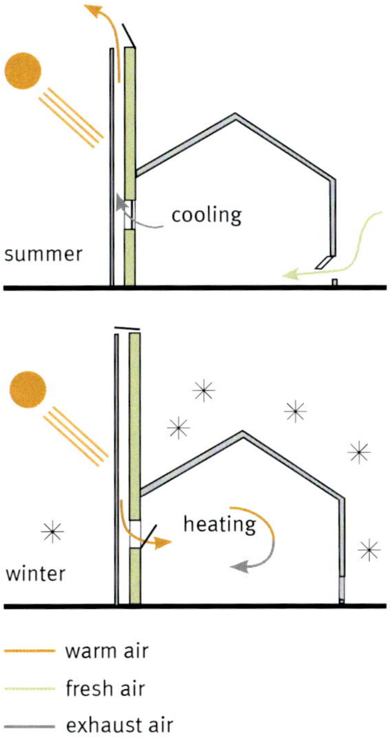

268

268 Solar chimney can either heat a space in winter or cool it in summer
269 Schematic of evaporative cooling tower
270 Solar tower used for power generation combining the passive ventilation with active energy production

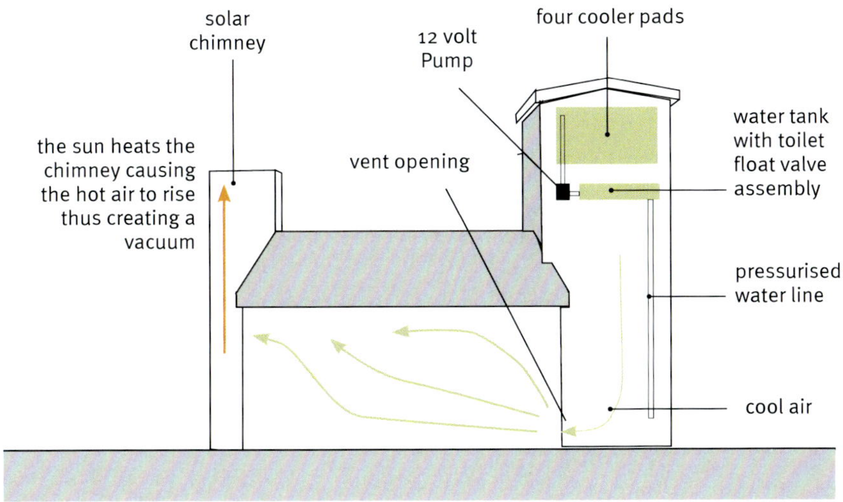

269

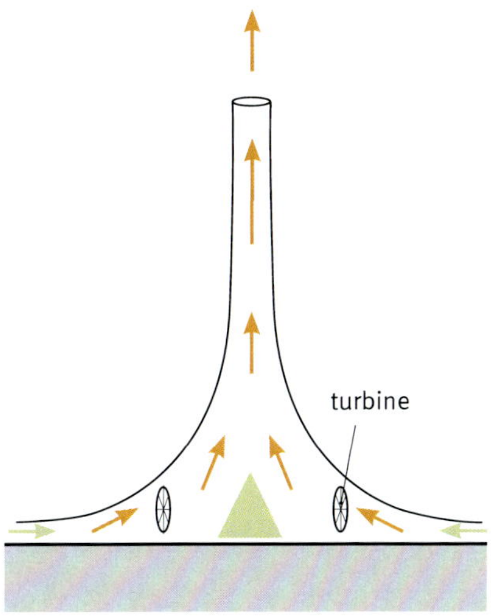

270

4.8 Passive building concepts

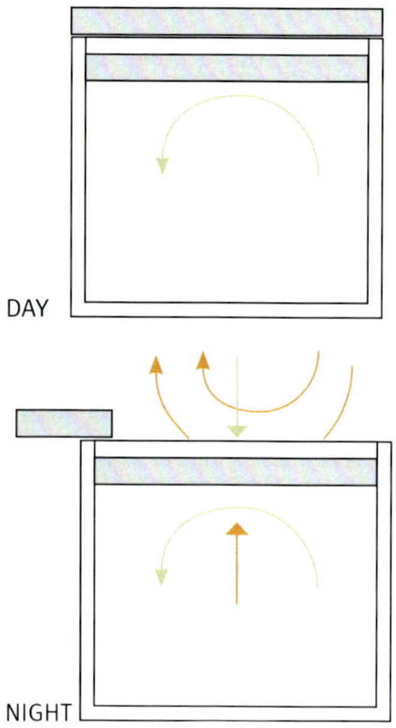

271

Trombe wall

A trombe wall is another ventilation system that can be used for summer cooling as well as winter heating. A trombe wall is fronted with glazing and consists of a storage wall with two openings; one in the bottom and one in the top.

In the winter, the outside cold air flows inside and beside the floor space. The cool air flows into the air space in between the trombe wall where it is heated by the thermal storage wall. Simultaneously, the air mixes with the internal exhaust air. The now warmed air rises and enters into the room from the top.

For summer cooling, the inside air flows through the trombe wall and out of the building. In this case, the trombe wall uses the solar chimney effect to cool the interior.

Double-skin facade

Today in ecological buildings, it is extremely common to use a double-skin facade. This is typical of high rise office buildings or in areas with high noise emissions or pollution. The double-skin facade system uses a double-layer for a variety of functions. The system allows ease of maintenance of the structure, it ensures noise and emission protection, provides natural ventilation and reduces energy consumption.

The double skin together with appropriate shading systems help to keep the interior of the building cool during the summer. Using the chimney effect, the air between the facades moves up and takes away heat. It can reduce the temperature of the surface and save energy.

In winter, the double facade works as a winter garden collecting passive solar gains, which heats up the interior spaces. It acts as a buffer layer between the interior and the cold outside air. The preheated air then enters the interior space, which helps to reduce the heat energy demand.

Ground source heat exchanger

The stable temperature of soil can be used to ventilate air via an air-ground heat exchanger. The air is brought into the building through a few pipes that are laid in the ground. In summer, the underground soil temperature is lower than the air temperature and the supply air is precooled by the soil.

This reduces the cooling needs of the active cooling systems. In winter, the soil temperature is higher than the air temperature and the supply air is preheated by the earth.

At this point, the incoming air is at a higher temperature than the outside air and the energy needs for heating are much lower.

271 Roof pond used to cool the building in summer – it is closed during the day protecting it from the sun's heat – during the night, it is opened and cooled from the outside air
272 Concept of a ground source heat exchanger
273 Key elements of passive cooling in summer

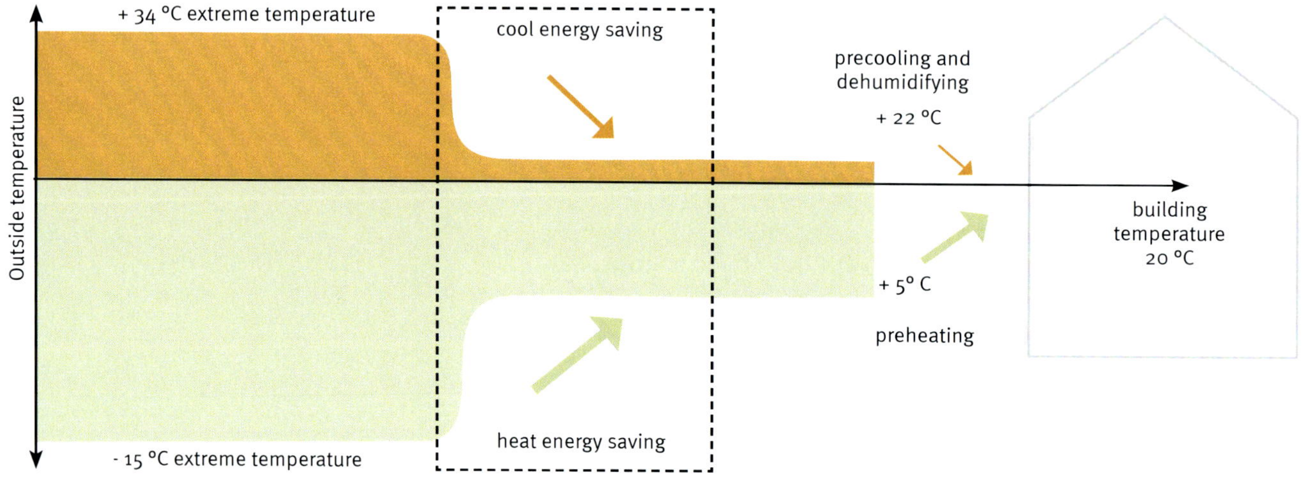

272

4.8.2 Passive cooling

Passive cooling is a method for cooling internal building environments with the use of design features or technologies that require no power consumption or mechanical devices.
The method of passive cooling uses the natural climatic conditions to its advantage and maximises the efficiency of the building envelope. Cooling a building passively will provide excellent thermal comfort and indoor air quality, while keeping a very low energy consumption.

Passive cooling uses basic concepts:

- heat prevention
- heat dissipation

Heat prevention – possible solutions:

- summer shading

To keep a home cool during the summer, windows exposed to the sun should be covered during the day. To restrict the sun from shining through the windows and heating indoor surfaces, we can use shutters, curtains and louvres. Plants and trees are also a very effective natural shading system.

- overhanging roofs

In summer, the sun angle is higher than in winter. Overhanging roofs can reduce direct summer sunlight while allowing the winter sun into the building.

- green roof and facade

In summer, plants on a roof or facade can absorb heat and keep the surrounding spaces cool. A green roof also acts as a good insulator, reducing heat energy gains.

- thermal insulation

A good thermal insulation keeps the building not only warm in winter but also cool in summer.

Heat dissipation – possible solutions

- thermal mass and night cooling

This is used for a climate that is cool at night and too warm in the day. Thermal mass can be strategically placed and insulated to slow the heating of the building when the sun is hot.

The windows are closed during the day and opened in the night. In the night, natural ventilation cools the thermal mass and stores cool energy, giving it back to the rooms during the day.

- water cooling

This involves evaporative cooling by using water. If a pool is positioned appropriately outside a building, hot summer wind can flow over the pool, be cooled by the evaporation effect of the cool water, and continue into the house.
Roof ponds are also a type of water cooling system. (see page 155 for the use of roof pond as passive heating)

- ground cooling

Ground cooling uses the stable temperature of the ground for cooling. (see also chapter '3.9 Earthsheltered architecture' page 126)

Several methods described in '4.8.1 Passive ventilation' can also be used for passive cooling.

Passive cooling in urban environments

Modern society is becoming increasingly more urbanized and as a result, the air temperature within the urban areas is rising dramatically.

This phenomenon is known as the 'Heat Island Effect' and occurs in developed areas due to greater heat gains from high amounts of stored radiation, cars, and the reduction of wind speeds.

The Heat Island effect has a great impact on the energy consumption of buildings for cooling. As well designing buildings that create their own microclimate, it is also very important to consider improvements to the overall urban development to fight against the effects of the heat island and temperature increases.

This may involve the use of more appropriate materials, increased use of green areas, use of cool sinks for heat dissipation, appropriate layouts of urban canopies, etc.

The idea of cooling the urban environment can be taken further by utilizing centralized or semi-centralized cooling ponds or distribution networks based on renewable energies and by harnessing the unwanted heat.

A successful example of this is the cooling pond within central Berlin. Its purpose is to not only to create a new ecosystem but to help fight against the rise in the districts overall urban heat.

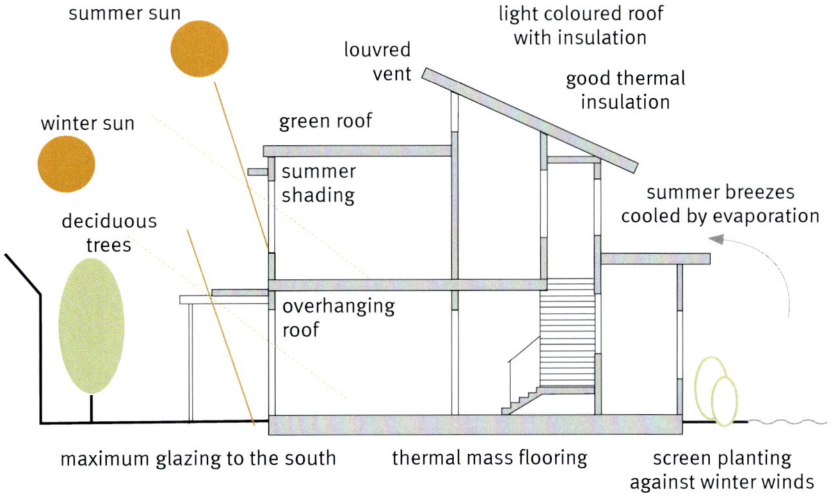

4.8 Passive building concepts

[55] *Arizona Solar Centre, Inc.;* Passive Solar Heating & Cooling Manual [http://www.azsolarcentre.org/tech-science/solar-architecture/passive-solar-design-manual/passive-solar-design-manual-heating.html] (08.11.2012)

274 Direct gain interior – a direct gain design with an interior water wall for heat storage, heat stored in the water wall is radiated into the living space at winter night

275 Indirect gain – Trombe wall stores heat during the day, excess heat is vented to the interior space – at night, Trombe wall vents are closed and the storage wall radiates heat into the interior space

276 Trombe wall in summer used for space cooling

277 A combination of methods to avoid heat losses in the winter is to plan zones and use buffer zones with direct solar gains to provide passive heating

278 Attached greenhouse with vented storage wall (masonry or water wall) – heat is stored in the wall during the day, excess heat is vented to the interior space, at winter night, the wall vents are closed and stored heat is radiated to both the greenhouse and the interior space

279 Heating cycle – roof ponds collect and store heat during the day, at night, roof ponds are covered and stored heat is radiated into the spaces below

- exhaust air
- cold air
- warm air

4.8.3 Passive heating

Passive solar design refers to the use of the sun's energy for heating living spaces. With this approach, the building itself or some elements of it, take advantage of the energy characteristics found within the material. Passive heating concepts are simple, requiring minimal maintenance and no mechanical assistance.

Section '4.4 Respecting the Sun' describes different methods on how to design according to a buildings orientation, sun angle, etc. Building elements, including windows, walls and floors are designed to collect, store and distribute heat energy from the sun in the winter and to protect the interior from heat gains in the summer. It is called passive design because it does not use mechanical or electrical systems. It works with the use of active solar heating elements.

The prevention of heat loss is critical for good passive heating – it is described in section '4.6 Heat transmissions loss/gain prevention' and '4.7 Heat ventilation loss/gain prevention'. Several methods described in '4.8.1 Passive ventilation', can also be applied for passive heating.

Passive solar heating design can use:

- direct radiation
- direct gain – e.g. interior heat mass storage
- indirect gain – Trombe wall
- attached greenhouse
- roof pond

Direct radiation

The simplest type of passive solar heating used in winter is allowing sunlight to penetrate into a room through window glazing. The interior air is heated and the temperature is increased. In the summer it is important to have appropriate shading mechanisms to avoid overheating.

Direct gain – e.g. interior heat mass storage

Heat energy from the sun enters the building and is stored via thermal mass, namely a water tank, floor or wall. Heat energy is released in the night, maintaining the temperature of the room. With this approach, the thermal mass heat storage performance must be high, in combination with high window insulation.

Indirect gain – Trombe wall

Fresh air is preheated from sun radiation within the trombe wall prior to flowing into the interior spaces. The Trombe wall concept is described in 'passive ventilation' (page 152).

Attached Greenhouse

"The attachment of a greenhouse to the south side of a building ena-

Water wall – winter

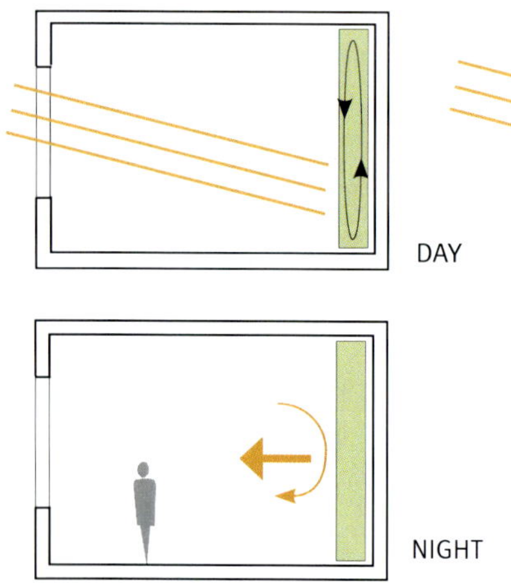

274

Trombe wall – winter

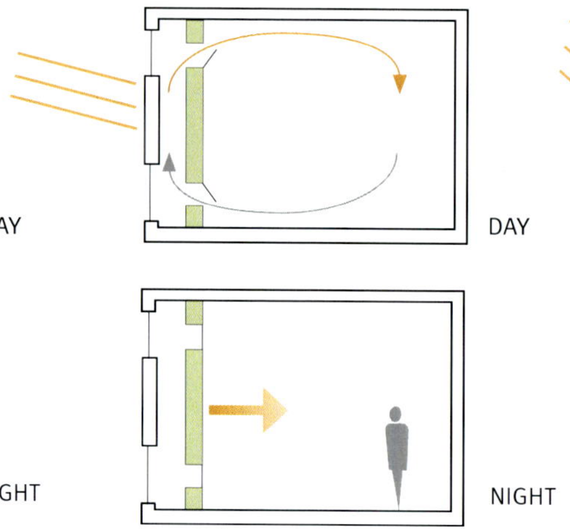

275

Trombe wall – summer

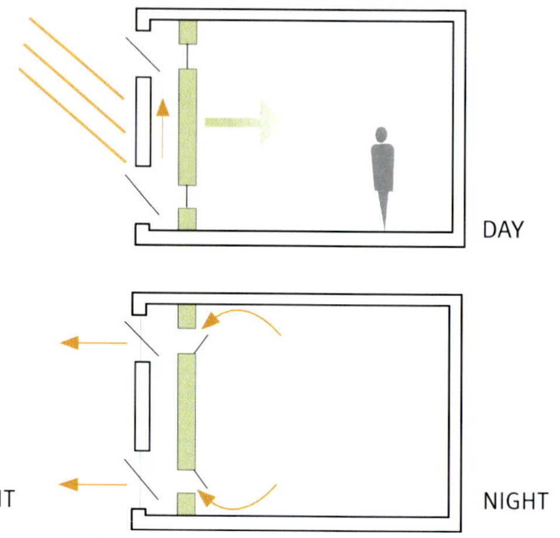

276

bles the structure to benefit from the normal heat collecting greenhouse operation. The greenhouse collects heat due to its solar exposure. This heat can be conducted through a thermal storage wall separating house and greenhouse, or can be convected to the interior space of the building. In this way the greenhouse serves both as a heat collector, and a solarium for people and plants. (...)

The common wall between the greenhouse and the building interior can be constructed of thermal mass materials (masonry, water, etc.). The greenhouse side of common walls should be dark in colour (better absorber) and should receive maximum sunlight throughout the day. Wall vents and/or operable windows can be used to allow heated air directly into the interior space during the daytime." [55]

Roof pond

Roof ponds can be used for heating in winter and cooling in summer. They consist of a waterproofed roof structure filled with water. There is a movable insulation layer above, which protects the pond from the weather and regulates the heating or cooling. In the wintertime, insulation is opened and solar radiation heats the water. The water heats the roof structure and it radiates the heat into the spaces below. At night, the insulation is closed, storing the heat gathered by the ponds.

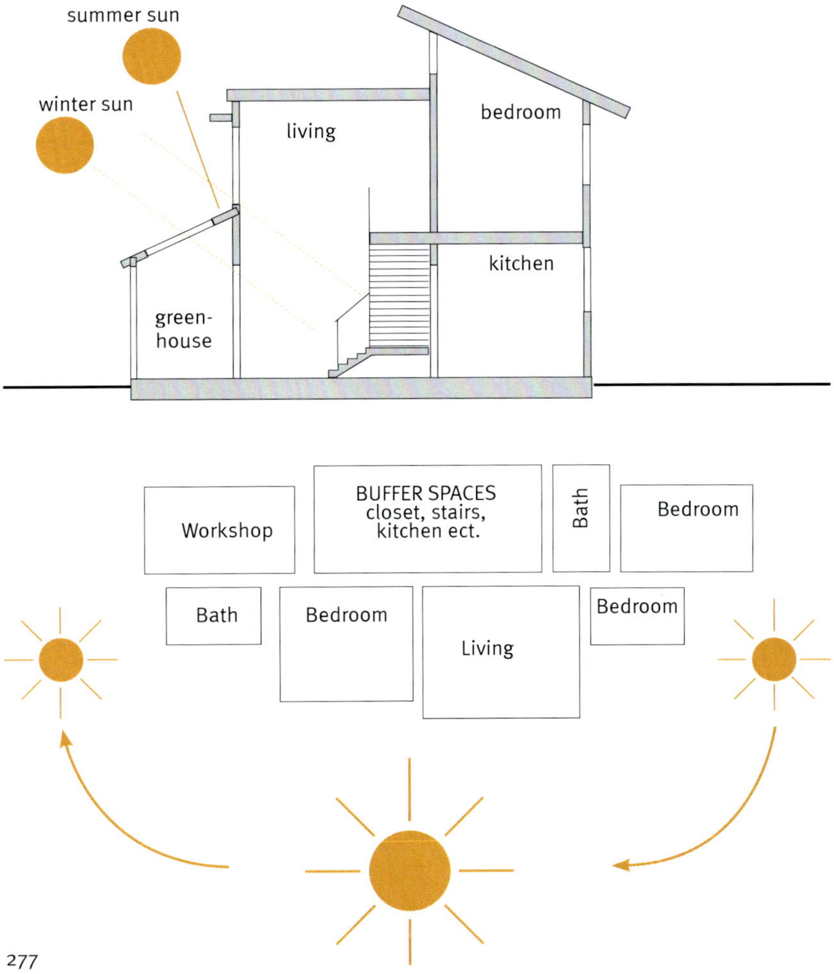

277

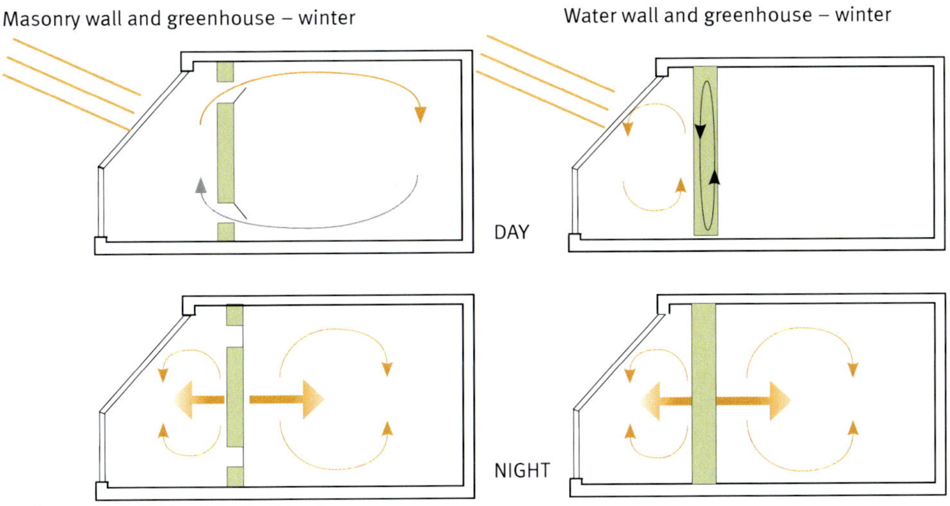

278

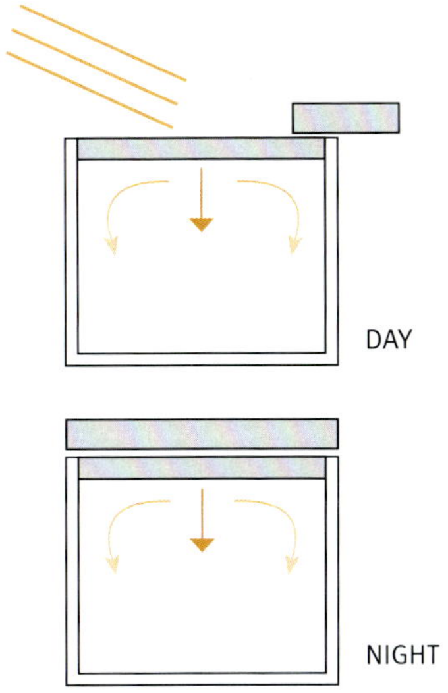

279

4.8 Passive building systems

280

[56] *Passive Lighting;* Why choose LED lighting? [http://www.passivelighting.com.au/] (08.11.2012)

280 *Skylight to provide natural light in the wide-span sporting hall, Germany*
281 *Artificial lighting wall inside the building in New York, USA*
282 *Atrium of the Jin Mao building, student excursion in Shanghai city, China*
283 *Light shelves – devices and forms – distribute light evenly inside a room*
284 *The placement and dimension of openings has big influence on the entering of daylight into the room*
285 *Smart design of the north-orientated classrooms and school corridor in Plus Energy School Rostock allows daylight enter the building*

4.8.4 Passive lighting

Energy used for electricity is a vital energy source, which needs to be saved. Most of the electricity sourced from the public grid uses fossil energy sources and a high primary energy. The best solution is to light the interior spaces with natural daylighting. This is not only environmentally friendly but also energy and material cost savings because of the unnecessary need to buy and maintain equipment. For this reason, a number of concepts to bring daylight into the interior spaces have been developed.

Passive solar lighting

Passive solar lighting design uses natural illumination (direct, diffused or reflected sunlight) to illuminate the building interior. The goal is to use as much daylight as possible and to reduce the artificial lighting demand.

By designing with daylight, the appropriate orientation, placement and size of windows must be considered. The larger the horizontal openings, the more daylight will enter the building.

Another way is by using different surface materials, which reflect the daylight inside. For reflecting elements, different light shelves, lightly coloured walls and floors, mirrored wall sections, interior walls with upper glass panels, clear or translucent doors or even snow in winter can be used.

Light redirected to interior spaces without natural daylight possibilities

In dark interior spaces where it is not possible to create a window opening (e.g. in earth-sheltered architecture or deep rooms), the daylight can be brought inside through skylights, atriums, light pipes, light tubes or light channels. These are placed in the roof and bring daylight into the interior.

Heliostat mirrors can be used to reflect the daylight into the interior. They move automatically to reflect sunlight as the sun moves across the sky. These mirrors can be placed on the roof, beside the building, as well as in the interior, for example as a mirror curtain along the staircase bringing the light deep to the building.

Smart glass

Smart glass can change appearance from transparent, opaque, translucent, reflective or retro- reflective. The light shaft elements, e.g. the windows or skylights can be made of smart glass and can be used to control suitable indoor lighting quality.

Optical fibre

Optical fibre cables act as light pipes which transmit light between the two ends of the fibre. The fibres are placed within solid walls and daylight can pass directly through from outside to the interior.

281

282

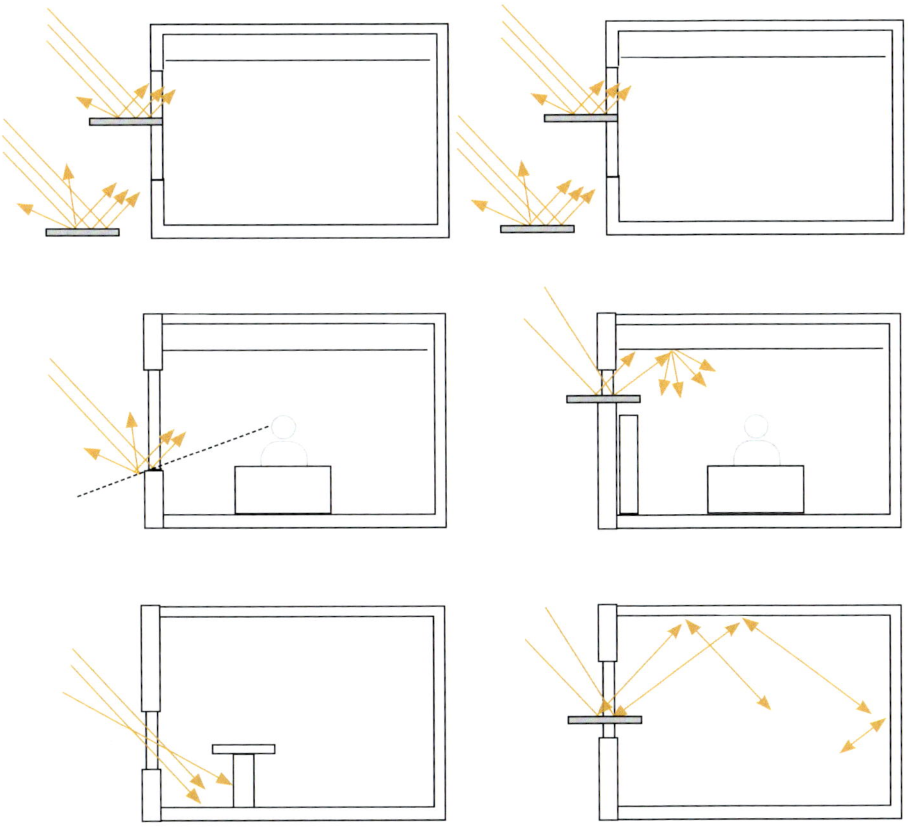

283

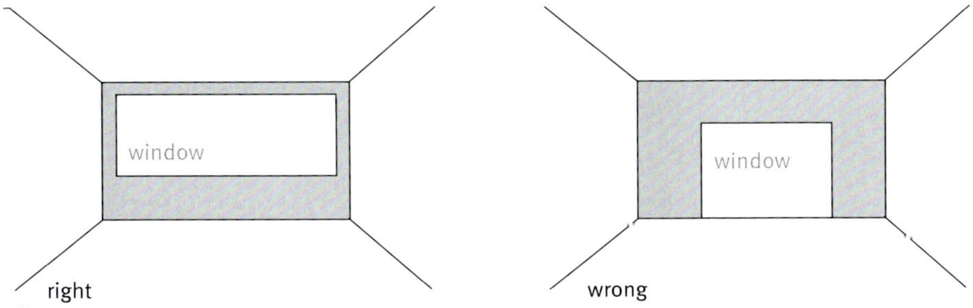

284

285

LED lighting

In the case that artificial lighting is needed, high energy saving systems should be used, such as LED lighting.

"An LED or Light-Emitting Diode is a semiconductor-based electronic light source which transforms power into light with over 90 % efficiency. A typical LED lamp consists of a semiconductor chip mounted in a reflecting cavity on metal leads, then encapsulated in clear epoxy.

LEDs are available in many different colours, and the luminaires have many distinct advantages over conventional lighting.

- They generally use around 75 % less power than most conventional lighting.
- They do not emit high levels of heat or carbon dioxide. In the luminaires there are very efficient and highly effective heat sinks which ensure long life.
- They last ten to twenty times longer and require less maintenance than most other types of lighting.
- They are not so much affected by vibration and are more tolerant to lower and some higher temperatures, making them ideal for use in a wide range of applications including mining, industrial and other situations too numerous to mention." [56]

4.9 Summary

As mentioned previously, passive energy-saving concepts are the simplest, cheapest and most effective method to save energy in order to achieve a comfortable healthy indoor environment. The appropriate combination with active components or systems can increase their efficiency.
There are many possibilities of such combinations. An example is aquaponics.

Aquaponics is a polyculture of fish farming and cultivation of useful plants that is integrated with the water cycle. The name comes from aquaculture (fish farming) and Hydroponic (plant production in water, without soil).

There are several types of systems, most of which use floating planters for the production of leafy vegetables such as salads, spinach, tomatoes and for short-lived plant species. The fish farmed are typically tilapia, carp, catfish and others.

The primary goal is to recycle the nutrients contained in the fish water. This is achieved by beginning with a fish tank and a container of plants. The water in the fish tank contains ammonia extracted from the fish feces. The content of ammonia that is found here can be dangerous for fish, however it is an important nutrient for plant growth therefore the water is transferred to the plant container.
Here, the plants extract the ammonia that is needed for growth, leaving clean water, which is returned via pipes to the fish container, completing the cycle.

Aquaponics does not require large areas and is therefore very suitable for urban areas with limited land. It is a very simple system and does not require a long time to harvest.

Example: Student Project in Hamburg, Germany – Aquaponics in Architecture

The aim of the project was to create awareness for alternative, sustainable architecture for the future. The concept was adapted to a set of existing tower blocks on the outer boundary of Hamburg's old city.
The concept was based on the principals of reuse and recycling to create a building that was self-sustaining. The aquaponic system was integrated within the existing form of the building, providing the primary source of food production while creating a passive cooling and heating system for the occupied spaces.

In addition, the proposition focused on three other key elements - building continuity, public accessibility and the retaining of commercial space.
The design also focused on creating a stronger relationship between the surrounding urban spaces and the function of the building to allow a greater interaction with the public.

286 Interior perspectives of aquatank and vegetable growing pods
287 Flow chart of general system components arrangement

286

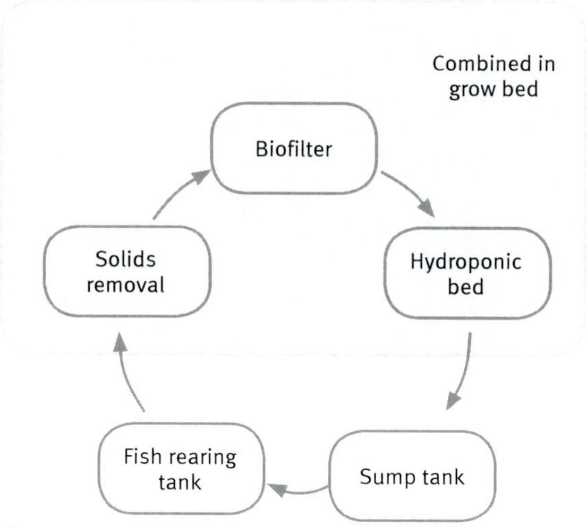

287

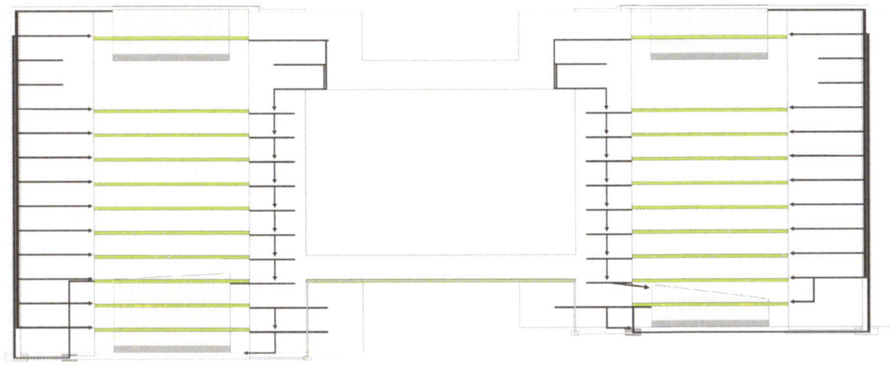

288

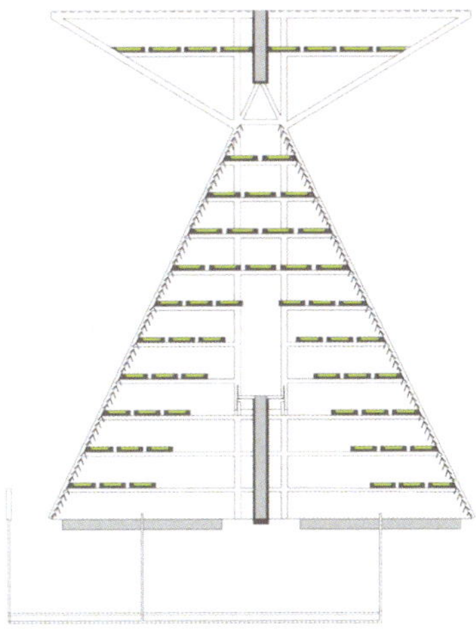

289

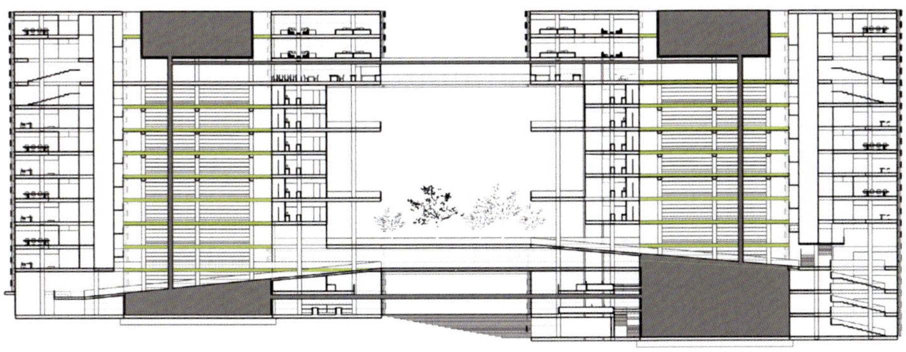

290

288 Cross section of building showing the water cycle from the top tank through the vegetable and into the main aquatank at the bottom
289 Cross section showing the aquaponic system components integrated within the building
290 New internal atrium between the existing tower blocks, designed to create a chimney affect for the air while maximizing the surface area in direct contact with daylight
291 Passive heating system using warm water from the aqua tanks to circulate through the building floors
292 Passive cooling system that forces cooler air from the storage pond into pipes between the vegetable growing pods to be circulated through the offices

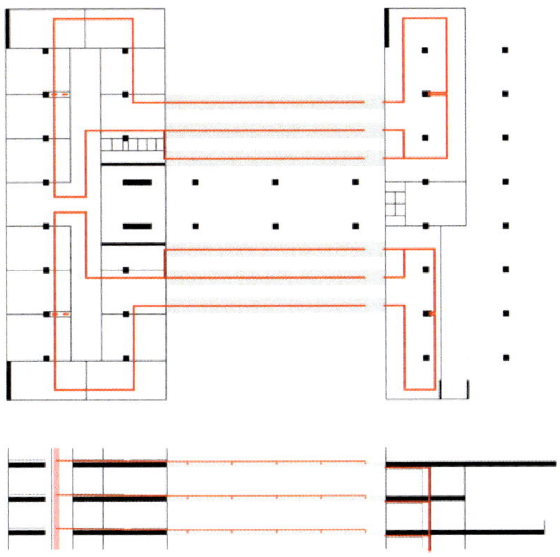

291

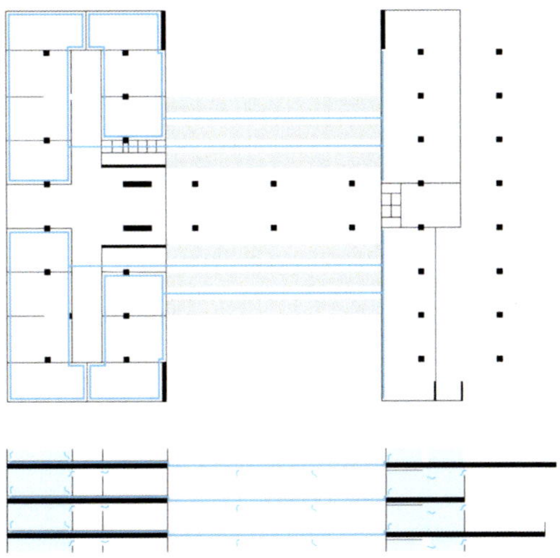

292

293

293 *Integrated photovoltaics shading system as an active energy-saving element on the Southern facade of the kindergarten "Plappersnut", Wismar, IGEL-Institut*

Life time design

5.0 Active energy-saving concepts (high-tech)

5.0 Active energy-saving concepts

5.1 Introduction

The saving of operation energy needed to provide required comfort levels in a building (ventilation, cooling, heating, lighting) are considered within the third building life cycle – building operation. There are two main components that deal with this topic – passive and active energy-saving concepts. In this chapter, one may find descriptions of the active concepts.

A common discussion of the 21st century considers the effective use of energy. Energy is required in all aspects of our life including the construction of housing, traffic, working, shopping, agriculture and industry.
The first steps one should consider in saving energy is the inclusion of passive concepts expressed throughout the architecture and within the structure. The main idea is to reduce the energy required to a bare minimum by reducing heat loss within a building, by effective use of daylighting and by natural ventilation. These passive concepts, as described in the previous chapter, are low-tech system and therefore require null or little active energy.

Active systems should only be introduced in the case that greater energy levels are required. It is important to choose the technology carefully as cheaper systems are of lower quality and sustainability. Investing in a high quality and efficient system will decrease the payback period.

Active integrated systems are mostly based on the use of natural renewable energy (such as sun, wind, air, soil, biomass, biogas, etc.) or on the effective use of waste energy. They are dependent on technical support which help them to retrieve, store and transfer energy. Respectively, these technologies are rather modern and are continually being developed into better solutions. These technologies are used mostly for heating, warm water generation, cooling, ventilation and power generation for lighting and equipment.

Energy storing is of high importance due to the difference in energy captured and the resulting energy demand.

Intelligent building

IIt is possible not only to save energy by installing energy-saving technology, but also being actively aware as an individual to reduce energy use. Alternatively, special monitoring or controlling systems can be built in to replace human control. Such buildings are called intelligent or smart buildings, which have integrated and automated systems of monitoring, regulating and controlling safety services, heating systems, cooling, ventilation, lighting and shading systems. These systems can be controlled on the main panel within the house or via the internet.

294 Charging station for electric cars, HafenCity Hamburg
295 Control panel of Efficiency House Plus with electric mobility, Germany, architect Werner Sobek

294

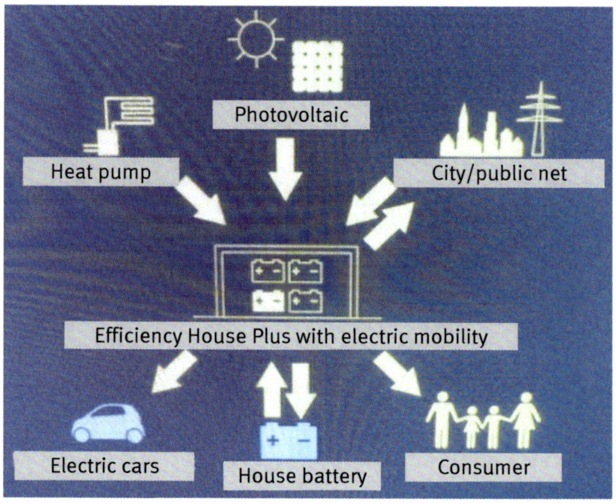

295

Example: Academy Mont Cenis, Sodingen district, Herne, Germany

The Mont Cenis academy is the result of an architectural competition organised by IBA (Internationale Bauaustellung – International Building Exhibition), Emscher Park and the land of North-Rhine Westphalia in 1990/1991 as ideas for the further development of the former mining area of Mont Cenis. The redevelopment of the old coal mine played an important part.

The majority of the reclaimed area was regenerated into a district park to improve the quality of life in the Ruhr region in Germany. Space used as recreation for the locals is encouraged and the academy is the core of the complex.
The new residence was built with 250 flats, including new offices, shops and surgeries.
The architectural concept was a building within a building, encapsulated under a micro-climatic glass capsule. The climate created inside imitates that of Nice, in France, following the seasons of the Mediterranean.
The unique energy concept uses heritage elements (mine gas combined heat and power station) with future technologies (block-type thermal power station, solar and energy storage technologies). The building is an architectural milestone for environmental protection and low energy consumption.

296

296 Elevations – Energy Park at Academy Mont Cenis, HHS planner + architects in cooperation with Jourda & Perraudin architects
297 Site plan with energy concept – Energy Park at Academy Mont Cenis, HHS planner + architects in cooperation with Jourda & Perraudin architects

Technical dates:
10,000 m² photovoltaic module surface
3,185 solar panels

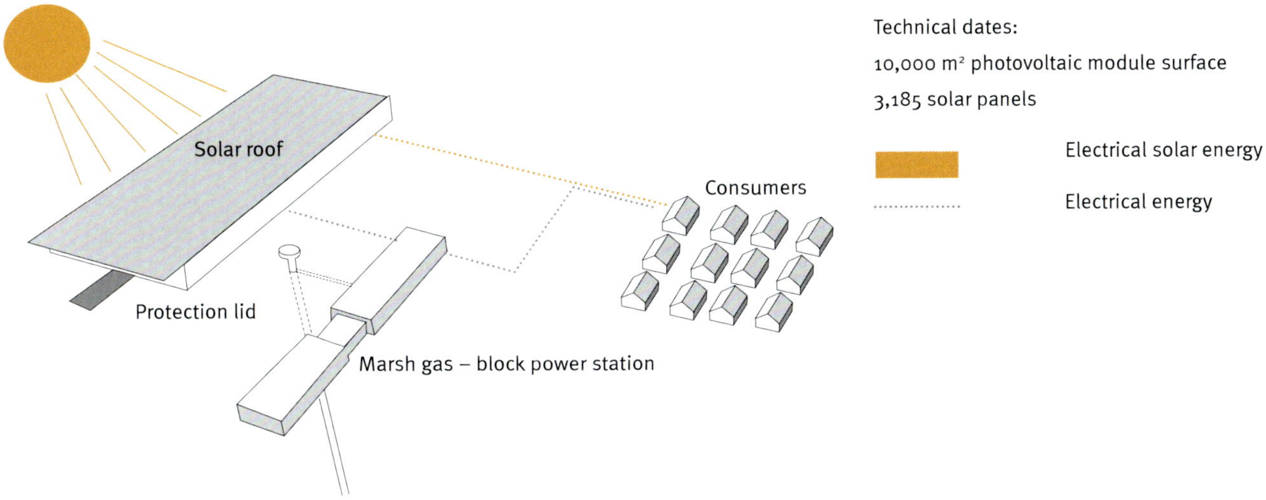

297

5.2 Active building concepts

298

298 *The hybrid decentral, moist-guided air exhaust ventilation system in kindergarten "Plappersnut" – the amount of air that is sucked out is dependent on the relative air humidity*
299 *The decentral fresh and exhaust air system with heat recovery from Eurotherm – the fan pushes the exhaust air through a heat recovery system and therefore warms the air, after approximately 70 seconds, the fan changes the direction and then preheats the fresh air that is brought back into the room – the air vents are working in pairs, therefore simultaneous draft-free cross-ventilation can be achieved*

5.2.1 Active ventilation systems

Active ventilation requires additional, mostly electrical energy and is only used when natural ventilation is not efficient. There are two main types of active ventilation:

- decentralised
- central

Decentralised ventilation is installed only within rooms, where ventilation is required, e.g. in the bathroom or kitchen. They can be integrated to an existing building because they require less additional construction.

There are three groups of decentralised ventilation systems:

- exhaust air system

Exhaust air system is used e.g. in bathrooms. The system consists of a fan which creates a negative pressure in the room and sucks the poor and moist air out.

The operation of the system can be manually activated by an ambient light, or by moisture and CO_2 sensors. Sensors in this case are most energy-efficient, since they are only operated when required.

The air supply is passively provided. This is done either by simple ventilation flaps or louvres in door.

- fresh and exhaust air systems without heat recovery

These systems require an interface to the outside air, mostly near the windows. Technically, these devices are made up of fans and dampers. The devices can be driven at a default interval, so there is always a supply and an exhaust phase.
Furthermore, there are devices that can also operate at the same time. These devices can be manually controlled by the light switch or by humidity and CO2 sensors, whereby the detectors are the most energy-efficient measure when connected with the exhaust systems. To free the air supply of allergens and dirt particles, filters are used in the equipment.

- fresh and exhaust air systems with heat recovery

This system can recover 70-75% of the energy from the exhaust air. Recuperators or regenerators are used for the heat recovery. When the supply and exhaust work simultaneously, a plate recuperator is used. The warm exhaust air transfers its heat to the cooler supply air and heats it.
If a ventilation system's fan alternates operation for supply and exhaust air, regenerators are used. In this case, a thermal storage mass is heated during the exhaust phase, so that it is able to heat the cold supply air.
If these devices are placed in bedrooms or children's rooms, it should use low-noise fans.

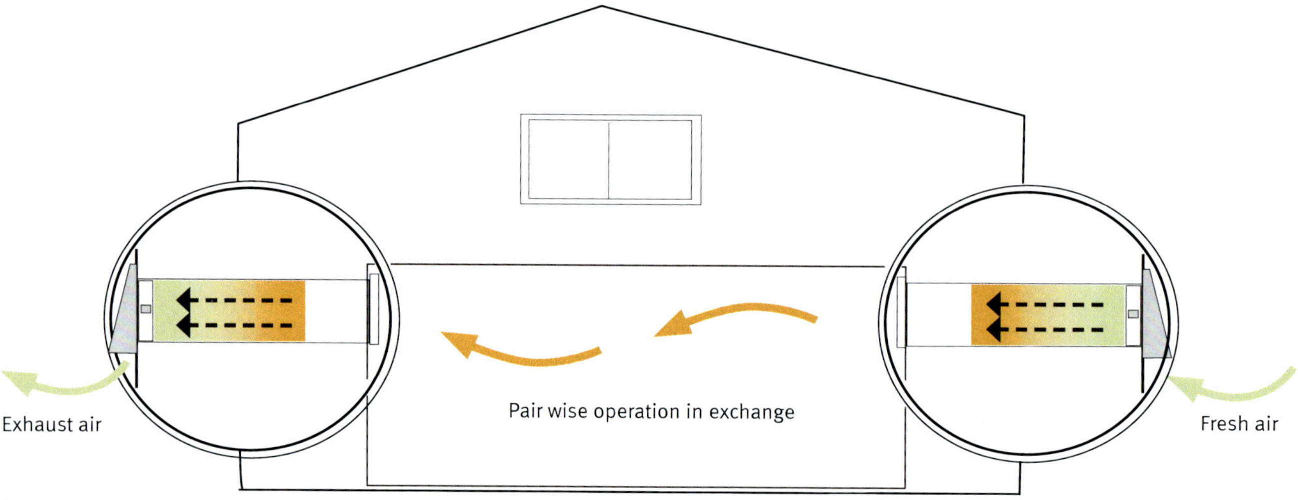

299

Central ventilation systems are mostly used in new construction and can have a high degree of heat recovery. The system is similar to a decentralised ventilation, exhaust air system, fresh and exhaust air system, with the option of heat recovery.

Central fresh and exhaust air system with heat recovery

Heat recovery ventilation is an energy recovery ventilation system that uses heat recovering equipment, which enables the transformation of heat energy from exhaust air to supply air. Heat recovery ventilation provides fresh air and improved climate control while also saving energy by reducing heating requirements. The efficiency varies where some units can have over 90 % efficiency. Efficiency depends on the particular design of the unit, the indoor and outdoor temperature, humidity and fan speed.

There are different types of heat-recovery cores:

- flat-plate cores

These consist of several thin metal plates. Supply air and exhaust air pass over the different sides of the plates so that both airflows do not mix together. This means that there is no transfer of odours, particles and bacteria. The heat is transferred through the plates from the exhaust warm air to the cool fresh air.
In turn, the warm energy from the exhaust air is not lost but transferred to the supply air. The flat-plate cores can be made of plastic, aluminium or specially treated paper.
There are cross flow flat-plate cores which have air-streams moving at 90° to each other. Other counter flow flat-plate cores have the air-streams moving in opposite directions.

- rotary cores

These have a special wheel that rotates between the fresh and stale air-streams. The disadvantage of this system is that the supply and exhaust air can be mixed. These are made of plastic.

- heat-pipe cores

These consist of sealed tubes filled with a refrigerant that transfers heat from one air-stream to the other. These are made of metal.

Seasonal bypassing

The efficiency of heat recovery ventilation differs between seasons. In some seasons it can be thermally efficient to bypass the heat recovery ventilation.
In winter, the heat recovery ventilation reuses the warm energy from the waste air. And in summer, there is no need for heating and therefore no need to gain warm energy.
However, the heat recovery should be bypassed as there is a need to cool the building.

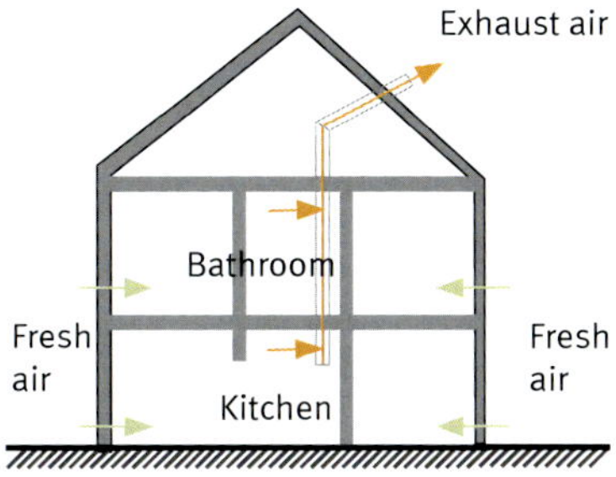

300

300 Central exhaust air ventilation schematic
301 Different types and functional Schematic of flat-plate heat exchanger
302 Schematic of rotary heat exchanger
303 Heat exchanger within an integrated circuit

cold air
warm air

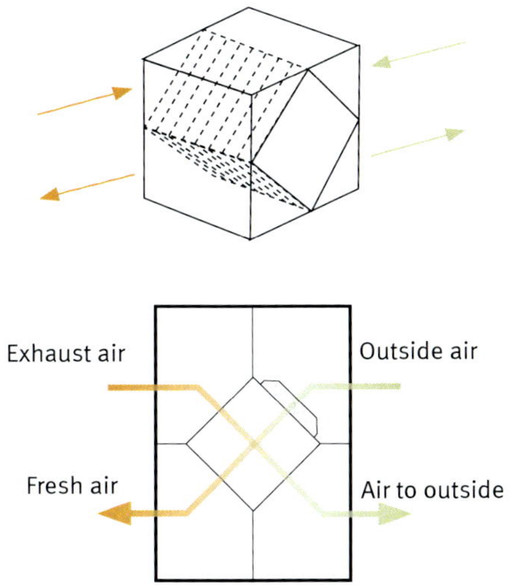

301

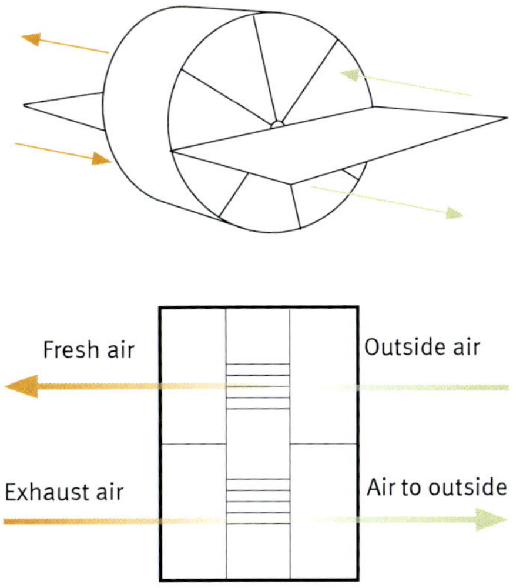

302

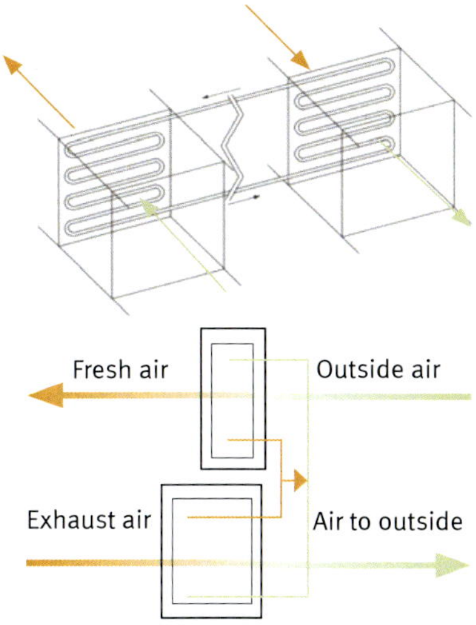

303

5.2 Active building concepts

5.2.2 Active cooling systems

The cooling of buildings is also very important – buildings that mostly require air-conditioning are offices, hospitals or industrial buildings. Energy-saving air-conditioning systems are therefore of high importance.

Adiabatic evaporative cooling is one type of air-conditioning that uses water to cool the air and requires no additional energy for cooling. The airflow in the ventilation system is humidified and cooled down.

The cooling of the outside air is possible down to 10 °C. Locations with very high exterior temperatures use additional air-conditioning supporting systems to help reach the ideal room temperature values.

There are three possibilities of adiabatic cooling in ventilation and air conditioning systems:

- supply air humidification

The outside air is directed via a humidifier and cooled in the process. The generation of air within the indoor comfort zone is possible only with very dry external air, which is rare in Central Europe. For this reason, direct supply air humidification is not efficient in local climates.

- exhaust air humidification with heat recovery

Here, the exhaust air can be humidified by the humidifier and is therefore the coolest. The internal comfort zone does not need to be considered. The cooled exhaust air flows through a heat recovery system, that is connected to the supply air flow.
The supply air is cooled in the heat recovery unit and pushes the warm energy out the exhaust. It can also be referred to as "cool recovery" instead of "heat recovery". Only high heat recovery systems using a flat-plate or heat-pipe core system can be used, so the humidity of the supply air will not be affected by the exhaust air.
The cooling of outside air is realistic to approx. 6 °C. Rainwater can be used to humidify the exhaust air.

- supply air humidification with upstream air drying

The temperature decreases by adiabatic cooling, dependent on the water absorption of the humidified air (about 2.5 °C per gram of evaporated water). The absolute water absorption capacity of air depends on the inlet air humidity before the humidifier, so that a definite prediction of the initial moisture can be assessed. In addition, there are such air conditions possible in which the adiabatic cooling of the exhaust air does not reach the desired cooling effect.
This problem is avoided when the air is dried to a desired moisture level before it enters into the humidifier. Solar energy can be used to warm and dry the air. This is called desiccant evaporative cooling.

304 The principle of an adiabatic evaporative cooling system with a heat recovery unit
305 The principle of an adiabatic evaporative cooling system from Menerga, with a direct water sprinkler and double plate heat exchanger that can reach cooling of 10 °C

rainwater
cold air
warm air

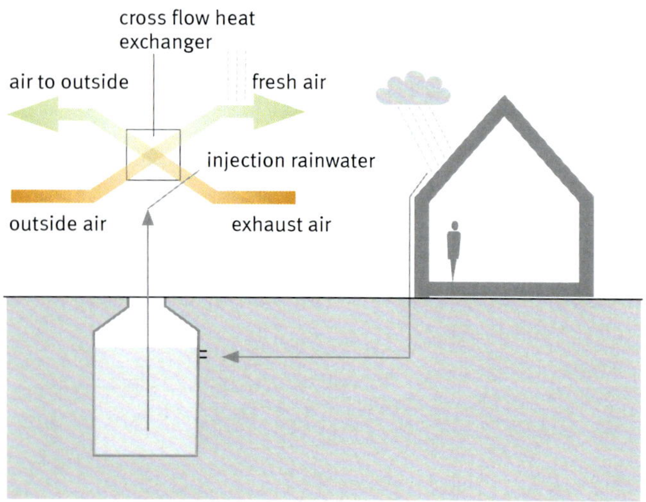

304

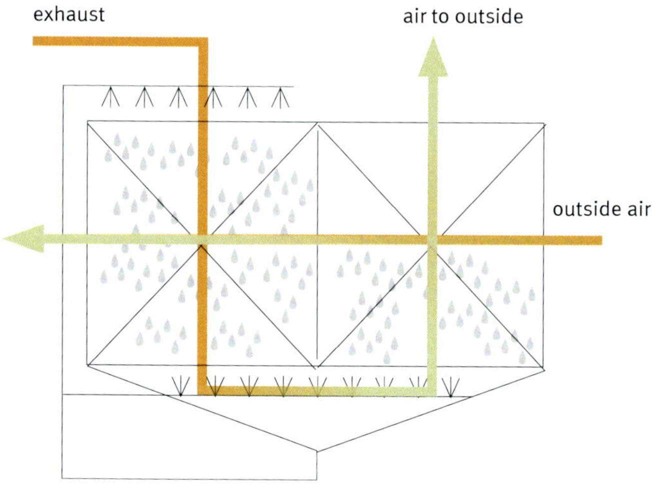

305

Solar cooling is another type of alternative cooling using natural resources. Solar thermal energy can not only be used for water heating and heating support but also for solar cooling.

The method of **adsorption and absorption chillers** can be used.
If solar thermal energy is used for heating support and hot water generation, the energy plants in the summer are used very little when most of the solar heat accumulates. However, during the summer the demand for solar cooling is increased.
By using the solar thermal energy for cooling it allows the high solar yield to be used as it is collected. Because of the parallel cooling demand and solar radiation during the day no large storage systems are necessary.
The basis of solar-thermally driven cooling is the thermo-chemical process of sorption: a liquid or gaseous substance is either attached to a solid, porous substance (adsorption) or absorbed by a liquid or solid substance (absorption).
In absorption chillers the most commonly paired substances are water/lithium bromide and ammonia/water.
In adsorption chillers water/silica gel and water/zeolite are mostly used.
Coefficient of Performance (CoP) is a key indicator of such plants and shows the ratio of driving heat and stored cold energy.
Closed absorption chillers are usually operated in Germany in combination with heat and power but can also be supported by vacuum tube collectors (drive temperature above 80 °C).
The heat ratio (COP) is 0.6 - 0.75 for 1-stage procedure or up to 1.2 for 2-stage procedure.

Closed adsorption chillers normally work with vacuum pipes or flat solar collectors. Nevertheless, these systems are still the most expensive.

The principle of solar cooling

The refrigerant is supplied with heat generated by solar thermal energy and at the same time is deprived of water so that steam is produced. This vapour condenses (it once again becomes liquid) in an adjacent container and is sprayed under vacuum conditions into a heat exchanger, where it evaporates again. The water that flows through the heat exchanger vaporises because of the heat. The water cools off by about 6 °C and can be used for air conditioning.
Then the evaporated refrigerant is liquefied again, mixed with water, and the cycle repeats.
The thermal cooling is not possible without the use of solar energy. It is not the most ecological solution due to its low performance factor, but in comparison to conventional electrical air conditioning it can save resources, energy and costs.

306 *Schematic of a solar chiller*

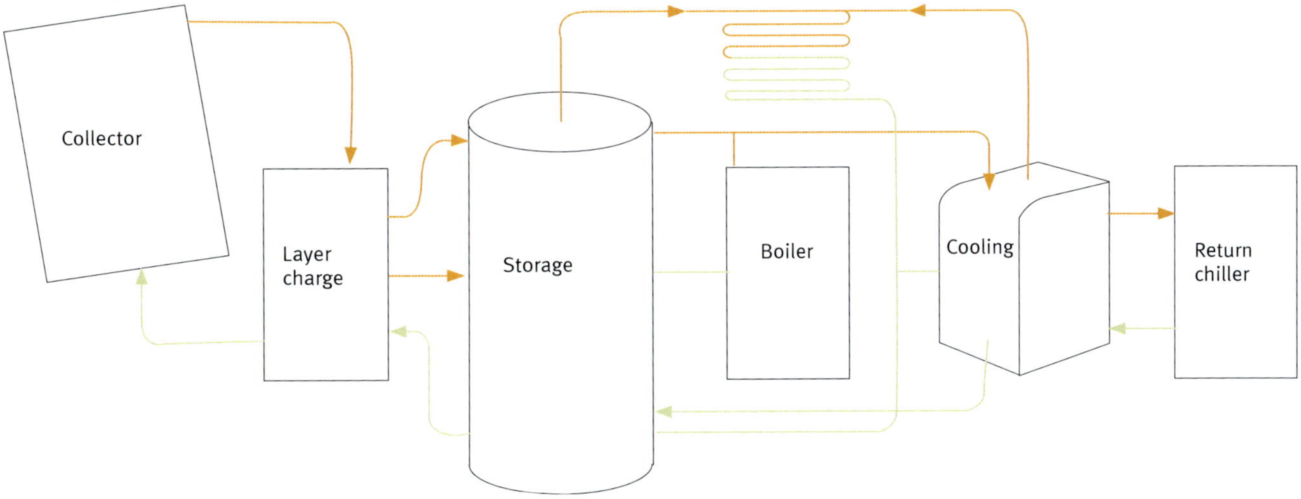

306

5.2 Active building concept

Heat pumps consume only 25 % of the electricity, the rest is heat transferred. This means that to obtain 1 kW of heat, only 0.25 kW of electrical energy is needed.

To operate a heat pump more ecologically, other fuel instead of electrical energy can be used. Heat pumps that work on biogas or other renewable energies can be a very sustainable heating solution.

307 Principle of a heat pump
308 Different types of heat pump

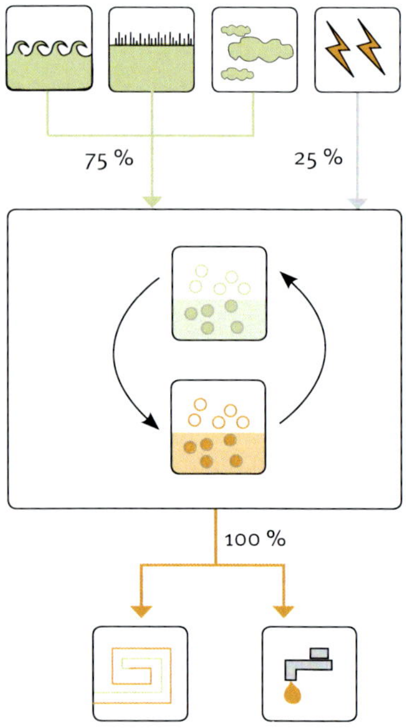

307

5.2.3 Active heating and warm water systems

Active heating and warm water systems generate warm energy. In order to achieve a zero or low primary energy value, renewable energies are to be used.

Warm energy gained from renewable resources normally have a low temperature, meaning radiation heating (e.g. surface heating) which requires lower temperatures can be used. Conventional air heating is not possible.
Warm water generated by renewable energies, e.g. sun, is normally stored within a buffer storage, where it is additionally heated up to 60 °C.

Heat pump

The heat pump is a device that uses low temperature heat which is an unlimited source found all around us. The heat taken from the air (outside or exhaust air), soil, earth (geothermal well) and water, transfers from a lower level to a higher temperature. This means that the heat pump does not produce energy, it pumps it to a higher temperature level by the consumption of a certain quantity of electricity.
Heat pumps can be used to generate heat energy and warm water and can also be used in the summer for cooling. Normally, an additional system (e.g. electric heating) is required to cover the peak loads.

Heat sources and types of heat pump

- heat taken from soil

These heat pumps are able to extract thermal energy from the environment in two ways:

- horizontal collectors
- vertical collectors, i.e. wells

Horizontal collectors are placed in the ground at a depth of about 1.2-1.5 m to extract heat from the ground. It is then passed through the heat transfer fluid (water-glycol) within the heat pump. Heat pumps with compressor circuits absorb the heat to a higher temperature level, followed by the distribution of heating and radiation into the space. This system requires large collector planes, two to three times larger than the area to be heated.

The principle of **vertical wells** is similar to the horizontal collector but with a probe (two tubes or more) placed in boreholes 30-100 meters deep. By using the heat transfer fluid (water-glycol) which circulates down the pipes, the heat is collected and transmitted from the ground to the heat pump. Vertical geothermal probes require very little space and are more stable than horizontal collectors.

- heat collected from the bottom and surface water

The most efficient heat source is groundwater. The temperature remains almost unchanged throughout the year, ranging from 9-14 °C. With these temperatures the heat pump can achieve higher performances with lower consumption, saving operating costs when compared to horizontal or vertical tube collectors.

The principle consists of pumping groundwater from boreholes (well) to the heat pump where the heat energy is collected and then discharged into the infiltration boreholes (wells). Drilling distance depends on the substrate and the amount of pumping water in order to prevent interference with influencing wells. In ordinary houses this distance should be at least 10 m.

- heat taken from the air

Generating heat from air in terms of installation and use is the simplest and often economically the best solution because air source is unlimited. The disadvantage is that there is a wide range of temperatures throughout the seasons with very low temperatures in the winter.
In the past, heat pumps could function effectively only in temperatures over -5 °C. Todays technology allows some heat pumps the use of water to air systems at high efficiency, to -20 °C. Air-water heat pumps are used to full capacity and are the most widely used alternative heating system.

Ground coupled closed cycle heat pumps

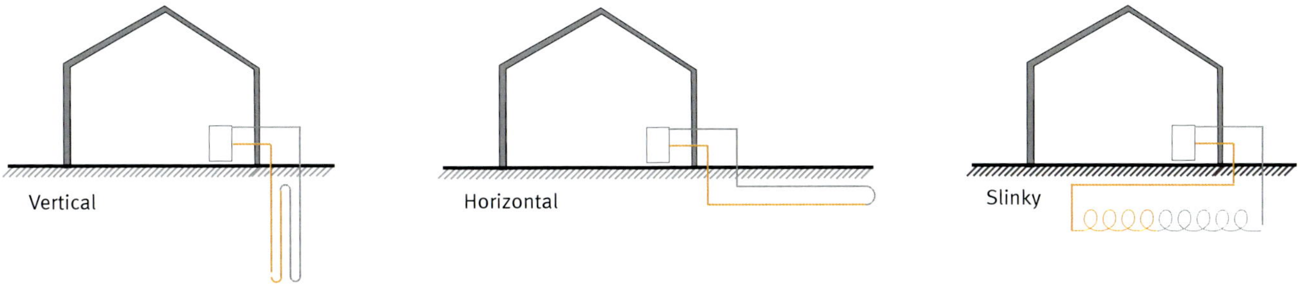

Groundwater open cycle heat pumps

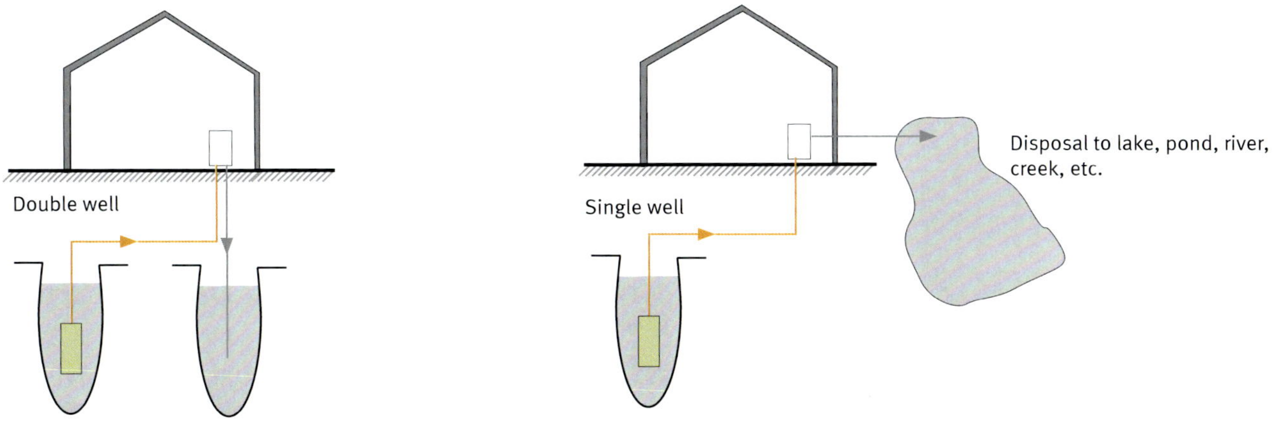

Surface water heat pumps - closed and opened cycle

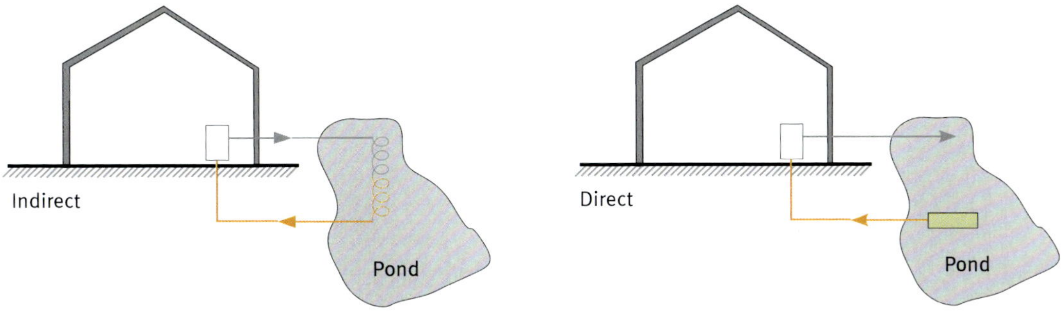

Air source heat pump for both heating in winter and cooling in summer

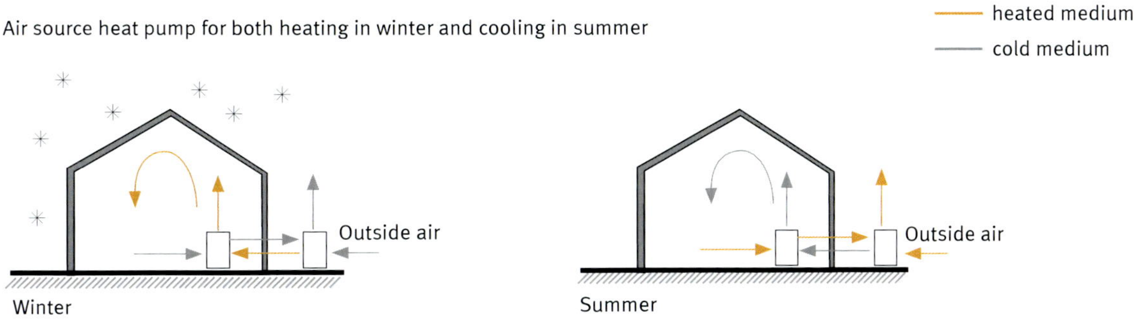

308

5.2 Active building concept

309

Solar thermal collectors

“Solar thermal collectors collect heat by absorbing the sunlight. There are two basic types of active solar heating systems based on the type of fluid – either liquid or air – that is heated in the solar energy collectors.
Liquid-based systems heat water or an antifreeze solution in a ‘hydronic’ collector, whereas air-based systems heat air in an air collector.
Both of these systems collect and absorb solar radiation then transfer the solar heat directly to the interior space or to a storage system, from which the heat is distributed.

If the system cannot provide adequate space heating, an auxiliary or back-up system provides the additional heat. Liquid systems are more often used when storage is included, and are well suited for radiant heating systems, boilers with hot water radiators, and even absorption heat pumps and coolers.” [57]

Solar thermal collectors are mostly used for warm water generation and heating support. A solar system that is designed correctly can provide annually 50 % to 65 % of the hot water demand.

Types of solar heat collectors

- flat plate collectors
- evacuated tube collectors
- concentrating collectors

Flat plate collectors

A flat plate collector is an insulated and weatherproofed box, which consists of a dark absorber metal plate under one or more transparent/translucent covers. Water or other fluid runs in pipes (mostly copper) that are attached to the metal sheet for heat exchange. As the fluid flows through the pipes it is heated and used for domestic purposes.

Evacuated tube collectors

This type of solar collector system consists of rows of parallel glass tubes that are well insulated by a vacuum within the glass. The series of glass tubes are arranged in the form of a solar panel and serve as a solar thermal collector system.
There are several types of evacuated tube collectors – glass-glass, glass-metal, glass-glass with water flow path.

Concentrating collectors

Concentrating solar collectors use shaped mirrors or lenses to provide higher temperatures than flat plate collectors. They are usually parabolic. This type of solar collector is generally only used for commercial power production applications due to very high temperature capabilities. It is however reliant on direct sunlight and therefore does not perform well in overcast conditions.

[57] *The Worlds of David Darling;* active solar energy system [http://www.daviddarling.info/encyclopedia/A/AE_active_solar_energy_system.html] (08.10.2012)

309 Evacuated tube solar collectors on the south facade of a family house
310 Processes occurring within a flat-plate collector
311 Principle of an evacuated tube collector
312 Schematic of a solar thermal heating system

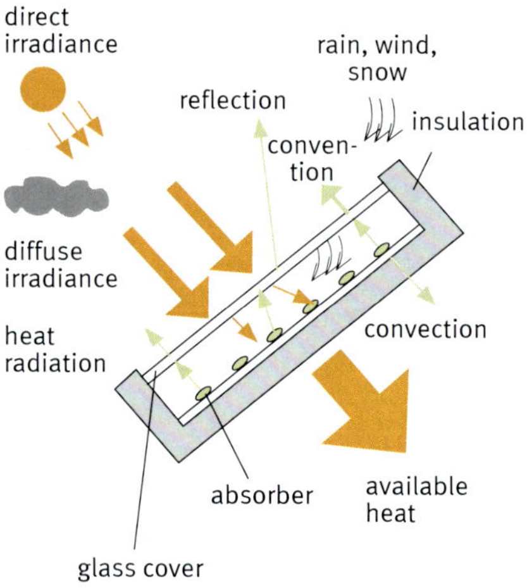

310

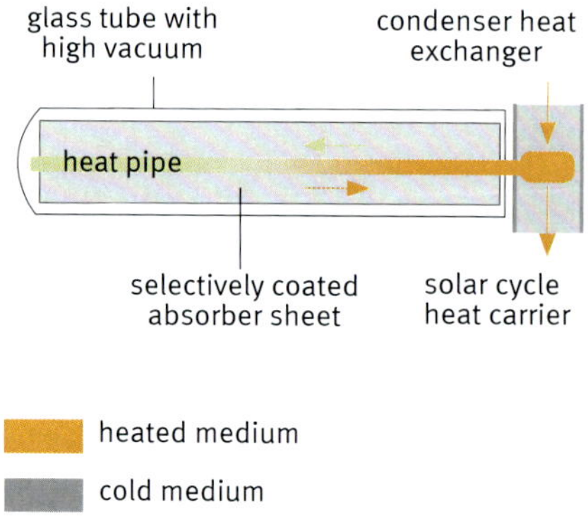

311

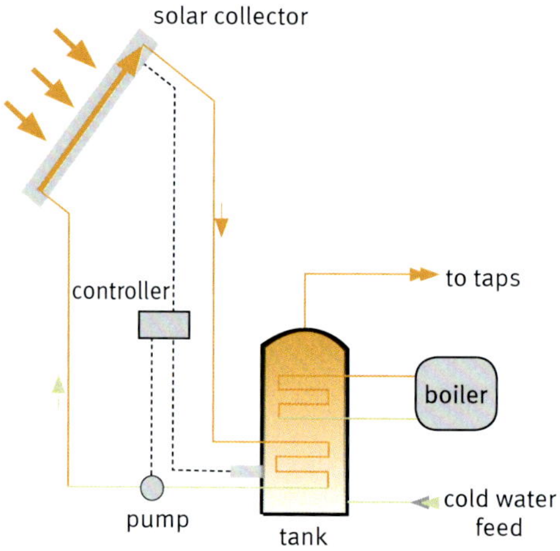

312

Waste water heat recovery

"In a busy, modern, working family household, up to 90 % of hot water consumption is for showering. Most of that heat goes straight down the drain with the waste water.
Shower-Save is a very simple grey water heat recovery system which can reclaim over 60 % of the heat that would normally be lost down the drain whenever you shower.
The waste water from the shower runs through a heat exchanger on its way to the drain. The cold water feeding the shower and the hot water cylinder/ combi boiler passes through the heat exchanger and picks up the waste heat. Only the heat is transferred, the waste water never comes into contact with the fresh water." [58]

"Drain water heat recovery technology works well with all types of water heaters, especially with demand and solar water heaters. Also, drain-water heat exchangers can recover heat from the hot water used in showers, bathtubs, sinks, dishwashers, and clothes washers. Water enters the home between 5-12 °C and is heated to 50 °C in the hot water tank. Showerhead temperature is approximately 41 °C and this water is flushed down the drain at 37 °C." [59]

The fresh cold water flowing through the waste water heat exchanger is warmed by the hot drain water to 25 °C, achieving around 14 °C heat recovery.

The advantages of waste water heat recovery are:

- money saving

The initial costs are relatively low and the payback is very quick. There are costs also saved for the water heating because the fresh water is already preheated by the heat exchanger.

- reduce carbon foot print

The system saves high amounts of CO_2 emissions because of saved energy for heating. The carbon dioxide emission savings depend on how often the shower is used and what fuel is used for water heating.

- reliability

It is a simple and low maintenance system. Heat exchangers are made from copper construction and can last for many years.

- performance

60 % of the energy used when showering can be recovered.

- other benefits

The time required for water heating is reduced as the fresh water that enters has already been preheated.

- applicability

The system works well with standalone showers and bath showers, however not with baths that are filled and emptied non-simultaneously.

[58] *1 World Solar Ltd;* Shower Save [http://shower-save.com/] (18.10.2012)

[59] *Sunandwindenergy;* Waste water heat [http://www.sunandwindenergy.ca/wastewaterheat.html] (18.10.2012)

313 Schematic of waste water heat exchanger integrated into shower base

hot water
warm water
cold water

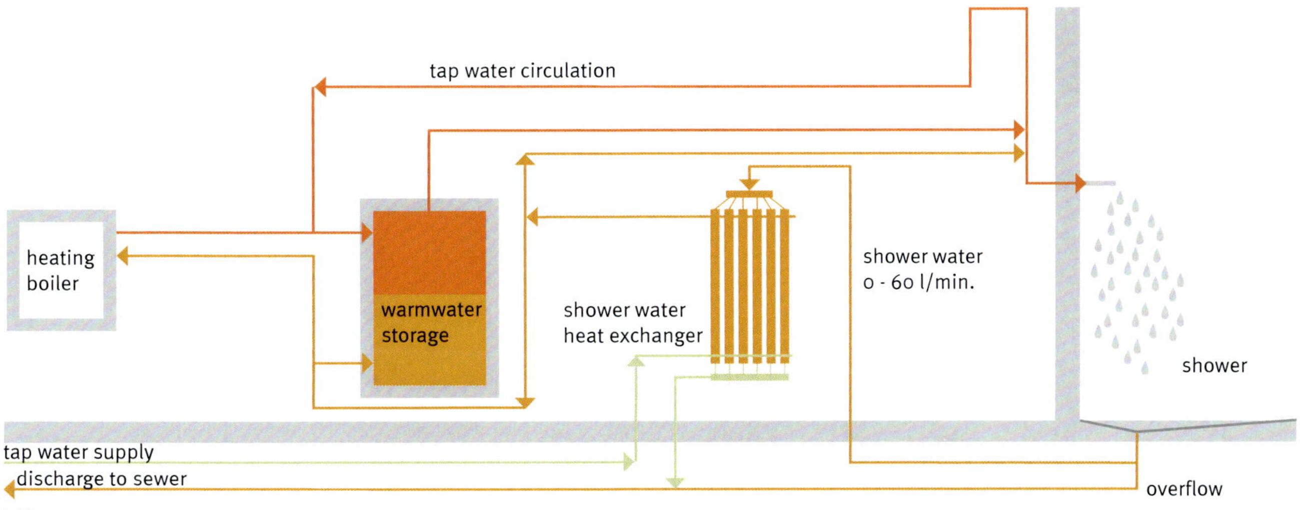

313

5.2 Active building concepts

314

5.2.4 Active power systems

The generation of electricity is a popular topic. The majority of public power is generated by nuclear or fossil energies resulting in a high primary energy value. The use of renewable resources to generate electricity is therefore of high importance.

Photovoltaics

"Photovoltaics is the direct conversion of light into electricity at the atomic level. Some materials exhibit a property known as the photoelectric effect that causes them to absorb photons of light and release electrons. When these free electrons are captured, an electric current results that can be used as electricity. (...)

PV cells are made of the same kinds of semiconductor materials, such as silicon, used in the microelectronics industry. For solar cells, a thin semiconductor wafer is specially treated to form an electric field, positive on one side and negative on the other. When light energy strikes the solar cell, electrons are knocked loose from the atoms in the semiconductor material. If electrical conductors are attached to the positive and negative sides, forming an electrical circuit, the electrons can be captured in the form of an electric current - that is, electricity. (...)

A number of photovoltaic cells electrically connected to each other and mounted in a support structure or frame is called a photovoltaic module. Modules are designed to supply electricity at a certain voltage, such as a common 12 volts system. The current produced is directly dependent on how much light strikes the module.

Multiple modules can be wired together to form an array. In general, the larger the area of a module or array, the more electricity that will be produced." [60]

"Types of PV cell materials

PV cells are made of semiconductor materials. The major types of materials are crystalline and thin films, which vary from each other in terms of light absorption efficiency, energy conversion efficiency, manufacturing technology and cost of production.

Crystalline materials

- single-crystal silicon

Single-crystal silicon cells are the most common in the PV industry. The main technique for producing single-crystal silicon is the Czochralski method. High-purity polycrystalline is melted in a quartz crucible. A single-crystal silicon seed is dipped into this moulten mass of polycrystalline. As the seed is pulled slowly from the melt, a single-crystal ingot is formed. The ingots are then sawed into thin wafers about 200-400 micrometers

314 *Photovoltaics power station*
315 *PV-Collectors as shading element*

315

thick. The thin wafers are then polished, doped, coated, interconnected and assembled into modules and arrays.

A single-crystal silicon has a uniform molecular structure. Compared to noncrystalline materials, its high uniformity results in higher energy conversion efficiency. (...) The conversion efficiency for single-silicon commercial modules ranges between 15-20%. Not only are they energy efficient, single-silicon modules are highly reliable for outdoor power applications. (...)

- polycrystalline silicon

Consisting of small grains of single-crystal silicon, polycrystalline PV cells are less energy efficient than single-crystalline silicon PV cells. The grain boundaries in polycrystalline silicon hinder the flow of electrons and reduce the power output of the cell. The energy conversion efficiency for a commercial module made of polycrystalline silicon ranges between 10 to 14 %.

A common approach to produce polycrystalline silicon PV cells is to slice thin wafers from blocks of cast polycrystalline silicon. Another more advanced approach is the "ribbon growth" method in which silicon is grown directly as thin ribbons or sheets with the approach thickness for making PV cells. Since no sawing is needed, the manufacturing cost is lower. The most commercially developed ribbon growth approach is EFG (edge-defined film-fed growth).

Compared to single-crystalline silicon, polycrystalline silicon material is stronger and can be cut into one-third the thickness of single-crystal material. It also has slightly lower wafer cost and less strict growth requirements. (...)

- Gallium Arsenide (GaAs)

A compound semiconductor made of two elements: gallium (Ga) and arsenic (As), GaAs has a crystal structure similar to that of silicon.
An advantage of GaAs is that it has high level of light absorptivity. (...) Also, GaAs has a much higher energy conversion efficiency than crystal silicon, reaching about 25 to 30 %.

Its high resistance to heat makes it an ideal choice for concentrator systems in which cell temperatures are high. GaAs is also popular in space applications where strong resistance radiation damage and high cell efficiency are required.

The biggest drawback of GaAs PV cells is the high cost of the single-crystal substrate that GaAs is grown on. Therefore it is most often used in concentrator systems where only a small area of GaAs cells is needed. (...)

Cell type	Efficiency grade
Monocrystalline	20 %
Polycrystalline	16 %
Amorphous silicon	8 %
CIS cells	12 %
GaAS cells	25 %
Pigment cells	2-3%

316

[60] *NASA: Netting,R.;* How do Photovoltaics Work? [http://science.nasa.gov/science-news/science-at-nasa/2002/solarcells/] (18.11.2012)

[61] *National Solar Power Research Institute, Inc.: Mah,O.;* Fundamentals of Photovoltaics Materials [http://userwww.sfsu.edu/ciotola/solar/pv.pdf] (08.11.2012)

316 Efficiency of various PV cell types
317 Testing of different PV-Systems
318 Single crystal solar cells in panel

317

318

5.2 Active building concepts

319

Thin film materials

- amorphous Silicon (a-Si)

Amorphous silicon is a noncrystalline form of silicon i.e. its silicon atoms are disordered in structure. A significant advantage of a-Si is its high light absorption, about 40 times higher than that of single-crystal silicon. This means that only a thin layer of a-Si is sufficient for making PV cells (about 1 micrometer thick as compared to 200 or more micrometers thick for crystalline silicon cells). Also, a-Si can be deposited on various low-cost substrates including steel, glass and plastic, and the manufacturing process requires lower temperatures, thus less energy. The total material and manufacturing costs are therefore lower per unit area compared to those of crystalline silicon cells.

Despite the promising economic advantages, a-Si has two major roadblocks to overcome. One is the low cell energy conversion efficiency that ranges between 5-9 %, and the other is the issue of outdoor reliability where the efficiency degrades within a few months due to sunlight exposure and losing about 10 to 15 %.

- Cadmium Telluride (CdTe)

As a polycrystalline semiconductor compound made of cadmium and tellurium, CdTe has a high light absorptivity level – only about a micrometer thick can absorb 90 % of the solar spectrum. Another advantage is that it is relatively easy and cheap to manufacture by processes such as high-rate evaporation, spraying or screen printing. The conversion efficiency for a CdTe commercial module is about 7 %, similar to that of a-Si.

The instability of cell and module performance is one of the major drawbacks of using CdTe for PV cells. Another disadvantage is that cadmium is a toxic substance. Although very little cadmium is used in CdTe modules, extra precautions must be taken in the manufacturing process.

- Copper Indium Diselenide ($CuInSe_2$, or CIS)

A polycrystalline semiconductor compound of copper, indium and selenium, CIS (...) which has the highest conversion efficiency of 17.7 % is not only the best among all of the existing thin film materials, but also came close to the 18 % research efficiency of the polycrystalline silicon PV cells. (...) CIS is also one of the most light-absorbent semiconductors – 0.5 micrometers can absorb 90 % of the solar spectrum.

CIS is an efficient but complex material. Its complexity makes it difficult to manufacture. Also, safety issues might be another concern in the manufacturing process as it involves hydrogen selenide, an extremely toxic gas." [61]

319 Photovoltaics as shading system – solar PV louvres
320 Roof integrated Photovoltaics

320

Applying photovoltaics

- power stations
- building integrated photovoltaic (BIPV)
- in transport
- standalone devices
- rural electrification
- solar roadways
- solar power satellites

Building-integrated photovoltaics

BIPV are photovoltaic materials that are used to replace conventional building materials in parts of the building envelope such as the roof, skylights, or facades.

Forms of BIPV:

- shading systems

External shades can be fixed or adjustable, metal or glass, large or small and can also be incorporated into the maintenance walkway systems.
The term 'louvres' refers to adjustable and fixed shading devices.

- rain screen systems

Rainscreens are an over-cladding system which can be used for new buildings as well as the replacement of old building envelopes.
The outer leaf that acts as a rainscreen provides the major barrier to rain penetration, while the inner leaf of the wall forms the air barrier. Vertical cladding rails or fixing brackets are bolted on to the backing wall ready to receive the outer rainscreen panels.

- stick-system curtain walls

The stick system, also known as mullion/transom system, is a fairly common form of curtain-wall construction.
Stick-system curtain walls are widely used for low-rise buildings where a low-medium size system is required.

- unitised curtain walls

Unitised systems are particularly suited to highly articulated facades providing visual interest which are often finished in heavy materials, i.e. natural stone.
They tend to be used on more prestigious city-centre commercial developments where the cladding would be of custom nature and therefore in the middle to high cost range.

- double-skin facades

Between the heat-insulated inner facade and the outer skin is an unheated thermal buffer zone which is ventilated if required and can incorporate movable solar shading devices.
Double-skin facades are designed to adapt to ambient conditions and balance out seasonal climate fluctuations.
The outer facade is extremely suitable for integrating photovoltaics as it consists of single glazing and the modules can provide solar shading.

- atriums and canopies

Canopies are similar to atrium spaces which consist of horizontal or gently inclined faces high on a building which provide good opportunities for PV integration.

321 Photovoltaic roof

321

5.2 Active building concepts

322

322 *Building integrated horizontal-axis wind turbine*
323 *Wind turbines used in connection to the building; Savonius vertical-axis, modern horizontal-axis and Giromill/ Darrieus vertical-axis wind turbine*

Wind power

The use of wind energy depends on the location. The most suitable locations receive constant high wind speed throughout the whole year. Areas with high wind speeds include the coast, hilltops, open plains and valleys. The electricity produced from wind power can be variable at several time scales: hourly, daily or seasonally.

Wind power is the conversion of wind energy into useful energy. A tall tower with a large propeller on top can generate and produce electricity when the wind blows and turns the propeller. Windmills are also used to produce mechanical power and wind pumps can be used for pumping water or sails to propel ships.

Almost all large wind turbines have similar designs represented by a vertical tower with a horizontal axis, and a wind turbine with an upwind rotor with three wings.
To use wind energy has many advantages. Wind is a renewable resource and is free without the need of fossil fuels. Wind is plentiful, widely distributed and clean because it produces no waste or greenhouse gases. It does not use up land and can be further used for agriculture or integrated into a building. The environmental effects of wind power are minimal in comparison to other traditional energy sources.

Wind farms

Multiple wind turbines that are used for the production of electricity are called wind farms. They can be located on the ground while using the land below for agriculture or they can be located on large water bodies such as at sea – such wind farms are called offshore wind farms. The wind above water bodies is more frequent, more powerful and the offshore wind farms have no impact on the landscape. However, construction and maintenance is of higher cost.

The individual turbines within a wind farm are interconnected by a power collection system which has a medium voltage. Through transformers it is then connected to a high voltage electric power transmission system.

Small-scale wind power

These are wind generation systems with the capacity to produce up to 50 kW of electrical power. This can be an alternative for isolated communities or individuals to produce electricity and reduce their dependence from the use of the electricity grid or to reduce their carbon footprint.
There are two possibilities for wind turbine use for households or other buildings; they can be connected with battery storage or into the grid. Grid-connected domestic wind turbines use grid energy storage.

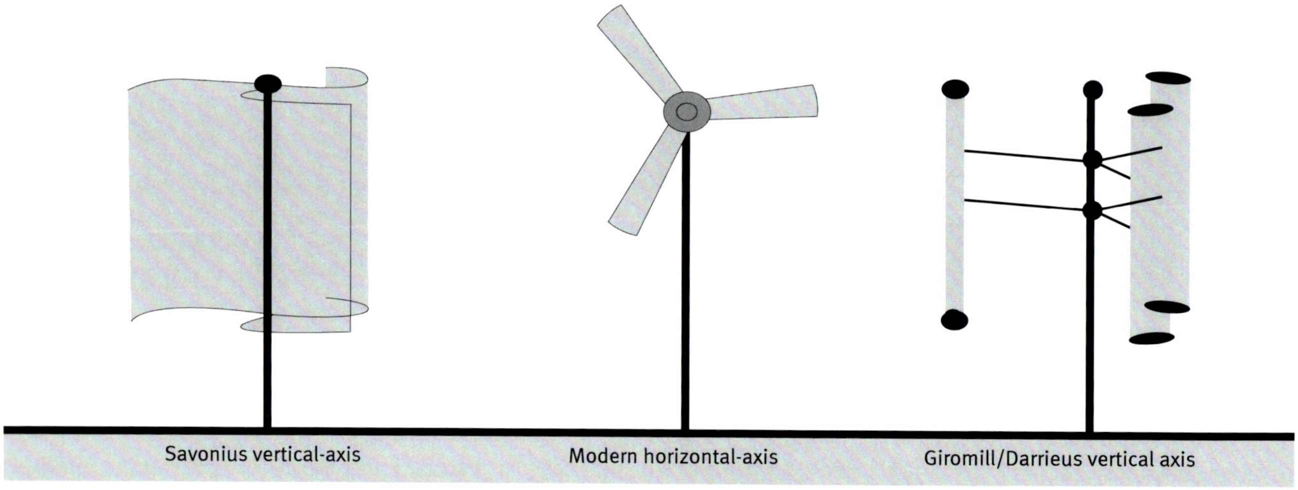

323

Wind turbines used in buildings

Today, an accumulating number of wind turbines are being used in buildings. The future of wind power is growing around the world. Architects should therefore consider and develop methods of how to integrate wind power within building design in the future.

Wind turbines can rotate on either a horizontal or vertical axis.
Vertical-axis wind turbines have the main rotor shaft arranged vertically. A key advantage of this arrangement is that the turbine does not need to point into the wind to gain efficiency. This is an advantage on sites where the wind direction is highly variable, and when integrated into buildings. Vertical plants can run at low wind speeds and produce electricity.
With a vertical axis, the generator and gearbox can be placed near the ground or the turbine can be mounted on a rooftop, so also the maintenance of the most maintenance-intensive components is easier.
Vertical axis wind turbines are quieter and are therefore suitable for residential areas and cities.

A major disadvantage of vertical small wind turbines is lower efficiency. Horizontal systems often produce significantly more power than vertical systems. Vertical turbines can also cause strong vibrations and are best located near to the ground.

324

325

324 Wind power farms in California
325 Wind turbines integrated into the building, HafenCity Hamburg
326 Applying of small wind turbines

					Wind hybrid									Single wind turbine			
			Wind hybrid								Single wind turbine						
	Wind home system									Build integrated							
P < 1 kW	X	X	X	X	X	X	X			X	X	X	X				
1 kW < P < 7 kW	X	X	X	X	X	X	X	X			X	X	X	X	X	X	X
7 kW < P < 50 kW					X	X	X	X	X				X	X	X	X	X
7 kW < P < 50 kW								X	X						X	X	X
Small wind system applications	Sailboats	Signalling	Street lamp	Remote houses/ dwellings	Farms	Water pumping	Seawater desalina-tion	Village power	Mini-grid	Street lamp	Buildings rooftop	Dwellings	Public centres	Car parking	Industrial	Industrial	Farms
	Off-grid applications									On-grid applications							

326

5.2 Active building concepts

Organic Rankine Cycle process

The substance in the vaporiser begins to boil at temperatures lower than water. As the first step of the cycle, octamethyltrisiloxane (OMTS) is filled into a container called the vaporiser.
The vaporiser is heated up. For this process various kinds of thermal energy can be used.
By applying this energy to the substance it begins to boil and creates a pressure of approximately 10 bars.
The pressure is released over an ORC-turbo - generator and is transferred into electricity.
After the OMTS-steam leaves the ORC-turbo - generator, it flows into the condenser. In the condenser is a low pressure of approximately 0.1 bars where it is liquefied by cool pipe bundles, and rains down to the bottom of the container.
After a certain level is filled, the medium is drawn by a pump and pressed into the recuperator where it takes energy from the hot steam leaving the turbine, and then flows back into the vaporiser to close the cycle.

[62] *Emispec;* Organic Rankine Cycle (ORC) type external combustion engine [http://emispec.ca/en/external-combustion-engine-type-organic-rankine-cycle.php] (08.11.2012)

5.2.5 Active combined systems

Active combined systems generate heat energy and power simultaneously. These systems are very efficient as they use the waste energy produced from power generation for heating or warm water, or by transferring the warm energy generated during non-peak hours (e.g. in summer) to electrical energy.

This method uses the energy which would be normally unused waste energy to become a valuable energy that can be used in a building.

Organic Rankine Cycle (ORC)

The ORC process can produce both heat and power energy from a single plant based on low temperature heat (e.g. geothermal energy, industrial waste heat, biomass, solar energy) using the principle of a steam circuit.

The ORC process is a thermodynamic process similar to a conventional steam cycle in which circulates a low-boiling organic substance as working fluid, instead of water.

The major advantage of using an organic fluid instead of water is that the fluids can be used below a temperature of 400 °C and do not need to be overheated.

"The organic media is compressed and circulated in a closed loop by a pump. It will be evaporated in a shell and tube heat exchanger by absorbing the thermal heat of the thermal oil primary circuit.

The organic vapour expands in a special designed turbine which drives the electrical generator and will be condensed in another heat exchanger by using a cooling media like water.

The condensate will then be compressed again by the circulation pump, which closes the thermodynamic cycle." [62]

With organic rankine cycle systems it is possible to economically convert even small sources of thermal energy into electricity.

The ORC process can be used for the generation of electrical energy from solar collectors. In the summer, when the solar collectors generate more heat energy than needed, the additional energy, with the help of the ORC system, can be converted into electricity.

327 Organic Rankine Cycle process

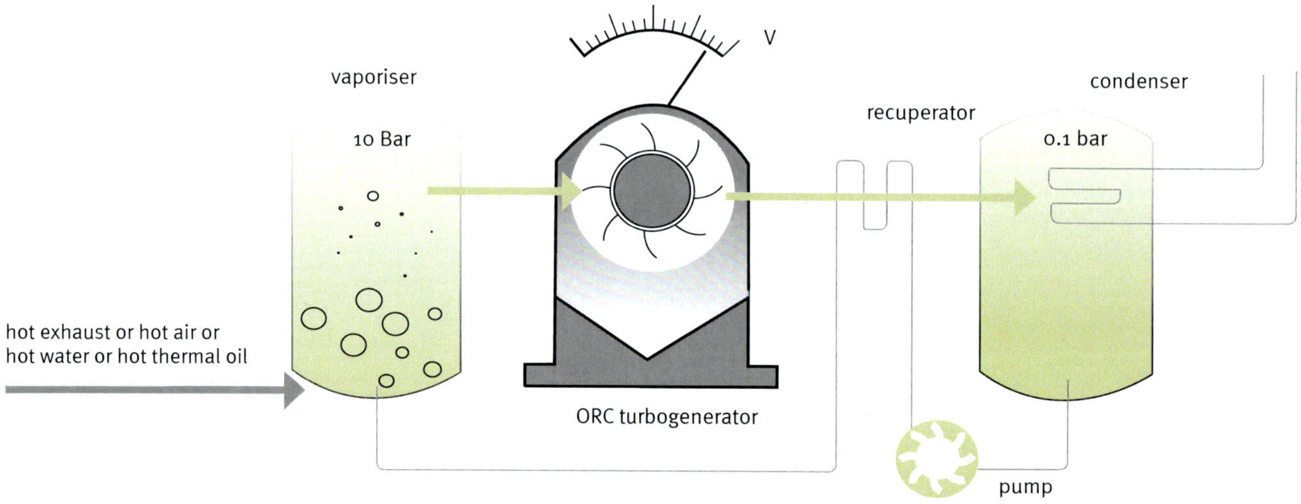

327

Kalina cycle

In the 1970s, the process of the Kalina cycle was developed by Russian engineer Alexander Kalina. He developed a heat exchange process to produce steam at a low temperature level to generate energy.
Conventional steam turbines require steam at temperatures of several hundred degrees Celsius in order to ensure a viable energy. At geothermal power plants, this is accessible only by deep, expensive drilling.
To make use of the water temperatures of 90 °C, Kalina developed a circuit where the heat of the water is discharged to an ammonia-water mixture. The steam already formed at much lower temperatures is then used to drive turbines. Compared with an Organic Rankine Cycle, the efficiency can be between 10-60 % higher depending on the application. In this way, even at lower depths a geothermal power plant can be operated. It can be used to industrially process heat, geothermal energy, solar energy, and the use of waste heat from power plants (Bottoming cycle).
The process is protected by various patents which are held by the Californian company Exergy. However, Siemens Industrial Solutions and Services in Europe hold licenses for one type of process, called the SG1 Cycle, and the more advanced SG2 cycle is held by the construction company M + W Zander.

At present, only a few worldwide geothermal power plants operate on this principle of action, and the best known being Husavik facility in Iceland. Two others found in Germany are the Unterhaching facility, the first of its kind in Southern Germany, and Brushal facility.

The Ecogen units are designed for the Japanese hot spring market and can be found at Matsunoyama Onsen hot spring in Tokamachi, Niigata, Japan.

The Kalina cycle power plants using recoverable heat from industrial processes are the Kashima Steel Works, operated by Sumitomo Metals and The Tokyo Bay Oil Refinery, operated by Fuji Oil.

328 Geothermal Power Station in Hellisheiði, Iceland – the largest geothermal power plant in the world

328

5.2 Active building concepts

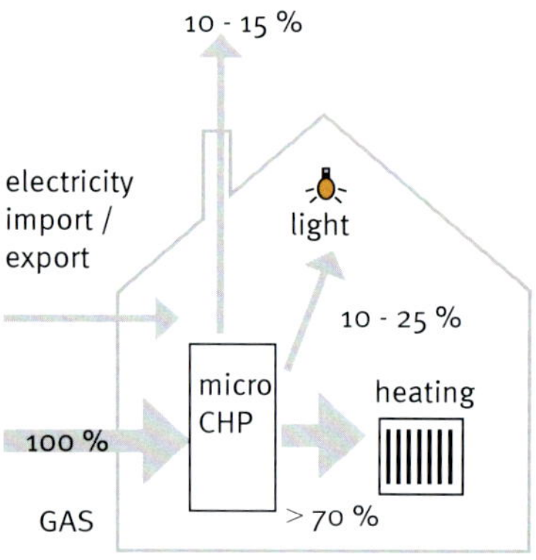

329

Combined heat and power (CHP)

In a combined heat and power system (CHP), also known as cogeneration, power and heat is produced in the same time from a single fuel source.

In this coupling system, the input energy (e.g. natural gas, biomass, biogas, coal, waste heat, or oil) is used much more efficiently than in conventional production by separate facilities. The main advantage, besides the reduction of CO_2 emissions, is that a significant amount of primary energy is saved.

The waste heat from power generation is used directly at the place of its generation. The efficiency of power generation, depending on the system size, is between 25-50 %.

The primary energy is used from 80 % to over 90 % thanks to the local use of waste heat. Consequently, CHP can save up to 40 % of primary energy.

Combined heat and power systems are an efficient use when there is a uniform and simultaneous demand for electricity and heating/cooling throughout the year. Combined heat and power plants are usually used as a base load in addition to the hot water demand or in combination with absorption chillers for cooling requirements.

Plants with combined heat and power should be used more than 5,000 hours per year in order to operate economically.

The heat energy generated by CHP can almost cover the basic heat energy requirements. When the generated heat energy is not required it can be stored to compensate future peak loads, or covered by an additional system.

In combined heat and power plants, the power is generated from the steam turbine process and fed into a district heating network.

Heat is operated preferably at the location of the heat consumption, but also useful heat can be fed into a district heating network.

Cogeneration heat and power plants work with a gasoline or diesel engine which drives a generator. Fuel cell systems for heating and power generation operate with hydrogen. Due to the use of solar-produced hydrogen, they provide future solutions for decentralised and non-fossil heating.

"The benefits of CHP

- efficiency benefits

CHP requires less fuel to produce a given energy output, and avoids transmission and distribution losses that occur when electricity travels over power lines.

[63-64] *EPA – U.S. Environmental Protection Agency;* Combined Heat and Power Partnership: Basic Information [http://www.epa.gov/chp/basic/index.html] (22.11.2012)

329 Concept of Micro CHP
330 Gas turbine or engine with heat recovery unit

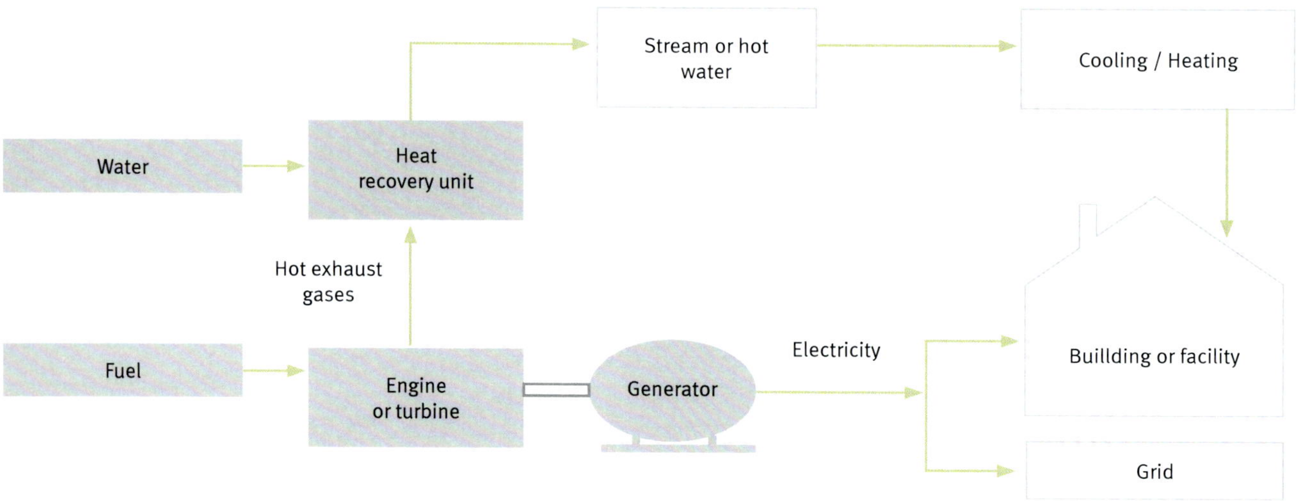

330

- reliability benefits

CHP can be designed to provide high-quality electricity and thermal energy to a site regardless of what might occur on the power grid, decreasing the impact of outages and improving power quality for sensitive equipment.

- environmental benefits

Because less fuel is burned to produce each unit of energy output, CHP reduces air pollution and greenhouse gas emissions.

- economic benefits

CHP can save facilities considerable money on their energy bills due to its high efficiency and can provide a hedge against unstable energy costs." [63]

Two most common CHP system configurations:

- "gas turbine or engine with heat recovery unit
- steam boiler with steam turbine

Gas turbine or engine with heat recovery unit

Gas turbine or reciprocating engine CHP systems generate electricity by burning fuel (natural gas or biogas) to generate electricity. They then use a heat recovery unit to capture heat from the combustion system's exhaust stream. This heat is converted into useful thermal energy, usually in the form of steam or hot water. Gas turbines/engines are ideally suited for large industrial or commercial CHP applications requiring ample amounts of electricity and heat.

Steam boiler with steam turbine

Steam turbines normally generate electricity as a by-product of heat (steam) generation, unlike gas turbines and reciprocating engine CHP systems, where heat is a by-product of power generation.

Steam turbine-based CHP systems are typically used in industrial processes where solid fuels (biomass or coal), or waste products are readily available to fuel the boiler unit.

Biomass CHP

CHP can be powered by biomass (plant material, vegetation, or agricultural waste) or biogas (methane produced by the aerobic or anaerobic digestion of biomass).

In the current environment of high fossil fuel costs, using an opportunity fuel such as agricultural residuals or tree trimmings might provide the best economics for a project, as well as allow the project to qualify for additional incentives due to the renewable and clean attributes of the fuel." [64]

The CHP modules have an electrical service between five kW and five MW. Under 50 kW is also called **mini-CHP**, under 15 kW **micro-CHP**. Mini- and micro-CHP can be used in single and multi-family homes, on farms and in settlements.

The combined heat and power is also used in thermal power plants, typically with electrical outputs of several hundred MW.

331 Steam boiler with steam turbine

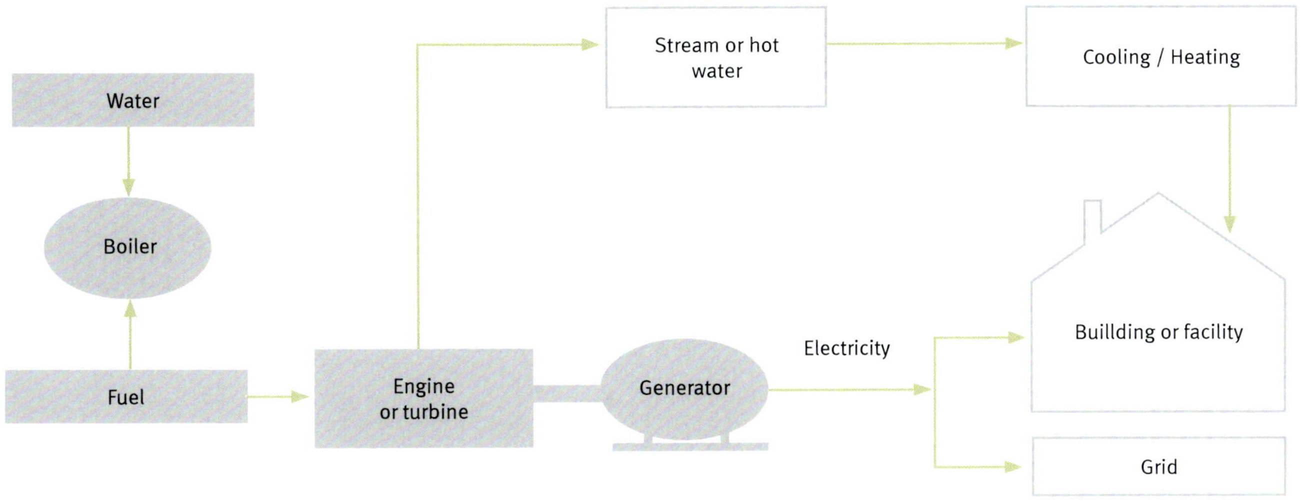

331

5.3 Alternative energy fuels

Examples of alternative fossil energy fuels for active building systems are waste, biomass and biogas. Such alternatives are unlimited but are normally treated as a waste resource. The burning of alternative fossil fuels can achieve higher temperatures, which are not possible from renewable energies such as the sun, water and wind.

However, we must carefully use such alternative systems as a material to generate energy. Covering large areas of fields with plants for energy generation takes away valuable earth surface normally used for food production.

Biomass

Biomass is a renewable energy source that can grow over a relatively short time period. The use of biomass as an energy source reduces many kinds of air pollution and carbon emissions. Biomass can be grown and harvested in ways that protect soil quality, avoid erosion, and maintain wildlife habitat.

Biomass can be a good solution to reduce the need of imported fossil fuels from other states. It can be grown everywhere, resulting in eliminated costs and offering economic benefits.

"With increasing biomass development, farmers and forest owners gain valuable new markets for their crop residues, new energy crops and forest residues." [65]

Basic biomass categories

- "virgin wood – from forestry, arboricultural activities or from wood processing
- energy crops – high yield crops grown specifically for energy applications
- agricultural residues – from agriculture harvesting or processing
- food waste – from food and drink manufacturing, preparation and processing, post-consumer waste
- industrial waste and co-products from manufacturing and industrial processes" [66]

Converting biomass to biopower

- direct combustion

Biomass is converted into electricity by burning to produce steam, which turns a turbine that produces electricity. During this process, much energy is wasted, causing some pollution.

- co-firing

Biomass is mixed together with coal and burnt at a power plant designed for coal. This solution has lower operating costs and lower CO_2 emissions.

- repowering

"Coal plants can also be converted to run entirely on biomass.

- combined heat and power (CHP)

Direct combustion of biomass produces heat that can also be used to heat buildings or for industrial processes. (...) Because they use heat energy that would otherwise be wasted, CHP facilities can be significantly more efficient than direct combustion systems." [67]

- biomass gasification

Syngas is a mixture of hydrogen and carbon monoxide which is converted from biomass. The syngas can be used to produce electricity or further processed to make liquid biofuels and other useful chemicals.

- anaerobic digestion

Biomass is used to produce biogas which can be burned for heat and power.

332 Comparison of a one-way process of increasing CO_2 in the atmosphere from fossils fuels to burning wood and other biomass that also release CO_2 which can stay in life cycle

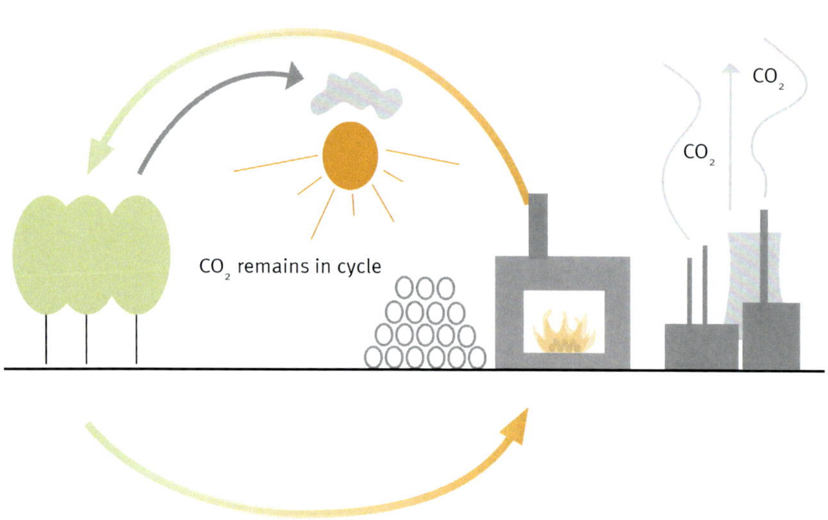

332

[65,67] *Union of Concerned Scientists USA;* How Biomass Energy Works [http://www.ucsusa.org/clean_energy/our-energy-choices/renewable-energy/how-biomass-energy-works.html] (22.11.2012)

[66] *Biomassenergycentre.org.uk;* Biomass Energy [http://www.biomassenergycentre.org.uk/portal/page?_pageid=76,15049&_dad=portal] (22.11.2012)

Biogas

Biogas is a renewable energy carrier with a chemical composition of which methane is its main component. Biogas originates from biogenic material and is a type of bio fuel. It is produced by the microbial degradation of organic matter (biomass), which commonly used forms are agricultural substrates such as manure and energy crops (corn, rye, sugar beets, etc.), but also organic waste, e.g. grass clippings, food waste and by-products of food production.
The information contained in this organic matter based energy (bio-chemical binding energy) is dependant on the ability of plants to convert incident light energy from the sun into bio-chemical energy (photosynthesis). Biogas technology is therefore an indirect use of solar energy that is represented in biogas plants (also called fermentation plants). This energy is used for controlling the absence of air (anaerobic) to generate electricity.
In hermetically sealed vats – called fermenters – biogas is produced by the use of bacteria fermentation. The bacteria are similar to those found in the digestive tract of a cow.
Biogas can be used as a fuel in any country, for any heating purpose. It can also be used in anaerobic digesters where it is typically used in a gas engine to convert energy within the gas into electricity and heat. Biogas can be compressed, much like natural gas, used to power motor vehicles.

Biogas plant

"In biogas plant, biomass is converted to electricity, heat and fertilizer. For this, the biomass (mainly liquid manure and plant components, in some case also conferments – waste products of the food industry) are crushed and homogenised in a pre-treatment tank. Disinfection through heating to 70 °C is sometimes required. In the fermenter (fermentation tank, reactor), the biomass is converted through bacterial processes into biogas and fouled substrate.

The biogas is conveyed from the fermenter via gas pipes to a gas treatment system and the combined heat and power unit. The CHP burns the gas and generates electricity and heat. The electricity is usually fed into the public electricity network, while the heat is used as local heat for heating adjoining buildings. In pilot plants, biogas that has already been purified is fed into the public natural gas network or is compressed to be used as vehicle fuel.

A wide variety of technically possible solutions are available for adapting a plant to the general conditions in the individual case (e.g. type and amount of the substrates, energy utilisation concepts)." [68]

[68] *HDI-Gerling Sicherheitstechnik GmbH*; Risk Engineering Guideline. Biogas Plants. Hazards and safety measures for generation and utilisation of biogas. Hannover: HDI-Gerling Sicherheitstechnik GmbH 2009, page 2

333 The first sea grass facade which can produce biomass and heat energy, Smart Material House in IBA 2013 (International Building Exhibition) in Hamburg-Wilhelmsburg, Splitterwerk Architekten (Graz), Arup GmbH (Berlin), Ingenieure B+G (Frankfurt) and Immosolar GmbH (Hamburg)
334 Detail of the sea grass facade element, Smart Material House in IBA 2013 (International Building Exhibition) in Hamburg-Wilhelmsburg, Splitterwerk Architekten (Graz), Arup GmbH (Berlin), Ingenieure B+G (Frankfurt) and Immosolar GmbH (Hamburg)

333

334

5.4 Energy storing

335

336

Power-to-Gas is a long-term storage system where surplus power from renewable energies uses chemical reactions to be transformed into fuel gas.

335 Batteries to store power generated by photovoltaics system
336 Electric bicycles can be loaded by power during parking
337 Solar, in combination with buffer storage for heating support and warm water generation, can heat the warm water to a certain temperature, however additional systems are required to help warm the water to 60 °C
338 Schematic for the long-term thermal storage in Hannover-Kronsberg

The decentralized storing of energy is always important to consider when creating an energy concept. Despite other methods on how to use renewable energy sources, the highest yields can be expected by using a decentralized system.

To store excess solar energy during the year, four methods of memory technology can be used:

- chemical storage

stores thermal or electrical energy by chemical reactions, e.g. with the help of water and methane.

- mechanical storage

works with the aid of a mechanical process, e.g. compressed air storage, pumped power plant storage, flywheels.

- electrical storage (e.g. condensers, magnetic storage, batteries)
- thermal storage (e.g. water, fat, ice, salt storage)

Through the use of chemical, mechanical, electrical and thermal storage technologies, it is possible to increase the proportions covered by renewable energies. Building-integrated air buffer zones can also be an effective method to save energy and reduce fossil fuels.

Methods for energy saving does not only refer to how the energy is stored and the technologies used but also the various storage periods. The storage periods can range from a few hours to several months:

Week thermal storage

The core of this technology is the buffer memory which, when correctly dimensioned, is able to store the energy obtained by the solar panels for a lengthened period. In combination with an additional electrical heater for higher temperatures, an efficient resource-saving heat support and warm water supply is possible. For the efficient use of this technology, a collector area of approximately 7 m² per dwelling unit and a storage volume of approximately 240 l/m² are necessary.

Monthly thermal storage

Longer-term storage of energy over a several month period (seasonal storage) is in principle no different to short-term storage of energy. The only difference is the area required to collect energy and the size of the storage volume.

Innovative seasonal storage – an example of ice storage technology

An interesting and effective example of seasonal storage technology is the ice storage system, which enables the storage of recovered energy with high efficiency, and delivers that energy when it is most needed. By using ice storage technology several "natural forces" are harnessed simultane-

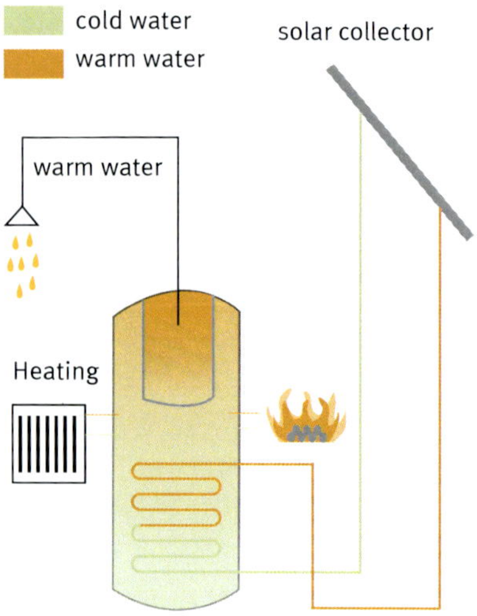

337

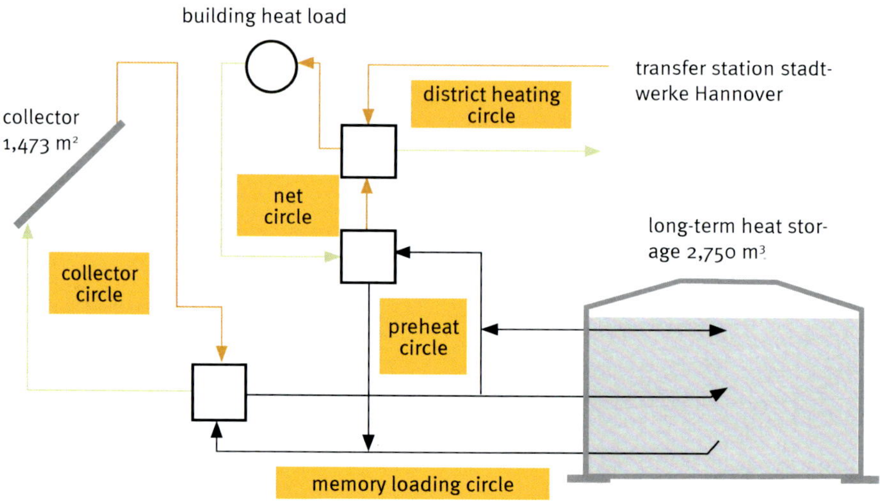

338

ously: the sun, air, earth, water and ice. The central element is the ice storage. It is an insulated tank that is inserted into the ground at a depth of approximately 4 m. The capacity ranges from approximately 10 m³ for a single family home up to thousands for a commercial building.

The principle is simple: When water freezes into ice, the molecules are no longer able to move freely and the so-called crystallization heat takes place which essentially heats the hot water in the building with the help of a heat pump, providing the building with heat and hot water.

The principle of ice storage technology can be applied for heating during the winter period and also cooling during the summer season.
In this case the winter ice is removed from the energy storage and fed back using a heat exchanger from the heat pump to act as a heating/refrigerant circuit. This technology can be extremely effective when used during winter and summer.

For example, a family house with 120 m² requires approximately 10 m³ of ice storage. Half of the cost to heat will in turn save 99 % of the cost for summer cooling. The initial investment cost for an ice storage required for the 120 m² house is approximately 10,000 to 15,000 euros.
The fat storage system works similar to that of ice storage.

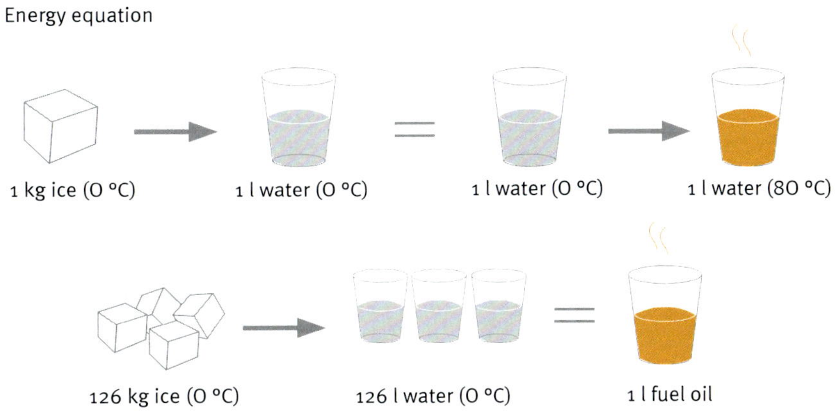

339

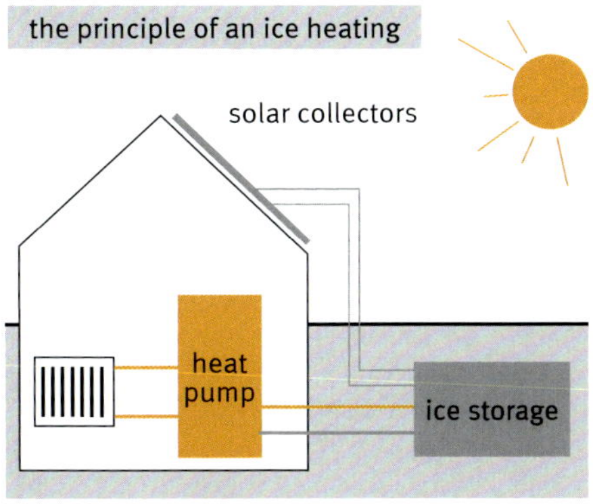

340

339 The energy efficiency of ice storage technology – the melting of 1 kg of ice uses approximately the same amount of energy as if you were to heat 1 l of water to 80 °C
340 The principle of an ice storage heating
341 Working principle of an ice storage system depending on the season and time of day/night

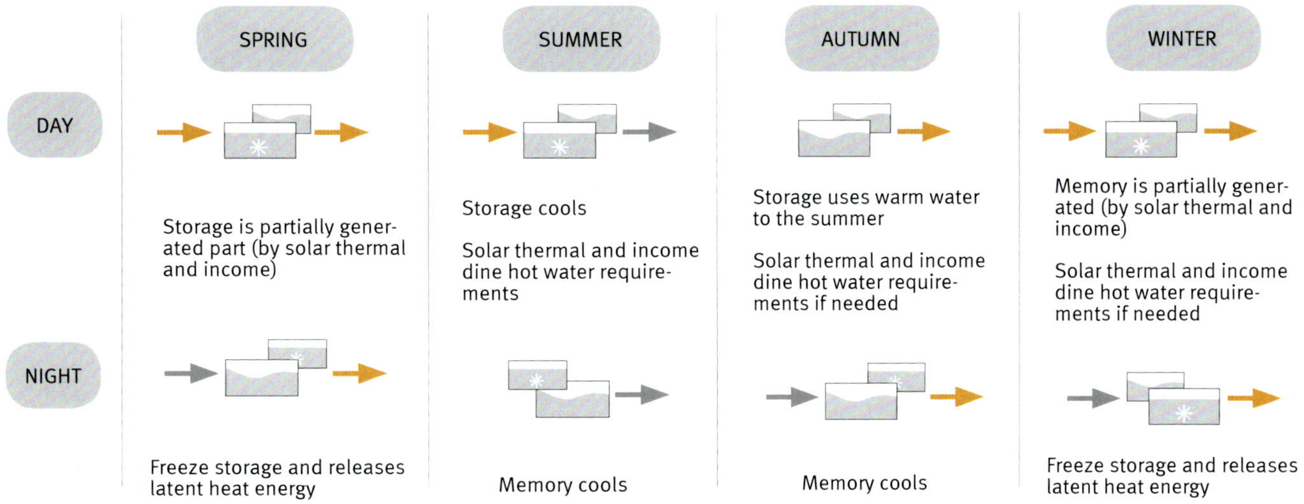

341

5.5 Summary

As described in the previous chapter, passive energy-saving concepts should be the first option when designing. Active systems are also useful as they can offer alternative solutions for conventional systems. They are often combined with other systems, including passive systems, e.g. to cover the peak loads of the energy demand for power and heat.
The transition between systems is clear however an understanding of the classifications is often very difficult. These systems in their individual components are composed and developed after an intensive analyse of their demands.

Individual concepts for different situations are required, which are conceived and optimised through a selection process in relation to its special demands.
The efficiency of the systems has a high transferring loss compared to what is required. Research by the government and various institutes and organisations investigate how these systems can be further developed.

There is a lot of research conducted in the different active technology fields to help increase efficiency. E.g., research concerning how to achieve a higher photovoltaic efficiency with new types of photovoltaics being developed, e.g. double skin photovoltaic modules by Solar-Fabrik, that could achieve 25 % higher efficiency.

Example: Dealing with heritage protected warehouses in the old harbour of Wismar in Green building course

The use of only active energy-saving concepts is not the best solution when approaching the re-designing of the building. Different possibilities must be analysed and proven in order to find the best solution. Energy-saving concepts along with resource-saving concepts must be considered.

In the Green Building course, different possibilities of handling an existing building was analysed by the students. The existing building is the heritage-protected warehouse "Kruse Speicher" in the old harbour of Wismar.

Four main concepts developed by students:

- building conversion following the heritage protection law and EnEV 2014

The first group of students kept the building's heritage facade untouched by using internal thermal insulation, heat recovery ventilation and CHP for heat and power generation. This achieved the EnEV 2014 standard.

- the energy renovation of the building with the focus on passive principals (reducing heat loss)

The second group of students chose to re-function the building with a hotel,

342 The first student´s group design – building conversion following the heritage protection law and EnEV 2014
343 The second student´s group design – the energy renovation of the building with the focus on passive principals
344 The third student´s group design – energy renovation of the building with the focus on active principals
345 The fourth student´s group design – replacing with a new construction in passive house standard

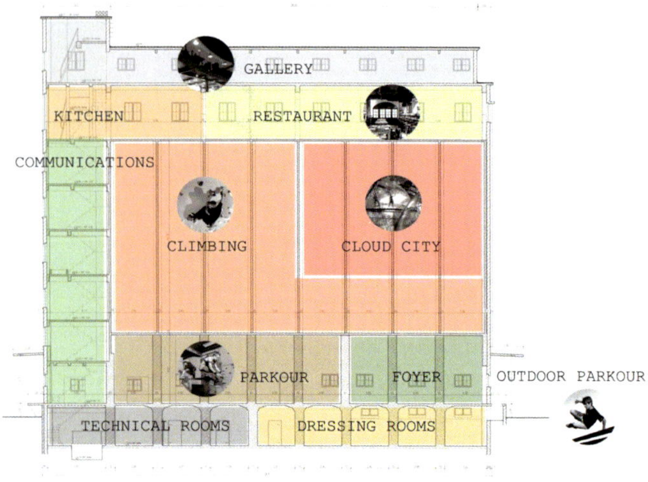

342

bars and restaurants on the roof. To achieve this, the large indoor storage spaces were divided by adding ceilings. The passive concept used a courtyard space to gain natural light and as a buffer zone for the preheating and cooling of air. The additional glass facades were added to the southern facade to act as a Trombe wall.

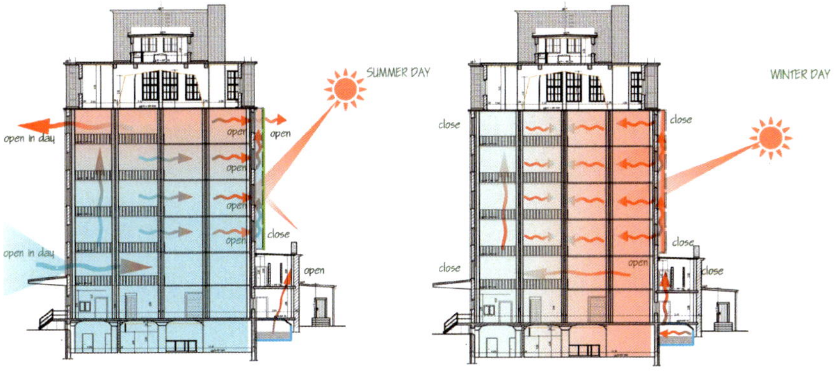

343

- energy renovation of the building with the focus on active principals

The third group of students focused on the active use of solar, hydro and wind energy by using technology such as solar thermal collectors, photovoltaic, water pumping power turbines, wind turbines and flywheels. For the thermal and electrical energy, the old storage tanks were re-functioned as a water pumping power plant, which was possible due to the original tanks being used to store corn, which has a similar density to that of water. The systems integrated into the building would be able to generate a total of 367 MWh/a of power.

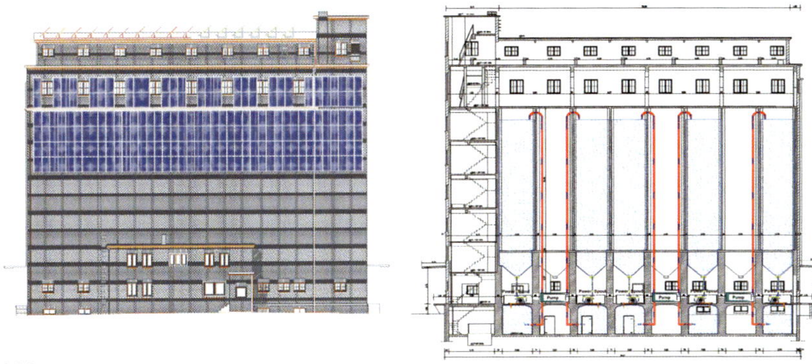
344

- replacing with a new construction in passive house standard

The fourth group of students focused on achieving a very low energy demand according to the passive energy standard. Because it was not possible to achieve this by renovating the building, students decided to destroy the building. The new building should be entirely built out of wood and serve as an exhibition space for the wooden building industry and also have a coffee shop. The building should be heated and cooled by the surrounding sea water with the help of a brine operated water source heat exchanger and heat recovery system.

345

346 The utilization of old building parts and elements within the design of the kindergarten "Kunterbunt", Sassnitz, IGEL-Institut

Life time design

6.0 Active resource-saving concepts (hard-tech)

6.1 Introduction

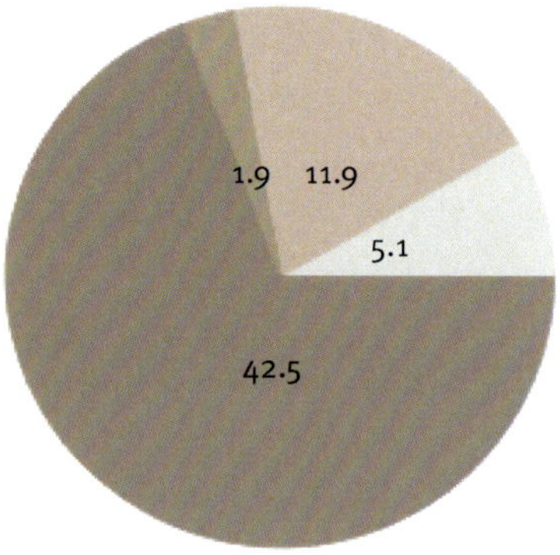

- other use
- earth works
- concrete surcharge
- road construction

347

347 Use of recycled building materials, Germany 2000, total 61.4 Mio. t
348 Testing of exterior wall from recycled materials, designed and built by students of Hochschule Wismar
349 Cover of the book Cradle to Cradle
350 Recycling processes before and after the useful phase of the material

The fifth life step of the building considers what happens after the end of the building's life, including the waste materials generated from building demolition – if the building elements and materials used in the building should be reused, recycled or disposed.

In the case of building demolition, the ideal situation would be if the building could be removed from site without leaving a trace. In addition, the connections between the building elements as well as the connections to the ground are designed so that they can be easily disassembled and separated from each other.

In this way, the landscape after building demolition remains untouched and the easily separable building elements can be recycled. All materials can be reused without the need to load landfills with new waste.

Untouched landscape with zero waste production is the goal of resource-saving concepts. Such concepts reduce raw material consumption, waste generation, energy use, air and water pollution, and also the costs.

In the chapter, '3.0 Passive resource-saving concepts', the reuse of the whole building (restoration, renovation, conversion) or building elements were discussed.

This topic is used for passive concepts, due to their relatively low energy input required to adapt to their new function.
Passive and active concepts are closely connected and are sometimes not easy to distinguish.

Material recycling (mainly down-cycling) belongs to "Active resource-saving concepts", because relatively high amounts of energy and technology are needed for the re-production of new products from the old materials (e.g. breaking concrete parts to granulates for the production of new concrete parts). Recycling refers to the utilization of waste.

The ecological effectiveness of recycling also demands input energy. E.g., there is a lot of energy required to recycle concrete to become new structural material and therefore it may be more environmentally friendly to use clay bricks, which can easily decompose.It is important to define different types of recycling:

Down-cycling is the process, in which waste materials are converted into new materials with lower quality and reduced functionality. E.g., down-cycling includes plastic recycling where the recycled plastics have a lower quality grade. However, most recycling can be considered down-cycling.

348

The down-cycling of some materials requires almost the same or a greater amount of energy than what is required to produce the material. It should be considered whether or not the recycling in such cases is efficient and sustainable.

Up-cycling is the process of which a higher quality of the old products is obtained. This is the opposite of down-cycling. The up-cycled products provide the environment with better aesthetic or functional quality. For example, old products can be used to create pieces of art.

The main goals concerning the treatment of resources should always be:

- resource-saving
- waste avoidance
- waste as a valuable material

Other methods of waste treatment can also be thermal recovery which is discussed in the chapter '5.0 Active energy-saving concepts' and in chapter '5.3 Alternative energy fuels'.

This considers the use of waste materials for generating thermal or electrical energy.

Sustainable water concepts

While material handling discussed above is important, the sustainable association with water should also be an important part of the passive building concepts.

Water is a vital resource required for all living organisms. Only 3 % of the earth's water is fresh water however most of this is frozen in glaciers and polar ice caps. In reality, only 0.3 % of all fresh water is available to use.

In many countries freshwater is highly scarce and it is astonishing to know that developed countries with general high standards of living, consume high levels of fresh water while also polluting water resources.

The actual handling of fresh water and waste water results in the overuse of natural water resources.

It is therefore important to develop new sustainable concepts for handling water that are incorporated into the urban and architectural planning.

349

In the book **"Cradle to Cradle: Remaking the Way We Make Things"**, William McDonough and Michael Braungart discuss the different terms of recycling.
The book shows how it is possible to achieve "Cradle to cradle" design by switching from cradle to grave industry patterns.
It classifies two ways of how to use products after they have reached the end of their useful life - they become either "biological nutrients" or "technical nutrients".
"Biological nutrients" can be returned back into the environment. "Technical nutrients" remain within the closed industrial cycle and are reused or recycled.

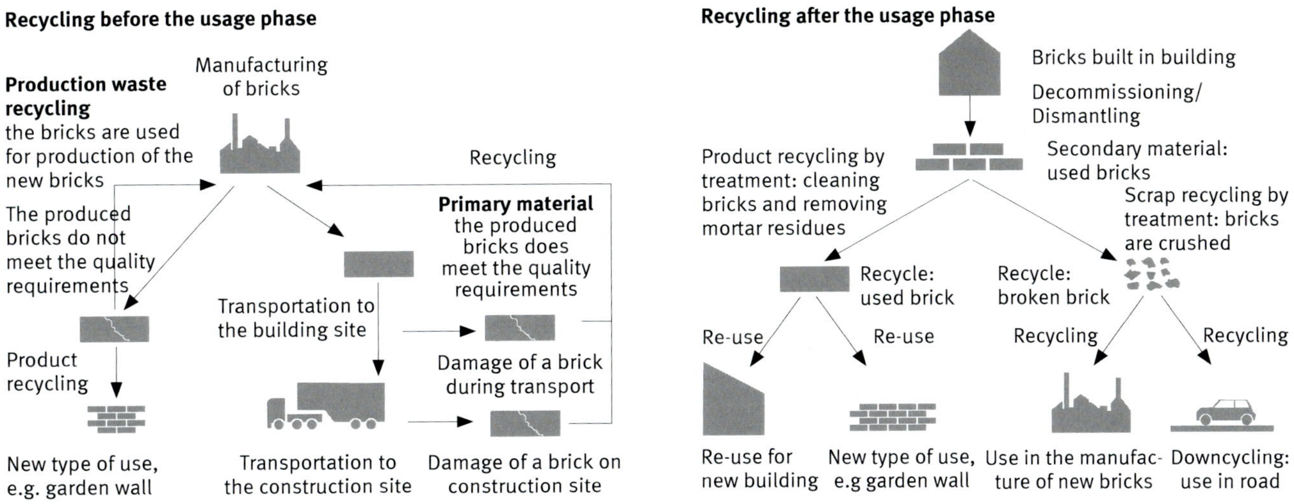

350

6.2 Recycling of building materials

351

6.2 Recycling of building materials
6.2.1 Brick/stone/clay recycling

The reuse of old bricks from demolished buildings has already been discussed in the chapter '3.0 Passive resource-saving concepts' under the subtitle "Component reuse".

The simplest form of brick recycling is when bricks, taken from old buildings, are cleaned of old mortar and other contaminations and reused again to build another building.

When brick walls are mechanically demolished, the brick can instead be re-used as a natural bulk or sub-base material for roads or landscaping, or as a raw material for the construction of noise barriers.

Demolished bricks can also be used as an aggregate for mortar and plaster, with broken brick currently being the only recycled material from masonry building materials that is a lightweight aggregate for concrete.

It can be used, for example as a lightweight aggregate for concrete blocks of ceramic chimneys.

Brick sand and broken pieces can also be used as landscape substrates or as a drainage layer on a multi-layer green roof.

Natural stone can be recycled in a similar way. The stones can be reused as a whole component (e.g. for landscape architecture) or crushed and used as a substrate similar to that of bricks.

The energy input required for brick and stone recycling depends on the method of recycling.

For example to crush the material, special crushing machines are required.

Clay is another material which can be easily recycled – clay bricks can be reused as a substance for new constructions.

The clay can be easily brought back to nature after its end of life span or crushed to be used as a substance for creating new clay building bricks, plaster or rammed-earth construction. Special heavy machinery is not required to crush clay walls as it can be easily deconstructed and reused again, for the construction of a new house, oven or for other building parts.

351 Recycling from history - white limestone slabs originally cladded the Chefren pyramid approximately 4550 years ago and were reused in medieval times to build houses around Cairo, parts of the limestone slabs remained only on the top of Chefren pyramide
352 Ningbo Historic Museum in China was built from salvaged stone and roof tiles from building debris, designed by Wang Shu, Amateur Architecture Studio, who were awarded the Pritzker Architecture Prize in 2012

352

6.2.2 Wood recycling

Since 2005, waste materials that consist of more than 5 % organic material, can not be disposed of in landfills. This also refers to wood and wood products.

There are several different methods to recycle wood. Old wood can be made into chips to make pellets for heating or used as raw material for the making of chipboard. There are already many companies that deal with wood recycling.

An example is the company Pfleiderer AG, who have developed a process in which wood is recycled and reused in production without any energy losses.

The research project is called "Integrated environmental protection in the timber industry" and it is funded by the Federal Ministry for Education and Research (BMBF).

Pfleiderer Rheda (North Rhine-Westphalia), also created a chipboard recycling plant that uses a process patented by the company. The process enables a continuous thermo-hydrolytic cleavage in a closed system. The chip material is supplied directly to the particleboard machine, manufactured locally without any energy losses. This method is possible in any particleboard plant.

By using the thermo-hydrolysis method, all resin based particleboards – over 90 % – are recycled. First, they are pre-crushed into fragments of a few centimetres in size. Magnets and search coils then remove impurities.

The thermo-hydrolytic cleavage process then follows in a closed system under a water vapour atmosphere, at temperatures of 120 °C to 180 °C. Under these conditions, the resin splits into its components, so that the cohesion dissolves in the plate and the chips separate.

As part of the funding priority "Integrated environmental protection in the field of wood industry", the BMBF supports research in the areas of timber product manufacturing, timber, sawmills, wood remuneration and adhesive technology.

The environmentally friendly applications of the renewable resource wood, should be demonstrated and used.

To find out more about this and other projects within the funding program, visit the website www.holz-and-umwelt.de.

The website was created and is maintained within the framework of project-related knowledge and technology transfer by the German Society for Wood Research.

353

353 Construction of the building for the Fachagentur Nachwachsende Rohstoffe (FNR) e.V. (Foundation of Renewable Resources), Gülzow, designed by Matrix Architects, the structural facade is covered with reused oak wood
354 Fachagentur Nachwachsende Rohstoffe (FNR) e.V. (Foundation of Renewable Resources), Gülzow, Matrix Architects

354

6.2 Recycling of materials

355

Another example of paper recycling is the system of cellulose thermal insulation, which consists of cellulose fibres from the recycling of old newspapers. It is available in the form of sheets or as a loose fibre. In cellulose insulation boards, the fibres are pressed with water vapour to form the sheets. Loose cellulose fibres are easily dried following the conclusion of the pulping process and blown into the roof/wall construction, at the building site.

355 Cellulose fibre thermal insulation blown into the wall
356 Recycled paper products that can be used in architecture – paper boards

6.2.3 Paper recycling

Recycled paper tubes and cores can have many advantages when used as architectural materials:

- paper is durable

Paper tubes made as industrial products and from recycled paper have high stable qualities and are extremely durable.

- paper is light

Paper tubes used as structural materials are much lighter than wood, let alone steel or concrete. Lightweight structures for ease of handling and transportation can be achieved.

- paper can return to nature

Paper tubes are easily manufactured and recyclable.

- paper is beautiful

Paper tubes are simple, powerful and beautiful. They have a soft, gentle texture which is different from that of steel or concrete. Paper tubes can create a rhythmic visual feeling.

- easy-made paper construction

Paper tubes can be joined by simple metal joints, welded at two angle joints.

Examples from history

The first use of the paper tube was seen in an installation project at an exhibition of Alvar Aalto's work in 1986. An involved Japanese architect, named Shigeru Ban, was unable to use the favourite wood material of Aalto due to limited resources, so he used the paper tube as an alternative. From this experience, he was surprised to discover that the strength of the paper tube was much better than he had imagined. The material explorations in this design exhibit mark the beginning of "paper architecture".
He later designed several paper tube constructions, e.g.:

- Paper arbor, Nagoya, Japan 1989

consists of 48 tubes, which were treated with paraffin water-proofing and fitted onto a concrete base

- Paper house, Yamanashi, Japan, 1995

consists of 110 paper tubes – it was the first project in which paper tubes were authorised for use as the structural basis in a permanent building

- Japan pavilion, EXPO, Hannover, 2000

suited the main theme of the Hannover Expo (environment), as a structure that produced as little industrial waste as possible when dismantled (it was possible to recycle or reuse almost all of the building materials)

- Paper theatre, Amsterdam/Utrecht, Holland, 2003
- Paper bridge, Remoulin, France, 2007

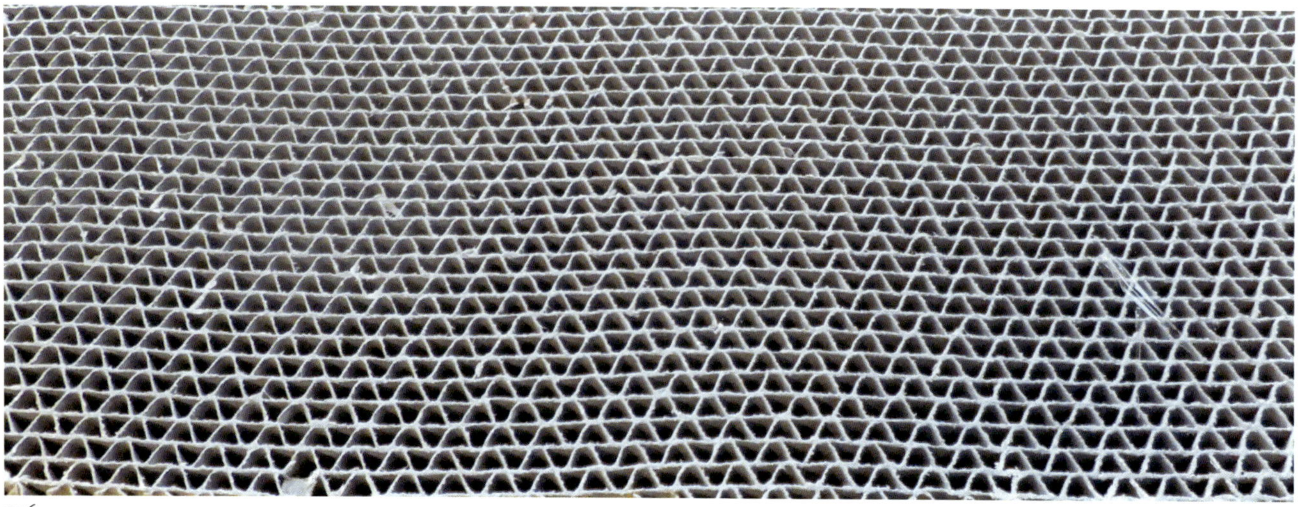

356

6.2.4 Glass recycling

Glass is widely used in architecture. It is a transparent material that enables internal light penetration and therefore an important material for natural daylighting.

It is commonly used for windows but can also be used for flooring, glass curtains, and kitchen plates or in other parts of the building. It is an amorphous solid material, which consists of inorganic elements.

Glass is a large part of waste, usually in the form of old bottles, broken glassware and other items. Glass is very easy to recycle, as recycling uses less energy than the initial manufacturing from sand, lime and soda.

Recycled glass has a wide range of uses. In the building industry, glass can be used as aggregate in concrete, giving it a greater long term strength and better thermal insulation.

Recycled glass can be used in insulation products, in ceramic sanitary ware production, as a flux agent in brick manufacturing, in astroturf and related applications (e.g. top dressing, root zone), material or golf bunker sand, in recycled glass countertops, as water filtration media, as an abrasive, as an aggregate and many more. It can substitute pea gravel or crushed rock for pipe bedding placed around sewers, storm water or drinking water pipes to transfer weight from the surface and to protect the pipes.

Not all forms of glass are easy to recycle. For example, window glass is very complex, having highly complicated parts and high-tech material.

The window glass that can be recycled can be coated (depending on its original use), printed, enamelled, filled with gases, colored etc. The purification of the glass is a complicated process and is not economically viable.

The recycling of window glass is similar to the recycling of glass bottles; they are ground and melted, however the material cannot be reused as glass for windows.

Foam glass

Foam glass is an example of a construction material that is made from recycled glass and which has high heat insulation properties. Foam glass has high compressive strength, it is vapour tight even in extreme conditions and it is a good thermal insulation material.

Foam glass is waterproof and pressure resistant. It is an environmental material that is lightweight, fire resistant and rot resistant. It is a good material for heat insulation in the foundation of a building, but it can also be used in roofs, terraces, exterior walls and interior walls.

357

357 Foam glass gravel made out of recycled glass
358 Glass bottle house in Calico Ghost Town California, USA

358

6.2 Recycling of materials

6.2.5 Concrete recycling

Concrete is a mineral building material and creates most of the construction waste. During the demolition of a building, concrete recycling is a good way to save energy and costs.

Instead of transporting the concrete to the landfill for disposal, recycling has many advantages. Recycling concrete saves high levels of energy and natural resources compared to mining, processing and transporting new aggregates.

By not land-filling, one will save landfill space. Using recycled material as gravel reduces the need for gravel mining. Recycled concrete aggregate is good quality and is actually lighter in weight comparable to a pure solid concrete product.

The production costs for recycled concrete is generally more or less even in comparison to normal concrete. One factor is the reduction of transportation and freight charges.

Recycled building materials from the processing of mineral waste are primarily used for technical buildings, such as in earth and road works.

After demolition, concrete parts can be reused as structural elements for other buildings or, for example as anti-erosion or supporting walls.

Concrete can be broken, crushed and have the steel removed by magnets to be used as new aggregate for other products. There are portable crushers that enable crushing on site, which reduces costs and pollution made during transportation.

It is important for quality-assurance when dealing with the quantity of mineral recycled building materials. The objective of the treatment of construction waste is to achieve a quality standard for primary raw materials.

The demolition process of concrete structures includes:

- mechanical processes (clearing, milling, grinding, tapping, cutting, sawing, drilling, pressing, hammering, turning, pushing, tearing)
- hydrodynamic processes (high-pressure water jets)
- thermatic processes
- chemical processes (blasting)

During the selective demolition process, all techniques can be applied. The goal is to separate the different types of pollutants and pure building materials.

359 Headquarters of the German Federal Trust Fund Environment (DBU) in Osnabrück, designed by architect Prof. Erich Schneider-Wessling, the internal building elements are built from recycled concrete
360 Quality assurance for the production and processing of recycled concrete (quality chain)
361 Energy input required for different types of concrete from demolition to construction processes
362 Concrete in combination with other building materials – when the cement screed is placed directly on a concrete ceiling, it is difficult to separate and therefore has to be crushed together – an insulating layer in between makes the selective dismantling of the material possible

359

Recycled concrete applications

"In general, applications without any processing include:

- many types of general bulk fills
- bank protection
- base or fill for drainage structures
- road construction
- noise barriers and embankments

Most of the unprocessed crushed concrete aggregate is sold 37.5 mm or 50 mm fragments for pavement sub bases.

After removal of contaminants through selective demolition, screening, and/or air separation and size reduction in a crusher to aggregate sizes, crushed concrete can be used as:

- new concrete for pavements, shoulders, median barriers, sidewalks, curbs, gutters, and bridge foundations
- structural grade concrete
- soil-cement pavement bases
- lean-concrete or econo-crete bases
- bituminous concrete" [69]

Larger pieces of recycled concrete can be used as a substitute for landscaping stone or mulch. Wire gabions can also be filled with crushed concrete to create retaining walls which are extremely economical.

Demolition

Construction rubble

Preparation — Conformity proof

Testing and monitoring in accordance to DIN 12620, suplement ZA

Concrete sand

Recipe development — Conformity proof for concrete properties according to DIN 206-1 / DIN 1045-2

Mixing concrete — Testing and monitoring of concrete properties and of the concrete construction, monitoring class 2

Concrete for use in construction

360

[69] *Portlant Cement Association;* CCT aggregates recycled [http://www.cement.org/tech/cct_aggregates_recycled.asp] (20.06.2014)

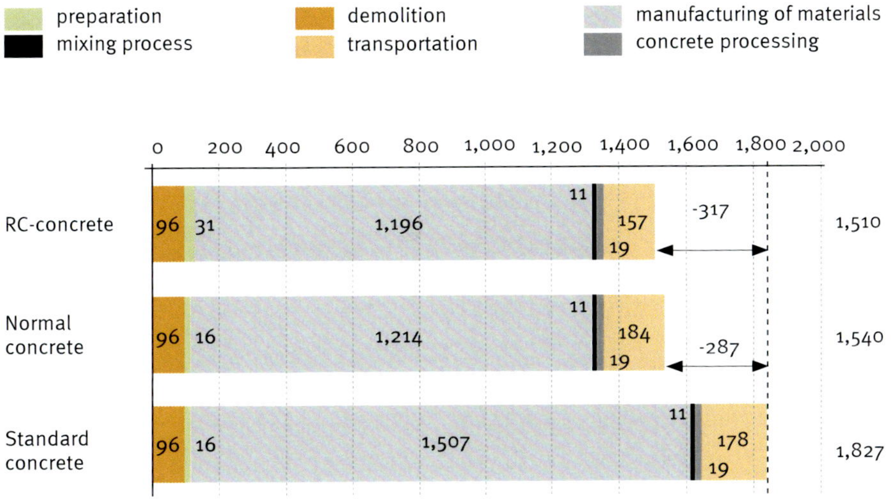

361

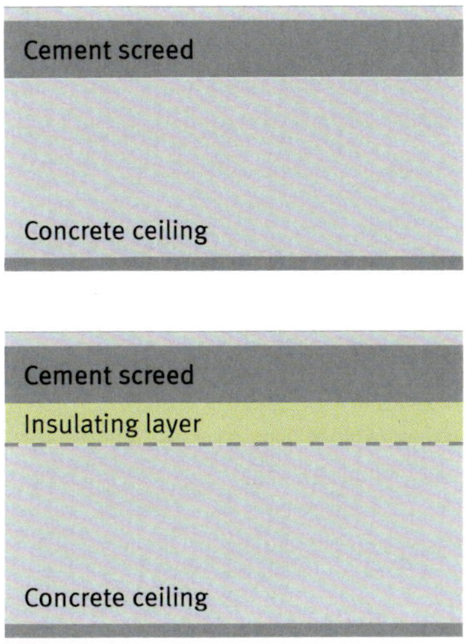

362

6.2 Recycling of materials

6.2.6 Metal recycling

The visible use of iron was initially only accepted for bridges, industry buildings and railway stations. Later, cast iron was used for its load efficiency and montage in buildings for the world exhibitions in London and Paris. Examples include the "Crystal Palace" in London designed by Joseph Paxton and Gustave Eiffels "Eiffel Tower" in Paris.

Iron's high load carrying properties allowed the construction of high rise buildings. Today, metal is used more commonly as a structural material for halls, high rise buildings or for reinforcement within concrete. It can also be used as wall cladding, roofs, gutters, pipes, tubing, fittings, fixing parts and for technical elements.

Metals have high density, strength, a high melting point and a good heat and electrical conductivity. They can be formed and can even be magnetic. Metals used for building (e.g. iron, aluminium, copper) are produced through a series of different processes and it is only the noble metals such as gold, silver and platinum that can be obtained directly from nature.

Metals can be melted down repeatedly without any loss in quality. This makes them ideal for recycling because they can be used again and again.

Recycling scrap metal reduces greenhouse gas emissions and uses less energy than making metal from natural ore. Metal recycling also conserves natural resources. For example, the primary energy used when recycling iron is only 20-40 % in comparison to new production. By recycling aluminium, around 75-90 % of primary energy use is saved and when recycling copper, 86 % of primary energy use is saved.

Recycling metal decreases environmental damages caused by mining resulting in less land wasting and less water pollution.

Metal recycling has become very developed. More frequently recycled materials are steel, iron, lead, aluminium, copper and zinc.

Some of the main recyclable products are cans, appliances, car parts, windows, doors made from aluminium, bridge parts, structural frames or appliances made of steel.

Metal is not limited to recycling. Where common methods are to melt the metal material and remould, alternatively it can be re-used in its entirety. As you can see in the examples provided below, elements salvaged from kitchen units, traffic signs, old phone boxes and entire shipping containers can be used to create interesting and dynamic facades and building constructions.

363 Art inside of German federal environment office in Dessau made out of recycling metal and other material

363

6.2.7 Plastic recycling

Plastic materials are used in our daily lives. They are used in the electronic industries, car industries, and also in the building industry. They are used in all areas of building including flooring, facade cladding, waterproofing, insulation and in installations.
Plastic material characteristics include low density, low thermal conductivity, high tensile strength, good electrical isolation and resistance against water, flammability and many chemicals.
Plastic recycling is the process of recovering waste plastic and reprocessing it into useful products. Sometimes this can be in a completely different form from its original state. Typically, plastic is recycled into another type of plastic and recycled plastic products are often non-recyclable.
There are four recycling possibilities:

- reuse

Here, the plastic parts are reused in whole, e.g parts in the car industry. In the building industry, PVC windows can be reused. There is also potential to reuse facade cladding and insulation.

- down-cycling

This is the mechanical deformation of used plastics into directly reusable regrinds or recyclates where the chemical structure remains unchanged. As a result, the quality of the recycled material decreases.

- feedstock recycling

This is the splitting of the polymer chains within plastic through warming and solvents. The results are petrochemical based materials such as oils and gasses which are used to produce new plastics or for other purposes.

- energy recycling

Old plastics have high heat values due to their high carbon content. Using them for energy gain instead of using fossil fuels is also a very ecological and economical solution.

Different plastic recycled products find different fields of use. For example, recycled PET can be used to create strong and durable fabrics for the clothing industry (e.g jackets, coats, shoes, bags, hats and accessories). They can also be used to produce new containers, strapping tape or even building materials.

Recycled high-density polyethylene can be downcycled into plastic lumber, tables, roadside curbs, benches, truck cargo liners, trash bins and stationery (e.g. rulers).
Recycled and expanded polystyrene can be added to EPS insulation sheets and other EPS materials for construction applications.

It can also be used in clothes hangers, park benches, flower pots, toys, stapler bodies, containers, picture frames, ...

In the early 1990's there was an annual collection systems established for PVC building products. The collected waste is processed by various organisations, e.g.:

- Plastic Pipes – Plastic Pipe Association with a nationwide collection system
- PVC flooring – AG Flooring Recycling (AgPR)
- PVC roofing membranes – AG PVC roofing membrane recycling Ltd.
- PVC plastic window – Rewindo GmbH

364 Wood Plastic Composite (WPC) are tiles made from recycled plastic and wood fibres and can be used as external floor tiles

364

6.2 Recycling of materials

365

6.2.8 Rubber recycling

"The tire-house can be a very practical method of building a bermed, passive-solar residence, using mostly renewable and free building materials that draw little from the Earth's energy resources (that haven't already been drawn). They are easy and pleasant to live in, though quite a bit different than stick-framed houses. They are also low maintenance and cost effective to construct. Due to their continuous invisible carbon footprint, they give back to the Earth in a much larger sense, for the life of the home.
As the construction method itself provides thermal storage (thick, heavy walls), no thermal mass needs to be imported into the structure to store the heat gained by the solar array of south-facing windows, as is necessary in stick-framed passive solar homes. This inherent thermal mass storage and the almost continuous addition of vast amounts of heat via the solar windows, keeps the inside temperature relatively consistent within "normal" living temperatures, once the thermal mass of the house "charges" with heat. (...)

As a result of the large amount of thermal mass in the house, the ambient temperature doesn't fluctuate as it would in a stick-framed home with no heat. Even with the wood-stove going, the inside temperature doesn't go up but one or two degrees because of the large amount of "stabilized" mass. The thermal mass of the home literally pulls heat out of the air. Then when the air temperature of the room goes below the temperature of the walls, the heat comes out of the walls to keep the room relatively warm and stable.
Peripheral drains, insulation and plastic film vapour barrier are placed in the earth berms that are built-up to the tire walls, in a configuration that amplifies the capture of thermal mass storage, prevents heat loss/gain and allows normal drainage to avoid the home's interior. This stabilized interior can be obtained in any climate, by placing insulation while facing and shading windows.

Tire bales are a product of the tire recycling business and limited space. They are big "rubber bricks" composed of roughly 100 used tires, compressed under great pressure and wrapped with steel wires, weigh-in at a ton and are sometimes even free to the end user!! They produce a thermal mass wall with exactly the same characteristics as a rammed-earth tire wall." [70]
Tire walls are a very strong method of construction, they are earthquake resistant and can bear very high loads. It is a very sustainable construction method because it reduces waste material from the planet which would otherwise need a lot of energy to be recycled or disposed.
The result is a construction method with a negative carbon footprint.

[70] *Touch the Earth Ranch;* Tire houses: An Efficient Construction Method. Exploring the Benefits of Using Earth-friendly Materials [http://www.touchtheearthranch.com/tirestart.htm] (20.04.2014)

365 *Building protection matting from recycling rubber granules*
366 *Students building chair from old bicycle wheels*
367 *Examples of old CDs used for building structure – for columns, walls or building cladding*
368 *Images from the second design group – coloured facades made from reused doors and windows*
369 *Images from the first design group – building materials of old pallets and magazines, used also for furniture*

366

6.2.9 Examples of recycling concepts

During the course "Recycled design" at the faculty of Architecture and Design at the University of Wismar, students were tasked with finding the best solution to re-design the campus cafeteria out of recycled or reused materials. Some examples are shown:

The concept from the **first group** was to build the **cafeteria from old, used pallets and magazines.** The wall construction consisted of pallets as the main structure and filled with magazines as the thermal insulation. The furniture was also designed from these materials by stacking magazines to form chairs, grouping cardboard to form lamps, and using pallets as chairs, benches and tables.

After calculating the entire building, approximately 1,216 old pallets would be required along with 86,000 old magazines.

The **second design** used **old empty bottles and cans** as the design element for the walls that were inspired by mosaic ceramic. The old windows and doors became the main elements for the facades.

Other designs proposed to use containers for the building construction or the exterior envelope from containers as building elements. Proposals were also made to use old CDs to form columns or wall elements.

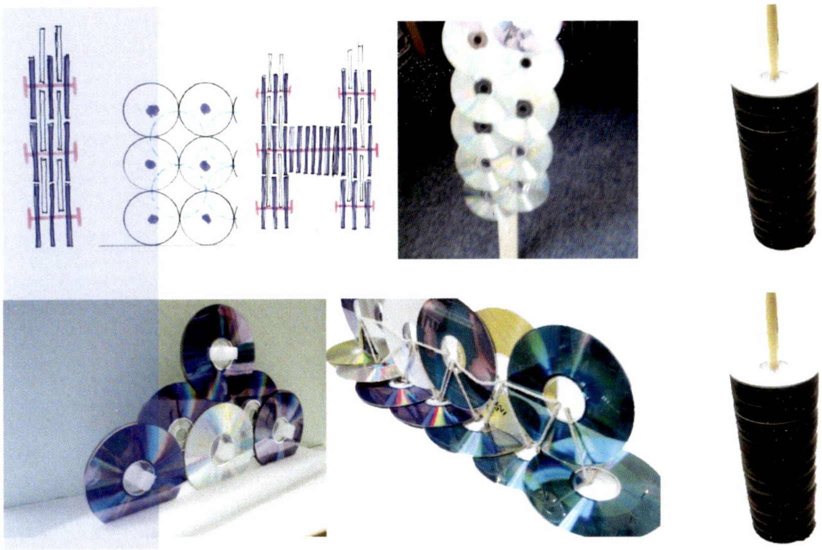

367

368

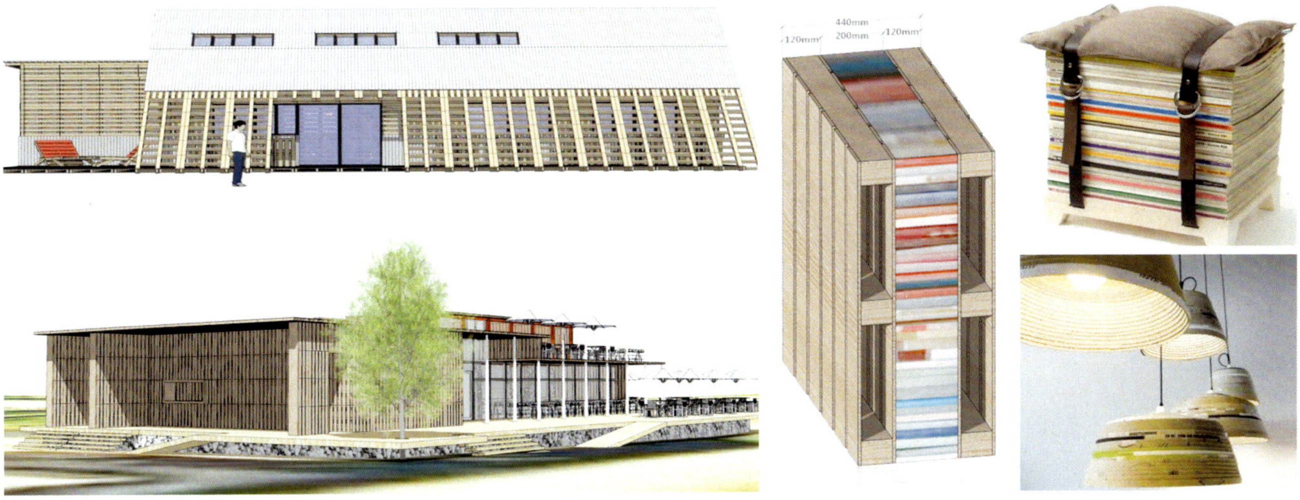

369

6.3 Active water-saving concepts

Domestic wastewater carries used water from houses and apartments.
There are a few kinds of domestic wastewater:

- Grey water

is wastewater generated from domestic activities such as the laundry, dish washing and bathing. It is easy to be cleaned and re-used.

- Black water

is wastewater from the toilets that contains faeces.

- Yellow water

is wastewater from the toilets that contains urine.

Industrial wastewater is used water from manufacturing or chemical processes.
Service water is water not requiring drinking quality, e.g. for watering the gardens, toilet flushing, cleaning and washing.

370 Means and ways for a sustainable association with water, the boxes highlighted in orange show active action water-saving concepts

Active water saving concepts include potable water saving through the recycling of rainwater and a natural wastewater recycling management.

Active potable water savings

Substituting drinking water with domestic waste water for specific use (water recycling, rainwater recycling).

Water recycling

Water recycling consists of rainwater recycling, grey water recycling and black water recycling. It is important to separate the various waste waters because they have various ways of being recycled and different forms of future use due to different consistencies. For example, it is easier to purify grey water than black water because black contains faeces.

Purified grey water can be used after treatment as service water or brought back into the natural water cycle.

Ideally, black water should be separated from yellow water as it contains nutrients which can be used as fertiliser in agriculture.

There are **technical and nature-oriented techniques** for grey water recycling.
Environmentally friendly techniques feature low costs and simple installation, however they require a lot of space outside the building.

Technical systems are expensive and require regular inspections, however they do not need as much space.

Natural wastewater management

Wastewater is water that has been altered through utilisation. It also includes water run off and water collected in canals. Wastewater should be considered as a valuable resource.

The alternative wastewater treatment is based on:

- decentralised 'natural' waste water treatment where appropriate, which can serve an individual building or small group of buildings
- the separate treatment of waste water with different levels of contamination (the separation of domestic and industrial/commercial waste water and the differentiated treatment of black and grey water)
- the recovery of valuable nutrients such as nitrogen, phosphorus and potassium (used as fertiliser in agriculture)

The several stages of wastewater treatment include mechanical sedimentation, biological treatment, post-purification, and UV treatment. There are natural and technical processes for biological purification.

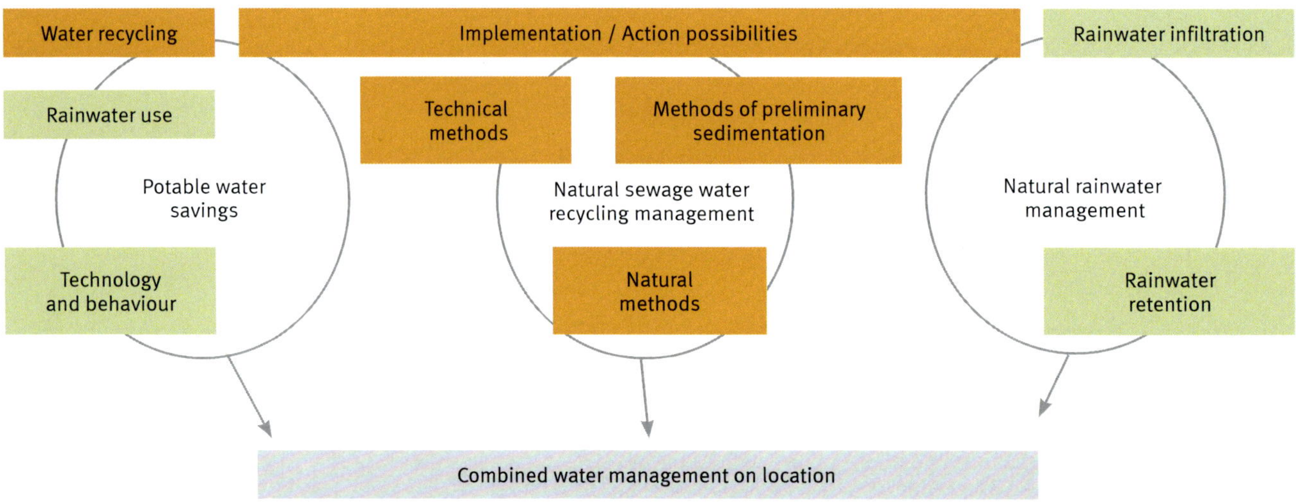

370

371

371 A view into an ecological settlement Flintenbreite Lübeck
372 The three water systems used in the settlement project Flintenbreite Lübeck – the black water from vacuum toilets is used for biogas production, which drives the CHP for electricity and heat generation, designed by OtterWasser GmbH, Lübeck

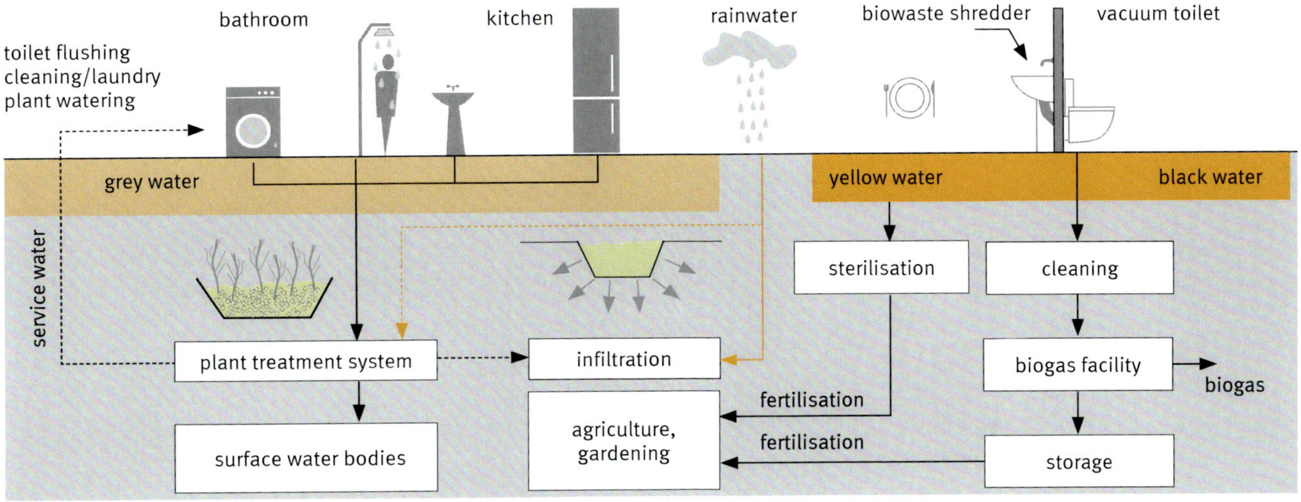

372

6.4 Summary

The main goal of resource-saving is to avoid landfilling. If a building element cannot be reused, it should be proven that it cannot be up or down cycled before it becomes landfill. This is valid for all building materials/elements.

A building's waste management is of high importance – very often the organisation of the construction site influences the need for landfilling. All building materials/elements should be kept on site. When a building is renovated/demolished, a selective decomposition should be provided.

This refers to the building abortion with prior site clearance including any claims for species-specific detection and disposal of demolition material.

The recycled material should also be used directly on the site or within the neighbourhood. By providing a recycling centre on site, the need for long transportation of recycled materials is avoided.

The ground excavation should also be kept on the site and reused, for example for landscaping.

Reusing and up cycling is always the best alternative. If down cycling is required, than the energy demands and expenditures for providing down cycling should be minimized and reduced as much as possible.

With new construction, reused components and fittings or recycled materials/elements are preferred over new manufactured ones. Before the dismantling of a building, the potential of objects should be identified.

This is part of the "inventory and initial assessment" and the "technical analysis".

Such tools are still mostly theoretical and are not commonly practiced in reality.

The EU Construction Products Regulation (CPR) now specifies that the landfilling of solid material should be forbidden and each material must be brought back to its original cycle.

This will provide new methods to identify construction products and the sustainability of buildings, represented by life cycle of a preparation, article and in the sum.

Resource utilisation, primary energy use, CO_2 accountability, declaration of risk and hazardous substances are the essential factors for the reorganisation of the European Construction Products Directive in the field of hygiene, health and environmental protection.

This was formulated by the European Parliament (EP) on the 13th March 2009 and will be shown as a "declaration of performance" in the CE-marking.

373 Increase of investments made in the construction sector, compared to new building and renovation
374 Recyclable building – the way how new constructions and buildings should be designed and built

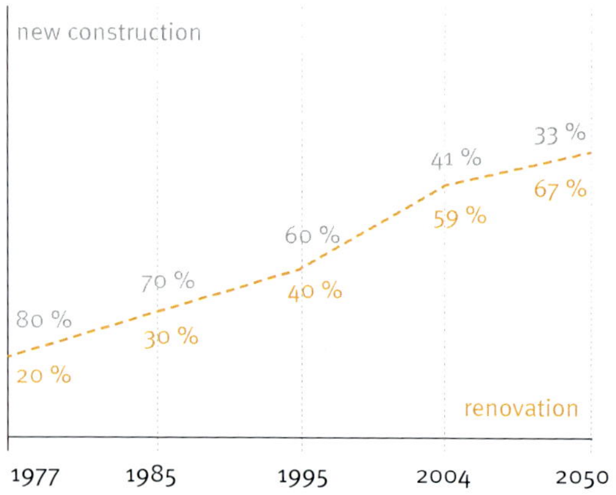

373

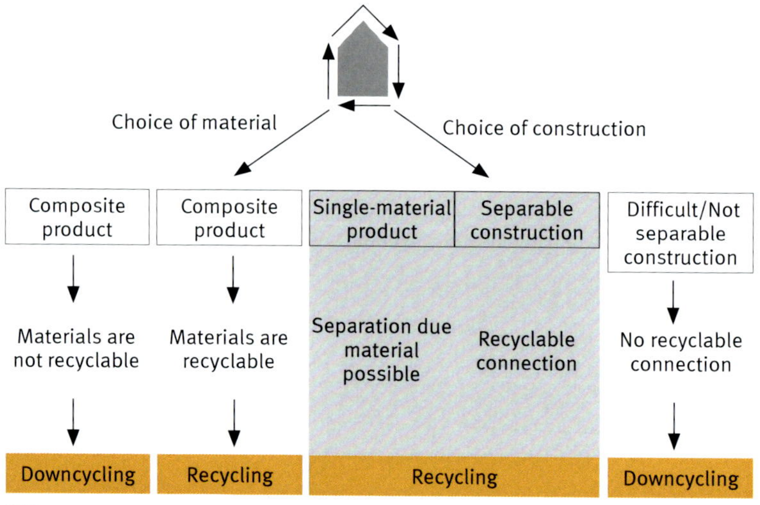

374

The goal is that building materials must be evaluated for their environmental and health risks, and implemented in the planning and construction process in order to create a sustainable building.

Other regulating bodies in Europe and internationaly are:

- Europa 2020 – Leitinitiative "Resource-saving Europa", Roadmap resource-efficiency (09/2011)
- UNEP: International Resource Panel – "Decoupling" study (05/2011)
- Rio plus 20 (06/2012) – focus in green economy

The Federal Ministry of Transport, Building and Urban Affairs, Germany and the Federal Ministry of Defence, Germany published Working aids for recycling "Arbeitshilfen Recycling" outlining the main goals for a waste-free construction sector.

Despite the efforts and regulations supporting resource-saving through reuse and recycling, there are still many problems and restrictions.

For example, large quantities of mineral building debris is used for road construction, not because we need road construction, but for political reasons. This leads to a waste-oriented society.

Many types of potentially reusable construction materials often do not correspond to the current legal standards and therefore become the owner's responsibility as there is no warranty for such building materials.

In addition, newly recycled products require licensing and sometimes it is very difficult to get a license.

From an organisational point of view, it is preferable to source reusable construction materials from the immediate environment, but this is difficult to achieve.

This problem is related to long-term material procurement difficulties, such as expensive store keeping, transport costs (self-pick up), cleaning (e.g. mortars of masonry units, nails from timber beams), old elements often not meeting the current standards (e.g. dimensions, static maximum stress) and less work planning security.

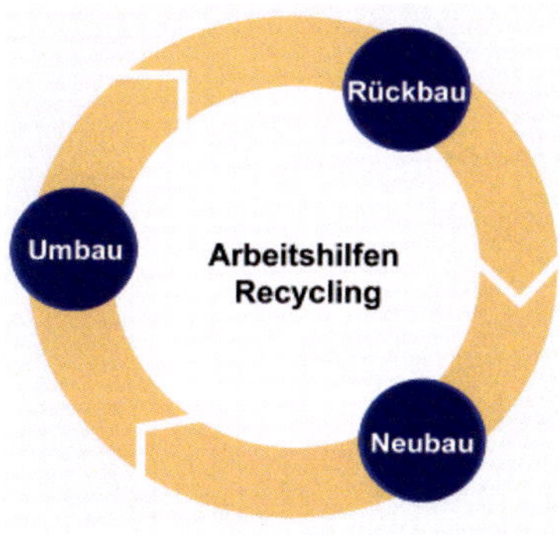

375

375 The cover of the Working aids recycling "Arbeitshilfen Recycling" published by the Federal Ministry of Transport, Building and Urban Affair, Germany and the Federal Ministry of Defence, Germany
376 The validity area of Working aids recycling "Arbeitshilfen Recycling"

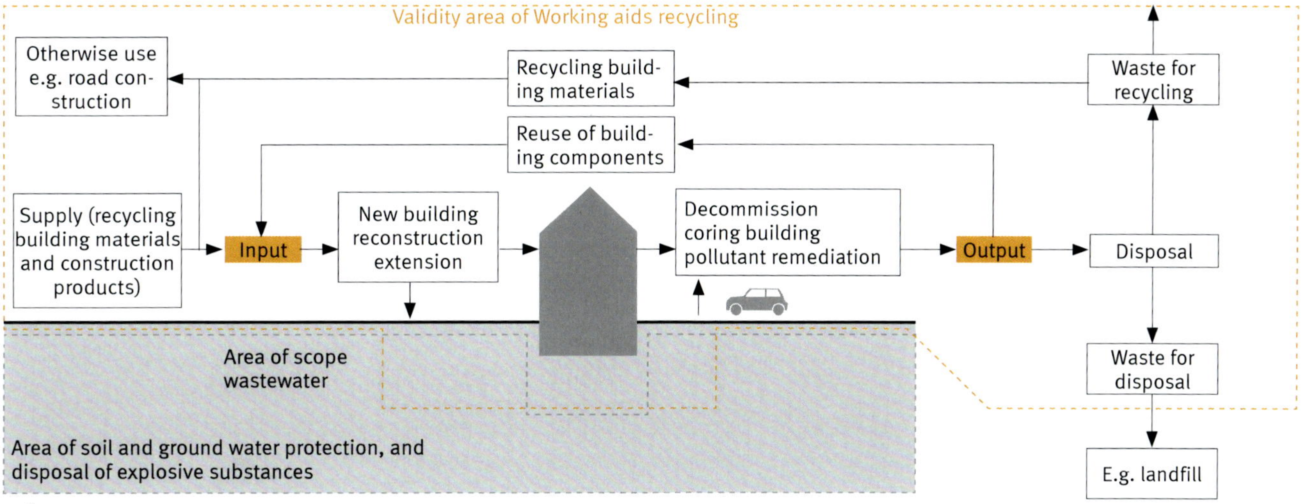

376

377

377 Combination of low and high-tech energy-saving features within a building – highly efficient LED lighting and an unheated courtyard used as a buffer zone – Plus energy school, Reutershagen - Rostock, IGEL-Institut

Life time design

7.0 Buildings for a long life span

7.0 Building for a long life span

7.1 Introduction

Durability is the resistance of a building material or element to external influences (through weather, chemical or mechanical effects). It is an important factor to be considered when designing a long life span building.
Durable building materials/elements without the need of change/repair should be used on buildings with long life spans.
The aging capability refers to the capability of a building material/element to be of a high quality for a long life span. Maintaining the material/element during its use will extend past its life span, e.g. painting or vanishing wood.

Long life span buildings are designed specifically to suit a location. These can also be called "immobility", because the building is permanently bound to one original site.

Regarding life cycle, building occupancy is the most important phase. Buildings should be designed so that when in operation (in-use), or when requiring cleaning or maintenance, as little energy as possible is used. Energy regeneration, e.g. using renewable resources is also important and very desirable. It is because of this that the different requirements of different functions should be considered in order to reduce required operation energy.

It is of the uttermost importance that the operating energy is as low as possible, e.g. passive energy use and well insulated external surfaces for low energy consumption). According to external conditions, rather than the construction method, it is the climate zoning of rooms that becomes more useful. In regards to total costs, the minimization of life cycle costs should also be considered. However, this excludes pure construction costs and the maintenance costs, e.g. costs to operate (cooling, heating, warm water, ...).

In former times, the highest primary energy needs and associated costs were due to operational use, e.g. the heating and supply of warm water. Today, this has shifted towards production and maintenance. This is due to advances in technology and construction which provide a drastic reduction in heating energy needs. However, this has resulted in an increase in maintenance costs.
A long life span building should be designed for change and growth to keep up with constant changes in the external environment. A building's surroundings are changing, populations are increasing, as well as the space, technology and aesthetic requirements that follow cultural movements.

When materials, context, occupants and technology need to change, the building should be able to flex and adapt along side them.
It should be expandable and adaptable for new functions. In the case of renewing or disassembling a building, we should first consider refurbishment.
During design, the building's post life should also be considered. Ideally, the building should be easily disassembled and recycled, without a trace on the landscape.

Different building types that are designed for a long life span include:

- Traditional buildings
- Unique buildings
- Variable buildings
- Building renovation
- Building conversion

378 Standing for almost 2,000 years – the Pantheon is a preserved Ancient Roman monument built in Rome, Italy

378

Examples of long life span buildings are **heritage buildings** from different historical time periods that have withstood the test of time; from ancient times, e.g. monuments in old Rome or Athens which now serve as museums and as a place to visit, or historical wooden storage houses that are reused for new functions.

Other examples of buildings with long life spans include the building type **"Starter Homes"**. Starter homes are affordable single family houses designed for first time buyers.

They are usually arranged as terraced houses in urban areas and as detached homes in suburban and rural areas. They have a basic **neutral floor plan** that is flexible and changeable by the user.

Small show homes are often built to display the property's investment value and to provide an expansion module. These buildings may also be temporarily inhabited.

The construction time is extremely short due to prefabricated building elements that are produced in the factory and assembled on site. These housing types consume very little energy.

The buildings are designed so that alterations and extensions are possible according to the user's demands and financial situation.

379

379 House on insel Poel, Wollensak architects – an example that expresses a rational supporting system layout, carefully chosen and applied materials, as well as the neutral floorplan that allows it to be adapted to different functions during its life time

380 Neutral floorplan of House on insel Poel, Wollensak architects

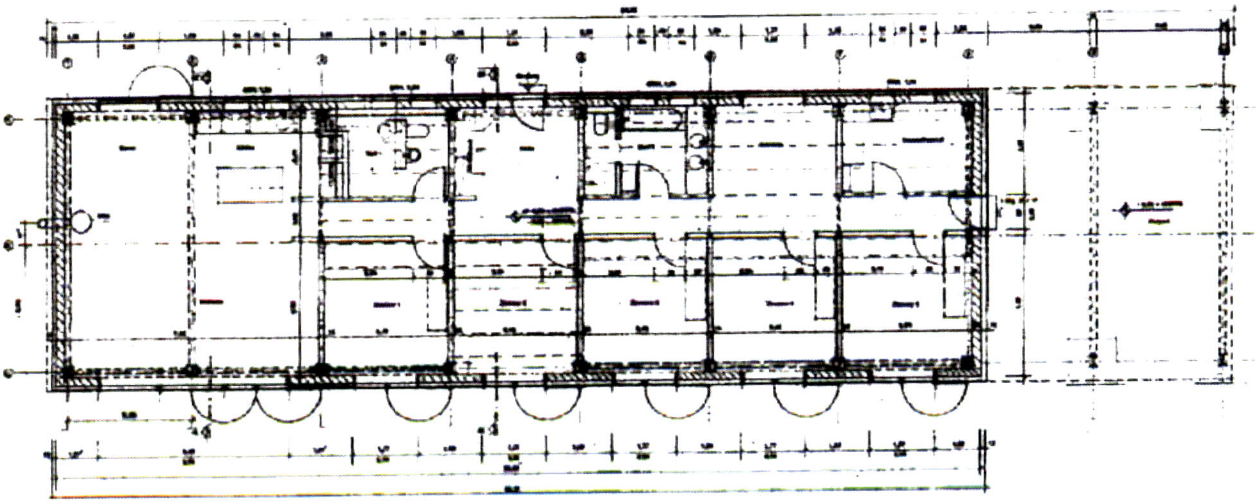

380

7.2 Traditional building

Traditional buildings are typical examples of long life span buildings. These buildings are specially built for the site and follow the local climate conditions.

They are built out of local materials and according to the building traditions of the location.

Traditional architecture and passive energy saving was discussed during the introduction of chapter '4.0 Passive energy-saving concepts'.

Traditional buildings normally stand for more than one hundred years. There are also historical heritage buildings that stand for thousands of years.

Traditional buildings are normally the result of an analysis of different local conditions with the design following the restrictions of the climate and site.

It is typical that different regions have their own architectural form, which is repeated without the focus being strictly on the design.

From the view point of design, two main types of architecture must be considered:

- regional architecture
- regionalistic architecture

Regional, also know as vernacular architecture, is a traditional architecture where the design follows the climatic conditions and regional specifications of the location.

Here, most of the traditional architectural forms come from history.

Regionalism is a type of modern architecture, which follows the functional, regional requirements to create a design.

The goal is to consider local specifications in relation to international styles.

Building restoration must be considered when approaching historical or traditional architecture.

It is a process where the existing building is conserved, leaving as much material untouched as possible along with repair work to bring the building to a historically accurate condition and the replacement of missing elements.

Building restoration was highlighted in chapter '2.0 Building life time' and chapter '3.0 Passive resource-saving concepts'.

381 Mecklenburg-Vorpommern land prize awarded in 2013 for a house designed in Warnemünde, Germany, by Löser Lott architects, as an example for regionalistic architecture

381

The “Future house” concept is based on the traditional Hutong building structure where the main houses are located around a central courtyard.
The single houses are flexible and can be adapted to suit different residential housing types e.g. generation housing, living for singles and couples, luxurious residential housing, living for families with higher requirements, etc.

The construction and material concept is based on a wood frame structure. The main structure consists of wooden columns and beams which provide spacial flexibility.
Regarding the energy concept, creating space zoning is important where the secondary spaces create the north zone of the building with small windows, which bring required daylighting.

This zone is a buffer zone that does not require warmer temperatures and separates the living zones from the exterior.

These zones include staircases, bathrooms and storages. The middle zone is the living zone that is separated from the buffer zone with an installation layer. Main living areas are located here, including kitchen, living room and bedrooms.
A winter garden creates the southern zone where the sun’s rays are able to enter the building, optimising passive solar gains in the winter.

388

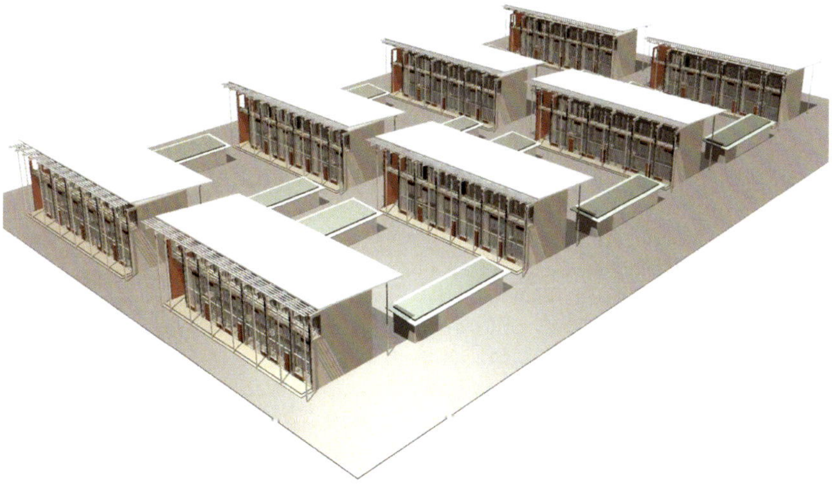

389

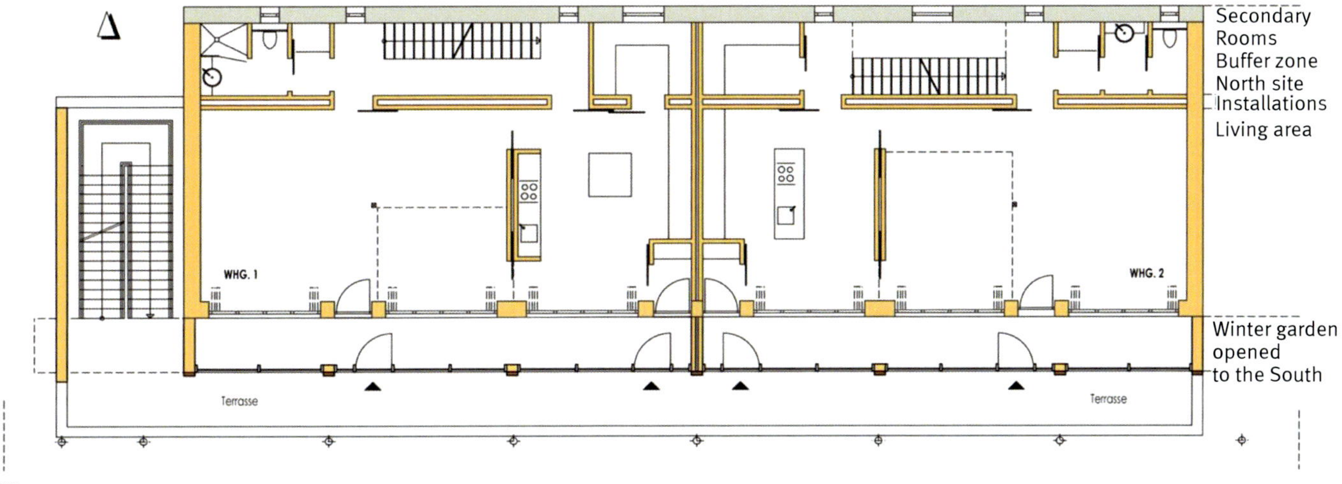

390

7.5 Building renovation

391 Image of the case study object – single family house and office in Nagold-Hochdorf, Germany
392 Student example – renovation concept, goals and limits – material and energy related renovation
393 Student example – energy independent house – energy source in 2040
394 Student example – building aging
395 Student example – life span analysis of individual building elements

391

Building renovation keeps the original function and makes the building ready for further use, revitalization of the existing building.
Building renovation was already described in chapter '2.0 Building life time' and chapter '3.0 Passive resource-saving concepts'.

Student example: Family house and office in Nagold-Hochdorf, Germany

This single-family house consists of three levels with an office. The scenario is that the building changes owner after 20 years and the new owner must make some investigations into the building.

The goal is to find out what developments are useful and necessary to extend the building's life time by 30 years

In 30 years time, the building should use zero fossil fuels. The price for fossil fuel energy and power will have increased over this time. Buildings after 2018 must cover their own energy needs and therefore plus energy will become a minimum requirement.
The building consists of many elements with different life times, which will need to be renewed. During the renovation of the building it is important to consider that the building materials have low grey energy.
The focus after 30 years is on the renovation of the building envelope and the building technology.

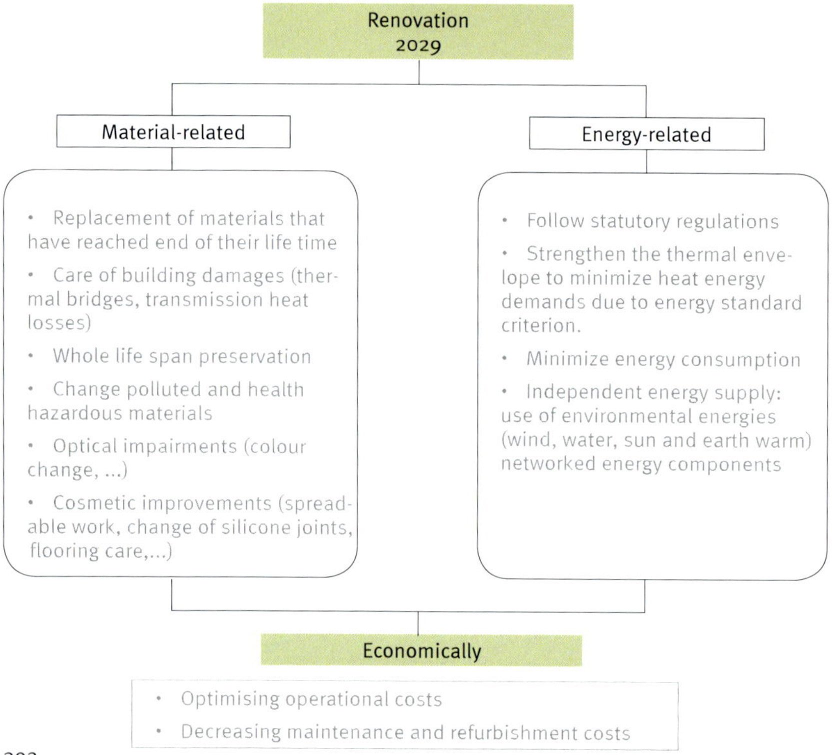

392

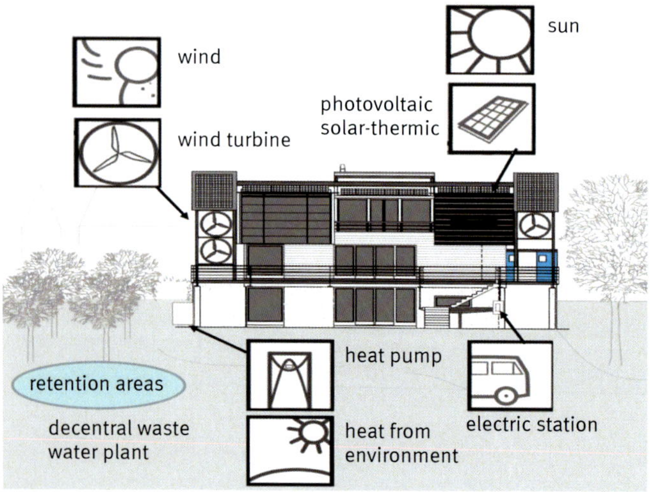

393

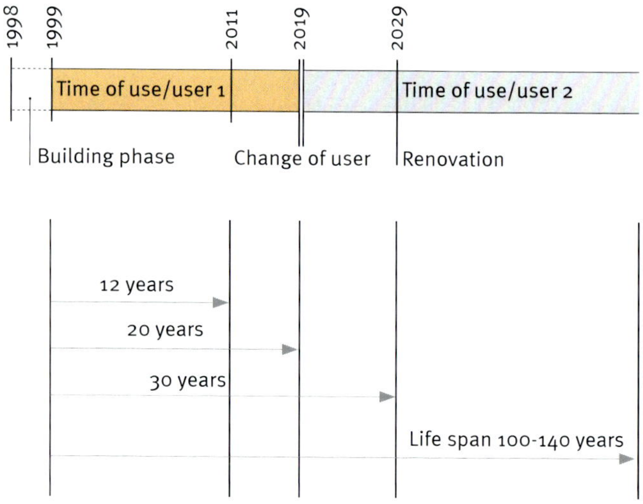

394

Building element	Building element catalogue BMVBS	Individual assessment in years	Comment	Replacement after 30 years of use (2029)	Replacement after 50 years of use (2049)
Construction					
Concrete	70 - 100	100		-	-
Steel beam	80 - 120	100		-	-
Masonry	90 - 100	100		-	-
Stairs (inside) concrete	80 - 100	100		-	-
Foundation reinforced concrete	80 - 120	100		-	-
Reinforced concrete ceiling		100		-	-
Exterior coverings					
WDVS exterior plaster	25 - 45	40		x	x
Weatherboarding larch	40 - 50	40		-	x
Larch unhandled	40 - 50	40		-	x
MDF plates, coating	40 - 50	40		-	x
Corrugated sheet profile		80 - 100		-	-
Douglas, fluted	80			-	-
Windows and doors					
Wooden frames	20 - 50	30		x	-
Handle	20 - 35	30		x	-
Double glazing	20 - 30	30		x	-
Windowsill aluminium	30 - 60	60		as required	-
Roof skin					
Flat roof waterproofing	20 - 40	30		x	
Heat insulation	20 - 40	30		x	
Roof drainage	20 - 40	30		x	
Interior construction					
Wooden wall racks		40	abrasions		x
Translucent glass		60		-	-
Inside wood doors		40	abrasions		x
Plexiglas panels/hollow chamber panels		30		x	repair, coating needed
Metal sheet		100		-	-
Concrete elements	80 - 100	100		-	-
Floor construction					
Cement screed	60 - 100	80		-	-
Mastic asphalt	60 - 100	100	stair covering inside		beauty repairs repair needed
Cobblestones	50 - 100	70		-	-
Granite stones	50 - 100	70		-	beauty repairs repairs of joints needed
Carpet synthetic fibre	5 - 15	15		x	x
Epoxy resin coating				beauty repairs	beauty repairs
Parquet	30 - 70	50		sanding and sealing every 10 years	sanding and sealing every 10 years
Technology					
Hot water pipes	15 - 30	40	deposit by high lime water	-	questionable
Cold water pipes	30 - 60	40	deposit by high lime water	-	questionable
Basic pipes	30 - 40	40		-	questionable
Sanitary Objects	20 - 30	30		x	-
Heating	15 - 25	30		x	-
Heating pipes	30 - 50	60		x	-
Electrical pipes	15 - 25	50		-	-

395

7.6 Building conversion

Building conversion, also called adaptive reuse, occurs when the original function is changed.

The building is renewed in order to fulfil the new functional requirements.

Building conversion was already described in chapter '2.0 Building life time' and chapter '3.0 Passive resource-saving concepts.

Student example: Family house with office in Nagold-Hochdorf, Germany

The case project is a single-family house with office use on the first floor. A new highway passes near to the building.

Noise emission of the existing residential use is in question. The building should be reused and converted.

After an analysis of possible new building functions, the conversion of the office building into a medical centre was the final decision.

The analyses showed many options for possible reuse for many functions.

The analysis of the static conditions, location of fixed points (building service pipes) and room heights are important for building conversion.

A new energy supply concept must be developed and the fire and noise protection for the new function must be examined.

A cheap, green facade was designed for the highway-side of the building.

The conversion of the building allowed the existing building elements to be reused. Only necessary elements would be new.

The design has zero waste and is very resource friendly.

396 Student example – construction in the existing building and possible extensions
397 Student example – alternative with office use in the first floor
398 Student example – alternative with ambulance in the first floor
399 Overview of the reuse possibilities

Structurally fixed points

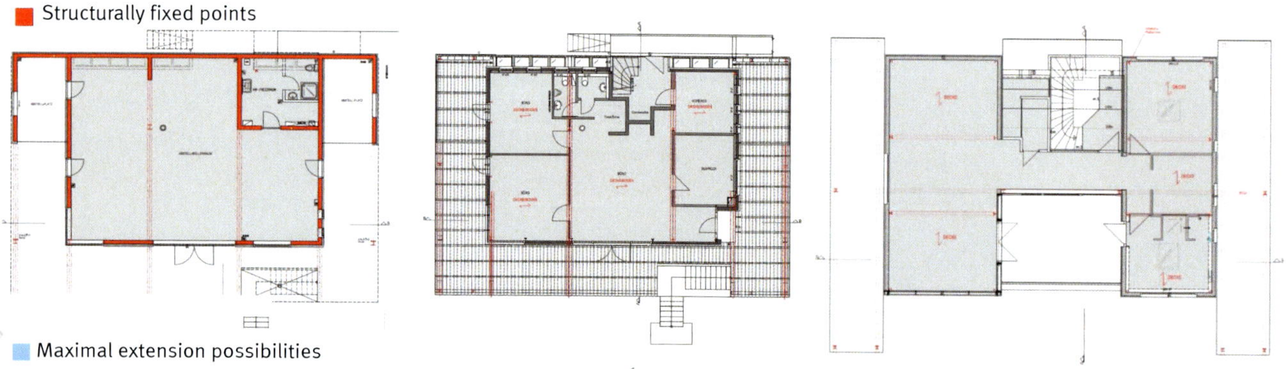

Maximal extension possibilities

Basement: there are high costs for the extension works – thermal insulation for the ground plate, facade elements, heat insulation

First floor: the plates are hung between the steel beam plates – with or without heat insulation

Second floor: the steel construction already exists in atrium, quick and flexible extension possible, both roofs are because of the surface difficult to be built

396

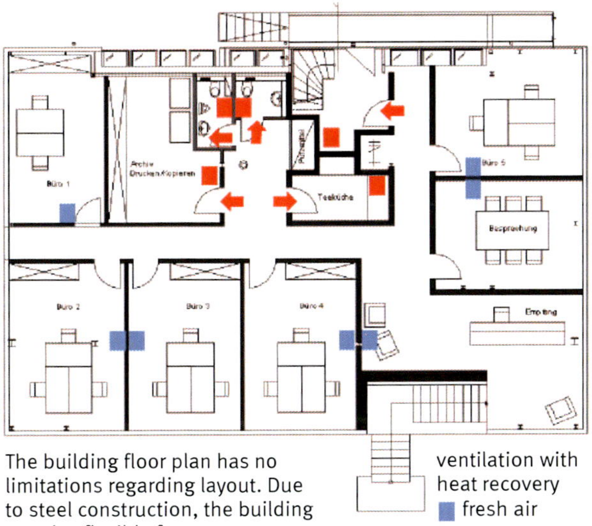

The building floor plan has no limitations regarding layout. Due to steel construction, the building remains flexible for reuse.

ventilation with heat recovery
fresh air
exhaust air

397

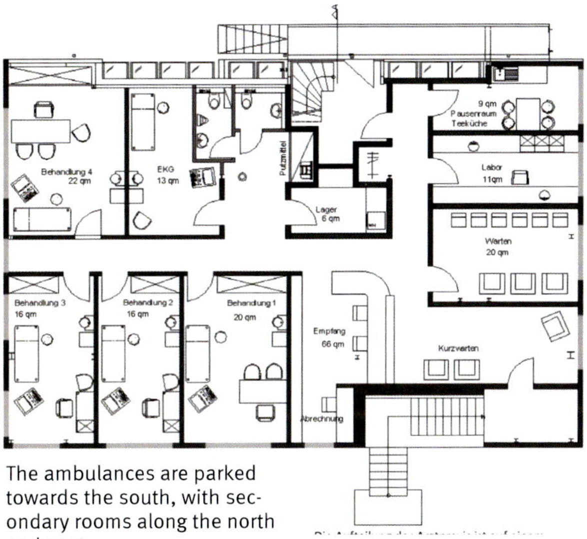

The ambulances are parked towards the south, with secondary rooms along the north and east.

398

👍 = possible 👎 = difficult

Possibilities	Functional change – building and architecture	Flexibility of construction	Urban planning use depended on airport	Surfaces using	Economy of the use	Architecture
Car repair with electric loading station	👍 G F: workshop, electric stat. 1 F: storage 2 F: office	👍	👎 gas station exists	👎 parking for customers	depends on offer and demand	👎 billboards
Fast food	👍 G F: kitchen, WC 1 F: restaurant 2 F: office elevator needed for the people and for the food	👍 extension on all layers needed	👎 fast food already exists	👎👎 surface sealing for parking, drive thru and waste	👎 logistic over two storey – costly with elevators and installations	👎 billboards design of fast food restaurants
Hotel	👍 G F: reception, breakfast room, kitchen 1 F + 2 F: rooms 2 F: office	👍 extension on all layers needed	👎 many hotels already exist	👎👎 surface sealing for parking and waste	👎 too small to operate the hotel economically	👍 existing
Office building	👍👍 G F: tea kitchen, offices, conference room 1 F + 2 F: office rooms 2 F: office	👍 extension on all layers needed	👍 renting to the service providers	👎 surface sealing for parking	depends on supply and demand	👍 existing
Textile cleaning	👍 G F: dirty clothes 1 F: cleaning 2 F: office transport elevator needed	👍 extension of G F and 1 F needed	👍 decentral cleaning for hotel and restaurant at airport	👎 surface sealing for delivering	👍 short distances to users depends on offer and demand	👍 existing
Beauty centre	👍 G F: reception, coffee 1 F: treatment 2 F: office	👍	👍 short length of stay, ideal for airline crew	👎 parking for customers	depends on supply and demand	👎 billboards
Medical centre	👍 G F: reception, office 1 F: ambulance 2 F: ambulance	👍	👍	👎 parking for customers	depends on supply and demand	👍 existing

399

7.7 Summary

Various building certifications, for example the German Green Building certification system DGNB are designed for long life span buildings. The certification considers buildings that have a life span of 50 years or more.

The aim of designing should always be to build sustainably and for a long life span. When designing a new building, the first question should be – Is it possible to renovate or reuse the existing building?

This often requires extensive planning. When designing a long life span building, the time spent for planning should also be considered.
Investing more time into the planning, in order to design a long life span building of a higher quality, saves the additional costs and resources, which could arise due to poor planning.
However, the regulations for architects and engineers should adapt to the planning of longer life span designs. Architects and engineers are currently forced to shorten the planning time in order to work economically, which can cause higher costs during the building's construction and utilization phase.

The regulations in Germany do not consider the different building specifications for a longer life span design, but only the degree of building difficulty. They should be revised to enable a longer planning phase, which the designing of sustainable buildings require.

Regulations concerning the legal bases of long life span buildings should also be considered, as the liability of construction companies for the building realization is generally between three and five years in Germany. It is contradictory to the long life span of building.
Another problem is building permits for building renovation or conversion. The permits for the original building are only valid for minor building changes with all original functions remaining.

However, a new building permit is required when changing the function or doing larger alterations (e.g. adding of a new building storey). Because of the new norms and regulations from when the building was originally built, this can cause unsolvable problems.
For example, when new statical calculations are made according to new legal norms, the old building construction may not meet the new standards.

This would then require a redesign of the original structure or the design of a new structural system, which results in high building costs.
Another example are buildings that are unusable. These are buildings that were designed and built for a long life span, but due to various reasons (e.g. invariable or inadaptable to a new function) the building must be demolished.

Such examples are very unsustainable and cause wasting of resources and energy and the generation of huge amounts of building debris waste.

400 A lot of material is wasted when a building is not used for the life time that it was planned – example of a swimming pool centre closed because of salmonella disease
401 Due to strict regulations, many existing buildings remain abandoned

400

401

402

402 The material selection and construction connections must be thoroughly analysed in order to avoid demolition waste that is generated at the end of a buildings life span – this is similar with the products

Life time design

8.0 Buildings for a short life span

8.0 Building for a short life span

8.1 Introduction

Building types that are designed for a short life span include:

- Building as a product
- Building as a function
- Disposable building
- Mobile building
- Exhibition building
- Flying building
- Floating building

Considering population growth and the changing requirements of building users, future space requirements are ever increasing.
While the number of inhabitants in Germany between 1950 and 1993 grew over approx. 50 %, the energy consumption has exploded by almost five times over the required floor space per person.

Compared to Switzerland with 45 m²/Person, the German citizen has approximately 37 m²/Person, the largest floor space consumption in Europe.

This is one reason that the economic life span of a building is shortening. The options to overcome this are either a drastic refurbishment or demolition of a new construction.
An intermediate solution would be the development of a building with a predetermined life span in agreement with the client and the predetermined period of use.

For example, the average life span of China's residential buildings is approx. 25-30 years. Buildings with short lives create huge waste. In China, construction waste comprises 30 to 40 percent of total urban waste. Consideration should be made during the planning process to design for a certain lifetime. What happens after the life of the building should be considered to minimize waste and resources.

Considering life cycle, the first and fifth are the most important as we should try to save resources more than energy required for operation.
Choosing materials is important as they should be easily recyclable without producing waste. The resource-saving concepts play a more important role here than energy-saving concepts.

These buildings types stay only for a short time so it is of high importance to find solutions that will allow the rejuvenation of the landscape after the building removal. The consideration of foundation systems is therefore of a high importance.
Most short life span buildings are not connected to the specific site and are movable, and therefore also called "mobile". They can be moved wherever and at any time.
Examples of such buildings are houses-to-go, a house on wheels which can be moved by car to different locations.

These houses are built with a light structure with a minimalistic design that provides good quality of living comfort.

Various concepts and solutions that will help with the design of sustainable, short life span buildings are discussed in chapter '3.0 Passive resource-saving concepts' and chapter '6.0 Active resource-saving concepts'.

403 Student example S.haus – alternative of floor plans design with open living, cooking and eating space, the secondary rooms are situated to North
404 Student example S.haus – the easy separable facade enables changes during the building life span
405 Student example S.haus – life cycle schematic of a single-family house
406 Student example S.haus – life cycle schematic of an S.haus in comparison to the life cycle of a conventional single family house
407 Student example S.haus – designed like recyclable building, only 8 m³ of soil has to be excavated for foundation system and the landscape stays untouched after dismantling

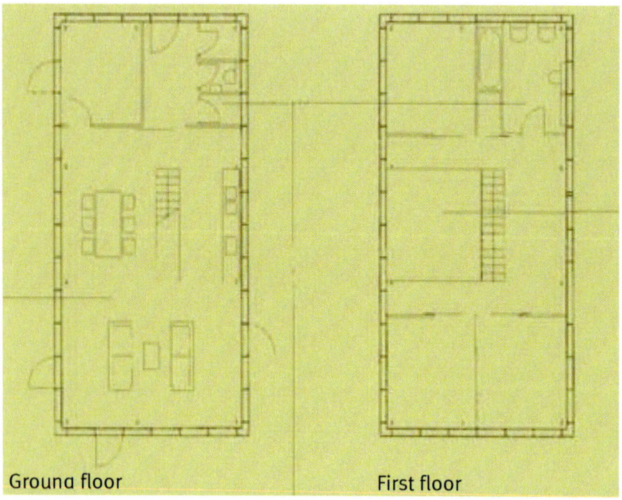

403

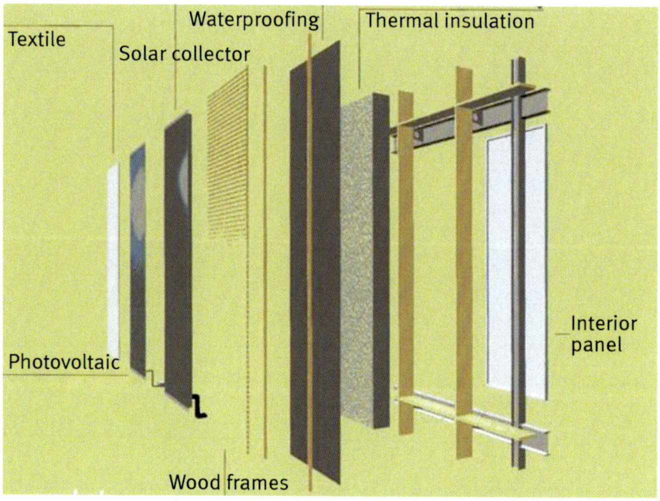

404

Student example: S.house – house for 20 years

The idea of this project considers the real use time of a single-family house. The real use time is around 20 years, and when we design the house for 20 years, we also use the land for such a time. By designing for a short life span we satisfy needs without the need to think about the future. In this way we are able to save costs, resources and energy.

The lifetime of the building consists of more than just this step. The S.haus uses only the first step of 20 years. S.haus is a light building with a steel structure. The foundation is a point foundation system that requires no excavation and the ground remains green and untouched. After 20 years the building is dismantled without impacting the direct site. The building elements are easily separable and therefore easy to recycle.

To use sun energy, most of the windows are situated on the south facade of the house. To minimize warm energy loss, there should be few windows at the north facade.

One should also consider possible shadows created by neighbouring buildings and trees. The arrangement of the rooms in connection to sun shine hours are also to be considered when analysing where and at which time the sun will shine within the building during the day.

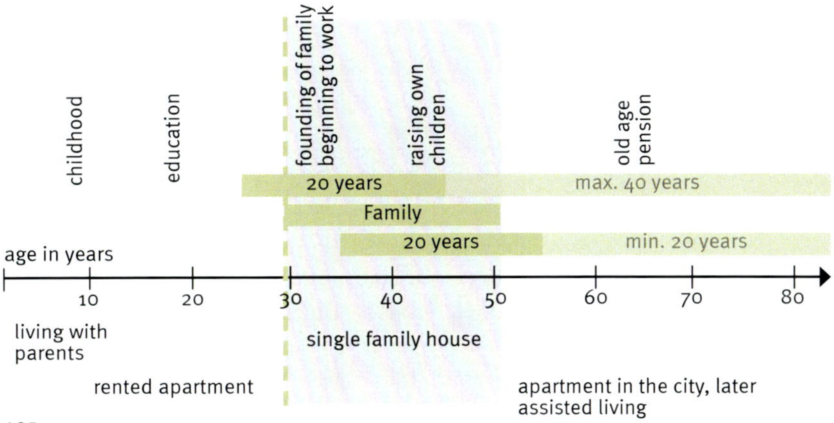

405

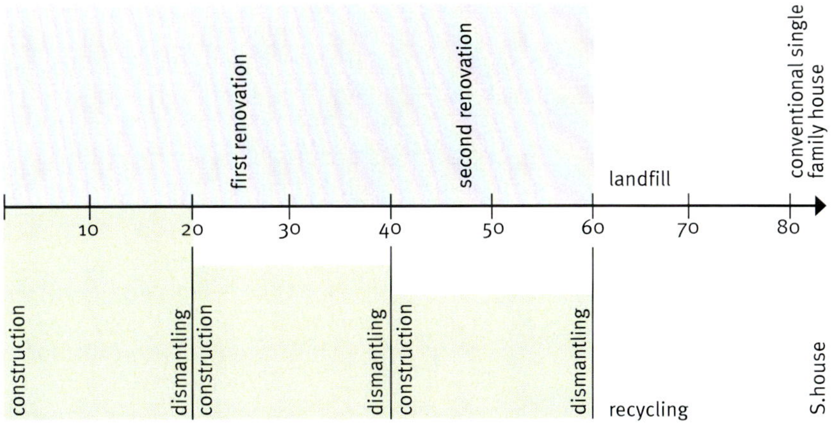

406

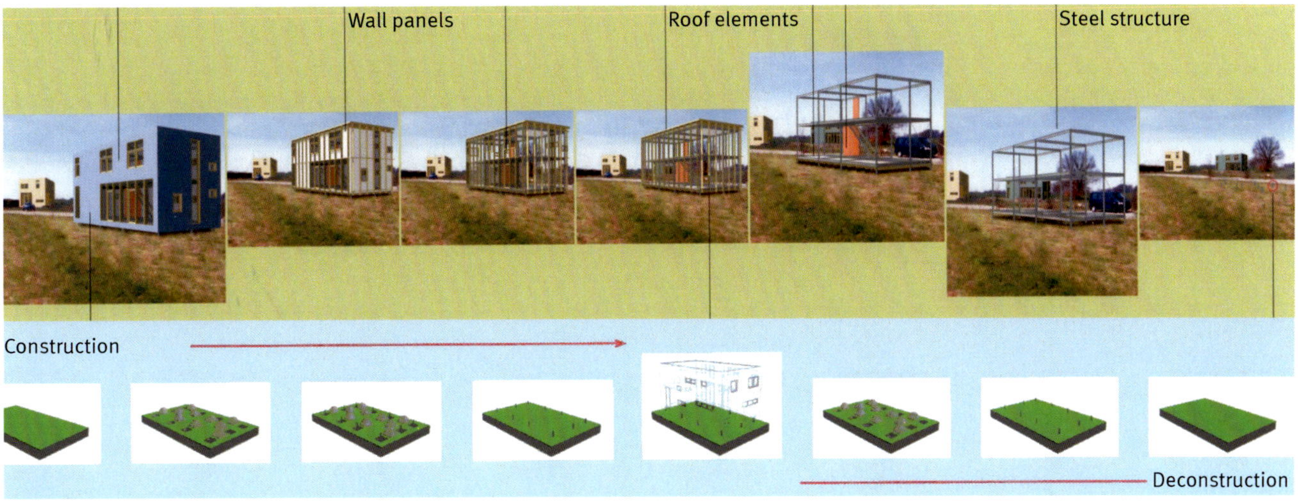

407

8.2 Building as a product

408

Product Definition

"1. A good, idea, method, information, object or service created as a result of a process and serves a need or satisfies a want. It has a combination of tangible and intangible attributes (benefits, features, functions, uses) that a seller offers a buyer for purchase.
For example a seller of a toothbrush not only offers the physical product but also the idea that the consumer will be improving the health of their teeth.

2. Law: A commercially distributed good that is (1) tangible personal property, (2) output or result of a fabrication, manufacturing, or production process, and (3) passes through a distribution channel before being consumed or used.

3. Marketing: A good or service that most closely meets the requirements of a particular market and yields enough profit to justify its continued existence. As long as cars are manufactured, companies that produce tires fill the market need and continue to be profitable." [71]

Products can be tangible objects, services, persons, places and ideas. They can be consumed in short time (food, etc.) or in a longer time, and repeatedly used. Services are intangible and changeable.
Certain products are nowadays designed for a shorter time – mobile phones, printers, etc. are made for a certain time of validity. The companies shorten the validity time of their products.
Components with short life times are designed to be a part of the products. To repair the product is nearly impossible, or the components are too expensive.
These products are designed to be thrown away after a certain time of use. This mentality is often referred to as throw-away society and it has a big impact on the environment – the landfills are growing and new resources are used.

Building as a product

Building as a product can also be referred to as "mobile" because it is not connected to any one place. These buildings are adjustable, possible to build or to move anywhere. They are designed without any connection to the building site and are composed as one single product.
It can be built in series, i.e. more buildings with the same design in order to build economically and fast. The buildings are made for a short lifetime, but we must make their lifetimes as long as possible.

Many products are designed for short life times because they are often changed and updated with newer and more developed products. A fridge for example must be replaced after time because older fridges use high levels of electricity. Buying a new fridge saves power and supports the production industry.
A building as a product is not designed to be refurbished or reused. Such buildings become waste after their time of use. They are designed for the life time of the materials and the building parts without having to change them.
These buildings should be designed to be recyclable after use. Important is the choice of materials and technologies used to build the buildings. Connections between different building materials and components must be easily demountable.

Examples of such buildings include high rise blocks of flats, schools and other public buildings designed around the time of communism, built in many European cities. These building types were built multiple times and in multiple places. Other examples include catalogue houses, which are pre-designed houses where the investor may choose a design from the catalogue that can be built in almost any location.

[71] BusinessDictionary.com; Product [http://www.businessdictionary.com/definition/product.html] (04.09.2012)

408 Example of the building as a product – it is produced in series and can be bought and placed everywhere
409 Student master thesis showing building as a function – a contemporary hotel for Hansa sail as a blow up building that can easily be blown up and easily transported to another location

8.3 Building as a function

Buildings with a special function are designed for short life spans and cannot be reused for other functions. Function becomes more important than the building form, which results in the internal connection of different spaces.
Such buildings include industrial buildings that express a form, resulting from the industrial processes inside.

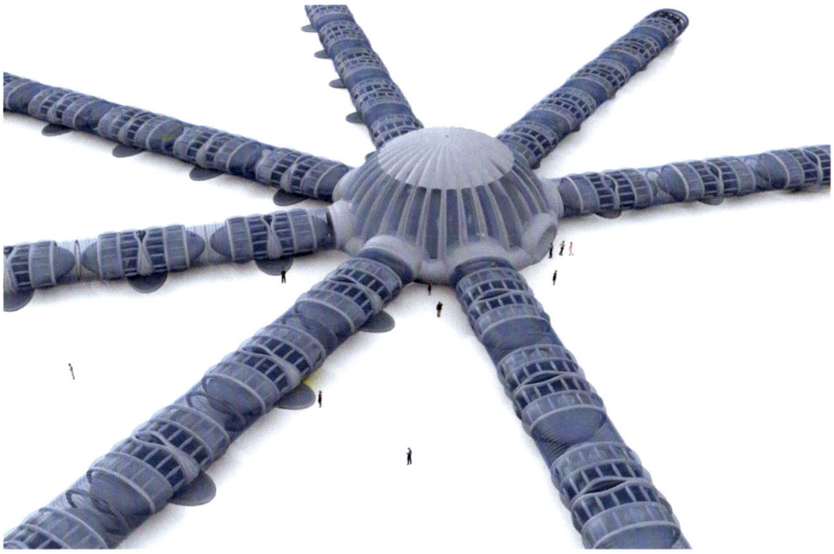

An extreme example, i.e. the factory for microchip production where very high requirements for air cleanliness is required in order to not contaminate the microchip elements. This building has a large technology area for ventilation and air cleaning in comparison to the final production area.

Other situations are working spaces and parts or entire buildings designed following the workflow management system. This refers to the space that is organised depending on the activity that occurs there.
For example the organisation of kitchen elements in relation to the workflow (storing-washing-cutting-cooking).

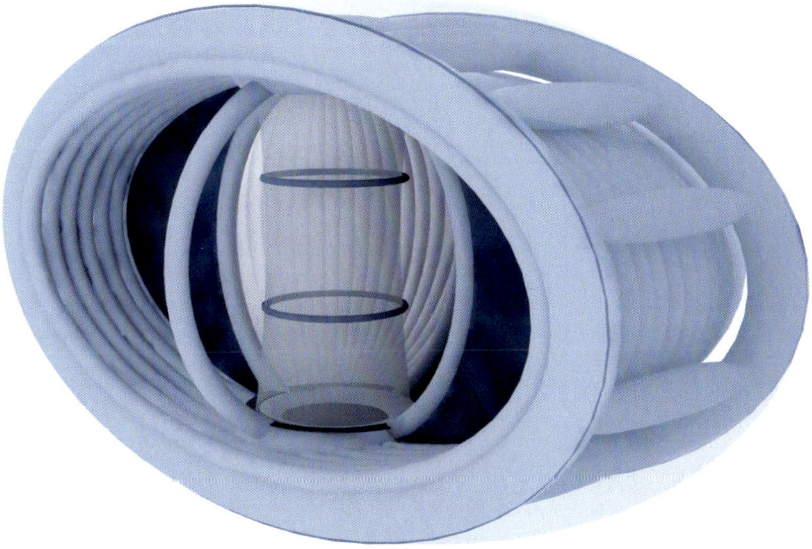

Event buildings are also short life span buildings that are connected with their function. They are often demountable and can be built again in another place. These types of buildings are called blow up buildings because they consist of a pneumatic construction which is fulfilled with air.

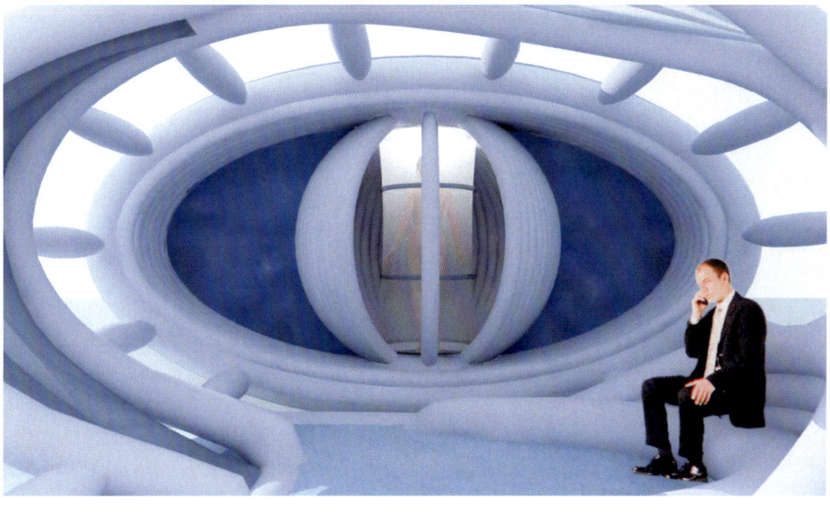

8.4 Disposable building

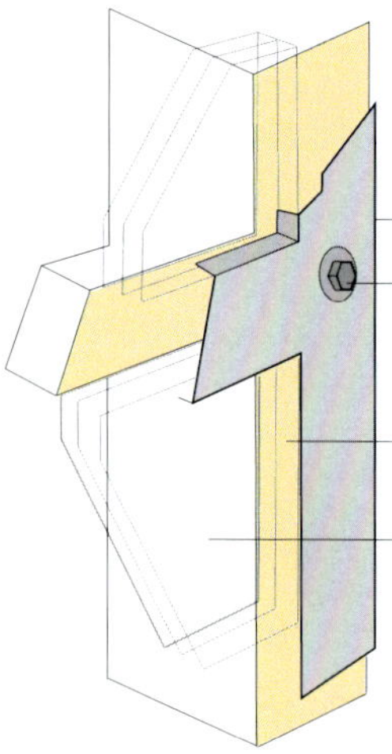

410

Buildings for short life spans become waste after their use time. Such buildings are called disposable buildings.

These buildings should be industrialized and optimised in terms of resource consumption. The impact of their components on the environment must be as little as possible, and if possible from renewable resources.

Use of building materials, with those in production that process little waste (foil-packed masonry units) and/or use fewer energy and raw materials should be used.

Most importantly, one should keep the energy used for building construction as low as possible.

In this case, energy consumption during the building operation and consideration of EnEV are not as important.

After their life time, the buildings should continue to be waste-free and recyclable. This can be achieved by using natural materials which can be easily brought back to the nature (chapter '3.0 Passive resource-saving concepts') or by using recyclable materials, which can be reused after the end of a buildings life.

The landscape should also be considered. The foundations of the building should be easily demolished, leaving the land untouched.

Below are general construction principles that make a building easily recyclable after the building lifetime:

- reduction/minimization of material diversity
- avoidance of composites that are intractable or difficult to be solved
- separability of materials that cannot be recycled together
- disuse of composites
- constructive separability of components and materials with different lifetimes, for example, construction and material finishes, bearing and non-load-bearing materials
- avoid plastics in general (e.g. polyurethane, adhesive, bitumen)
- design construction to avoid the use of chemically preserved products
- component separation of different functions (weather protection/insulation/bearing function)

410 Screwed instead of glued – triple glazing with aluminium-cladding from exterior, easily demountable
411 Disposable material for furniture in sustainable pavillion, HafenCity

411

8.5 Mobile building

A typical example of a mobile building is a caravan that people live in during their holidays. The biggest advantage of this type of house is that it is not connected to one place and can be driven anywhere at any time.
Many people take advantage of mobile houses, not only for short periods such as holidays, but also for longer periods.

Mini mobile houses or comfortable caravans can be used for various purposes. They can be used as a main residence or attached studio, guest house, holiday residence, mobile office, therapy room, or even kindergarten or workshop.

The increasing demand for mini mobile houses is known as the tiny house movement, which refers to living in small houses. The houses have a reduced living area to that of an average flat however they still have all necessary spaces while offering a comfortable living.

In the U.S.A, the Small House Society was founded in 2002 by Jay Shafer and Gregory Johnson which popularized mobile houses. In 2005, after Hurricane Katrina, many small mobile houses were developed as a solution for the disaster zone. Small houses also became more popular in the times of the financial crisis.
There are many companies developing and selling mobile house products all over the world.

412

412 Mobile house for shopping
413 Caravan is a mobile home equipped as travelling living quarters
414 A mobile house on the roads of California

413

414

8.6 Exhibition building

415

Exhibition architecture are systems that are designed to provide space in which something can be shown. Exhibitions usually occur within museums, galleries or exhibition halls.

Generally, exhibition halls are light constructions designed for a short life span.

Other concepts include architectural expositions that show a building itself as an exhibition. An example of this is the World Architecture Exposition Expo.

The first World Expo took place in London in 1851. After, this event occurred in different cities over the world every few years.

After the World Expo in Chicago in 1933, the concept to have a theme followed in the consecutive years, each with special topics.

The most recent Expo in Shanghai, China 2010, had the topic “Better City, Better Life”. The next expo will be in Milano, Italy in 2015.

Pavilions are free-standing structures that are often providing functional elements that are relaxing, for pleasure or for commercial purposes.

The focus here should also be on the use of sustainable building materials and the preventing of waste.

416

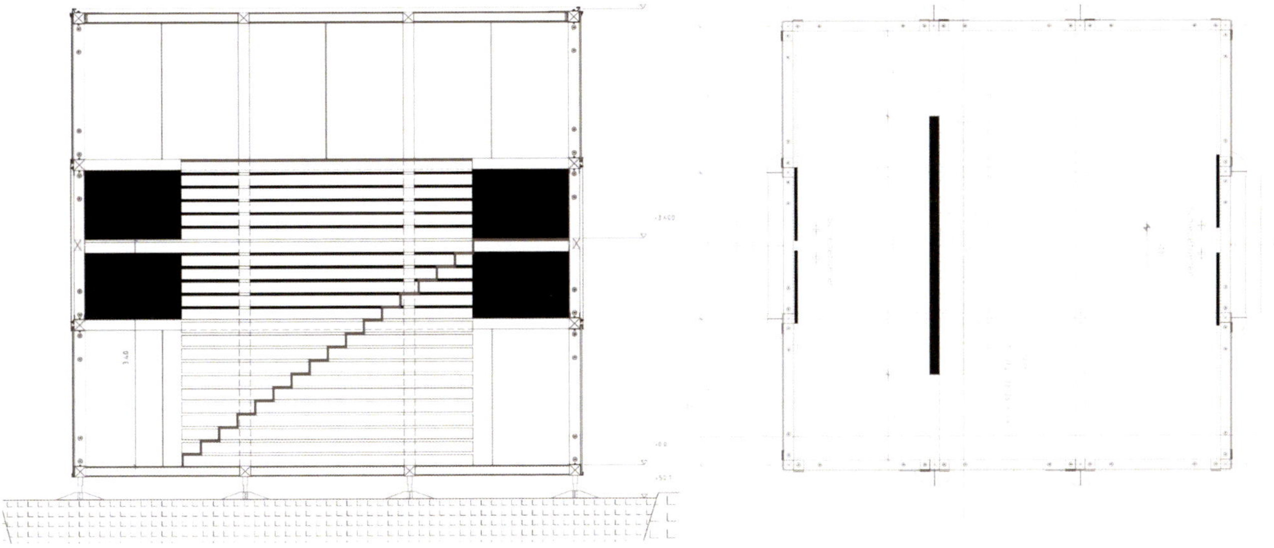

417

415 Infopavilion as attention catching cube for Art museum Ahrenshoop designed by a student of HS Wismar
416 German pavilion, Expo 2010 in Shanghai, China
417 Pavilion of HS Wismar for landscape exhibition, designed and built by students of HS Wismar – planning
418 Pavilion of HS Wismar for landscape exhibition, designed and built by students of HS Wismar

418

8.7 Flying building

"Flying building" or temporary structures are by definition of the relevant building regulations of the German states and the German Institute for Standardization (DIN) "physical structures that are suitable and intended to be repeatedly erected and dismantled." These are, for example carousel, non-stationary stands, amusement shops, booths, marquees, circus tents, temporary open-air stages and temporary stage roofs for concerts as well as temporary construction equipment for artistic performances in the air.

Flying architecture could be considered one of the best possible ways of future living by combining a house, a yacht, a private jet and a car – the often sought after luxury items that people wish they owned.

This way of living could be considered as a concept for future development – people may live and travel at the same time without leaving their own homes. Considerably high speeds to move from one place to another with the provision to land almost wherever desired without limitation of space is achievable – on a mountain top, at the beach, on the water and in the air.

These buildings could be stacked together to form collective structures or placed separately forming new communities or cities, anywhere and at anytime.

Traffic problems are reduced – there would be no need to own a car or to use other transportation means.

In addition, the buildings could provide autonomous systems including power production, warm energy, and water systems. They could also be used as a home, hospital or in cases of emergency as a school for refugees after world disasters.

These buildings can be designed for unique functions and also for a range of other functions. SkyLifter for example, is a vehicle building from an Australian company that resembles an alien space ship. It is 25 m in height and white in colour.

Although still in planning, SkyLifter is to be used for different purposes – to transport buildings to different places, carry heavy equipment or to take tourists to exotic locations.

Furthermore, it can pick up and carry loads of up to 150 tons. SkyLifter is powered by biodiesel and solar and does not produce downdraft or noise. Larger scale examples are entire cities raised as flying cities. These are huge airships that consist of housing, offices, laboratories and entertainment sectors, all of which are powered by the use of renewable resources.

Another group of flying buildings are structures in space, used by astronauts to fly above the atmosphere, allowing them to live comfortably for a limited time period.

Such structures allow humans to discover the universe while supporting space science.

Due to current technology and functionality, flying buildings can only be considered as short life span buildings.

They remain only a utopian dream of the future, which depends on further developments in the technical and mechanical fields.

419 Roof of exhibition area constructed from textile membrane

419

8.8 Floating building

Floating architecture is another type of short life span design.

There are many contributing factors that have lead to the idea of floating houses and their continued existence. Possibly the most important of these is the relation to climate change and global warming.

Floating homes are designed to adapt to rising sea levels, continuing to provide habitable spaces that survive afloat on water level rather than the unliveable flooded floor level.

Of the European countries, the Netherlands is the most vulnerable to rising sea levels, which is why it is a common topic for Dutch architects.

The Dutch are developing different city platforms that can rise with incoming waters such as the Rotterdam floating Pavilion, built in 2010 as a demonstration project to prove the viability of the technology.

Consisting of three connected and bubble-shaped transparent domes, it will stay anchored until 2015 and then moved to other waterfront areas in the Netherlands.

It is an exhibition for climate science and resource conservation while also serving as a meeting space. The idea is to extend the pavilion concept into an integrated urban district. The design will have offices, retail space and residences. The pavilion is powered by surface water, solar energy and has wastewater treatment.

Other Dutch architects, Waterstudio Architects, focus on designing floating buildings that also consider rising sea levels.

They build floating buildings all over the world with different functions including residence, hotels, restaurants, mosques, gardens, boulevards, car storages, water parks and even entire urban quarters.

Not only are rising sea levels an increasing issue but also the crisis of over-flooding of many areas in the world. Floating architecture is an ideal solution for areas that are permanently flooded. The idea is to accommodate to floodwaters, rather than to fight against them.

An example is the Nigerian floating school design in Lagos by architect Kunlé Adeyemi and NLE architects. The communities living along the water in Lagog have constant problems with flooding in the area.

This innovative floating school design ensures, that the children's education may continue no matter how high the water rises. The school will produce its own power via roof-mounted solar panels and use rainwater for the toilets.

420

420 "Water houses" in IBA Hamburg, Germany

8.9 Summary

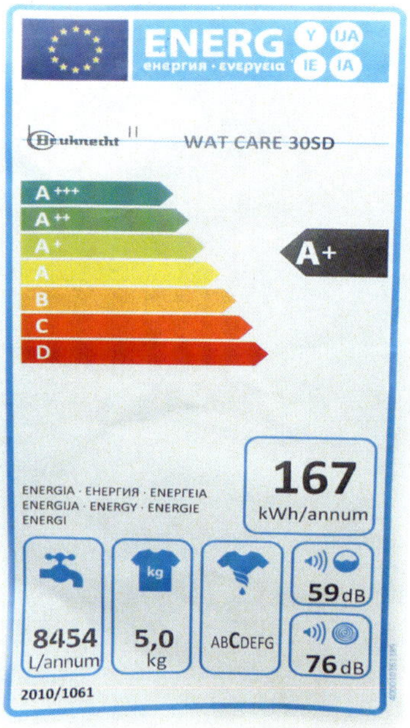

421

A Green Building certificate is not suitable for the certification of "building products" as the Green Building certificate only considers the life time of buildings. Therefore there is a need to develop a particular certification system that is suitable for short life span buildings with the focus on certifying building products.

421 "Energy pass" of a washing machine – could also become a method to certify "building products"
422 Prora, Rügen in Germany – example of a building built for a longer time span, but finally not used, very unsustainable for the environment

Short life span buildings normally have no connections to its location and region. They are products, similar to a fridge or furniture.
Normally, they require a shorter planning time than that of a long life span building. It often depends on the type of the short life span building:
unique product, e.g. Expo pavilion, was planned in a short time-frame and focuses mostly on architecture and resources
standard product, which is manufactured in a series, for example cars which requires a long planning process followed by the continuation of the development of the product.
It should be required to state the duration of a building that is going to be built. There is no general method to estimate how long a building will stand for.

It could be of interest if guidelines for the classification of a building's life time span were developed. It could help to estimate the building's life span over time and avoid the wasting of resources, energies and costs.
There have been many experiments to try and design mobile short life span buildings or building parts. Unfortunately most have failed because they were uneconomical and unsustainable.

The largest problem was the lack of flexibility because they are unable or are very difficult to change.
An example is the "Metastadt Wulfen" which was designed over 70 years by architects Richard J. Dietrich and Bernd Steigerwald. The idea was to build prefabricated steel units of 4.2 m in length and 3.6 m in height. They could be connected together when required to create a variety of spaces. They were built in 1973 and consisted of 100 flats.

The buildings were demolished in 1987 due to structural and physical defects. Also, the resources required to build such a buildings were far too high.

This was due to the doubling of required construction when several prefabricated units were connected together (e.g. ceiling of one unit connected to the floor of a unit above). It caused higher costs and was not at all sustainable.

Also, nonrenewable materials, which require high energy demands to be produced, were used (exhibition buildings) and therefore did not meet the recycling standards.
Another undesirable method occurrence is when a building that was planned for a certain time period stands for longer.
This brings great disadvantages because when it was built, it did not follow the principles for the design of a long life span building (no regional consideration). This is therefore very unsustainable.

422

The Solar Decathlon is an international award-winning program organised by U.S. Department of Energy. The idea is to design, build, and operate solar-powered houses that are cost-effective, energy-efficient, and attractive.

The first Solar Decathlon was held in 2002. The competition has since occurred in 2005, 2007, 2009, 2011 and 2014.

In 2009, the Solar Decathlon winner team was from Germany (Technical University of Darmstadt). Team Germany began with a "focus on the facade", creating a house that was essentially a two-storey cube.
The surface was covered with solar cells; a 11.1 kW photovoltaic (PV) system made of 40 single-crystal silicon panels on the roof and about 250 thin-film copper indium gallium selenide (CIGS) panels on the sides that were expected to produce an incredible 200 % of the energy required for the house.
The facade's highly insulating, custom vacuum insulation panels, plus the phase-change material within the drywall will maintain comfortable temperatures. Automated louvre-covered windows block unwanted solar heat.

In 2014, students from Hochschule Wismar also took part in the Solar Decathlon, with their simple one and half story house, south facade and roof covered with photovoltaic panels.

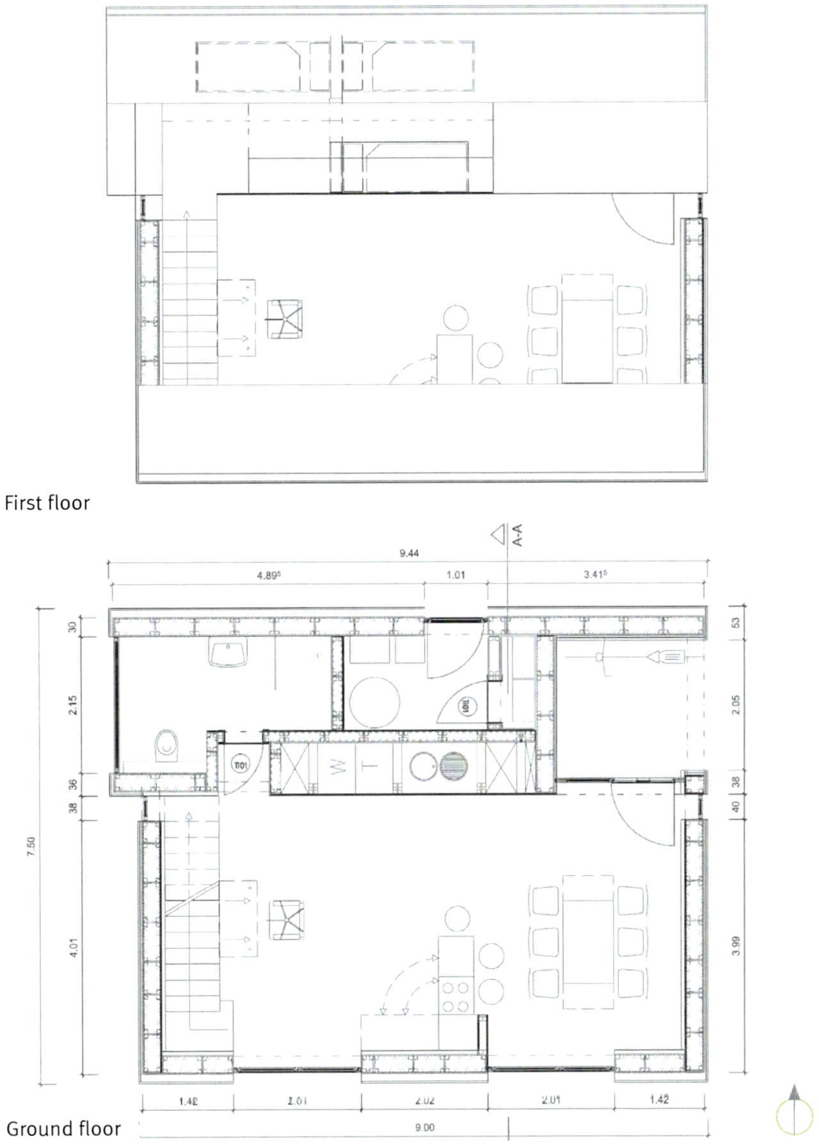

423

424

425

423 Project by students of Hochschule Wismar for Solar Decathlon – floor plans
424 Project by students of Hochschule Wismar for Solar Decathlon – view
425 Project by students of Hochschule Wismar for Solar Decathlon – east side

426

426 The development of a building concept is determined by various conditions - building function, space and functional requirements, user behaviour, building orientation, material and energy losses and the availability of sources - Passive house theatre, Wismar, IGEL-Institut

Life time design

9.0 Building concept

9.0 Building concept

9.1 Introduction

427

In the design phase, the basic concepts of sustainability are space, material, energy, water and costs. In order to prove and optimise these concepts, rough calculations may be used.

In this chapter, these formulas and rough calculations for development are shown. As you move into the following phases (for construction permission and building realization), exact calculations and simulations should be made.

In the chapter **'9.2 Space concept'**, structured methods are outlined to save resources and energy. To achieve a sustainable design, the most important of these methods to consider include space concept, appropriate space use and space saving.
Based on the desired life span of a building, the sustainable concept should be deciphered during the first design stages.

For **short life span buildings**, the first and fifth life cycles are important phases to consider. In order to save resources, an appropriate 'Material concept' should be developed.

In the first phase, it is important to consider which materials and methods are used for construction. In the fifth phase, at the end of the buildings life span, one should consider what happens to the building's structure and land after removal.

The goal of the 'Material concept' is to create intelligent resource saving construction with low environmental impacts and easily recyclable or reusable qualities without the production of waste. In addition, a smart foundation system should be deconstructible after the building's life, leaving the landscape untouched.

In the chapter **'9.3 Material concept'**, methods to estimate building element dimensions during the designing phase and methods to evaluate the ecological value of different materials are described. These estimates are then used to develop an appropriate material concept that will reduce resources and emissions.

The goals of a **long life span building** are different to that of a short life span. Materials are chosen to last longer, and land treatment is designed to withstand permanent structure. As operation time is longer, methods to reduce energy requirements are considered with an 'Energy concept'.
For long life span buildings, the material concept is also considered but in this case for their long life materials, maintenance and cleaning.

In the chapter **'9.4 Energy concept'**, methods are shown to estimate the energy demand for heating, cooling, warm water and ventilation power energy including how to dimension basic systems for energy generation and storing. On the other hand,

427 Double facade detail
428 Example of a simple building energy flow diagram with the balance of inputs and outputs
429 Eco system of a building
430 Determining conditions of building concept
431 To create a sustainable building concept, each aspects have to be considered – e.g. ease of maintenance and cleaning

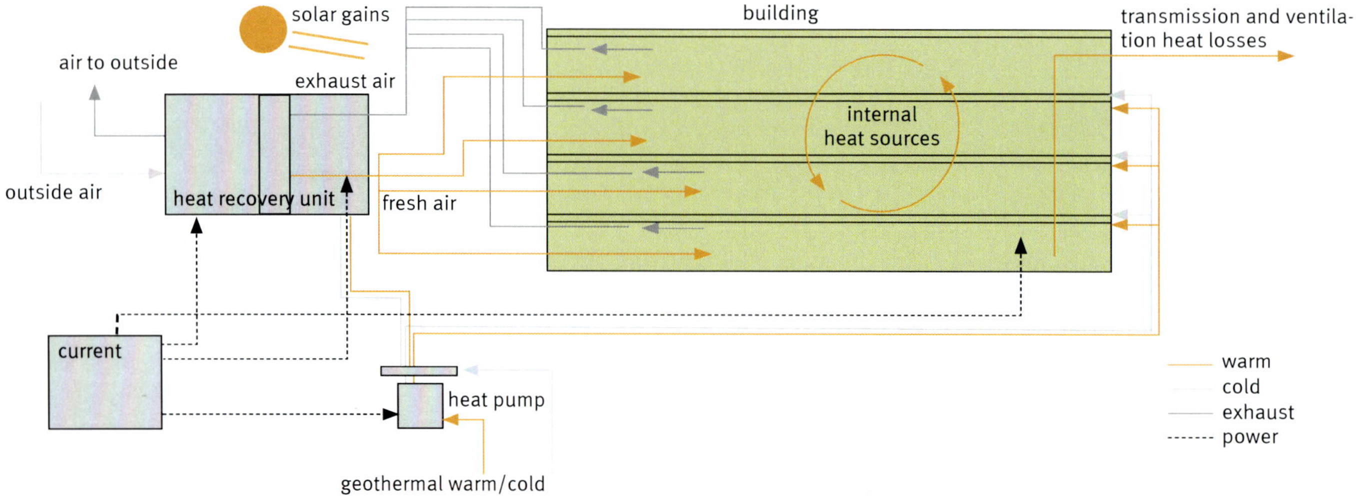

428

the ecological evaluation of different resources used to generate the energy encourages emission and primary energy savings.

An adequate **'Water concept'** will provide estimated potable water requirements and water recycling methods which will reduce water use and save on water resources.
Rough calculations made in the design phase are used to develop appropriate energy concepts that help to reduce energy use during building operation and provide intelligent energy management.

The **'Life cycle concept'** describes the whole buildings life outlined by a Life Cycle Assessment (LCA page 15 and 72) and Life Cycle Costing (LCC page 15 and 264).
Investors are attentive to Life Cycle Costing as this shows building costs not only during the building construction process, but also during the whole buildings life. Here, a building's rent-ability for initial investment can be found. Rough Life Cycle Cost calculations can be found in chapter **'9.6 Economy concept'.**

As a result of these calculations, the feasibility, advantages and cost saving benefits for additional investment to increase structural performance (i.e. better thermal insulation using modern building technology based on renewable resources) can be seen.

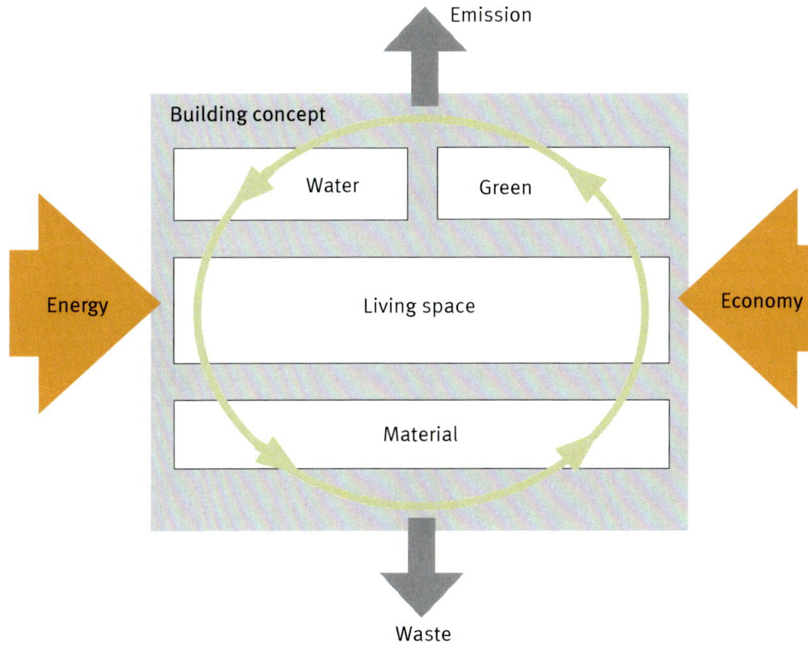

429

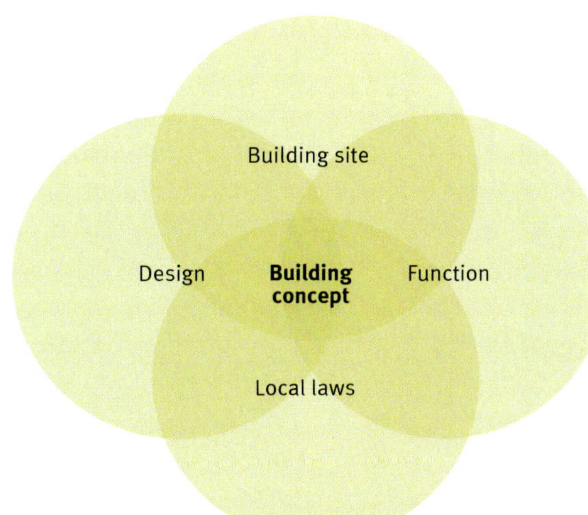

430

431

9.2 Space concept

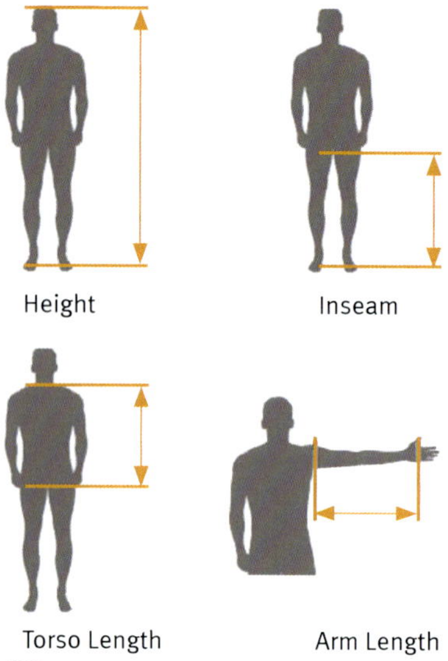

432

The aim of economical space management is to optimise the possibilities of small space consumption in consideration with ergonomic requirements. However, this varies for new or re-constructed buildings.

For **new constructions**, a space concept may be designed beginning with

1. An estimation of the required floor area, and depending on the buildings function.

Minimal floor areas, air volumes, room heights, dimensioning of toilets and other requirements for the workplace in Germany can be found in the 'Arbeitsstättenverordnung' (Workplace regulation). Values for these may be found in the table below.

Regulations for residential buildings in Germany may be found in the 'Wohnungsbaunormen' (Housing construction standards).

The DIN 18040 (barrier-free building) documents outline space demand values for disabled persons in different space functions.

Additional norms, regulations and guidelines for minimal, optimal and maximal space requirements for the dimensioning of building spaces are also included.

The Norm DIN 277 describes the calculation method for the buildings floor areas and volumes (page 17). Information obtained helps one to calculate areas that are required for different rooms and zones, e.g.

$$FA = FA_p \cdot N_p$$

where
FA – floor area [m²]
FA_p – required FA for one person [m²]
N_p – number of persons

Space requirements are based on the ergonomic principles of the person that uses that space, their age, type of activity they do and the furniture or equipment they require.

Children for example, have different space requirements compared to adults. Disabled people (depending on the type of disability) have higher space requirements for movement and access.

Understanding a persons scale, considering movability and reach distance as well as the dimension of furniture and equipment used in the rooms is a very important component of designing space appropriately.

When floor areas are estimated, they can be compared and evaluated against the space consumption of other homes, or companies with similar structures.

From these comparisons, evaluations can be found to clarify whether surfaces are adequate or alternatively, over dimensioned.

432 Good space management is required to meet and consider human scale requirements
433 Minimal light height of a room by different floor area, Germany
434 Floor area for different spaces in residential/office building, Germany

Working and break room Room light height [m]	**Floor area [m²]**
Min. 2.50	< 50
Min. 2.75	> 50
Min. 3.00	> 100
Min. 3.25	> 2.000
Dressing room, washing room	
Min. 2.30	< 30
Min. 2.50	> 30

433

Office building	**Floor area [m²/person]**
Computer workplace in single office	8 - 10
Computer workplace in group office	12 - 15
Computer workplace in landscape office	15 approx. 400 m² total
Conference, training	0.3 - 1.0
Entry hall	0.2 - 0.6
Toilets, wash room	0.6 - 0.8
Corridors	1.5 - 4.0
Stairs, elevator	0.8 - 2.0
Tea kitchen, canteen	0.8 - 1.5
Printer room, machine room, ...	0.6 - 1.5
Archive	0.4 - 1.0
Storage	0.4 - 1.5
Post office	0.3 - 0.5
Computer centre	0.5 - 1.5
Building technology	2.4 - 4.6
Building construction	1.9 - 3.8
Parking place	0 - 13.0

434

2. The analyse of a building and building parts use during different times (day/night use, week/weekend use, seasonal use). The possibility of double use rooms, building parts or the whole building is to be proofed. (diagrams page 142-143)

3. The correct organisation of different functional zones is also an important criteria.

Goals to achieve this include maximising the usable floor area (e.g. in office building the workplace area or in residential building the living area) and minimise the traffic area (e.g. corridors, stairs, elevators, ...) and secondary zones (e.g. technology, storage, ...).

Two additional elements also important to the space concept include the depth and structural grid of a building. For example, office buildings with irregular structural grids are found to have greater distances than required between internal walls resulting in wasted floor area. Buildings that increase floor plan depth are also decreasing their space utilization.

By creating a space concept for the reconstruction of a building, similar principles can be used.

First, the actual spatial demands are to be described. Then, the reality of spatial use is to be analysed and documented. From this analysis, the unused or less frequently used spaces as well as the functional and spatial organisation can be determined.

In respect, organisational issues are realized and thereafter space optimising proposals may be designed. Future function - if the functional use remains or if the building is reused for a new function, is also an important concept to be considered. In this case, the most suitable function must be considered for the future as this also helps with the analysis of the current concepts.

Rentable building spaces are an example of a properties strong economical gains. In these cases, space management is of even higher importance due to profit gained per m² for the owner.

435 An appropriate floor area of a flat or single family house based on determination of surface needs in residential building according to DIN 18022, DIN 18025-1 and DIN 18025-2, Germany
436 Air volume for a person in a working room in accordance with ArbStättV VO, Germany
437 Average flat floor area for different number of persons who live there

Type of room	**1 person**	**2 persons**	**3 persons**	**4 persons**	**5 persons**	**6 persons**
Living room		18 m²	18 m²	20 m²	22 m²	22 m²
Living bedroom	[25 m²]					
Living room with eating corner	20 m²	[20 m²]	[22 m²]	[25 m²]		
Eating corner		5 m²	6 m²	6 m²	8 m²	10 m²
Working corner	2 m²	2 m²	2 m²	2 m²	2 m²	2 m²
Bedroom	11 m²	15 m²	15 m²	15 m²	15 m²	15 m²
Child room - 1 bed			11 m²	11 m²	11 m²	11 m²
Child room - 1 bed				11 m²		11 m²
Child room - 2 beds				[14 m²]	14 m²	14 m²
Kitchen	7 m²	8 m²	8 m²	8 m²	8 m²	8 m²
Cooking corner	[5.5 m²]					
Household room					6 m²	6 m²
Bad	4 m²	4 m²	5 m²	5 m²	5 m²	5 m²
Additional toilet room					4 m²	4 m²
Corridor with storage	5 m²	6 m²	6 m²	7 m²	7 m²	7 m²
Floor area total		**58 m²**	**71 m²**	**85 m²**	**102 m²**	**115 m²**
Living bedroom	[45 m²]					
Living room with eating corner	47.5 m²	[60 m²]	[75 m²]	[87 m²]		

435

Working room Air volume for a person
Min. 12 m³ when mostly sitting activity
Min. 15 m³ when mostly non-sitting activity
Min. 18 m³ when hard body work

436

Number of persons	**Floor area [m²]**
1	45 - 50
2	60 or 2 living rooms
3	75 or 3 living rooms
4	85 - 90 or 4 living rooms
for each 1 person more	10 m² or 1 living room more

437

9.3 Material concept

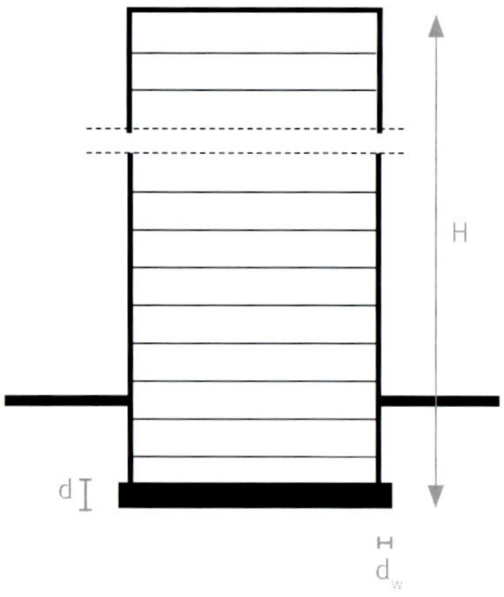

438

Material choice is considered as one part of the building's sustainable concept. Elements important to consider are the locality and availability of different materials, their physical characteristics (e.g. thermal conductivity, insulation or storing characteristic) and their ecological values.

Structural building element dimensions have a direct impact on resource and material savings.

A building's materials are generally categorized into the following groups:

- main structural bearing (foundation, walls, columns, beams, ...)
- non-bearing construction (walls, ceilings, roofs, ...)
- openings (doors, windows, ...)
- insulation materials (thermal, waterproof, acoustic, fire protection, ...)
- coating (flooring, paintings, cladding, roofing, ...)
- technology elements (equipment and piping for water, heating, lighting, electricity, ventilation, sanitary)

9.3.1 Rough structural dimensioning

Dimensioning of the buildings main structural elements are determined by the distances between components.

Efficient dimensioning increases resource savings – e.g. appropriate distances between columns can save material required for beams.

Basic values used to estimate structural elements can be found in the table 439.

These values are used as rough calculations at the beginning of the design phases. However, for exact dimensioning, static calculators should be used.

E.g. 1: Reinforced concrete ceiling with the span of 6,000 mm:
l/20 = 6,000 mm/20 = 300 mm
Height of the ceiling is 300 mm.
E.g. 2: Light wooden ceiling with the span of 6,000 mm:
l/20 = 6,000 mm/20 = 300 mm - 10% = 270 mm
Height of the ceiling is 270 mm.
E.g. 3: Wooden column with the height of 3,000 mm:
l/20 = 3,000 mm/20 = 150 mm
Column radius is 150 mm (cylindrical section), or 150 mm/150 mm (square section).

A buildings element dimensioning not only calculates the bearing characteristics but it is also an important aspect of overall **building physics** (page 16). To calculate the building material's physical characteristics quickly and easily for the buildings construction (e.g. thermal protection, moisture protection, condensation, overheating protection, ...), the web page u.wert.net may be used.

438 Reinforced concrete plate foundation dimensioning

d [cm] = H [mm]/30 ≥ 300 mm, or d [mm] = 100 . number of floors

439 Basic values to be used for rough estimation of building structure dimensions

440 Example – dimensioning of inteligent resource-saving trussed roof construction – the wooden beam height is estimated at l/40 and the steel substructure height of l/12

441 Example calculation of the ecological balance (construction and end of life) for a concrete stone wall with density 2,000 kg/m³ and dimension of 10 m³ = 20,000 kg – ecological values based on Ökobau.dat

Beam and ceiling	**Dimensioning**
Wooden beam	l/20
Steel construction beam	l/30
Wide-span steel lattice beam, parallel	l/10
Wide-span steel lattice beam, triangle form	l/8
Wide-span wood lattice beam, parallel	l/15
Wide-span wood lattice beam, triangle form	≥ l/10
Reinforced concrete ceiling	l/20
Lighter ceiling (e.g. light concrete, wooden ceilings)	- 10 %
Column	
Reinforced concrete column	l/20
Wooden column	l/20
Steel column	l/30

439

440

9.3.2 Ecological material evaluation

The ecological evaluation of a buildings materials decipher the global warming potential (GWP), ozone depletion potential (ODP), photochemical ozone creation potential (POCP), acidification potential (AP), eutrophication potential (EP), primary energy nonrenewable (PEnre), primary energy renewable (PEre) and water use in different building life cycles. These are the main indicators that tell us about the ecological characteristics of different materials.

While the ecological evaluation is required for building certification, it is also helpful to compare values of different materials, allowing one to choose ecologically.

The lower the number that can be calculated, the greater the ecological value of the material.

In addition, the ecological evaluation is considered a part of the LCA (page 15 and 72) which is used to assess the environmental impacts associated with all stages of a product's life. Calculations can be made manually, with an excel sheet, or with a range of software, such as Legep®.

The ecological evaluation of a building's construction and its successive end of life is based on values from ökobau.dat.

Ökobau.dat consists of different building material constructions and their associated ecological values for each unit of building material.

$Val_m = Val_{öko} \cdot N_m$

where

$Val_{öko}$ – value found in the ökobau.dat table

Val_m – value for amount of material

N_m – the amount of material used in the building [kg or m³]

For further information and values, visit the web page here: http://www.nachhaltigesbauen.de/baustoff-und-gebaeudedaten/oekobaudat.html

Ökobau.dat

"The Ökobau.dat, the development of the first German building material database for the determination of global, ecological effects, provides a simplified basis for data for the ecological evaluation of buildings. (...) The researcher had developed a number of data records in XML format for the further use in existing life cycle calculation tools with the support of the German Construction Materials Industry. Using so-called style sheets, currently around 650 construction materials or construction and transport processes are described in terms of their effects. For every data entry, alongside the ecological details, details are also given regarding the source data such as reference unit, validity, data quality etc." [73]

[73] *BMU;* Assessment System for Sustainable Building: Practical Aids and Tools [http://www.nachhaltigesbauen.de/sustainable-building-english-speaking-information/assessment-system-for-sustainable-building.html] (04.05.2014)

Inputs	Value (Ökobau.dat)	Percentage [%]	End of life – Construction waste treatment (Ökobau.dat)	Concrete wall construction calculation (value . 10 m³)	Concrete wall construction waste treatment calculation (end of life . 20,000 kg)
PEnre	0.682 MJ/m³		0.0535 MJ/kg	6.82 MJ	1,070 MJ
Lignite		27 %			
Hard coal		19 %			
Natural gas		10 %			
Petroleum		32 %			
Uranium		13 %			
PEre	0.0594 MJ/m³		0.00214 MJ/kg	0.594 MJ	42.8 MJ
Water power		16 %			
Wind power		35 %			
Solar energy		49 %			
Biomass					
Recovered fuels	0.362 MJ/m³		$3.1031E^{-6}$ MJ/kg	3.62 MJ	0.02062 MJ
Water	52.5 kg/m³		1.08325 kg/kg	525 kg	21,665 kg
Outputs					
EP	$3E^{-5}$ kg PO_4-Equiv./m³		$4.43234E^{-6}$ kg PO_4-Equiv./kg	3 E^{-4} kg PO_4-Equiv.	0.0887 kg PO_4-Equiv.
ODP	$9.6E^{-11}$ kg R_{11}-Equiv./m³		$1.897711E^{-12}$ kg R_{11}-Equiv./kg	$9.6E^{-10}$ kg R_{11}-Equiv.	$3.7954E^{-8}$ kg R_{11}-Equiv.
POCP	$2.014E^{-5}$ kg C_2H_4-Equiv./m³		$2.69195E^{-6}$ kg C_2H_4-Equiv./kg	$2.014E^{-4}$ kg C_2H_4-Equiv.	0.05384 kg C_2H_4-Equiv.
GWP	0.11 kg CO_2-Equiv./m³		0.00272 kg CO_2-Equiv./kg	1.1 kg CO_2-Equiv.	54.4 kg CO_2-Equiv.
AP	0.000211 kg SO_2-Equiv./m³		$2.53439E^{-5}$ kg SO_2-Equiv./kg	0.00211 kg SO_2-Equiv.	0.50698 kg SO_2-Equiv.

441

9.4 Energy concept

Air temperature [°C]	Relative air humidity [%]
20	80
22	70
24	62
26	55

442

All buildings require operational energy. Therefore the creation of an energy concept at the very beginning of a building's design helps to optimise the building energy balance and waste reduction. With a developed energy concept, rough calculations based on the average experienced values can be used to evaluate building energy flows.

Main goals and solutions for the building energy concept are specified during the first building design phase. Calculating exact building energy flows is the next step of building design, including building elements and technology.

There are two main parameters required to develop an energy concept:

- energy demand (losses/outputs)
- energy generation (gains/inputs)

In ideal conditions, the energy demand should equal the energy generation so that a balance is created between inputs and outputs.

Firstly, the buildings energy demand is to be calculated, depending on the buildings location, function, size and substance (renovation or new buildings, construction standard). The building requires energy to heat, cool and to create warm water, to ventilate the building and for power (including lighting and building equipment). The best way to describe the building's energy concept is by a simple schematic that shows energy requirements and energy generation systems (example table 431, 445).
Due to variations of building situation during the day/night or during seasonal periods, at least four sections (winter day, winter night, summer day, summer night) should be drawn in order to display the full extent of the building energy concept .

9.4.1 Boundary conditions of functional zones

Every building function or building zone has different boundary conditions depending on the day/night time use, hourly use, or days used per year. Different functions require ranging interior temperatures, lighting intensity and varied heat gains from the people or equipment inside. These are the factors to be considered while creating the energy concept.
Different functions also have different demands. For example the summer cooling in an office building is more important to consider than the heating for the winter, because it requires a larger amount of energy. On the other hand, the heating and warm water generation in residential buildings is more important than the summer cooling.
The classification of the functions needs to be done before creating an energy concept and should follow the main requirements of the function.

442 The maximum relative air humidity by different room temperatures in accordance to ArbStättV, Germany
443 Student example – four energy concept sections – winter day, winter night
444 Basic values for the boundary conditions of different functional zones based on the German norm DIN V 18599-10:2011-12, Germany
445 Student example – four energy concept sections – summer day, summer night

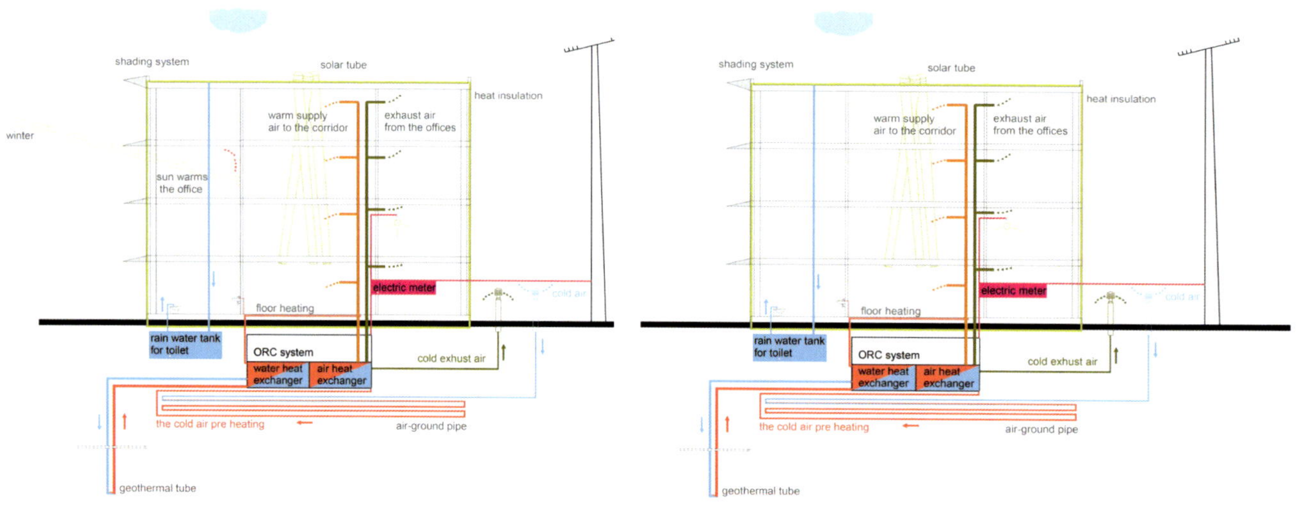

443

Type of usage	Use time [h]	Annual use time [d/a]	Lighting intensity [lux]	Relative absence	Heat sources persons [Wh/m²d]	Heat sources equipment [Wh/m²d]
Personal office (single occupant)	07:00-18:00	250	500	0.3	30	42
Group office (max. 6 workers)	07:00-18:00	250	500	0.3	30	42
Landscape office (min. 7 workers)	07:00-18:00	250	500	0	42	60
Conference, seminar	07:00-18:00	250	500	0.5	96	8
Classroom (school)	08:00-15:00	200	300	0.25	100	20
Lecture hall, auditorium	08:00-18:00	150	500	0.25	420	24
Canteen	08:00-15:00	250	200	0	177	10
Restaurant	10:00-00:00	300	200	0	236	14
Kitchen in nonresidential building	10:00-23:00	300	500	0	56	1,800
Kitchen – preparing, storage	10:00-23:00	300	300	0.5	56	180
Sanitary rooms in nonresidential building	07:00-18:00	250	200	0.9	0	0
Other living rooms	07:00-18:00	250	300	0.5	96	8
Secondary rooms	07:00-18:00	250	100	0.9	0	0
Traffic area (corridors, ...)	07:00-18:00	250	100	0.8	0	0
Storage, technology, archive	07:00-18:00	250	100	0.98	0	0
Server room, data centre	0:00-24:00	365	500	0.5	15	1,800
Workshop	07:00-16:00	250	500	0	28	245
Congress	09:00-18:00	150	300	0.5	138	12
Exhibition rooms and museum	10:00-18:00	250	200	0	28	0
Library – reading hall	08:00-20:00	300	500	0	168	0
Library – freehand area	08:00-20:00	300	200	0	42	0
Sporting hall	08:00-23:00	300	300	0.3	60	0
Shopping facility without cooled products	08:00-20:00	300	300	0	84	24
Shopping facility with cooled products	08:00-20:00	300	300	0	84	-170
Residential, bedroom	0:00-24:00	365	300	0	108	24
Single family house					50	
Multi-family house					100	
Hotel room	21:00-08:00	365	200	0.25	70	44
Theatre – audience	19:00-23:00	250	200	0	186	0
Theatre – foyer	19:00-23:00	250	300	0,5	88	0
Theatre – stage	13:00-23:00	250	1000	0	0	0
Parking house (office, private use)	07:00-18:00	250	75	0.95	0	0
Parking house (public use)	09:00-00:00	365	75	0.8	0	0

444

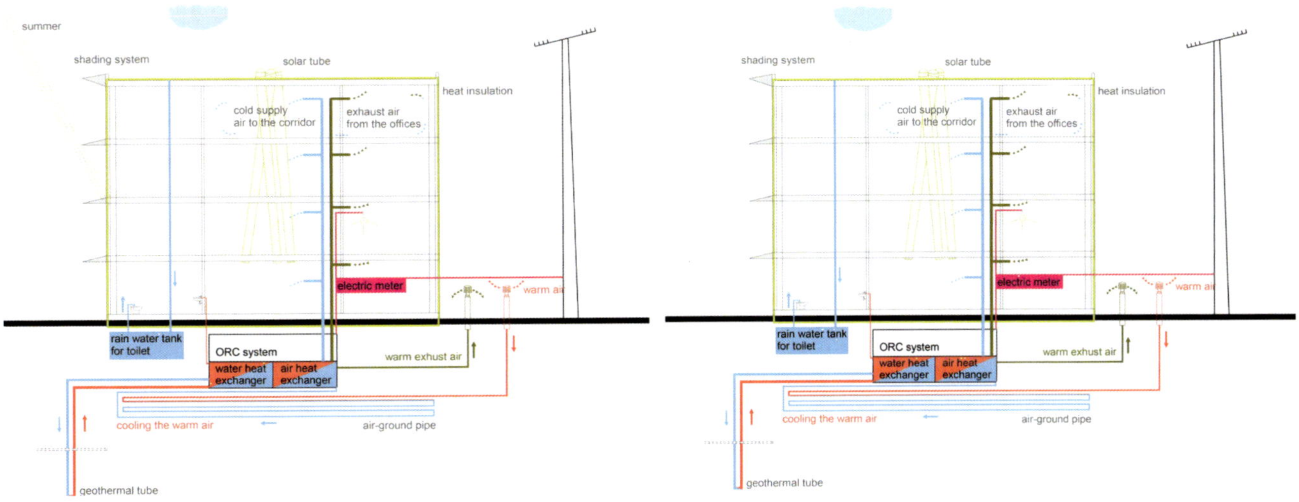

445

9.4 Energy concept

9.4.2 Rough estimation of energy demand

Heat energy demand Q_h [kWh/a]

First, one must decide which energy standard the building is to achieve. This can be found in the energy standards (page 10), of which shows the maximum heat energy demands for different energy standards per m² of useful building area.

Rough building energy demand can be calculated as following:

$$Q_h = Q_{hUFA} \cdot HFA$$

where

Q_h – heat energy demand [kWh/a]

Q_{hHFA} – area-specific heat energy demand [kWh/m²a]

HFA – heated floor area [m²]

Building design should follow the chosen energy standard (e.g. for the passive house standard, appropriate thermal insulation, air-tightness of the building envelope and heat recovery ventilation should be implemented within the building design).
Standard guides and methods, i.e. DIN 4701 in Germany are available to calculate exact heat demand. The calculation is based on the balance of thermal energy losses and gains.
Thermal energy losses are equal to thermal transmittance heat losses (via surrounding surface) and ventilation losses (heating of incoming outside air).

446 Determined dimension of the thermal lead wire connection due to the peak loads in the cold winter period, example weather of Hannover in December 2011

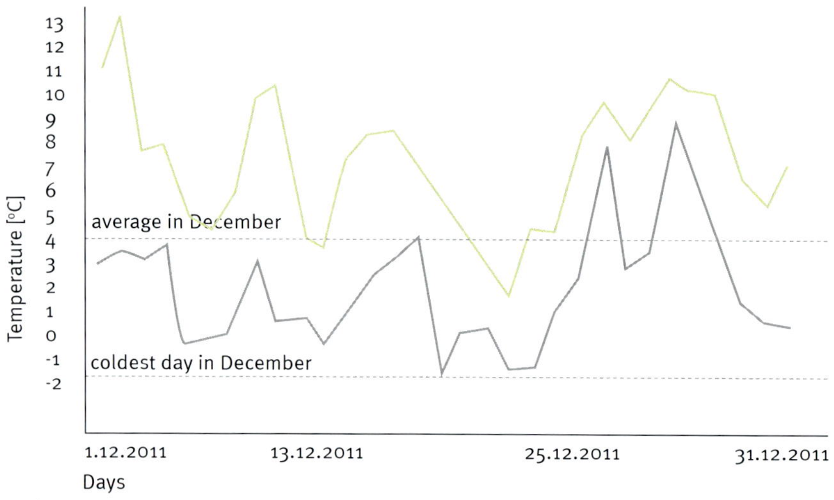

446

Thermal energy gains are equal to passive solar thermal gains (absorbed through windows and opaque surrounding surfaces) and passive internal gains (from the people and building equipment). The remaining energy required to balance the thermal energy losses must be gained by additional heating (an active item).

To dimension the heating system, **static heat energy and peak loads** during the extreme cold winter days and nights must be considered.

This requires the inside temperature to be stable (depends on function, e.g. 20 °C) not only during average outside temperatures, but also when the outside temperature is extremely cold, e.g. - 20 °C.

Peak loads dimensioning

The heating system should be dimensioned so that it can cover the peak loads, or so that an additional heating system may be provided for the moments of extreme cold weather conditions (e.g. a connection to the public network).

To determine an accurate assessment of the boiler and heating surfaces, calculations should be based on DIN EN 12831.

Rough estimation of the lead wire:

120 W/HFA – existing thermally uninsulated building
80 W/HFA – restored or renovated building, uninsulated new building
60 W/HFA – new building with standard thermal insulation
40 W/HFA – new building built in accordance to EnEV 2009
15 W/HFA – passive house
Additional capacity of 250 W/person is planned in the case that the heating system serves also for warm water.

Different software may be used to calculate the exact heat energy demand or heat load simulations. Some examples of software are introduced in the chapter '10.0 Methods and instruments'.

Warm water demand Q_w [kWh/a]

Warm water demands vary between building use depending not only on the building size or the number of people, but also the lifestyle, age, water installations and season.

In the table 449 below, details are outlined on warm water demand and temperatures for different building types, based on the empirical values of warm water consumption.

Values are presented per day and as m² of useful area or unit. To calculate the total whole year consumption, the following formula can be used:

$$Q_w = Q_{wUFA} \cdot UFA \cdot N_d \ / \ Q_w = Q_{wP} \cdot N_P \cdot N_d$$

where
Q_w – warm water demand [kWh/a]
Q_{wUFA} – area-specific warm water demand [kWh/m²d]
UFA – usable floor area [m²]
Q_{wP} – usage dependent warm water demand [kWh/person.d]
N_P – number of persons
N_d – number of usable days per year

Example: A school with 60 students use the shower facilities 200 days per year.

$Q_w = Q_{wP} \cdot N_P \cdot N_d =$
$= 1{,}5$ kWh/d . 60 students . 200 d $=$
18,000 kWh/year

Warm water demand of the school is 18,000 kWh/year.

447 The warm water demand and temperatures for different building types in accordance to German norm DIN V 18599-10:2011-12

Type of usage	Area-specific demand Q_{wUFA} [Wh/m²$_{UFA}$d]	Reference area [m²]	Usage dependent demand Q_{wP} [kWh/person (bed, seat, meal).d]	Usage dependent demand [l/person(bed).d]	Temperature [°C]
Office building, laboratory	30	office floor area	0.4	10 - 40	45 °C
Hospital, bedroom	530	wards and rooms	8.0	100 - 300	60 °C
School without showers	170	classrooms	0.5	5 - 15	45 °C
School with showers	500	classrooms	1.5	30 - 50	45 °C
Retail shop, department store	10	sales areas	1.0	10 - 40	45 °C
Workshop, industrial facility	75	workshop area	1.5		
Modest hotel	190	hotel bedrooms	1.5		
Medium-class hotel	450	hotel bedrooms	4.5		
Luxury-class hotel	580	hotel bedrooms	7		
Restaurant	1,250	public rooms	1.5		
Residential building	230	rooms	3.5		
Single-family house	12,000	useful area			
Multiple-family house	16,000	useful area			
Modest apartments				10 - 20	60 °C
Medium-class apartments				20 - 40	60 °C
Luxury-class apartments				40 - 80	60 °C
Sauna	235	sauna area	2.8		
Fitness	300	fitness area	1.5		
Sport facilities with shower			1.5	50 - 70	45 °C
Commercial kitchen, canteen			0.4		
Bakery			5.0	105 - 150	45 °C
Hairdresser			6.0	150 - 200	45 °C
Butcher with production			18.0	400 - 500	45 °C
Laundry			20.0 kWh/100 kg laundry	250 - 300 l/100 kg laundry	75 °C
Brewery with production			15.0 kWh/100 l beer	250 - 300 l/100 l beer	60 °C
Dairy			10.0 kWh/100 l milk	1 - 1.5 l/l milk	75 °C

447

9.4 Energy concept

Building type	Power demand [kWh/a]
Single flat	approx. 1,700
2 persons flat	approx. 2,900
3 persons flat	approx. 3,900
4 persons flat	approx. 4,500
Single family house	approx. 7,000 - 10,000

448

448 Values for the average electricity consumption of household per year (2008) in Germany
449 The factor for calculating power demand, based on the experience of different building types in Germany
450 The general capacity of different electrical equipment in the building, the exact capacity is always in manual instructions to the equipment

Building type or zone	Area-specific power demand P_{elNFA} [kWh/m²$_{NFA}$a]
Single family house	12
Multi-family house	16
Residential building	13
Public building (office building, sport building,...)	17.2
Gastronomy	200
Elevator	1.5
Heat pump	1 - 2

449

Power demand [kWh/a]

A buildings power supply is required for artificial lighting, electrical equipment (e.g. washing machine, dryer, fridge, freezer, dishwasher, electric stove, microwave, electric heater, television, computer,...), and for machine ventilation and cooling.

In some cases this also includes electrical warm water generation and heating (i.e. by heat pump).

Rough calculations to estimate the power demand:

1. The most simple rough building power demand estimation:

$W_{el} = W_{elNFA} \cdot NFA$
where
W_{el} – power demand [kWh/a]
W_{elNFA} – area-specific power demand [kWh/m²a]
NFA – net floor area [m²]

2. The calculation for household power demand was developed by the Association of Energy Consumers (Bund der Energieverbraucher) in Germany based on the analysis of Federal Ministry of Economics (Bundesministeriums für Wirtschaft). This method is based on the useful living area, occupancy and number of household appliances.
The following calculation is for a four person family, living in an 87 m² home with electrical equipment (.8) :

Equipment	Capacity [W/h]
Computer	400
Energy saving lamp	11
Television	70
Dishwasher	820
Stove oven	4,000
Coffee machine	1,000
Air conditioner	2,500
Fridge	26
Microwave	700
Vacuum cleaner	1,500
Stereo system	1,000
Washing machine, dryer	1,000
Hair dryer	2,000
Water heater	2,000

450

a) Living area (m²) . 9 kWh
(e.g. 87 m² . 9 kWh = 783 kWh)

b) Household occupancy . 200 kWh
(e.g. 4 persons . 200 kWh = 800 kWh)
Where warm water is electrically generated, 200 kWh increases to 550 kWh (e.g. 4 persons . 400kWh)

c) Number of household electrical equipment . 200 kWh
(e.g. 8 equip. . 200 kWh = 1,600 kWh)

d) The sum of numbers 1, 2, 3 results in the overall household power demand
(e.g. W_{el} = 783 kWh + 800 kWh + 1,600 = 3,183 kWh)

The calculated household requires 3,183 kWh of power in a year.

3. Separating the calculation of individual power demands, then adding the sum will provide you with a more overall and accurate power demand.

This procedure may be used for all building types.

Lighting power demand is calculated by multiplying lamp and lighting time. Additional methods to calculate lighting demand are described on the following page.

Example: 2 fluorescent lamps with the capacity P_{el} = 18 W/h and 12 hours of lighting a day used the whole year.

$W_{ellight}$ = 2 lamps . 18 W/h . 12 h . 365 d= 157.680 kWh/a

The following formula can be used to calculate an accurate power demand for electrical equipment:

$W_{elequip} = P_{el} \cdot t$
where
$W_{elequip}$ – equipment power demand [kWh/a]
P_{el} – equipment capacity [W/h]
t – time of use per year [h/a]

Power demand estimations for machine ventilation, cooling, electrical warm water and heating are described on the following pages.

Lighting energy demand [kWh/a]

The energy demand for lighting is one component of the overall power demand. When artificial lighting is present, the electric energy levels are required.

Table 451 below is a guide to calculate the building's lighting electric energy demand. It shows the limit and goal values for the artificial lighting capacity of different zones within a building.

To calculate the power demand for an artificially lighted zone, the following formula can be used:

$W_{ellight} = P_{ellight} \cdot t \cdot UFA$

where

$W_{ellight}$ – power demand for an artificial lighting of the zone [kWh/a]

$P_{ellight}$ – lighting electrical capacity of the zone [W/m²$_{UFA}$h]

t – time of use per year [h/a]

UFA – zones usable floor area [m²]

The result represents power demand for the whole functional zone. Demands of different zones may be combined to calculate the artificial lighting power demand for the entire building.

451 Lighting power demand for different building zones – limit and goal values – limit value boundary conditions are: room reflection grade 0.7; 0.5; 0.2, light bulb with light yield > 75 lm/W, light efficiency 70 %, window/floor surface ratio of 30 %, time control, daylight areas without presence detectors, other areas with presence detectors – goal value boundary conditions are: room reflection grade 0.8; 0.5; 0.3, light bulb with light yield > 90 lm/W, light efficiency 85 %, window/floor surface ratio of 30 %, daylight-based control, all areas with presence detectors

Type of usage	Limit $P_{ellight}$ [W/m²$_{UFA}$h]	Limit [h/a]	Limit [kWh/m²$_{UFA}$a]	Goal $P_{ellight}$ [W/m²$_{UFA}$h]	Goal [h/a]	Goal [kWh/m²$_{NGF}$a]
Single office	12	1,200	14.400	8	550	4.400
Group office (max. 6 workers)	12	1,550	18.600	8	750	6.000
Large space office (min. 7 workers)	11	2,200	24.200	7	1,950	13.650
Conference, seminar	13	1,600	20.800	8	550	4.400
Classroom (school)	7	650	4.550	4	400	1.600
Lecture hall, auditorium	12	1,050	12.600	7	650	4.550
Canteen	5	1,050	5.250	3	600	1.800
Restaurant	8	3,350	26.800	6	2,500	15.000
Kitchen in nonresidential building	14	2,850	39.900	8	2,350	18.800
Kitchen – preparing, storage	9	2,400	21.600	5	1,250	6.250
Sanitary rooms in nonresidential building	7	1,200	8.400	4	100	0.400
Other living rooms	8	1,550	12.400	5	550	2.750
Secondary rooms	4	400	1.600	2	250	0.500
Traffic area (corridors, ...)	4	1,600	6.400	2	650	1.300
Traffic area without daylight	4	2,550	10.200	2	2,250	4.500
Storage	3	1,850	5.550	2	200	0.400
Server room, data centre	15	2,700	40.500	8	1,100	8.800
Workshop	11	1,600	17.600	6	1,600	9.600
Congress	6	500	3.000	4	500	2.000
Exhibition rooms and museum	7	1,350	9.450	6	750	4.500
Library – reading hall	10	2,500	25.000	7	1,350	9.450
Library – freehand area	6	2,250	13.500	3	1,100	3.300
Sporting hall	7	2,600	18.200	4	1,050	4.200
Parking house (office and private)	3	1,500	4.500	1	200	0.200
Underground parking (office and private)	3	1,900	5.700	1	250	0.250
Parking house (public)	4	3,200	12.800	1	1,050	1.050
Underground parking (public)	4	4,050	16.200	1	1,300	1.300

451

9.4 Energy concept

Cooling energy demand

The best solution to cool a building in summer is to use passive concepts (chapter '4.0 Passive energy-saving concepts') to avoid overheating by reducing warm summer gains and by using natural cooling.

When passive, natural ways are insufficient, additional mechanical cooling must be added. The cooling equipment typically consumes electrical energy. As the cooling medium, air or water can be used.

In Germany, the calculation method to determine the cooling load is based on VDI 2078. The calculation considers different factors, e.g. volume flow, room dimensions and window surfaces. Cooling loads are considered by both exterior and interior factors. Exterior cooling loads are created with solar radiation and warm outside air temperature by transmission (through transparent and opaque building elements), radiation (solar radiation through opaque building elements) and ventilation.

Interior cooling loads are created by persons, lighting, equipment, activities, building elements, chemical reactions and from neighbouring rooms inside a building.

The cooling equipment capacity is equal to the amount of warm energy that must be removed from the room. The table 452 shows the limit and goal values for the cooling capacity of different zones within a building.

The following formula can be used to calculate the power demand for a mechanically cooled zone:

$$W_{elequip} = P_{elequip} \cdot t \cdot UFA$$

where

$W_{elequip}$ – power demand for cooling equipment within the zone [kWh/a]

$P_{elequip}$ – cooling electrical capacity within the zone [W/m²$_{UFA}$h]

t – time of use per year [h/a]

UFA – zones usable floor area [m²]

The result represents power demand for the whole functional zone. Demand of different zones may be combined to find the cooling energy demand for the entire building.

452 The cooling power demand for different functional zones in the building – limit and goal values – limit value boundary conditions: window surface of 60 %, outer sun protection, seasonal performance factor 4, cold water temperature 14/18 °C, multilevel control, without free cooling mode – goal value boundary conditions are: window surface of 40 %, outer sun protection, seasonal performance factor 4, cold water temperature 14/18 °C, multilevel control, with free cooling mode

Function	Limit $P_{elequip}$ [W/m²$_{UFA}$h]	Limit [h/a]	Limit [kWh/m²$_{UFA}$a]	Goal $P_{elequip}$ [m²$_{UFA}$h]	Goal [h/a]	Goal [kWh/m²$_{UFA}$a]
Single office	10	522	5.220	10	213	2.130
Group office (max. 6 workers)	11	542	5.962	10	211	2.110
Large space office (min. 7 workers)	14	690	9.660	14	212	2.968
Conference, seminar	21	351	7.371	21	189	3.969
Classroom (school)	17	132	2.244	17	114	1.938
Lecture hall, auditorium	46	121	5.566	45	113	5.085
Canteen	26	126	3.276	26	119	3.094
Restaurant	26	237	6.162	25	235	5.875
Kitchen in nonresidential building	130	258	33.540	129	266	34.314
Kitchen – preparing, storage	25	298	7.450	24	285	6.840
Sanitary rooms in nonresidential building	18	134	2.412	17	116	1.972
Other living rooms	15	296	4.440	14	236	3.304
Secondary rooms	5	265	1.325	5	194	0.970
Traffic area (corridors, ...)	3	257	0.771	3	84	0.252
Storage	5	236	1.180	5	166	0.830
Server room, data centre	41	6,301	258.341	40	1,532	61.280
Workshop	30	169	5.070	30	157	4.710
Congress	14	131	1.834	14	106	1.484
Exhibition rooms and museum	7	258	1.806	7	175	1.225
Library – reading hall	17	455	7.735	17	284	4.828
Library – freehand area	7	462	3.234	6	336	2.016
Sporting hall	8	387	3.096	8	312	2.496

452

Ventilation energy demand

Ventilation serves to renew the room's air by either natural or mechanical ventilation. Natural ventilation is achieved by opening a passage through a window, shaft, roof top or vents with support fans.

Natural ventilation can be achieved by methods that are either continuous, or airing. Airing ventilation is for a short time and involves an intensive air change (approx. 3 - 10 minutes) which takes place on a regular time schedule. For example, an office may be programmed to change air every 60 minutes, and a conference room every 20 minutes.

Mechanical ventilation is achieved by systems that create air movement and include air purification (filters) with at least one thermodynamic air treatment function (heating, cooling, humidifying, dehumidifying).

For mechanical ventilation, the electrical energy demand is also required and can be calculated with the limit and goal values for different zones within a building (table 453).

The following formula can be used to calculate the power demand for a mechanically ventilated zone:

$$W_{elvent} = P_{elvent} \cdot t \cdot UFA$$

where

W_{elvent} – power demand for mechanical ventilation within the zone [kWh/a]

P_{elvent} – ventilation electrical capacity within the zone [$W/m^2_{UFA}h$]

t – time of use per year [h/a]

UFA – zones usable floor area [m^2]

The result represents power demand for the whole functional zone. Demands of different zones may be combined to find the mechanical ventilation power demand for the entire building.

453 Power demand for ventilation of different functional zones in the building – limit and goal values – limit value boundary conditions are: hygienic minimum air exchange, cooling through water system, pressure loss max. 1,500 Pa, total efficiency 65 %, specific fan power max. 2,000 W/m³/s, 2-stage controlling – goal value boundary conditions are: hygienic minimum air exchange, cooling through water system, pressure loss max. 1,200 Pa, total efficiency 65 %, specific fan power max. 1,250 W/m³/s, continuously controlling

Type of usage	Limit [W/m²]	Limit [h/a]	Limit [kWh/m².a]	Goal [W/m²]	Goal [h/a]	Goal [kWh/m².a]
Single office	2.4	3250	7.800	1.4	3,250	4.550
Group office (max. 6 workers)	2.4	3,250	7.800	1.4	2,381	3.333
Large space office (min. 7 workers)	3.6	3,250	11.700	2.1	2,381	5.000
Conference, seminar	9.1	3,250	29.575	5.3	1,947	10.319
Classroom (school)	6.1	1,800	10.980	3.5	1,453	5.086
Lecture hall, auditorium	18.2	1,297	23.605	10.6	1,156	12.254
Canteen	10.9	1,412	15.391	6.4	1,245	7.968
Restaurant	10.9	2,788	30.389	6.4	1,096	12.134
Kitchen in nonresidential building	55	3,662	201.410	32	3,662	117.184
Kitchen – preparing, storage	9.1	3,326	30.267	5.3	3,327	17.633
Sanitary rooms in nonresidential building	3.8	3,250	12.350	2.2	3,250	7.150
Other living rooms	4.2	3,250	13.650	2.5	1,947	4.868
Secondary rooms	0.9	3,250	2.925	0.5	3,250	1.625
Traffic area (corridors, ...)	0	0	0	0	0	0
Storage	0.9	3,250	2.925	0.5	3,250	1.625
Server room, data centre	0.8	3,865	3.092	0.5	2,314	1.157
Workshop	12.1	2,750	33.275	7.1	2,750	19.525
Congress	4.2	1,147	4.817	2.5	1,147	2.868
Exhibition rooms and museum	1.2	6,000	7.200	0.7	4,842	3.389
Library – reading hall	7.9	2,188	17.285	2.8	2,284	6.395
Library – freehand area	1.2	2,188	2.626	0.7	2,284	1.599
Sporting hall	1.8	5,100	9.180	1.1	3,363	3.699
Parking house (office and private)	4.9	2,132	10.447	2.8	1,623	4.544
Parking house (public)	9.7	3,145	30.506	5.7	2,105	11.999

453

9.4 Energy concept

9.4.3 Ventilation dimensioning

Appropriate ventilation levels may be designed by calculating the amount of air volume requiring change.

Air exchange rates for different room types may be determined in the norm DIN V 18599-10:2011-12 (table 455).

Calculation of the required fresh air volume by free ventilation:

$V = q \, . \, N_{Pmax}$
where
V – required fresh air volume [m³/h]
q – fresh air supply [m³/h.person]
N_{pmax} – maximal number of persons

Dimensioning of the air change rate required for mechanical ventilation:

$V = n_{50} \, . \, V_{room}$
where
V – required fresh air volume [m³/h]
n_{50} – general air change rate (or with cooling as a part of ventilation) [h^{-1}]
V_{room} – rooms volume [m³]

General required fresh air volumes for mechanical ventilation are:

- 20 - 40 m³/h per person while in a seating activity
- 40 - 60 m³/h per person while in a non-seating activity
- over 65 m³/h per person while in hard body work

454 Allowed air speed, dependant on temperature and turbulent level in accordance to DIN EN 13779 (risk of draft air 15 %), Germany
455 Minimum natural outdoor-air supply volume flow rates for different room types and mechanical outdoor-air supply volume flow rates or air change rates general and air change rates with cooling by ventilation, in accordance to the DIN V 18599-10:2011-12, Germany

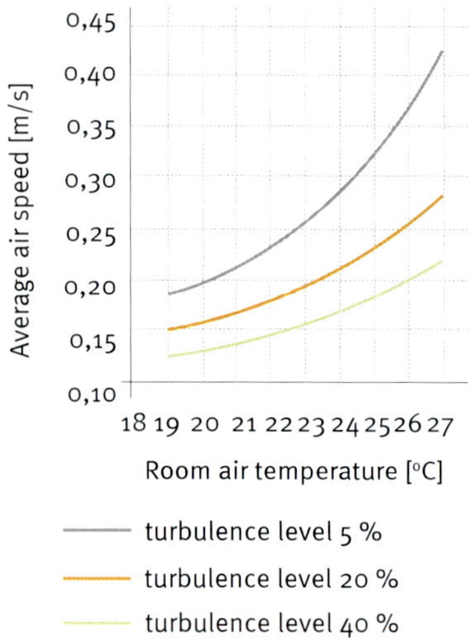

454

Type of room	Fresh air supply q [m³/h.person]	Mechanical air supply flow rates [m³/h.m^2_{NFA}]	Air exchange rate general n_{50} [h^{-1}]	Air exchange rate (with cooling) n_{50} [h^{-1}]
Single office, workgroup office	40	4	2 - 3	4 - 8
Landscape office (7+ workers)	60	6	2 - 3	4 - 8
Conference, meeting or seminar room	20	15	5 - 7	10 - 15
Bedroom (2-bed, in hospital)	-	4	-	-
Hotel room (double room)	30	-	-	-
Foyer	20	-	-	-
Retail shop/department store	20	-	-	-
Exhibition hall	20			
Classroom, lecture hall, auditorium	30	-	-	-
Restaurant, canteen	30	18	-	-
Kitchen in nonresidential building	-	90	15 - 25	-
Kitchen – preparing, storage	-	15	-	-
Toilets and sanitary facilities in non-residential building	-	15	-	-
Other habitable rooms	-	7	-	-
Auxiliary spaces	-	0.15	-	-
Traffic areas	-	0	-	-
Storeroom, technical equipment, archives	-	0.15	-	-
Server room, computer centre	40	-	-	-
Workshop, assembly, manufacturing	-	20	-	-
Cinema, theatre – audience	30	-	4 - 4.5	-
Theatre – stage	20	0.3	3 - 5	-
Fair, congress building	20	-	8	-
Exhibition rooms and museums	20	-	-	-
Library – reading rooms	20	-	-	-
Library – open stacks area	20	-	-	-
Sports hall	60	-	6	-
Garage buildings	-	8	-	-
Smoking room (DIN EN 13779)	90	-	-	-

455

In case of higher loads, e.g. smoke, odours or raised heat, a higher air change rate is required.
To avoid air drafting within a space, the room's air speed should be monitored.
The air speed of a naturally ventilated room depends on the positioning and dimensioning of the ventilation openings. In the table 456, average air speeds required to naturally ventilate different room activities with minimum opening dimensions are shown.

E.g., in a seated room with an average temperature of 20 °C, the air speed should not reach over 0.15 m/s. Where higher room temperatures apply, a higher air speed is acceptable.

Mechanical ventilation is required when natural ventilation is not possible. E.g., when the rooms dimensioning prohibits it, or the room is positioned with no possible natural ventilation (e.g. underground, surrounding buildings, ...), or has a special function (e.g. workplaces without openings, high interior loads, ...).
Mechanical ventilation should be designed so that no draft air should be created. The creation of draft air depends at most on the temperature of the air, the air speed and type of activity.

There is normally no risk of draft air with temperatures below 20 °C and with air speeds under 0.15 - 0.2 m/s.

Example – calculate the opening area of the tilt/turn window for natural ventilation in a 2 person office with the room area of 20 m², volume of 50 m³ and a room height h = 2.5 m:

the maximum depth for one sided ventilation = 2.5 . h_r = 6.25 m
for cross ventilation = 5 . h_r = 12.50 m

Continuous ventilation

The opening area calculation for continuous ventilation refers to the occupancy of the space. The opening area of a tilted window is given by:

$A_{til} = w \cdot a + 2 \cdot (h_w \cdot a)/2 = a \cdot (w + h_w)$
where
A_{til} – area of a tilted window [m²]
w – width of the window [m]
h_w – height of the window [m]
a – window gap width [m]

Airing ventilation

The opening area calculation for airing ventilation refers to the rooms floor area and it is given by:

$A_{shot} = w \cdot h_w = 1.2\ m^2$
where
A_{shot} – area of a window [m²]
w – width of the window [m]
h_w – height of the window [m]

For intermittent window ventilation, an opening of A_{shot} = 2.1 m² is required for a 20 m² room. This means that 2 windows of 1.20 m² are needed.
For cross-ventilation, an opening area of A_{shot} = 1.2 m² is required. This means that 2 windows of 0.6 m² are to be placed on opposite walls.

456 Ventilation cross sections for natural ventilation based on "Arbeitsstätten-Richtlinie Lüftung (ASR 5) Zu § 5 der Arbeitsstättenverordnung, Abschnitt 3" (Working space ventilation guidelines to § 5 of the Workplace regulation, Section 3, the openings area is the sum of fresh and waste air openings

System	Average air speed [m/s]	Light room height [h_r]	Max. room depth	Profile of fresh and waste air opening related to the m² of floor area [cm²/m²]			Opening area to secure the minimum air exchange	
				Sitting activity e.g. office	Mostly not sitting activity, e.g. sale rooms, barber shops	Mostly sitting or non sitting activity with high odour nuisance or hard body work	For continuous ventilation [m²/person]	For intermittent ventilation [m²/10 m^2_{FA}]
One-side ventilation, openings for fresh and waste air in one outside wall	0.08	< 4m	2.5 xh_r	200	350	500	0.35	1.05
Cross-ventilation, openings in opposite outer walls, or in outer wall and in the roof	0.14	< 4m	5.0 xh_r	120	200	300	0.20	0.60
Cross-ventilation, openings in outer wall and in opposite shaft, the shaft has profile of 80cm² and is 4m high	0.21	< 4m	5.0 xh_r	80	140	200		
Cross-ventilation with roof tops, e.g. dome, lantern, deflector and openings in an exterior wall or opposite outer walls	0.21	> 4m	5.0 xh_r	80	140	200		

456

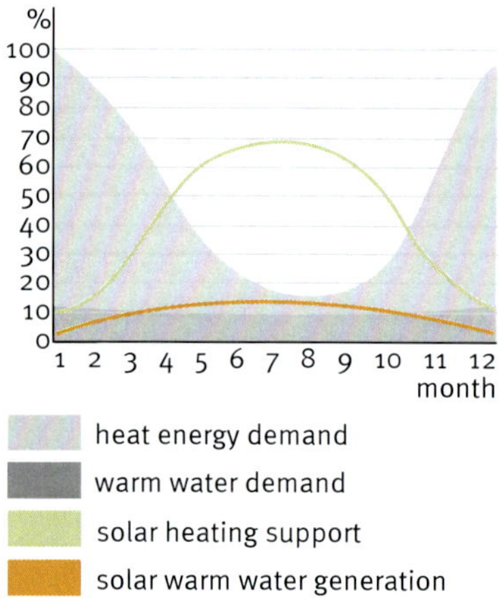

457

457 The relationship between warm water and heating demand and solar radiation during the whole year – the heat storage for summer and additional system for winter are necessary to cover the heating requirements
458 The solar radiation extends or decreases depending on angle and orientation of the surface in comparison to horizontal surface
459 Daily variation of solar gains and warm water demand in a residential building – each solar collector must find a good compromise between solar covering rate and the solar harvesting
460 Solar radiation in Germany
461 Diagram – dimensioning of solar thermal collector surface and hot water storage tank for warm water generation
462 Diagram – dimensioning of solar thermal collector surface and hot water storage tank for heating support and warm water generation

9.4 Energy concept

9.4.4 Rough estimations of energy generation

Solar thermal collectors

The heat generated by solar systems depends on building location, orientation, sun radiation, building type, occupancy, collector type and angle.

The most efficient positioning for a collector is orientated south with an angle of 40° - 60° in Germany. The sun should penetrate collectors without obstruction or shading.

For solar system dimensioning, the warm water demand is the most important item of information. The table for standard warm water requirements can be found on page 247.

When not all information can be obtained, the standard value of 30-50 l per person/day may be used for a single family house. Solar systems generate a warm water temperature of 60 °C.

1. A simple estimation for the surface of the solar thermal collector:

- $1 m^2$ of flat solar collectors = approx. 400 kWh/a
- $1 m^2$ of vacuum pipe solar collectors = approx. 600 kWh/a

The average values are for flat and vacuum pipe collectors with the best orientation and angle in Germany.

For other locations, dimensioning depends on the solar radiation during the year.
Another simple estimation that may be used for the dimensioning of solar systems for both warm water and heating supply:

2. Solar systems for warm water

Warm water solar systems are normally designed for 50-65 % of the warm water demand in a single family house, and for 30-40 % in a multi-residential building.

The formula used to design the dimension of the collector surface is:

- flat collector - approx. 1.5 m^2/person
- vacuum pipe collector - approx. 1.0 m^2/person

Another way of dimensioning of a solar thermal collector surface and the volume of a hot water storage tank can be found in table 461-462.

Example: A multi-residential unit with 30 persons in Kempten, south of Germany, middle covering, after heating with gas boiler:

From the diagram, the flat collectors surface is approx. 22 m^2, or vacuum pipe collectors surface approx. 18 m^2. The solar thermal storage volume is 1250 l (+ after heating approx. 750 l = storage total 2000 l).

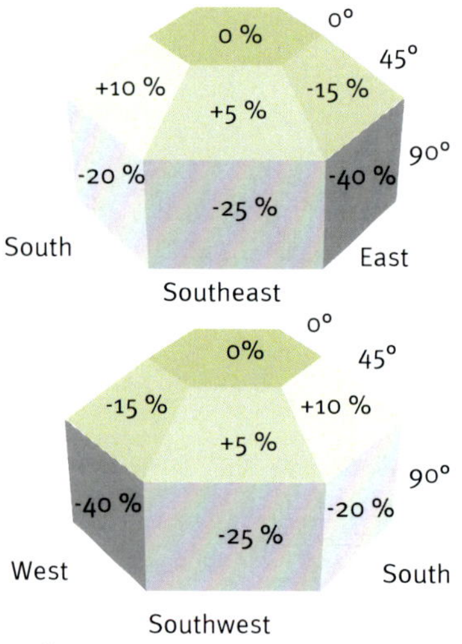

458

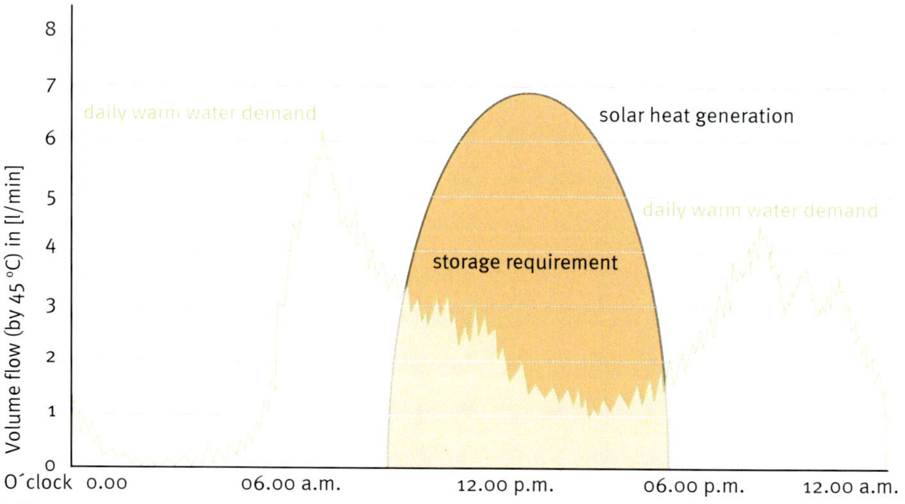

459

3. Solar systems for warm water and heating support

Solar systems for heating support can save up to 25-30 % of heating energy depending on the buildings location, building type and its heat protection. The system supports heating on cold summer days and throughout the transitional seasons.

The following formula is used to dimension a collector surface for a good insulated single family house:

- approx. 1.0 m² of a good flat collector for 10 m² of living surface
- approx. 0.6 m² of a vacuum pipe collector for 10 m² of living surface
- or 4 m² of collector per person

The volume of a storage tank (including buffer) should be 50 l per m² of collector surface, plus 50 l per person.

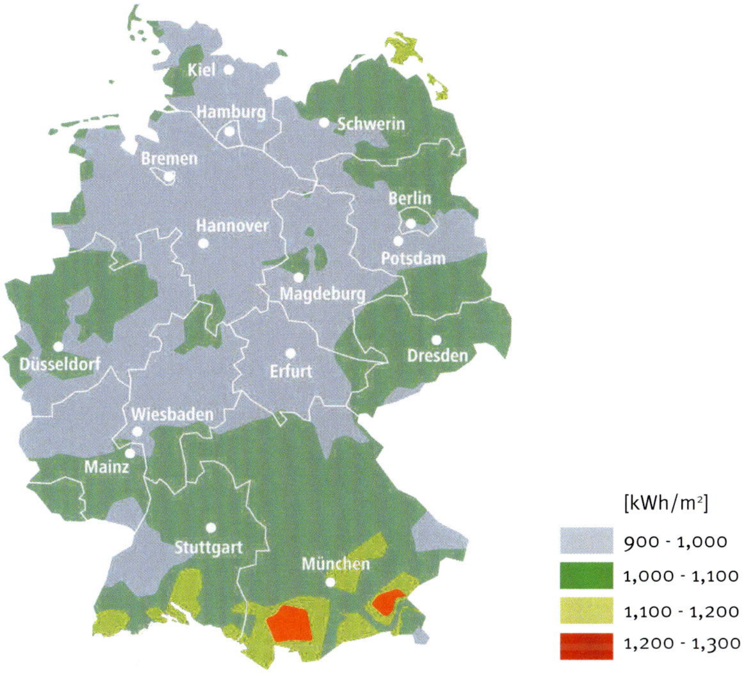

460

Solar thermal collector efficiency

The maximum efficiency is defined from optical efficiency grade and form maximal solar radiation of 1,000 W/m². By optical efficiency grade of 80 %, the maximal efficiency of 1 m² of solar collector is 0.8 kW.
In normal operation, as this value is rarely reached, the maximal efficiency is important to determine the safety technology.

The performed efficiency is used for planning of solar thermal collectors. The minimum is a specific collector efficiency of 500 W/m² as in VDI 6002.

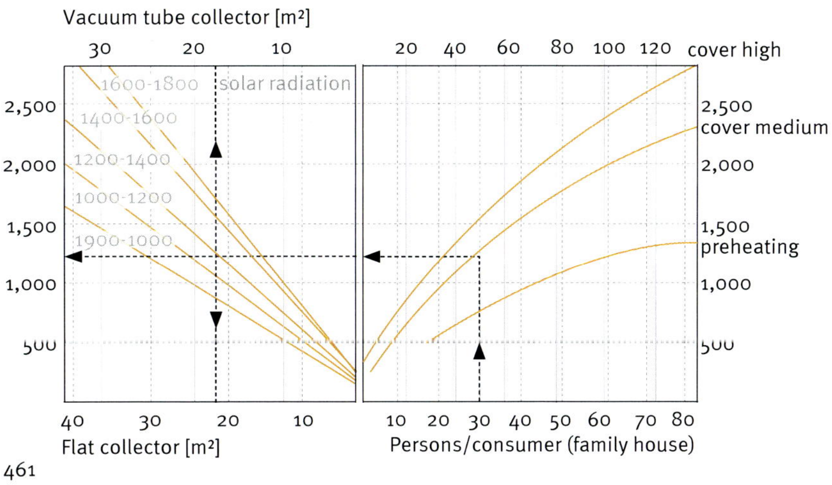

461

Storage

As the time of heat generation by solar collectors and heat consumption by users are almost always different, if in the day/night or seasonal consideration, the storing of heat energy is important. The storing dimensioning is in the table 464.

There are also different online calculators for dimensioning solar collectors.

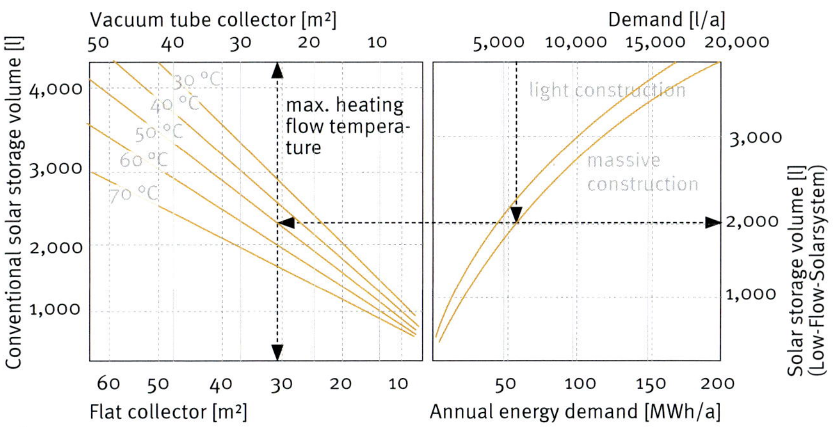

462

9.4 Energy concept

463 Monovalent heat pump operation – heat pump covers the whole heat load
464 Bivalent heat pump operation with additional electrical heating in storage
465 Bivalent heat pump operation with additional peak loads boiler

covered through heat pump
covered through additional heater
unused heat energy (can be stored or sold)

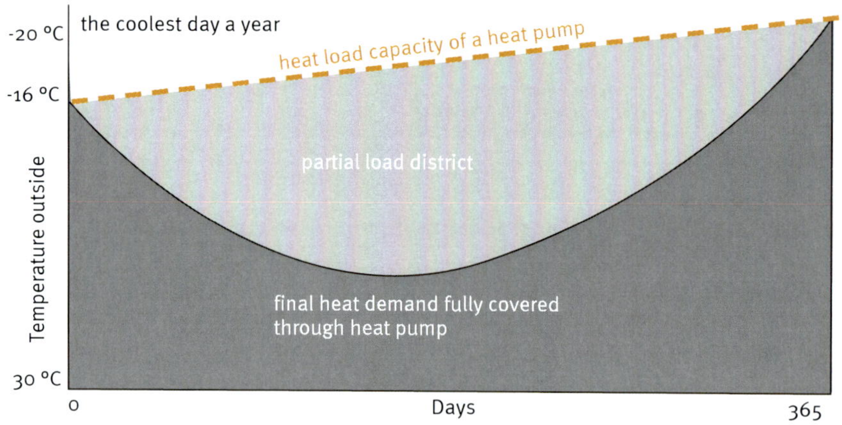

463

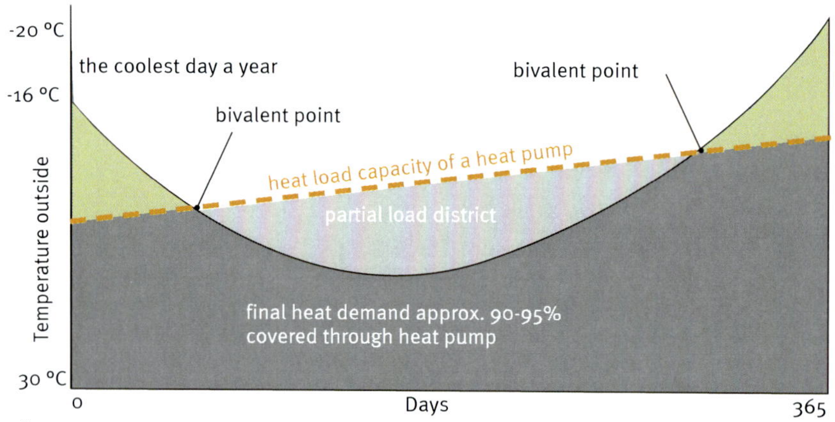

464

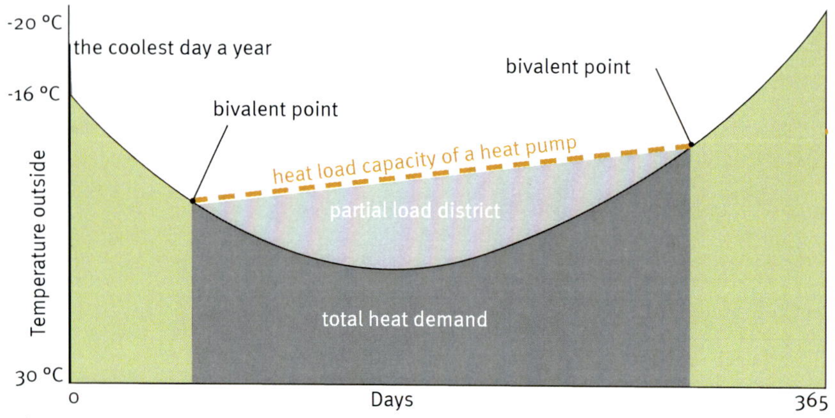

465

Heat pump capacity [kW]

To estimate the dimensions of a heat pump, the most important parameters to be considered are the heat energy demand (heating, warm water) of a building, the type of the heat pump, the flow temperature and the outside temperature.
If the flow temperature is < 55 °C, a low temperature heat pump is required. If the flow temperature is between 55 °C and 65 °C, it is considered middle temperature and from 65 °C to 75 °C a high temperature heat pump is required. In order to design the heat pump economically, the flow temperature for heating should not be over 55 °C and for warm water, 60 °C.

Under these conditions and when the heat pump covers the heat energy requirements also in the coldest day in a year, the monovalent operation of the heat pump is possible.
Due to a higher heat pump capacity, it is possible that the heat pump would be used inefficiently, especially in areas with periods of variable outside temperatures. In this case, the system is rentable only when the unused energy can be stored or sold.

In case of higher temperature requirements or if the heat pump is not enough for the total heat energy demand, a bivalent operation is required. Often planned for the additional heating in the coldest days is additional electrical heating in the storage.

The third possibility is to cover the higher energy demand with a peak load boiler, e.g. wood chip boiler. In this case, the boiler generates the entire heat energy during the coldest days and the heat pump is turned off.

The heat pump capacity is calculated with the help of peak loads dimensioning mentioned on the page 246:

$$Q_{hcap} = A_{HFA} \cdot Q_{load}$$

where
Q_{hcap} – heat pump capacity [kW]
A_{HFA} – Heated Floor Area
Q_{load} – specific lead wire heat demand

Combined Heat and Power [kW]

Normally the dimensioning of CHP is based on the heat demand of the object to be supplied. The thermal annual load duration curve is the basis and is used to decide how many hours per year at which capacity of CHP can be covered by the available heat and electricity.

As a rule, CHP is currently designed to cover the base load supply of an object, so that as many full-load hours per year as possible are guaranteed. However, in addition to a higher 'full load hours' number, the percentage covered by the CHP heat in relation to the total heat demand plays a crucial role.

The generic rule of thumb is that the thermal output of the cogeneration unit should be approximately 10-30 % of the properly designed heat boiler supply capacity. This means the CHP plant usually covers around 40-70 % of the heat demand of a supply object.

The peak load of the supply object is achieved by the significantly more cost-effective boiler plant. To ensure maximum availability of the system, special attention should be paid to good maintenance and repair of the cogeneration unit.

Biogas plant capacity [kW]

Today, many types of biogas plants are available on the market. A small biogas plant of 30 kW can cover the energy demand of a small farm or a single or multi-family house. The larger plants with a higher amount of MW are now able to supply any small town with electricity and heat. There are also numerous examples of plants in between.

On average in 2010, a biogas plant in Germany had a capacity of around 380 kW. The kW output is always dependent on the available amount of biomass. The factors that have a positive or negative influence on this are manifold, since the substrate used and its carbohydrate, fat or protein content, is as important as the size of the fermenter of the biogas plant.

The following are examples of biogas plant capacities:

- Small biogas plant for power generation:

biogas plant capacity of 100 kW by 7,500 h/a generates to 750 MWh/a

- Small biogas plant for heat generation:

biogas plant capacity of 300 kW by 7,500 h/a generates to 2,925 MWh/a

A biogas plant generation can be divided e.g. to 35 % of power and 65 % of heat energy.

466 Example of yearly line of required heat capacity for dimensioning of CHP – the more hours a year is CHP in use, the lower heat capacity can be covered

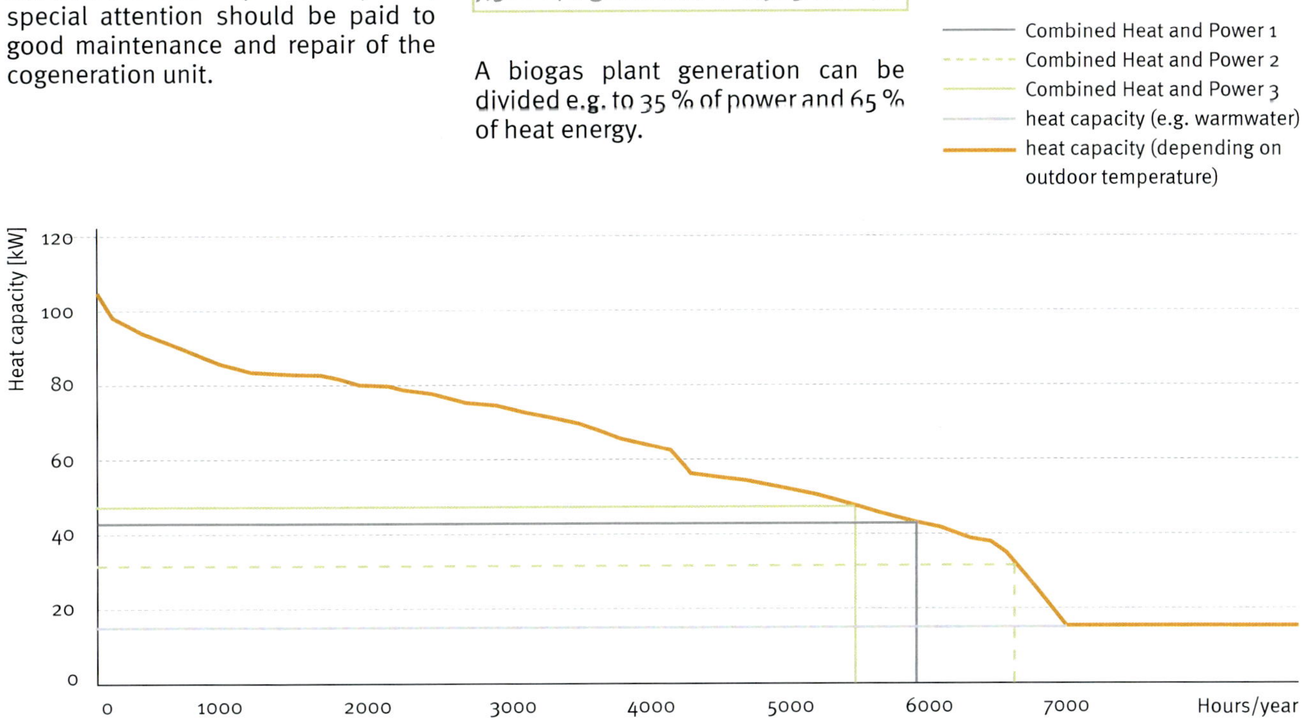

466

9.4 Energy concept

There are a lot of online calculation of PV system, e.g for Germany can be also done in webpage:

http://www.solarserver.de/service_tools/online_rechner/pv_anlage_online_berechnen.html

or calculation for Europe: http://re.jrc.ec.europa.eu/pvgis/apps4/pvest.php

Photovoltaic

To calculate the size of photovoltaics required, the following formula can be used:

5,5 m² of PV = 1 kWp = 950 kWh/a

The formula is optimal for Germany and is in relation to the best orientation and angle for PV. The angle of photovoltaic depends on the height of the sun throughout the seasons of a year. It is always best when the angles can be adjustable.

The most efficient angle for a fixed photovoltaic is 30°, orientated to the south for central Europe. In this configuration, the highest energy yield can be produced.

If the orientation is in a different direction to the sun, the expected energy yield is reduced. Locations that are oriented to the north, usually produce poor energy yields.

The amount of PV surface depends on the PV module; the formula above is for module E20 monocristaline that has a module efficiency of 327 W/module element (approx. 1,6 m²). This is related to the efficiency of the photovoltaic cell module. The efficiency is still developing and increasing due to technology.

A peak of 1 kW is a constant used to compare the module and describes the efficiency under test conditions. Gaining more kWh/a depends on the location, orientation, angle and material of PV.

Another factor that must be considered is shading – the shading of PV elements should be avoided. If there is partial shade on the PV element, the entire element will not work.

Normally, the electricity generated by a PV system is fed into the local power grid with the help of an inverter which changes the generated energy to the 230 Voltage.

In Germany, due to EEG (page 74), money is paid to the owner for feeding electrical energy to the public network. In the table 470, the recent payments in Cent/kWh are shown.

Another possibility is to use the energy required for the site and then transfer the remaining energy into the public network. Otherwise, batteries can be used to store the extra energy that will be used later on the site.

Today, the payment rates for electric energy from photovoltaics that are transferred to the public network are very low and therefore, undesirable. It is more common to store the energy on the site and use it when required. An example of dimensioning the battery storage capacity is shown in table 472.

Due to the fact that the generated or stored power cannot always meet the required consumption rate, the connection to a public grid cannot be avoided.

*467 The payment back for the PV systems for 2013/2014 in accordance to the EEG law, * the digression of the payment rates is 1.0 % monthly, ** the digression of the payment rates is 1.4 % monthly, Germany*

Commissioning	**Payment [Cent/KWh] for different installed plant capacity – PV roof and free surfaces systems**				
	< 10 KWp (100 %)	**10 - 40 KWp (90 %)**	**> 40 KWp (90 %)**	**1 - 10 MWp (100 %)**	**< 10 MWp (100 %)**
Since 01.04.2014*	13.28	12.60	11.23	9.19	9.19
Since 01.03.2014*	13.41	12.72	11.35	9.28	9.28
Since 01.02.2014*	13.55	12.85	11.46	9.38	9.38
Since 01.01.2014**	13.68	12.98	11.58	9.47	9.47
Since 01.12.2013**	13.88	13.17	11.74	9.61	9.61
Since 01.11.2013**	14.07	13.35	11.91	9.74	9.74

467

Wind power wheel

Small windmills are also a good alternative for power generation on site.

They can be situated on the ground or on the roof. The statics (foundation) should be considered.

There are two main types of small windmills – horizontal and vertical. The rated power of small windmills range from 2 kW to 10 kW.

The yearly generation of power depends on the location and wind conditions.

An example of various vertical windmills and their possible power generation are shown in table 469.

The transfer of power to the public network or storage of energy in batteries is similar to photovoltaic.

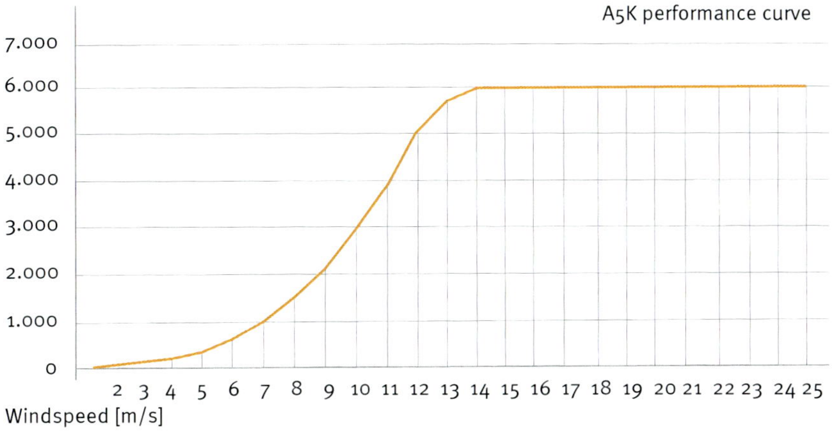

468

468 The rated power of small wind power wheel darrieus rotor of 5 kW by different wind speed
469 Example of different small wind power wheel types – darrieus rotors and their characteristic as well as possible annual power generation
470 The payment back for the wind power systems for 2013 according to thc EEG law

Type of small wind power wheel	Rated power [W]	Power generation [kWh/a]	Average yearly wind speed [m/s]	Height of rotor [m]	Perimeter of rotor [m]	High of the whole wind wheel [m]
Small wind power wheel 3 kW	3,000	approx. 2,000 - 5,000	6	3.6	3.0	8
Small wind power wheel 5 kW	5,000	approx. 6,000 - 10,000	6	4.6	4.0	8.7
Small wind power wheel 10 kW	10,000	approx. 15,000 - 18,000	6	6.2	6.0	10.5

469

Commissioning	Payment in Cent/KWh for on-shore wind power wheel < 50 kW				Payment in Cent/KWh for off shore wind power wheel		
	Start payment – first 5 years (§ 29 EEG)	Basic payment – after 5 years (§ 29 EEG)	System service bonus (§ 29 EEG)	Repowering bonus (§ 30 EEG)	Standard (§ 31 EEG)	Higher start payment	Basic payment
2013	8.80	4.80	0.47	0.49	15	19	3.5

470

9.4 Energy concept

9.4.5 Energy storing

The decentralize storage of energy is most important during the designing of an energy concept. This is because the highest energy requirements are dependent on the function and are not usually equal to the time of energy generation from renewable resources. There are many possibilities of energy storing and also a variety of storing mediums. Examples of possible energy storing are in page 184.

The following are examples of how to dimension the storage of energy with a water storing medium and for power storing.

Weekly water storage

For the efficient use of this technology a collector area of approx. 7 m^2 is suggested per dwelling to heat approx. 240 litres/m^2 of water.

The dimensions for a combined storage for solar collectors is based on:

- 60 l of storage for 1 m^2 of flat solar thermal collector
- 70 l of storage for 1 m^2 of vacuum pipe collectors

Diagrams on page 255 also show the dimensioning of thermal storages for solar collectors.

Monthly water storage

Storage capacity is 1.5 to 2.25 m^3 per m^2 of collector area (water equivalent) with a minimum of 1.000 m^3.

Power storage

For the storage of energy generated, for example from photovoltaic or windmills, storage batteries are used.

In certain new systems, the batteries from electrical cars are used for power energy storing.

The capacities of different power storage systems are shown in the table 472.

471 Dimensioning of solar thermal collector and hot water storage tank for warm water generation in Germany
472 Capacity of different power storage batteries

Number of consumers	Solar collector surface	Hot water storage tank volume
< 20 persons	1.0 - 1.5 m^2/Person	80 - 120 l/Person
20 - 100 persons	0.5 - 1.1 m^2/Person	60 - 90 l/Person
> 100 persons	0.4 - 0.8 m^2/Person	40 - 70 l/Person

471

Memory type/use	Discharge	Memory type	Storage capacity (how much power can be stored in 1 m^3)
Short time memory grid stabilization, network maintenance	Less than 1 second to a few minutes	Coil SMES	30 kWh
		Capacitors/Super Caps	52 kWh
		Flywheel mass storage	5 MWh
Long time memory peak demand coverage	2 to 24 hours	Compressed air storage mass storage	58 MWh
		pumped storage	848 MWh
Electrochemical memory reserve memory electromobility	1 hour to several days	Lithium-ion batteries	40 MWh
		Lead-acid batteries	50 MWh
		REdox-Flowbatteries	5 MWh
Hydrogen reserve memory long-term memory, great potential, not yet marketable			10 GWh

472

9.4.6 Ecological evaluation

The ecological evaluation of an energy concept is one part of the LCA (page 15, 72).

One possibility is to evaluate the GWP, ODP, POCP, AP, EP, PEnre, PEre in relation to the operation life time of a building with the help of ökobau.dat (page 243).

Ökobau.dat contains ecological values for different energy generation systems during the operation life time of a building.

The calculation works similar to the ecological evaluation of building construction (page 243):

$Val_e = Val_{öko} . N_e$

where

$Val_{öko}$ – value found in the ökobau.dat table

Val_e – value for yearly required energy

N_e – the amount of energy required to produce (i.e. power, heating, lighting, etc) [kWh/a]

For further information and values, visit the web page here:

http://www.nachhaltigesbauen.de/baustoff-und-gebaeudedaten/oekobaudat.html

Table 474 shows how to calculate ecological indicators such as a wood chip boiler with a capacity of 20-120 kW, used as a building's heating system.

First, the amount of heat energy requirement for the building is estimated (page 246). The table in ökobau.dat shows the ecological indicators for 3.6 MJ (3.6MJ=1kWh) of heat energy.

Therefore, the total heat energy demand [kWh/a] is to be multiplied with the ecological indicator of 1 kWh in order to get the ecological balance for the heating system.

The table 473 shows the CO_2 emissions generated (for 1 kWh of energy) and the primary energy factors for different energy supply materials.

Energy supply material	CO_2 Emission	Primary energy factor
Power-Mix	683 g CO_2/kWh	2.7
Natural gas	247 g CO_2/kWh	1.1
Fluid gas	272 g CO_2/kWh	1.1
Petroleum	311 g CO_2/kWh	1.1
Lignite	452 g CO_2/kWh	1.2
Hard coal	439 g CO_2/kWh	1.2
Distance heating	406 g CO_2/kWh	1.3 (system depending)
Wood chips	35 g CO_2/kWh	0.2
Wood pellet	43 g CO_2/kWh	0.2
Wood	6 g CO_2/kWh	0.2
Renewable	0 g CO_2/kWh	0.0

473

In this case, it is clear that by using renewable energies it is sustainable. This is due to its zero primary energy factor and because it releases no pollution into the environment.

Example: A natural gas boiler with the heat energy generation of 10,000 kWh/a generates during its operation:

- **emission: 247 g CO_2/kWh . 10,000 kWh = 2.47 t CO_2/a**
- **primary energy: 1,1 . 10,000 kWh = 11 MWh**

Once compared to the wood chip boiler, the CO_2 emissions for the same heat energy demand is 35 g CO_2/kWh . 10,000 kWh = 0.035 t CO_2/a. This is 70 times less compared to the natural gas boiler. The primary energy is 0.2 . 10,000 kWh = 2 MWh which is also 5.5 times smaller.

473 Basic values of CO2 emissions and primary energy factor for different energy supply materials based on GEMIS 4.13 Datenbank, Germany

474 An example of the calculation of an ecological indicator for a wood chip heating boiler with a heat demand of 10,000 kWh/a, the ecological indicator values are based on Ökobau.dat

Inputs	Value (Ökobau.dat)	Woodchip boiler ecological indicators calculation (value . 10.000 kWh)
PEnre	0.423 MJ/kWh	4,230 MJ = 1,175 kWh
PEre	5.44 MJ/kWh	54,400 MJ = 15,111 kWh
Secondary materials	$4.87E^{-5}$ kg/kWh	0.487 kg
Water	0.016 m^3/ kWh	160 m^3
Outputs		
EP	$8.27E^{-5}$ kg PO_4-Equiv./kWh	0.827 kg PO_4-Equiv.
ODP	$3.2E^{-11}$ kg R_{11}-Equiv./kWh	$3.2E^{-7}$ kg R_{11}-Equiv.
POCP	$5.19E^{-5}$ kg C_2H_4-Equiv./kWh	0.519 kg C_2H_4-Equiv.
GWP	-0.5 kg CO_2-Equiv./kWh	-5,000 kg CO_2-Equiv.
AP	0.000382 kg SO_2-Equiv./kWh	3.82 kg SO_2-Equiv.

474

9.5 Water concept

Type of usage	Potable water demand
Office building	20 - 25 l/d.person
Swimming pool	50 - 150 l/d.person
Sport facility	10 - 60 l/d.person
Educational building	10 - 15 l/d.person
Hospital	
150 - 300 beds	250 - 450 l/d.bed
300 - 600 beds	300 - 500 l/d.bed
Residential building	126 l/d.person

475

475 The value of potable water demand per day and unit in different building usage in Germany
476 The amount of water flows for different water installations in the building in Germany
477 Estimation of potable water demand and sewage generation and possibilities for optimization
478 Potable water demand for different functions in residential building per person per day in Germany
479 Runoff coefficient for different types of roof or payment surfaces, shows that green roof is not appropriate for intensive rainwater use

Installation	Water amount
Basin	0.15 l/s
WC	9 l/flushing
Urinal	3 l/flushing
Shower	0.25 l/s
Tee kitchen	0.25 l/s

476

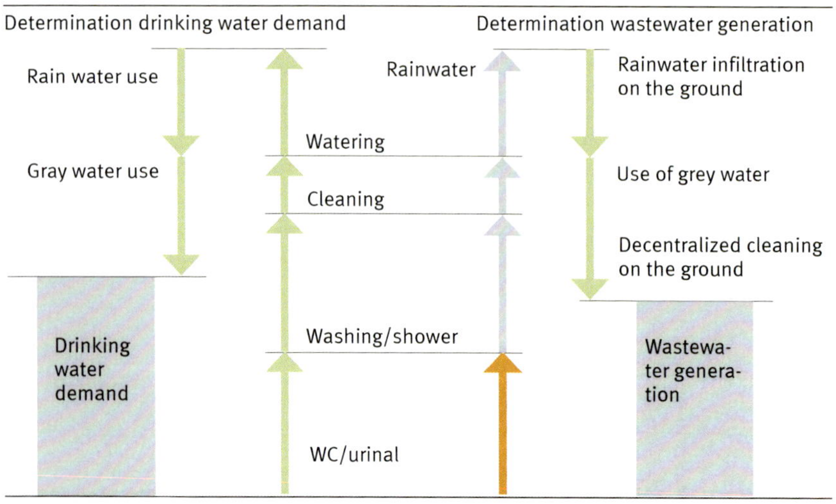

477

Potable water demand

The simplest potable water demand calculation is based on empiric values of water demand in different building types in l or m³ per day and unit (table 475):

$$PW = PW_p \cdot N_p \cdot N_d$$

where
PW – potable water demand [l/a]
PW_p – usage dependent potable water demand [l/d.person]
N_p – number of occupants
N_d – number of usage days per year

Example: Calculation of a potable water demand in a school with 60 children used 200 days a year.

$PW = PW_p \cdot N_p \cdot N_d$ = 15 l/d.person . 60 children . 200 d/a = 180,000 l/a

Generally, the water flows after its use to the sewage. **The sewage water from a house can be calculated by adding the used potable water with the rain water.**

In order to reduce the potable water consumption and sewage generation, different possibilities can be applied – shown in table 477 .

The optimization of user behaviour and water fitting technologies, along with the reuse of rainwater and grey water has a high influence on potable water saving.

The water can be reused for toilet flushing, cleaning, or for watering plants.

First, it should be made clear what the reused water will be used for. Then, the amount of the required reused water (e.g. for toilet flushing) has to be estimated. Following this, the average amount of rain or grey water that can be collected should be estimated. Only then, the calculation of the water tank is possible.

By reusing rain and grey water, the sewage generation is reduced. Other possibilities to reduce the sewage generation is to enable the water infiltration (page 128-129) on the site and avoid connection of rainwater with the canalisation.

General estimation of toilet flushing water demand based storage tank

The amount of toilet water depends on the type of WC flushing system, e.g. one flush requires an average of approx. 9 l/flushing, A WC with water saving flushing requires approx. 6-8 l/flushing (big business), or approx. 3-5 l/flushing (small business). A urinal requires approx. 3 l/flushing.
The amount of water flows in l/s for different water installations are shown in table 476.

The calculation depends on the number of occupants and how often they use the toilet.
Example: 35 office workers using a toilet 3 times a day with water saving flushing (1 large business, 2 small businesses and the office is used 250 days a year.

35 persons . (7l/flushing + 2 . 4,5l/flushing) . 250 d/a = 560 l/d = 140.000 l/a

$$V_{RW} = RW_p \cdot N_d$$

where
V_{RW} – rainwater storage requirement for the toilet flushing [l]
RW_d – daily rainwater consumption for toilet flushing [l/d]
N_d – longest average dry period [d]

Rough estimation of the amount of rainwater harvesting to determine the rainwater storage tank size

$$V_{RW} = R \cdot A \cdot RC \cdot FE \cdot 0.05$$

V_{RW} – rainwater collection volume [l]
R – annual rainfall [mm]
A_r – effective collection area (equal to the area of roof made from a hard surface that can be used to collect rainfall) [m²]
RC – runoff coefficient [%]
FE – filter coefficient (manufacturers usually advise that 90 % of the water flowing into the filter is retained so a filter coefficient of 0.9 can be used in the calculation) [%]

After knowing how much water you can collect, the next step is to estimate the size of the tank that is required. The general rule is that the tank size should be around 5 % of the annual rainwater supply, or annual demand.

Therefore a coefficient of 0.05 is applied to calculate 5 % of the annual rainwater supply.

This final step in the equation gives an estimate of the tank size required. The tank capacity is scaled to cover the demand for one, three or six months.

Rough estimation of grey water recycling

An example for a 4-person household:

Grey water generation calculation

- The water demand for a basin is approx. 7 l/d.person, so approx. 2,555 l/a.person.
- The water demand for showering and bathing is approx. 40 l/d.person, so approx. 14,600 l/a.person.
- Together it is approx. 47 l/d.person and approx. 17,155 l/a.person.
- In a 4-person household, it is therefore 188 l/d and 68.62 m³/a of grey water generation.

Service water demand calculation

- The demand for toilet flushing is approx. 34 l/d.person, which means approx. 12,240 l/a.person.
- The demand for a washing machine is approx. 15 l/d.person and approx. 5,400 l/a.person.
- The demand of water for cleaning is approx. 5 l/d.person and approx. 1,800 l/a.person.
- Together it is approx. 54 l/d.person and approx. 19,440 l/a.person.
- For a 4-person household, the service water demand is then 216 l/d, which is 77.76 m³/a.

The demand for service water is higher as the complete reuse of grey water is possible. The remainder can be then collected from rainwater.

Estimation of surface demand for rainwater infiltration

To estimate the surface demand for rainwater infiltration, the size and nature of the outflow effective areas as well as the permeability of the soil should be known.
The calculation can be easy done under:

http://www.dresden.de/regenwasser-versickerung/

or http://www.bottrop.de/stadtleben/downloads/umwelt/Versickerungsanlage.xls

water consumption per person per day [l]

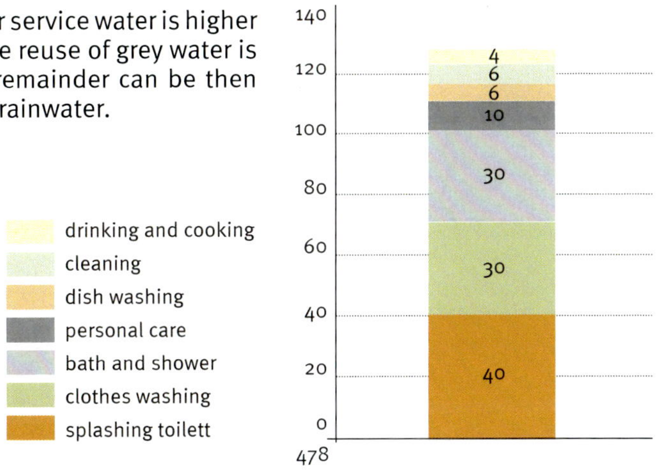

478

Material, surface	Type of area	Runoff coefficient
Pavement		
Asphalt		0.95
Concrete		0.95
Brick		0.85
Gravel		0.75
Porous concrete unit pavers	< 5 % slope	0.50
Porous concrete	< 5 % slope	0.30
Porous asphalt	< 5 % slope	0.40
Roof		
Asphalt, metal, glass, concrete	pitched roof flat roof (roof pitch up to 3° or approx. 5 %)	0.9 - 1.0
Roofing tiles, roofing paper	pitched roof	0.8 - 1.0
Roofing paper, gravel	flat roof (roof pitch up to 3° or approx. 5 %)	0.7 - 0.9
Humous	green roof (depth < 100 mm)	0.50
Humous	green roof (depth 100 - 200 mm)	0.30
Humous	green roof (depth 200 - 500 mm)	0.20
Humous	green roof (depth > 500 mm)	0.10

479

9.6 Economy concept

Economy, efficiency and contemplation
While creating an energy concept, the economy and efficiency of a system has to be proven. Normally the economy and efficiency calculation of various energy supply systems help to determine the most appropriate option.
The initial investment of energy systems and their maintenance and refurbishment (important is the efficient life time of the system) costs for a building's life time have to be estimated. In addition annual price increases and vise versa rates are to be considered.
By dividing the final costs by the number of years the building is in operation, the annual costs for the energy supply system is estimated. By comparing the costs of various energy supply systems, e.g. a system using renewable energies compared to systems connected to the public network, a more economically efficient system can be chosen.
The table 482 shows examples of the average investment costs for various energy supply systems.
The economy and efficiency contemplation also has to be considered. This refers to the renewable energy systems in Germany, founded by the government that give an option for back payments for renewable power that is fed back into the public network.

Life Cycle Costs (page 15)

The life cycle cost assessment can be done with various software, e.g. Legep, but can also be done manually or with the help of an excel sheet.

The calculated costs for the building construction and technical equipment are based on the cost groups as in DIN 276 described on page 17. These are to be actual costs of products or general costs, e.g., in Germany the BKI costs or Sirados costs.

The costs for energy, water and sewage water can be calculated with the help of table 480 per annum.

$C_e = Q_h$ (or W_{el} or PW) . C_u
where
C_e – energy, water or sewage water costs [€/a]
Q_h (or W_{el} or PW) – annual energy or water consumption [kWh/a or (m³/a)]
C_u – costs per unit [€]

If photovoltaic or other systems for energy generation are used, the energy demand onsite will be less.
When calculated for additional years, the table 481. can be used to calculate the annual price, also factoring in an increased rate or vise versa.

The costs for cleaning can be calculated with the aid of table 485. There are costs for the cleaning of the glazing, the cladding on the walls and flooring.

The calculation multiples the m² of windows (from both sides), doors, external wall cladding and flooring with the value from the table.
The final costs in the table are based on values of an office building, i.e. the cleaning of each floor 100 times/a. In other cases, e.g. kindergarten, the floors should be cleaned every working day. The table that shows examples of floor cleaning for various building types is 484.
Through this method, the costs can be calculated for a full year. To calculate the cleaning costs for additional years, the annual price increase and vise versa is to be used.

The maintenance costs can be calculated as a percentage of the building costs.
The table 483 shows different percentages for various building elements for a single year. Again, to calculate the maintenance costs for additional years, the annual price increase and vise versa is to be used.

Refurbishment costs are also calculated as a percentage, the useful life time of building element is important.
If the building is built for 50 years and the building's element has a duration e.g. of 30 years, it will have to be changed during the building's life time. The costs for the demolishing and new construction of the building elements are refurbishment costs (also with consideration to annual price increases and decreases).

Energy supply material	Unit	€ without tax
Power	kWh	0.17
Power for heating	kWh	0.11
Oil	l	0.65
Natural gas	m³	0.62
Wood pellets	kg	0.18
Lignite	kg	0.5
Hard coal	kg	0.7
Distance heating / CHP fossil	kWh	0.09
Distance heating / CHP renewable	kWh	0.07
Fresh water	m³	2.01
Waste water	m³	2.14
Rain water (paved building site area)	m²	1.10

480

General annual price increases	2%
Discount rate (nominal)	5.5%
Annual price increase for heating and electric power (nominal)	4%

481

Energy supply system	Investment costs
Solar thermal collector	approx. 300 €/m²
Solar thermal vacuum pipe	approx. 1,000 €/m²
Solar thermal collector storage, volume 300 l	approx. 1,200 €
Solar thermal collector storage, volume 1,000 l	approx. 2,000 €
Photovoltaic	1,700 €/kWp
Air-air-heat pump	approx. 7,000 - 10,000 €
Air-water-heat pump	approx. 13,000 - 16,000 €
Water-water-heat pump	approx. 17,000 - 19,000 €
Soil-water-heat pump, earth piles	approx. 14,850 - 19,850 €
Soil-water-heat pump, earth collector	approx. 11,500 - 15,000 €

482

Cost Group	Costs for maintenance [% from building costs/a]	Costs for refurbishment [% from building costs/a]
CG 300	0.1	the costs to be calculated depends on the useful life time of construction
CG 410 Gas, water and wastewater systems	0.7	0.55
KG 420 Heating		
Heat supply systems	0.9	0.5
Transfer to use	0	1
Distribution	0	1
Generation	1	2
Potable water heating		
Transfer to use	1	1
Distribution	0	2
Generation	1	2
Water treatment systems	1	1
CG 430 Ventilation		
Ventilation and air conditioning	2.05	2.4
Transfer to use	1	1
Heat recovery	10	2
Air conditioning	4	2
Cooling ceiling	1	1
Humidifier/dehumidifier	2	3
Distribution	0	1
CG 440 Power system	1.25	0.65
CG 460 Elevator	2.05	1.1

483

Cleaning of flooring	Cleaning [number/a]
Offices	100
Sanitary rooms	each working day (e.g. for office building 250)
Entrance hall	each working day (e.g. for office building 250)
Circulation	150
Secondary rooms	12
Hospital spaces	each working day 365
Kindergarten spaces	each working day 220

484

480 The net prices for different energy supply materials per unit, Germany
481 Annual price increases and discount rate, Germany
482 Examples of average investment and maintenance net prices for some energy supply systems, state January 2014, Germany
483 Cleaning net prices in office building, hourly rate: 15 €/h, Germany
484 The different amount of floor cleaning in different functions in year in Germany
485 The percentage from building costs for maintenance and refurbishment costs in office building, Germany

CG	Building element	Costs [€/m²]	Number per year	Costs [€/m²a]
CG 334	**Glazing**			
	Easily accessible	0.6	2	1.2
	Mildly accessible	0.75	2	1.5
	Difficult to access	1.15	2	2.31
CG 335	**External wall cladding (outer)**			
	Soft natural stone	13.04	0.25	3.26
	Aluminium, stainless steel, copper sheet, corrosion-protected steel	5.00	0.25	1.25
	Variable glass	0.75	0.25	0.19
	Ceramic, artificial stone, hard natural stone	2.5	0.25	0.63
CG 338	**Sun protection**	5.00	0.25	1.25
CG 344	**Inside doors and windows**	0.06	4	0.24
CG 352	**Flooring normal dirtying**			
	Ceramic tiles, soft natural and artificial stone	0.06	100	6.00
	Carpet	0.05	100	5.00
	Plastic to 2.5 mm, laminate, linoleum to 2.5 mm, parquet	0.04	100	3.75
	Flooring strong dirtying			
	Ceramic tiles, parquet	0.07	100	7.06
	Plastic over 2.5 mm, linoleum from 3.2 mm, hard natural and artificial stone, hard carpet	0.04	100	4.41
CG 410	**Sewage, water, gas installations**			
CG 412	Sanitation	0.07	250	7.06

485

9.7 Green concept

Season	Evaporation values [mm/d]	Water condition inside the growing media
Winter	0.1 - 0.5	well saturated, no frost
Spring/ autumn	0.6 - 1.5	well saturated
Summer wet	1.5 - 4.5	well saturated
Summer hot	0.0 - 0.2	dry substrate

486

486 Daily evaporation rate of a green roof in different seasons, Germany
487 Surface temperatures of bituminous and green roofs on 20.06.2001, Germany

A tree covers only a small piece of ground, but offers large usable surfaces. It is a home for birds or other organisms.

It cools its surrounding through the evaporation of rainwater. It absorbs pollutants and CO_2, creates shadows and it also looks attractive.

The evaporation of water is an effective way to cool the surroundings. The exterior walls of a building can be cooled down and the interior temperature can be reduced by 4 °C through the greening of the roof or facade with appropriate plants.

Green roofs can convert about 58 % of the solar radiation into the evaporation of water through the plant covering. Non-green roofs normally convert about 95 % of solar radiation into heat energy.

Estimation of cooling through evaporation of green roof and facade

There are different methods used to calculate evaporative cooling energy; depending on surrounding factors (wind speed, percolation, temperatures, solar radiation, ...) or on the building and plant factors (plant system, facade orientation, granulates, plant types and dimensions and amount of blades, ...).

Generally in Germany, the approx. evaporation between July and August is between 5.4 and 11.3 mm of water/d, depending on the building level. The evaporation of 1 m³ (= 1,000 l) rainwater generates an evaporative cooling energy of 680 kWh.

The following formula can be used to calculate evaporative cooling energy:

$$C_e = (A_p \cdot Ca_e \cdot N_d) \cdot E_e$$

Where
C_e – evaporative cooling [kWh/a]
A_p – area of plants [m_2]
Ca_e – evaporation capacity [m/d, 1 m = 1,000 mm]
N_d – vegetation period [d/a]
E_e – amount of evaporation energy [kWh/l, 1l = 0.001 m³]

Trees can be also used to restore the ecological balance that is negatively influenced by buildings, transportation, processes or people:

- **one tree binds approx. 12.5 kg CO_2/a, so e.g. 259 trees . 0.0125 t/a = 3,24 t/a**
- **one shrub binds approx. 6.25 kg CO_2/a, so e.g. 800 shrubs . 0.00625 t/a = 5 t/a**

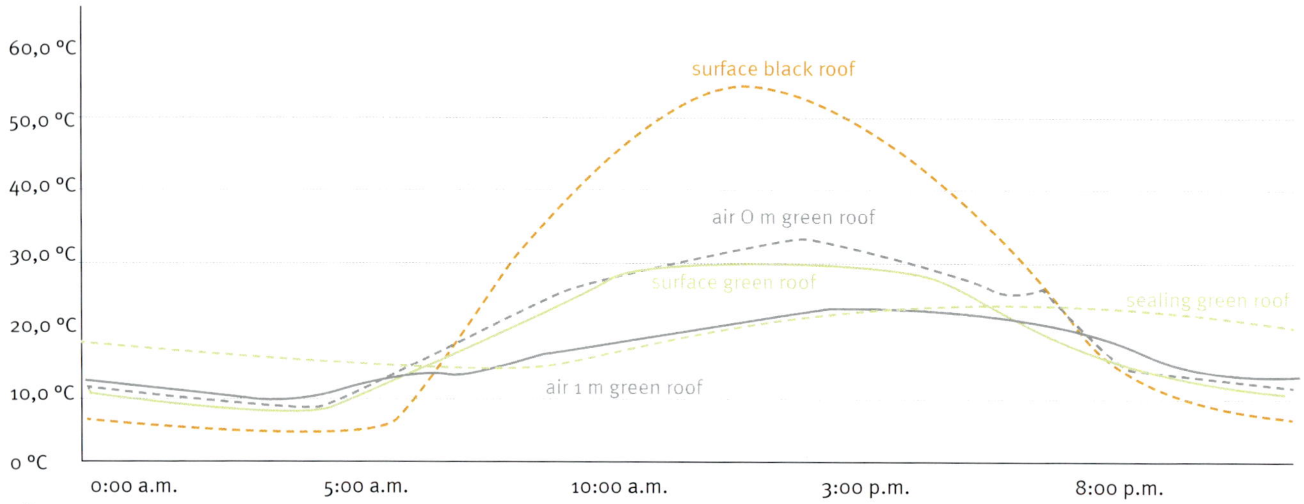

487

9.8 Waste concept

The waste concept is an important part of the building concept. Waste avoiding and then waste separation is preferable in order to reuse as much waste material as possible.

For the rough estimation of household waste generation, the statistic values from table 488 and 489 can be used.

Waste type	Waste generation [kg/a.person]	Disposed [1,000t/a]	Reused [1,000t/a]
Total	**456**	**11,781.5**	**24,940.4**
Household and bulky refuse	**193**	**11,314.6**	**4,258.4**
Household waste	164	9,990.9	3,221.9
Bulky refuse	29	1,323.8	1,036,5
Separately: organic waste	**113**	**12.4**	**9,083.1**
Biological waste	54	0.1	4,358.4
Biologically degradable waste (garden and park waste)	59	12.3	4,724.7
Separately: recyclable waste	148	392.9	11,525.0
Glass	24	0.6	1,908.2
Paper, cardboard, carton	72	9.2	5,828.6
Metal	3	0.0	253.3
Wood	14	16.2	1,105.8
Plastic	2	39.3	86.8
Textiles	1	0.4	99.5
Mixed recyclables/packaging (incl. lightweight packaging), composites	32	327.1	2,242.9
Other waste	**2**	**61.5**	**73.8**
Dangerous waste	1	27.7	20.8
Other waste	1	33.9	52.9

488

Waste type	Waste generation [kg/a.person]	Disposed [1,000t/a]	Reused [1,000t/a]
Total	**456**	**11,781.5**	**24,940.4**
Baden-Württemberg	445	7.6	4,695.6
Bayern	471	2,013.7	3,880.3
Berlin	413	452.5	940.5
Brandenburg	393	282.9	680.7
Bremen	439	127.0	160.1
Hamburg	454	1504.9	281.9
Hessen	466	749.5	2,056.2
Mecklenburg-Vorpommern	423	197.8	478.7
Niedersachsen	508	1,398.2	2,551.8
Nordrhein-Westfalen	470	4,180.1	4,077.7
Rheinland-Pfalz	512	131.6	1,912.6
Saarland	461	178.8	279.8
Sachsen	320	334.5	962.5
Sachsen-Anhalt	444	266.1	736.5
Schleswig-Holstein	480	572.3	774.6
Thüringen	394	384.0	470.9

489

488 Waste generation from household divided to the waste types in 2012, Germany
489 Waste generation from household divided to the region in 2012, Germany

9.9 Summary

The integral planning and development of concepts are important for the long and short life spans of buildings. Using a rule of thumb as a rough calculation tool is one method to develop an appropriate building concept.

Unfortunately, the integral planning and the designing of planning processes are not sufficient enough to be considered in the German sustainable building certification tools, because they focus mainly on process quality and the architectural competition.

Architectural competitions and their corresponding guidelines are often contradictory to the planning requirements for the sustainable development of a building.

An integral planning team should work together on a building's concept development from the very beginning, however this is not possible in the case of architecture competitions.

The creation of an appropriate building concept must consider all building elements (material, energy, water, waste, etc) and is the main goal of integral planning.

At the very beginning of the planning stage, it is not possible to design all concepts in detail. The ideas come from experience and are supported and proven by rough calculations based on rules of thumb.

In this chapter, we attempt to introduce how to form an entire building concept, covering different components to create a collection of rough estimations for partial concepts.

Some calculations and values are based on valid guidelines, regulations and norms, however some are the results from the experiences of developing building concepts.

The collection is not complete and requires more research and work. We would be thankful for your comments, tips and references that could help bring new knowledge to this field.
It should also be mentioned that it isn't always the best method to calculate and verify everything. Sometimes it is important to rely on past experiences and the overall goal of the building concept.

This depends on the location of the design and the building owners, different backgrounds of the decision makers. E.g. in China it is common for one main boss to make the decisions on the building design and concept. His decision is based on his own reasons and not on calculations.

On the other hand, in Germany it is normal that a larger group of people with different opinions make the decisions about the building concept. In these situations, the calculations and expertise can help to find the best solution where all participants agree.

490 A building concept is always a result of the various professionals work and processes – construction site of Egger's "New Entrance" in Wismar

490

Example "New Entrance"

Wood processing factory EGGER, Wismar

The entrance pavilion of the wood processing factory EGGER in Wismar was built in accordance to the design of a student from HS Wismar. The building was built together with the participation of students from HS Wismar, who supervised the whole design and construction process.

The students were able to take part of a real project process and were able to learn and influence building design and implementation. The pavilion was built in 3 months, from 20.06.2011 until 06.09.2011.

491 Impressions from the designing and construction process of Egger's "New Entrance" in Wismar

491

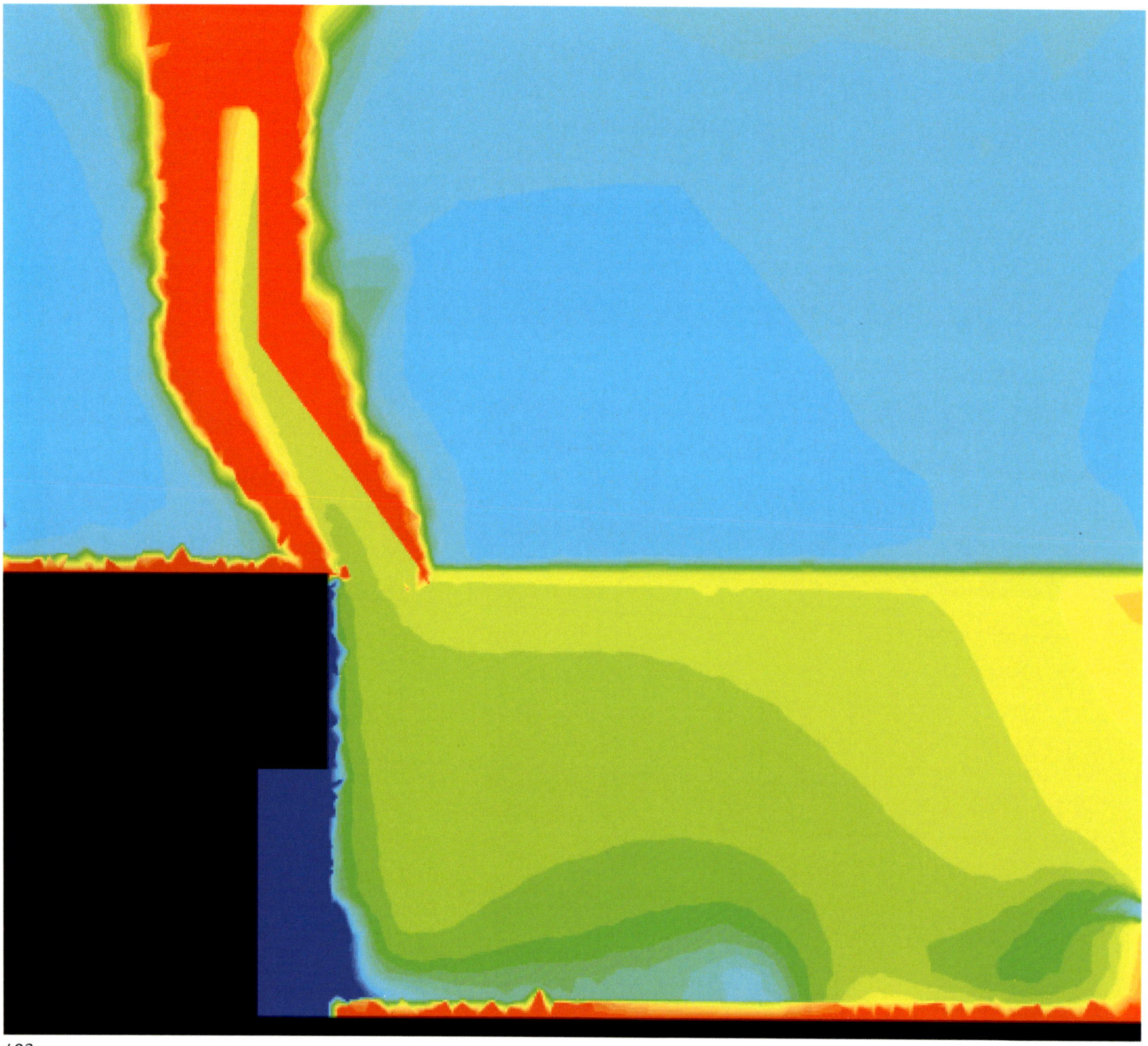

492

492 Building climate investigation during the developing of building energy renovation concept – Kindergarten "Burg", Luckenwalde, IGEL-Institut

Life time design

10.0 Methods and instruments

10.1 Introduction

In the previous chapter '9.0 Building concept', the main estimation methods to design building space, calculate the material, construction, energy, water, economy and green concept was based on a manual calculation with basic formulas or with the help of various sources.
To make exact calculations that support, prove and optimise the design requires special engineers. Some calculations can also be done with special software developed especially for these purposes.

In the chapter '10.0 Methods and instruments', some of the software for appropriate calculations are introduced. These calculations can be done during the design building phase in order to help prove different possibilities and develop the best concept from all points of view.
The calculations help to develop the appropriate building constructions and elements with the optimal building space and operation concept also by considering the economical impacts.

As an example, to make decisions about building materials in relation to their ecological characteristics and impacts, the ökobau.dat is a source for values required for the calculation. With the software Legep®, all ecological impacts of a building and its life cycle (LCA) can be calculated. The software Legep was developed also to calculate Life Cycle Costs (LCC).

There are also other documents that help to evaluate the ecological values of building materials, e.g. Environmental Product Declarations (EPD), WECOBIS, GISCODE, etc. Some of them are introduced in this chapter.

To consider the physical characteristic of a building's construction, the online source u-wert.net, that was introduced in the previous chapter can be used. Dämmwerk and WUFI® are examples of software that were developed specially for building physics, to evaluate designs or for EnEV calculation. This is used to calculate and simulate the thermal, moisture or acoustic characteristics of a building's constructions.
Lighting simulation software such as Relux®, Dialux help to design appropriate daylighting and artificial lighting for a building.

Thermal or flow simulations can be done with software such as Trnsys, TRNFlow, ANSYS Fluent, DesignBuilder, EnergyPlus, etc.
All of these programmes and many others help and support the design of different building concepts. They can be also used during the later phases of designing to prove and evaluate the final construction and technologies. They can be used by both architects or engineers.
However they do not replace engineers, who do precise calculations for the statics and technologies of the building.

493 The Blower Door Test is used to find out the leakages in the building envelope construction and to determine the building air tightness according to DIN V4108-7
494 Thermography is used to determine the surface temperature and quality of the building envelope by using thermal images made with a thermal imaging camera – the most accurate value is shown by thermography when the building is heated and the difference between exterior and interior temperature is at least 15 °C – thermography can be also used to test if the PV or solar collectors work efficiently

493

494

In order to reach an appropriate energy standard, a high quality of building and technology is necessary along with the interaction of building structure and building services using communication technology. This includes as a basis the intense collaboration between architects and engineers, clients and users in the planning phase and the involvement of the construction companies and craftsmen in the execution phase.

As a result of these processes, a functioning building that achieves all parameters and use properties is usually not immediate. An optimization process is necessary and can only be tackled in cooperation with all concerned, particularly the users.

The planning element of integration between the building envelope and the building services must be achieved and experienced in the transfer and utilization phase, until the technology achieves what was planned and the users have learned to use it properly. It should be noted that the users´ behaviour and the proper handling of the building can have a significant influence on this result and are thus included in the optimization process.

The use of monitoring and evaluating the energy consumption data by functionally separable building areas is thus an integral part of the design, construction and handover phase. Just as a successful planning and construction process includes quality assurance to ensure compliance with construction times and building qualities, so are monitoring plans, the measurement and evaluation as a part of quality management to achieve the energy objectives.

For the estimation of the energy values, it is necessary to collect the relevant energy flows for significant, separate functional units. The electrical energy consumption in the lighting, ventilation, water heating technology, various technology sectors (e.g power supply) and user-related consumption (e.g. copier, etc.) are divided into groups in order to examine the different fractions of the respective sectors.

As an alternative, in addition to the energy consumption measurements of individual strands and time sheets for times of use, uniform loads (e.g. lighting) can be used to reduce costs. Here, it is necessary to capture the passive heat gains (solar and internal heat gains, as well as waste heat utilization by heat recovery) and the additional demand on the heating.

In addition, monitoring of the local climate and the indoor climate are needed. The quality of the building climate, especially the thermal climate, but also the health and visual comfort of the users are to be analysed. With the help of example measurements, thermal and visual comfort, humidity, CO_2 content in the air should be checked at different times of the year and day in the selected areas.
Monitoring is already a part of various projects and it is also necessary to obtain different certifications, such as DGNB or BNB. In the future, the implementation of monitoring into the building's use phase will be an obligation.

495 Schematic of integration of monitoring within the building

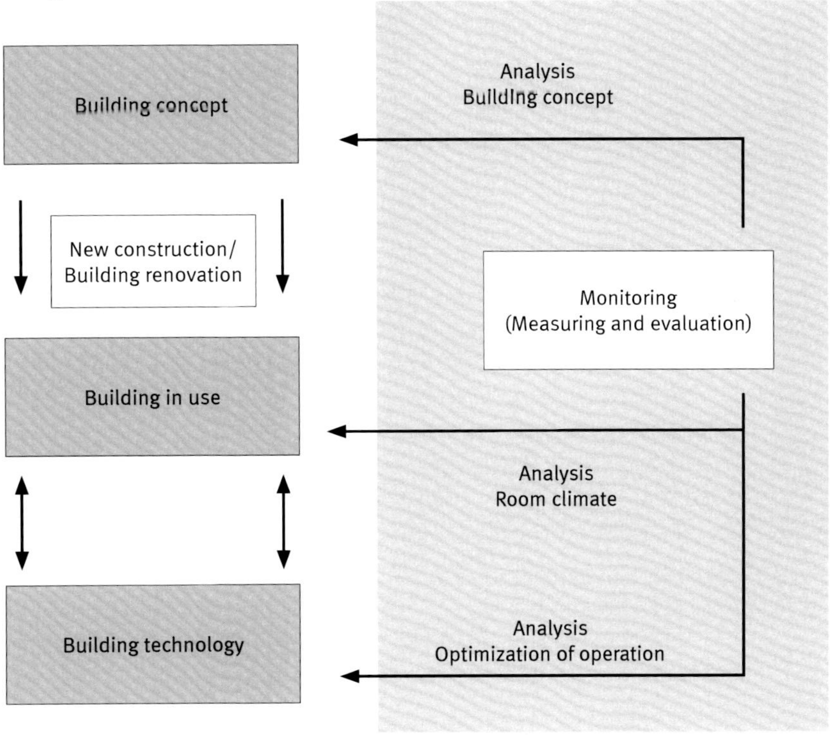

495

10.2 Calculation software Dämmwerk

496

[74]*DämmwerkBauphysik-Software;* Dämmwerk building physics software [http://www.bauphysik-software.de/en-GB/concept-english.html] (17.10.2012)
[75] *Dämmwerk Bauphysik-Software;* Designing Structural Elements [http://www.bauphysik-software.de/en-GB/elements-english.html] (17.10.2012)
[76] *Dämmwerk Bauphysik-Software;* EnEV 2007 – German Energy Saving Regulation [http://www.bauphysik-software.de/en-GB/enev-2007.html] (17.10.2012)

496 Example of student work calculation – IBA Smart Material House
497 Example of student work calculation – creating zones – floor plan divided into functional zones
498 Example of student work calculation – creating zones in the software

Building physics software can be used during design to improve the physical characteristics of a building. It can upgrade the thermal, moisture, sound and fire protecting characteristics of the building's structural elements including the walls, roofs and floors.

The aim of this software is to help design efficient buildings by calculating the building energy need for heating, warm water, lighting, ventilation and air-conditioning. Dämmwerk is one example that is used specifically for climate area in Germany.

It can be downloaded on the home page of **www.bauphysik.software.de** in German or English language.

"DÄMMWERK is specifically designed for building physicists, structure planners, construction experts, application technicians and students.

The comprehensive and interdisciplinary concept of the software makes it possible to perform building physical calculations for heat, moisture, sound and fire insulation of structural components or complete building projects. (...)

Innovation + Software Concept

- complex calculation of structural elements and complete structures.
- current European (and German) standards including information about the products of the building material industry.
- interdisciplinary utilisation and interpretation of data.
- import and export of data with simple interface : text or graphic
- variation of parameters in local context menus, collections of data are easily accessible and individually expandable.
- visual design and controlling, representative and meaningful diagrams, individual graphics design, coloured printouts." [74]

Inputs – Designing Structural Elements and creating a zone model

"The well sorted material assistant with various commercial products and DIN building-materials supports the creating of structural elements. DÄMMWERK is converting the choices into a cross section drawing, which serves to describe the calculations and to control the projects. Once constructed a structural element can be used for heat, moisture, noise and fire protection calculations - only one input is necessary." [75]

The next step after designing structural elements is to create different temperature zones. The floor plans of a building are divided into different zones due to their different characteristics, i.e. varying temperature, ventilation system, etc. The energy calculation is possible once the zones are created.

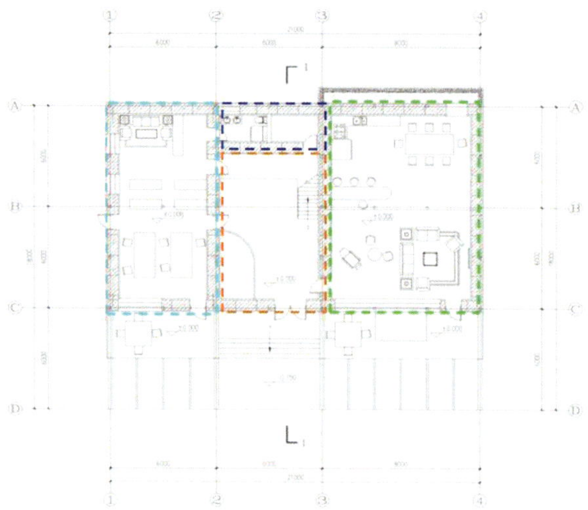

497

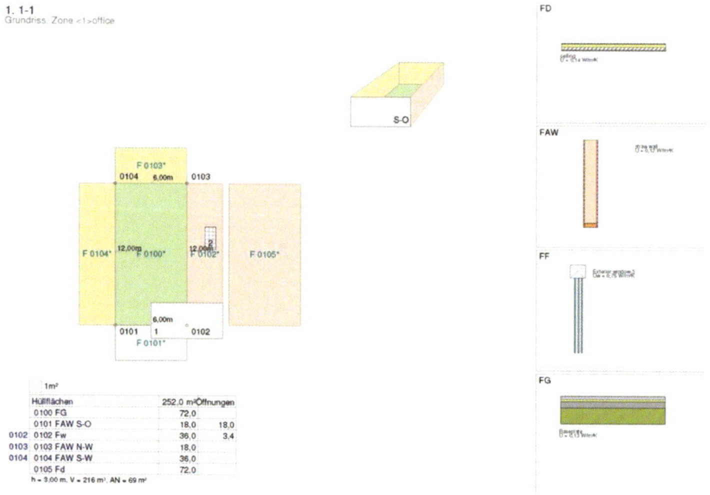

498

EnEV calculation

The main priority for use of this software is to produce the German EnEV (energy saving regulation) calculation – "monthly balance, period balance, procedures under public law, procedures for buildings with low inside temperatures and existing buildings.

- calculation of transmission heat losses using Fx-values, integration of thermal bridges, losses to the ground (including stationary or harmonious conductance), front buildings of glass
- Structural element relations with actualising function
- explicit calculation of thermal bridges, using of Ψ-values from the structural element calculation
- energy losses of integrated heating surfaces
- free ventilation, ventilation systems with/without heat recovery
- internal heat gains
- solar heat gains of windows, winter gardens, opaque structural units transparent heat insulation, radiation intensities and shading factors
- determination of the effective heat storage capacity, explicitly or flat
- heating interruption and calculation of nightly shut off
- Calculation of heat and warm water requirements
- facilities according to German DIN V 4701-10:2001, diagram procedure or detailed table procedure, warm water, ventilation and heating installations
- calculation of primary energy requirements and transmission energy losses, limiting values according to German EnEV 2014
- graphical preparation: monthly or periodical balances, energy profiles
- table/graphic comparison of two building and calculation varieties" [76]

An Energy Performance Certificate for the building is an output for completing this EnEV calculation.

Result analysis

- energy demand (DIN V 18599-1)
- primary energy demand due to the energy holder
- energy demand of zones
- ventilation
- lighting
- air-conditioning
- warm water
- heating
- useful energy
- final energy
- primary energy

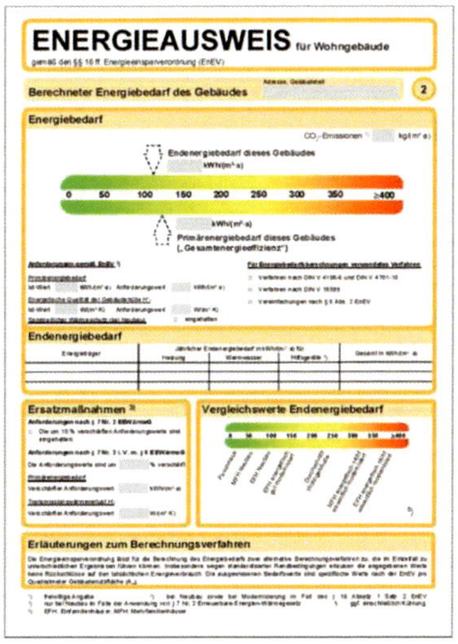

499

499 Energy performance certificate as a result of the EnEV calculation with software Dämmwerk
500 Example of student work calculation – Result analysis of the software
501 Example of student work calculation – choose the material; once determine the material and thickness of each part, the system can calculate the U-Factor and list the characters of each material

14.2 Endenergiebedarf nach Zonen
(Ref-No 5.14.2)

siehe Abschnitt Zone	m²	RLT 9 kWh/a	Beleucht. 10 kWh/a	Klima 11 kWh/a	Warmwasser 12 kWh/a	Heizung 13 kWh/a	Summe kWh/a
<1> office	56	253	797		-164		887
<2> bathroom	12	78	797				875
<3> garden	117	263	1751				2013
<4> living room	192	864	2709		-569		3003
<5> bedroom	50	307	1525		-199		1632
Gebäude	427	1766	7578		-933		8411

14.3 Aufteilung des Energiebedarfs (für den Energieausweis)
(Ref-No 5.14.3)

	RLT kWh/m²a	Beleucht. kWh/m²a	Klima kWh/m²a	Warmwasser kWh/m²a	Heizung kWh/m²a	Summe kWh/m²a
Nutzenergiebedarf	4.1	17.7	33.8	46.6	49.3	151.6
Endenergiebedarf	4.1	17.7	0.0	0.0	0.0	21.9
Primärenergiebedarf	10.8	46.1	0.0	0.0	0.0	56.9

500

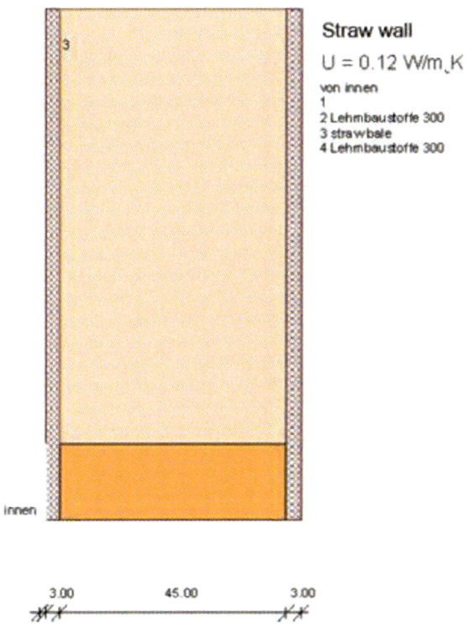

501

10.3 Calculation/simulation software WUFI®

502

The software WUFI® was developed by Fraunhofer-Institute for Building Physics IBP to calculate and simulate the hygrothermal building envelope performance and indoor climate.
WUFI® means Wärme und Feuchte instationär (Transient Heat and Moisture) and is validated by using data derived from outdoor and laboratory tests. It allows realistic calculations of the transient hygrothermal behaviour of multi-layer building components exposed to natural climate conditions.

Information, application examples and downloads can be found on the homepage www.wufi.de in various languages.

"WUFI® Pro (multilingual)

WUFI® Pro is the standard tool for one-dimensional hygrothermal evaluation of building envelopes. Previous methods (e.g. 'Glaser') consider only the risk of condensation under steady state conditions. Important physical phenomena like moisture storage and liquid transport are disregarded. The same is true for relevant climate effects like wind-driven rain and solar radiation.

WUFI® Pro calculates the dynamic hygrothermal behaviour of building assemblies using real climatic conditions. Thus you can analyse the performance of your design under any climate and predict:

- drying time of construction
- water absorption due to driving rain
- additional moisture entry due to rainwater leakages and vapour convection
- the influence of materials with variable diffusion resistance on the moisture balance
- moisture influence on thermal performance of the construction
- long-term system behaviour or hygrothermal consequences of construction modifications
- the hygrothermal behaviour of pipe insulation

WUFI® 2D (English)

Some constructions cannot be modelled accurately by one-dimensional simulation. In these cases two-dimensional calculations with WUFI® 2D should be performed. Application examples are:

- moisture conditions at structural and geometrical thermal bridges – especially if the hygrothermal conditions inside the structure and not only on the surface are evaluated
- simulation of joints, connections and corner details
- timber framed constructions with multiple insulation layers
- three dimensional simulation of punctual penetrations with radial symmetry

The input in WUFI® 2D and also the calculation is in comparison to WUFI® Pro more time-consuming. As far as two-dimensional problems can be solved one-dimensionally (incl. simple approaches for ventilation and rain water leakages) the simulation with WUFI® Pro is normally easier. Generally WUFI® 2D should be used in addition and not as an alternative to WUFI® Pro.

WUFI® Plus (English)

WUFI® Plus is a new holistic model that considers all hygrothermal interactions between the indoor air and the building envelope in detail. It analyses the wall, roof and basement components and the indoor conditions with different heating and air-conditioning approaches.

It employs the same GUI structure as WUFI® Pro to facilitate its application. In addition to the hygrothermal assessment of single components, WUFI® Plus allows evaluations such as

- appropriate ventilation to avoid mould growth
- shading strategies to reduce overheating
- influence of thermal and hygric inertia on building energy demand

[77] *WUFI®;* WUFI® Pro, 2D, Plus. Software for calculating the coupled heat and moisture transfer in building components [http://www.wufi.de/index_e.html] (07.04.2014)

502 Logo of WUFI®

and indoor environment
• hygrothermal performance of buildings with exceptional indoor conditions or intermittent operation" [77]

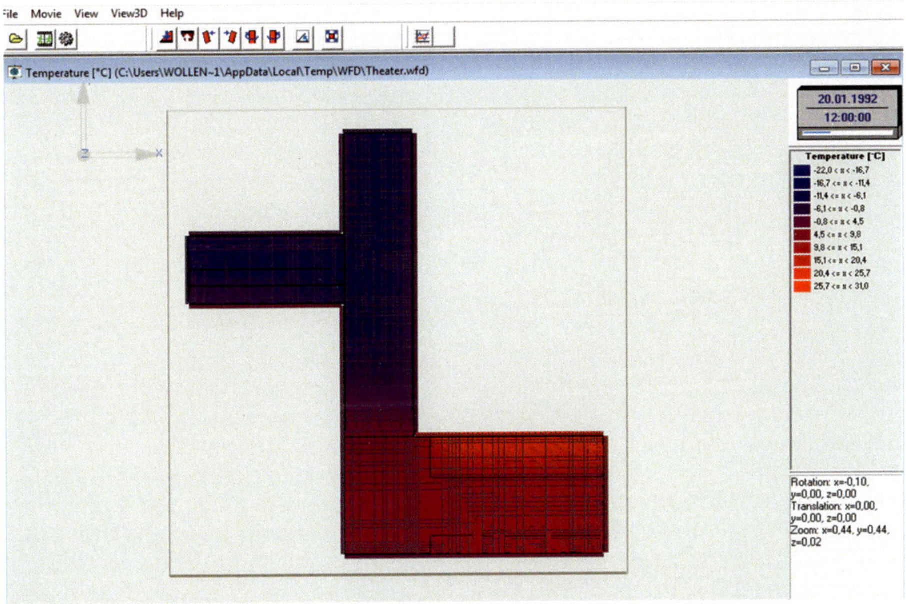

503

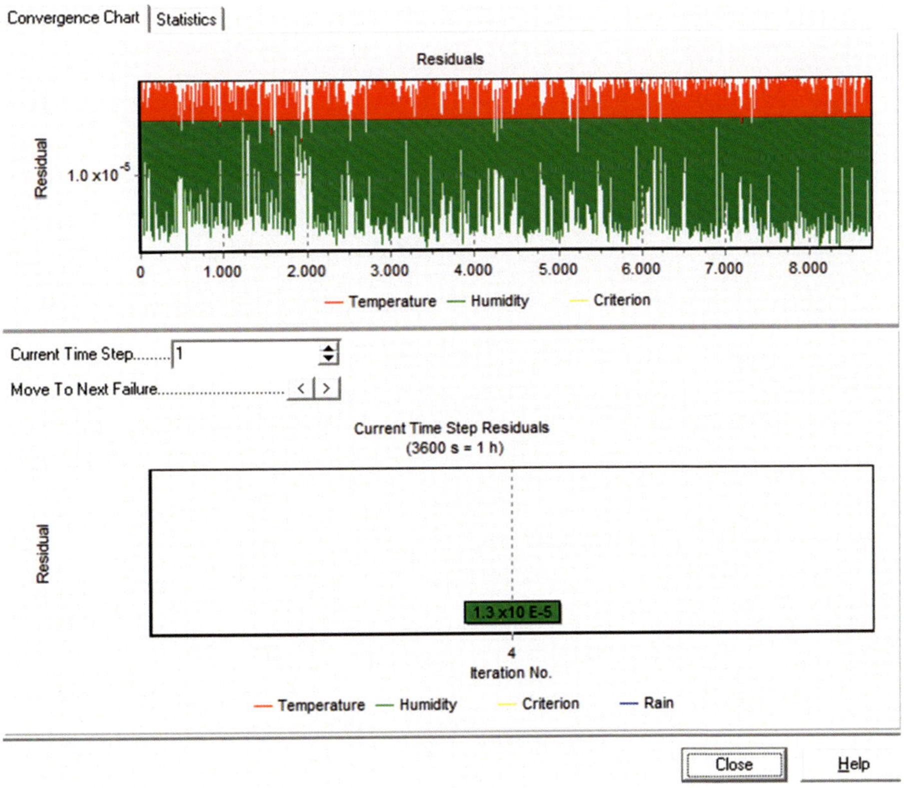

504

503 Example of simulation results from WUFI®2D – temperature flow in the building construction during the year
504 Example of simulation results from WUFI®2D – diagram of temperature and humidity flow in the building construction during the year

10.4 Calculation software Legep®

505

Buildings have five main life cycles – material production, building construction, building use, maintenance/refurbishment, and end of life (recycling, disposal). Evaluating the life cycle assessment (LCA) and life cycle costs (LCC) is a very important part of sustainable design. The Legep® software is a highly suitable program that is able to calculate building needs in order to design a sustainable building with low costs, energy and material needs for all parts of the building life-cycle, while decreasing ecological impacts on our environment.

"Legep® is a tool for integrated life-cycle analysis. It supports the planning teams in the design, construction, quantity surveying and evaluation of new or existing buildings or building products. The Legep® database contains the description of all elements of a building (based on DIN 276); their life cycle costs (LCC/WLC) based on DIN 18960 and the final report EU-TG4 LCC in Construction. All information is structured along life cycle phases (construction, maintenance, operation (cleaning), refurbishment and demolition. Legep® establishes the energy needs for heating, warm-water, electricity and their costs (following EnEV 2002 and EN 832). The environmental assessment comprises the material flows (input and waste) as well as an effect oriented evaluation based on ISO 14040-43.

Legep® is organised along four software tools, each with its own database. The method is based on cost planning by elements. The database is hierarchically organised, starting with the LCI-data at the bottom, building material data, work-process description, simple elements for material layers, composed elements like windows, and ends with macro-elements like building objects. The data are fully scalable and can be used either bottom-up or top-down.
Elements at each level contain all necessary data for cost, energy, and mass-flow and impact evaluation. A building can be described using either preassembled elements or defining elements from scratch. The user can also define a specific composition by exchanging layers or descriptions of the element. The advantage of the top down approach is its completeness: if an element is not explicitly changed or eliminated it will remain in the calculation. The costs of the elements are established by the Sirados® database, which is published each year. There are about 6,000 elements ready for use for the building fabric, technical equipment and landscape work. The LC Inventories are based on the Ecoinvent data and specific values from the Baustoff Ecoinventare (Kohler, N., Lützkendorf, Th. et al., Karlsruhe/Weimar/Zürich 1995).

Input in Legep®: A building can be described alternatively with 15 macro-elements, 40 complex elements, or approx. 150 simple elements. This corresponds to the increase in knowledge during the design and planning process allowing describing the building more and more in detail without loosing the overall framework. At each level a complete evaluation can be made and documented automatically.

Output of LEGEP®: at each phase a complete, interrelated set of cost, energy, mass-flow and environmental indicators. The number of indicators, which are displayed, can be chosen from the CML indicators (Green house potential 100 years, Acidification potential, Photochemical Ozone creation potential, Ozone depletion potential, Eutrophication potential, primary energy consumption renewable and nonrenewable, Ecoindicator etc.). Additional indicators are under implementation. It is possible to show separately specific indicators or all indicators, for each life cycle phase (new construction, operation, cleaning, maintenance, refurbishment, demolition) of the building. The different evaluations are represented in the form of tables and appropriated graphs. Through the use of Legep® the main effort of the designers and other specialists is shifted from the extremely cumbersome description of a building and extensive input of

[78] *Legep®*; Legep® [http://legep.de/?AktivId=1125] (17.10.2012)

505 Logo of Legep®
506 Life cycle of Legep® calculation
507 Material flows as input and output, identifying different European Waste Classes

data into a specific software to the interpretation of large number of synthetic results at each moment. The combined effects of changes can be immediately visualised; new methods of design can be founded on experience gained from LCA knowledge.

Legep® is used at present mainly for the design of new built buildings, taking into account the future life cycle. The information is highly appreciated by clients and facility managers. For existing buildings Legep® assists in the decisions on refurbishment operations and long term, sustainable management of buildings and building stocks." [78]

More information as well as downloads can be found on the homepage www.legep.de. The software is currently available only in the German language.

Legep® consists of three main modules:

- Project
- Cost planning
- Heat and power

The module "heat & power" can be used to create energy performance certificates for residential and non-residential buildings.

- Economy

The module "economy" can be used for the assessment of building measures in existing residential and non-residential buildings.

- Life-cycle costs

The module "Life-cycle costs" can be used for the creation of cost planning (LCC) for all life cycle phases of a building.

- Ecology

The module "ecology" can be used to create a life cycle assessment (LCA) for all life cycle stages of a building.

506

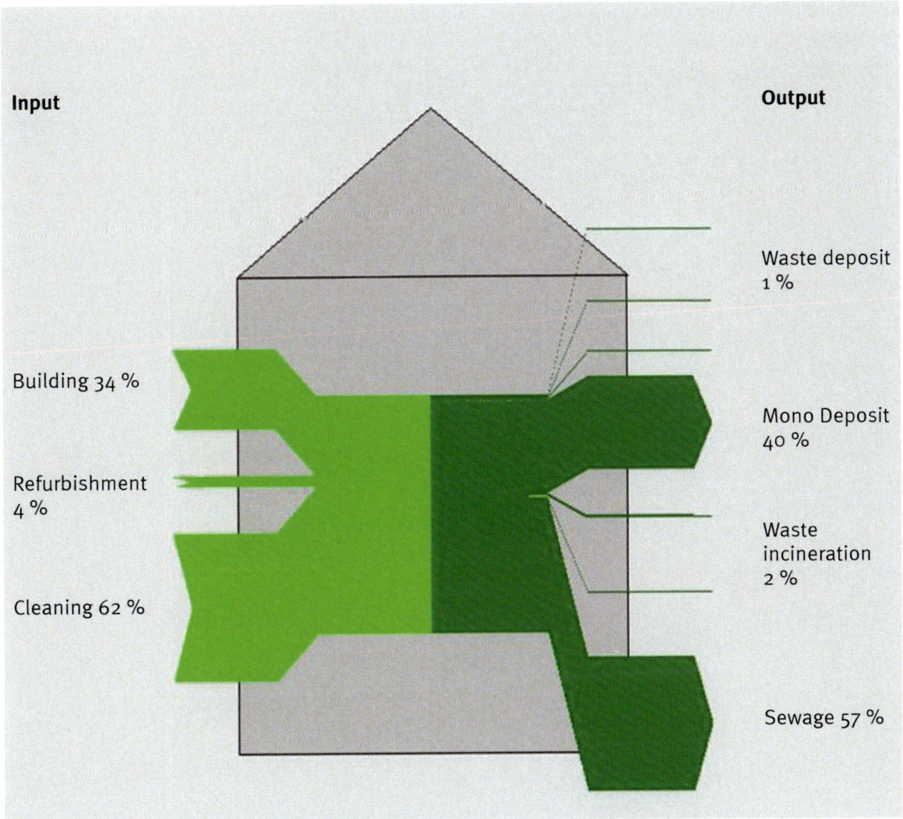

507

10.5 Light simulation software DIALux/Relux®

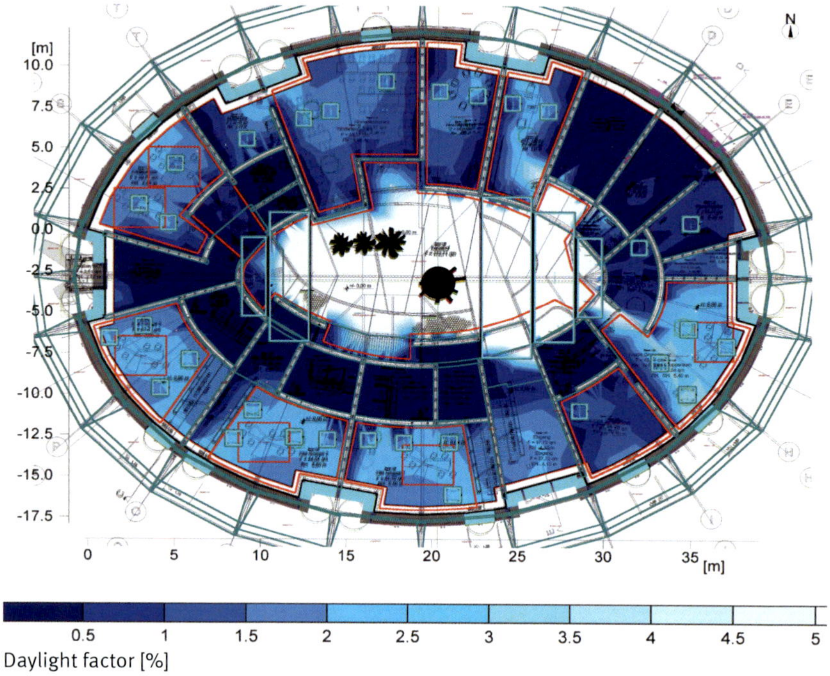

508

While planning the lighting of a building, a light simulation is necessary. This calculates how much daylighting the building gains via openings and is a good tool to design artificial lighting for the inside of the building.

With this simulation, the energy needed for lighting can be counted. There are two commonly used light simulation software – DIALux and Relux®.

DIALux

DIALux, the free and complete software for professional light planning is open to luminaires of all manufacturers.

It is a simple, effective and professional light planning software, created by planners, and for planners. DIALux is continuously being developed by a team of 20.

It is used for planning whole buildings as well as outdoor spaces. The software is free of charge and can be downloaded from the website in a variety of languages.

508 Simulation of daylight factor at user level 0.85 m, kindergarten "Wildblume"
509 Simulation of annual percentage of daylighting in working space, Kindergarten "Wildblume"

[79-80] Online: http://www.dial.de/DIAL/en/light/lighting-design-planning/projects.html (17.10.2012)
[65] Online: http://www.relux.biz/index.php?option=com_content&view=article&id=226&Itemid=211&lang=en (17.10.2012)
[65] Online: http://www.relux.biz/index.php?option=com_content&view=article&id=217&Itemid=200&lang=en (17.10.2012)

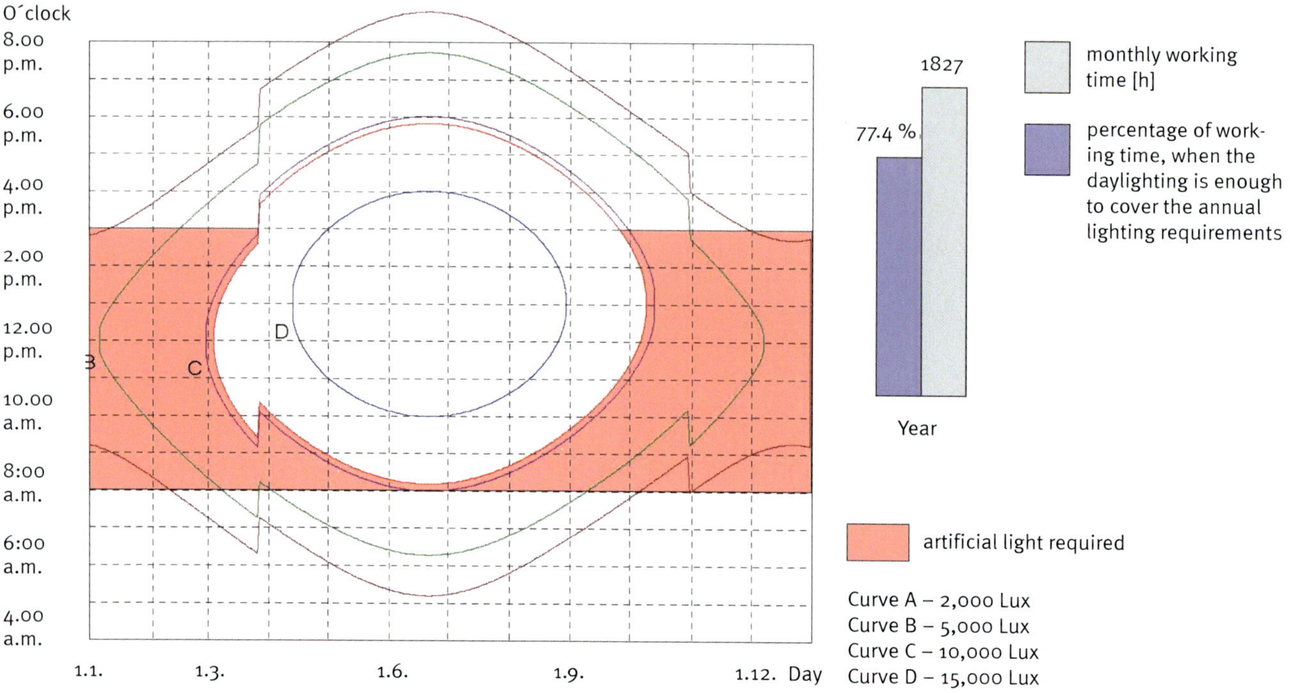

509

Relux

"For several years Relux® has been the embodiment of professional lighting planning software. (...) Relux® Informatik AG, located in Switzerland, is involved in development, production and distribution of the lighting planning software and product catalogues." [79]

The software is provided to the user free of charge. "The package contains the following programs: ReluxPro, ReluxSensor, ReluxOffer, ReluxEnergy, ReluxLum (Reader)." [80]

More information as well as downloads can be found on the homepage www.relux.biz in different languages.

[79] *Relux®;* Relux®, the standard in lighting planning [http://www.relux.biz/index.php?option=com_content&view=article&id=226&Itemid=211&lang=en] (17.10.2012)

[80] *Relux®;* ReluxSuite, the free lighting planning software for lighting and sensor planners [http://www.relux.biz/index.php?option=com_content&view=article&id=217&Itemid=200&lang=en] (17.10.2012)

510 Student example – simulation of space lighting with different lamp types for a project in Las Vegas

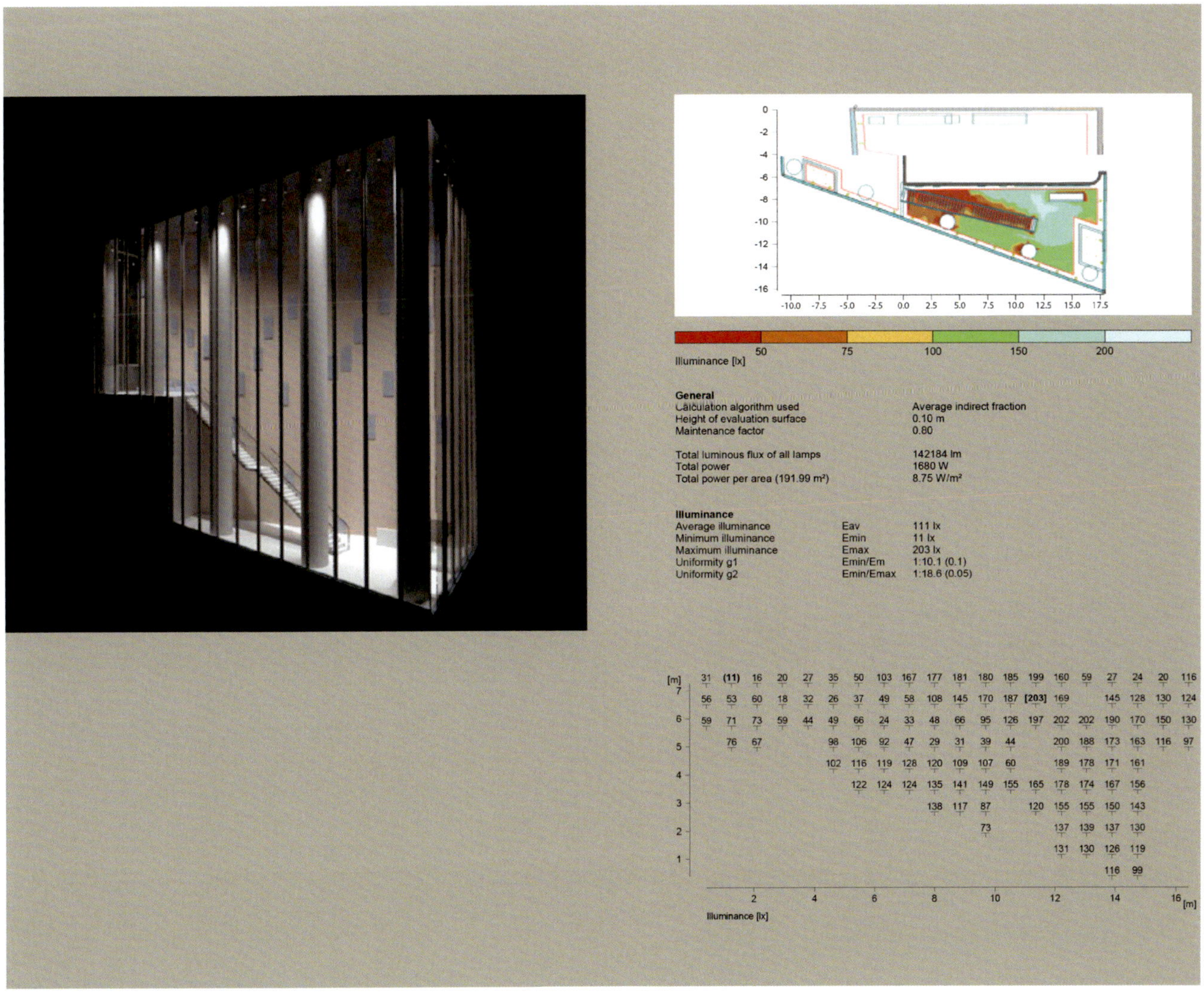

510

10.6 Simulation software TRNSYS/TRNFlow/ ANSYS Fluent

More information as well as downloads for TRNSYS and TRNFlow can be found on the homepage www.trnsys.de in German and English language and for ANSYS Fluent on www.ansys.com in different languages.

During the design of a building, the dynamic simulation is necessary to improve efficiency. Simulation software are able to simulate the thermal behaviour of a building, its air flows, different energy systems, light conditions, etc. Software used for simulation include examples such as TRNSYS, TRNSflow, Autodesk Ecotect, Design builder and EnergyPlus.

TRNSYS

"TRNSYS is a complete and extensible simulation environment for the transient simulation of thermal systems including multi-zone buildings.

It is used by engineers and researchers around the world to validate new energy concepts, from simple solar domestic hot water systems to the design and simulation of buildings and their equipment, including control strategies, occupant behaviour, alternative energy systems (wind, solar, photovoltaic, hydrogen systems), etc." [81]

"The TRNSYS package consists of a suite of programs:

- TRNSYS Studio – a graphical front-end that houses all aspects of the TRNSYS simulation procedure
- TRNBuild – a graphical input program for describing multi-zone buildings
- TRNEdit – an editor of the TRNSYS input file

In TRNSYS each physical component e.g. a solar collector is represented as a so called TYPE. The standard component library contains the following TYPEs:

- utility subroutines
- solar collectors
- thermal storage
- controllers
- hydronics
- electrical components
- auxiliary heating and cooling
- building loads and structures
- heat exchangers
- physical phenomena
- output devices" [82]

TRNFlow – airflow simulation

"TRNSYS thermal multi-zone building model, type 56, requires air flows between zones as input values. However, in natural ventilation systems these depend on the wind pressures and the inside and outside temperatures. To account for this situation, a coupling with an air flow model is absolutely necessary.

TRNFLOW integrates the multi-zone air flow model COMIS into the type 56. An internal solver, optimised for this task, iterates in each time step between the two models until their solutions are consistent. The existing GUI TRNBuild was extended in such a way that data for the air flow model can be entered. (...)

[81] *Transsolar Energietechnik GmbH;* Trnsys – The Universal Tool for Climate Engineering [http://www.transsolar.com/__software/docs/trnsys/trnsys_uebersicht_en.htm] (17.10.2012)
[82] *Transsolar Energietechnik GmbH;* Trnsys – Components – Trnsys Standard Package[http://www.transsolar.com/__software/docs/komponenten/komponenten_standard_en.htm] (17.10.2012)
[83] *Transsolar Energietechnik GmbH;* Trnflow – Airflow Simulation in Buildings [http://www.transsolar.com/__software/docs/trnflow/trnflow_uebersicht_en.htm] (17.10.2012)
[84] *Ansys;* Ansys [http://www.ansys.com/Products/Simulation+Technology/Fluid+Dynamics/ANSYS+Fluent] (17.10.2012)

511 Interface view of software TRNSYS
512 Thermal simulation made in software TRNSYS – exterior temperature and temperature in different building zones in case of extreme cold winter, Germany

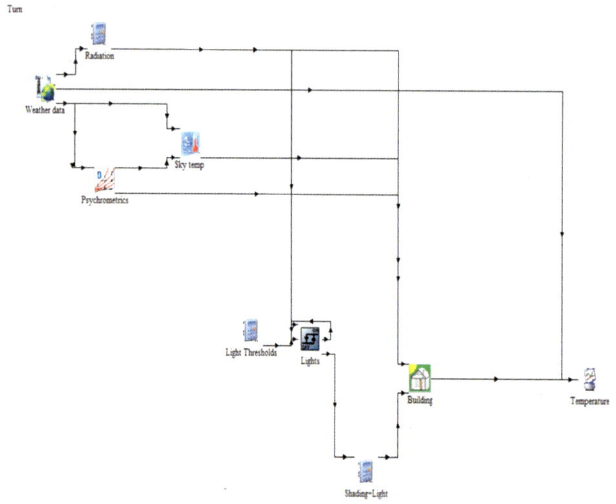

511

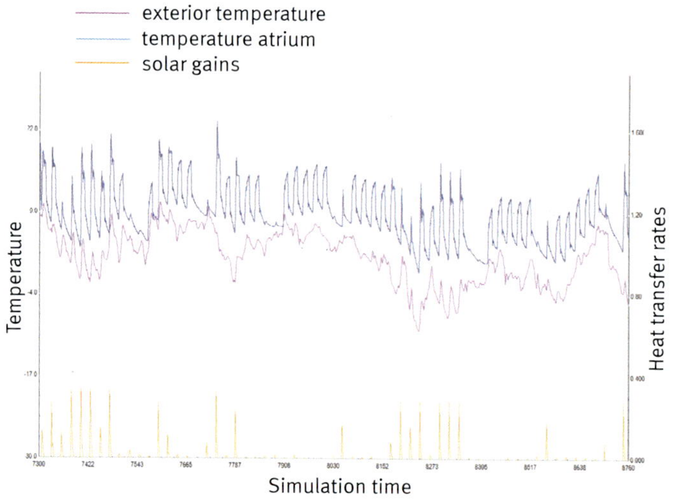

512

TRNFlow is a tool which allows an easy calculation of natural ventilation, passive night cooling, double facades and exhaust air shafts quite fast." [83]

ANSYS Fluent

"ANSYS Fluent software contains the broad physical modelling capabilities needed to model flow, turbulence, heat transfer, and reactions for industrial applications ranging from air flow over an aircraft wing to combustion in a furnace, from bubble columns to oil platforms, from blood flow to semiconductor manufacturing, and from clean room design to wastewater treatment plants. Special models that give the software the ability to model in-cylinder combustion, aero-acoustics, turbo-machinery, and multiphase systems have served to broaden its reach. (...)

Advanced solver technology provides fast, accurate CFD results, flexible moving and deforming meshes, and superior parallel scalability. User-defined functions allow the implementation of new user models and the extensive customisation of existing ones. The interactive solver setup, solution and post-processing capabilities of ANSYS Fluent make it easy to pause a calculation, examine results with integrated post-processing, change any setting, and then continue the calculation within a single application. Case and data files can be read into ANSYS CFD-Post for further analysis with advanced post-processing tools and side-by-side comparison of different cases.

The integration of ANSYS Fluent into ANSYS Workbench provides users with superior bidirectional connections to all major CAD systems, powerful geometry modification and creation with ANSYS DesignModeler technology, and advanced meshing technologies in ANSYS Meshing. The platform also allows data and results to be shared between applications using an easy drag-and-drop transfer, for example, to use a fluid flow solution in the definition of a boundary load of a subsequent structural mechanics simulation.

The combination of these benefits with the extensive range of physical modelling capabilities and the fast, accurate CFD results that ANSYS Fluent software has to offer results in one of the most comprehensive software packages for CFD modelling available in the world today. A native two-way connection to ANSYS structural mechanics products allows capture of even the most complex fluid-structure interaction (FSI) problems in the same easy-to-use environment, saving the need to purchase, administer or run third-party coupling software. Other multi-physics connections include electromagnetic-fluid coupling." [84]

513 Example of the simulation with software ANSYS Fluent, temperature and speed of the air, kindergarten "Burg"

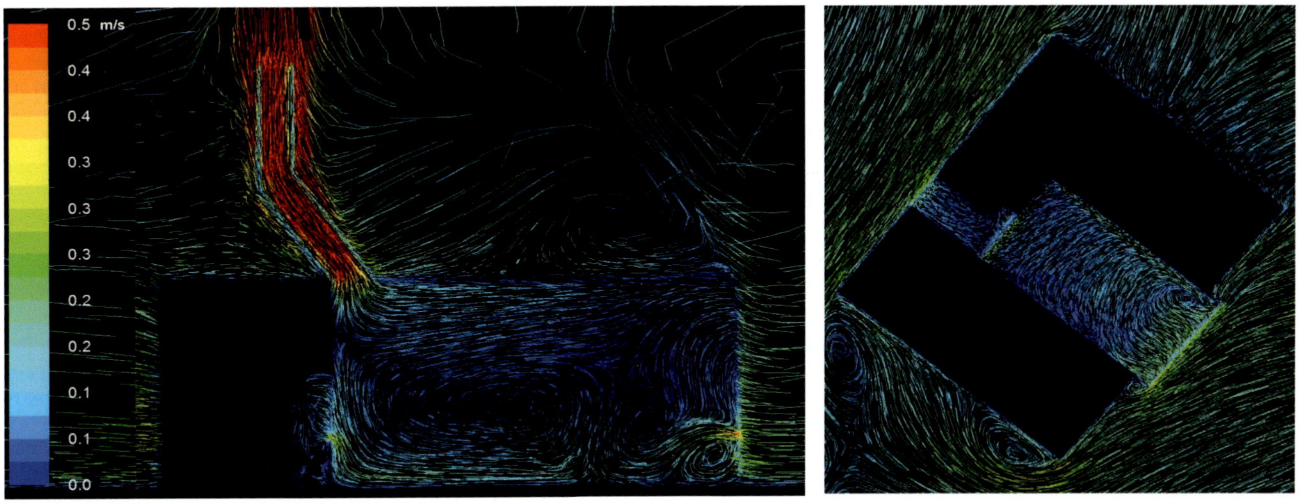

513

10.7 Simulation software Autodesk Ecotect/ DesignBuilder/EnergyPlus

514

Autodesk Ecotect

"Autodesk Ecotect Analysis sustainable design analysis software is a comprehensive concept-to-detail sustainable building design tool. Ecotect Analysis offers a wide range of simulation and building energy analysis functionality that can improve performance of existing buildings and new building designs. Online energy, water, and carbon-emission analysis capabilities integrate with tools that enable to visualise and simulate a building's performance within the context of its environment.

- Whole-building energy analysis – calculate total energy use and carbon emissions of your building model on an annual, monthly, daily, and hourly basis, using a global database of weather information.
- Thermal performance – calculate heating and cooling loads for models and analyse effects of occupancy, internal gains, infiltration, and equipment.
- Water usage and cost evaluation – estimate water use inside and outside the building.
- Solar radiation – visualise incident solar radiation on windows and surfaces, over any period.
- Daylighting – calculate daylight factors and luminance levels at any point in the model.
- Shadows and reflections – display the sun's position and path relative to the model at any date, time, and location." [85]

After 20.03.2015, Autodesk Ecotect licenses are not more available. Key Ecotect solutions are now available in the Revit environment.

DesignBuilder

"DesignBuilder combines rapid building modelling and ease of use with state of the art dynamic energy simulation.
DesignBuilder is easy to use. Its innovative productivity features allow even complex buildings to be modelled rapidly by nonexpert users.
DesignBuilder is the first comprehensive user interface to the EnergyPlus dynamic thermal simulation engine.

DesignBuilder features an easy-to-use OpenGL solid modeller, which allows building models to be assembled by positioning, stretching and cutting 'blocks' in 3D space. Realistic 3D elements provide visual feedback of actual element thickness and room areas and volumes and there are no limitations on geometric form or surface shape.

You can import 3D CAD models from ArchiCAD, Microstation, Revit and any other BIM software supporting the gbXML standard.
Data templates allow you to load common building constructions, activities, HVAC & lighting systems

[85] Autodesk, Inc.; Autodesk Ecotect Analysis [http://usa.autodesk.com/ecotect-analysis/] (17.10.2012)

[86] Design Builder Software Ltd.; DesignBuilder Simulation [http://www.designbuilder.co.uk/content/view/7/13/] (17.10.2012)

[87] U.S. Department of Energy; EnergyPlus Energy Simulation Software [http://apps1.eere.energy.gov/buildings/energyplus/] (17.10.2012)

514 Logo of EnergyPlus
515 Daylight planning with software DesignBuilder, Client ABSA Barcleys, Consultant WSP Green by Design

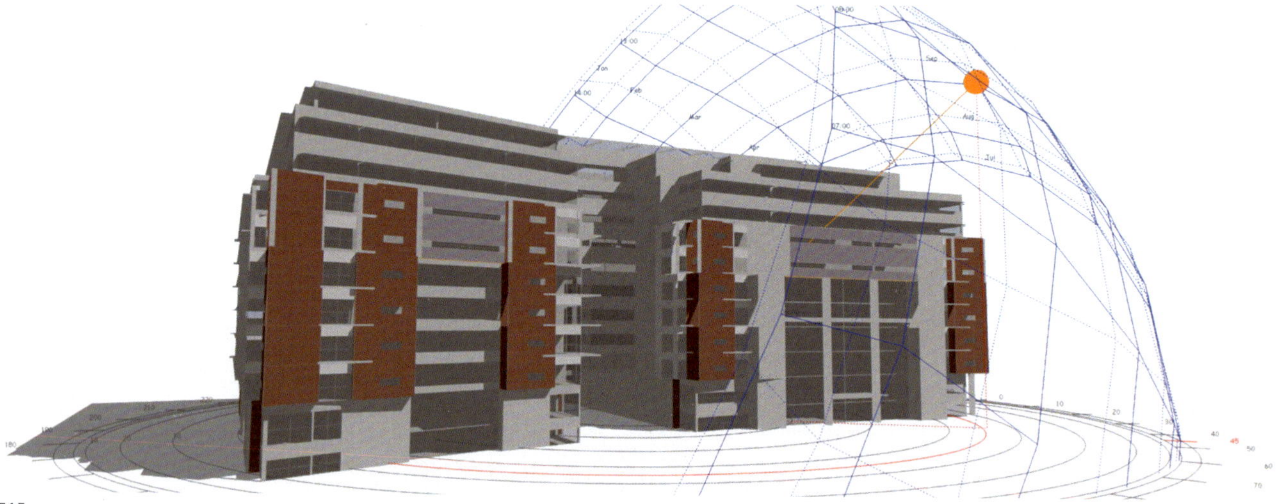

515

into your design by selecting from drop-down lists. You can also add your own templates if you often work on similar types of buildings. This, combined with data inheritance, allows global changes to be made at building, block or zone level. You can also control the level of detail in each building model allowing the tool to be used effectively at any stage of the design or evaluation process." [86]

More information as well as downloads for DesignBuilder can be found on the homepage www.designbuilder.co.uk in different languages.

EnergyPlus

"EnergyPlus is a whole building energy simulation program that engineers, architects, and researchers use to model energy and water use in buildings. Modelling the performance of a building with EnergyPlus enables building professionals to optimise the building design to use less energy and water. Each version of EnergyPlus is tested extensively before release.

EnergyPlus models heating, cooling, lighting, ventilation, other energy flows, and water use. EnergyPlus includes many innovative simulation capabilities: time-steps less than an hour, modular systems and plant integrated with heat balance-based zone simulation, multi-zone air flow, thermal comfort, water use, natural ventilation, and photovoltaic systems." [87]

DesignBuilder

516

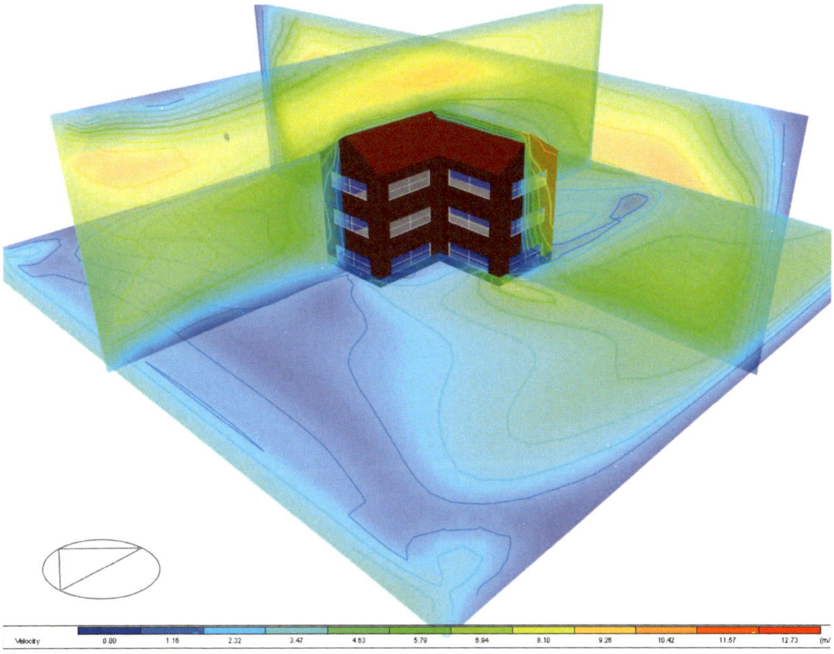

517

516 Logo of DesignBuilder
517 Analysis of wind external presure and velocity with DesignBuilder
518 Analysis of temperatures in Atrium with DesignBuilder
519 Analysis of air temperature and speed, as well as the influence of radiators in the room with DesignBuilder

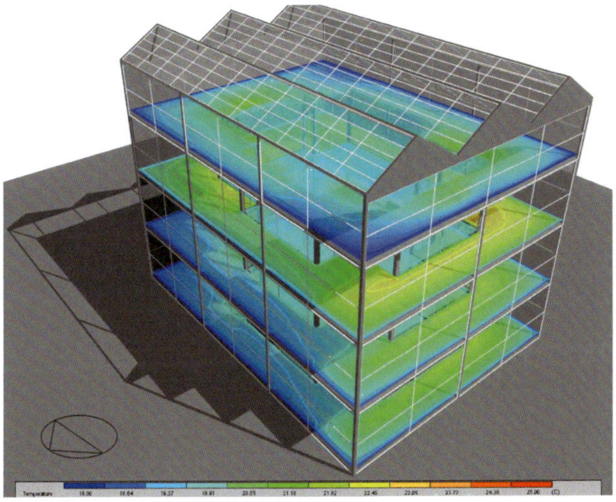

518

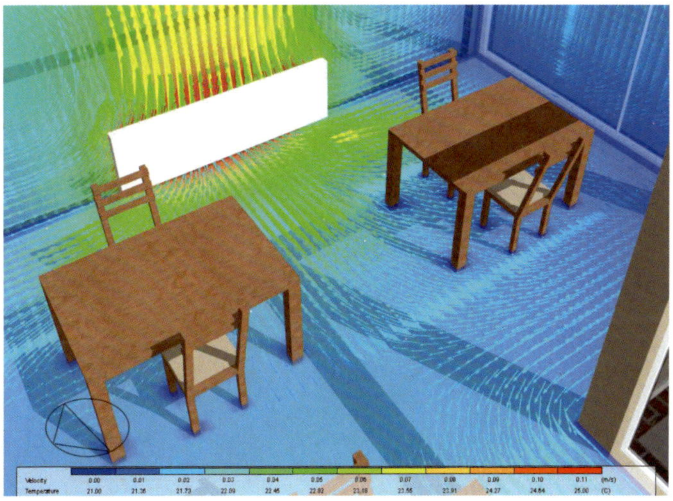

519

10.8 Building material evaluation

To evaluate a building's sustainability, diverse basic data of the building materials and that of the whole building are required. There are some useful instruments available as aids to complete the life cycle analysis, however it is easier to include sustainable aspects within the planning and construction phases.
Ökobau.dat was previously documented on page 243 . However, below are some other instruments for the sustainable evaluation of materials:

Ökologischer Bauteilkatalog (ecological building elements catalogue)

The catalogue is a tool to spread awareness of ecological inputs of building elements as a collection of elements that are ecologically evaluated. It encourages designers to consider future operational, maintenance and refurbishment costs already in the planning phase of the building. It also considers the demolition life cycle up until disposal or recycling.

EPD® (Environmental Product Declaration)

Environmental Product Declarations are the basic data required for an ecological building evaluation. They are based on ISO norms and are therefore internationally valued. The declaration describes energy and resource consumption and information regarding the product's ecological indicators. The EPD also contains the technical characteristics of a product's life span, heat and acoustic insulation and influence on interior air quality.

"WECOBIS (Web-based Ecological Building Material Information System)

offers comprehensive, structured, neutral information to health and ecological aspects of construction products and also online links with further sources of data. The system supports the observation of life cycle phases with information regarding the choice of raw products, creation, treatment, use and re-use." [88]

GISCODE

GISCODE is a classification system formed in 1993 by manufacturers and German Builders' Trade Associations (GISBAU) for promoting protection of workers when dealing with chemical products in construction work.
It assigns products to product groups. With the help of this code, it is possible to group together products with similar health risks. The GISCODE groups are identified by appropriate abbreviations. The GISCODE is signed on the packaging of the product with the technical information on the safety data sheet.

Other documents

Other documents for material and product descriptions for specific industry regulations (e.g. RAL, VdL-guidelines) are documented for different markets or for coating technologies that describe the general accepted, manufacturing usage.
Additional are certifications (e.g. The Blue Angel, EmiCode®) which are environmentally-related labels for products and services that are awarded only to products, which are considered beneficial to the environment while meeting high standards of serviceability, health and user protection.
"The Blue Angel – Transparency and independence; The Federal Ministry for the Environment, Nature Conservation, Building and Nuclear Safety is the owner of the label. The Blue Angel is a Type-1 environmental label according to ISO 14024. It thus meets the highest requirements when it comes to the standards it sets, the relevance of the award criteria and the independence, management and transparency of the development and award processes." [89]
"EmiCode® is a quality control scheme which awards labels to modern, solvent-free, low-emission building materials. Extensive testing and continuous monitoring is assured by GEV-Association for the Control of Emissions in Products for Flooring Installation, Adhesives and Building Materials." [90]

[88] *BMU;* Assessment System for Sustainable Building: Practical Aids and Tools [http://www.nachhaltigesbauen.de/sustainable-building-english-speaking-information/assessment-system-for-sustainable-building.html] (04.05.2014)

[89] *Umweltbundesamt;* The Blue Angel – Transparency and independence. Dessau: 12/2015

[90] *EMICODE®;* What is EMICODE® [www.emicode.com] (07.12.2015)

520

521

522

Building physics characteristic				
Building physics - construction	**Unit**	**Variant 1**	**Variant 2**	**Variant 3**
Thickness	cm	46	46	46
Heat transmission coefficient	W/m²K	0.36	0.34	0.36
Sound protection	dB	67	67	67
Fire resistance class		F90	F90	F90
Condensation / dehydration	kg/m²a	-/>5	-/>5	-/>5
Saving effective interior mass	kg/m²	90	90	90

Ecological characteristic				
Construction clam-shell brickwork	**Mass [kg/m²]**	**PE_{nre} [MJ/m²]**	**GWP 100 [kg CO_2-Äquiv.]**	**AP 100 [g SO_x-Äquiv.]**
Brick	216.0	585	53.4	203
Mortar	40.0	56	7.2	24
Flax with polyester (Var.1)	3.1	164	2.0	40
Glass wool (Var.2)	2.4	76	3.8	20
Cellulose fibre-plates (Var.3)	9.0	197	9.3	71
Lumber, timber	9.0	42	-13.9	20
Steel, low alloyed (dowel)	0.3	13	0.9	4
Steel, low alloyed (anchor)	0.4	17	1.2	6
Perforated brick, pored	127.5	335	17.1	49
Mortar	58.0	81	10.4	35
Clay plaster	17.0	8	-1.0	3
Total amount Variant 1	471.3	1,302	77.3	383
Total amount Variant 2	461.6	1,172	93.0	343
Total amount Variant 3	468.2	1,293	98.5	394

523

Var 1 [cm]	Var 2 [cm]	Var 3 [cm]	Construction from exterior to interior
12.0	12.0	12.0	Brick
4.0	4.0	4.0	Air gap
12.0			Flax
	12.0		Glass wool
		12.0	Cellulose
17.0	17.0	17.0	Pored brick
1.0	1.0	1.0	Clay plaster
46.0	46.0	46.0	Thickness

Building physics characteristic				
Building physics- construction	**Unit**	**Variant 1**	**Variant 2**	**Variant 3**
Thickness	cm	32	32	32
Heat transmission coefficient	W/m²K	0.27	0.27	0.29
Sound protection	dB	45	45	45
Fire resistance class		F60	F60	F60
Condensation / dehydration	kg/m²a	-/0.1	-/0.1	-/0.1
Saving effective interior mass	kg/m²	24	24	24

Ecological characteristic				
Construction wood stud wall	**Mass [kg/m²]**	**PE_{nre} [MJ/m²]**	**GWP 100 [kg CO_2-Äquiv.]**	**AP 100 [g SO_x-Äquiv.]**
Lumber, wood board	10.0	36	-15.5	20
Lumber, timber	2.3	11	-3.5	5
Lumber, timber	1.0	5	-1.5	2
Building paper	0.3	6	0.1	4
Lumber, timber	9.0	33	-13.9	18
Lumber, timber	12.0	56	-18.6	26
Rockwool (Var.1)	3.7	64	4.4	19
Sheepwool (Var.2)	4.1	50	-1.1	19
cellulose fiber (Var.3)	7.5	31	1.7	18
Polyethylene	0.3	26	0.7	5
Lumber, timber	1.5	7	-2.3	3
Plasterboard-2x	27.0	61	2.8	27
Total amount Variant 1	67.0	304	-47.3	129
Total amount Variant 2	67.4	290	-52.8	128
Total amount Variant 3	70.8	271	-50.0	128

524

Var 1 [cm]	Var 2 [cm]	Var 3 [cm]	Construction from exterior to interior
2.0	2.0	2.0	Wood
3.0	3.0	3.0	Battens 3/5
4.0	4.0	4.0	Battens 4/4
0.02	0.02	0.02	Paper foil
2.0	2.0	2.0	Wood
16.0			Rockwool
	16.0		Sheepwool
		16.0	Cellulose
0.02	0.02	0.02	PE foil
2.0	2.0	2.0	Battens 2/5
3.0	3.0	3.0	Gypsum fiber
32.0	32.0	32.0	Thickness

520 Logo of GEV-EmiCode® EC1 for very low emission products
521 Logo of The Blue Angel
522 Logo of WECOBIS
523 Clam-shell brickwork evaluation with the help of "Ökologischer Bauteilkatalog"
524 Wood stud wall evaluation with rear-ventilated front side with the help of "Ökologischer Bauteilkatalog"

10.9 Summary

Ecological footprint

The evaluation of an ecological footprint is also a method, which considers all the resources that are needed for everyday life, and shows how much land is needed to provide all the energy and raw materials available.
The result of ecological footprint is equivalent to the amount of earth planets required to cover the living standard of the person (or a city, country, ...) doing the evaluation.
Everybody can calculate their ecological footprint with the help of various online ecological footprint calculators.

525 Extract from monitoring report; CO_2 concentration values in interior spaces during the day of 25.02.2015
526 Extract from monitoring report; Exterior and interior temperature values during the week 01.12.-08.10.2014
527 Examples of diagrams from Theater monitoring

The building ownership has changed considerably nowadays, with more associations, cooperative organisations or public holders assuming the function of a building investor.
The function of a building investor is therefore often perceived as accountable for justifying their decisions. The reasons behind their decisions are very important for the construction activities and become increasingly important during the planning process.

The building planning process has changed considerably from subjective decisions to having to prove and verify each decision. The building certification, analysing, calculating and simulating is therefore a logical consequence of this development. This will cause extensive structural changes within the planning process. The development of different regulations and certifications has increased, making it often very difficult to keep up and follow them all. The need for regular specialisations creates a contradiction to the integral planning process. However, the demand for specialist consultants still grows.

If someone were to have a different specialisation, it would not follow the goal of synergy. This problem has already begun and will continue to develop through globalization and internationalization of the market. It will cause the need for more specialization in the architecture profession.

This means that a small architecture office will not be able to carry out all phases of the building planning, beginning with creating a concept, building development and until handing over a built construction.

Only large companies consisting of multiple departments will be able to follow the entire building planning and performance phases. Smaller offices need to be specialized in certain planning phases and therefore only focus on one specialisation. The building process known from history is not possible anymore, where he architect, who created the building concept, usually followed the planning and construction from the very beginning until the end when the building was handed over.

Various energy, thermal or light calculations and simulations are also specializations that are today required for the design of a building. Previously, only engineers would provide these calculations. However, nowadays it is very important that architects begin to assume these rules while still creating functional building concepts together with the aesthetically pleasing idea.
For example, thermal, lighting and functional qualities should not only be considered through decision making in relation to the openings on a building facade, but the facade should also be considered in relation to the aesthetics and design principals.

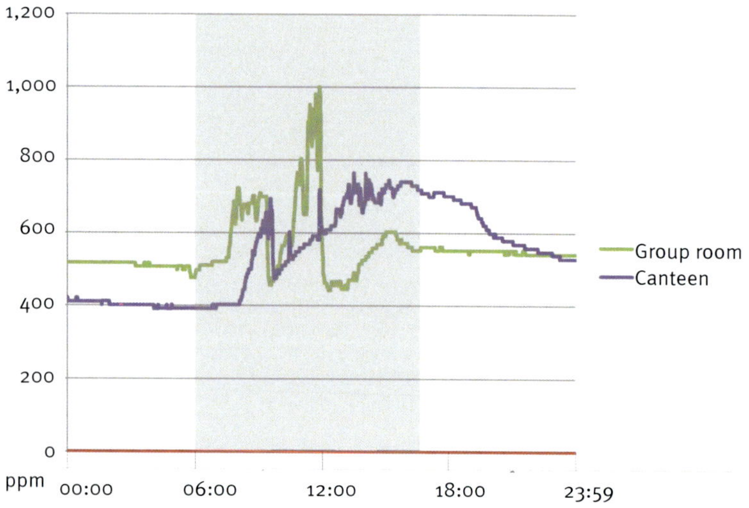

525

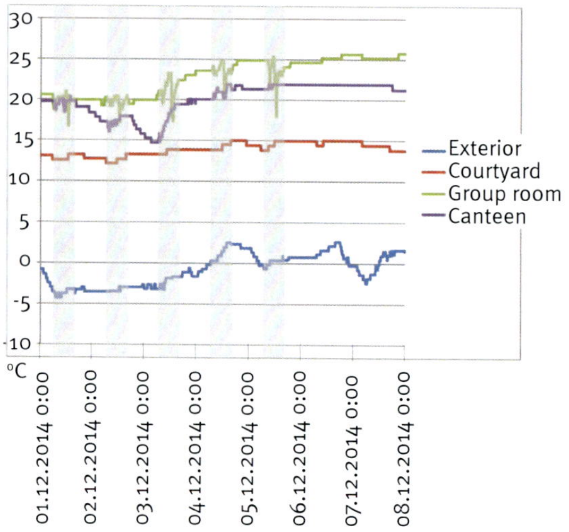

526

Auditorium
tag1=val1,tag2=val2
Custom
6/1/2015, 15:56:00
10/14/2015, 16:56:00
Ort
RK
Saal
Pod Name
Room air temperature
10. Jun
17. Jun
27. Jun
8. Jul
17. Jul
30. Jul
18. Aug
1. Sep
12. Sep
22. Sep
30. Sep
4. Oct
9. Oct
14. Oct
25
Bottom
Balcony
Ceiling
3 / 3
Medium
Line
Room air humidity
4. Jun
14. Jun
24. Jun
2. Jul
10. Jul
18. Jul
28. Jul
8. Aug
20. Aug
1. Sep
12. Sep
24. Sep
6. Oct
14. Oct
40
30
Bottom
Balcony
Ceiling
CO2-concentration
8. Jun
15. Jun
22. Jun
29. Jun
6. Jul
13. Jul
20. Jul
27. Jul
3. Aug
10. Aug
17. Aug
24. Aug
31. Aug
7. Sep
14. Sep
21. Sep
5. Oct
12. Oct
1000
500
Ceiling
Bottom
Balcony
3 / 3
Medium
Line

527

528

528 The architectural aesthetic that follows the sustainable idea and building concept at the kindergarten "Wellenreiter", Wismar, Wollensak architects

11.0 Examples

11.1 Introduction

529

This chapter shows the different Realisations and projects designed by Prof. Wollensak and his team that show different aspects of designing, following sustainable criterion.

The first question in design is the relationship between the building and its surroundings. An example of this is the new construction of a primary school in the city – Erfelden, which was designed as part of the urban structure, following the city regulations. The building has a great connection to the exterior with approx. half-interior, half-exterior spaces.

The primary school also answers the difficult question in reference to the treatment of heritage or historical building structures – the result is to keep all parts where possible (depending on their structural, functional and aesthetical conditions), or renew them and add new parts if required – but to work in harmony with the older elements to respect their heritage, and also show that they were added in another time period.

Additional projects that work in harmony with modern and historical architecture, is the example renovation of Orangery – castle, Weikersheim "Modern within heritage architecture" or Office building for the housing association, Bützow "Sustainable Renovation and conversion".

Other projects, New House on Poel, Kirchdorf/Poel "Modern as answer to tradition" is a new construction, however the form is based on the traditional architecture from the island of Poel. Therefore, the modern structure respects the history and tradition of the area and responds to its conditions.

Different projects for kindergarten renovations show how the treatment of old prefabricated buildings from the time of the German Democratic Republic can serve as demonstration projects for other buildings of the same type in East Germany.
The concepts exemplify not only how to treat old structures but also how to improve their quality from all points of view – ecological, economical, social, resource-saving, energy-saving and also aesthetical.
Such examples include the Kindergarten "Plappersnut", Wismar "Sustainable renovation" or Kindergarten "Sonnenschein", Wismar "Sustainable renovation".

Other kindergarten projects with new constructions have different goals. The planning of the new Kindergarten "Wellenreiter", Wismar was based on the life cycle analysis of the building - considering not only the building use timeline, but also the extraction of materials that were used for the building construction and their end of life. The result is a very light, resource-saving building that requires very little energy for operation.

529 The heritage wooden beams of office building in Bützow
530 Image of Plus Energy School in Rostock after the first construction step – the new building construction and courtyard in contrast to the unrenovated existing building
531 Orangery – castle, Weikersheim – The roof construction was completed with the respecting contrast to the original heritage building in the contemporary architectural way

530

531

The new construction of the **Kindergarten "Wildblume", Garz/Rügen** follows the goals of the construction Three-Zero-Concept. This means – zero energy, zero emission and zero waste. Only natural materials were used that can be returned to its natural form after the building's life.

The project **Plus energy school, Reutershagen – Rostock** adapts all sustainable principals for designing – from resource-saving designing (Cobiax ceilings) to energy-saving operation (Plus energy concept).

The project **EnEff: In the town of Luckenwalde** is an example of how sustainable and energy-based renovations within an existing town can succeed. As a pilot project for Luckenwalde, the energy renovation of multiple buildings in the **towns district "Burg"** was introduced.

The building project for the energy renovation was based on a block of residential buildings and a kindergarten. These were exemplar projects for the energy renovation of existing prefabricated building types.

Another city district project is the sustainable renovation of **Wismar university campus "Campus 2020"**. This is based on the renovation and development concept for the university campus, dependant on space saving, the double-use of buildings and areas, resource and energy saving and creating user awareness. This project is now in the planning stage and is partially realized; however it will be implemented before 2020.

The sustainable renovation of the **theatre on the university campus** is a project based on the double-function of its spaces. It is now in Realization and will be finished at the end of 2014.

Further projects of sustainable building designing is the **Eco-kindergarten – renovation and extension of the kindergarten in Stadtweide Rostock**, following the principles of low, light and high tech architecture and the renovation of a **sporting hall in Rostock Schmarl** as an energy plus sporting hall and youth club.

The 4 standards of sustainability for the renovation of the **kindergarten "Kunterbunt" in Sassnitz** introduces sustainable renovation based on its own developed standard – land saving, energy saving, material saving and water saving.

In response to the demographic (re) development in Germany, a sustainable project to renovate and convert a former primary school into a **senior residence was realized in Bützow**.

A **vacuum bottle house** is an exemplar project for energy saving designing, based on vacuum-insulated bearing walls.

532

532 Detail of the facade of house on island Poel – respecting the traditional architecture of the environment
533 The courtyard of the Kindergarten "Wellenreiter" – as light and low tech architecture connected to the nature
534 The outside view of Kindergarten "Wildblume", Garz/Rügen

533

534

11.2 Realisations

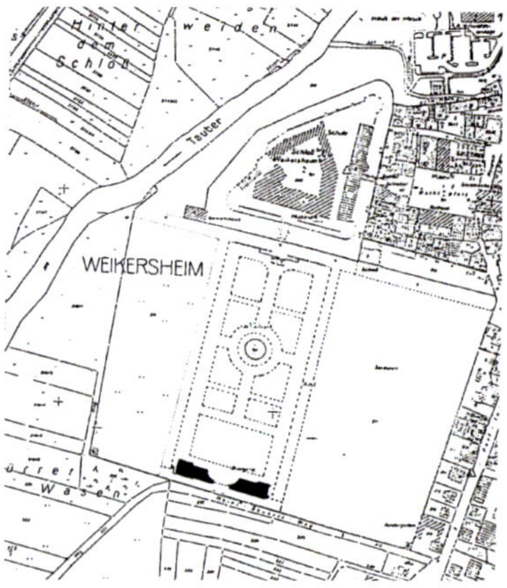

535

Architects
Wollensak architects, Stuttgart

Construction
1995 – 1997

11.2.1 Modern within heritage architecture: Renovation Orangery – castle, Weikersheim

The orangery is originally a building from 1719, built by Johann Christian Lüttich. The project is a reconstruction of the abandoned heritage building of orangery castle Weikersheim for winter accommodation of exotic plants and for summer events – concerts, exhibitions, and celebrations.
The building is located at the south end of the castle and encloses the castle garden with the landscape. The building is from the Baroque period and consists of two nearly mirrored building parts with a view from the castle to the landscape of Taubertal, through quarter-circle concaves. The decorated facade of the castle is orientated to the north and is under heritage protection. The facade is orientated to the southern landscape of Taubertal.

During the planning stage, the roof and windows were nonexistent and the floor was void. Existing building elements were obtained in their original condition or were re-built. Building elements that were missing or unusable, were replaced by contemporary architectural elements that contrasted the original building.
The building is a good example of handling heritage buildings by respecting the requirements and the historical building elements in connection with new parts.

535 Site plan of the orangery in Weikersheim
536 Elevation of the orangery in Weikersheim after renovation

536

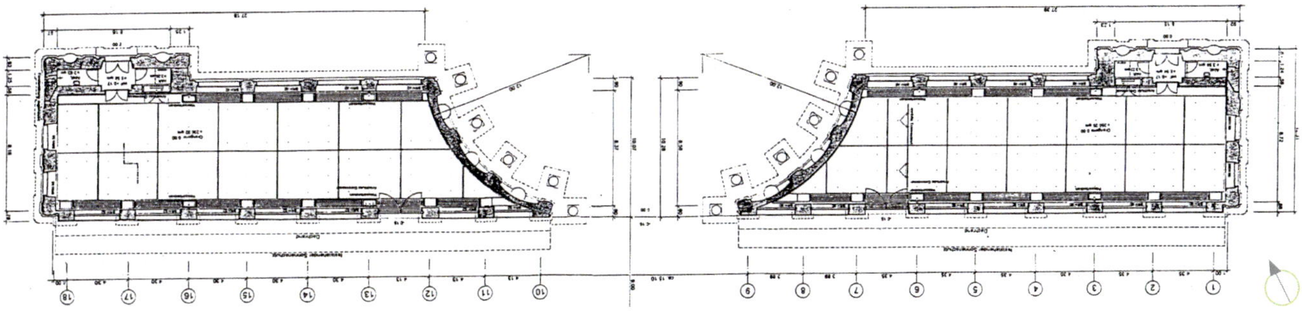

537

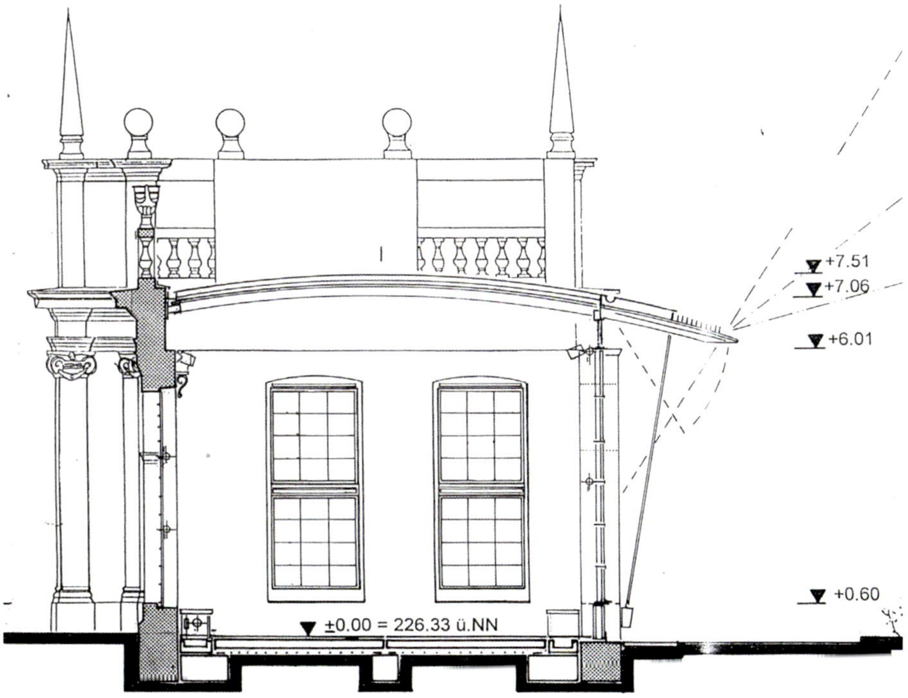

538

537 The planning design of ground floor plan of the orangery in Weikersheim
538 The roof construction was completed with the respecting contrast to the original heritage building in the contemporary architectural way – section
539 Photos from the building site – the modern elements of the architecture gentle follows the traditional building form of the orangery

539

11.2 Realisations

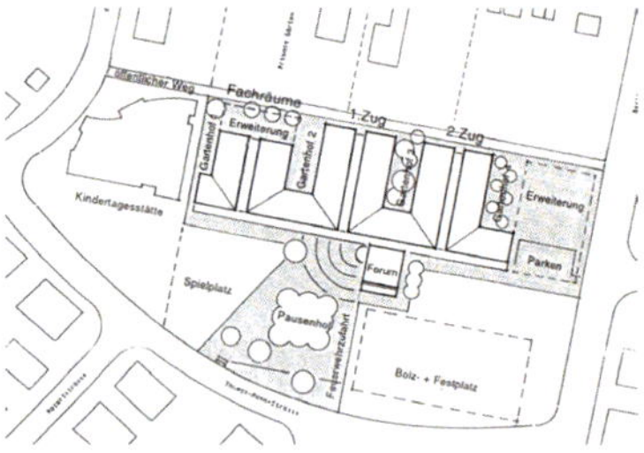

540

Architects
Wollensak architects

Planning and construction
01/1995 – 11/1998

540 Site plan of the primary school in Reed city – Erfelden
541 The shading concept
542 Outside views on the primary school in Reed city – Erfelden

11.2.2 Building as a part of urban structure: New Primary school, Reed city - Erfelden

The construction of a single-storey primary school in the middle of a residential area on the eastern border of Erfelden. Additional functions within the site of the primary school is the – kindergarten, playing area, football field and a celebration area.

The buildings are arrangement in the form of a comb, creating small gardens and courtyards between the classrooms. As a result, a strong connection between the interior and exterior spaces is created.

This not only creates valuable spaces but also benefits the building climatic conditions - all classrooms have two facades, allowing natural daylight from both sides along with natural cross ventilation.

In addition, all secondary rooms have daylight.

The building technology follows the low energy concept:

- the southern main circulation area is fully glazed in order to have passive heat gains
- decentralized ventilation equipment with heat recovery and air distribution
- rainwater use for toilet flushing
- rainwater infiltration for exterior

Shading in summer

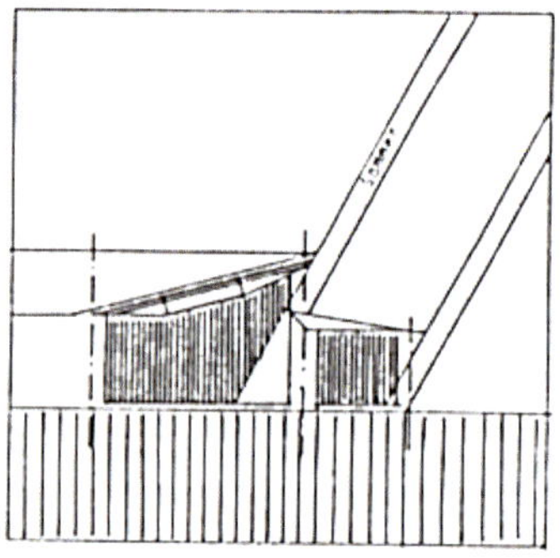

Partial shade in spring/autumn

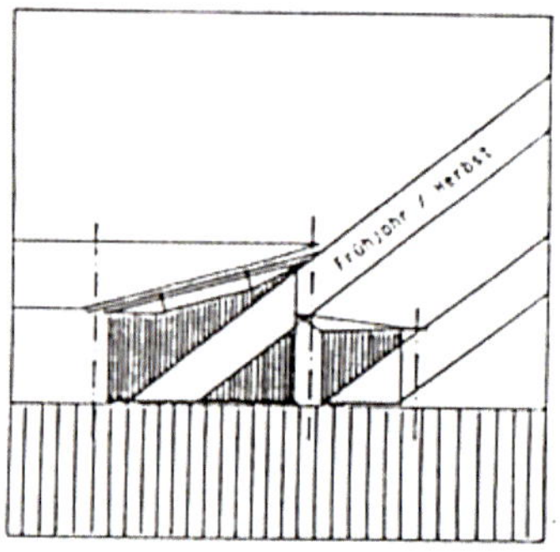

Sun in winter

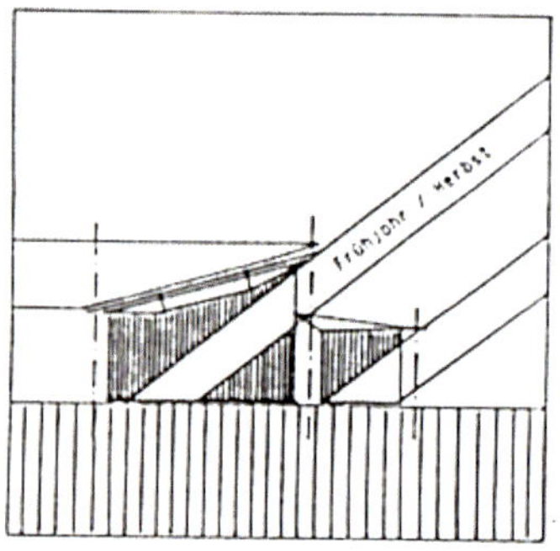

541

542

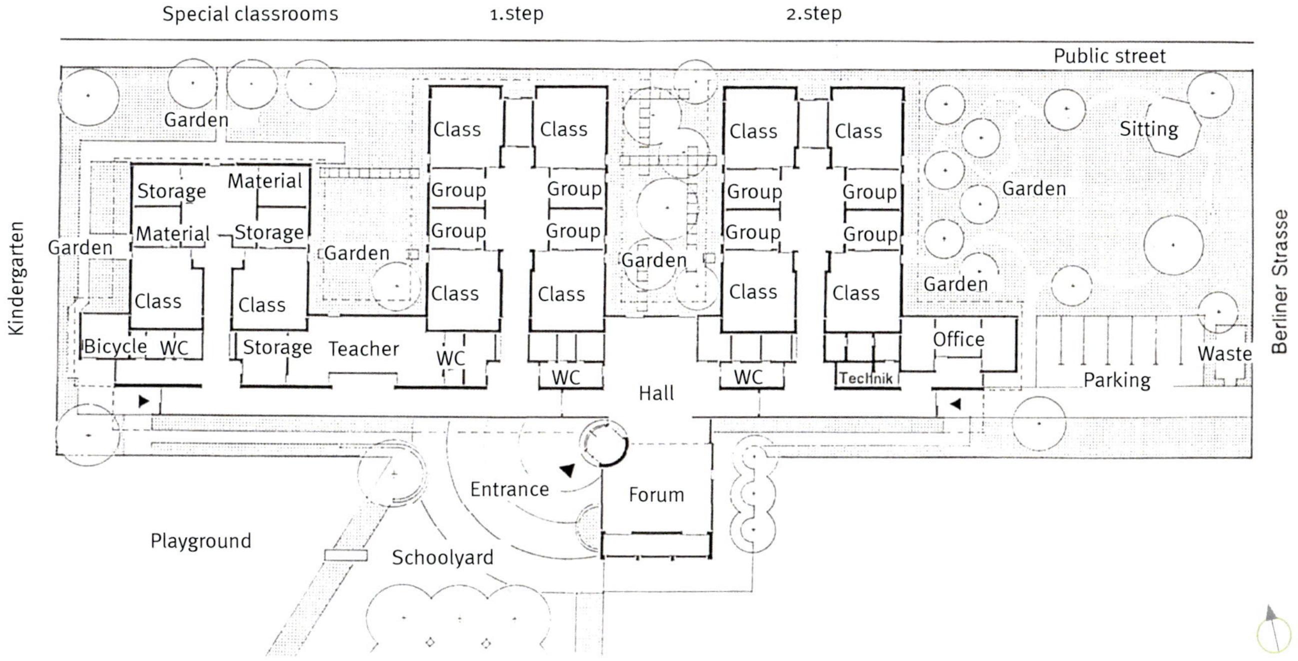

543

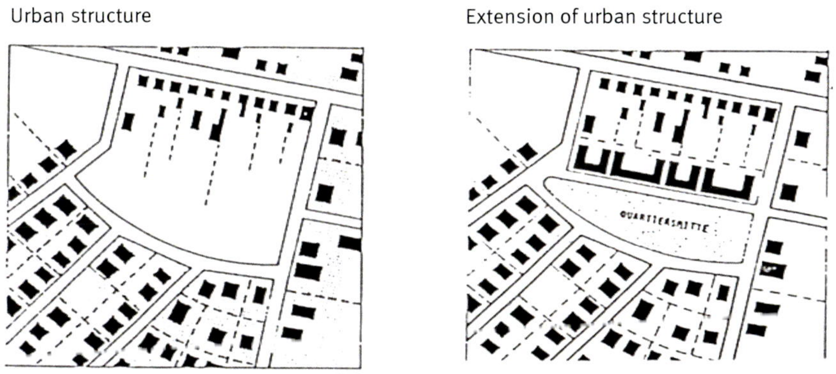

544

543 *Ground floor plan of the primary school in Reed city – Erfelden*
544 *Alignment into the urban area – the area structure and its coherence*
545 *The Primary school in Erfelden – connection between interior and exterior*
546 *Synergy between building technology and design – ventilation pipe designed to suit the environment*

545

546

11.2 Realisations

Architects
Wollensak architects, Wismar

Construction
03/2002 – 08/2002

11.2.3 Modern as answer to tradition: New House on Poel, Kirchdorf/Poel

The Island of Poel in the Wismar bay is an attractive place for visitors and holiday guests. It contains traditional architecture from the Baltic region that should not be disturbed by new structures.

Building technologies and materials are constantly evolving along with requirements for people in residential building, e.g. requests for light rooms, energy saving and environmentally orientated buildings.

The New House on Poel connects tradition with modern architecture:

- the proportions and colours are traditional – a long rectangular, single storey building with a roof angle of 30°
- red brick was used for the walls with an anthracite coloured roof
- building construction and expression is modern – no large walls, column structure allows for large openings to the lake
- rather than handmade brick, elements of brick plate were used

The building is divided into two zones: The zone to the street contains all of the wet and storage rooms (bathroom, kitchen, technology).

The zone facing the garden contains all of the living and sleeping rooms.

The galleries face the street and can be entered from the sleeping rooms and used as additional areas, without disturbing the views to the landscape.

The main goal was to have a short construction time and create modern architecture. Therefore, modular construction was used.

The primary structure is steel frames with red brick. The exterior walls are thermally insulated and have ventilated facade plates.

The interior walls use light construction and can be moved or changed if required in the future.

The wooden beams in the gallery ceilings sit on steel columns. OSB (oriented strand board) panels were used for the flooring of the galleries and the roof sheathing.

The sanitary connections are located on the street side and the electrical cabling is only located within the interior walls and gallery ceilings.

547 Original traditional house from island Poel – outside view
548 House on insel Poel – outside view

547

548

549

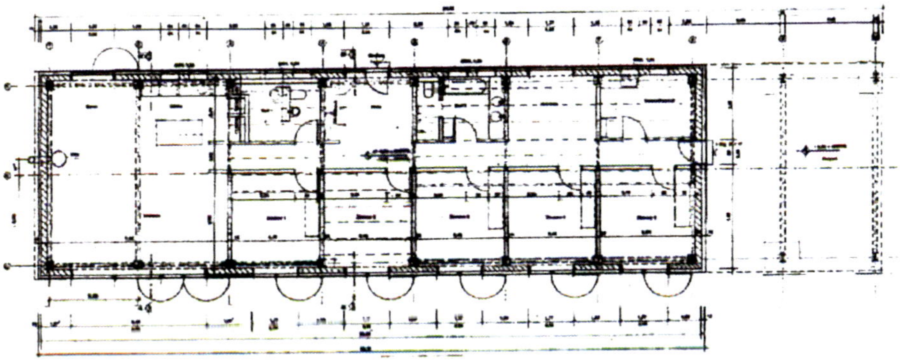

550

549 *Impressions of the house – exterior facade*
550 *Ground floor plan of the house on island Poel*
551 *Impressions of the house – interior life*

551

11.2 Realisations

552

Architects
IGEL-Institut, Wismar

Construction
01/2004 – 01/2005

Awards
Building physics award 2005
State building award Mecklenburg Vorpommern (Landesbaupreis M-V) 2006

552 The elevation of renovated kindergarten "Plappersnut" in Wismar – with better compactness and quality
553 Renovation concept – transformation from a prefabricated building with A/V ratio of 0.56 to a compact green building with an A/V ratio of 0.41

11.2.4 Sustainable renovation: Kindergarten "Plappersnut", Wismar

The renovation project of the kindergarten "Plappersnut" is a model project in the program "Energy efficient refurbishment of buildings" that is founded by the German Federal Ministry of Economic Affairs and Energy (ENSAN BMWI).

The kindergarten was built in 1972 and is one of 300 prefabricated building types with a combined nursery/kindergarten. The main axis orientation is east-west. It has an interesting plan organisation, which enables lighting and ventilation from both sides of the classrooms. The disadvantages are its relatively large surface to volume ratio, inadequate thermal protection of the building envelope, problematic indoor climate, inflexible room structure and high operational costs.
The main issue was the high-energy needs required for heating the corridors of the existing building. The corridors were demolished and the common spaces in between were covered with a foil roof construction. This created a more compact building with an optimised A/V ratio. Reduction of ventilation losses due to less heated surface is around 24 %.

The unheated atrium serves as a buffer zone and acts as a preheating function in winter and a precooling function in the summer. The space becomes better architecturally and functionally, with new possibilities for children. The walls to the atrium contain no thermal insulation and serve also as heat storage mass. Preheating of air in the atrium contributes approx. 50 % of heat costs.

With adaptations, the transmission heat loss was reduced via direct insulation of the external components. The east and west facades have vacuum panel insulation and the other longitudinal facades are insulated with mineral wool. Transom windows in the atrium enable solar gains even in the winter. The development of a "low-tech" timber cladding in the courtyard gives the buildings shade in summer while improving acoustics.

Technologies used in the building are heat recovery ventilation, a heat pump and solar thermal collectors for heat generation. PV systems used for power generation and shading were designed for the southern facade. Motion sensors for the lighting are used to help save additional energy.
The energy needs rapidly reduced through clever and useful building design, together with new technology. The energy consumption was reduced by 65 % in the first year after reconstruction. Because of smart designing, the costs for the renovation were only 531 $€/m^2_{UFA}$ and 120 $€/m^3_{NRV}$.
The illness rate after the renovation also reduced greatly from 10 % to 4 % for employees and from 11 % to 6 % for children.

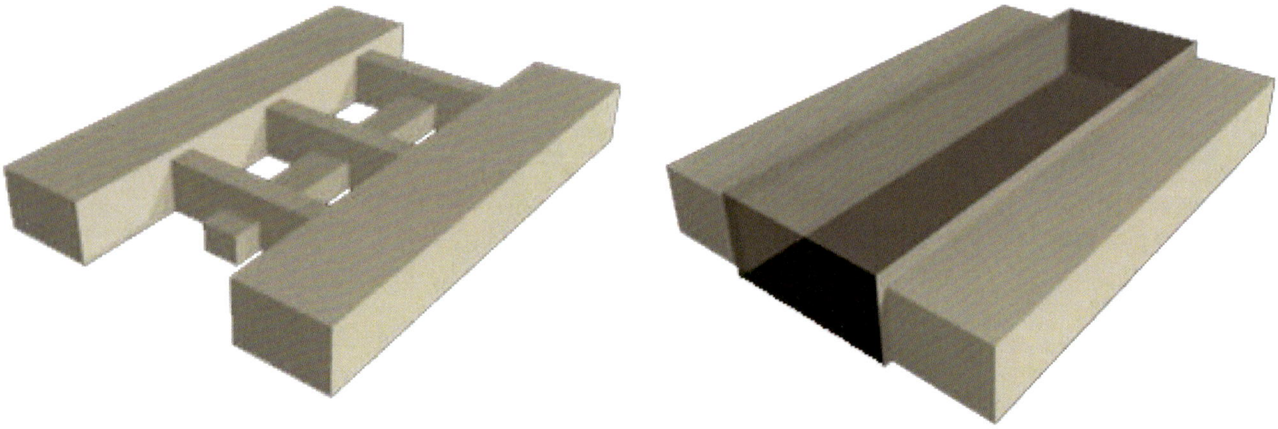

553

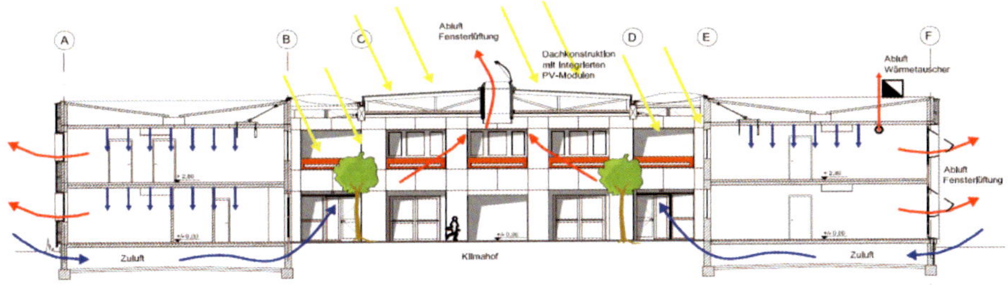

Summer day

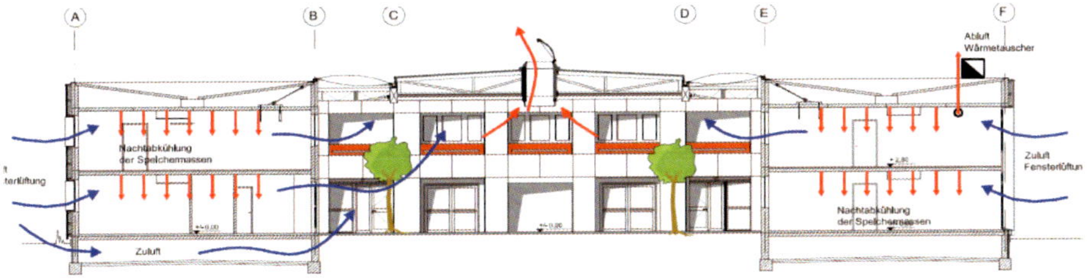

Summer night and morning

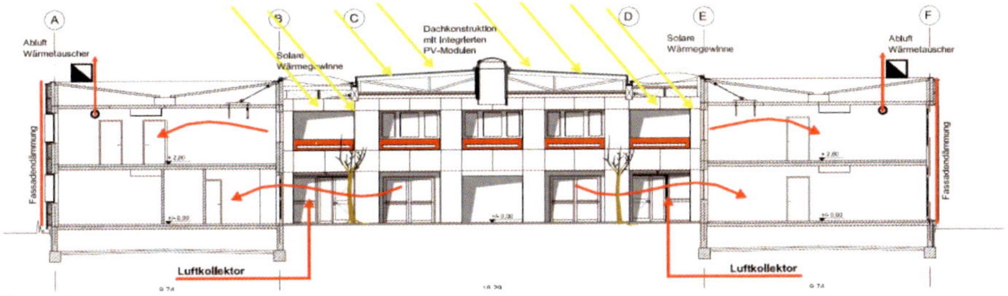

Winter day

Winter night and morning
567

568

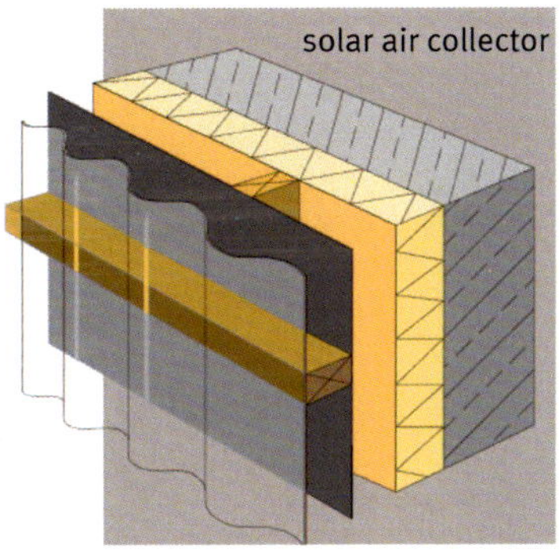

569

sun rays
warm air
cold air

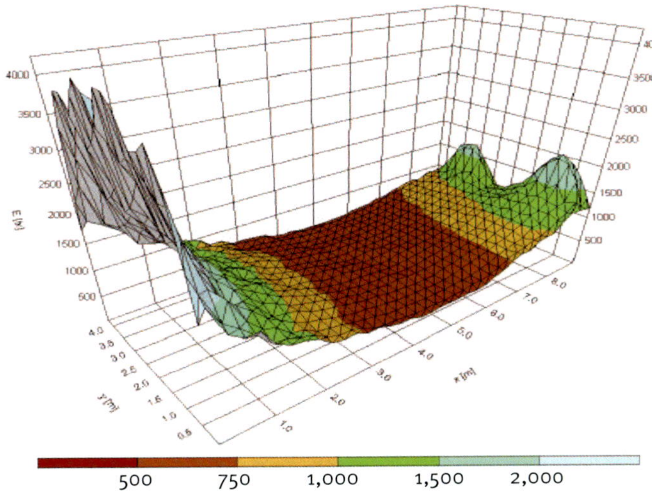

570

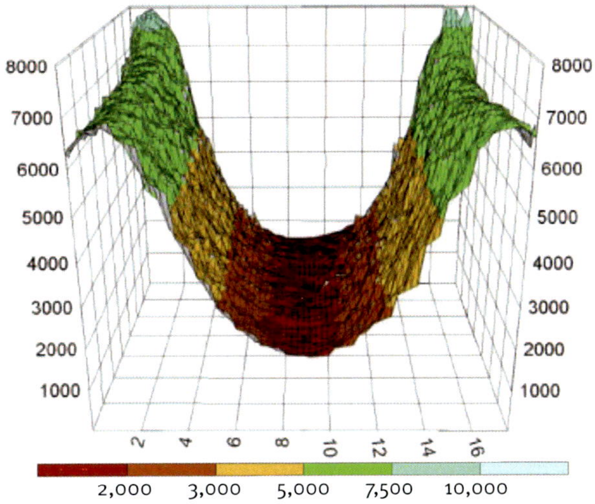

571

11.2 Realisations

572

Architects
IGEL-Institut, Wismar

Construction
11/2010 – 10/2011

572 The site plan of the building
573 The former situation of existing building
574 The new street facade image based on the registered design of Bützow

11.2.7 Sustainable renovation and conversion of heritage residential house for office building of housing association, Bützow

The conversion and renovation of an existing residential building in Wollenweber street, Bützow into a main administration building of BÜWO (housing association in Bützow).
The building is heritage as and is situated in the historical, mixed-use city centre of Bützow. The south street facade is composed of two, separate two-storey building elements from various years of origin.
The building site is approx. 1,400 m². Parking possibilities are limited; however, adding parking on the building site would enable a shorter distance to the building.

The main idea was to make the differences between the old and the new building elements visible in order to respect the historical value of the building. The most important aspect when treating historical buildings is to restore the older elements that are in good condition and add the new parts required for the new function. The old and new parts should be different; however, still work in harmony and together create a balanced design. The basic concept was to restore the facade and roof adjacent to the street. Wood preservation analyses determined which wood construction could be kept and which was no longer structurally sound. The heavily damaged areas of the building were demolished but the street-facing facade was restored. The roof was rebuilt with respect to the old design. Within the older building, the oak timber construction of the back facade had to be partially replaced. Therefore a new foundation for this facade and the renewing of the floor plate (mainly the waterproofing) was required. It was important to enable enough daylighting for the offices, which are situated to the courtyard. In addition, the ceilings had construction problems and would also have to be renewed.

The concept was to get more space and public areas within the building; therefore, the southern internal walls on the ground and first floor were to be demolished. This created a generously open entrance foyer. This also allowed a vertical connection through the building with a staircase in the gallery. The new organisation of the plan also optimised the northern facade for daylighting.

The new floor plan connects to the northern rooms that remain in the existing room structure. The existing internal walls were repaired and new walls are added where necessary.
The gable walls needed to be rebuilt. This was achieved with limestone bricks in order to carry greater loads. The street facade was saved and covered with clay plaster. All windows were renewed.

573

574

575

576

575 The new function in the building divided into customer zone, director with secretary, 9 employee offices, consulting rooms, workshop and supporting spaces – ground floor plan, first floor plan and roof floor plan, the demolished parts are in yellow colour
576 Schematic ground floor plan – concept of the building renovation – the southern street facade as well as the stable wooden building parts are kept, the building parts with the risk of collapsing are demolished
577 New north courtyard facade design
578 Interior image after the renovation – the heritage ceilings are preserved; however, they have only decorative function, the interior plaster of the southern street wall is made by natural straw-clay

577

578

11.2 Realisations

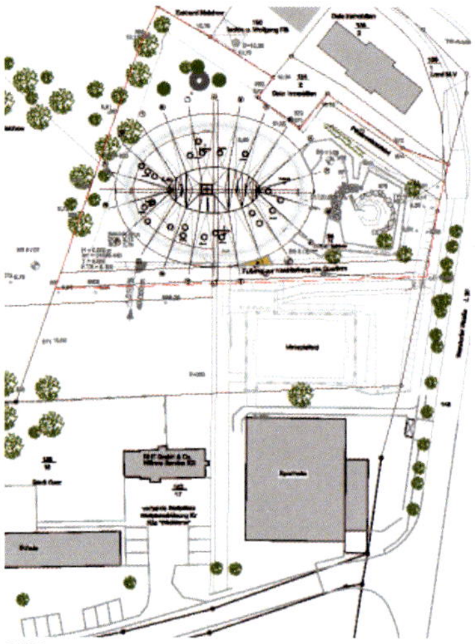

579

Architects
IGEL-Institut, Wismar

Construction
05/2012 – 07/2014
www.kita-wildblume.hs-wismar.de

579 Building site plan – the main entrance is from the south side where also other education buildings are located
580 Courtyard in the middle, is the pulsing heart of life in the kindergarten
581 Ground floor plan – the oval form is advantageous for energy and resource saving, the south and north sides are longer than east and west following the energy concept of the kindergarten
582 Sections showing the energy concept of the kindergarten
583 The outside image of the kindergarten – the extended roof covered with sustainable roof covering protects the clay-straw walls and supports the strictly introversion of the building

11.2.8 Three-Zero-Concept construction: New Kindergarten "Wildblume", Garz/Rügen

Three-Zero-Concept

The three-zero-concept can be seen throughout the entire building lifecycle starting from ecological building materials until an environmentally friendly deconstruction. The building reduces the level of possible harmful emissions, it burdens neither air nor ground and minimises consumption of fossil fuel energy and other resources.

The use of recyclable materials is given priority, in particular, the use of organic materials, clay and wood, which create no problems for necessary building disposal in the later phases. They are harmless in their effects on the environment and they are easily recyclable. Composite materials and parts, which are difficult to separate, are avoided. When the building function is changed from a kindergarten to something else, the building can be easily converted due to the flexibility of the floor plan and the support system.

The basic concept of the kindergarten consists of significant elements from the fields of low, light and high-tech design for overall energy-efficiency. Due to the introverted form and the central courtyard, the building fits perfectly within the building site. Additionally, the building's form blocks the acoustic noise from the surroundings while optimising the A/V ratio.

Clay and wood as structural elements

The key element of the building a wooden structure that is filled with clay bricks and covered with multiple layers of clay plaster. This creates positive effects of a good indoor climate, low transmission loss and low production costs.

Ecologically, if one compares a standard building construction, the wood-clay exterior walls that are made from local building materials require much less primary energy for the production, transport, work and energy.

Additionally, positive outputs are achieved through the use of clay as a building material including an activated thermal mass.

Innovative energy sources

The reduction of CO_2 emissions is a cornerstone of the Triple-Zero concept. During the entire service life of the building, highly efficient plants minimize the annual heating demand achieving low transmission and ventilation heat losses.

Used for this purpose is a simple heat recovery and controlled air conditioning system. When combined, the heat generated by the heat pump can be brought to a higher temperature level which covers heat supply for the building.

580

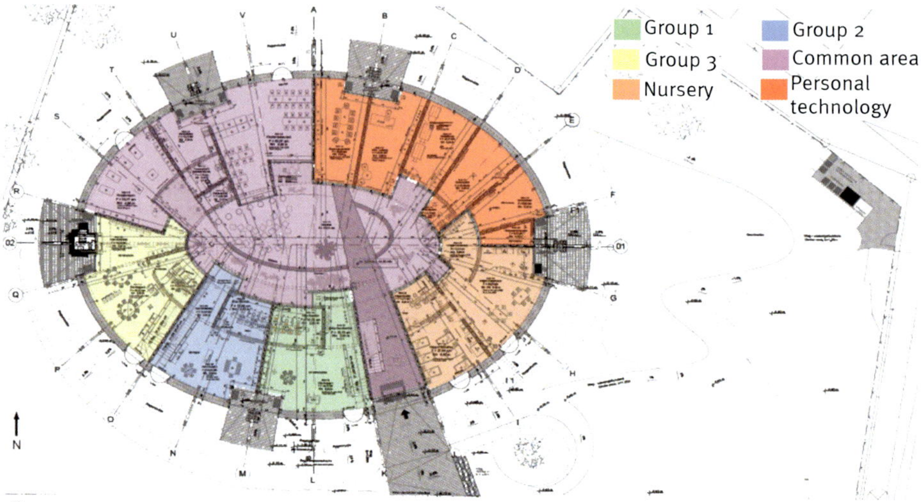

581

Courtyard as a storage buffer

The idea of the film-covered courtyard is to act as a buffer which collects the thermal energy during the day and delivers to the adjoining rooms at night. Via the earth heat exchanger, the courtyard is filled with preheated air creating an intermediate climatic zone which reduces the temperature difference between the inside and outside.

This also creates additional opportunities for passive solar energy while solar thermal flat plate collectors support supply of hot water. With a planned annual heat energy need of less than 15 kWh/m² and primary energy of 57 kWh/m², the kindergarten "Wildblume" will easily meet the sustainable requirements for an environmentally friendly building.

Monitoring in the real operation

For the users and builders within the region, this project will be an exemplary building. The project will be valued with the evaluation system for sustainable building (BNB) by BMVBS. The goals identified in advance are continuously tested through calculations and by simulations at the Hochschule Wismar. After building completion, planned monitoring will continue in order to help reach ambitious energy saving plans during real operation. The project results will then be documented and published by interested organisations and institutions.

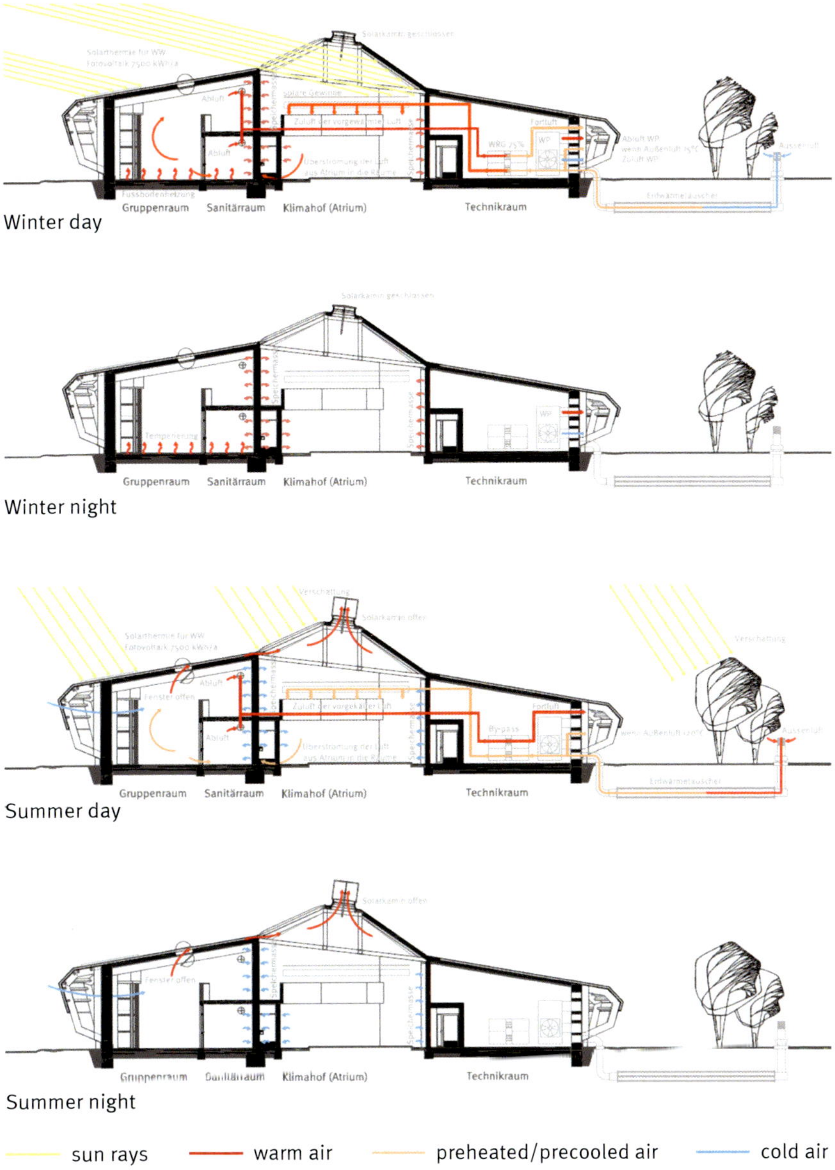

582

583

11.2 Realisations

Existing Buildings:

- 2 schools of the same type

Heat energy - approx. 126.3 kWh/m²a

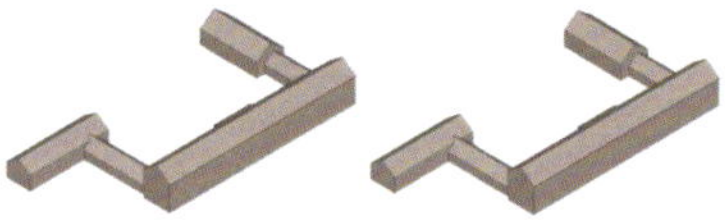

Planning:

- 1 school

Heat energy - approx. 42.8 kWh/m²a

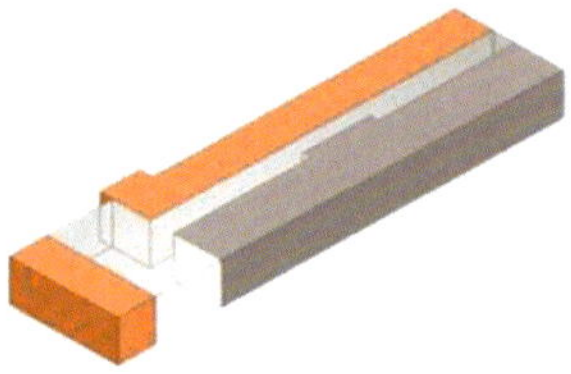

- Reduction of heat energy need at approx. 2/3 or 66 %

584

Architects
IGEL-Institut, Wismar

Construction
1. step: 10/2009 – 10/2011
2. step: 03/2012 – 12/2015

Award
School 2030 – Learning with energy (Schule 2030 – Lernen mit Energie), BMWE

11.2.9 Plus energy renovation: Plus Energy School, Reutershagen Rostock

The project, plus energy school is a pilot construction project for the energy-efficient renovation of a school building founded by the program EnEff:Schule. Public buildings, such as the school building are of public interest due to their exposure and function. They are exemplar for appropriate design standards. Moreover, they constitute an important part of our architecture culture, and reflect the self-understanding of our society. The students and teachers, as the future users of the building, must also be energy conscious conservative in the handling of natural resources and materials available. The aim of the demonstration building project is to reach a maximum reduction of energy consumption through the active and passive use of renewable energies. The school is situated in two similar but separate buildings, which has a high energy demand – primary school and gymnasium.

Here, not only the external and internal structure and shape of the building are to be improved, but also the potential to extend uses of the school system. The result formulated this holistic approach to planning quality on an energy, architectural and usage-specific level.

Here, the applications of energy measurements are expressed visually in order to demonstrate the conceptual ideas and building technology to all users and visitors.

An essential foundation for an energy balance improvement is to simplify the shape of the building by reducing the building envelope while creating new useful areas. This is achieved by the removal of the two additional wings, and replacing them with the addition of new areas including the recreation hall, staff room and classrooms. These additions are arranged parallel to the main building creating a compact structure. By reducing the outer surfaces, a decrease in heat loss is reached and the renovation expenditure for greater external insulation ensures a consistent internal environment.

As a result, the proportion of access areas in relation to the total area of the building is reduced.
This is because the existing collar type building is replicated and placed side by side. The new building acts as a second collar building and the area in-between functions as a climate buffer zone.

The south-facing facade of the new atrium space is weather-protected but unheated, which adds possibilities of active and passive solar energy gains while also acting as a tempered intermediate climate zone.
With the use of the buffer zone, problems of overheating in the summer

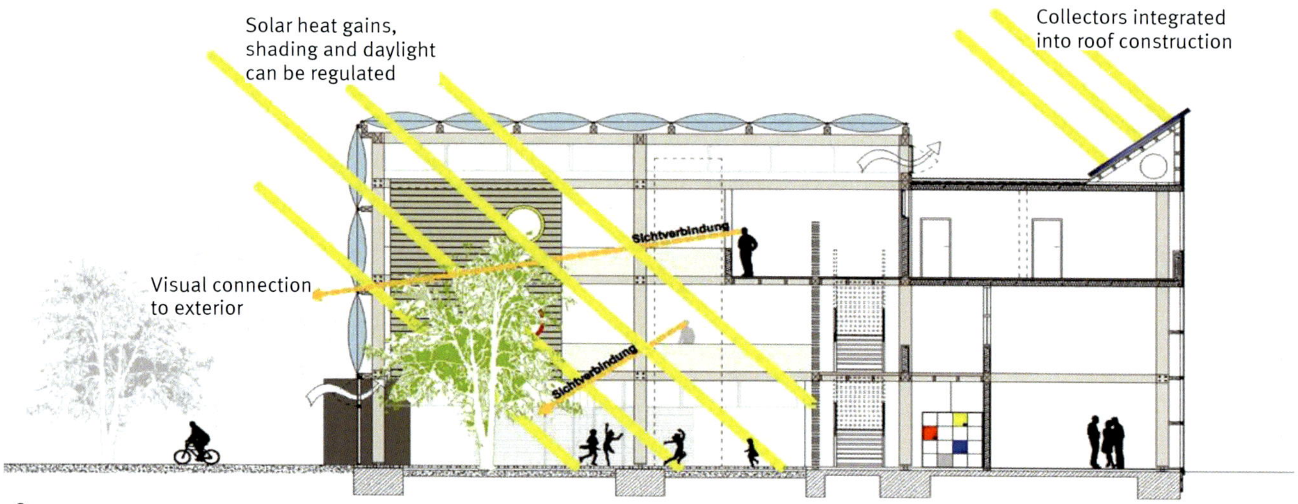

585

are reduced while providing heating in the winter. However, this area is also a valuable addition to the classroom units. The supplementary outside space represents life and is a usable space for both the children and youth to experience and create new possibilities together.

As a result, the air and general atmosphere (temperature, lighting, sound) was significantly improved. In addition to the building's structural measures for energy use and production, renewable energy sources were considered. The building is supplied with sufficient levels of solar and wind power. The additional and unused energy from both systems is recovered and fed back into the public grid. As a compact structure, with a mix of both new and old building parts, areas with different features are divided into different climatic zones. The old parts of the building are left in their basic structure in order to express the newer elements.

The new buildings are optimised accordingly to energy and use-specific requirements (lighting, ventilation, energy balance). This gives the building a high level of internal differentiation, guaranteeing many indoor climate improvements including acoustics and use-related problems. Reconciling these measures together with the measures of direct energy use ensures the plus.

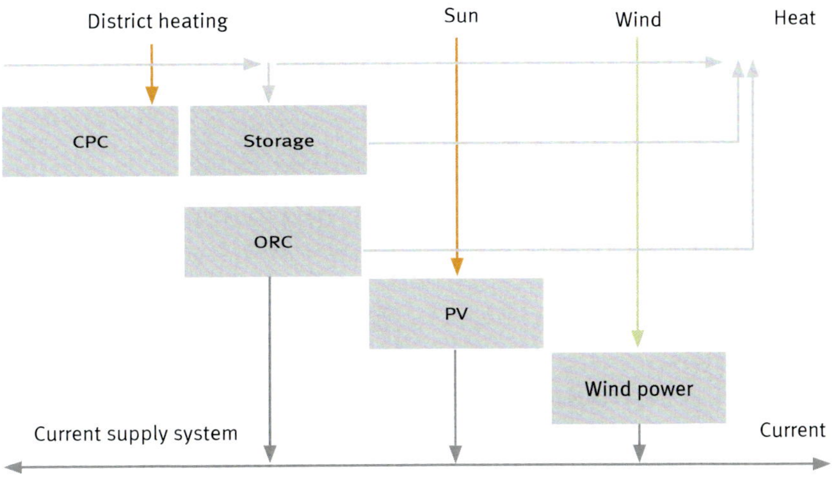

586

New use of surfaces:

- Building integrated PV arrangements
- Integration of a top performance-thermo solar arrangement
- Low temperature – ORC – Solar thermal collectors
- Double use of stairwell construction that integrate two small wind turbines

584 The design concept – from two non-compact existing buildings into one compact building
585 Section of the courtyard with a schematic introduction of passive and active solar use
586 Schematic of the energy supply concept of Plus Energy School in Rostock
587 Some impressions from the construction of Plus Energy School

587

11.3 Projects – urban planning

Architects
IGEL-Institut, Wismar

Planning
2008

588 The energy redevelopment of town Luckenwalde divided into 3 steps:
1.step – demonstration projects 2008–2012, here is the pilot project town district renovation of settlement "Burg", founding of cooperative energy organisation and energy renovations of public buildings in other town districts – the CO_2 emission reduction at around 22 %
2.step – inclusion of the biggest energy consumers 2012-2015, here is the energy efficiency renovation of second residential district "Weichpfuhl", energy renovation of trade and industry buildings and following of energy renovations of public buildings in other town districts – the CO_2 emission reduction at around 46 %
3.step – more density 2016, following energy renovation of trade and industry buildings and public buildings in other town districts, renovation of private buildings, reduction of CO_2 emissions at around 50 %

town facility
geothermal power station
decentral energy supply
energy-efficient planning
trade

11.3.1 EnEff:Stadt: Application town Luckenwalde

Luckenwalde is a small town in the north-east of Germany near Berlin in the region of Brandenburg. It has 20,324 inhabitants (statement from 2007, however is showing a decrease) and 46.75 km² of surface area. The approx. age is 45.1 years and the percentage under the age of 18 is 13.3 % and over the age of 60 is 30.0 %.

The economy is based on metal processing, automotive, the food industry from small businesses, biotechnology and tourism. The unemployment rate is 12.7 %.

It is a town of short distances, with a medieval centre with administration buildings and a perimeter wall. Around the old town are districts divided into block arrangements and settlements from the 20s and 30s.

In the northeast and northwest are a number of prefabricated buildings and in the south, the city's industrial and commercial area is concentrated. The main energy and heat supply is from the public Städtische Betriebswerke Luckenwalde GmbH (Urban depots Luckenwalde GmbH) and from the company eon-edis. The natural gas supply is through a 84.3 km long gas network. 3,400 apartments and 31 other institutions are supplied by distance heating.

The power consumption of the town is around 80,280 MWh and consumption of natural gas is 180,729.6 MWh.

Analysis of energy problems:
The emigration of young people and the decline in the birth rate (a decrease of around 20 %) leaves large apartments empty, public infrastructure is no longer rentable and high-energy surpluses which cause high energy costs.

A high rate of un-renovated buildings (around 50 %) causes high energy losses and demands.

Due to vacancies and rehabilitation requirements, the living environment becomes less attractive, the districts lose their image, life quality decreases and the town body is abandoned along with settlements of single-family houses and industrial areas outside the town. This trend continues to create greater distances, unstructured public areas, and a lack of quality open space.

CO_2 fossil fuel emissions for power are around 27,000 t CO_2/a and gas is around 30,000 t CO_2/a. Distance heating requires around 10,000 t CO_2/a.

The goal of the concept is to reduce the CO_2 emissions through building renovations to help reduce the energy demands and bring new activity to the area.

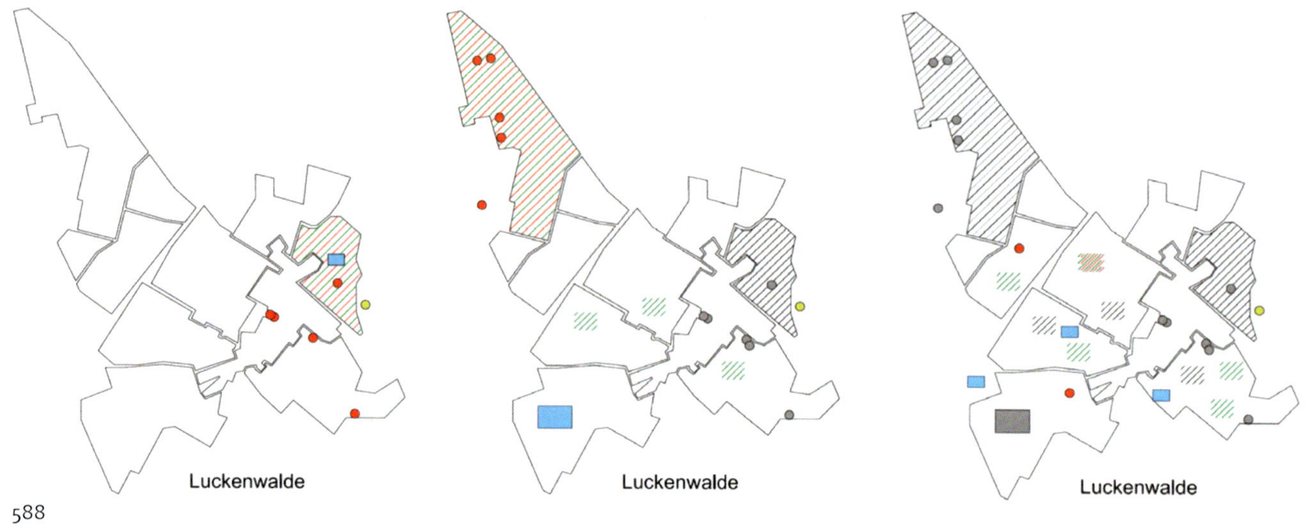

588

The following steps show how this goal is possible:

1. The reduction of energy demands from existing buildings by thermally insulating the building's envelope. Also, the construction of new buildings in order to gain compact building forms, design of the secondary and circulation rooms as thermal buffer zones, modernisation of building technology, heat recovery, improvement of daylight harvesting and awareness of the user.

2. The flexibility of energy supply systems that use renewable energies - the central supply system can be from e.g. a geothermal station provided by the town's supply, decentralized energy supply systems from wind turbines, solar thermal collectors and photovoltaic that are provided by building owners, private persons or organisations.

3. The development of space by controlled demolition to improve the living environment - using abandoned land in or near to city centre, improvement of pedestrian and bicycle network, renewing of town lighting.

4. The founding of cooperative energy organisations:
Creation of energy rules ensures compliance with the energy policy objectives of the town and structural changes of all buildings. The creation of energy consulting – information and advice on the requirements and possibilities of the implementation of the energy rules, assistance and promoting groups from private builders to builder communities and cityscapes in a cooperative manner.
The promotion of privately organised energy saving committees, advising and supporting the production and operation of decentralized energy supply systems.
Establishment of an energy council to ensure that all participants follow the objectives in developing renewable energy for the town. These include: town administration, housing associations, utilities, trade, and industries. This will ensure control over the proposed measures in terms of their energy efficiency and the development of the saving values/total energy balance for the entire town.
As a pilot project, an energy concept for the renovation of the town district settlement "Burg" was designed. It is described in the following pages.

Some other features of the town are:

- soft locations, with possibilities for leisure activities
- a centre
- presence of all types of schools
- centre for professional sport
- variation of cultural landscape
- seat of government and provincial authorities (district court, district administration, chamber of commerce, agency for labour, tax office, theatre, cinema, library, community college)

589 The energy supply system and values of CO_2 emissions after 2.step of town redeveloping, reducing of CO_2 emissions at around 46 %

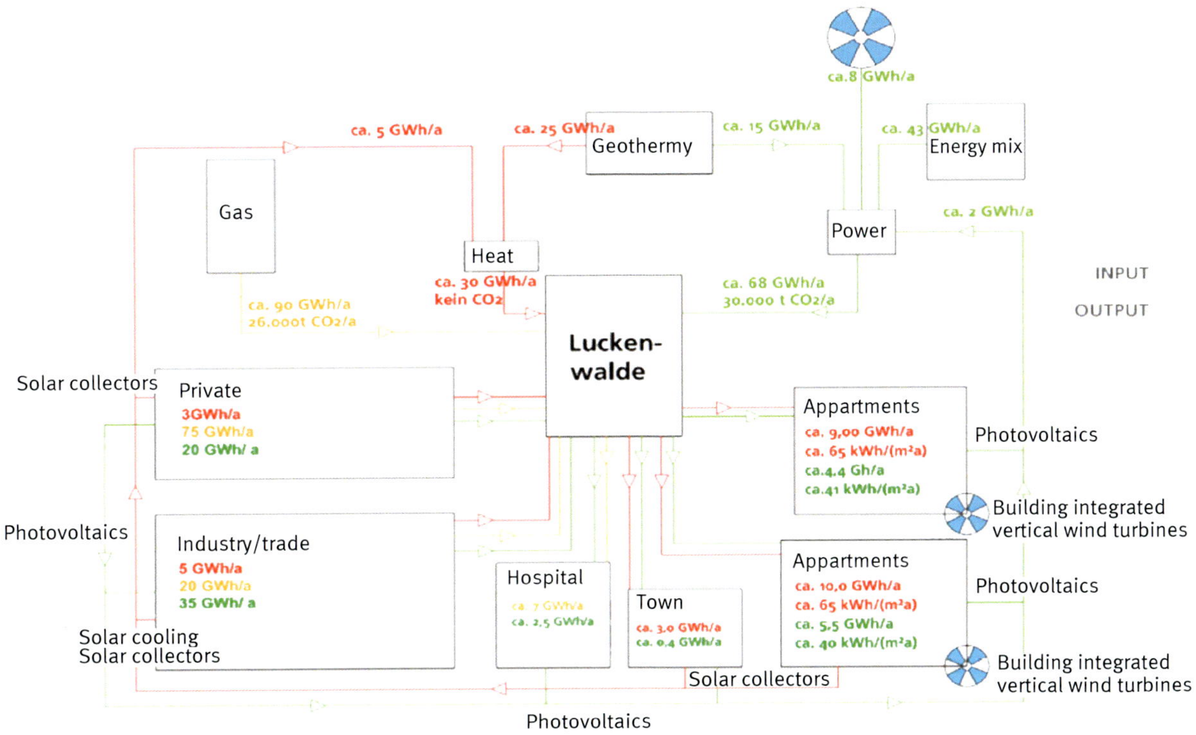

589

11.3 Projects – urban planning

- Services
- Residences
- Services under construction
- Kindergarten "Burg"
- Citizen and neighbourhood meeting
- Residences with commercial facilities in ground floor

590

Architects
IGEL-Institut, Wismar

Planning
2008

590 The site plan with built and free area of the town district and the usage – existing situation
591 Energy flow in the city district "Burg" – existing situation
592 Energy flow in the city district "Burg" after the energy renovation of existing buildings and switching of energy generation to renewable energies

11.3.2 Town district energy renovation: Settlement "Burg", Luckenwalde

The town district energy renovation of the settlement "Burg" is a part of the common program "Town renovation" in Luckenwalde. This settlement consists of 4 and 5 storey prefabricated residential buildings – around 750 flat units, 17 % of which are not used and of the 19 commercial units, 5 % are unused.

Also in the area is the "Brother Heinrich" foundation, kindergarten "Burg", citizen and neighbourhood meeting place and newly built supermarket; all one and two storey buildings. There is a high amount of free areas in the settlement. There are sufficient parking places, mainly in the shopping centre area and around the streets.

The short-time parking places around kindergarten "Burg" are missing. There are many green surfaces, but most are poor quality and unused. The town district is in the neighbourhood of the town centre.

The issue of the town district is also the consistency of the inhabitants; the average age is approx. 44 years. The young people move out and the older people remain. The existing residential buildings are not good for the new requirements. The old ages of inhabitants are increasing the need for elevators and other elements.

The energy renovation also considers the energy components in addition to traditional, social, structural, space and infrastructure components. The main opportunity is to reduce energy waste through the use of waste warm energy and flexible decentralised supply systems, which uses renewable energies.

The focus is also on activating the regional cycles and the support of density inside the town. Around 50 % of existing buildings are renovated – mainly improvements of thermal insulation characteristics of building envelopes.

The town district "Burg" is supplied by power, gas and warm energy through the district energy supply of Luckenwalde. The energy generation is through combined heat and power (gas) and peak load boiler (gas). The regenerative energy for warm energy is around 23 % and for power around 26 %.

The energy requirement is approx. 3,700,000 kWh/a of power and approx. 4,400,000 kWh of warm energy. The biggest user is the supermarket, mainly for cooling.

Goals

- improvement of the town district to attract new families and inhabitants – new development of residential buildings

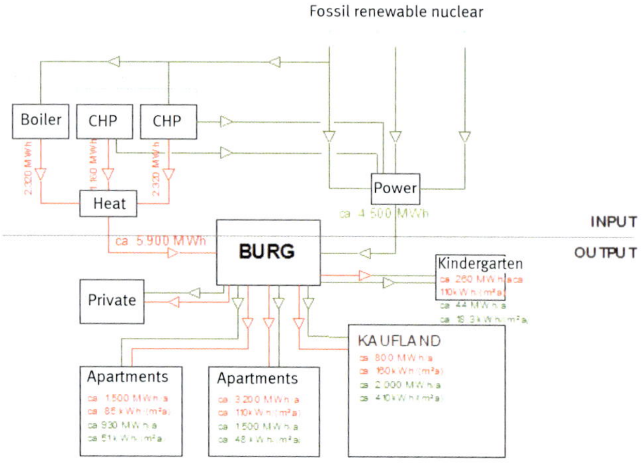

591

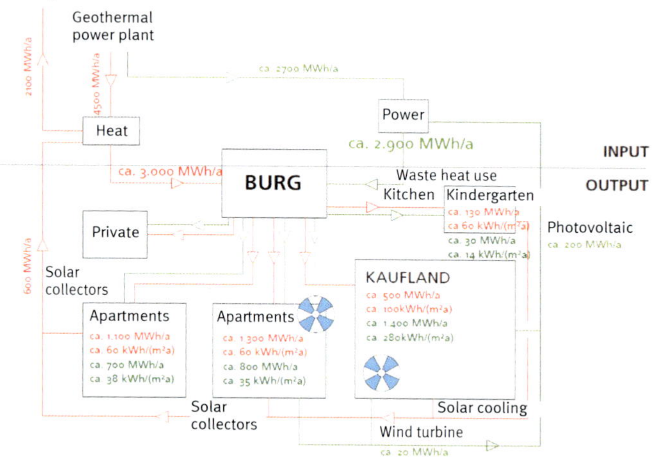

592

- old-age friendly residences for the seniors currently living there
- attractiveness and quality of green spaces – reuse of landscape after demolished buildings, the design of streets and courtyards
- better orientation, space structure and circulation – better bicycle connections and parking, supporting of public transportation
- improvement of pedestrian streets
- barrier-free
- energy saving plan with a high amount of renewable energies and rainwater usage
- reduce energy demand of unrenovated buildings and kindergarten
- reduction of transmission heat loss through thermal insulation of buildings, optimization of Surface/Volume ratio, optimization of building technology with possibility of heat recovery
- improvement of daylighting
- use of central energy supply system based on geothermal
- decentral additional energy supply based on wind, solar thermal and photovoltaic system
- solar cooling for supermarket
- use of waste heat energy
- street lighting concept

Strengths	**Weaknesses**
Short distance to the town centre	Old age of people and few families
Good shopping potential	Some parts are not renovated
Mixture of use	No social mixture
Sufficient free space	No diversity of green spaces
Good building scale and compactness	Bad orientation
Sufficient parking	Not enough bicycle streets and parking
Distance energy supply through CHP	Not barrier-free

593

Strengths	**Weaknesses**
Distance energy supply through CHP	High energy demand of non-renovated buildings
Some buildings are renovated	Small amount of renewable energies
Compactness of buildings	Utilization problems with demolition
Orientation	No internal coordination
Efficient water supply	No solar thermal systems
	No use of rainwater

594

595

593 SWOT analysis – space and function
594 SWOT analysis – energy
595 New design of the city district – the east border consists of green space – west site is to town centre – north and south is river Nuthe, the river should be connected with two artificial water ways flowing through district
596 Pedestrian streets in the district, new design of courtyards

596

11.3 Projects – urban planning

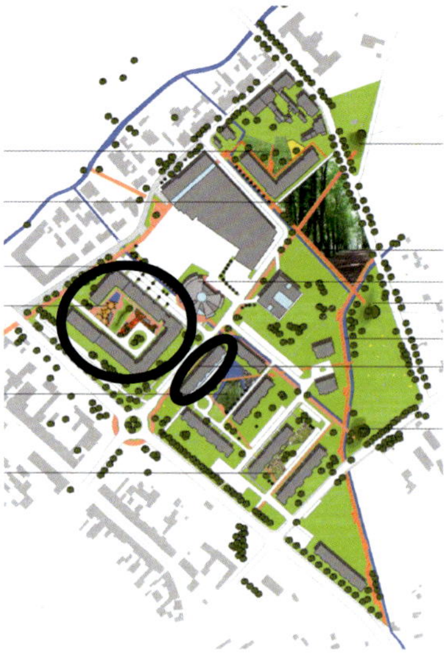

597

Architects
IGEL-Institut, Wismar

Planning
2008

597 The site plan settlement "Burg" Luckenwalde with the marked position of considered block of flats buildings
598 Existing situation – first group of block of flats buildings
599 The concept of functional reorganisation of the building

11.3.3 Energy renovation: Block of flats buildings "Burg", Luckenwalde

The first group of residential-flat buildings is situated in a very good location between the supermarket and town centre. The prefabricated buildings were built in 1987 and are commonly found in many other cities.

The buildings are in their original state without any renovations and an entire energy renovation is needed. The thermal insulation of the building envelopes is insufficient to building regulations. The main weak points are roofs, walls, basement ceilings and windows. The heat and warm water supply is through distance heating and the flats have plate heaters. The kitchen and baths are ventilated through exhaust ducts.

The heating energy demand is approx. 115 kWh/m²a and the total warm energy demand (heating + warm water) is 145 kWh/m²a.

There are also many functional problems – not senior / disabled friendly, small residential units, poor image and housing conditions, upper floors are empty (because of no elevator).

The building advantages are a good urban location, simple construction and compactness. Also, the renovation of existing buildings is more sustainable than new construction.

The main goals are:

- warm energy demand of 60 kWh/(m²a) – reduction of 45%
- power energy demand of 34,84 kWh/(m²a) – reduction of 32 %
- friendly to seniors, disabled people and families
- inexpensive living
- optimization of thermal insulation of building envelope
- controlled ventilation
- better surface/volume ratio
- optimization of building technology
- better daylighting
- new design of building envelopes with use of existing building elements

The design works with four elevators (rather than placing an elevator in each flat group) in the middle points between the buildings, connected with the middle corridors or with the corridors attached to the facade. This solution reduces costs, materials and labour.

There are many alternatives for inside reorganisation (minimal and maximal). The main idea is to create a few maisonette flats with the possibility of connection to the exterior (garden) for families. Other flats would be more senior and disabled friendly and the remaining flats for the socially weak.

The second considered group of residential-flat buildings is next to the

598

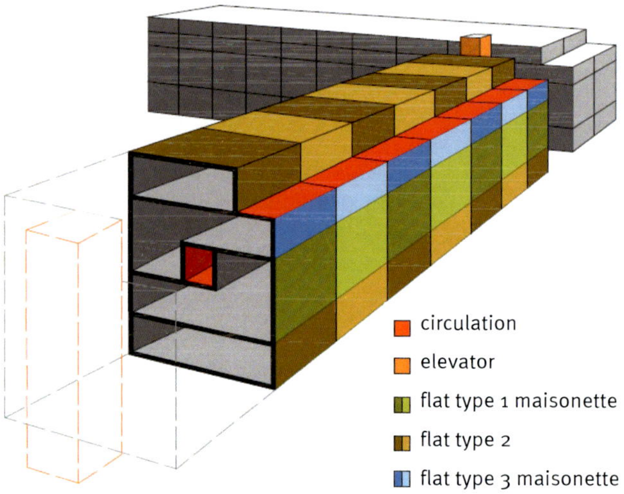

599

first group. It was partially renovated in 1997 with new thermal insulation in the façade and basement ceiling, new waterproofing on the roof, new windows, new drinking water piping, new sanitary rooms, new distance heating connection pipes, new radiators and new electro-installations.

The heating energy demand is approx. 62 kWh/m²a and total warm energy demand (heating + warm water) is approx. 81 kWh/m²a. The new design should be lowered to 60 kWh/m²a warm energy (30 %) and 38 kWh/m²a power (25 %).

The energy supply situation, ventilation and functional problems as well as advantages are similar to the first building group. The design also follows the same goals.

The whole block of flats should be connected with one elevator, situated in the middle of a buffer zone for passive energy usage.

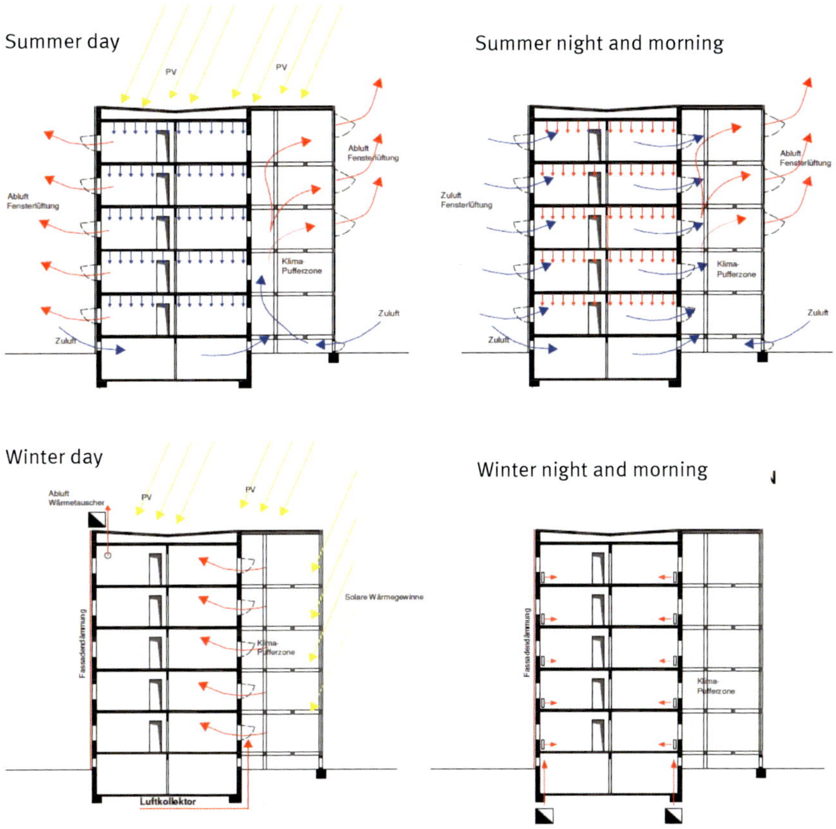

600

sun rays
warm air
cold air

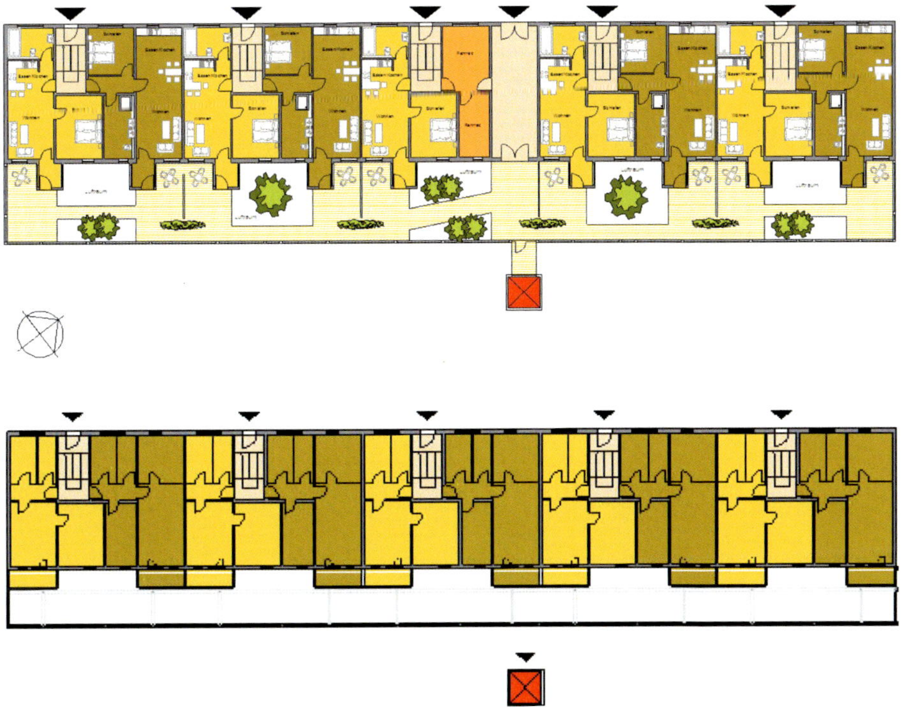

601

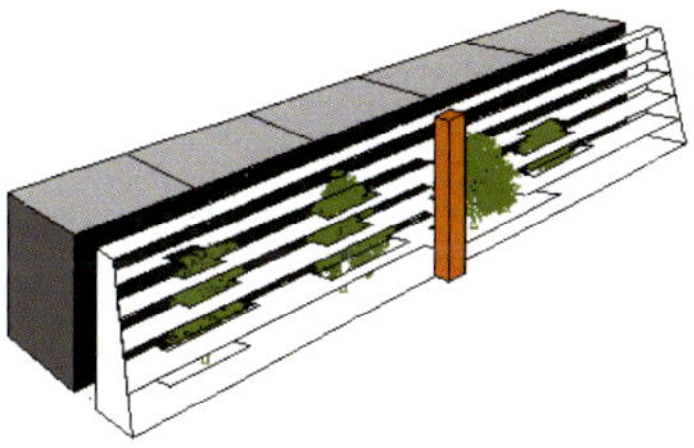

602

600 Energy concept of residential houses
601 Ground floor plan – maximal and minimal alternative – minimal alternative has no changes in the ground floor plan
602 Schematic of the elevator connection with the building – maximal and minimal alternative

11.3 Projects – urban planning

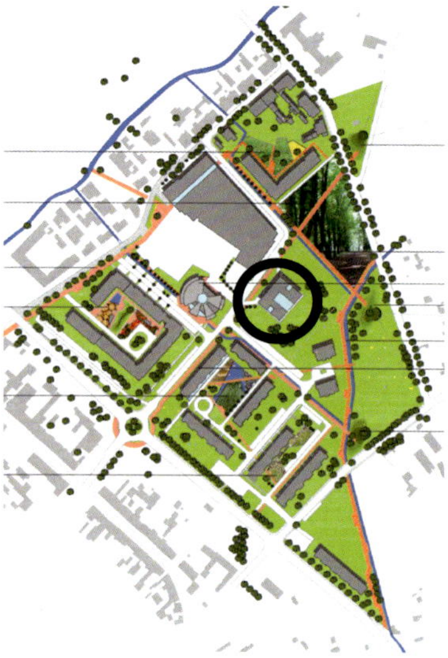

603

Architects
IGEL-Institut, Wismar

Planning
2008

603 The site plan settlement "Burg" Luckenwalde with the marked position of the kindergarten
604 Final functional design of the kindergarten – in steps

11.3.4 Energetic renovation: Kindergarten "Burg", Luckenwalde

This type of prefabricated building is from 1985. Many such buildings exist in east Germany, consisting of four, three-storey buildings connected with tree-storey connection building.

The existing situation of the kindergarten is good from a functional point of view. There had been previous renovation works of the sanitary rooms and lighting. The remainder of the building had not been renovated, except for a few windows.

The main functional problems are the difficult connection and orientation, no multifunctional rooms, only a few individual and social spaces, and only a few common spaces.

The energy-based problems are high transmission losses through building envelope, high ventilation losses – no control ventilation, one-sided ventilation and day lighting, bad surface/volume ratio and the resulting high operational costs.

The goals are:

- enhancement of user possibilities
- maximum lowering of energy requirements to: 60 kWh/m²a heat (around 46 %) and 14 kWh/m²a power (around 25 %)
- better compactness of the building – improving of A/V ratio
- optimization of technology
- heat recovery
- passive/active solar energy use
- improvement of daylighting
- appropriate design of new building envelope including the existing building elements

The design follows three concepts:

Concept 1 – compact building with courtyard buffer zone

- the kitchen zone and connection buildings are demolished
- the A/V ratio is optimised
- more buffer zones
- optimization of existing facades
- new entrances with elevator

Concept 2 – usage extension

- the kitchen zone and connection building are demolished
- the A/V ratio is optimal
- central buffer zone
- optimization of existing facades

Concept 3 – minimal alternative

- improvement of A/V ratio
- creating of two buffer zones
- connection building foyer
- optimization of existing facades
- new functional organisation

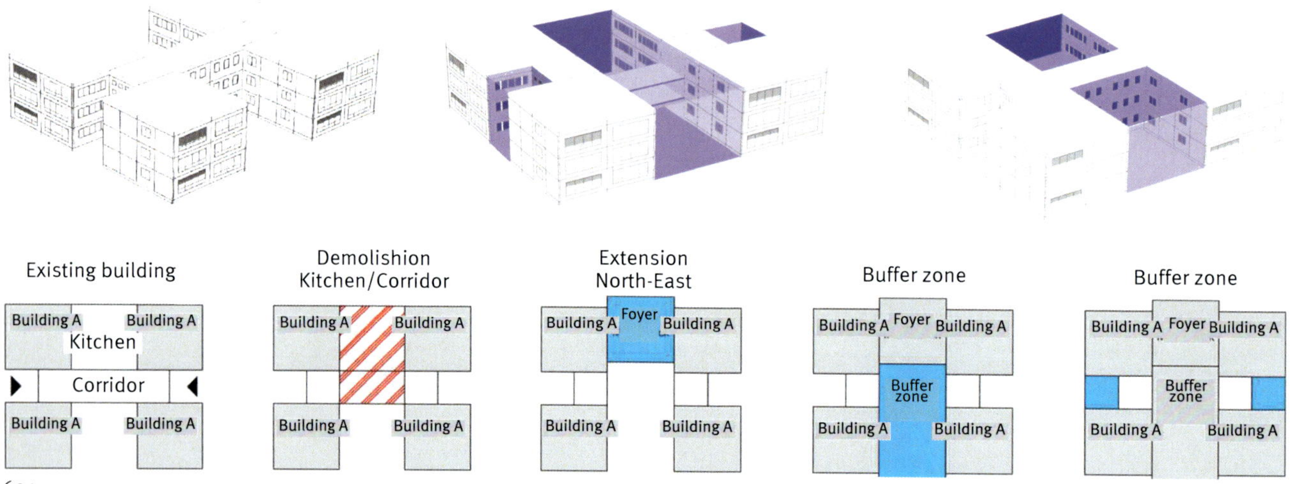

604

605

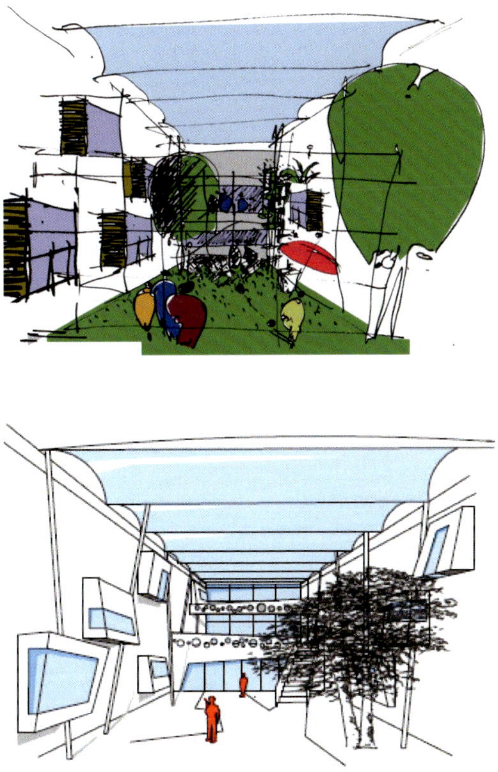

606

605 Ground plan from planning stage
606 Sketches of different courtyard designs
607 Ventilation concept – summer and winter

sun rays
warm air
cold air

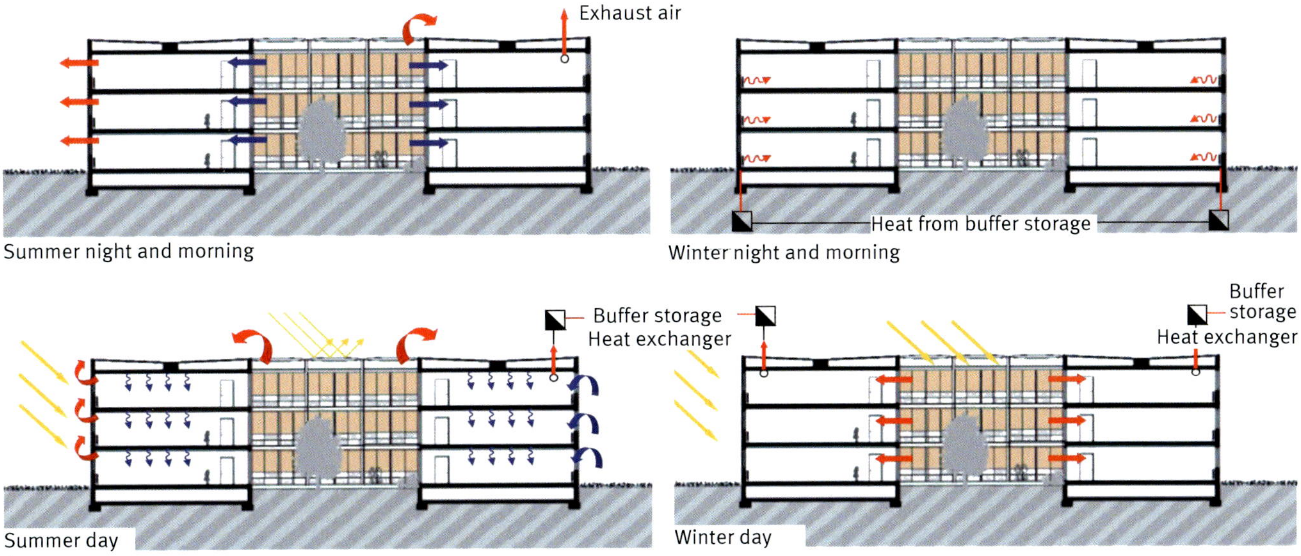

607

11.3 Projects – urban planning

Architects
M.A. Maluschak, Prof. Römhild and Prof. Wollensak with students of Hochschule Wismar

Planning
2008

The common concept consists of partial concepts:

- 1. energy – CO_2 neutral campus
- 2. use – space efficiency
- 3. traffic – car free campus
- 4. water – careful treatment of resources
- 5. rain water – use and infiltration of rainwater
- 6. free space – respect of living space
- 7. building materials and elements – sustainable use
- 8. waste – reduction through separation
- 9. developing of environmental management system

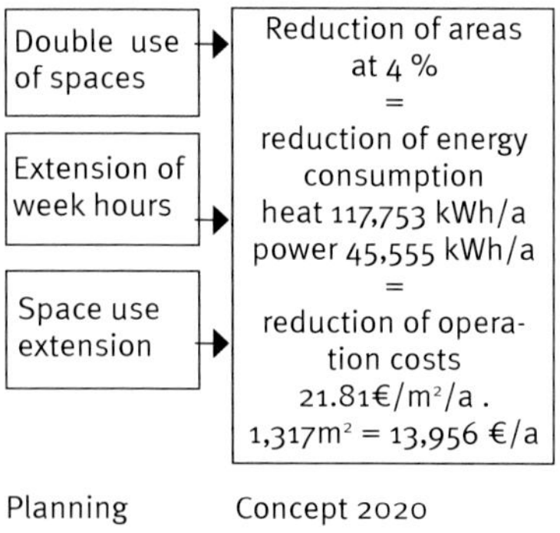

608

11.3.5 Campus 2020 – development concept for university campus Wismar

Campus of Wismar University has 89,310 m² and is located in a former military barrack area. The centre of the area consists of the main buildings with a large outdoor multifunctional free space in the centre. Buildings are partially military barracks – plastered massive buildings with purlin slope roofs. The area is extended by different provisor, unstructured buildings. The newer buildings are the library, canteen, kindergarten "Wellenreiter", theatre foyer and faculty of architecture and design.

The university consists of three faculties – faculty of engineering sciences, faculty of economic sciences, faculty of architecture and design. Also Wings is a distance study program of architecture and environment.
The goal was to design a sustainable renovation, development and use concept for the university campus of Wismar, exemplar for developments of other campus areas.

First, the existing situation is to be analysed and methods and measurements for development of concepts created. The concept of the whole campus consists of partial concepts for individual buildings, based on energy consumption in all life cycles.
The former heating system consists of three gas boilers and two pumps situated in building 20. The flow temperature is 90 °C and return temperature is 70 °C. The main problem is the long distances of piping. The canteen, kindergarten and theatre have their own heat supply system.
The power comes from the town Schwerin. The energy mix is 9 % of atom energy, 76 % of fossil fuels and 15 % renewable energy. Two transformer buildings are on the campus site. The fresh water supply is from the city network. The waste water is collected through the sewage system in campus and brought to the municipal sewage treatment. The rain water is collected separately from sewage water and flows into the retention basins.

The main goal for energy is the drastic reduction of CO_2 emissions and energy consumption. The primary energy consumption should be drastically reduced. The focus should be on use of renewable energies, e.g. passive and active solar energy, wind energy. The design concept also considers a new heat supply system, e.g. through combined heat and power with biogas for the basic needs and a wood pellet boiler for peak loads.
Other considerations are optimising the use of space, sustainable development planning, functional structure/ centre use, short distances and spatial identity. The heat energy demand should also be reduced by the renovation of buildings, partial demolitions and new constructions. The awareness of users and optimised user behaviour is of high importance.

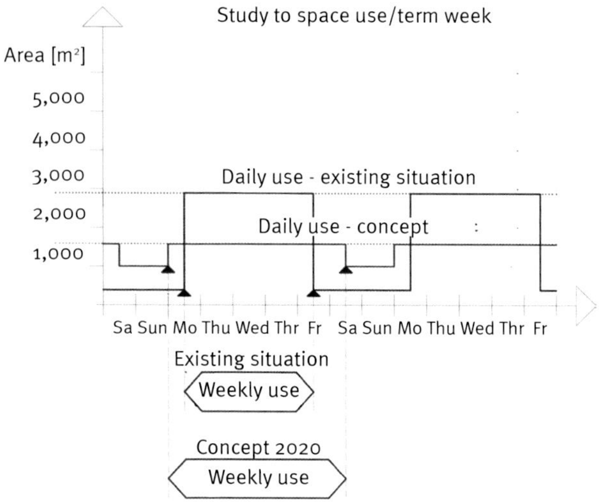

609

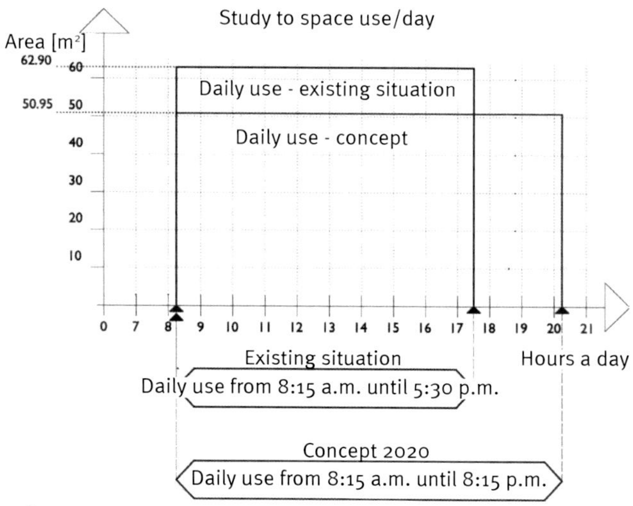

610

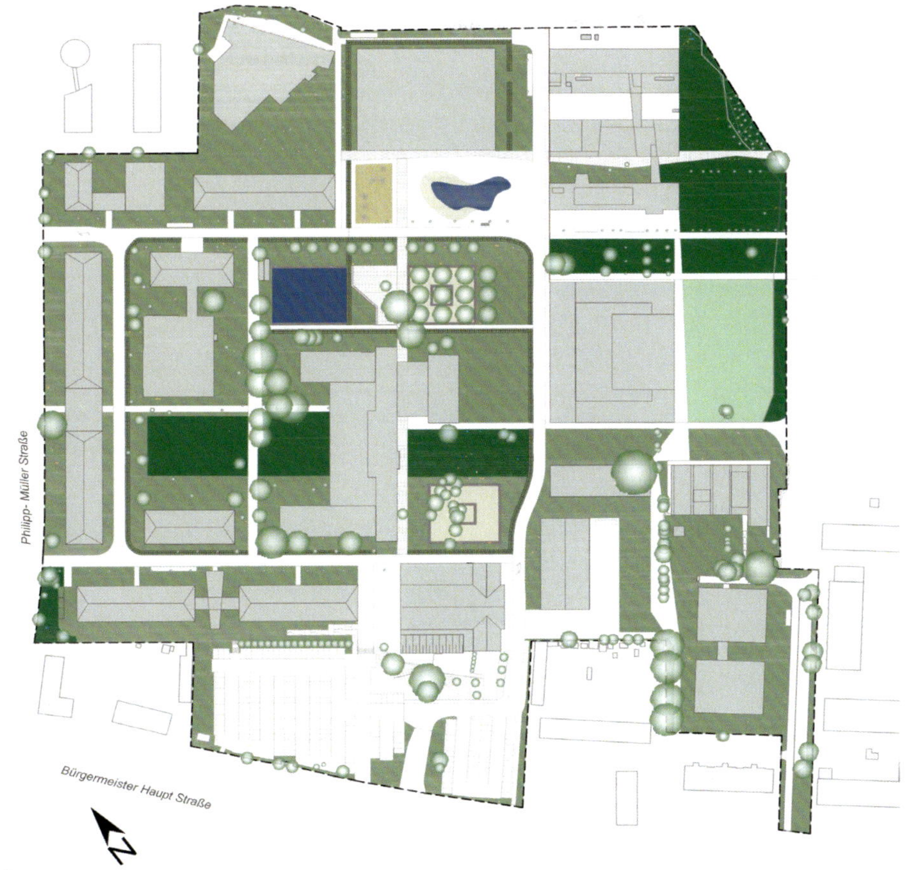

611

612

608 The plan of the campus after redevelopment
609 Goal of the concept 2020 in the field of action use
610 The analyse of the space utilization of seminar rooms for term week – it shows the space potential is used only up to 63.84 %
611 The analysis of the space utilization of seminar rooms during the day
612 Campus area of Wismar university
613 The energy consumption in 2008
614 Optimised energy consumption due to new concept in 2020 based on use of CHP, solar, wind energy for power generation and CHP, solar and energy of biomass

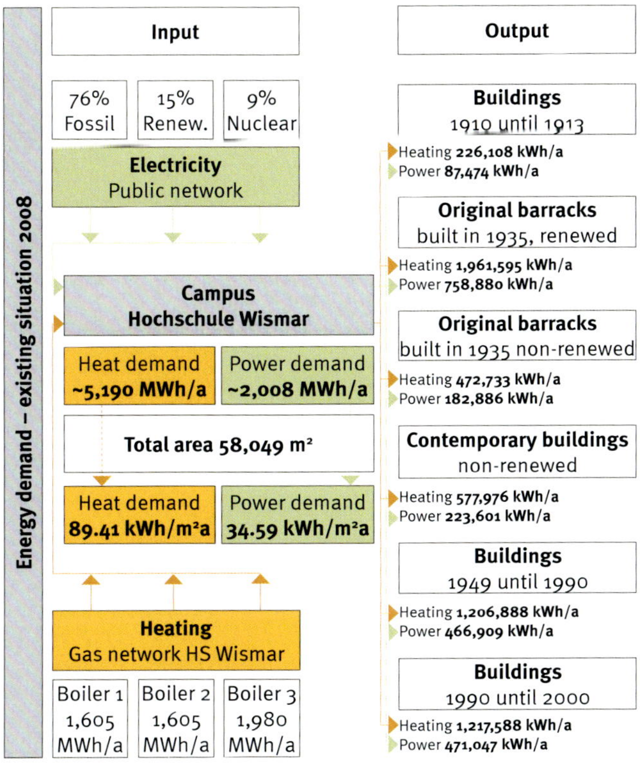

613

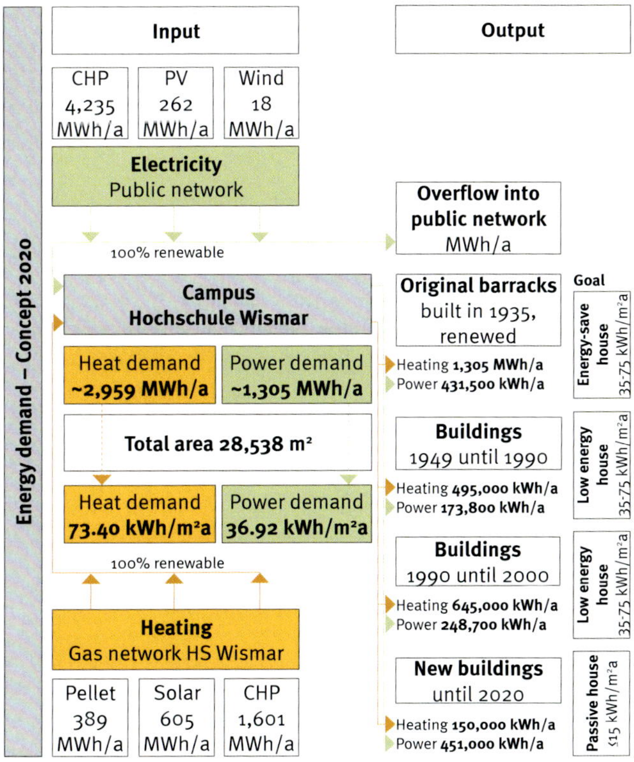

614

11.4 Projects – building

615

Architects
IGEL-Institut, Wismar

Planning
since 2003

Construction
Foyer 10/2006 – 04/2008
main building and the secondary spaces 2012 – 12/2014

umweltgerechte-buehne.hs-wismar.de

615 New foyer construction of passive house theatre – outside view
616 Energy and time concept of the theatre renovation – from a building with large outside surface to the compact energy-saving building

11.4.1 Passive house concept: Sustainable renovation theatre, Wismar

The theatre Wismar is situated in the campus of Hochschule Wismar and is used by both the town and the university. It was originally built over 60 years ago as part of a military compound. Its sustainable renovation is part of the greater concept for Hochschule Wismar 2020, which consists of the renovation of buildings on the university campus. In addition to a fundamental restructuring of the university, the buildings will be sustainable and ecologically rehabilitated. The theatre should become the first theatre in Germany with passive house standard.

The existing theatre consisted of an entrance hall, main auditorium hall, stage house and some additional buildings that served as service rooms and chamber stages.
Following the planning stage, the additional buildings were demolished and the entrance hall, auditorium and stage house were renovated. Two additional buildings were added to the main auditorium hall - the well-insulated service rooms at the north-east corner of the site are of passivhaus standard with the glazed entrance hall acting as a climate buffer with solar heat gains to the south-west.

By placing the additional buildings around the existing brick walls of the main theatre hall, a compact structure with an improved A/V ratio is created. The longitudinal outer walls of the existing hall building become partial interior walls. Some exterior walls and windows are not surrounded by the additional buildings and therefore receive additional insulation.

The outer walls of the new building in the north for the chamber/puppet theatre, theatre bar, dressing rooms and technical rooms are to be highly insulated according to the passive house standard. The new windows are designed with heat-insulating glass. At the lower flat-roof areas where connected to the old building, the exterior walls are fully insulated and plastered.
The south-western and north-west facade of the already completed lobby are designed to match the new theatre. The facade elements are fully glazed, consisting of window units framed with wood/aluminium construction and steel sections for horizontal wind bracing.

The pitched roofs of the additional buildings are to be fully insulated. The flat roof areas will be fully insulated to reduce transmission heat losses. These will be accessible for the purpose of building maintenance.

The energy concept is based on efficient technologies along with the reduction of transmission losses, through highly insulated building ele-

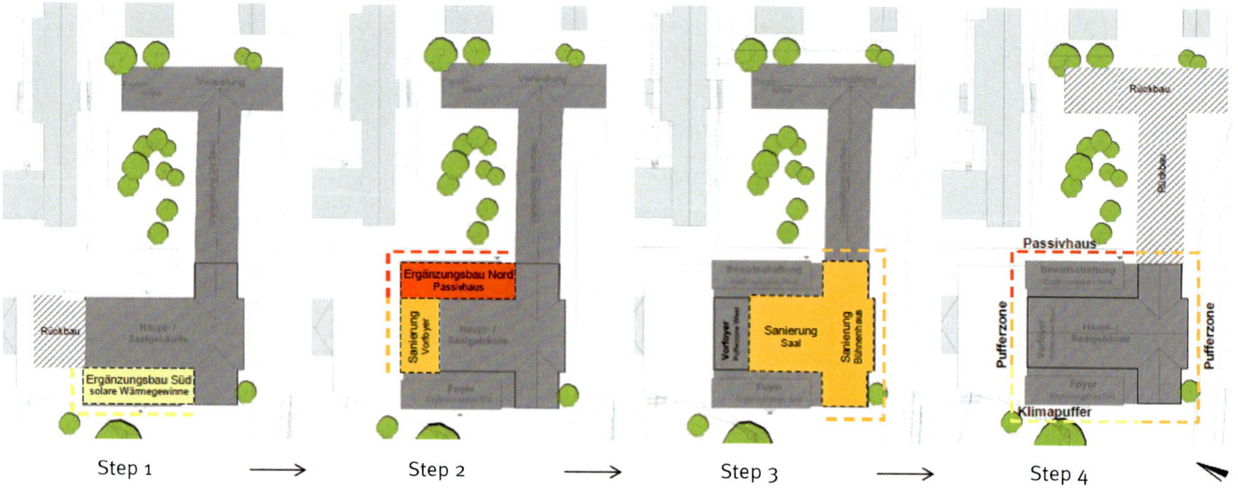

616

ments. Thermal insulation is to be improved with the use of new equipment and increased insulation. In addition, sustainability is achieved through the double use of the theatre building; a university lecture hall during the day and a public theatre during the evening. The double use of the building contributes to resource and energy saving design.

Reduce ventilation heat losses of the south extension building/lobby

A very simple ventilation system was chosen, which uses the heat gain of the foyer space. The foyer is ventilated via window openings including strip windows that were arranged to ensure proper air movement.

In summer during the daytime, the foyer either remains closed or the vents are opened. Due to the consistent wind in Wismar, the foyer is sufficiently ventilated. Designed for the use of solar heat gains, the set room temperature increases in correspondence to the local radiation intensity. Thus, the additional heating requirements of the rooms are reduced.

Reduce ventilation heat losses of the building's northern extension

To minimise ventilation heat losses, a ventilation system with heat recovery is installed. The ventilation system runs with a low pressure drop. The entire building is served by cross-ventilation, with demand-dependent air change rates. For winter, in the case of required air renewal, an air flow rate is set. The air volume can be adjusted through variable working volume controllers, with air flow specifically influenced by flaps.

Active use of solar energy

The building's shed roof for the dressing rooms (passive house) have a roof-integrated PV and solar thermal system for domestic hot water, and space heating. The south-facing roof of the hall building and the shed roof construction of the passive houses are equipped with a roof-integrated PV system.

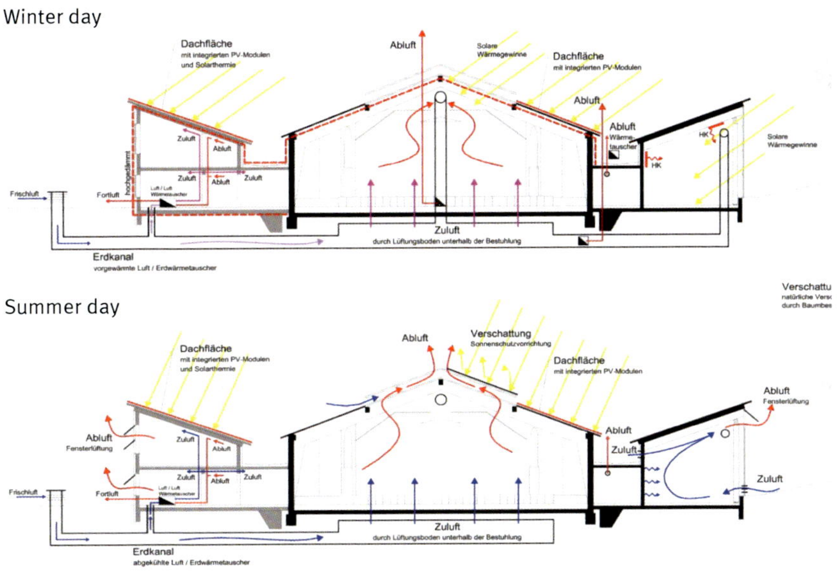

617

- sun rays
- warm air
- cold air
- preheated air
- well insulated envelope

617 Energy concept of passive house theatre – winter day, summer day
618 Floor plans of theatre

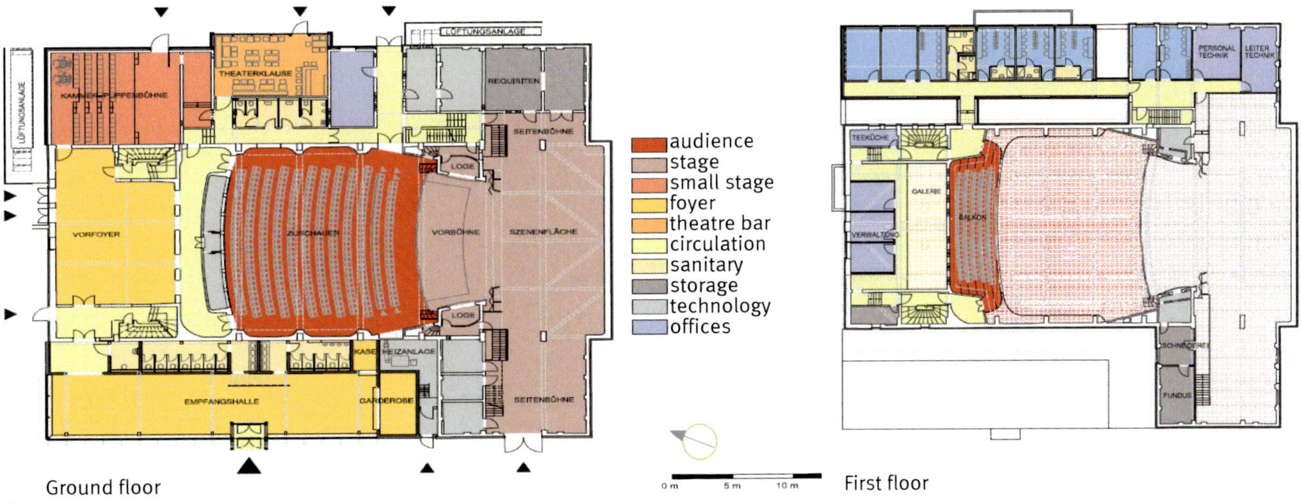

618

11.4 Projects – building

Architects

IGEL-Institut, Wismar

Planning

2004

619 Section of the vacuum bottle house
620 Perspective of vacuum bottle house – galvanized steel or rusted steel envelope

11.4.2 Vacuum bottle house: Demonstration pavilion for vacuum insulation

The main concept is the transformation of the vacuum insulation bottle principle; a vessel with a vacuum cavity and enclosed walls – developed in 1903 by Reinhold Burger in building construction.

The design of the building is similar to an upturned vacuum bottle. The basement is for building technology, the ground floor is the entrance and wardrobe and the three upper floors are for living purposes. The diameter is 5 m and the storey height is 2.75 m.

The global efforts for CO_2 emission reduction and for the digressive use of primary energy results in the continual increase of requirements for the winter protection of buildings.

Because of the nonlinear coherence between thermal insulation layer thickness and the thermal insulation capability, the large amount of thermal insulation material is not uncommon (e.g. by passive houses, the thermal insulation layer has around 400 mm thickness).

Vacuum thermal insulation elements reach up to ten times better thermal insulation values with a relatively small thickness. Vacuum thermal insulation is the future of thermal insulation.

The location of the vacuum bottle house is not determined. The ring-like foundation can also have an optional basement made of prefabricated concrete. The building can be used as a residential house or for different functions. For demonstration purposes, there is a possibility for the development of a mobile home.

The cost for realizing one building is approximately 500.00 €/m^2_{UFA}.

The preliminary cost estimate is based on the experience in construction of steel tubes in the manufacturing of wind turbines.

For the foundations, glazing and building construction, standard values were used which were determined on the basis of the calculated masses and comparison costs from the BKI construction cost database.

Today, there are two types of vacuum thermal insulation products:

- VIP – vacuum insulated panel (element of an envelope from alu-foil), which can be used only as non-bearing element for building thermal protection
- VIS – vacuum insulated sandwich (element of an envelope from stainless steel), which can be used as the building thermal protection element but also as bearing building construction

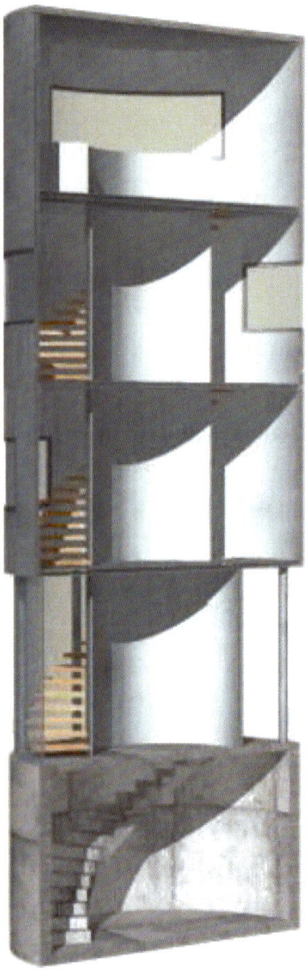

619

620

VIS – System description

A gas-tight welded steel shell, consisting of surface cover plates and a circumferential membrane wrapped snugly, supports a core consisting either of extruded polystyrene or fumed silica.

The vacuuming takes place by means of a vacuum pump, connected to the vacuuming flange located in one of the two cover shells.

A bearing support between the inner core and outer shell must be integrated into the panel. The construction of the vacuum bottle house has the advantage of the vacuum to atmospheric pressure by the shape stability of the shell to absorb and to achieve the desired insulating effect, without the additional braces similar to a thermos.

Material construction consists of cover sheets/cover plates, membrane profile and a vacuuming flange made of mild steel (preferably stainless steel to reflect the outstanding permeation resistance.

For architectural reasons, it can be applied to steel cover plates and other materials, for example wood, stone, plasterboard, plaster surfaces etc.

From a statics perspective, a VIS is a system of two tension members (shell 1 and 2) without its own bending stiffness and a shear-flexible core (supporting core material), which are connected physically together in shear, fixed in the evacuated state by atmospheric pressure.

Due to the vacuum, the structural behaviour of the three individual layers is changed to a system with a significant bending stiffness.

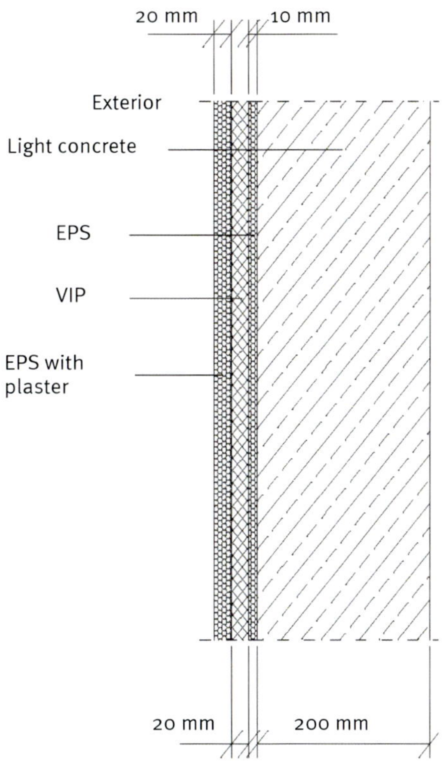

621

621 Thicknesses of only 20 mm of the high performance vacuum insulation panel is required for west facade of Kindergarten Plappersnut in Wismar, Wollensak architects
622 Picture of a VIP element
623 Vacuum insolation for ground floor renewing of Plus Energy School in Rostock, IGEL-Institut

622

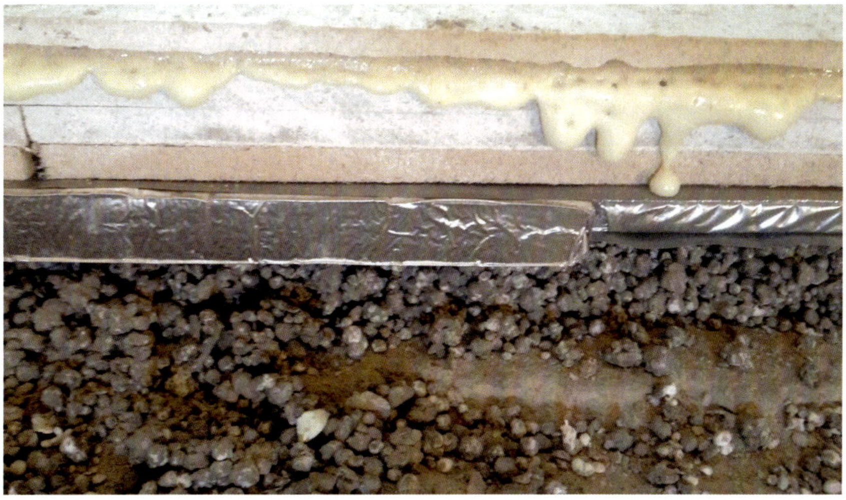

623

11.4 Projects – building

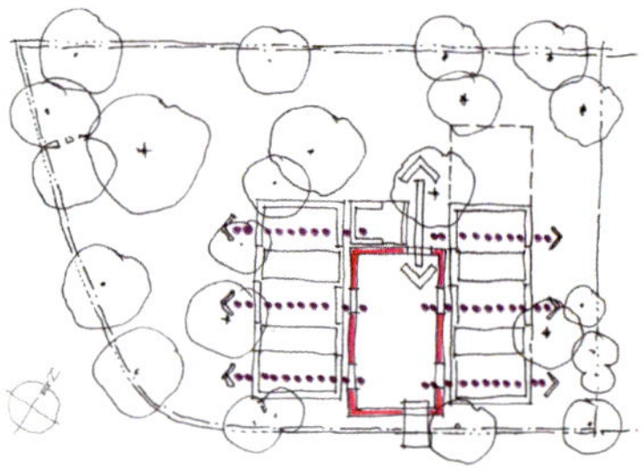

624

Architects
IGEL-Institut, Wismar

Planning
2005

624 Site plan of the eco – kindergarten with the concept of different view possibilities and relationships
625 The design concept in steps – the envelope of the existing building is kept, the former outside walls change to the interior walls of the unheated courtyard space covered with light foil construction placed on the existing building, the new construction of nursery borders to the east side and the kindergarten groups and kitchen rooms borders the west side

11.4.3 Eco-kindergarten: Renovation and extension of kindergarten, Stadtweide Rostock

The concept is a small kindergarten with a pleasant atmosphere in the middle of nature, where children and parents can feel comfortable.

The project's focus is on the mediation of natural and environmental topics.

The space conditions also enables the treatment of integrating children.

The main ecological concepts:

- resource-saving design
- recycling and reuse of the existing building and elements
- new construction – light construction and minimal material use (wood frame construction)
- compact building construction
- as little technology as possible
- use of high quality and efficient technology (e.g. ventilation, heating, photovoltaics for power generation)
- rainwater use
- passive solar energy use
- friendly treatment of surrounding
- all trees are kept
- environmental education
- use of natural materials
- natural garden
- small animals treatment
- nutrition-balanced kitchen
- familiar community
- working with eco-farmers
- pedagogic concept based on experience, curiosity, appreciation of nature, recognizing the consequences of own actions, education for activity, initiative, responsibility and energy awareness

The building concept is to use the bones of the existing building. The outside walls, windows and doors are kept as a part of the whole concept. They act as an energy storage mass for the building. The resulting courtyard is covered with a transparent foil roof at a height of 6 m.

This climatic buffer zone is heated by solar radiation and the passive energy gains supports the energy cycle of building. The walls are created from clay plates in the lower level and from wood panels (for acoustical requirements) in the upper level.

The children experience the large courtyard space through the main entrance. From the courtyard, they can enter the group rooms. In addition to energy saving, the courtyard is also a valuable space for children to experience, play and touch.

The educational value is experienced via warm rooms of group spaces adjacent to the courtyard. It is an additional life space, supporting a higher quality of educational processes.

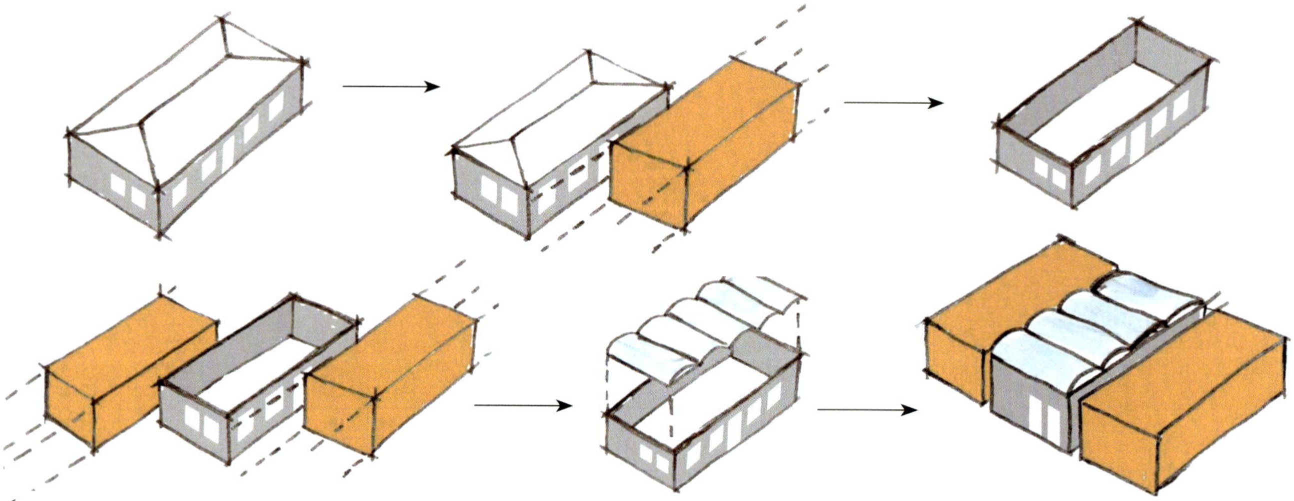

625

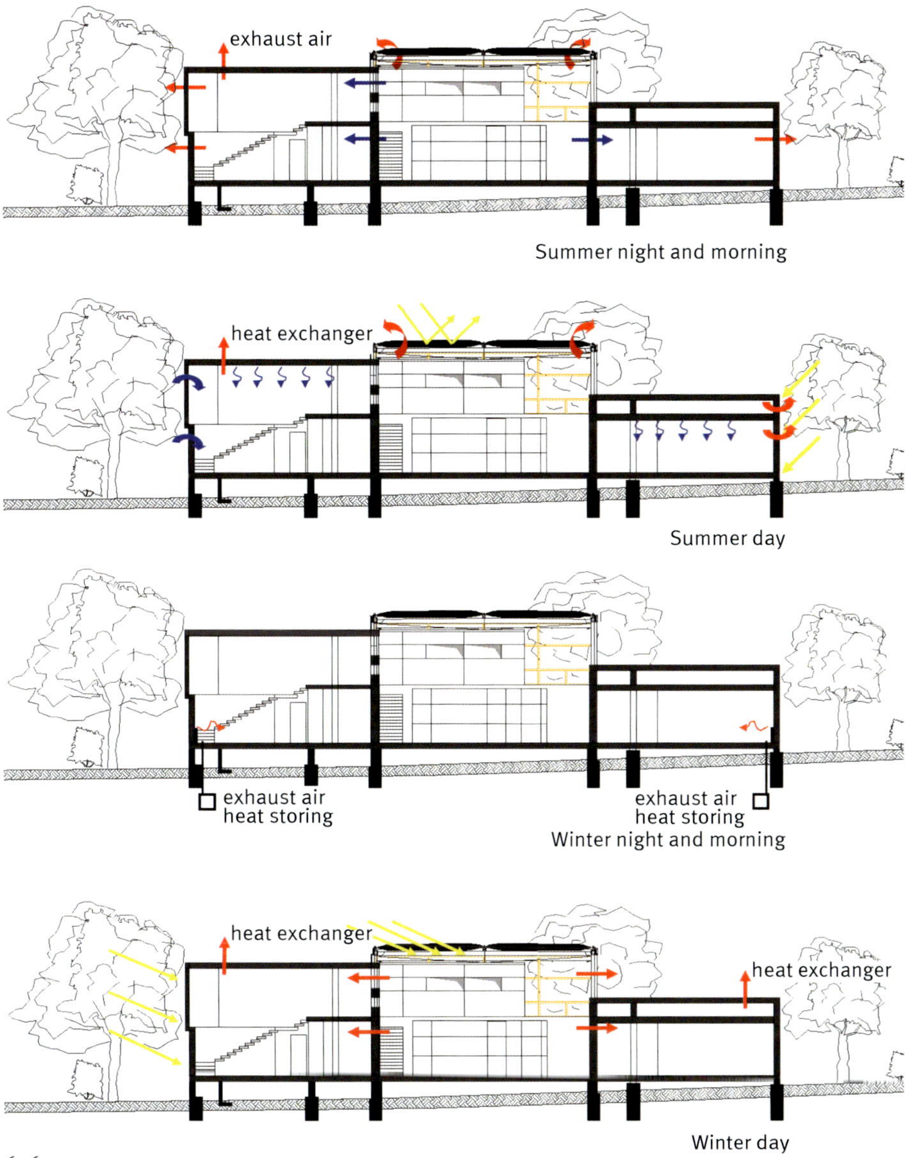

626

626 The energy concept sections – winter day and winter night, summer day and summer night
627 The final visualisation of eco – kindergarten in Stadtweide Rostock

627

11.4 Projects – building

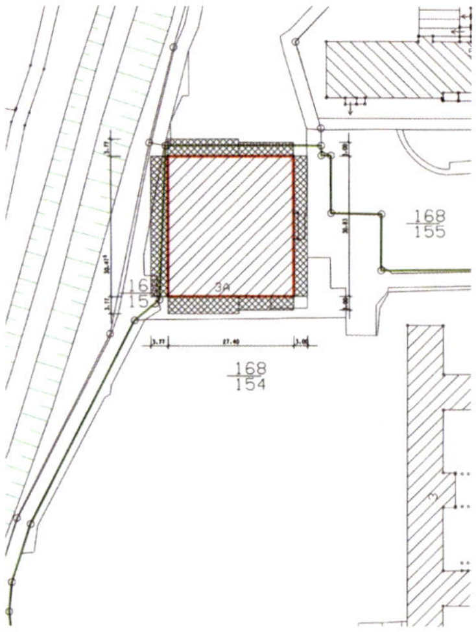

628

Architects

IGEL-Institut, Wismar

11.4.4 Energy plus concept: Sporting hall and youth club, Rostock Schmarl

The existing sporting hall building in Schmarl Rostock is in very bad condition (functional, energy, architectonic). The building envelope is not thermally insulated, the surface/volume ratio is poor, there is high transmission, and there are ventilation losses in winter and overheating in summer. The building technology is outdated. The building has a high heat energy demand, primary energy need and also high operational costs.

The goals are:

- reduction of operational costs
- reduction of energy demand
- reduction of primary energy need
- architectural quality
- variable usage surfaces
- ecological building construction
- CO_2 neutral

Energy concept:

- controlled natural ventilation
- heat recovery
- use of earth temperature
- passive solar energy use through skylights
- active solar energy use through solar thermal collectors, photovoltaics, ORC for warm water and power
- controlled building technology
- compact building form (A/V ratio)
- thermal insulation of building envelope

Input

Solar gains: roof and window openings, solar thermal collectors
Internal gains:
Heat from people and technology
Primary energy: Distance heating gas CHP
Power: eco power from city network
Process gains:
ORC with solar thermal collectors
Environmental gains: Air earth exchanger

Use

Heating: 90 % with fresh air from earth exchanger, 10 % from distance heating through ceiling radiators
Cooling: cold fresh air from earth exchanger
Artificial light: 90 % ORC with solar thermal collectors, 10 % eco-power
Warm water: 90 % ORC with solar thermal collectors, 10 % distance heating

Output

Ventilation: individual controlled ventilation
Transmission through building envelope: high compactness
Building technology losses: Piping for fluids and air
Conversion losses: artificial light

629

628 The site plan settlement of sporting hall and youth club – Rostock Schmarl – existing situation
629 Energy balance
630 The design of the sporting hall and youth club – outside image with the wooden facade, roof ETFE foil and roof photovoltaic foil covering

630

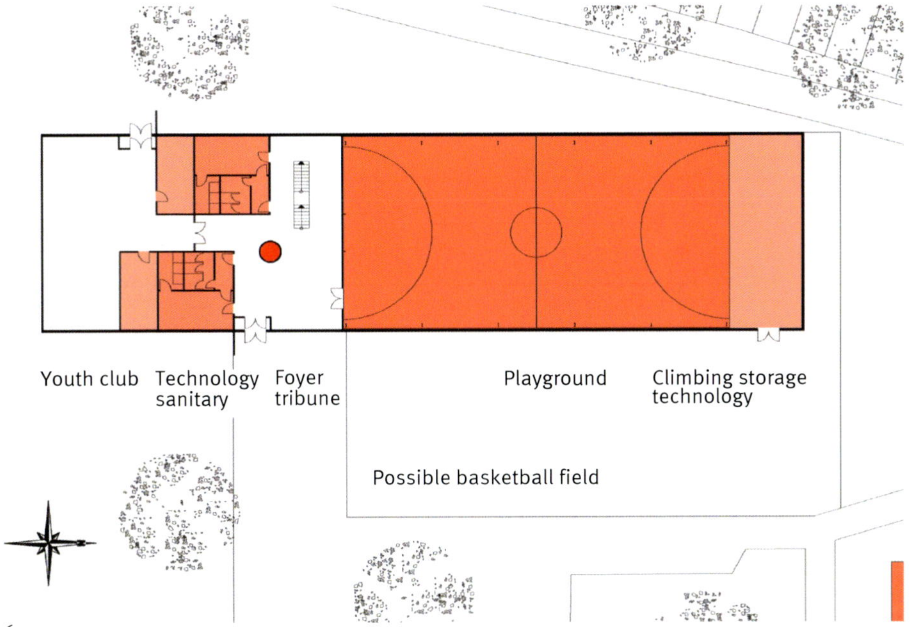

631

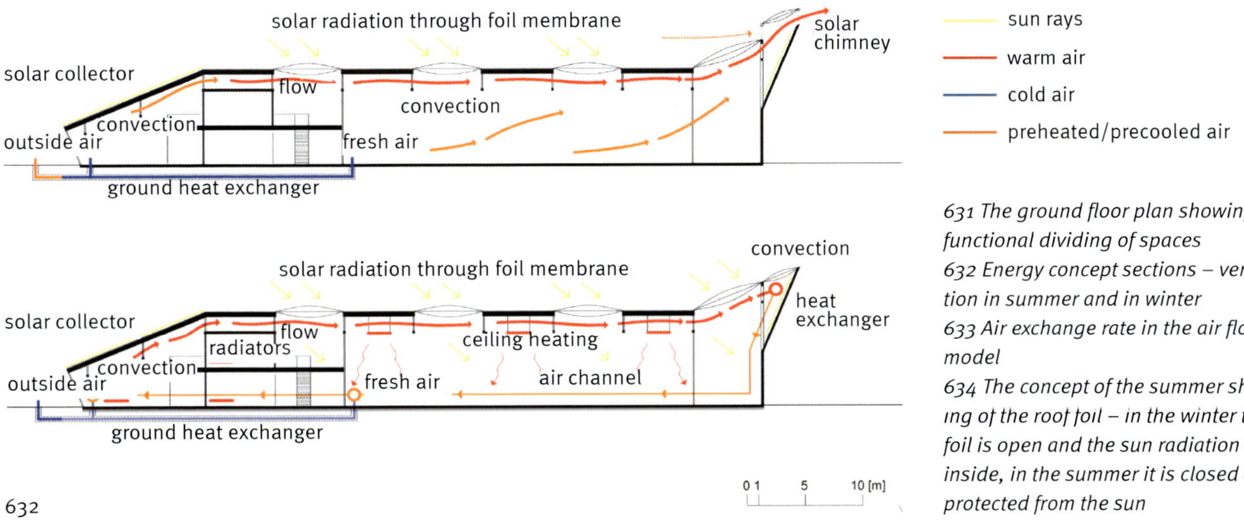

632

631 The ground floor plan showing the functional dividing of spaces
632 Energy concept sections – ventilation in summer and in winter
633 Air exchange rate in the air flow model
634 The concept of the summer shading of the roof foil – in the winter the foil is open and the sun radiation is let inside, in the summer it is closed and protected from the sun

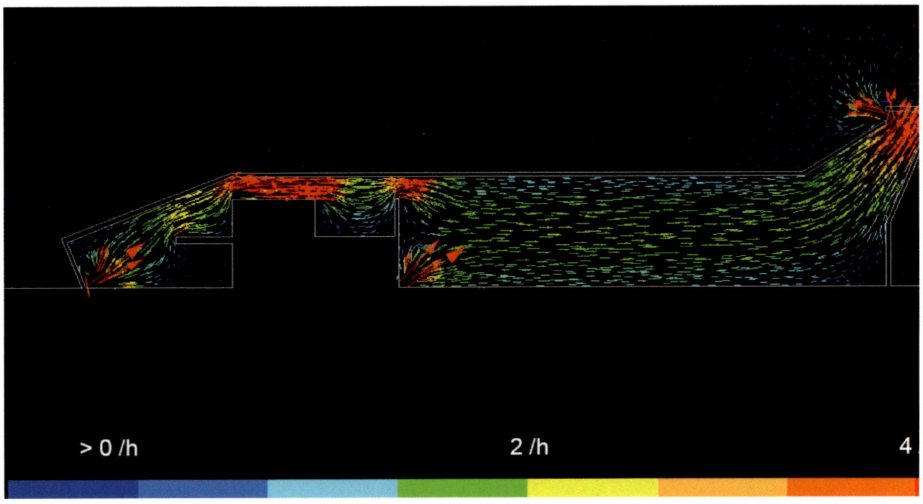

633

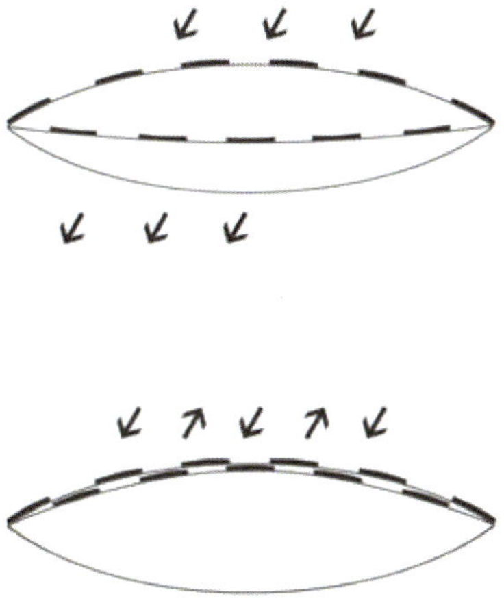

634

11.4 Projects – building

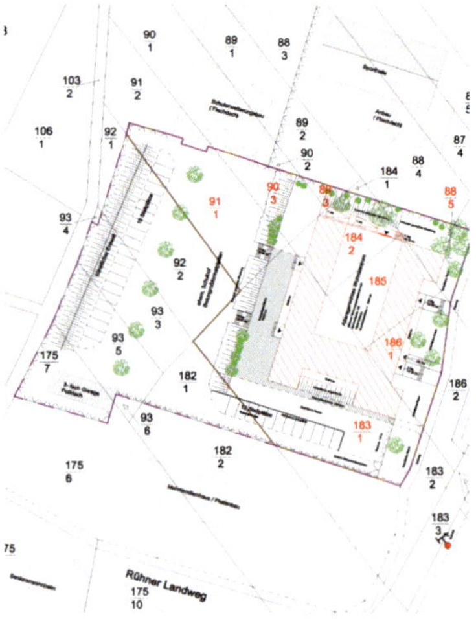

635

Architects
IGEL-Institut, Wismar

Planning
09/2009 – 08/2011

635 Site plan of the senior residence
636 Schematic of the concept – partial demolition and creation of atrium
637 Ground floor plan with common use areas in middle courtyard
638 Visualisation of the facade design
639 Visualisation of the atrium

11.4.5 Sustainable renovation and conversion: Senior residence in class rooms, Bützow

Reuse and redevelopment of the former prefabricated Regional School "Käthe Kollwitz" (from 1970) into a senior's residential centre, including commercial use and community facilities. This is due to the current political, economical and ecological situation.

As a part of an integrated planning model, the following project shows how the existing buildings of Käthe Kollwitz School can be converted sensibly in both an economical and ecological sense.

General goals

- higher technical equipment
- upgrade of the building's static substance use, and changed for the new purpose
- energy renovation of the building envelope to comply with the new EnEV regulation
- use of ecological materials

The number of inhabitants is decreasing in Bützow each year; however, the proportion of seniors is growing. Seniors make up more than one quarter of the inhabitants in the town. The number of children and young people in school is very small. This results in empty school buildings that are no longer used anymore because of the demographic change.

The existing school building is partially renovated and divided into two main 4-storey buildings connected by two 3-storey buildings. The building has a good structure and interior space and is also located between the residential and recreation area.

The project aims to meet the demands of a senior-friendly housing complex with a balanced and individually customized care plan for the immediate residential area and the entire region in and around Bützow. The goal is to create high-quality yet affordable senior housing.

The integration of commercial space and community facilities responds to the needs of elderly people while further improving the site-based care of residents. Due to the formation of the new residential centre, an element of potential future urban development will also be pursued.

Within the courtyard, an intermediate climate zone is established for functional use as well as energy gains. The additional space creates a liveable courtyard, an extended lounge, resident employment and communication facilities and also spaces for the caregivers and visitors. It is a valuable addition to the individual residential units, creating a weather-independent space in the centre of the building.

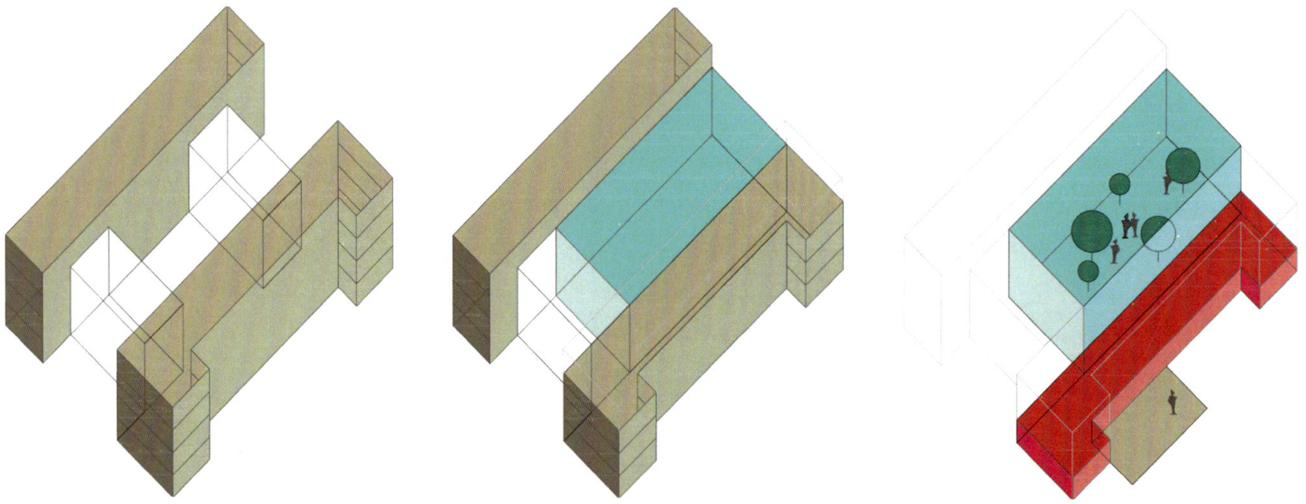

636

new walls
existing walls
daycare station
services doctors
common areas
flats

637

638

639

11.4 Projects – building

640

Architects
IGEL-Institut, Wismar

Planning
2013

640 Site plan of the kindergarten
641 Thermal picture – shows the main thermal problems and heat bridges of the existing kindergarten
642 Recycling concept – the demolished crushed concrete from corridors will be used as facade cladding in form of gabions, the old radiators and lamps will be also reused

11.4.6 4 Save standard renovation: Kindergarten "Kunterbunt", Sassnitz

This sustainable renovation project of a prefabricated building (similar building type as kindergarten "Plappernut" and "Sonnenschein") follows the 4 save standard – land saving, energy saving, material saving and water saving. The key to the project's success is recycling.
The existing building and room structure has many advantages – two storey building, rooms with daylight from two sides and with cross ventilation possibilities. Disadvantages include poor consistency of existing building with no architectural quality, unwelcoming entrance area, lack of larger multipurpose rooms, lack of orientation and a lack of visual internal/external references. The room and building scales are not appropriate for children. The building also has energy problems – high transmission losses, bad thermal protection, large outer wall surface area – small space volume generates quick heating in summer and quick cooling in winter. High window percentage creates glare and overheating. Necessary ventilation leads to heat losses, the structural is in poor condition and the building's technology is outdated. Therefore, the operation requirements and costs are extremely high. Also, the pedagogic concept is not respected in the building, the spaces are ugly, impersonal, inflexible, and there is no possibility to identify with the building.

The main goals for the renovation are:

- improve A/V ratio through compact building form – courtyard as buffer zone
- improve thermal insulation – lowering of transmission heat loss
- better functional possibilities – new additional intersecting areas, e.g. through new courtyard
- support of residential quarters
- better orientation in the building and stronger identity of user
- lowering of primary energy demand and operational costs
- heat recovery and passive/active solar energy use
- active solar energy usage through collector system and solar ice storage system
- lowering of overheating in summer through sun protection and natural air conditioning
- optimization of building technology
- new design of outside envelope with use of existing elements
- exemplar to other similar type kindergartens
- the excavated soil needed for new foundation reused on the building site as landscape-forming element
- use of photovoltaics and earth warm energy
- green facade

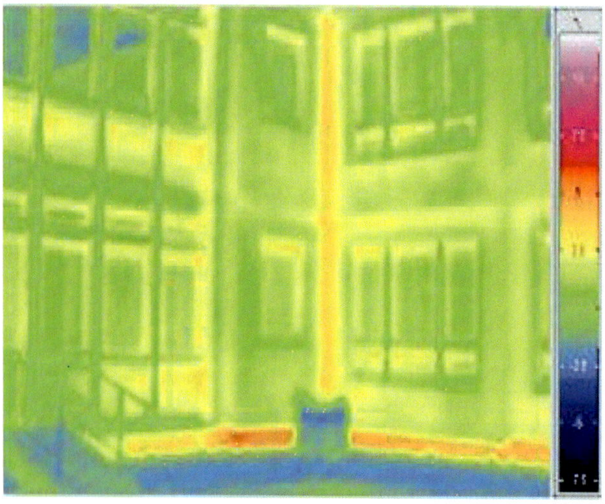

641

642

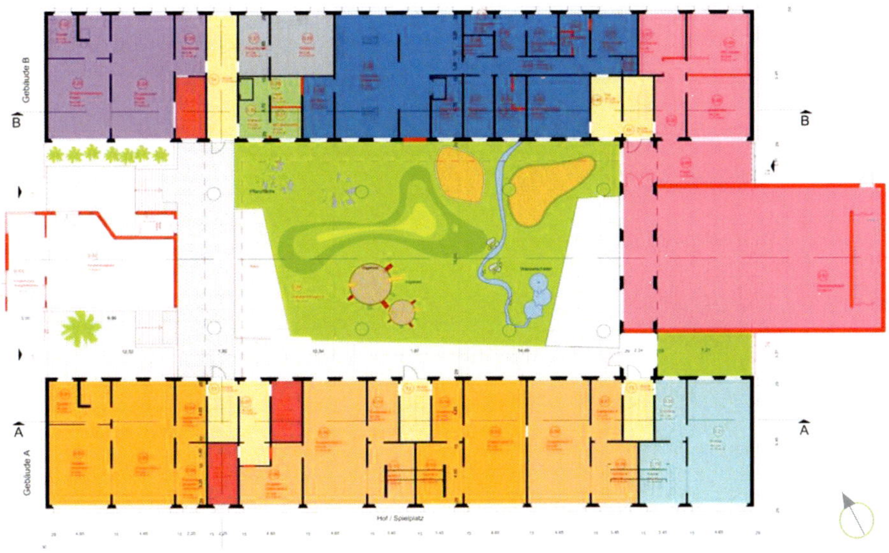

643

643 *The ground plan achieved through demolition of corridors in the middle, keeping the two side wings with classrooms and creating the new multifunctional room and buffer courtyard area with solar chimney in the middle space*
644 *Section of the kindergarten – the solar chimney has a second function as an elevator*
645 *Energy concept of the kindergarten*

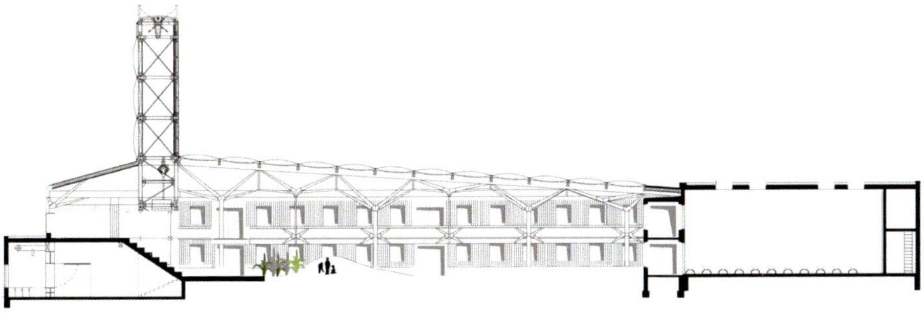

644

sun rays
warm air
cold air
preheated/precooled air

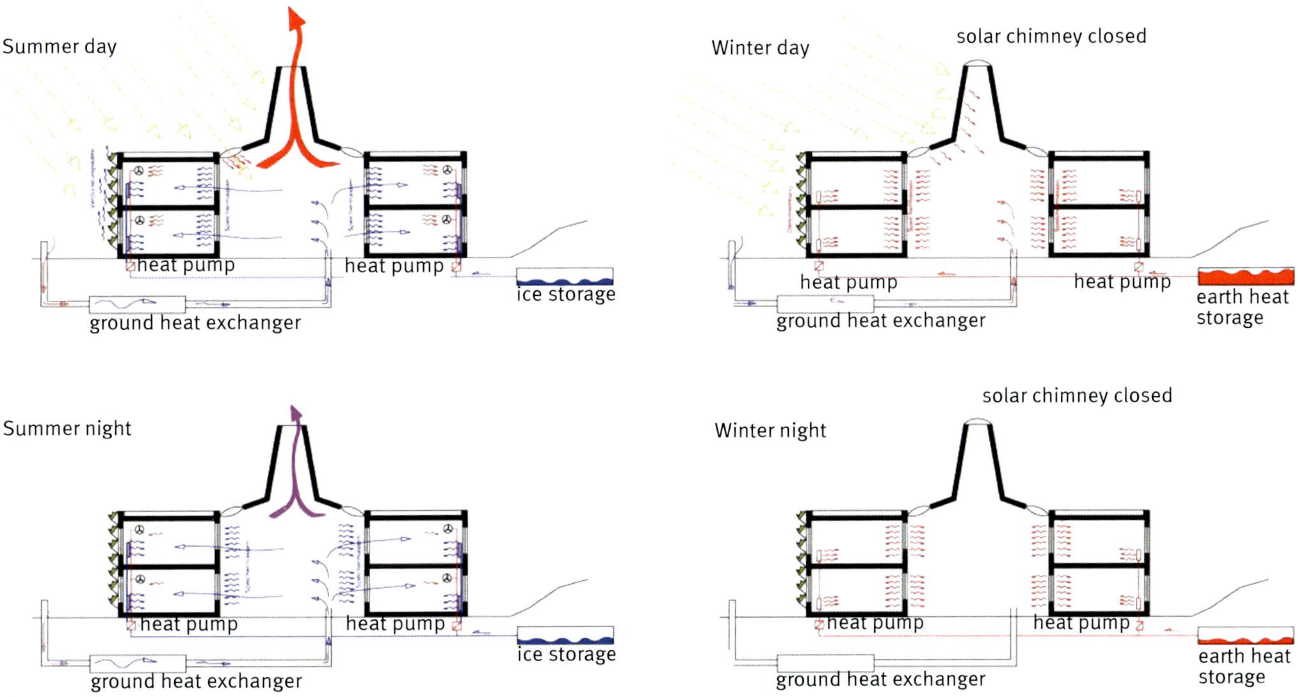

645

11.5 Summary

The history of architecture has continuously evolved and is often characterized by various styles and design methods. The austere and simple compositions alternate with pompous styles, depending on the social characteristics of the times.

Even traditional architecture is characterized by sustainable methods, but consciously sustainable design has recently occurred concurrently with the financial and resource crisis. A look at the recent history of architecture, specifically at the end of the massive post-modernism period of the 80s shows us clearly for the first time the common features of crisis and sustainability. At the beginning of the crisis-ridden 90s, the British high Tec and Scandinavian eco-house emerged.

At that time, the former began to technically toughen up the building envelope and the first solar cells and wind turbines on houses were sighted. The protagonists of that time were people like Richard Rogers, Norman Foster, Renzo Piano, who all sought to work closely with engineers.

The latter insulated houses with extremely thick walls and used intensive green roofs turned to the sun. An architect from Freiburg, Rolf Disch, even made one of his buildings rotatable so that it could follow the course of the sun like a sunflower.

The current period, which is starting to be characterized by sustainability, is also bringing new aesthetics into architecture, such as simple shapes, local materials, no false standards, autonomy and project development in the context of the policy, while taking into account the location and task.

Examples in this chapter show that a sustainable building designed in accordance to the principles of life cycle planning does not reflect a clear architectural aesthetic style.
A sustainable building arrises from the process of a certain method, where the surrounding is considered as a main influence on the building. The architectural aesthetic is then a result of the developing process. Therefore, sustainable building looks different in Germany than in China, but can also vary between two different locations in the same city.
Still, there is a possibility to find similarities in such projects, as opposed to formal architectural projects, e.g. in the approach with materials, technology and colour.

Thereby, durable architectural aesthetics result, specially developed for the location.
Likewise, a sensitive method is common to the projects, that is not manifested in a formal solitaire aesthetics, but is gently designed up to scale with user-friendly aspects.

646 Sustainable architecture can have similarities, but speaks with different dialects in different regions and with different languages in different countries

Abbreviations

General

AG (Arbeitsgemeinschaft) – working group
approx. – approximately
BIM – Building Information Modeling
BIPV – Building Integrated Photovoltaic
BKI (Baukostenindex) – Building Costs Index
BMS – Building Management System
CAD – Computer-Aided Design
CA (in German VF) – Communication Area
CCS – Carbon Capture and Storage
CE mark – conformity marking for a product
CFA (in German KGF) – Construction Floor Area
CFD – Computational Fluid Dynamics
CG – Cost Group
CHP (in German BHKW) – Combined heat and power
DALY – Disability-Adjusted Life Year
E – East
Eco – Ecological
EE (Erneurbare Energien) – renewable energies
EEA – European Economic Area
EFG – Edge-defined Film-fed Growth
e.g. (exempli gratia) – for example
EPS – Expanded Polystyrene
equiv. – equivalent
etc. (Et cetera) – and other things
EU – European Union
e.V. (Eingetragener Verein) – registered association
FA – Floor Area
FSI – Fluid-Structure Interaction
GbR (Gesellschaft bürgerlichen Rechts) – civil law association
gbXML – the Green Building XML schema
GFA (in German BGF) – Gross Floor Area
GmbH (Gesellschaft mit beschränkter Haftung) – limited liability company
GRV (in German BRI) – Gross Room Volume
GUI – Graphical User Interface
HFA – Heated Floor Area
HVAC – heating, ventilation, and air conditioning
IDA – indoor air category
IEQ – Indoor Environmental Quality
i.e. (id est) – that is
Inc. – Incorporation
Incl. – Including
inter alia – among other things
LED – Light-Emitting Diode
Low-E – Low-Emissivity
LP (Leistungsphase) – phase of performance
Ltd. – Private Company Limited by Shares
max. – maximum
MENA – Middle East, North Africa
micro (micrós) – small
M-V (Mecklenburg-Vorpommern) – Mecklenburg-West Pomerania
N – North
NE – Northeast
NFA (in German NGF) – Net Floor Area
No – Number
NRV (in German NRI) – Net Room Volume
NW – Northwest
NZ – New Zealand
ORC – Organic Rankine Cycle
OSB – Oriented Strand Board
PV – Photovoltaic
ref – reference
R&D – Research and Development
S – South
SE – Southeast
SMEs – Small and medium enterprises
SW – Southwest
TFA (in German TF) – Technical Floor Area
TG – Task Group
UAE – United Arab Emirates
UFA (in German NF) – Usable Floor Area
UK – United Kingdom
USA, U.S. – United States of America
VIP – Vacuum Insulated Panel
VIS – Vacuum Insulated Sandwich
W – West
XPS – Extruded Polystyrene
2D – two dimensional
3D – three dimensional
& – and
§ – paragraph, section sign
® – registered sign

Building physics

A – surface area [m²]
AP – Acidification Potential [kg SO_2-Equiv./m^2_{NFA}a]
A/V ratio – surface-area-to-volume ratio
C – cooling energy [kWh/a]
Ca – capacity [m/d, 1 m = 1,000 mm]
DF – daylight factor [-]
E – energy [kWh]
EP – Eutrophication Potential [kg PO_4-Equiv./m^2_{NFA}a]
fp – primary energy factor [-]
GWP – Global warming potential [kg CO_2-Equiv./m^2_{NFA}a]
h – height [m]
H – overall heat loss [W]

HT – heat loss due to transmission [W]
HT-value – overall heat transmission coefficient [W/m²K]
HV – heat loss caused by ventilation [W]
l – construction span [mm]
λ-value (lambda value) – thermal conductivity [W/mK]
m – construction condensation [kg/m²]
μ-value (mi) – diffusion resistance factor [-]
N – number, amount (e.g. N_m – amount of material)
n_{50} – air exchange rate, related to heated building volume [h^{-1}]
ODP – Ozone Depletion Potential [kg R_{11}-Equiv./m^2_{NFA}a]
P_{el} – electrical capacity [W/h]
PE – primary energy [MJ/kg, 1 kWh = 3.6 MJ]
PE_{nre} – primary energy non renewable [MJ/kg, 1 kWh = 3.6 MJ]
PE_{re} – primary energy renewable [MJ/kg, 1 kWh = 3.6MJ]
POCP – Photochemical Ozone Creation Potential [kg C_2H_4-Equiv./m^2_{NFA}a]
PW – potable water demand [l/a]
Ψ-value (psi) – linear thermal transmittance [W/mK]
Q – overall heat gains [W]
Q_e – final energy demand [kWh/a, 1 kWh = 3.6 MJ]
Q_h – heating demand [kWh/a, 1 kWh = 3.6 MJ]
Q_I – internal heat gains [W]
Q_P – primary energy demand [kWh/a, 1 kWh = 3.6 MJ]
Q_S – solar heat gains [W]
Q_w – warm water demand [kWh/a, 1 kWh = 3.6 MJ]
q – fresh air supply [m³/h]
q_{50} – air permeability, related to building envelope area [m/h]
R – annual rainfall [mm]
R_a – colour rendering index [-]
RC – runoff coefficient [%]
RW – rainwater water amount [l]
ρ (rho) – volumetric mass density [kg/m³]
S – sun entry parameter [-]
T – reverberation time [s]
t – time [1 h = 3600 s]
U-value – heat transmission coefficient [W/m²K]
ΔU_{WB} – thermal bridge surcharge [W/m²K]
V – Volume [m³]
Val – Value (e.g. $Val_{öko}$ - value from ökobau.dat)
VOC – Volatile Organic Compound [μg/m³]
w – width [m]
W_{el} – power demand [kWh/a, 1 kWh = 3.6 MJ]

Chemicals and Units

a – year (unit of time, 1 a = 365.25 d)
a-Si – amorphous Silicon
CCS – Carbon Capture and Storage
CdTe – Cadmium Telluride
CO_2 – carbon dioxide, absolute CO_2 concentration in the indoor air [ppm]
$CuInSe_2$ (or CIS) – Copper Indium Diselenide
C_2H_4 – ethylene
d – day
GaAs – Gallium Arsenide
h – hour (unit of time, 1 h = 3600 s)
h^{-1} – per hour
ha – hectare (a metric unit of area, 1 ha = 10,000 m²)
HDPE – High-Density Polyethylene
K – Kelvin (unit of measurement for temperature, 247.15 K = 1°C)
kg – kilogram (the base unit of mass, 1 kg = 1,000 g)
kWh – kilowatt hour (a unit for energy, 1 kWh = 1,000 Wh or 3,6 MJ)
l – litre (a unit of volume, 1 l = 10-3 m³)
lx – lux (a unit of light strength)
m – meter (fundamental unit of length)
m² – square meter (a unit of area defined as the area of a square whose sides measure exactly one meter)
m³ – cubic meter (a unit of volume defined as volume of a cube with edges 1 m in length)
MJ – Megajoule (a unit for energy, 1 kWh = 3,6 MJ)
NO – nitric oxide
NO_2 – nitrogen dioxide
NO_x – generic term for the mono-nitrogen oxides NO and NO_2
Pa – Pascal, unit of pressure
PO_4 – phosphate
PU – polyurethane
PVC – polyvinylchlorid
R_{11} – trichlorofluoromethane
s – second
SO_2 – sulphur dioxide
W – Watt (derived unit of power, measures the rate of en energy conversion or transfer (1 GW=1,000 MW, 1 MW = 1,000W)
°C – degree Celsius (unit of measurement for temperature)
% – percent sign (a number of ratio as a fraction of 100)
€ – Euro
$ – Dollar

Abbreviations

Institutions

AgPR – AG Flooring Recycling
BBR (Bundesamt für Bauwesen und Raumordnung) – Federal Institute for Building and Regional Planning, Germany
BBSR (Bundesinstitut für Bau-, Stadt- und Raumforschung) – Federal Office for Building, Urban Affairs and Spatial Research, Germany
BDA (Bund Deutscher Architekten) – Association of German Architects
BMBF (Bundesministerium für Bildung und Forschung) – Federal Ministry for Education and Research, Germany
BMU (Bundesministerium für Umwelt, Naturschutz, Bau und Reaktorsicherheit) – Federal Ministry for the Environment, Nature Conservation and Nuclear Safety, Germany
BMVBS (Bundesministerium für Verkehr, Bau und Stadtentwicklung) – Federal Ministry of Transport, Building and Urban Affair, Germany
BMVg (Bundesministerium der Verteidigung) – Federal Ministry of Defense, Germany
BMWI or BMWE (Bundesministerium für Wirtschaft und Energie) – Federal Ministry of Economic Affairs and Energy, Germany
BÜWO - Housing Association in Bützow, Germany
CEN (Comité Européen de Normalisation) – European Committee for Standardisation
CENELEC (Comité Européen de Normalisation Èlectrotechnique) – European Committee for Electrotechnical Standardisation
DBU (Deutsche Bundesstiftung Umwelt) – German Federal Trust Fund Environment
DENA (Deutsche Energie-Agentur) – German Energy Agency
DESTATIS (Statistisches Bundesamt Deutschland) – Federal Statistical Office Germany
DGNB (Deutsche Gesellschaft für Nachhaltiges Bauen) – German Sustainable Building Council (GeSBC)
DIN (Deutsches Institut für Normung) – German Institute for Standardisation
DIN EN (Deutsches Institut für Normung, Europäische Norm) – German Institute for Standardisation, European Norm
DIN V (Deutsches Institut für Normung, Vornorme) – German Institute for Standardisation, Prestandard
DLR (Deutsches Zentrum für Luft- und Raumfahrt) – German Centre for Aerospace
EC – European Commission
EC – European Community
ECOBINE – Ecological Building Net
EDUCATE – Environmental Design in University Curricula and Architectural Training in Europe
EEC – European Economic Community
EFRE (Europäischer Fonds für regionale Entwicklung) – European Regional Development Fund
EG (Europäische Gemeinschaft) – European Community
ENSAN – Energy Efficient Refurbishment of Buildings
EOTA – European Organisation for Technical Approvals
EP – European Parliament
EPA U.S. – U.S. Environmental Protection Agency
FfE – Forschungsstelle für Energiewirtschaft
FNR (Fachagentur für Nachwachsende Rohstoffe e.V.) – Foundation for Renewable Resources e.V
Fraunhofer IBP (Fraunhofer-Institut für Bauphysik) – Fraunhofer Institute for Building Physics, Germany
Frauenhofer ISE (Fraunhofer-Institut für Solare Energiesysteme) – Fraunhofer Institute for Solar Energy Systems, Germany
FSC – Forest Stewardship council
GBC – Green Building Council
GBLMO – Green Building Label Management Office, China
HS (Hochschule) – College, University
IBEC – Institute for Building Environment and Energy Conservation, Japan
iBR – Shenzhen Institute of Building Research, China
IGEL-Institut (Institut für Gebäude-, Energie- und Lichtplanung) – Institute for Building, Energy and Lighting Design, Wismar
IHK zu Schwerin (Industrie- und Handelskammer) – Chamber of Industry and Commerce to Schwerin
JSBC – Japan Sustainable Building Consortium
ISO – International Organisation for Standardisation
KfW (Kreditanstalt für Wiederaufbau) – Loan for rebuilding, Germany
MLIT – Ministry of Land, Infrastructure, Transport and Tourism, Japan
MOHURD – Ministry of Housing and Urban-Rural Development, China
NASA – National Aeronautics and Space Administration
RAL (Reichs-Ausschuß für Lieferbedingungen) – German Institute for Quality Assurance and Certification
SOWARLA (Solare Wasserreinigungsanlage) – Solar Water Cleaning Plant Technology
SRIBS – Shanghai Research Institute of Building Sciences, China
SYJU – Shenyang Jianzhu University, China
TRCA – Toronto and Region Conservation Authority, US
TU (Technische Universität) – University of Technology
VDI (Verein Deutscher Ingenieure) – Association of German Engineers
VdL (Verband der Lackindustrie e.V.) – Association of Paint Industry
WorldGBC – World Green Building Council
WWF – World Wildlife Fund

Documents, standards, regulations, instruments

BBodSchG (Gesetz zum Schutz vor schädlichen Bodenveränderungen und zur Sanierung von Altlasten) – The Federal Land Protection and Residual Contamination Ordinance, Germany
BGG (Behindertengleichstellungsgesetz) – Law for the equalization of disabled persons, Germany
BNB (Bewertungssystem Nachhaltiges Bauen) – Rating System for Sustainable Building, Germany
BREEAM – Building Research Establishment Environmental Assessment Method
CASBEE – Comprehensive Assessment System for Building Environmental Efficiency
CoC – Certificate of Conformity
CPD – Construction Products Directive
CPR – The EU Construction Products Regulation
DGNB (Deutsches Gütesiegel Nachhaltiges Bauen) – The DGNB German Sustainable Building Certificate
DIN 18024 (Barrierefreies Bauen) – Norm: Barrier-free construction, Part 1: Streets, squares, paths, public transport and parks and playgrounds; Planning Principles, Germany (DIN 18070 is in preparation as replacement for DIN 18024-1)
DIN 18040 (Barrierefreies Bauen) – Norm: Barrier-free construction, Part 1: Public buildings, Part 2: Residential buildings, Germany
DIN 276 (Kosten im Bauwesen) – Norm: Building costs
DIN 277 (Grundflächen und Rauminhalte von Bauwerken im Hochbau) – Norm: Surface areas and volumes of structures in building construction, Germany
DIN 4108 (Wärmeschutz im Hochbau) – Norm: Heat insulation in buildings, Germany
DIN 4108 supplement 2 (Wärmeschutz und Energie-Einsparung in Gebäuden – Wärmebrücken– Planungs- und Ausführungsbeispiele) – Norm: Thermal protection and energy saving in buildings – thermal bridges – design and construction examples, Germany
DIN 4109 (Schallschutz im Hochbau) – Norm: Sound insulation in buildings, Germany
DIN EN 12207 (Fenster und Türen – Luftdurchlässigkeit – Klassifizierung) – Norm: Windows and doors – Air permeability – Classification, EU
DIN EN 13829 (Wärmetechnisches Verhalten von Gebäuden – Bestimmung der Luftdurchlässigkeit) – Thermal performance of buildings – Determination of the permeability to air of buildings, EU
DIN EN 15251 (Eingangsparameter für das Raumklima zur Auslegung und Bewertung der Energieeffizienz von Gebäuden – Raumluftqualität, Temperatur, Licht und Akustik) – Indoor environmental input parameters for design and assessment of energy performance of buildings addressing indoor air quality, thermal environment, lighting and acoustics, EU
DIN EN ISO 14040 – „Environmental management – Life cycle assessment – Principles and framework, EU
DIN EN ISO 14044 – Environmental management – Life cycle assessment– Requirements and guidelines, EU
DIN V 18599 (Energetische Bewertung von Gebäuden) – Energy efficiency of buildings (11 parts), Germany
DoP – Declaration of Performance
EADs – European Assessment Documents
EEG (Erneuerbare Energien Gesetz) – Renewable Energy Sources Act, Germany
EEWärmeG (Erneuerbare Energien Wärme Gesetz) – Heat Act, Germany
EnEV (Energieeinsparverordnung) – Energy Conservation Ordinance, Germany
EPD – Environmental Product Declaration
ES-Bau (Entscheidungsunterlage Bau) – ES-building (decision support construction)
ESD Guide – Ecologically Sustainable Design Guide
ETAs – European Technical Assessments
EU SDS – EU Strategy for Sustainable Development
EW-Bau (Entwurfsunterlage Bau) – EW-construction (design documents construction)
GISCODE (Gefahrstoff-Informationssystem) – Hazardous Materials Information System
GISBAU – (Gefahrstoff-Informationssystem der Bauberufsgenossenschaften) – Hazardous Materials Information System of the German Builders' Trade Association
hENs – harmonised European product standards
HOAI (Honorarordnung für Architekten und Ingenieure) – Honorarium rules for architects and engineers, Germany
HTS (Hightech-Strategie für Deutschland) – The High-Tech Strategy for Germany
LCA – Life Cycle Assessment
LCC – Life Cycle Costing
LCI – Life Cycle Inventory
LEED – Leadership in Energy and Environmental Design
PEFC – Programme for the Endorsement of Forest Certification Schematics
PHPP (Passivhaus Projektierungs-Paket) – Passive House Planning Package, Germany
RBBau (Richtlinien für die Durchführung von Bauaufgaben des Bundes) – Guidelines for the implementation of federal construction projects, Germany
RIS (Regionale Innovationsstrategie) – Regional Innovation Strategy
ROG (Raumordnungsgesetz) – Spatial Planning Act
SiGe (Sicherheits- und Gesundheitsschutz) – Safety and Health Protection
UNEP – United Nations Environment Programme
WECOBIS – Web-based Ecological Building Material Information System
WSVO (Wärmeschutzverordnung) – Thermal insulation ordinance, Germany

List of figures

Key words, energy standards and norms

1 *Lampe, S.;* Wismar , Germany 12/2013

2 *Own representation;* Wismar, Germany 2014

3 *Own representation;* Wismar, Germany 2014

4 *Own representation, inspired by Passipedia;* Planning a Passive House [http://passipedia.passiv.de/passipedia_en/_media/picopen/passive_house_section_400.jpg] (20.09.2012)

5 *Own representation, inspired by Green Energy+Haus Planungsgruppe;* Nullenergiehaus [http://www.nullenergiehaus.com/download_de.php] (20.09.2012)

6 *Own representation;* Wismar, Germany 2014

7 *Klopp, E.;* Berlin, Germany 01/2012

8 *Klopp, E.;* Berlin, Germany 01/2012

9 *Own representation, inspired by BMVBS;* Energieausweis für Gebäude - nach Energieeinsparverordnung (EnEV 2009). Informationsbroschüre des Bundesministeriums für Verkehr, Bau und Stadtentwicklung. Berlin: BMVBS 01.12.2009, page 12

10 *Own representation, inspired by Netzwerk Energieberater;* Primärenergiefaktor [http://www.netzwerk-energieberater.de/wiki/Primärenergiefaktor] (20.09.2012)

11 *Own representation;* Energieausweis für Gebäude - nach Energieeinsparverordnung (EnEV 2009). Wismar, Germany 2014

12 *Own representation, inspired by Georgia Institute of Technology;* AIA Guide to Building Life Cycle Assessment in Practice. New York: American Institute of Architects 2010, page 15

13 *Own representation;* Wismar, Germany 2014

14 *Own representation, inspired by Georgia Institute of Technology;* AIA Guide to Building Life Cycle Assessment in Practice. New York: American Institute of Architects 2010, page 54

15 *Own representation, inspired by European Commission;* Lifecycle costing [http://ec.europa.eu/environment/gpp/lcc.htm] (20.08.2014)

16 *Own representation, inspired by BMVBS;* Kostensätze für Externe Kosten. Externe Kosten im Hochbau. BMVBS 10/2010, page 31

17 *Own representation;* Wismar, Germany 2014

18 *Own representation;* Wismar, Germany 2014

19 *Own representation;* Wismar, Germany 2014

20 *Own representation, inspired by DIN 277;* Wismar, Germany 2014

21 *Own representation, inspired by Grote,S.;* Spezifischer Transmissionswärmeverlust HT [http://www.daemmen-sanieren.de/fileadmin/DAM/Energie/ht.pdf] (16.05.2014)

1.0 Strategies and regulations

22 *Wollensak architects;* Wismar, Germany 2010

23 *Own representation;* Wismar, Germany 2014

24 *Student project (Baiyang, Y., Dasong, W., Yichen, Y., Zhuoya, Q);* Future City: Transforming into Wildness. Faculty of Architecture and Design, Hochschule Wismar, Germany, SS 2014

25 *Own representation;* Wismar, Germany 2014

26 *Own representation, inspired byTriplepundit;* SD Model [http://cdn5.triplepundit.com/wp-content/uploads/2010/12/Sustainable-Development-Model.jpg] (20.09.2012)

27 *Own representation, inspired by Genesisalliance corporation;* SD [http://genesisalliancecorp.com/assets/images/emerging_tech/sustainable_development_small.jpg] (on 20.09.2012)

28 *World Green Building Council;* Logo of World Green Building Council. London, United Kingdom 02/2016

29 *World Green Building Council;* The map of World Green Building Council. London, United Kingdom 02/2016

30 *Own representation;* Wismar, Germany 2014

31 *Institute for Building Environment and Energy Conservation (IBEC)* Secretary of Japan GreenBuild Council/Japan Sustainable Building Consortium

32 *Own representation, inspired by CASBEE ranking;* [http://blog-imgs-30-origin.fc2.com/d/a/n/dantodanto/210px-CASBEE_ranking_graph.png] (30.07.2012)

33 *Höhnk, J-H.;* Sidney, Australia 08/2015

34 *Own representation, inspired by Green Building Council Australia;* Introducing Green Star. Sidney, Australia 01/2015

35 *Own representation;* Wismar, Germany 2014

36 *Piatov, D.;* Auckland, New Zealand 11/2015

37 *Oberfrancova, L.;* Hafencity Hamburg, Germany 06/2015

38 *Fan, Y.;* Shanghai, China 09/2014

39 *German Sustainable Building Council;* Stuttgart, Germany 12/2015

40 *Own representation, inspired by DGNB;* Presentation of DGNB International. Stuttgart, Germany: DGNB 2010

41 *Own representation, inspired by DGNB;* Presentation of DGNB International. Stuttgart, Germany: DGNB 2010

42 *Own representation, inspired by DGNB;* Presentation of DGNB International. Stuttgart, Germany: DGNB 2010

43 *German Sustainable Building Council;* Stuttgart, Germany 12/2015

44 *German Sustainable Building Council;* Stuttgart, Germany 12/2015

45 *Oberfrancova, L.;* Rostock, Germany 10/2015

46 *Own representation, inspired by BNB;* Gewichtung und Bedeutungsfaktoren. BMVBS 2011_1

47 *Own representation, inspired by student presentation (Glatzel, M., Stanelle, K.);* DGNB evaluation of a new office construction in Wismar harbour, Germany. Hochschule Wismar, Faculty of Architecture and Design, Green Building class WS 2012/2013

48 *Own representation, inspired by student presentation (Glatzel, M., Stanelle, K.);* DGNB evaluation of a new office construction in Wismar harbour, Germany. Hochschule Wismar, Faculty of Architecture and Design, Green Building class WS 2012/2013

49 *Own representation, inspired by student presentation (Glatzel, M., Stanelle, K.);* DGNB evaluation of a new office construction in Wismar harbour, Germany. Hochschule Wismar, Faculty of Architecture and Design, Green Building class WS 2012/2013

50 *Own representation, inspired by student presentation (Glatzel, M., Stanelle, K.);* DGNB evaluation of a new office construction in Wismar harbour, Germany. Hochschule Wismar, Faculty of Architecture and Design, Green Building class WS 2012/2013

51 *Own representation, inspired by student presentation (Glatzel, M., Stanelle, K.);* DGNB evaluation of a new office construction in Wismar harbour, Germany. Hochschule Wismar, Faculty of Architecture and Design, Green Building class WS 2012/2013

52 *Own representation, inspired by student presentation (Glatzel, M., Stanelle, K.);* DGNB evaluation of a new office construction in Wismar harbour, Germany. Hochschule Wismar, Faculty of Architecture and Design, Green Building class WS 2012/2013

53 *Own representation, inspired by student presentation (Glatzel, M., Stanelle, K.);* DGNB evaluation of a new office construction in Wismar harbour, Germany. Hochschule Wismar, Faculty of Architecture and Design, Green Building class WS 2012/2013

54 *Own representation;* Wismar, Germany 2014

55 *Own representation, inspired by student presentation (Ribovicová, M.);* DGNB evaluation of a new office construction in Wismar harbour, Germany. Hochschule Wismar, Faculty of Architecture and Design, Green Building class WS 2012/2013

56 *Own representation, inspired by student presentation (Olexáková, M.);* DGNB evaluation of a new office construction in

Wismar harbour, Germany. Hochschule Wismar, Faculty of Architecture and Design, Green Building class WS 2012/2013

57 *Own representation;* Wismar, Germany 2014

58 *Own representation, inspired by DGNB;* Neubau Büro- und Verwaltungsgebäude. Steckbrief 18 Thermischer Komfort im Winter. DGNB: Version 2009

59 *Own representation, inspired by DGNB;* Neubau Büro- und Verwaltungsgebäude. Steckbrief 19 Thermischer Komfort im Sommer. DGNB: Version 2009

60 *Own representation, inspired by Daniels,K.;* Low-Tech Light-Tech High-Tech. Bauen in der Informationsgesellschaft. Berlin: Birkhäuser 1998, page 91

61 *Own representation, inspired by DGNB;* Neubau Büro- und Verwaltungsgebäude. Steckbrief 20 Innenraumhygiene. DGNB: V 2009

62 *Own representation, inspired by DGNB;* Neubau Büro- und Verwaltungsgebäude. Steckbrief 20 Innenraumhygiene. DGNB: V 2009

63 *Own representation, inspired by DGNB;* Neubau Büro- und Verwaltungsgebäude. Steckbrief 22 Visueller Komfort. DGNB: V 2009

64 *Own representation, inspired by DGNB;* Neubau Büro- und Verwaltungsgebäude. Steckbrief 22 Visueller Komfort. DGNB: V 2009

65 *Student presentation (Yichun, K.);* DGNB evaluation of a new office construction in Wismar harbour, Germany. Hochschule Wismar, Faculty of Architecture and Design, Green Building class WS 2012/2013

66 *Own representation;* Wismar, Germany 2014

67 *Höhnk, J-H.;* Sidney, Australia 10/2015

68 *Oberfrancová, L.;* Ribnitz-Dammgarten, Germany 10/2015

69 *Oberfrancová, L.;* Rostock, Germany 10/2015

70 *Own representation, inspired by DGNB;* Neubau Büro- und Verwaltungsgebäude. Steckbrief 30 Fahrradkomfort. DGNB: Version 2009

71 *Own representation, inspired by DGNB;* Neubau Büro- und Verwaltungsgebäude. Steckbriefe 35 Wärme- und feuchteschutztechnische Qualität der Gebäudehülle. DGNB: Version 2009

72 *Own representation, inspired by DGNB;* Neubau Büro- und Verwaltungsgebäude. Steckbriefe 35 Wärme- und feuchteschutztechnische Qualität der Gebäudehülle. DGNB: Version 2009

73 *Own representation, inspired by DGNB;* Neubau Büro- und Verwaltungsgebäude. Steckbriefe 35 Wärme- und feuchteschutztechnische Qualität der Gebäudehülle. DGNB: Version 2009

74 *Own representation;* Wismar, Germany 2014

75 *Oberfrancová, L.;* Park Lingezegen, Netherlands 07/2010

76 *Own representation;* Wismar, Germany 2014

77 *Oberfrancová, L.;* Rostock, Germany 05/2015

78 *Own representation;* Wismar, Germany 2014

79 *Own representation;* Wismar, Germany 2014

80 *Schachtschneider, S.;* Berlin, Germany 09/2014

81 *Schachtschneider, S.;* Berlin, Germany 09/2014

82 *Own representation, inspired by DGNB;* DGNB Systemgrundlagen. Nutzungsprofil Neubau Stadtquartiere. DGNB: Version 2012

83 *Wollensak, M.;* Berlin, Germany 09/2014

84 *Own representation, inspired by Criteria and Issues of Urban Planning;* Thüringen

85 *Schoenen, D.;* Freiburg, Germany

86 *Own representation;* Wismar, Germany 2014

87 *Own representation;* Wismar, Germany 2014

88 *IGEL-Institut;* Wismar, Germany 2008

89 *IGEL-Institut;* Wismar, Germany 2008

90 *Oberfrancová, L;* Hamburg, Germany 06/2015

91 *Wollensak, M.;* California, USA 08/2011

92 *European Union;* [http://www.clubofrome.at/events/2006/brussels/files/img_sustainability-strategy-2001-booklet.jpg] (10.10.2012)

93 *Worldmapper Limited;* United Kingdom

94 *Worldmapper Limited;* United Kingdom

95 *Worldmapper Limited;* United Kingdom

96 *BMU;* Guideline for Sustainable Building. Berlin: BMU 02/2016

97 *Wollensak, M.;* Dessau, Germany 11/2015

98 *Own representation, inspired by BMVBS;* Leitfaden Nachhaltiges Bauen. Berlin: BMVBS April 2013, page 47

99 *Own representation, inspired by BMVBS;* Guideline for Sustainable Building. Berlin: BMVBS January 2001, page 6

100 *BMWI, BMU;* Energy Concept for an Environmentally Sound, Reliable and Affordable Energy Supply. Berlin: BMWi, BMU 09/2010

101 *Own representation, inspired by BMWI;* Energieszenarien für ein Energiekonzept der Bundesregierung. Projekt Nr. 12/10. Basel, Köln Osnabrück: Prognos AG, EWI, GWS 08/2010, page 6

102 *Own representation, inspired by Germanwatch e.V.;* [http://germanwatch.org/klima/nes1g.jpg] (30.07.2012)

103 *BMBF;* The High-Tech Strategy for Germany. Berlin: BMBF 2006

104 *Own representation, inspired by BMBF;* The High-Tech Strategy for Germany. Berlin: BMBF 2006, page 12, 17

105 *Own representation, inspired by BMBF;* Die Hightech-Strategie 2020 für Deutschland vorantreiben [http://www.bmbf.de/de/19870.php] (11.10.2012)

106 *Common Sense for the World;* Manifesto for sustainable architecture and civil engineering issued by architects, engineers and town planners in Germany. [http://www.klima-manifest.de/fileadmin/templates/klima-manifest/images/BDAKlimaManifestENGLISCH.pdf] (30.07.2012)

107 *Ministerium für Wirtschaft, Arbeit und Tourismus M-V;* Energieland 2020. Gesamtstrategie für Mecklenburg – Vorpommern. Schwerin: Ministerium für Wirtschaft, Arbeit und Tourismus M-V 04/2009

108 *Own representation, inspired by Ministerium für Wirtschaft, Arbeit und Tourismus M-V;* Energieland 2020. Gesamtstrategie für Mecklenburg – Vorpommern. Schwerin: Ministerium für Wirtschaft, Arbeit und Tourismus M-V 04/2009 , page 116

109 *Own representation, inspired by Ministerium für Wirtschaft, Arbeit und Tourismus M-V;* Energieland 2020. Gesamtstrategie für Mecklenburg – Vorpommern. Schwerin: Ministerium für Wirtschaft, Arbeit und Tourismus M-V 04/2009, page 82

110 *Own representation;* Wismar, Germany 2014

111 *Own representation, inspired by* Energy Performance Certificate in England & Wales

112 *Construction products association;* Guidance Note on the Construction Products Regulation [http://www.constructionproducts.org.uk/publications/industry-affairs/display/view/construction-products-regulation/](11.04.2014)

113 *Own representation, inspired by Bezirksregierung Düsseldorf;* [http://www.brd.nrw.de/planen_bauen/marktueberwachung/Bilder/CE.JPG](11.04.2014)

114 *Own representation;* Wismar, Germany 2014

115 *Own representation, inspired by Food and Agriculture Organisation of the United Nations;* [http://www.fao.org/docrep/004/Y3609E/y3609e1.gif] (11.04.2012)

116 *Own representation;* Wismar, Germany 2014

117 *Own representation;* Wismar, Germany 2014

List of figures

118 *BMU;* EEG – The Renewable Energy Sources Act. Berlin: BMU 07/2007, page 16

119 *Own representation, inspired by DLH GmbH;* [http://haar24.com/images/stories/Presse/EEG/Anteil_EE.jpg] (11.06.2013)

120 *Own representation, inspired by dena;* [http://www.zukunft-haus.info/fileadmin/zukunft-haus/erneuerbare_energien/Presseinfo_EEWaermeG/Infografik_EEWaermeG.jpg] (11.06.2013)

121 *Own representation, inspired by BUBW (Betrieblicher Umweltschutz in Baden-Württemberg);* [http://www.umweltschutz-bw.de/images/Schreiner/Produktverantwortung/enev_verbrauchsentwicklung.jpg] (11.06.2013)

122 *Own representation, inspired by ENVISYS;* [http://www.envisys.de/energieberatung/fileadmin/envisys/media/news/HStrichT.png] (11.06.2013)

123 *Own representation, inspired by Deutsches Institut für Normung e.V.;* DIN V 18599-1:2005-07 Energetische Bewertung von Gebäuden. Berechnung des Nutz, End und Primärenergiebedarfs für Heizung, Kühlung, Lüftung, Trinkwarmwasser und Beleuchtung. Teil 1: Allgemeine Bilanzierungsverfahren, Begriffe, Zonierung und Bewertung der Energieträger

124 *Own representation, inspired by Bundesministerium der Justiz und für Verbraucherschutz;* Gesetz zur Förderung der Kreislaufwirtschaft und Sicherung der umweltverträglichen Beseitigung von Abfällen (Kreislaufwirtschafts- und Abfallgesetz – KrW-/AbfG) [http://www.gesetze-im-internet.de/krwg/] (12.10.2012)

125 *Oberfrancová, L.;* Rostock, Germany 10/2015

126 *Oberfrancová, L.;* Athens, Greece 2006

127 *Own representation, inspired by WoldPress. gesichtspunkte.de;* [http://gesichtspunkte.de/wp-content/uploads/2012/12/BSR_Der.Flyerpng.Rueckseite.png] (11.06.2013)

128 *von Zadow, A.;* Wismar, Germany 03/2014

129 *von Zadow, A.;* Wismar, Germany 03/2014

130 *Students presentation;* Workshop „Green Univer-City Wismar", Germany. Hochschule Wismar, Faculty of Architecture and Design, 03/2014

131 *Students presentation;* Workshop „Green Univer-City Wismar", Germany. Hochschule Wismar, Faculty of Architecture and Design, 03/2014

2.0 Building life time

132 *IGEL-Institut;* Wismar, Germany 2012

133 *Own representation;* Wismar, Germany 2014

134 *Own representation, inspired by BMVBS;* Leitfaden Nachhaltiges Bauen. Berlin: BMVBS 04/2013, page 31

135 *Own representation, inspired by BMVBS;* Leitfaden Nachhaltiges Bauen. Berlin: BMVBS 04/2013, page 41

136 *Own representation, inspired by VDI Zentrum Ressourceneffizienz. Becker, N.;* Kurzanalyse Nr.2. Resourceneffizienz der Tragwerke. Berlin: 01/2013, page 9

137 *Own representation, inspired by Mück, W.;* Baustoffe- und Bautechnik: Baustoffwerte [http://www.gesundbauen.at/BER3-BTE.htm] (04.05.2013)

138 *Own representation, inspired by wired.com;* [http://www.wired.com/images_blogs/wiredscience/2010/08/anthromes_v2_area_change_1700_2000.png] (15.05.2012)

139 *Oberfrancová, L.;* Wismar, Germany 02/2016

140 *Own representation, inspired by Umwelt Bundesamt;* [http://www.umweltbundesamt.de/indikator-anstieg-der-siedlungsverkehrsflaeche] (15.05.2014)

141 *Own representation, inspired by eon-mitte.com;* [http://www.eon-mitte.com/admin/userimages/Image/privatkunden/energiebedarfsrechner/energiebedarfsrechner_grafik.gif] (15.05.2012)

142 *Own representation, inspired by TU Wien;* [http://www.tuwien.ac.at/fileadmin/t/tuwien/fotos/pa/download/70_2008/lifecycle-cost_bosh-1.jpg] (15.05.2012)

143 *Own representation;* Wismar, Germany 2014

144 *Own representation;* Wismar, Germany 2014

145 *Own representation, inspired by BBSR;* Nutzungsdauern von Bauteilen für Lebenszyklusanalysen nach Bewertungssystem Nachhaltiges Bauen (BNB). Berlin: BBSR 03.11.2011

146 *Own representation, inspired by oikos®;* [http://www.oikos.com/library/waste/Waste.gif] (15.05.2012)

147 *Own representation, inspired by BMU, BMVg;* Arbeitshilfen Recycling. Arbeitshilfen zum Umgang mit Bau- und Abbruchabfällen sowie zum Einsatz von Recycling – Baustoffen auf Liegenschaften des Bundes. Berlin: BMU, BMVg 31.10.2008, page 18

148 *Own representation, inspired by DESTATIS;* Composition of waste generated in Germany in 2005. Wiesbaden: 2007

149 *Oberfrancová, L.;* Rostock, Germany 09/2014

150 *Own representation, inspired by Wuppertal In. Bringezu,S.;* 1993

151 *Own representation, inspired by Hahn, E.;* Presentation Urban ecology at Workshop „Green Univer-City Wismar" , Germany. Hochschule Wismar, Faculty of Architecture and Design, 03/2014

152 *Own representation; picture Oberfrancová, L.;* Karitena 2006

153 *Own representation; picture Wollensak, M.;* Shanghai, China 06/2012

154 *Own representation; picture Student project (Baiyang, Y., Dasong, W., Yichen, Y., Zhuoya, Q);* Future City: Transforming into Wildness. Germany, Hochschule Wismar, Faculty of Architecture and Design, SS 2014

3.0 Passive resource-saving concepts (light tech)

155 *IGEL-Institut;* Wismar, Germany 02/2014

156 *Own representation;* Wismar, Germany 2014

157 *Wollensak, M.;* München, Germany 07/2012

158 *Oberfrancová, L.;* München, Germany 2006

159 *Oberfrancová, L.;* Lübeck, Germany 2011

160 *Oberfrancová, L.;* Lübeck, Germany 2011

161 *Lampe, S.;* Sevilla, Spain 2011

162 *Wollensak, M.;* Germany 2007

163 *Oberfrancová, L.;* Athens, Greece 2006

164 *Wollensak, M.;* New York, USA 08/2011

165 *Hochschule Wismar (Wollensak, M., students: Glaß, Ch., Zimmermann, J.);* Concept 2020. Wismar, Germany 2012

166 *Schoblocher, P.;* Master Thesis: Bestand erhalten - Teilrückbau, Umbau und Erweiterung - Abbruch und Neubau? Investitionsüberlegungen und Entscheidungsprozesse zum Nachhaltigen Bauen - Vergleichende Untersuchungen unter Berücksichtigung der „Externen Kosten" am Beispiel „Neubau Rathaus Thannhausen". Wings at Hochschule Wismar, Distance Study Program Architecture and Environment: Thannhausen 11/2011, page 30

167 *Own representation, inspired by Schoblocher, P.;* Master Thesis: Bestand erhalten - Teilrückbau, Umbau und Erweiterung - Abbruch und Neubau? Investitionsüberlegungen und Entscheidungsprozesse zum Nachhaltigen Bauen - Vergleichende Untersuchungen unter Berücksichtigung der „Externen Kosten" am Beispiel „Neubau Rathaus Thannhausen". Wings at Hochschule Wismar, Distance Study Program Architecture and Environment: Thannhausen 11/2011, page 56

168 *Own representation, inspired by Schoblocher, P.;* Master Thesis: Bestand erhalten - Teilrückbau, Umbau und Erweiterung - Abbruch und Neubau? Investitionsüberlegungen und Entschei-

dungsprozesse zum Nachhaltigen Bauen - Vergleichende Untersuchungen unter Berücksichtigung der „Externen Kosten“ am Beispiel „Neubau Rathaus Thannhausen“. Wings at Hochschule Wismar, Distance Study Program Architecture and Environment: Thannhausen 11/2011, page 55

169 *Schoblocher, P.;* Master Thesis: Bestand erhalten - Teilrückbau, Umbau und Erweiterung - Abbruch und Neubau? Investitionsüberlegungen und Entscheidungsprozesse zum Nachhaltigen Bauen - Vergleichende Untersuchungen unter Berücksichtigung der „Externen Kosten“ am Beispiel „Neubau Rathaus Thannhausen“. Wings at Hochschule Wismar, Distance Study Program Architecture and Environment: Thannhausen 11/2011, page 44

170 *Schoblocher, P.;* Master Thesis: Bestand erhalten - Teilrückbau, Umbau und Erweiterung - Abbruch und Neubau? Investitionsüberlegungen und Entscheidungsprozesse zum Nachhaltigen Bauen - Vergleichende Untersuchungen unter Berücksichtigung der „Externen Kosten“ am Beispiel „Neubau Rathaus Thannhausen“. Wings at Hochschule Wismar, Distance Study Program Architecture and Environment: Thannhausen 11/2011, page 34

171 *Own representation, inspired by Schoblocher, P.;* Master Thesis: Bestand erhalten - Teilrückbau, Umbau und Erweiterung - Abbruch und Neubau? Investitionsüberlegungen und Entscheidungsprozesse zum Nachhaltigen Bauen - Vergleichende Untersuchungen unter Berücksichtigung der „Externen Kosten“ am Beispiel „Neubau Rathaus Thannhausen“. Wings at Hochschule Wismar, Distance Study Program Architecture and Environment: Thannhausen 11/2011, page 66

172 *Own representation, inspired by Schoblocher, P.;* Master Thesis: Bestand erhalten - Teilrückbau, Umbau und Erweiterung - Abbruch und Neubau? Investitionsüberlegungen und Entscheidungsprozesse zum Nachhaltigen Bauen - Vergleichende Untersuchungen unter Berücksichtigung der „Externen Kosten“ am Beispiel „Neubau Rathaus Thannhausen“. Wings at Hochschule Wismar, Distance Study Program Architecture and Environment: Thannhausen 11/2011, page 66

173 *Own representation, inspired by Schoblocher, P.;* Presentation of Master Thesis: Bestand erhalten - Teilrückbau, Umbau und Erweiterung - Abbruch und Neubau? Investitionsüberlegungen und Entscheidungsprozesse zum Nachhaltigen Bauen - Vergleichende Untersuchungen unter Berücksichtigung der „Externen Kosten“ am Beispiel „Neubau Rathaus Thannhausen“. Wings at Hochschule Wismar, Distance Study Program Architecture and Environment: Thannhausen 11/2011, page 27

174 *Own representation, inspired by Schoblocher, P.;* Presentation of Master Thesis: Bestand erhalten - Teilrückbau, Umbau und Erweiterung - Abbruch und Neubau? Investitionsüberlegungen und Entscheidungsprozesse zum Nachhaltigen Bauen - Vergleichende Untersuchungen unter Berücksichtigung der „Externen Kosten“ am Beispiel „Neubau Rathaus Thannhausen“. Wings at Hochschule Wismar, Distance Study Program Architecture and Environment: Thannhausen 11/2011, page 27

175 *Wollensak, M.;* Germany 2010

176 *Gill-May, N.;* Christschurch, New Zealand 2014

177 *Fuchs, N.;* Master-Thesis: Recycling in der Architektur. Hochschule Wismar, Faculty of Architecture and Design: Wismar SS 2013, page 54, 55

178 *Fuchs, N.;* Master-Thesis: Recycling in der Architektur. Hochschule Wismar, Faculty of Architecture and Design: Wismar SS 2013, page 61

179 *Fuchs, N.;* Master-Thesis: Recycling in der Architektur. Hochschule Wismar, Faculty of Architecture and Design: Wismar SS 2013, page 56

180 *Own representation, inspired by Daniels, K.;* Low-Tech Light-Tech High-Tech. Bauen in der Informationsgesellschaft. Berlin: Birkhäuser 1998, page 136

181 *Oberfrancová, L.;* Wismar, Germany 10/2014

182 *IGEL-Institut;* Rostock, Germany 06/2012

183 *Wollensak, M.;* Friedrichshafen, Germany 2007

184 *Own representation;* Wismar, Germany 2014

185 *Klopp, E.;* Germany 11/2015 and *Oberfrancová, L.;* Wismar, Germany 10/2014

186 *Oberfrancová, L.;* Rostock, Germany 11/2015

187 *Own representation, inspired by Gerber, U-T.;* Master Thesis: Systemtrennung beim Amt für Grundstücke und Gebäude des Kantons Bern. Untersuchung von nutzungsflexiblen Planungsvorgaben anhand von amtlichen Vorgabedokumenten, Literatur, Umfragen und von geplanten Gebäuden. Wings at Hochschule Wismar, Distance Study Program Architecture and Environment: Wismar, Germany 11/2009 page 23

188 *Own representation, inspired by Gerber, U-T.;* Master Thesis: Systemtrennung beim Amt für Grundstücke und Gebäude des Kantons Bern. Untersuchung von nutzungsflexiblen Planungsvorgaben anhand von amtlichen Vorgabedokumenten, Literatur, Umfragen und von geplanten Gebäuden. Wings at Hochschule Wismar, Distance Study Program Architecture and Environment: Wismar, Germany 11/2009 page 15

189 *Own representation;* Wismar, Germany 2014

190 *Own representation;* Wismar, Germany 2014

191 *Own representation;* Wismar, Germany 2014

192 *Oberfrancová, L.;* IBA Hamburg, Germany 06/2015

193 *Own representation;* Wismar, Germany 2014

194 *Own representation;* Wismar, Germany 2014

195 *Own representation;* Wismar, Germany 2014

196 *Own representation, inspired by Hestia Service GmbH;* Thünensche Kreise [http://wordpress.hestia.de/wp-content/gallery/cache/1__500xfloat=left_zeiten.jpg] (08.05.2014)

197 *Wollensak, M.;* Germany 05/2007

198 *Own representation, based on Arbeitsgemeinschaft Holz e.V. (publisher); Informationsdienst Holz:* Holzbausysteme. Arbeitsgemeinschaft Holz e.V.: Düsseldorf 12/2000 and *IGEL-Institut;* Rostock 11/2015 and *Wollensak, M.;* Germany 5/2007 and *Klopp, E.;* 11/2015 and *own representation*

199 *Wollensak, M.;* China 2012

200 *IGEL-Institut;* Wismar, Germany 09/2008

201 *Wollensak, M.;* China 2012

202 *Oberfrancová, L.;* Wismar, Germany 2010

203 *Klopp, E.;* Germany 06/2011

204 *Oberfrancová, L.;* Garz/Rügen, Germany 2014

205 *Oberfrancová, L.;* Atsicholos, Greece 2006

206 *Oberfrancová, L.;* Hannover, Greece 08/2014

207 *Tucek, I.;* Yazd, Iran 2006

208 *Oberfrancová, L.;* Wismar, Germany 06/2014

209 *Own representation, inspired by InspirationGreen.com;* Rammed Earth [http://www.inspirationgreen.com/assets/images/Blog-Building/Rammed%20Earth/rammedearth-1.jpg] (05.04.2014)

210 *Oberfrancová, L.;* Wismar, Germany 11/2015

211 *Oberfrancová, L.;* München, Germany 2007

212 *Own representation, inspired by Kuhn, M.;* Glossar zum Leichtbau [www.archplus.net/download/artikel/1080/] (08.06.2014)

213 *Jeserig, J.;* Harbin, China 2011

214 *Wollensak, M.;* New York, USA 08/2011

215 *Hagendorf, O.;* Glaumbær, Iceland 06/2015

216 *Oberfrancová, L.;* Copenhagen, Denmark 2010 and Springe, Germany 2010

List of figures

217 *Own representation, inspired by Evolution hostings;* [http://538357.cache1.evolutionhosting.com/images/wofati_rain.gif] (08.05.2011)

218 *Own representation, inspired by blogger.com;* [http://photos1.blogger.com/blogger/17/2396/320/pahs.jpg] (08.05.2011)

219 *Own representation, inspired by Universität bür Bodenkultur Wien;* [http://www.baunat.boku.ac.at/fileadmin/data/H03000/H87000/H87200/3Arbeitsgruppen/Hydrogeologie/pantherm/image008.gif] (08.05.2011)

220 *Own representation;* Wismar, Germany 2014

221 *Xinchen, P.;* Student project: Back to Nature. Climb the tree, Burrow into the ground. Hochschule Wismar, Faculty of Architecture and Design, Germany 2013

222 *Own representation, inspired by Glücklich, D.;* [http://ecologic-architecture.org/main/] (08.03.2012)

223 *Own representation, inspired by Glücklich, D.;* [http://ecologic-architecture.org/main/] (08.03.2012)

224 *Oberfrancová, L.;* Hannover, Germany 08/2014

225 *Schachtschneider, S.;* Berlin, Germany 09/2014

226 *IGEL-Institut;* Wismar, Germany 05/2005

227 *Own representation, inspired by Schoblocher, P.;* Presentation of Master Thesis: Bestand erhalten - Teilrückbau, Umbau und Erweiterung - Abbruch und Neubau? Investitionsüberlegungen und Entscheidungsprozesse zum Nachhaltigen Bauen - Vergleichende Untersuchungen unter Berücksichtigung der „Externen Kosten" am Beispiel „Neubau Rathaus Thannhausen". Wings at Hochschule Wismar, Distance Study Program Architecture and Environment: Thannhausen 11/2011, page 37

228 *Own representation, inspired by Schoblocher, P.;* Presentation of Master Thesis: Bestand erhalten - Teilrückbau, Umbau und Erweiterung - Abbruch und Neubau? Investitionsüberlegungen und Entscheidungsprozesse zum Nachhaltigen Bauen - Vergleichende Untersuchungen unter Berücksichtigung der „Externen Kosten" am Beispiel „Neubau Rathaus Thannhausen". Wings at Hochschule Wismar, Distance Study Program Architecture and Environment: Thannhausen 11/2011, page 37

229 *IGEL-Institut;* Wismar, Germany 05/2005

230 *IGEL-Institut;* Wismar, Germany 05/2005

4.0 Passive energy-saving concepts (low tech)

231 *IGEL-Institut;* Wismar 2011

232 *Oberfrancová, L.;* Levanto, Italy 2008

233 *Own representation, inspired by boqueteweather.com;* [http://www.boqueteweather.com/images/world_climate_map.jpg] (21.03.2013)

234 *Tucek, I.;* Yazd, Iran 2006

235 *Own representation, inspired by Hegger, M., Fuchs, M., Stark, T., Zeumer, M.:* Energie Atlas. Nachhaltige Architektur, München 2008, page 51

236 *Own representation, inspired by Hegger, M., Fuchs, M., Stark, T., Zeumer, M.:* Energie Atlas. Nachhaltige Architektur, München 2008, page 51

237 *Own representation;* Wismar, Germany 2014

238 *Own representation;* Wismar, Germany 2014

239 *Own representation, inspired by Hegger, M., Fuchs, M., Stark, T., Zeumer, M.:* Energie Atlas. Nachhaltige Architektur, München 2008, page 69

240 *Own representation;* Wismar, Germany 2014

241 *Own representation, inspired by Hegger, M., Fuchs, M., Stark, T., Zeumer, M.:* Energie Atlas. Nachhaltige Architektur, München 2008, page 69

242 *Own representation;* Wismar, Germany 2014

243 *Own representation;* Wismar, Germany 2014

244 *Own representation;* Wismar, Germany 2014

245 *Own representation;* Wismar, Germany 2014

246 *Own representation;* Wismar, Germany 2014

247 *Own representation;* Wismar, Germany 2014

248 *Own representation;* Wismar, Germany 2014

249 *Own representation;* Wismar, Germany 2014

250 *Own representation, inspired by educate-sustainability.eu;* [https://www.educate-sustainability.eu/portal/index.php?q=img_assist/popup/766] (21.03.2013)

251 *Own representation, inspired by educate-sustainability.eu;* [https://www.educate-sustainability.eu/portal/index.php?q=img_assist/popup/768] (21.03.2013)

252 *Own representation, inspired by educate-sustainability.eu;* [https://www.educate-sustainability.eu/portal/index.php?q=img_assist/popup/769] (21.03.2013)

253 *Own representation;* Wismar, Germany 2014

254 *Own representation, inspired by Hegger, M., Fuchs, M., Stark, T., Zeumer, M.:* Energie Atlas. Nachhaltige Architektur, München 2008, page 69

255 *Own representation;* Wismar, Germany 2014

256 *Own representation;* Wismar, Germany 2014

257 *Own representation;* Wismar, Germany 2014

258 *Wollensak, M.;* Germany 2007

259 *Own representation;* Wismar, Germany 2014

260 *Own representation, inspired by Hegger, M., Fuchs, M., Stark, T., Zeumer, M.:* Energie Atlas. Nachhaltige Architektur, München 2008, page 85

261 *Own representation, inspired by Hegger, M., Fuchs, M., Stark, T., Zeumer, M.:* Energie Atlas. Nachhaltige Architektur, München 2008, page 91

262 *Own representation, inspired by Tuschinski, M.;* EnEV 2014 - die neue Energieeinsparverordnung [http://www.enev-online.com/enev_2014_volltext/index.htm] (12.04.2014)

263 *Autridge, S.;* Student project: Old brewery. Hochschule Wismar, Faculty of Architecture and Design, Germany 2013

264 *Oberfrancová, L.;* Lübeck, Germany 2011

265 *Tucek, I.;* Yazd, Iran 2006

266 *Own representation, based on* [http://passivesolar.weebly.com/uploads/3/4/1/4/341482/4885581.gif] (08.03.2012)

267 *Own representation;* Wismar, Germany 2014

268 *Own representation, inspired by Autodesk®, Inc.;* Autodesk Sustainability Workshop: Concepts and tools for sustainable design [http://sustainabilityworkshop.autodesk.com/sites/default/files/images/solar%20chimney%20cooling%2C%20no%20labels_0.jpg] (08.11.2012)

269 *Own representation, inspired by* [http://ars.els-cdn.com/content/image/1-s2.0-S0960148108000931-gr2.jpg] (08.03.2012)

270 *Own representation, inspired by Green planet – solar energy;* Solar tower [http://www.green-planet-solar-energy.com/images/chimney_operation_2.gif] (08.11.2012)

271 *Own representation;* Wismar, Germany 2014

272 *Own representation;* Wismar, Germany 2014

273 *Own representation, inspired by smarterhomes.org.nz;* [http://www.smarterhomes.org.nz/uploads/pics/design_overview_01.jpg] (08.11.2012)

274 *Own representation, inspired by azsolarcentre.org;* [http://www.azsolarcentre.org/images/articles/design/fig5.gif] (08.11.2012)

275 *Own representation, inspired by Autodesk®, Inc.;* Autodesk Sustainability Workshop: Concepts and tools for sustainable design [http://sustainabilityworkshop.autodesk.com/sites/default/files/images/Solar%20chimney%20vs%20Trombe%20wall_0.jpg] (08.11.2012)

276 *Own representation, inspired by azsolarcentre.org;* [http://www.azsolarcentre.org/images/articles/design/fig7.gif] (08.11.2012)

277 *Own representation, inspired by azsolarcentre.org;* [http://www.azsolarcentre.org/images/articles/design/fig14.gif] (08.11.2012)

278 *Own representation, inspired by azsolarcentre.org;* [http://www.azsolarcentre.org/images/articles/design/fig9.gif] (on 08.11.2012) and [http://www.azsolarcentre.org/images/articles/design/fig10.gif] (08.11.2012)

279 *Own representation, inspired by azsolarcentre.org;* [http://www.azsolarcentre.org/images/articles/design/fig11.gif] (08.11.2012)

280 *Wollensak, M.;* Germany 06/2012

281 *Wollensak, M.;* New York, USA 06/2012

282 *Wollensak, M.;* Shanghai, China 06/2012

283 *Own representation, inspired by new-learn.info;* [http://www.new-learn.info/packages/clear/interactive/matrix/images/37.jpg] (08.11.2012)

284 *Own representation;* Wismar, Germany 2014

285 *Oberfrancová, L.;* Rostock, Germany 10/2015

286 *Bailey, S.;* Master Thesis: Aquaponics in Architecture. Project in Hamburg, Germany. Hochschule Wismar, Faculty of Architecture and Design WS 2011/2012

287 *Bailey, S.;* Master Thesis: Aquaponics in Architecture. Project in Hamburg, Germany. Hochschule Wismar, Faculty of Architecture and Design WS 2011/2012

288 *Bailey, S.;* Master Thesis: Aquaponics in Architecture. Project in Hamburg, Germany. Hochschule Wismar, Faculty of Architecture and Design WS 2011/2012

289 *Bailey, S.;* Master Thesis: Aquaponics in Architecture. Project in Hamburg, Germany. Hochschule Wismar, Faculty of Architecture and Design WS 2011/2012

290 *Bailey, S.;* Master Thesis: Aquaponics in Architecture. Project in Hamburg, Germany. Hochschule Wismar, Faculty of Architecture and Design WS 2011/2012

291 *Bailey, S.;* Master Thesis: Aquaponics in Architecture. Project in Hamburg, Germany. Hochschule Wismar, Faculty of Architecture and Design WS 2011/2012

292 *Bailey, S.;* Master Thesis: Aquaponics in Architecture. Project in Hamburg, Germany. Hochschule Wismar, Faculty of Architecture and Design WS 2011/2012

5.0 Active energy-saving concepts (high tech)

293 *IGEL-Institut;* Wismar, Germany 2008

294 *Oberfrancová, L.;* HafenCity Hamburg, Germany 06/2015

295 *Klopp, E.;* Berlin, Germany 01/2012

296 *Lampe, S.;* Herne, Germany 2007

297 *Own representation, inspired by Akademie Mont-Cenis Herne;* [http://www.akademie-mont-cenis.de/en/] (08.12.2013)

298 *IGEL-Institut;* Wismar, Germany 2004

299 *Own representation, inspired by Eurotherm GmbH;* [http://www.eurotherm-gmbh.de/images/banner_funktion_lueftung.jpg] (08.07.2014)

300 *Own representation;* Wismar, Germany 2014

301 *Own representation, inspired by Höcker Polytechnik®;* [http://www.hoecker-polytechnik.de/produkte/windsichtungsanlagen-lueftungsanlagen/waermerueckgewinnung.html] (08.07.2014)

302 *Own representation, inspired by Höcker Polytechnik®;* [http://www.hoecker-polytechnik.de/produkte/windsichtungsanlagen-lueftungsanlagen/waermerueckgewinnung.html] (08.07.2014)

303 *Own representation, inspired by Höcker Polytechnik®;* [http://www.hoecker-polytechnik.de/produkte/windsichtungsanlagen-lueftungsanlagen/waermerueckgewinnung.html] (08.07.2014)

304 *Own representation, inspired by* [http://www.mall.info/fileadmin/_processed_/csm_Adiabate_Abluftkuehlung_beschriftet_00d39f370b.jpg] (08.07.2014)

305 *Own representation, inspired by Energieagentur NRW;* [http://www.energieagentur.nrw.de/virtuell/downloads/adiabate_kuehlung.pdf] (08.07.2014)

306 *Own representation;* Wismar, Germany 2014

307 *Own representation, inspired by BTK;* [http://www.btk.sk/images/tepcer-02.gif] (05.06.2012)

308 *Own representation, inspired by eere.energy.gov;* [http://www1.eere.energy.gov/tribalenergy/guide/images/photo_ghp_types.jpg] (05.06.2012)

309 *Oberfrancová, L.;* Wismar, Germany 12/2015

310 *Own representation, inspired by Quaschning,V.;* [http://www.volker-quaschning.de/articles/fundamentals4/figure1.gif] (05.06.2012)

311 *Own representation, inspired by Quaschning,V.;* [http://www.volker-quaschning.de/articles/fundamentals4/figure2.gif] (05.06.2012)

312 *Own representation, inspired by Darling,D.;* [http://www.david-darling.info/images/active_solar_heating_system.gif] (05.06.2012)

313 *Own representation, inspired by Shower-save.com;* [http://shower-save.com/pdfs/Commercial%20grey%20water%20heat%20recovery.pdf] (05.06.2012)

314 *Oberfrancová, L.;* Wismar, Germany 02/2016

315 *Oberfrancová, L.;* Hamburg, Germany 06/2015

316 *Own representation, inspired by photovoltaik.org;* [http://www.photovoltaik.org/wissen/photovoltaik-wirkungsgrad] (05.06.2012)

317 *Oberfrancová, L.;* Wismar, Germany 2015

318 *Oberfrancová, L.;* Wismar, Germany 2015

319 *Oberfrancová, L.;* Rostock, Germany 2015

320 *Wollensak, M.;* Rostock, Germany 2015

321 *Wollensak, M.;* Academy Mont-Cenis, Germany 2007

322 *Oberfrancová, L.;* Rostock, Germany 08/2014

323 *Own representation, inspired by Dr. Van-Tran Consulting Trading Co.;* [http://dvt-consulting.com/datapic/image005.jpg] (05.06.2012)

324 *Wollensak, M.;* Californien, USA 08/2011

325 *Oberfrancová, L.;* HafenCity Hamburg, Germany 06/2015

326 *Own representation, inspired by wind-energy-the-facts.org;* [http://www.wind-energy-the-facts.org/images/fig/chap1/Table_6.2.PNG] (05.06.2012)

327 *Own representation, inspired by GMK;* [http://www.gmk.info/popup_en.php] (05.06.2012)

328 *Hagendorf, O.;* Hengill, Iceland 06/2015

329 *Own representation, inspired by BUY ability;* [http://www.buy-ability.co.uk/wp-content/uploads/MicroCHP.jpg] (05.06.2012)

330 *Own representation, inspired by U.S: Environmental Protection Agency;* [http://www.epa.gov/chp/basic/index.html] (05.06.2012)

331 *Own representation, inspired by U.S: Environmental Protection Agency;* [http://www.epa.gov/chp/basic/index.html] (05.06.2012)

332 *Own representation, inspired by s1.hubimg.com;* [http://s1.hubimg.com/u/3466120_f520.jpg] (05.06.2012)

333 *Oberfrancová, L.;* Hamburg, Germany 06/2015

334 *Fuchs, M.;* Hamburg, Germany 2013

335 *Oberfrancová, L.;* Island Poel, Germany 09/2014

List of figures

336 *Lampe, S.;* Sevilla, Spain 2011

337 *Own representation, inspired by Steiner Haustechnik GmbH;* [http://www.steiner.net/bilder/skombipuffer.gif] (05.06.2012)

338 *Own representation, inspired by Schlosser, M.;* Vortragsreihe:„Zukunft der Wärmeversorgung - Kommunale Nahwärmenetze". TU Hannover, Institut für Gebäude und Solartechnik. 02/05/2011

339 *Own representation, inspired by* Planning of IGEL-Institut 2012

340 *Own representation, inspired by gartino - Haus und Garten;* [http://www.gartino.de/wp-content/uploads/2013/01/prinzip_eisheizung.jpg] (05.06.2012)

341 *Own representation, inspired by* Planning of IGEL-Institut 2012

342 *Student presentation (Gallová, K., Richnavská, H., Skrabák, Z.);* Treatment of a heritage warehouse in Wismar harbour, Germany. Hochschule Wismar, Faculty of Architecture and Design, Green Building class SS 2014

343 *Student presentation (Junhui,W.,Lin,W., Shuang,L., Shuyang,Z., Yingdong,M., Xiaoyin,Y.);* Treatment of a heritage warehouse in Wismar harbour, Germany. Hochschule Wismar, Faculty of Architecture and Design, Green Building class SS 2014

344 *Student presentation (Kryeziu, B., Milad, A., Rrahmani, V., Shoeybi, M., Xhigoli, J.);* Treatment of a heritage warehouse in Wismar harbour, Germany. Hochschule Wismar, Faculty of Architecture and Design, Green Building class SS 2014

345 *Student presentation (Boelsterly, F., Mullinger, S., Ovcharova, V.);* Treatment of a heritage warehouse in Wismar harbour, Germany. Hochschule Wismar, Faculty of Architecture and Design, Green Building class SS 2014

6.0 Active resource-saving concepts (hard tech)

346 *IGEL-Institut;* Wismar, Germany 2012

347 *Own representation, inspired by Ecobine;* [http://www.ecobine.de/print.php?SESSID=5d7092d85d384778d6c3226dcb5d3204&id=4.5.1.1.6&kurs=11&l=de] (23.06.2014)

348 *Oberfrancová, L.;* Wismar, Germany 06/2015

349 *Siebold, D.;* Wismar, Germany 02/2016

350 *Own representation, inspired by Linden, W.;* Presentation: Baustoffe. Instrumente der Bewertung: Fachhochschule Lübeck, Fachbereich Bauwesen

351 *Belánová, E.;* Hurghada, Egypt 2009

352 *Fan, Y.;* Ningbo, China 08/2014

353 *Klopp, E.;* Gülzow, Germany 04/2011

354 *Klopp, E.;* Gülzow, Germany 04/2011

355 *IGEL-Institut;* Garz/Rügen, Germany 2014

356 *Oberfrancová, L.;* Wismar, Germany 10/2014

357 *Oberfrancová, L.;* Wismar, Germany 2014

358 *Wollensak, M.;* California, USA 08/2011

359 *Oberfrancová, L.;* Osnabrück, Germany 2010 and *Križánková, A.;* Osnabrück 2016

360 *Own representation, inspired by Linden, W.;* Presentation: Baustoffe. Instrumente der Bewertung: Fachhochschule Lübeck

361 *Own representation, inspired by Linden, W.;* Presentation: Baustoffe. Instrumente der Bewertung: Fachhochschule Lübeck

362 *Own representation, inspired by Linden, W.;* Presentation: Baustoffe. Instrumente der Bewertung: Fachhochschule Lübeck

363 *Wollensak, M.;* Dessau, Germany 11/2015

364 *Oberfrancová, L.;* Mühlenteich Wismar, Germany 12/2015

365 *Oberfrancová, L.;* Wismar , Germany 02/2016

366 *Student presentation (Wiebe, B., Podzimkova, F., Renowden, N.);* Recycled Furniture. Germany, Hochschule Wismar, Faculty of Architecture and Design, Green Building class SS 2015

367 *Student presentation (Pliss, M.);* Recycling building design. Hochschule Wismar, Faculty of Architecture and Design WS 2012

368 *Student presentation (Xiaoyang, F.);* Recycling building design. Hochschule Wismar, Faculty of Architecture and Design WS 2012

369 *Student presentation (Liu, S.);* Recycling building design. Hochschule Wismar, Faculty of Architecture and Design WS 2012

370 *Own representation, inspired by Glücklich, D.;* [http://ecologic-architecture.org/main/] (08.03.2012)

371 *Oberfrancová, L.;* Flintenbreite, Germany 06/2015

372 *Own representation, inspired by OtterWasser GmbH;* [http://www.otterwasser.de/english/concepts/imge3/img4-eng.gif] (05.06.2012)

373 *Own representation, inspired by BMU, BMVg;* Arbeitshilfen Recycling. Arbeitshilfen zum Umgang mit Bau- und Abbruchabfällen sowie zum Einsatz von Recycling – Baustoffen auf Liegenschaften des Bundes. Berlin: BMU, BMVg 31.10.2008, page 17

374 *Own representation, inspired by Linden, W.;* Presentation: Baustoffe. Instrumente der Bewertung: Fachhochschule Lübeck

375 *BMU, BMVg;* Arbeitshilfen Recycling. Arbeitshilfen zum Umgang mit Bau- und Abbruchabfällen sowie zum Einsatz von Recycling – Baustoffen auf Liegenschaften des Bundes. Berlin: BMU, BMVg 31.10.2008

376 *Own representation, inspired by BMU, BMVg;* Arbeitshilfen Recycling. Arbeitshilfen zum Umgang mit Bau- und Abbruchabfällen sowie zum Einsatz von Recycling – Baustoffen auf Liegenschaften des Bundes. Berlin: BMU, BMVg 31.10.2008, page 1

7.0 Building for a long life span

377 *IGEL-Institut;* Wismar, Germany 2012

378 *Oberfrancová, L.;* Rome, Italy 2005

379 *Wollensak architects;* Wismar, Germany 2002

380 *Wollensak architects;* Wismar, Germany 2002

381 *Oberfrancová, L.;* Warnemünde, Germany 10/2015

382 *Oberfrancová, L.;* Athens, Greece 2006

383 *Wollensak, M.;* California, USA 08/2011

384 *Student presentation (Fan, Y.);* Hybrid house for IBA Hamburg, Germany. Hochschule Wismar, Faculty of Architecture and Design, SS 2010

385 *Student presentation (Fan, Y.);* Hybrid house for IBA Hamburg, Germany. Hochschule Wismar, Faculty of Architecture and Design, SS 2010

386 *Student presentation (Fan, Y.);* Hybrid house for IBA Hamburg, Germany. Hochschule Wismar, Faculty of Architecture and Design, SS 2010

387 *Scheffler, M.;* Master thesis: „Future house" Beijing. Germany, Hochschule Wismar, Faculty of Architecture and Design, 2005

388 *Scheffler, M.;* Master thesis: „Future house" Beijing. Germany, Hochschule Wismar, Faculty of Architecture and Design, 2005

389 *Scheffler, M.;* Master thesis: „Future house" Beijing. Germany, Hochschule Wismar, Faculty of Architecture and Design, 2005

390 *Scheffler, M.;* Master thesis: „Future house" Beijing. Germany, Hochschule Wismar, Faculty of Architecture and Design, 2005

391 *Schneider, D.;* Homework: Bauen im Bestand - Analyse. Germany, Wings at Hochschule Wismar, Distance Study Program Architecture and Environment: WS 2010/2011, page 5

392 *Schneider, D.;* Homework: Bauen im Bestand - Analyse. Germany, Wings at Hochschule Wismar, Distance Study Program Architecture and Environment: WS 2010/2011, page 83

393 *Schneider, D.;* Homework: Bauen im Bestand - Analyse. Germany, Wings at Hochschule Wismar, Distance Study Program Architecture and Environment: WS 2010/2011, page 85

394 *Schneider, D.;* Homework: Bauen im Bestand - Analyse. Germany, Wings at Hochschule Wismar, Distance Study Program Architecture and Environment: WS 2010/2011, page 77

395 *Schneider, D.;* Homework: Bauen im Bestand - Analyse. Germany, Wings at Hochschule Wismar, Distance Study Program Architecture and Environment: WS 2010/2011, page 80-82

396 *Schneider, D.;* Homework: Bauen im Bestand - Analyse. Germany, Wings at Hochschule Wismar, Distance Study Program Architecture and Environment: WS 2010/2011, page 67

397 *Schneider, D.;* Homework: Bauen im Bestand - Analyse. Germany, Wings at Hochschule Wismar, Distance Study Program Architecture and Environment: WS 2010/2011, page 69

398 *Schneider, D.;* Homework: Bauen im Bestand - Analyse. Germany, Wings at Hochschule Wismar, Distance Study Program Architecture and Environment: WS 2010/2011, page 70

399 *Schneider, D.;* Homework: Bauen im Bestand - Analyse. Germany, Wings at Hochschule Wismar, Distance Study Program Architecture and Environment: WS 2010/2011, page 65-66

400 *Oberfrancová, L.;* Bojnice, Slovak Republic 2004

401 *Oberfrancová,L.;* Germany 2015

8.0 Building for a short life span

402 *Solto, P.;* Bratislava, Slovak Republic 2004

403 *Seyler, S.;* Master thesis: „s.haus“ Lebensabschnittshaus für 20 Jahre. Hochschule Wismar, Faculty of Architecture and Design

404 *Seyler, S.;* Master thesis: „s.haus“ Lebensabschnittshaus für 20 Jahre. Hochschule Wismar, Faculty of Architecture and Design

405 *Own representation, inspired by Seyler, S.;* Master thesis: „s.haus“ Lebensabschnittshaus für 20 Jahre. Hochschule Wismar, Faculty of Architecture and Design

406 *Own representation, inspired by Seyler, S.;* Master thesis: „s.haus“ Lebensabschnittshaus für 20 Jahre. Hochschule Wismar, Faculty of Architecture and Design

407 *Seyler, S.;* Master thesis: „s.haus“ Lebensabschnittshaus für 20 Jahre. Hochschule Wismar, Faculty of Architecture and Design

408 *Wollensak, M.;* Californien, USA 08/2011

409 *Altmann, S.;* Master Thesis: Ein temporäres Hotel für die Hanse Sail. Germany, Hochschule Wismar, Faculty of Architecture and Design

410 *Bredenbals, B., Willkomm, W.;* Neue Konstruktionsalternativen für recyclingfähige Wohngebäude. Stuttgard: Frauenhofer IRB Verlag 1996

411 *Oberfrancová, L.;* HafenCity Hamburg, Germany 06/2015

412 *Wollensak, M.;* Californien, USA 08/2011

413 *Oberfrancová, L.;* Wismar, Germany 12/2015

414 *Wollensak, M.;* Californien, USA 08/2011

415 *Daniel, D.;* Ahrenshoop, Germany 2008

416 *Yichen, Y.;* Shanghai 2010

417 *Students project;* Hochschulpavillon. Studienprojekt für die Landesgartenschau Wismar. Germany, Hochschule Wismar, Faculty of Architecture and Design 2002-2004

418 *Students project;* Hochschulpavillon. Studienprojekt für die Landesgartenschau Wismar. Germany, Hochschule Wismar, Faculty of Architecture and Design 2002-2004

419 *Wollensak, M.;* Germany 11/2007

420 *Oberfrancová, L.;* IBA Hamburg, Germany 06/2015

421 *Oberfrancová, L.;* Wismar, Germany 10/2014

422 *Oberfrancová, L.;* Rügen, Germany 08/2014

423 *Students project (Delgado-Krüger, A., Detjens, A., Höper, K., Kruse-Fölster, L., Koch, S., Korthals, A., Lorenzen, Ch., Mau, J., Müller, J., Schulz., R, Siebold, D., Wiehagen, T.);* Solar Decathlon. Hochschule Wismar, Faculty of Architecture and Design 2014

424 *Students project (Delgado-Krüger, A., Detjens, A., Höper, K., Kruse-Fölster, L., Koch, S., Korthals, A., Lorenzen, Ch., Mau, J., Müller, J., Schulz., R, Siebold, D., Wiehagen, T.);* Solar Decathlon. Hochschule Wismar, Faculty of Architecture and Design 2014

425 *Students project (Delgado-Krüger, A., Detjens, A., Höper, K., Kruse-Fölster, L., Koch, S., Korthals, A., Lorenzen, Ch., Mau, J., Müller, J., Schulz., R, Siebold, D., Wiehagen, T.);* Solar Decathlon. Hochschule Wismar, Faculty of Architecture and Design 2014

9.0 Building concept

426 *IGEL-Institut;* Wismar, Germany 2010

427 *Wollensak, M.;* Germany 11/2007

428 *Own representation;* Wismar, Germany 2014

429 *Own representation;* Wismar, Germany 2014

430 *Own representation;* Wismar, Germany 2016

431 *Oberfrancová, L.;* Wismar, Germany 11/2015

432 [http://toolboxes.flexiblelearning.net.au/demosites/series8/802/content/lo/lo_drawings/images/ergonomics2.gif] (13.06.2013)

433 *Own representation, inspired by Wöhrmann,W.;* Facility Mamagement. Flächen Management [http://www.cafm-mit-visio.de/Flaechenmanagement_Flaechenbedarfsermittlung.html] (03.07.2014)

434 *Own representation, inspired by Wöhrmann,W.;* Facility Mamagement. Flächen Management [http://www.cafm-mit-visio.de/Flaechenmanagement_Flaechenbedarfsermittlung.html] (03.07.2014)

435 *Own representation, inspired by HyperJoint GmbH* [http://nullbarriere.de/wohnflaechen.htm] (03.07.2014)

436 *Own representation, inspired by Bundesanstalt für Arbeitschutz und Arbeitsmedizin* [http://www.baua.de/de/Themen-von-A-Z/Arbeitsstaetten/ASR/ASR.html] (03.07.2014)

437 *Own representation, inspired by HyperJoint GmbH* [http://nullbarriere.de/wohnflaechen.htm] (03.07.2014)

438 *Own representation, inspired by Schulz, J.-U.;* Tragwerkslehre: Vordimensionierung. Hochschule Ostwestfalen-Lippe

439 *Own representation;* Wismar, Germany 2014

440 *Oberfrancová, L.;* HafenCity Hamburg, Germany 06/2015

441 *Own representation, inspired by BMU;* Ökobau.dat 2013 [http://www.nachhaltigesbauen.de/baustoff-und-gebaeudedaten/oekobaudat.html] (04.05.2014)

442 *Own representation, inspired by Steinborn,V.;* Verordnung über Arbeitsstätten (ArbStättV). Stuttgart: Kohlhammer Verlag 2005, page 92

443 *Student presentation (Skrabák, Z., Vechterová, A.);* Office building for Wings on Campus Wismar, Germany. Hochschule Wismar, Faculty of Architecture and Design, Green Building Class WS 2013/2014

444 *Own representation, inspired by Deutsches Institut für Normung e.V.;* Energetische Bewertung von Gebäuden DIN V 18599-10:2011-12

445 *Student presentation (Skrabák, Z., Vechterová, A.);* Office building for Wings on Campus Wismar, Germany. Hochschule Wismar, Faculty of Architecture and Design, Green Building Class WS 2013/2014

List of figures

446 *Own representation, inspired by Schachtschneider, S.;* Energiekonzept für die Entwicklung des Geländes „Alte Brauerei Schwerin". Germany, Wismar: Hochschule Wismar, Faculty of Architecture and Design 02/2013

447 *Own representation, inspired by Deutsches Institut für Normung e.V.;* Energetische Bewertung von Gebäuden DIN V 18599-10:2011-12

448 *Own representation, inspired by stromverbrauch-haushalt.de;* [http://www.stromverbrauch-haushalt.de] (04.05.2014)

449 *Own representation;* Wismar, Germany 2014

450 *Own representation, inspired by stromspartipps.net* [http://www.stromspartipps.net/stromverbrauch/stromsparpotentiale] (04.05.2014)

451 *Own representation, inspired by BMVBS;* Leitfaden Nachhaltiges Bauen. Berlin: BMVBS 04/2013, Appendix page 31

452 *Own representation, inspired by BMVBS;* Leitfaden Nachhaltiges Bauen. Berlin: BMVBS 04/2013, Appendix page 34

453 *Own representation, inspired by BMVBS;* Leitfaden Nachhaltiges Bauen. Berlin: BMVBS 04/2013, Appendix page 33

454 *Own representation, inspired by Finke, U., Fitzner, K.;* Lüftungsregeln für freie Lüftung. Dortmund/Berlin/Dresden 2012

455 *Own representation,inspired by Deutsches Institut für Normung e.V.;* Energetische Bewertung von Gebäuden DIN V 18599-10:2011-12

456 *Own representation, inspired by Abschnitt 3 ASR 5 - 3 Bundesrecht;* Arbeitsstätten-Richtlinie Lüftung (ASR 5) Zu § 5 der Arbeitsstättenverordnung [http://www.baua.de/de/Themen-von-A-Z/Arbeitsstaetten/ASR/pdf/ASR-A3-6.pdf?__blob=publicationFile&v=4] (12.04.2014)

457 *Own representation;* Wismar, Germany 2014

458 *Own representation, inspired by Viessmann;* Planungshandbuch Solarthermie. Allendorf: Viessman Werke 11/2008, page 23

459 *Own representation, inspired by Viessmann;* Planungshandbuch Solarthermie. Allendorf: Viessman Werke 11/2008, page 57

460 *Own representation, inspired by solera.de* [http://www.solera.de/solera/images/stories/content/Sonneneinstrahlung/sonneneinstrahlung_gross.jpg] (04.04.2013)

461 *Own representation, inspired by elco.ch* [http://www.elco.ch/pdf/3td_sys_02_solatron_d.pdf] (04.04.2013)

462 *Own representation, inspired by elco.ch* [http://www.elco.ch/pdf/3td_sys_02_solatron_d.pdf] (04.04.2013)

463 *Own representation, inspired by solarbayer.de* [http://www.solarbayer.de/Planungshilfe-Waermepumpen.html] (04.04.2013)

464 *Own representation, inspired by solarbayer.de* [http://www.solarbayer.de/Planungshilfe-Waermepumpen.html] (04.04.2013)

465 *Own representation,inspired by solarbayer.de* [http://www.solarbayer.de/Planungshilfe-Waermepumpen.html] (04.04.2013)

466 *Own representation;* Wismar, Germany 2014

467 *Own representation, inspired by photon-solar.de* [http://www.photon-solar.de/index.php?seite=einspeiseverguetung] (04.04.2013)

468 *Own representation, inspired by CET Technology* [http://www.cet-technology.de/Download/winDual_V-WKA_A5K.pdf] (04.04.2013)

469 *Own representation, inspired by CET Technology* [http://www.cet-technology.de/] (04.04.2013)

470 *Own representation, inspired by sharepoint.infra-fuerth.de* [https://sharepoint.infra-fuerth.de/unbundling/verguetungssaetze_eeg_pv_2013.pdf] (04.04.2013)

471 *Own representation;* Wismar, Germany 2014

472 *Own representation, inspired by stromtip.de* [http://www.stromtip.de/UserFiles/Image/grafiken/Stromspeicher_Kapazitaet1000x500.jpg] (04.04.2013)

473 *Own representation, inspired by GEMIS 4.13 Datenbank;* Germany

474 *Own representation, inspired by BMU;* Ökobau.dat 2013 [http://www.nachhaltigesbauen.de/baustoff-und-gebaeudedaten/oekobaudat.html] (04.05.2014)

475 *Own representation, inspired by Energiemanagement der Stadt Frankfurt;* [http://www.energiemanagement.stadt-frankfurt.de/Betriebsoptimierung/Seminarprogramm/Seminar-Teil-4-Wasser.pdf] (14.04.2013)

476 *Own representation, inspired by DGNB;* Neubau Büro- und Verwaltungsgebäude. Steckbrief 14 Trinkwasserbedarf und Abwasseraufkommen. DGNB: Version 2009

477 *Own representation, inspired by DGNB;* Neubau Büro- und Verwaltungsgebäude. Steckbrief 14 Trinkwasserbedarf und Abwasseraufkommen. DGNB: Version 2009

478 *Own representation;* Wismar, Germany 2014

479 *Own representation, inspired by Glücklich, D (publisher);* Ecological Architecture [http://ecologic-architecture.org/main/] (08.10.2012)

480 *Own representation, inspired by DGNB;* Neubau Büro- und Verwaltungsgebäude. Steckbrief 16 Gebäudebezogene Kosten - Lebenszykluskosen. DGNB: Version 2009

481 *Own representation, inspired by DGNB;* Neubau Büro- und Verwaltungsgebäude. Steckbrief 16 Gebäudebezogene Kosten - Lebenszykluskosen. DGNB: Version 2009

482 *Own representation, inspired byheizsparer.de;* [http://www.heizsparer.de/heizung/heizungssysteme/waermepumpe/waermepumpen-kosten] (on 14.08.2014) and solaranlage.eu; [http://www.solaranlage.eu/solar/solaranlagen-preise] (14.08.2014)

483 *Own representation, inspired by DGNB;* Neubau Büro- und Verwaltungsgebäude. Steckbrief 16 Gebäudebezogene Kosten - Lebenszykluskosen. DGNB: Version 2009

484 *Own representation;* Wismar, Germany 2014

485 *Own representation, inspired by DGNB;* Neubau Büro- und Verwaltungsgebäude. Steckbrief 16 Gebäudebezogene Kosten - Lebenszykluskosen. DGNB: Version 2009

486 *Own representation, inspired by Köhler, M., Schmidt, M.;* Benefits for Sustainable Water Management - Green roof technology. World Green Roof Congress. London: 16.-19. September

487 *Own representation, inspired by Schmidt, M.;* Die Reduzierung des Energieverbrauchs für Kühlung und Belüftung [http://www.gebaeudekuehlung.de/SunAndSense2008.pdf] (22.09.2014)

488 *Own representation, inspired by Statistisches Bundesamt;* Umwelt. Erlebung über Haushaltsabfälle (bei den öffentlich-rechtlichen Entsorgungsträgern) [https://www.destatis.de/DE/ZahlenFakten/GesamtwirtschaftUmwelt/Umwelt/UmweltstatistischeErhebungen/Abfallwirtschaft/Tabellen/ErgebnisberichtHaushaltsabfaelle.pdf;jsessionid=CC57896384B35918665A17E7F7C4A0A5.cae3?__blob=publicationFile] (22.09.2014)

489 *Own representation, inspired by Statistisches Bundesamt;* Umwelt. Erlebung über Haushaltsabfälle (bei den öffentlich-rechtlichen Entsorgungsträgern) [https://www.destatis.de/DE/ZahlenFakten/GesamtwirtschaftUmwelt/Umwelt/UmweltstatistischeErhebungen/Abfallwirtschaft/Tabellen/ErgebnisberichtHaushaltsabfaelle.pdf;jsessionid=CC57896384B35918665A17E7F7C4A0A5.cae3?__blob=publicationFile] (on 22.09.2014)

490 *Students (Chalmers, J., Riebort, A., Schachtschneider, S.);* Ein Projekt von Holzwerkstoffe EGGER Werk Wismar in Zusammenarbeit mit der Hochschule Wismar. Germany, Hochschule Wismar, Faculty of Architecture and Design 06.09.2011

491 *Students (Chalmers, J., Riebort, A., Schachtschneider, S.);* Ein Projekt von Holzwerkstoffe EGGER Werk Wismar in Zusammenarbeit mit der Hochschule Wismar. Germany, Hochschule Wismar, Faculty of Architecture and Design 06.09.2011

10.0 Methods and instruments

492 *IGEL-Institut;* Wismar, Germany 2010

493 *Oberfrancová, L.;* Garz/Rügen, Germany 2014

494 *Oberfrancová, L.;* Garz/Rügen, Germany 2014

495 *Own representation;* Wismar, Germany 2014

496 *Student project (Rudai, S.);* Smart Material House. Germany, Hochschule Wismar, Faculty of Architecture and Design SS 2010

497 *Student project (Rudai, S.);* Smart Material House. Germany, Hochschule Wismar, Faculty of Architecture and Design SS 2010

498 *Student project (Rudai, S.);* Smart Material House. Germany, Hochschule Wismar, Faculty of Architecture and Design SS 2010

499 *BMVBS;* Energieausweis für Gebäude - nach Energieeinsparverordnung (EnEV 2009). Informationsbroschüre des Bundesministeriums für Verkehr, Bau und Stadtentwicklung. Berlin: BMVBS 01.12.2009, page 60

500 *Student project (Rudai, S.);* Smart Material House. Germany, Hochschule Wismar, Faculty of Architecture and Design SS 2010

501 *Student project (Rudai, S.);* Smart Material House. Germany, Hochschule Wismar, Faculty of Architecture and Design SS 2010

502 *Fraunhofer-Institut für Bauphysik IBP;* Logo WUFI®. Valley, Germany 02/2016

503 *Oberfrancová, L.;* Wismar, Germany 2014

504 *Oberfrancová,L.;* Wismar, Germany 2014

505 *Ascona Gesellschaft für ökologische Projekte. König, H.;* Legep®. Gröbenzell, Germany12/2015

506 *Ascona Gesellschaft für ökologische Projekte. König, H.;* Legep®. Gröbenzell, Germany 12/2015

507 *Ascona Gesellschaft für ökologische Projekte. König, H.;* Legep®. Gröbenzell, Germany 12/2015

508 *Sachdev, S.;* Wismar, Germany 03/2013

509 *Sachdev, S.;* Wismar, Germany 03/2013

510 *Student project (Mahendra, A.);* Las Vegas project. Germany, Hochschule Wismar, Lighting Design study program

511 *Oberfrancová, L.;* Wismar, Germany 2012

512 *Oberfrancová, L.;* Wismar, Germany 2012

513 *IGEL-Institut;* Wismar, Germany 2012

514 *Energy.gov. Office of Energy Efficiency & Renewable Energy. Building Energy Modeling;* 12/2015

515 *DesignBuilder Software Ltd;* London, United Kingdom 12/2015

516 *DesignBuilder Software Ltd;* London, United Kingdom 12/2015

517 *DesignBuilder Software Ltd;* London, United Kingdom 12/2015

518 *DesignBuilder Software Ltd;* London, United Kingdom 12/2015

519 *DesignBuilder Software Ltd;* London, United Kingdom 12/2015

520 *GEV - Gemeinschaft Emissionskontrollierte Verlegewerkstoffe, Klebstoffe und Bauprodukte e.V.;* EMICODE®. Düsseldorf, Germany 11/2015

521 *Umweltbundesamt. FG III 1.3 Ökodesign, Umweltkennzeichnung, Umweltfreundliche Beschaffung;* The Blue Angel. Dessau, Germany 12/2015

522 *Federal Institute for Research on Building, Urban Affairs and Spatial Development within the Federal Office for Building and Regional Planning. Division II 6 Construction and Environment;* WECOBIS. Berlin, Germany 12/2015

523 *Own representation, inspired by Waltjen, T., Mötzl, H., Mück, W., Torghele, K., Zelger, T.;* Ökologischer Bauteilkatalog. Wien: Springer; 1999, page 58

524 *Own representation, inspired by Waltjen, T., Mötzl, H., Mück, W., Torghele, K., Zelger, T.;* Ökologischer Bauteilkatalog. Wien: Springer; 1999, page 42

525 *Oberfrancová, L.;* Monitoring Kindergarten "Wildblume". Wismar , Germany 04/2015

526 *Oberfrancová, L.;* Monitoring Kindergarten "Wildblume". Wismar, Germany 04/2015

527 *Oberfrancová, L.;* Monitoring Theater Wismar. Wismar 12/2015

11.0 Examples

528 *Wollensak architects;* Wismar, Germany 2010

529 *IGEL-Institut;* Bützow, Germany 2011

530 *IGEL-Institut;* Wismar, Germany 2013

531 *Wollensak architects;* Weikersheim, Germany 1998

532 *Wollensak architects;* Island Poel, Germany 2002

533 *IGEL-Institut;* Wismar, Germany 2010

534 *IGEL-Institut;* Wismar, Germany 2014

535 *Wollensak architects;* Stuttgart, Germany 1995

536 *Wollensak architects;* Weikersheim, Germany 1998

537 *Wollensak architects;* Stuttgart, Germany 1995

538 *Wollensak architects;* Stuttgart, Germany 1995

539 *Wollensak architects;* Weikersheim, Germany 1996

540 *Wollensak architects;* Stuttgart, Germany 1995

541 *Wollensak architects;* Stuttgart, Germany 1995

542 *Wollensak architects;* Erfelden, Germany 1998

543 *Wollensak architects;* Stuttgart, Germany 1995

544 *Wollensak architects;* Stuttgart, Germany 1995

545 *Wollensak architects;* Erfelden, Germany1998

546 *Wollensak architects;* Erfelden, Germany 1998

547 *Wollensak architects;* Wismar, Germany 2002

548 *Wollensak architects;* Wismar, Germany 2002

549 *Wollensak architects;* Wismar, Germany 2002

550 *Wollensak architects;* Wismar, Germany 2002

551 *Wollensak architects;* Wismar, Germany 2002

552 *IGEL-Institut;* Wismar, Germany 2005

553 *IGEL-Institut;* Wismar, Germany 2005

554 *IGEL-Institut;* Wismar, Germany 2005

555 *IGEL-Institut;* Wismar, Germany 2005

556 *IGEL-Institut;* Wismar, Germany 2005

557 *IGEL-Institut;* Wismar, Germany 2005

558 *Wollensak architects;* Wismar, Germany 2007

559 *Wollensak architects;* Wismar, Germany 2007

560 *Wollensak architects;* Wismar, Germany 2007

561 *Wollensak architects;* Wismar, Germany 2006

562 *Wollensak architects;* Wismar, Germany 2006

563 *Wollensak architects*; Wismar, Germany 2006

564 *IGEL-Institut;* Wismar, Germany 2010

565 *IGEL-Institut;* Wismar, Germany 2010

566 *IGEL-Institut;* Wismar, Germany 2010

567 *IGEL-Institut;* Wismar, Germany 2010

568 *IGEL-Institut;* Wismar, Germany 2010

569 *IGEL-Institut;* Wismar, Germany 2010

570 *IGEL-Institut;* Wismar, Germany 2010

571 *IGEL-Institut;* Wismar, Germany 2010

572 *IGEL-Institut;* Wismar, Germany 2011

573 *IGEL-Institut;* Wismar, Germany 2011

574 *IGEL-Institut;* Wismar, Germany 2011

575 *IGEL-Institut;* Wismar, Germany 2011

576 *IGEL-Institut;* Wismar, Germany 2011

577 *IGEL-Institut;* Wismar, Germany 2011

578 *IGEL-Institut;* Wismar, Germany 2011

579 *IGEL-Institut;* Wismar, Germany 2014

580 *Oberfrancová, L.;* Garz/Rügen, Germany 05/2015

List of figures

581 *IGEL-Institut;* Wismar, Germany 2014
582 *IGEL-Institut;* Wismar, Germany 2014
583 *Oberfrancová, L.;* Garz/Rügen, Germany 2014
584 *IGEL-Institut;* Wismar, Germany 2010
585 *IGEL-Institut;* Wismar, Germany 2010
586 *IGEL-Institut;* Wismar, Germany 2010
587 *IGEL-Institut;* Wismar, Germany 2010
588 *IGEL-Institut;* Wismar, Germany 2008
589 *IGEL-Institut;* Wismar, Germany 2008
590 *IGEL-Institut;* Wismar, Germany 2008
591 *IGEL-Institut;* Wismar, Germany 2008
592 *IGEL-Institut;* Wismar, Germany 2008
593 *IGEL-Institut;* Wismar, Germany 2008
594 *IGEL-Institut;* Wismar, Germany 2008
595 *IGEL-Institut;* Wismar, Germany 2008
596 *IGEL-Institut;* Wismar, Germany 2008
597 *IGEL-Institut;* Wismar, Germany 2008
598 *IGEL-Institut;* Wismar, Germany 2008
599 *IGEL-Institut;* Wismar, Germany 2008
600 *IGEL-Institut;* Wismar, Germany 2008
601 *IGEL-Institut;* Wismar, Germany 2008
602 *IGEL-Institut;* Wismar, Germany 2008
603 *IGEL-Institut;* Wismar, Germany 2008
604 *IGEL-Institut;* Wismar, Germany 2008
605 *IGEL-Institut;* Wismar, Germany 2008
606 *IGEL-Institut;* Wismar, Germany 2008
607 *IGEL-Institut;* Wismar, Germany 2008
608 *Students project;* Konzept 2020: Konzept zur nachhaltigen baulichen Weiterentwicklung der Hochschule Wismar zum umweltgerechten Campus der Zukunft. Germany, Wismar: Hochschule Wismar, Faculty of Architecture and Design 2008
609 *Students project;* Konzept 2020: Konzept zur nachhaltigen baulichen Weiterentwicklung der Hochschule Wismar zum umweltgerechten Campus der Zukunft. Germany, Wismar: Hochschule Wismar, Faculty of Architecture and Design 2008
610 *Students project;* Konzept 2020: Konzept zur nachhaltigen baulichen Weiterentwicklung der Hochschule Wismar zum umweltgerechten Campus der Zukunft. Germany, Wismar: Hochschule Wismar, Faculty of Architecture and Design 2008
611 *Students project;* Konzept 2020: Konzept zur nachhaltigen baulichen Weiterentwicklung der Hochschule Wismar zum umweltgerechten Campus der Zukunft. Germany, Wismar: Hochschule Wismar, Faculty of Architecture and Design 2008
612 *Students project;* Konzept 2020: Konzept zur nachhaltigen baulichen Weiterentwicklung der Hochschule Wismar zum umweltgerechten Campus der Zukunft. Germany, Wismar: Hochschule Wismar, Faculty of Architecture and Design 2008
613 *Students project;* Konzept 2020: Konzept zur nachhaltigen baulichen Weiterentwicklung der Hochschule Wismar zum umweltgerechten Campus der Zukunft. Germany, Wismar: Hochschule Wismar, Faculty of Architecture and Design 2008
614 *Students project;* Konzept 2020: Konzept zur nachhaltigen baulichen Weiterentwicklung der Hochschule Wismar zum umweltgerechten Campus der Zukunft. Germany, Wismar: Hochschule Wismar, Faculty of Architecture and Design 2008
615 *Oberfrancová, L.;* Wismar, Germany 02/2016
616 *IGEL-Institut;* Wismar, Germany 2008
617 *IGEL-Institut;* Wismar, Germany 2008
618 *Oberfrancová, L.;* Wismar, Germany 2013
619 *IGEL-Institut;* Wismar, Germany 2004
620 *IGEL-Institut;* Wismar, Germany 2004
621 *IGEL-Institut;* Wismar, Germany 2004
622 *Oberfrancová, L.;* Wismar, Germany 10/2014
623 *IGEL-Institut;* Rostock, Germany 2015
624 *IGEL-Institut;* Wismar, Germany 2005
625 *IGEL-Institut;* Wismar, Germany 2005
626 *IGEL-Institut;* Wismar, Germany 2005
627 *IGEL-Institut;* Wismar, Germany 2005
628 *IGEL-Institut;* Wismar, Germany 2005
629 *IGEL-Institut;* Wismar, Germany 2005
630 *IGEL-Institut;* Wismar, Germany 2005
631 *IGEL-Institut;* Wismar, Germany 2005
632 *IGEL-Institut;* Wismar, Germany 2005
633 *IGEL-Institut;* Wismar, Germany 2005
634 *IGEL-Institut;* Wismar, Germany 2005
635 *IGEL-Institut;* Wismar, Germany 2011
636 *IGEL-Institut;* Wismar, Germany 2011
637 *IGEL-Institut;* Wismar, Germany 2011
638 *IGEL-Institut;* Wismar, Germany 2011
639 *IGEL-Institut;* Wismar, Germany 2011
640 *IGEL-Institut;* Wismar, Germany 2013
641 *IGEL-Institut;* Wismar, Germany 2013
642 *IGEL-Institut;* Wismar, Germany 2013
643 *IGEL-Institut;* Wismar, Germany 2013
644 *IGEL-Institut;* Wismar, Germany 2013
645 *IGEL-Institut;* Wismar, Germany 2013
646 *IGEL-Institut;* Wismar, Germany 2010 and *IGEL-Institut;* Garz/Rügen, Germany 2014

Literature

Key words, energy standards and norms

Baulexikon; Wärmeschutzverordnung [http://www.baulexikon.de/NEWS_web/Bauordnung/Waermeschutzverordnung/Waermeschutzverordnung_start.htm] (20.09.2012)

BMVBS; Energieausweis für Gebäude - nach Energieeinsparverordnung (EnEV 2009). Informationsbroschüre des Bundesministeriums für Verkehr, Bau und Stadtentwicklung. Berlin: BMVBS 01.12.2009

BMVBS; Externe Kosten im Hochbau. BMVBS-Online-Publikation Nr. 17/2010. Berlin: BMVBS 10/2010

Das-Energieportal; 3-Liter-Haus [http://www.das-energieportal.de/wohneigentuemer/3-liter-haus] (20.09.2012)

Das-Energieportal; Niedrigenergiehaus [http://www.das-energieportal.de/wohneigentuemer/niedrigenergiehaus/] (20.09.2012)

Deutsches Institut für Normung e.V.; Energetische Bewertung von Gebäuden DIN V 18599 (11 parts). Edition 2011-12

Deutsches Institut für Normung e.V.; Grundflächen und Rauminhalte von Bauwerken im Hochbau DIN 277 (3 parts). Edition 2005

Deutsches Institut für Normung e.V.; Kosten im Bauwesen DIN 276 Teil 1: Hochbau. Edition 2008-12

Deutsches Institut für Normung e.V.; Wärmeschutz im Hochbau DIN 4108.

Deutsches Institut für Normung e.V.; Wärmeschutz und Energie-Einsparung in Gebäuden - Wärmebrücken - Planungs- und Ausführungsbeispiele DIN 4108 Beiblatt 2. Edition 2006-03

ECEEE - European Council for an Energy Efficient Economy; Steering through the maze #2. Nearly zero energy buildings: achieving the EU 2020 target. Stockholm/Schweden: ECEEE Secretariat 08.02.2011

Hegger,M., Fuchs,M., Stark,T., Zeumer,M.; Energie Atlas. Nachhaltige Architektur. München: Birkhäuser 2008

Kanzlei Dr. Bruck - Ingenieurkonsulent für technische Physik, Österreichisches Ökologie Institut für angewandte Umweltforschung; Externe Kosten im Hochbau Band I-V. Wien: Bundesministerium für Wirtschaft und Arbeit 05/2002

KfW-Konzern; KfW: Bank aus Verantwortung [https://www.kfw.de/kfw.de.html] (on 20.09.2012)

Netzwerk Energieberater; Primärenergiefaktor [http://www.netzwerk-energieberater.de/wiki/Prim%C3%A4renergiefaktor] (20.09.2012)

Passipedia; Planning a Passive House [http://passipedia.passiv.de/passipedia_en/planning] (20.09.2012)

Passivhaus Institut; Passivhaus Institut [http://www.passiv.de/] (20.09.2012)

Planungsgruppe Green Energy+Haus; Energieeffiziente Gebäudeplanung [http://www.nullenergiehaus.com/index.php] (20.09.2012)

Rolf Disch SolarArchitektur; Das Ziel ist Plusenergie [http://www.plusenergiehaus.de/index.php?p=home&pid=8&L=0&host=1] (20.09.2012)

Schoblocher,P.; Master Thesis: Bestand erhalten - Teilrückbau, Umbau und Erweiterung - Abbruch und Neubau? Investitionsüberlegungen und Entscheidungsprozesse zum Nachhaltigen Bauen - Vergleichende Untersuchungen unter Berücksichtigung der „Externen Kosten“ am Beispiel „Neubau Rathaus Thannhausen“. Wings at Hochschule Wismar, Distance Study Program Architecture and Environment 11/2011

Sobek,W.; Triple Zero® [http://www.wernersobek.de/index.php?page=392] (20.09.2012)

Tuschinski,M.; EnEV 2014 - die neue Energieeinsparverordnung [http://www.enev-online.com/enev_2014_volltext/index.htm] (12.04.2014)

Wikipedia; Energiestandard: Deutschland [http://de.wikipedia.org/wiki/Energiestandard] (20.09.2012)

Wikipedia; KfW (Kreditanstalt für Wiederaufbau) [http://de. wikipedia.org/wiki/KfW_Bankengruppe] (20.09.2012)

Wikipedia; Life-cycle assessment [http://en.wikipedia.org/wiki/Life-cycle_assessment] (20.09.2012)

Wikipedia; Wärmeschutzverordnung [http://de.wikipedia.org/wiki/Wärmeschutzverordnung] (20.09.2012)

1.0 Strategies and regulations

[http://www.constructionproducts.org.uk/publications/industry-affairs/display/view/construction-products-regulation/] (11.04.2014)

[http://www.nachhaltigkeit.info/media/1285831803phpz9Rqi2.pdf?sid=c450b23a7df80836eea8441c40af9957] (11.10.2012)

Baunetz Wissen; Nachhaltig Bauen: DGNB Zertifizierung für Stadtquartiere [http://www.baunetzwissen.de/standardartikel/Nachhaltig-Bauen-DGNB-Zertifizierung-fuer-Stadtquartiere_2402803.html] (24.09.2012)

Bezirksregierung Düsseldorf; Allgemeines zur Marktüberwachung harmonisierter Bauprodukte [http://www.brd.nrw.de/planen_bauen/marktueberwachung/1_Allgemeine_Informationen.html] (11.04.2014)

BMBF; Die Hightech-Strategie 2020 für Deutschland vorantreiben [http://www.bmbf.de/de/19870.php] (11.10.2012)

BMBF; High-Tech-Strategy [http://www.bmbf.de/en/6618.php] (11.10.2012)

BMBF; The High-Tech Strategy for Germany. Berlin: BMBF 2006

BMU; Bewertungssystem Nachhaltiges Bauen (BNB) [https://www.bnb-nachhaltigesbauen.de/] (04.08.2014)

BMU; EEG-The Renewable Energy Sources Act. Berlin: BMU 07/2007

BMU; EU Strategy for Sustainable Development [http://www.bmu.de/english/sustainability_globalisation/current/doc/35355.php] (10.10.2012)

BMU; Guideline for Sustainable Building. Berlin: BMU 03/2014

BMU; Leitfaden Nachhaltiges Bauen. Guideline for Sustainable Building [www.nachhaltigesbauen.de] (10.10.2013)

BMU; The Renewable Energies Heat Act [http://www.bmu.de/english/renewable_energy/downloads/doc/42351.php] (12.10.2012)

BMU; Waste management [Online: http://www.bmu.de/english/waste_management/doc/3432.php] (12.10.2012)

BMVBS; Energieausweis für Gebäude - nach Energieeinsparverordnung (EnEV 2009). Informationsbroschüre des Bundesministeriums für Verkehr, Bau und Stadtentwicklung. Berlin: BMVBS 01.12.2009

BMVBS; Energieeinsparverordnung [http://www.bmvbs.de/DE/BauenUndWohnen/EnergieeffizienteGebaeude/Energieeinsparverordnung/energieeinsparverordnung_node] (12.10.2012)

BMVBS; Guideline for Sustainable Building. Berlin: BMVBS 01/2001

BMVBS; Leitfaden Nachhaltiges Bauen. Berlin: BMVBS 04/2013

BMWI, BMU; Energy Concept for an Environmentally Sound, Reliable and Affordable Energy Supply. Berlin: BMWi, BMU 09/2010

BMWI; Act on the promotion of renewable energies in the heat sector [http://www.erneuerbare-energien.de/en/unser-service/mediathek/downloads/detailview/artikel/act-on-the-promotion-of-renewable-energies-in-the-heat-sector-heat-act-eewaermeg/] (12.10.2012)

BMWI; Energieszenarien für ein Energiekonzept der Bundesregierung. Projekt Nr. 12/10. Basel, Köln Osnabrück: Prognos AG, EWI, GWS 08/2010

BREEAM®; BREEAM 2008 Award Winners [http://www.breeam.org/filelibrary/BREEAM%20Awards/BREEAM_Awards_2008_PRESS.pdf] (30.07.2012)

BREEAM®; Evaluation with BREEAM [http://www.qed-energy.com/breeam.html] (30.07.2012)

Literature

BREEAM®; The world´s leading design and assessment method for sustainable buildings [www.breeam.org] (on 30.07.2012)

BREEAM®; What is BREEAM? [http://www.breeam.org/about.jsp?id=66] (30.07.2012)

Brindabella Business Park; 8 Brindabella Circuit [http://airportbusinessparks.com.au/brindabella/properties/?view=2830] (30.07.2012)

Building Regulations Advisory Body; Information Note on the Construction Products Regulation [http://www.environ.ie/en/Publications/DevelopmentandHousing/BuildingStandards/FileDownLoad,30649,en.pdf] (11.04.2014)

Bundesministerium der Justiz und für Verbraucherschutz; Gesetz zur Förderung der Kreislaufwirtschaft und Sicherung der umweltverträglichen Beseitigung von Abfällen (Kreislaufwirtschafts- und Abfallgesetz – KrW-/AbfG) [http://www.gesetze-im-internet.de/krwg/] (12.10.2012)

Business-on.de; Zusammenarbeit von Wirtschaft und Wissenschaft in der in neuer EU-Förderperiode [http://www.business-on.de/meck-pomm/industriepolitische-konferenz-zusammenarbeit-von-wirtschaft-und-wissenschaft-in-der-in-neuer-eu-foerderperiode-_id3626.html] (30.05.2014)

CASBEE®; Comprehensive Assessment System for Built Environment Efficiency: An Overview of CASBEE [http://www.ibec.or.jp/CASBEE/english/overviewE.htm] (30.07.2012)

CASBEE®; Comprehensive Assessment System for Built Environment Efficiency [http://www.ibec.or.jp/CASBEE/english/index.htm] (30.07.2012)

China GB; China Green Building [http://www.chinagb.net/chinagbc/] (30.07.2012)

China GB; China Three Star Green Building Standard [http://www.sue-chen.com/lqlab/china-three-star-green-building-standard.html] (30.07.2012)

Common Sense for the World; Manifesto for sustainable architecture and civil engineering issued by architects, engineers and town planners in Germany. [http://www.klima-manifest.de/fileadmin/templates/klima-manifest/images/BDAKlimaManifestENGLISCH.pdf] (30.07.2012)

Construction products association; Guidance Note on the Construction Products Regulation

Deutsches Institut für Normung e.V.; Energetische Bewertung von Gebäuden DIN V 18599 (11 parts). Edition 2011-12

DGNB; Deutsche Gesellschaft für Nachhaltiges Bauen. German Sustainable Building Council [www.dgnb.de] (09.10.2012)

DGNB; DGNB at a glance [http://www.dgnb.de/dgnb-system/de/aktuell/news/detail.php?we_objectID=4406] (09.10.2012)

DGNB; DGNB System: Nutzungsprofile: Zertifizierungsvoraussetzungen Stadtquartiere [http://www.dgnb-system.de/dgnb-system/de/nutzungsprofile/ueber-nutzungsprofile/zertifizierungsvoraussetzungen_Stadtquartiere.php] (24.09.2012)

DGNB; DGNB Systemgrundlagen. Nutzungsprofil Neubau Stadtquartiere. DGNB: Version 2012

DGNB; German sustainable building certificate. Structure – Application – Criteria. Stuttgart: DGNB 03/2009

DGNB; Impuls 2013: Stadtquartiere erfolgreich zertifizieren: Grundlagen und Praxisbericht [http://www.dgnb.de/fileadmin/de/dgnb_ev/Veranstaltungen/eigene_veranstaltungen/dgnb-impuls/Vortraege_Impuls/Praesentation_Impuls_Stadtquartiere.pdf] (24.07.2014)

DGNB; Neubau Büro- und Verwaltungsgebäude. Steckbriefe 01-61. DGNB: Version 2009

DGNB; Presentation of DGNB. Stuttgart: DGNB 2008

DGNB; Presentation of DGNB International. Stuttgart: DGNB 2010

Die Bundesregierung; Energiewende weiter voranbringen [http://www.bundesregierung.de/Content/DE/Artikel/2014/01/2014-01-09-energiewende-im-koalitionsvertrag.html] (24.04.2014)

Die Bundesregierung; High-Tech-Strategy [http://www.hightech-strategie.de/en/index.php] (11.10.2012)

Drees & Sommer AG; Referenzen: Potsdamer Platz [http://www.dreso.com/german/referenzen/Potsdamer_Platz.asp] (24.09.2012)

Ecocity Builders; Why Ecocities? [http://www.ecocitybuilders.org/why-ecocities/] (10.10.2012)

EnEff:Stadt; EnEff:Stadt. Forschung für die energieeffiziente Stadt [http://www.eneff-stadt.info/en/research-initiatives/] (10.10.2012)

EnEff:Stadt; Heating and cooling networks: Projects: Intelligent network of urban infrastructures – Smart Power Hamburg [http://www.eneff-stadt.info/en/heatingcooling-networks/project/details/intelligent-network-of-urban-infrastructures-smart-power-hamburg/] (10.10.2012)

EnEff:Stadt; Heating and cooling networks: Projects: Intelligent network of urban infrastructures – Smart Power Hamburg [http://www.eneff-stadt.info/en/heatingcooling-networks/project/details/intelligent-network-of-urban-infrastructures-smart-power-hamburg/] (10.10.2012)

EnEff:Stadt; Pilot projects: Climate-neutral campus at Leuphana University Lüneburg [http://www.eneff-stadt.info/en/pilot-projects/project/details/climate-neutral-campus-at-leuphana-university-lueneburg/] (10.10.2012)

European Commission; European Commission: Sustainable Development[http://ec.europa.eu/environment/eussd/] (10.10.2012)

European Union; Europa. Summaries of EU legislation: Energy performance of buildings [http://europa.eu/legislation_summaries/internal_market/single_market_for_goods/construction/en0021_en.htm] (11.10.2012)

European Union; Europa. Summaries of EU legislation: Waste management [http://europa.eu/legislation_summaries/environment/waste_management/ev0010_de.htm] (11.05.2014)

European Union; Europa: Zusammenfassungen der EU-Gesetzgebung [http://europa.eu/legislation_summaries/employment_and_social_policy/eu2020/growth_and_jobs/index_de.htm] (10.10.2012)

ForschungsInformationsSystem; Ökobilanz nach DIN EN ISO 14040 und 14044 [http://www.forschungsinformationssystem.de/servlet/is/349763/](11.04.2014)

Green Building Council Australia; Green Star: What is Green Star? [www.gbca.org.au/green-star/green-star-overview/] (30.07.2012)

IHK zu Schwerin; Regionale Innovationsstrategie [http://www.ihkzuschwerin.de/ihksn/Presse/Daten/2013/04/pm13_IHKsMV07.html] (30.05.2014)

International Centre for Quality Certification; CE Marking Decision 768/2008/EC (93/68/EEC) [http://www.icqc.co.uk/en/CE-marking-process.php] (11.04.2014)

Lewis,G.; China Green Buildings: A blog about green buildings and related sustainability topics in China. [http://chinagreenbuildings.blogspot.de/] (30.07.2012)

Lexikon der Nachhaltigkeit; Energiekonzept 2050 [http://www.nachhaltigkeit.info/artikel/deutsches_energiekonzept_2050_2010_1432.htm] (11.10.2012)

Lexikon der Nachhaltigkeit; Energiekonzept für eine umweltschonende, zuverlässige und bezahlbare Energieversorgung

Ministerium für Energie, Infrastruktur und Landesentwicklung M-V; Leitlinien „Energieland 2020“[http://www.regierung-mv.de/cms2/Regierungsportal_prod/Regierungsportal/de/vm/Themen/Energie/Leitlinien_Energieland_2020/index.jsp] (30.07.2012)

Ministerium für Wirtschaft, Arbeit und Tourismus M-V; Energieland 2020. Gesamtstrategie für Mecklenburg – Vorpommern. Schwerin: Ministerium für Wirtschaft, Arbeit und Tourismus M-V 04/2009

Müller,Ch. (publisher); Urban Gardening: Über die Rückkehr der Gärten in die Stadt [http://www.urban-gardening.eu/] (10.10.2012)

New Zealand Green Building Council; About Green Star [http://www.nzgbc.org.nz/index.php?option=com_content&view=article&id=17&Itemid=117] (30.07.2012)

New Zealand Green Building Council; New Zealand Green Building Council [www.nzgbc.org.nz] (30.07.2012)

New Zealand Green Building Council; Rating Tools: Green Star: Certified Projects: Office: 92 Albert Street [http://www.nzgbc.org.nz/index.php?option=com_content&view=article&id=154&Itemid=276] (30.07.2012)

Post Carbon Pathways; German Government: Energy Concept [http://www.postcarbonpathways.net.au/transition-strategies/german-government/] (11.10.2012)

PPMG Potsdamer Platz Management Gmbh; Potsdamer Platz [http://potsdamerplatz.de/de/quartier/daten-und-fakten/] (24.09.2012)

Results of students work (Autridge,S., Gill-May,N., Glatzel,M., Jancáryová,V., Jiangning,L., Ma,N., Olexáková,M., Ribovicová,M., Richel,K., Song,X., Stanelle,K., Wang,Ch., Xinchen,P., Yan,Z., Yang,L., Yichun,K., Yixuan,X., Zhang,Ch.,); DGNB evaluation of a new office construction in Wismar harbour, Germany. Hochschule Wismar, Faculty of Architecture and Design, Green Building class WS 2012/2013

Results of students work; Workshop “Green Univer-City Wismar”. Hochschule Wismar, Faculty of Architecture and Design, “Green Univer-City Wismar” workshop 2014

SEB Asset Management; Potsdamer Platz Berlin mit DGNB Nachhaltigkeitszertifikat ausgezeichnet [http://www.sebassetmanagement.de/de/presse/pressebereich/pressemitteilungen/pressemitteilungen-einzelansicht/news/potsdamer_platz_berlin_mit_dgnb_nachhaltigkeitszertifikat_ausgezeichnet/] (24.09.2012)

Sidwell Friends School; Environmental Stewardship: Green Buildings: Middle School [http://www.sidwell.edu/about_sfs/environmental-stewardship/green-buildings/ms-green-building/index.aspx] (30.07.2012)

Takenaka Corporation; Takenaka Corporation main office [http://www.takenaka.co.jp/takenaka_e/service_e/solutions/] (30.07.2012)

The Chemical Company; Eco-Efficiency Analysis and SEEBALANCE. Quantifying Sustainability. Ludwigshafen

Tuschinski,M.; EnEV 2009 [http://www.enev-online.org/enev_2009_volltext/index.htm] (12.10.2012)

Tuschinski,M.; EnEV 2014 - die neue Energieeinsparverordnung [http://www.enev-online.com/enev_2014_volltext/index.htm] (12.04.2014)

USGBC; LEED [http://www.usgbc.org/leed] (on 30.07.2012)

USGBC; U.S. Green Building Council [www.usgbc.org] (30.07.2012)

Wikipedia; Mülltrennung [http://de.wikipedia.org/wiki/M%C3%BClltrennung] (10.05.2014)

Wikipedia; Sustainable city [http://en.wikipedia.org/wiki/Sustainable_city] (10.10.2012)

World Green Building Council; MENA Regional Network [http://www.worldgbc.org/site2/green-building-councils/regional-networks/mena] (08.10.2012)

World Green Building Council; Regional Networks of World GBC [http://www.worldgbc.org/site2/index.php?cID=102] (08.10.2012)

World Green Building Council; The Africa Regional Network [http://www.worldgbc.org/site2/green-building-councils/regional-networks/africa/] (08.10.2012)

World Green Building Council; The Americas Regional Network [http://www.worldgbc.org/site2/green-building-councils/regional-networks/americas/] (08.10.2012)

World Green Building Council; The Asia Pacific Regional Network [http://www.worldgbc.org/site2/green-building-councils/regional-networks/asiapacific] (08.10.2012)

World Green Building Council; The Europe Regional Network [http://www.worldgbc.org/site2/green-building-councils/regional-networks/europe] (08.10.2012)

World Green Building Council; The introduction of GBC

World Green Building Council; World Green Building Council [www.worldgbc.org] (30.07.2012)

2.0 Building life time

BBSR; Nutzungsdauern von Bauteilen für Lebenszyklusanalysen nach Bewertungssystem Nachhaltiges Bauen (BNB). Berlin: BBSR 03.11.2011

BMU, BMVg; Arbeitshilfen Recycling. Arbeitshilfen zum Umgang mit Bau- und Abbruchabfällen

BMU; Assessment System for Sustainable Building: Practical Aids and Tools [http://www.nachhaltigesbauen.de/sustainable-building-english-speaking-information/assessment-system-for-sustainable-building.html] (04.05.2014)

BMU; Bewertungssystem Nachhaltiges Bauen (BNB) [https://www.bnb-nachhaltigesbauen.de/] (04.05.2014)

BMU; Guideline for Sustainable Building. Berlin: BMU 03/2014

BMU; Leitfaden Nachhaltiges Bauen. Guideline for Sustainable Building [www.nachhaltigesbauen.de] (10.05.2014)

BMVBS; Leitfaden Nachhaltiges Bauen. Berlin: BMVBS 04/2013

Bock,S., Hinzen,A., Libbe,J. (publisher); Nachhaltiges Flächenmanagement –in der Praxis erfolgreich kommunizieren. Ansätze und Beispiele aus dem Förderschwerpunkt REFINA. Berlin: Deutsches Institut für Urbanistik GmbH (Difu) 2009

DESTATIS; Waste management: Much reutilisation, hardly any landfilling of waste. Wiesbaden: DESTATIS 28.11.2007

Energy Recovery Council; Waste-to-Energy and Recycling Are Compatible [http://www.energyrecoverycouncil.org/waste-energy-recycling-compatible-a2975] (04.05.2014)

EPA U.S.; Energy Recovery from Waste [http://www.epa.gov/waste/nonhaz/municipal/wte/] (04.05.2014)

Hegger,M., Auch-Schwelk,V., Fuchs,M., Rosenkranz,T.; Baustoff Atlas. München: Institut für international Architektur-Dokumentation GmbH&Co.KG 2005

Heinlein,K., Hilka,M., Hilka,M.; HOAI [http://www.hoai.de/online/HOAI-Text/teil_2.php] (04.05.2014)

Lexikon der Nachhaltigkeit; Schutz des Menschen und der Umwelt: Ziele und Rahmenbedingungen [http://www.nachhaltigkeit.info/artikel/13_bt_ek_mensch_umwelt_664.htm] (04.05.2014)

König,H., Kohler,N., Kreißig,J., Lützkendorf,T.; Lebenszyklusanalyse in der Gebäudeplanung. Grundlagen Berechnung Planungswerkzeuge. München: Institut für internationale Architektur-Dokumentation GmbH&Co.KG 2009

Mück,W.; Baustoffe- und Bautechnik: Baustoffwerte [http://www.gesundbauen.at/BER3-BTE.htm] (04.05.2013)

Profu; Evaluating waste incineration as treatment and energy recovery method from an environmental point of view [http://www.cewep.eu/media/www.cewep.eu/org/med_454/172_profuslides.pdf] (04.05.2014)

Sustainable Sources; Construction Waste Recycling [http://constructionwaste.sustainablesources.com/] (04.05.2014)

Waltjen, T., Mötzl,H., Mück, W., Torghele,K., Zelger,T.; Ökologischer Bauteilkatalog. Wien: Springer; 1999

Literature

3.0 Passive resource-saving concepts (ligh-tech)

[http://www.bbsr.bund.de/BBSR/DE/FP/AO/Standortentwicklung/AkteursorientierteHandlungsstrategien/03_Ergebnisse.html?nn=425600] (05.05.2014)

[http://www.bbsr.bund.de/BBSR/DE/Veroeffentlichungen/BMVBS/WP/2007/2007_Heft51.html?nn=395966] (05.05.2014)

[http://www.enev-im-bestand.de/downloads/leseproben/sanierung-denkmalgeschuetzter-gebaeude.pdf] (10.06.2014)

[http://www.thueringen.de/de/genialzentral/landesinitiative/] (05.05.2014)

Advameg, Inc.; Cork [http://www.madehow.com/Volume-5/Cork.html] (08.11.2012)

Anderson,J.; Umbrella Homes [http://www.norishouse.com/PAHS/UmbrellaHouse.html] (8.11.2012)

Arbeitsgemeinschaft Holz e.V. (publisher); Informationsdienst Holz: Holzbausysteme. Arbeitsgemeinschaft Holz e.V.: Düsseldorf 12/2000

Bambus.com; Bambus.com - das Bambusportal [http://www.bambus.com/] (10.05.2013)

bauingenieur24; Holzbau: Spanloses Verformen Verfestigt Holz [http://www.bauingenieur24.de/fachbeitraege/holzbau/spanloses-verformen-verfestigt-holz] (08.11.2012)

BBSR; Flächenrecycling in suburbanen Räumen: Akteursorientierte Handlungsstrategien und Arbeitshilfen

BBSR; Kreislaufwirtschaft in der städtischen/stadtregionalen Flächennutzung

BBSR; Nutzungsdauern von Bauteilen für Lebenszyklusanalysen nach Bewertungssystem Nachhaltiges Bauen (BNB). Berlin: BBSR 03.11.2011

BMU (publisher); Kategorie 3/2. Umweltfreundliche Technologien - Preisträger 2: Prof. Dr.-Ing. Peer Haller von der Technischen Universität Dresden [http://www.iku-innovationspreis.de/preistraeger-09/kategorie-3-2/] (11.09.2014)

BMU, BMVg; Arbeitshilfen Recycling. Arbeitshilfen zum Umgang mit Bau- und Abbruchabfällen

BMU; Bewertungssystem Nachhaltiges Bauen (BNB) [https://www.bnb-nachhaltigesbauen.de/] (04.08.2014)

BuildingGreen, Inc.; The Next Great Building Material? [http://www.buildinggreen.com/auth/article.cfm/1995/5/1/Straw-The-Next-Great-Building-Material/] (08.11.2012)

Cappadocia Turkey; Underground Cities [http://www.cappadociaturkey.net/undergroundcities.htm] (08.11.2012)

Cobiax®; Benefits [http://www.cobiax.ch/en/benefits.html] (08.11.2012)

Cobiax®; Cobiax®: Betondecken leicht gemacht [http://www.cobiax.com/startseite] (11.09.2014)

Cobiax®; Concept [http://www.cobiax.ch/en/concept.html] (08.11.2012)

Cornell University; Sustainable Campus [http://www.sustainable-campus.cornell.edu/pages/about] (05.05.2014)

Daniels,K.; Advanced Building Systems. A Technical Guide for Architects and Engineers. Basel: Birkhäuser 2003

Daniels,K.; Low-Tech Light-Tech High-Tech. Bauen in der Informationsgesellschaft. Berlin: Birkhäuser 1998

DGNB; Neubau Büro- und Verwaltungsgebäude. Steckbriefe 15 Flächeninanspruchnahme. DGNB: Version 2009

Dierks,K., Wormuth,R.; Baukonstruktion. Köln: Werner Verlag 2012

EarthbagBuilding.com; Earthbag Building [http://www.earthbag-building.com/index.htm] (08.11.2012)

Earthshelters.com; Earthshelter architecture [http://www.earthshelters.com/] (08.11.2012)

Earth Structures; Rammed Earth [http://earthstructures.com.au/rammed-earth-construction/] (11.11.2013)

ECOBINE; Ecological Building Net [http://www.ecobine.de/index.php?l=en] (08.06.2014)

Federal Environmental Agency (publisher); The Future lies on Brownfields. Reactivation of Urban Land Reserves – Redevelopment Potentials and Practical [http://www.umweltbundesamt.de/sites/default/files/medien/publikation/long/3051.pdf] (05.05.2014)

Flontex; Flontex: Textile Architektur [http://www.flontex.de/de/etfe-folien-in-der-architektur] (08.06.2014)

FNR e.V.; Nachwachsende Rohstoffe im Überblick [http://www.nachwachsenderohstoffe.de/basisinfo-nachwachsende-rohstoffe/ueberblick/] (08.11.2012)

FORUM Verlag Herkert GmbH; Sanierung denkmalgeschützter Gebäude: Wo liegen die Grenzen der Energieeinsparung?

Fuchs,N.; Master-Thesis: Recycling in der Architektur. Hochschule Wismar, Faculty of Architecture and Design SS 2013

Gerber,U-T.; Master Thesis: Systemtrennung beim Amt für Grundstücke und Gebäude des Kantons Bern. Untersuchung von nutzungsflexiblen Planungsvorgaben anhand von amtlichen Vorgabedokumenten, Literatur, Umfragen und von geplanten Gebäuden. Wings at Hochschule Wismar, Distance Study Program Architecture and Environment 11/2009

Gil,L.; Cork as a Building Material: Technical Manual [http://apcor.pt/userfiles/File/Caderno%20Tecnico%20F%20EN.pdf] (08.11.2012)

Glücklich, D (publisher); Ecological Architecture [http://ecologic-architecture.org/main/] (08.10.2012)

Glücklich, D (publisher); Ökologisches Bauen. Von Grundlagen zu Gesamtkonzepten. München: Deutsche Verlags-Anstalt 2005

Green Building magazine; Cork for building [http://www.building-forafuture.co.uk/autumn02/focus_on_cork.php] (08.11.2012)

Hegger,M., Auch-Schwelk,V., Fuchs,M., Rosenkranz,T.; Baustoff Atlas. München: Institut für international Architektur-Dokumentation GmbH&Co.KG 2005

Inhabitat: Chino,M.; Underwater Skyscraper is a Self-Sufficient City at Sea [http://inhabitat.com/underwater-skyscraper-is-a-self-sufficient-city-at-sea/] (08.06.2014)

Inhabitat: Pham,D.; Take a Peek at a Stunning Secret Swiss Villa Hidden Into a Mountainside! [http://inhabitat.com/a-luxury-swiss-villa-nestled-beneath-the-earth/] (08.06.2014)

InsipirationGreen; Rammed Earth [http://www.inspirationgreen.com/rammed-earth.html] (11.11.2013)

Institut Wohnen und Umwelt: Cmella-Emrich,E.; Anpassbare Gebäude - Definitionen und Terminologie [http://www.akndsakademie.de/pub/IWU_Bericht_Anpassbare_Gebaeude.pdf] (30.10.2012)

Kuhn,M.; Glossar zum Leichtbau [www.archplus.net/download/artikel/1080/] (08.06.2014)

Littlegreenseed; Adaptable Nature: Adaptable Architecture [http://littlegreenseed.wordpress.com/tag/green-building/] (30.10.2012)

Minke,G.; Lehmbau- Handbuch. Der Baustoff Lehm und seine Anwendung. Ökobuch 05/2001

Mück,W.; Baustoffe- und Bautechnik: Lehmbau [http://www.gesundbauen.at/BER3-LEH.htm] (08.11.2012)

Nationale Genossenschaft für die Lagerung radioaktiver Abfälle (publisher); Kohle – Bioabfall liefert Energie [http://www.erdwissen.ch/2012/04/kohle-bioabfall-liefert-energie/] (8.05.2014)

Naturally:wood®; Key Features of Wood [http://www.naturally-wood.com/design-environment] (08.11.2012)

Ontario Association of Architects: Gorgolewski,M.; Reusing Buildings and Components [http://www.oaa.on.ca/professional%20resources/sustainable%20design/reusing%20buildings%20and%20component] (on 05.03.2014)

Peacock Irrigation; Rainwater Harvesting Systems [http://www.peacock-irrigation.co.uk/rainwater.html] (08.10.2012)

Permaculture: Wheaton,P.; wofati eco building [http://www.richsoil.com/wofati.jsp] (08.11.2012)

Preservation Green Lab: National Trust for Historic Preservation; The Greenest Building: Quantifying the Environmental Value of Building Reuse. Preservation Green Lab: National Trust for Historic Preservation

Rammed Earth Constructions; What is Rammed Earth? [http://www.rammedearthconstructions.com.au/] (11.11.2013)

Rex,M., Reinschmidt,J.; Presentation Bauen mit Ballen – Einführung in den Strohballenbau. Hochschule Wismar, Faculty of Architecture and Design 2007

RWTH Aachen; Bamboo as a building material [http://bambus.rwth-aachen.de/eng/PDF-Files/Bamboo%20as%20a%20building%20material.pdf] (10.05.2013)

Schoblocher,P.; Master Thesis: Bestand erhalten - Teilrückbau, Umbau und Erweiterung - Abbruch und Neubau? Investitionsüberlegungen und Entscheidungsprozesse zum Nachhaltigen Bauen - Vergleichende Untersuchungen unter Berücksichtigung der „Externen Kosten" am Beispiel „Neubau Rathaus Thannhausen". Wings at Hochschule Wismar, Distance Study Program Architecture and Environment 11/2011

Sustainable Build; Stone Construction [http://www.sustainable-build.co.uk/constructionstone.html] (08.11.2012)

Sustainable Sources.com; Earth Materials [http://earth.sustainablesources.com/] (11.11.2013)

Thüringer Ministerium für Bau, Landesentwicklung und Verkehr; Genial zentral. Entwicklung innerstädtischer Brachflächen

Umwelt Bundesamt; Grünlandumbruch [http://www.umweltbundesamt.de/daten/umweltdaten/public/theme.do?nodeIdent=2898] (05.05.2014)

Vetsch architektur AG.; Erdhäuser [http://www.erdhaus.ch/main.php?fla=y&lang=de&cont=start] (08.11.2012)

Waltjen, T., Mötzl,H., Mück, W., Torghele,K., Zelger,T.; Ökologischer Bauteilkatalog. Wien: Springer; 1999

Wikipedia; Bamboo [http://en.wikipedia.org/wiki/Bamboo] (10.05.2013)

Wikipedia; Cork (material) [http://en.wikipedia.org/wiki/Cork_%28material%29] (08.11.2012)

Wikipedia; Lehmbau [http://de.wikipedia.org/wiki/Lehmbau] (08.11.2012)

Wikipedia; Vakuum [http://de.wikipedia.org/wiki/Vakuum] (08.06.2014)

Windimnet: Haller,P.; Holz [http://www.windimnet.de/holz] (08.11.2012)

World Buildings Directory; Project in Detail: India Pavilion, Expo 2010 Shanghai China [http://www.worldbuildingsdirectory.com/project.cfm?id=2765] (8.11.2012)

4.0 Passive energy-saving concepts (low-tech)

[https://www.educate-sustainability.eu/portal/de/content/educate-portal] (10.06.2014)

Aquaponics4you.com; Step-By-Step How To Build Your Own Aquaponics System [http://www.aquaponics4you.com/] (on 08.11.2012)

Arizona Solar Centre, Inc.; Passive Solar Heating & Cooling Manual [http://www.azsolarcentre.org/tech-science/solar-architecture/passive-solar-design-manual/passive-solar-design-manual-heating.html] (08.11.2012)

Autodesk®, Inc.; Autodesk Sustainability Workshop: Concepts and tools for sustainable design [http://sustainabilityworkshop.autodesk.com/] (08.11.2012)

Autodesk®, Inc.; Autodesk Sustainability Workshop: Concepts and tools for sustainable design [http://sustainabilityworkshop.autodesk.com/resource/passive-ventilation-strategies] (08.11.2012)

Bailey,S.; Master Thesis: Aquaponics in Architecture. Project in Hamburg, Germany. Hochschule Wismar, Faculty of Architecture and Design WS 2011/2012

Blog pada WordPress.com; What's aquaponic?[http://myaquaponic.wordpress.com/] (08.11.2012)

BMU; Bewertungssystem Nachhaltiges Bauen (BNB) [https://www.bnb-nachhaltigesbauen.de/] (04.08.2014)

BMU; Guideline for Sustainable Building. Berlin: BMU 03/2014

BMU; Leitfaden Nachhaltiges Bauen. Guideline for Sustainable Building [www.nachhaltigesbauen.de] (10.05.2014)

BMVBS; Leitfaden Nachhaltiges Bauen. Berlin: BMVBS 04/2013

City of Melbourne; CH2 Council House [http://www.melbourne.vic.gov.au/Sustainability/CH2/aboutch2/Documents/CH2_How_It_Works.pdf] (04.08.2014)

Daniels,K.; Advanced Building Systems. A Technical Guide for Architects and Engineers. Basel: Birkhäuser 2003

Daniels,K.; Low-Tech Light-Tech High-Tech. Bauen in der Informationsgesellschaft. Berlin: Birkhäuser 1998

de Saldahna,M., Hausladen,G., Liedl,P.; ClimaSkin. Konzepte für gebäudehüllen, die mit weniger Energie mehr leisten. München: Callwey 2006

DGNB; Modul 01: Nachhaltige Architektur. DGNB: 2009

DGNB; Modul 09: Energieeffiziente Gebäudehülle. DGNB: 2009

DGNB; Neubau Büro- und Verwaltungsgebäude. Steckbriefe 01-61. DGNB: Version 2009

ECOBINE; Ecological Building Net [http://www.ecobine.de/index.php?l=en] (08.06.2014)

EDUCATE; Environmental Design in University Curricula and Architectural Training in Europe

Glücklich, D (publisher); Ecological Architecture [http://ecologic-architecture.org/main/] (08.10.2012)

Glücklich, D (publisher); Ökologisches Bauen. Von Grundlagen zu Gesamtkonzepten. München: Deutsche Verlags-Anstalt 2005

Green planet – solar energy; Solar tower [http://www.green-planet-solar-energy.com/solar-tower.html] (08.11.2012)

Hegger,M., Fuchs,M., Stark,T., Zeumer,M.; Energie Atlas. Nachhaltige Architektur. München: Birkhäuser 2008

König,H., Kohler,N., Kreißig,J., Lützkendorf,T.; Lebenszyklus-analyse in der Gebäudeplanung. Grundlagen Berechnung Planungswerkzeuge. München: Institut für internationale Architektur-Dokumentation GmbH&Co.KG 2009

Passive Lighting; Why choose LED lighting? [http://www.passive-lighting.com.au/] (08.11.2012)

Wikipedia; Daylighting [http://en.wikipedia.org/wiki/Daylighting] (08.06.2014)

Wikipedia; Natural ventilation [http://en.wikipedia.org/wiki/Natural_ventilation] (08.06.2014)

Wikipedia; Passive solar building design [http://en.wikipedia.org/wiki/Passive_solar_building_design] (08.06.2014)

5.0 Active energy-saving concepts (high-tech)

World Solar Ltd; Shower Save [http://shower-save.com/] (18.10.2012)

[http://www.energieagentur.nrw.de/virtuell/downloads/adiabate_kuehlung.pdf] (04.05.2014)

Literature

[http://www.solare-kuehlung.info/Projekte/Projekte/Planungsleitfaden_V12_18092013.pdf] (04.05.2014)

Aereco; Aereco: bedarfsgeführte Lüftung [http://www.aereco.de/] (04.05.2014)

Aerosolarsystems; Solarwater: Types of solar collectors [http://www.aesolarsystems.com/solarwater/types-of-solar-collectors.html] (08.10.2012)

Betriebsgesellschaft Akademie Mont-Cenis Herne; Akademie Mont-Cenis Herne: Architecture [http://www.akademie-mont-cenis.de/en/] (04.05.2014)

Biomassenergycentre.org.uk; Biomass Energy [http://www.biomassenergycentre.org.uk/portal/page?_pageid=76,15049&_dad=portal] (22.11.2012)

BMU; Bewertungssystem Nachhaltiges Bauen (BNB) [https://www.bnb-nachhaltigesbauen.de/] (04.08.2014)

BMU; Guideline for Sustainable Building. Berlin: BMU 03/2014

BMU; Leitfaden Nachhaltiges Bauen. Guideline for Sustainable Building [www.nachhaltigesbauen.de] (10.05.2014)

BMVBS; Leitfaden Nachhaltiges Bauen. Berlin: BMVBS 04/2013

Boxer-Infodienst Regenerative Energie; Biogas [http://www.boxer99.de/biogas.htm] (22.11.2012)

Bývanie Teplo Klimatizácia; Tepelné cerpadlá [http://www.btk.sk/tepelne-cerpadla.php] (08.10.2012)

Daniels,K.; Advanced Building Systems. A Technical Guide for Architects and Engineers. Basel: Birkhäuser 2003

Daniels,K.; Low-Tech Light-Tech High-Tech. Bauen in der Informationsgesellschaft. Berlin: Birkhäuser 1998

Deutsche Bundestiftung Umwelt; Projektdatenbank [www.dbu.de] (22.06.2014)

Deutsche Energie-Agentur; Strom in Gas wandeln [http://www.powertogas.info/] (22.06.2014)

DGNB; Modul 01: Nachhaltige Architektur. DGNB: 2009

DGNB; Modul 09: Energieeffiziente Gebäudehülle. DGNB: 2009

DGNB; Modul 09: Energieoptimierte Gebäudetechnik. DGNB: 2009

DGNB; Neubau Büro- und Verwaltungsgebäude. Steckbriefe 01-61. DGNB: Version 2009

ECOBINE; Ecological Building Net [http://www.ecobine.de/index.php?l=en] (08.06.2014)

Elektro Technische Dienstleistungen Glahr GmbH; Grundlagen Photovoltaik [http://www.etd-glahr.de/photovoltaikanlagen/grundlagen-photovoltaik] (08.11.2012)

Emispec; Organic Rankine Cycle (ORC) type external combustion engine[http://emispec.ca/en/external-combustion-engine-type-organic-rankine-cycle.php] (08.11.2012)

EnergieAgentur.NRW: Kabus,M.; Adiabate Kühlung – „Kühlen ohne Strom“

Energieheld; Dezentrale oder zentrale Wohnraumlüftung? [http://www.energieheld.de/heizung/klimaanlage-und-lueftung/lueftungsanlage] (04.05.2014)

Energieportal24.de; Chemische Energiespeicher [http://www.energieportal24.de/cms1/wissensportale/energiespeicherung/chemische-speicher/] (22.06.2014)

Energieportal24.de; Mechanische Energiespeicher [http://www.energieportal24.de/cms1/wissensportale/energiespeicherung/mechanische-speicher/] (22.06.2014)

Energy.gov: Office of Energy Efficiency&Renewable Energy; Geothermal [http://energy.gov/eere/renewables/geothermal] (08.10.2012)

Energy.gov: Office of Energy Efficiency&Renewable Energy; Geothermal [http://energy.gov/eere/renewables/geothermal] (08.10.2012)

EnergyGroove.net; Heat Pumps [http://www.energygroove.net/technologies/heat-pumps/] (08.10.2012)

EPA – U.S. Environmental Protection Agency; Combined Heat and Power Partnership: Basic Information [http://www.epa.gov/chp/basic/index.html] (22.11.2012)

Eurotherm GmbH; Intelligente Lüftung [http://www.eurotherm-gmbh.de/de/lueftung.html] (04.05.2014)

Fachverband Biogas e.V.; Die Verdauung macht‘s [http://www.biogas-kanns.de/links/Einfach-Biogas/Element-Biogas/460/] (22.11.2012)

Frauenhofer ISE; Planungsleitfaden Solare Kühlung

Frauenhofer ISE; Presseinformationen [http://www.ise.fraunhofer.de/de] (22.06.2014)

Glücklich, D (publisher); Ecological Architecture [http://ecologic-architecture.org/main/] (08.10.2012)

Glücklich, D (publisher); Ökologisches Bauen. Von Grundlagen zu Gesamtkonzepten. München: Deutsche Verlags-Anstalt 2005

GMK; Organic Rankine Cycle (ORC) [http://www.gmk.info/ORC.603.html] (08.11.2012)

GtV-Bundesverband Geothermie e.V.; Kalina cycle [http://www.geothermie.de/wissenswelt/glossar-lexikon/k/kalina-cycle.html] (08.11.2012)

HDI-Gerling Sicherheitstechnik GmbH; Risk Engineering Guideline. Biogas Plants. Hazards and safety measures for generation and utilisation of biogas. Hannover: HDI-Gerling Sicherheitstechnik GmbH 2009

Hegger,M., Fuchs,M., Stark,T., Zeumer,M.; Energie Atlas. Nachhaltige Architektur. München: Birkhäuser 2008

Jüttemann, P.; Vertikale Windkraftanlagen im Vergleich mit horizontalen Anlagen[http://www.klein-windkraftanlagen.com/news/vertikale-windkraftanlagen-im-vergleich-mit-horizontalen-anlagen/] (08.11.2012)

König,H., Kohler,N., Kreißig,J., Lützkendorf,T.; Lebenszyklusanalyse in der Gebäudeplanung. Grundlagen Berechnung Planungswerkzeuge. München: Institut für internationale Architektur-Dokumentation GmbH&Co.KG 2009

MANNVIT; Kalina [http://www.mannvit.com/GeothermalEnergy/GeothermalPowerPlants/GeothermalProjectKalina/] (08.11.2012)

Münch,Ch.; Solare Kühlung [http://www.solarthermie.net/solare-kuehlung] (04.05.2014)

NASA: Netting,R.; How do Photovoltaics Work?[http://science.nasa.gov/science-news/science-at-nasa/2002/solarcells/] (18.11.2012)

National Solar Power Research Institute, Inc.: Mah,O.; Fundamentals of Photovoltaics Materials [http://userwww.sfsu.edu/ciotola/solar/pv.pdf] (08.11.2012)

Photovoltaic.org; Photovoltaik Wirkungsgrad [http://www.photovoltaik.org/wissen/photovoltaik-wirkungsgrad] (08.11.2012)

Results of students work (Boelsterly,F., Gallová,K., Junhui,W., Kryeziu,B., Lin,W., Milad,A., Mullinger,S., Ovcharova,V., Richnavská,H., Rrahmani,V., Shoeybi,M., Suang,L., Shuyang,Z., Skrabák,Z., Xhigoli,J., Xiaoyin,Y., Yingdong,M.); Dealing with heritage protected warehouses in the old harbour of Wismar, Germany. Hochschule Wismar, Faculty of Architecture and Design, Green Building class SS 2014

Reysa,G.; Solarwater: Build It Solar: Concentrating Solar Collectors [http://www.builditsolar.com/Projects/Concentrating/concentrating.htm] (08.10.2012)

Roberts,S., Guariento,N.; Building Integrated Photovoltaics: A Handbook. Birkhäuser 09/2009

Solaranlage.com.; Photovoltaikanlagen – PV Anlagen nach Ihren Vorstellungen. Ökologische und ökonomische Stromproduktion, die Sinnvoll ist und sich rechnet! [http://www.solaranlage.com/photovoltaik/] (08.11.2012)

SolarServer; Mit Sonnenwärme kühlen: Das Interesse an solarer Klimatisierung wächst [http://www.solarserver.de/solarmagazin/artikeljuni2002.html] (04.05.2014)

Sunandwindenergy; Waste water heat [http://www.sunandwindenergy.ca/wastewaterheat.html] (18.10.2012)

Sustainable Sources; Sustainable Sources[http://sustainablesources.com/] (22.06.2014)

Tec-concept.com; ORC-Technologie - Verstromung solarer Wärme [http://www.tec-concept.com/orc_technologie_verstromung_solarer_warme.asp] (08.11.2012)

The Healthy House Institute, LLC.; Heat Recovery Ventilators – Getting technical [http://www.healthyhouseinstitute.com/a_985-Heat_Recovery_Ventilators_Getting_Technical] (04.05.2014)

The Worlds of David Darling; active solar energy system [http://www.daviddarling.info/encyclopedia/A/AE_active_solar_energy_system.html] (08.10.2012)

TU Braunschweig, Institut für Gebäude und Solartechnik: Schlosser,M.; Solarsiedlungen mit Langzeitwärmespeicher - Stand der Technik und Perspektiven. Hannover: Veranstaltung „Zukunft der Wärmeversorgung Kommunale Nahwärmenetze" 02.05.2011

Union of Concerned Scientists USA; How Biomass Energy Works [http://www.ucsusa.org/clean_energy/our-energy-choices/renewable-energy/how-biomass-energy-works.html] (22.11.2012)

Wikipedia; Biogas [http://en.wikipedia.org/wiki/Bio_fuel] (22.11.2012)

Wikipedia; Blockheizkraftwerk [http://de.wikipedia.org/wiki/Blockheizkraftwerk] (22.11.2012)

Wikipedia; Heat pump [http://en.wikipedia.org/wiki/Heat_pump] (08.10.2012)

Wikipedia; Heat recovery ventilation [http://en.wikipedia.org/wiki/Heat_recovery_ventilation] (04.05.2014)

Wikipedia; Kalina cycle [http://en.wikipedia.org/wiki/Kalina_cycle] (18.11.2012)

Wikipedia; Photovoltaics [http://en.wikipedia.org/wiki/Photovoltaics] (18.11.2012)

Wikipedia; Solar thermal collector[http://en.wikipedia.org/wiki/Solar_thermal_collector] (08.10.2012)

Wikipedia; Wind power [http://en.wikipedia.org/wiki/Wind_power] (18.11.2012)

Wind energy the facts; Chapter 6: Small wind turbines [www.wind-energy-the-facts.org/en/part-i-technology/chapter-6-small-wind-turbines/markets-and-applications-for-small-wind-turbines.html] (08.11.2012)

6.0 Active resource-saving concepts (hard-tech)

BauNetz Media GmbH; Recycling von Glas [http://www.baunetzwissen.de/standardartikel/Fenster-und-Tueren_Recycling-von-Glas_155383.html] (20.04.2013)

BBSR; Nutzungsdauern von Bauteilen für Lebenszyklusanalysen nach Bewertungssystem Nachhaltiges Bauen (BNB). Berlin: BBSR 03.11.2011

BMU, BMVg; Arbeitshilfen Recycling. Arbeitshilfen zum Umgang mit Bau- und Abbruchabfällen

BMU; Bewertungssystem Nachhaltiges Bauen (BNB) [https://www.bnb-nachhaltigesbauen.de/] (04.05.2014)

BMU; Guideline for Sustainable Building. Berlin: BMU 03/2014

BMU; Leitfaden Nachhaltiges Bauen. Guideline for Sustainable Building [www.nachhaltigesbauen.de] (10.05.2014)

BMVBS; Leitfaden Nachhaltiges Bauen. Berlin: BMVBS 04/2013

Braungart,M., McDonough,W.; Cradle to Cradle: Remaking the Way We Make Things. United States: North Point Press 2002

Bredenbals,B., Willkomm,W.; Neue Konstruktionsalternativen für recyclingfähige Wohngebäude. Stuttgard: Frauenhofer IRB Verlag 1996

ConreteNetwork.com; Recycling concrete [http://www.concretenetwork.com/concrete/demolition/recycling_concrete.htm] (20.06.2014)

Daniels,K.; Advanced Building Systems. A Technical Guide for Architects and Engineers. Basel: Birkhäuser 2003

Daniels,K.; Low-Tech Light-Tech High-Tech. Bauen in der Informationsgesellschaft. Berlin: Birkhäuser 1998

DGNB; Modul 07: Resourcenschonendes Bauen. DGNB: 2009

DGNB; Neubau Büro- und Verwaltungsgebäude. Steckbriefe 01-61. DGNB: Version 2009

ECOBINE; Abfallvermeidung [http://www.ecobine.de/print.php?SESSID=5d7092d85d384778d6c3226dcb5d3204&id=4.5.1.1.6&kurs=11&l=de] (08.06.2014)

ECOBINE; Ecological Building Net [http://www.ecobine.de/index.php?l=en] (08.06.2014)

European Union; Verordnung EU Nr. 305/2011 des Europäischen Parlaments und des Rates vom 9.3.2011 zur Festlegung harmonisierter Bedingungen für die Vermarktung von Bauprodukten und zur Aufhebung der Richtlinie 89/106/EWG des Rates

Glücklich, D (publisher); Ecological Architecture [http://ecologic-architecture.org/main/] (08.10.2012)

Glücklich, D (publisher); Ökologisches Bauen. Von Grundlagen zu Gesamtkonzepten. München: Deutsche Verlags-Anstalt 2005

Hegger,M., Auch-Schwelk,V., Fuchs,M., Rosenkranz,T.; Baustoff Atlas. München: Institut für international Architektur-Dokumentation GmbH&Co.KG 2005

Idw – Informationsdienst Wissenschaft; Holzwerkstoffrecycling durch thermohydrolytische Spaltung [https://idw-online.de/de/news41904] (15.06.2014)

König,H., Kohler,N., Kreißig,J., Lützkendorf,T.; Lebenszyklusanalyse in der Gebäudeplanung. Grundlagen Berechnung Planungswerkzeuge. München: Institut für internationale Architektur-Dokumentation GmbH&Co.KG 2009

Lee,E.; Chinese Paper Brick House at Architecture Biennale [http://inhabitat.com/chinese-pavilion-paper-brick-house/] (15.06.2014)

Linden,W.; Presentation: Baustoffe. Instrumente der Bewertung: Fachhochschule Lübeck

Meinhold,B.; Building Made Entirely of Recycled Kitchen Sinks [http://inhabitat.com/building-made-entirely-of-kitchen-sinks/ktichen-sink-building-9/] (20.06.2014)

Peacock Irrigation; Rainwater Harvesting Systems [http://www.peacock-irrigation.co.uk/rainwater.html] (20.04.2014)

Portlant Cement Association; CCT aggregates recycled [http://www.cement.org/tech/cct_aggregates_recycled.asp] (20.06.2014)

Results of students work (Junjie,R., Pliss,M., Shiti,L., Xiao,L., Xiaoyang,F.); Recycling design of a café shop, Germany. Hochschule Wismar, Faculty of Architecture and Design, Recycling Design class WS 2011/2012

Rewindo; Rewindo. Fenster-Recycling-Service [http://www.rewindo.de] (20.04.2014)

Shigeru Ban Architects; Paper Tube Structures [http://www.shigerubanarchitects.com/works.html#paper-tube-structure] (15.06.2014)

Student presentation (Zhen,R.); Paper Architecture. Hochschule Wismar, Faculty of Architecture and Design, Green Building class SS 2010

Touch the Earth Ranch; Tire houses: An Efficient Construction Method. Exploring the Benefits of Using Earth-friendly Materials [http://www.touchtheearthranch.com/tirestart.htm] (20.04.2014)

Waltjen, T., Mötzl,H., Mück, W., Torghele,K., Zelger,T.; Ökologischer Bauteilkatalog. Wien: Springer; 1999

WebUrbanist.com; 5 Recycled Buildings Made from Bottles, Cans, Bales & Tires [http://weburbanist.com/2007/10/23/5-kinds-of-creative-recycled-architecture-cans-bottles-and-other-unusual-building-materials/] (20.04.2013)

Wikipedia; Concrete recycling [http://en.wikipedia.org/wiki/Concrete_recycling] (08.11.2012)

Wikipedia; Cradle to Cradle: Remarking the Way We Make Things [http://en.wikipedia.org/wiki/Cradle_to_Cradle:_Remaking_the_Way_We_Make_Things] (22.11.2012)

Wikipedia; Glass recycling [http://en.wikipedia.org/wiki/Glass_recycling] (08.11.2012)

Wikipedia; Plastic recycling [http://en.wikipedia.org/wiki/Plastic_recycling] (on 08.11.2012)

Wikipedia; Schaumglas [http://de.wikipedia.org/wiki/Schaumglas] (08.11.2012)

Wikipedia; Scrap [http://en.wikipedia.org/wiki/Scrap] (08.11.2012)

Williams,M.; What Metals Can Be Recycled? [http://greenliving.nationalgeographic.com/metals-can-recycled-3128.html] (20.06.2014)

7.0 Buildings for a long life span

BBSR; Nutzungsdauern von Bauteilen für Lebenszyklusanalysen nach Bewertungssystem Nachhaltiges Bauen (BNB). Berlin: BBSR 03.11.2011

BMU; Bewertungssystem Nachhaltiges Bauen (BNB) [https://www.bnb-nachhaltigesbauen.de/] (04.05.2014)

BMU; Guideline for Sustainable Building. Berlin: BMU 03/2014

BMU; Leitfaden Nachhaltiges Bauen. Guideline for Sustainable Building [www.nachhaltigesbauen.de] (10.05.2014)

BMVBS; Leitfaden Nachhaltiges Bauen. Berlin: BMVBS 04/2013

Daniels,K.; Low-Tech Light-Tech High-Tech. Bauen in der Informationsgesellschaft. Berlin: Birkhäuser 1998

DGNB; Modul 01: Nachhaltige Architektur. DGNB: 2009

DGNB; Modul 03: Wertstabilität. DGNB: 2009

DGNB; Modul 07: Resourcenschonendes Bauen. DGNB: 2009

Dias,W.P.S.; Useful life of buildings. Moratuwa: Department of Civil Engineering University of Moratuwa 06/2003

Little Green Seed; Adaptable Nature: Adaptable Architecture [http://littlegreenseed.wordpress.com/tag/green-building/] (20.04.2013)

naumann.architektur; S(ch)austall [http://www.fnp-architekten.de/projekte/swe/pr001.html] (20.04.2013)

Preservation Green Lab, National Trust for Historic Preservation; The Greenest Building: Quantifying the Environmental Value of Building Reuse. 2011

Scheffler,M.; Master thesis: „Future house" Beijing. Hochschule Wismar, Faculty of Architecture and Design 2005

Schneider,D.; Homework Bauen im Bestand – Analyse. Wings at Hochschule Wismar, Distance Study Program Architecture and Environment WS 2010/2011

Student project (Fan,Y.); Hybrid house. Hochschule Wismar, Faculty of Architecture and Design SS 2010

Wikipedia; Adaptive reuse [http://en.wikipedia.org/wiki/Adaptive_reuse] (30.10.2012)

8.0 Buildings for a short life span

[http://inhabitat.com/high-flying-algae-airships-are-self-sufficient-airborne-cities/] (03.09.2012)

[https://www.educate-sustainability.eu/portal/de/content/educate-portal] (10.06.2014)

Archigram; Archigram. München: Birkhäuser 1991

Bahamón,A., Sanjinés,M.C..; Rematerial. From Waste to Architecture. Barcelona: Norton 2008

Baumer,K., Lubin,G.; Check Out The Australian Flying Saucer That Can Transport Buildings [http://www.businessinsider.com/skylifter-flying-saucer?op=1] (03.09.2012)

BBSR; Nutzungsdauern von Bauteilen für Lebenszyklusanalysen nach Bewertungssystem Nachhaltiges Bauen (BNB). Berlin: BBSR 03.11.2011

BMU; Bewertungssystem Nachhaltiges Bauen (BNB) [https://www.bnb-nachhaltigesbauen.de/] (04.05.2014)

BMU; Guideline for Sustainable Building. Berlin: BMU 03/2014

BMU; Leitfaden Nachhaltiges Bauen. Guideline for Sustainable Building [www.nachhaltigesbauen.de] (10.05.2014)

BMVBS; Leitfaden Nachhaltiges Bauen. Berlin: BMVBS 04/2013

Bredenbals,B., Willkomm,W.; Neue Konstruktionsalternativen für recyclingfähige Wohngebäude. Stuttgard: Frauenhofer IRB Verlag 1996

BusinessDictionary.com; Product [http://www.businessdictionary.com/definition/product.html] (04.09.2012)

ChinaHush; Most constructions in China only have life span of 25-30 years? [http://www.chinahush.com/2010/04/11/most-constructions-in-china-only-have-life-span-of-25-30-years/] (10.10.2012)

Chino,M.; High-Flying Algae Airships are Self-Sufficient Airborne Cities

Daniels,K.; Low-Tech Light-Tech High-Tech. Bauen in der Informationsgesellschaft. Berlin: Birkhäuser 1998

designboom®; Tiny houses [http://www.designboom.com/contemporary/tiny_houses2.html] (10.10.2012)

DGNB; Modul 01: Nachhaltige Architektur. DGNB: 2009

DGNB; Modul 03: Wertstabilität. DGNB: 2009

DGNB; Modul 07: Resourcenschonendes Bauen. DGNB: 2009

Earthtechling; Floating Architecture [http://www.earthtechling.com/tag/floating-architecture/] (04.09.2012)

Earthtechling; Nigerian Floating School Design Echoes `Beasts` [http://www.earthtechling.com/2013/02/nigerian-floating-school-design-echoes-beasts/] (04.09.2012)

EDUCATE; Environmental Design in University Curricula and Architectural Training in Europe

EuroEkonóm.sk; Co je to produkt [http://www.euroekonom.sk/marketing/produkt-a-produktova-politika/co-je-to-produkt/] (04.09.2012)

Flying Architecture; Architecture unchained! [http://www.flyingarchitecture.com/architecture-unchained-visualization-contest/] (03.09.2012)

Flying House Media; Flying House: Floating high tech residential building [http://flyinghouseproject.blogspot.de/2012_02_01_archive.html] (03.09.2012)

Hoyoung,F.K.; future architecture [http://fra-dab810.blogspot.de/2012/08/future-architecture.html] (03.09.2012)

Momtastic Web Ecoist; 10 Surprising Reclaimed&Recycled Building Materials [http://webecoist.momtastic.com/2010/03/29/10-surprising-reclaimed-recycled-building-materials/] (04.09.2012)

Pawley,M.; Future Systems. Die Architektur von Jank Kaplicky und Amanda Levete. Basel-Berlin-Boston: Birkhäuser Verlag 1993

Seyler,S.; S.haus - house for 20 years. Hochschule Wismar, Faculty of Architecture and Design

Solar Decathlon Europe; Solar Houses 2012 [http://www.sdeurope.org/?lang=en] (10.10.2012)

Students project; Hochschulpavillon. Studienprojekt für die Landesgartenschau Wismar. Hochschule Wismar, Faculty of Architecture and Design 2002-2004

Topham,S.; blow up. Inflatable Art, Architecture and Design. München: Prestel-Verlag 2002

U.S Department of Energy; Solar Decathlon [http://www.solardecathlon.gov/about.html] (10.10.2012)

Waterstudio.NL; Waterstudio.NL. Architecture [http://www.waterstudio.nl/] (04.09.2012)

WebUrbanist.com; The Futuro House: Space Age UFO Architecture Comes Home [http://weburbanist.com/2010/01/10/the-futuro-house-space-age-architecture-comes-home/] (04.09.2012)

Wikipedia; List of building types [http://en.wikipedia.org/wiki/List_of_building_types] (30.10.2012)

Wikipedia; Metastadt [http://de.wikipedia.org/wiki/Metastadt_%28Architektur%29] (30.10.2012)

9.0 Buildings concept

[http://www.solarserver.de/service_tools/online_rechner/solaranlage_online_berechnen.html] (12.04.2014)

BBSR; Nutzungsdauern von Bauteilen für Lebenszyklusanalysen nach Bewertungssystem Nachhaltiges Bauen (BNB). Berlin: BBSR 03.11.2011

Betzler,F.; Master Thesis: Konzept für eine zukunftweisende Klimaarchitektur am Beispiel der geplanten Bebauung der Simon-von-Utrecht-Strasse in Hamburg. Wings at Hochschule Wismar, Distance Study Program Architecture and Environment SS 2009

BHKW-Infozentrum GbR; BHKW-Berechnung [http://www.bhkw-berechnung.de/bhkw-berechnung_allgemeine_erlaeuterungen.html] (18.09.2014)

Bmt-solutions; Kostenlose Berechnung [http://www.solar-berechnung.de/calc.php] (12.04.2014)

BMU, BMVg; Arbeitshilfen Recycling. Arbeitshilfen zum Umgang mit Bau- und Abbruchabfällen

BMU; Assessment System for Sustainable Building: Practical Aids and Tools [http://www.nachhaltigesbauen.de/sustainable-building-english-speaking-information/assessment-system-for-sustainable-building.html] (04.05.2014)

BMU; Bewertungssystem Nachhaltiges Bauen (BNB) [https://www.bnb-nachhaltigesbauen.de/] (04.05.2014)

BMU; EEG – The Renewable Energy Sources Act. Berlin: BMU 07/2007

BMU; Guideline for Sustainable Building. Berlin: BMU 03/2014

BMU; Leitfaden Nachhaltiges Bauen. Guideline for Sustainable Building [www.nachhaltigesbauen.de] (10.05.2014)

BMU; The Renewable Energies Heat Act [http://www.bmu.de/english/renewable_energy/downloads/doc/42351.php] (12.10.2012)

BMU; Ökobau.dat 2013 [http://www.nachhaltigesbauen.de/baustoff-und-gebaeudedaten/oekobaudat.html] (04.05.2014)

BMVBS; Leitfaden Nachhaltiges Bauen. Berlin: BMVBS 04/2013

BMWI; Act on the promotion of renewable energies in the heat sector [http://www.erneuerbare-energien.de/en/unser-service/mediathek/downloads/detailview/artikel/act-on-the-promotion-of-renewable-energies-in-the-heat-sector-heat-act-eewaermeg/] (12.10.2012)

Bottrop.de; Versicherungsanlage [http://www.bottrop.de/stadtleben/downloads/umwelt/Versickerungsanlage.xls] (12.04.2014)

Bundesministerium für Wirtschaft und Arbeit; Informationen zur Angemessenheit der Unterkunftskosten im Rahmen des Arbeitslosengeldes II [http://www.pressrelations.de/new/standard/result_main.cfm?r=163128&aktion=jour_pm] (03.07.2014)

Bundesrecht; Arbeitsstätten-Richtlinie Lüftung (ASR 5) Zu § 5 der Arbeitsstättenverordnung [http://www.baua.de/de/Themen-von-A-Z/Arbeitsstaetten/ASR/pdf/ASR-A3-6.pdf?__blob=publicationFile&v=4] (12.04.2014)

CasaFan Ventilatoren; Luftmengenermittlung mittels Luftwechselraten [http://www.ventilator.de/luftmengenermittlung-mittels-luftwechselraten] (12.04.2014)

CasaFan Ventilatoren; Luftmengenermittlung nach der personenbezogenen Außenluftrate [http://www.ventilator.de/luftmengenermittlung-nach-der-personenbezogenen-aussenluftrate] (12.04.2014)

CET Technology; Clean Energy Transform Technology [http://www.cet-technology.de/] (12.04.2014)

check24.net; Stromverbrauch Berechnen in Vier Schritten [http://www.stromverbrauchberechnen.com/] (12.04.2014)

Cornell University; Sustainable Campus [http://www.sustainablecampus.cornell.edu/pages/about] (05.05.2014)

DAA Deutsche Auftragsagentur GmbH; Wenige kW bis mehrere MW - die Leistung von Biogas Anlagen [http://www.heizungsfinder.de/bhkw/biogasanlage/leistung] (18.09.2014)

Daniels,K.; Advanced Building Systems. A Technical Guide for Architects and Engineers. Basel: Birkhäuser 2003

Deutsches Institut für Normung e.V.; Barrierefreies Bauen DIN 18040 (part 1 and 2).

Deutsches Institut für Normung e.V.; Barrierefreie Wohnungen DIN 18025 (part 2).

Deutsches Institut für Normung e.V.; Energetische Bewertung von Gebäuden DIN V 18599 (11 parts). Edition 2011-12

Deutsches Institut für Normung e.V.; Grundflächen und Rauminhalte von Bauwerken im Hochbau DIN 277 (3 parts). Edition 2005

Deutsches Institut für Normung e.V.; Küchen, Bäder und WCs im Wohnungsbau. Planungsgrundlagen DIN 18022.

Deutsches Institut für Normung e.V.; Lüftung von Nichtwohngebäuden – Allgemeine Grundlagen und Anforderungen für Lüftungs- und Klimaanlagen und Raumkühlsysteme DIN EN 13779. Edition 09/2007

Deutsches Institut für Normung e.V.; Verfahren zur Berechnung der Norm-Heizlast DIN 12831. Edition 08/2003

Deutsches Institut für Normung e.V.; Verfahren zur Berechnung der Norm-Heizlast DIN 4701. Edition 08/2003

Deutsches Institut für Normung e.V.; Wohnungen für Rollstuhlbenutze DIN 18025 (part 1).

DGNB; Neubau Büro- und Verwaltungsgebäude. Steckbriefe 01-61. DGNB: Version 2009

elco; Planungsunterlagen Solarenergie [http://www.elco.ch/pdf/3td_sys_02_solatron_d.pdf] (12.04.2014)

Elektro Technische Dienstleistung Glahr; Grundlagen Photovoltaik [http://www.etd-glahr.de/photovoltaikanlagen/grundlagen-photovoltaik] (12.04.2014)

European Comission, Joint Research Centre; Photovoltaic Geographical Information System - Interactive Maps [http://re.jrc.ec.europa.eu/pvgis/apps4/pvest.php] (12.04.2014)

Finke,U., Fitzner,K.; Lüftungsregeln für freie Lüftung. Dortmund/Berlin/Dresden: 2012

Freie und Hansestadt Hamburg Umweltbehörde (publisher); Wasserpraxis. Ein praktischer Leitfaden zum Wassersparen. Hamburg: 09/2001

Gailfuß,M.; BHKW-Consult – Ingenieurbüro für BHKW-Planung und KWK [http://www.bhkw-consult.de/] (18.09.2014)

Holschemacher,K.; Entwurf- und Berechnungstafeln für Bauingenieure. Berlin: Bauwerk Verlag 2005

HyperJoint GmbH; Bedarfsermittlung von Wohnflächen nach VDI 6000 Blatt 1, DIN 18025-1 und DIN 18025-2 [http://nullbarriere.de/wohnflaechen.htm] (03.07.2014)

IBS Ingenieurbüro für Haustechnik Schreiner; Klima- und Kühlanlagen [http://energieberatung.ibs-hlk.de/planLuK_klimaanl.htm] (12.04.2014)

Institut für Arbeitschutz der Deutschen Gesetzlichen Unvallversicherung; GESTIS-Stoffdatenbank: 4.13 Datenbank

Köhler,M. (publisher); Handbuch Bauwerksbegrünung. Planung - Konstruktion - Ausführung. Köln: Verlagsgesselschaft Müller 10/2012

König,K.W., Töpfer,K.; Grauwassernutzung. Ökologisch notwendig - ökonomisch sinnvoll. Troisdorf: iWater Wassertechnik 2013

Landeshauptstadt Dresden; Flächenbedarf für Versickerung [http://www.dresden.de/regenwasser-versickerung/] (12.04.2014)

Länderausschuss für Arbeitsschutz und Sicherheitstechnik (publisher); Kenngrößen zur Beurteilung raumklimatischer Grundparameter. 09/2001

PE International; Methodische Grundlagen. Ökobilanzbasierte Umweltindikatoren im Bauwesen. 09/2011

Photon Solar; Einspeisevergütung (Photovoltaik ab 01.08.2014 [http://www.photon-solar.de/index.php?seite= einspeiseverguetung] (12.04.2014)

Schachtschneider,S.; Energiekonzept für die Entwicklung des Geländes „Alte Brauerei Schwerin". Wismar: Hochschule Wismar, Faculty of Architecture and Design 02/2013

Schmidt,M.; Institut für Physik in Berlin - Adlershof: Ein stadtökologisches Modellvorhaben [www.gebaeudekuehlung.de] (22.09.2014)

Schulz,J.-U.; Tragwerkslehre: Vordimensionierung. Hochschule Ostwestfalen-Lippe

Schweizer,A.; Lüftungstechnik – Volumenstromermittlung [http://www.schweizer-fn.de/lueftung/volumenstrom/volumenstrom.php] (12.04.2014)

Seminarprogramm für die Energiebeauftragten der Stadt Frankfurt am Main; Senkung der Wasserkosten in öffentlichen Gebäuden [http://www.energiemanagement.stadt-frankfurt.de/Betriebsoptimierung/Seminarprogramm/Seminar-Teil-4-Wasser.pdf] (12.04.2014)

Solaranlage.com; Dimensionierung einer Photovoltaikanlage [http://www.solaranlage.com/photovoltaik/dimensionierung.html] (12.04.2014)

Solaranlagenportal; Warmwasser mit der Solaranlage erzeugen - Die Werte [http://www.solaranlagen-portal.de/solarthermie/solaranlagen-warmwasser.html] (12.04.2014)

Solarbayer; Planungshilfe für Luft/Wasser-Wärmepumpen [https://www.solarbayer.de/Planungshilfe-Waermepumpen.html] (12.04.2014)

SolarServer; Kostenlose Berechnung thermischer Solaranlagen

SolarServer; Photovoltaikanlage online berechnen [http://www.solarserver.de/service_tools/online_rechner/pv_anlage_online_berechnen.html] (12.04.2014)

Statistisches Bundesamt; Umwelt. Erlebung über Haushaltsabfälle (bei den öffentlich-rechtlichen Entsorgungsträgern) [https://www.destatis.de/DE/ZahlenFakten/GesamtwirtschaftUmwelt/Umwelt/UmweltstatistischeErhebungen/Abfallwirtschaft/Tabellen/ErgebnisberichtHaushaltsabfaelle.pdf;jsessionid=CC57896384B35918665A17E7F7C4A0A5.cae3?__blob=publicationFile] (22.09.2014)

Steinborn,V.; Verordnung über Arbeitsstätten (ArbStättV). Stuttgart: Kohlhammer Verlag 2005

Students (Chalmers,J., Riebort,A., Schachtschneider,S.); Ein Projekt von Holzwerkstoffe EGGER Werk Wismar in Zusammenarbeit mit der Hochschule Wismar. Hochschule Wismar, Faculty of Architecture and Design 06.09.2011

Tuschinski,M.; EnEV 2014 - die neue Energieeinsparverordnung [http://www.enev-online.com/enev_2014_volltext/index.htm] (12.04.2014)

Viessmann; Planungshandbuch Solarthermie. Allendorf: Viessman Werke 11/2008

Volkmer & Buhlmann GbR; Stromverbrauch und Stromkosten berechnen [http://www.allesumrechnen.de/de/stromverbrauch] (12.04.2014)

Waltjen, T., Mötzl,H., Mück, W., Torghele,K., Zelger,T.; Ökologischer Bauteilkatalog. Wien: Springer; 1999

Wöhrmann,W.; Facility Mamagement. Flächen Management [http://www.cafm-mit-visio.de/Flaechenmanagement.html] (03.07.2014)

Wöhrmann,W.; Flächenbewirtschaftung in Verwaltungs- und Bürogebäuden. Expert Verlag 22.03.2007

10.0 Methods and instruments

Ansys, Inc.; Ansys [http://www.ansys.com/Products/Simulation+Technology/Fluid+Dynamics/ANSYS+Fluent] (17.10.2012)

Autodesk, Inc.; Autodesk Ecotect Analysis [http://usa.autodesk.com/ecotect-analysis/] (17.10.2012)

BMU; Assessment System for Sustainable Building: Practical Aids and Tools [http://www.nachhaltigesbauen.de/sustainable-building-english-speaking-information/assessment-system-for-sustainable-building.html] (04.05.2014)

BMU; GISCODE [http://www.nachhaltigesbauen.de/baustoff-und-gebaeudedaten/epd.html] (04.05.2014)

BMU; Ökobau.dat 2013 [http://www.nachhaltigesbauen.de/baustoff-und-gebaeudedaten/oekobaudat.html] (04.05.2014)

BMU; Ökobau.dat 2013 [http://www.wecobis.de/service/lexikon/giscode-lex.html] (04.05.2014)

BMVBS; Energieausweis für Gebäude - nach Energieeinsparverordnung (EnEV 2009). Informationsbroschüre des Bundesministeriums für Verkehr, Bau und Stadtentwicklung. Berlin: BMVBS 01.12.2009

BMVBS; Energieeinsparverordnung [http://www.bmvbs.de/DE/BauenUndWohnen/EnergieeffizienteGebaeude/Energieeinsparverordnung/energieeinsparverordnung_node] (12.10.2012)

Design Builder Software Ltd.; DesignBuilder Simulation [http://www.designbuilder.co.uk/content/view/7/13/] (on 17.10.2012)

DIALux; Software DIALux. By planners for planners [http://www.dial.de/DIAL/en/dialux.html] (17.10.2012)

Dämmwerk Bauphysik-Software; Designing Structural Elements [http://www.bauphysik-software.de/en-GB/elements-english.html] (17.10.2012)

Dämmwerk Bauphysik-Software; Dämmwerk building physics software [http://www.bauphysik-software.de/en-GB/concept-english.html] (17.10.2012)

Dämmwerk Bauphysik-Software; EnEV 2007 - German Energy Saving Regulation [http://www.bauphysik-software.de/en-GB/enev-2007.html] (17.10.2012)

EMICODE®; Was ist EMICODE®? [http://www.emicode.com/] (04.05.2014)

EPD®International Ltd.; The International EPD® System - a communications tool for international markets [http://www.environdec.com/] (04.05.2014)

Institut für Arbeitschutz der Deutschen Gesetzlichen Unvallversicherung; GESTIS-Stoffdatenbank. Gefahrstoffinformationssystem der Deutschen Gesetzlichen Unfallversicherung [http://www.dguv.de/ifa/Gefahrstoffdatenbanken/GESTIS-Stoffdatenbank/index.jsp] (04.05.2014)

Jugend im Bund für Umwelt und Naturschutz Deutschland e.V. (BUNDjugend); Passt dein Fuß auf diese Erde? [http://www.footprint-deutschland.de/inhalt/start] (22.09.2014)

Legep®; Legep [http://legep.de/?AktivId=1125] (on 17.10.2012)

Relux; Relux, the standard in lighting planning [http://www.relux.biz/index.php?option=com_content&view=article&id=226&Itemid=211&lang=en] (17.10.2012)

Relux; ReluxSuite, the free lighting planning software for lighting and sensor planners [http://www.relux.biz/index.php?option=com_content&view=article&id=217&Itemid=200&lang=en] (17.10.2012)

Student project (Rudai,S.); Smart Material House. Hochschule Wismar, Faculty of Architecture and Design SS 2010

Transsolar Energietechnik GmbH; Trnflow – Airflow Simulation in Buildings [http://www.transsolar.com/__software/docs/trnflow/trnflow_uebersicht_en.htm] (17.10.2012)

Transsolar Energietechnik GmbH; Trnsys – Components – Trnsys Standard Package [http://www.transsolar.com/__software/docs/komponenten/komponenten_standard_en.htm] (17.10.2012)

Transsolar Energietechnik GmbH; Trnsys – The Universal Tool for Climate Engineering [http://www.transsolar.com/__software/docs/trnsys/trnsys_uebersicht_en.htm] (17.10.2012)

Tuschinski,M.; EnEV 2009 [http://www.enev-online.org/enev_2009_volltext/index.htm] (12.10.2012)

Tuschinski,M.; EnEV 2014 - die neue Energieeinsparverordnung [http://www.enev-online.com/enev_2014_volltext/index.htm] (12.04.2014)

U.S. Department of Energy; EnergyPlus Energy Simulation Software [http://apps1.eere.energy.gov/buildings/energyplus/] (17.10.2012)

Waltjen, T., Mötzl,H., Mück, W., Torghele,K., Zelger,T.; Ökologischer Bauteilkatalog. Wien: Springer; 1999

WUFI®; WUFI® Pro, 2D, Plus. Software for calculating the coupled heat and moisture transfer in building components [http://www.wufi.de/index_e.html] (07.04.2014)

11.0 Examples

ATP Sphere GmbH: Mark,M.; Von der Ästetik der Nachhaltigkeit [http://www.sphere.ag/projektdetails-forschen/items/%C3%A4sthetik_der_nachhaltigkeit.html] (22.09.2014)

IGEL-Institut - Archive of the projects. Wismar

Students project; Konzept 2020: Konzept zur nachhaltigen baulichen Weiterentwicklung der Hochschule Wismar zum umweltgerechten Campus der Zukunft. Wismar: Hochschule Wismar, Faculty of Architecture and Design 2008

Wissenschaftliche Begleitung at the HS Wismar - Archive of the projects. Wismar

Wollensak Architects - Archive of the projects. Wismar

Outlook

When we started to collect all the presentations, we never planned to write a whole book. The goal was to create a collection of all the presentations about sustainable architecture focusing on a building's whole life time. "Life time design".

Without a clear structure, it was not possible to present the main idea – that a building is not only a beautiful architectural creation that is used and enjoyed by people, but that a building is more complicated and consists of various processes, inputs and outputs.

All these processes are affected by numerous influences and some of them are the various available strategies, regulations, or laws. This book presents their main overview as well as the different methods of building sustainably – by considering the building's whole life time.

Passive and active methods of saving resources and energy should be helpful to design for the building's whole life time. We have attempted to create guidelines and to describe how to develop the whole overarching building concept including space, material, energy, water, economy, green and waste concepts.

The examples show the implementation of these ideas in real building projects.

But this should not be the end. It is not enough to think of one building as being solitary – a building is always a part of a bigger complex with relationships to its closer and larger surroundings. Hence the book's subtitle – "of a building in urban areas".

As the surroundings influence the building and the building influences the surroundings, they collaborate together in order to create a completely sustainable surrounding, because a sustainable building in unsustainable surroundings or vice versa does not create a sustainable society.

As previously mentioned, there is no recipe to build sustainably. There is no sustainable building style, as we know from different historical architectural styles. It is also not a modern style. Each sustainable building is different, looks different and works differently, because it reflects the conditions of the urban area it is situated in.

Therefore it is of great importance to consider urban areas when designing. Eco City, city quarters, urban gardening or new certification of urban areas, e.g. DGNB sustainable city quarters, are some examples.

Thinking locally can save a lot by focusing on energy, resources, water and costs, e.g., the waste energy from one building can be used as valuable energy in another one, cooperation of the buildings with different functions, double use and decentralized water concepts for group of buildings, ...

"Life time urban planning" could include the continuation of the book you now have in your hands.

Ing. arch. Lucia Oberfrancová